# Microeconometrics
## of International Trade

## World Scientific Studies in International Economics

(ISSN: 1793-3641)



---

Vol. 42 Developing Countries in the World Economy
*by Jaime de Melo (FERDI, France & University of Geneva, Switzerland)*

Vol. 43 Farm Policies and World Markets: Monitoring and Disciplining the International Trade Impacts of Agricultural Policies
*by Tim Josling (Stanford University, USA)*

Vol. 44 Non-Tariff Barriers, Regionalism and Poverty: Essays in Applied International Trade Analysis
*by L. Alan Winters (University of Sussex, UK)*

Vol. 45 Trade Law, Domestic Regulation and Development
*by Joel P. Trachtman (Tufts University, USA)*

Vol. 46 The Political Economy of International Trade
*by Edward D. Mansfield (University of Pennsylvania, USA)*

Vol. 47 Trade-Related Agricultural Policy Analysis
by *David Orden (Virginia Polytechnic Institute and State University, USA)*

Vol. 48 The New International Financial System: Analyzing the Cumulative Impact of Regulatory Reform
*edited by Douglas Evanoff (Federal Reserve Bank of Chicago, USA), Andrew G. Haldane (Bank of England, UK) & George Kaufman (Loyola University Chicago, USA)*

Vol. 49 The Economics of International Migration
*by Giovanni Peri (UC Davis)*

Vol. 50 The Legal and Economic Analysis of the WTO/FTA System
*by Dukgeun Ahn (Seoul National University, Korea)*

Vol. 51 The Political Economy of Trade Policy: Theory, Evidence and Applications
*by Devashish Mitra (Syracuse University, USA)*

Vol. 52 Microeconometrics of International Trade
*by Joachim Wagner (Leuphana University Lueneburg, Germany)*

The complete list of the published volumes in the series can be found at
http://www.worldscientific.com/series/wssie

52 World Scientific Studies in International Economics

# Microeconometrics of International Trade

Joachim Wagner
Leuphana University Lueneburg, Germany

World Scientific
NEW JERSEY • LONDON • SINGAPORE • BEIJING • SHANGHAI • HONG KONG • TAIPEI • CHENNAI • TOKYO

*Published by*

World Scientific Publishing Co. Pte. Ltd.
5 Toh Tuck Link, Singapore 596224
*USA office:* 27 Warren Street, Suite 401-402, Hackensack, NJ 07601
*UK office:* 57 Shelton Street, Covent Garden, London WC2H 9HE

**British Library Cataloguing-in-Publication Data**
A catalogue record for this book is available from the British Library.

**World Scientific Studies in International Economics — Vol. 52**
**MICROECONOMETRICS OF INTERNATIONAL TRADE**



ISBN 978-981-3109-68-1

Desk Editor: Alisha Nguyen

Typeset by Stallion Press
Email: enquiries@stallionpress.com

*To Gabi and Nele*

# Biography

Joachim Wagner (1954*) studied economics at the University of Hannover (Germany) where he received his Diploma in 1979, his Doctoral degree in 1984, and his Habilitation in 1990. Since 1993 he is Professor of Economics at Leuphana University Lüneburg (Germany). His main areas of research are international firm activities and applied microeconometrics. He is an editor of the *Journal of Economics and Statistics*, and a co-editor of *Economics — The Open-Access, Open-Assessment E-Journal*, and he is a research fellow at IZA (Bonn, Germany) and CESIS (Stockholm, Sweden).

# Contents

# Acknowledgments

I am happy to have had the opportunity to work with several co-authors over the past 25 years on topics from the microeconometrics of international firm activities. Many thanks to all of you — I learned a lot from our collaborations, and I got by with more than a little help from my friends! In alphabetical order, I thank Andrew B. Bernard, Nils Braakmann, Helmut Fryges, Sourafel Girma, Holger Görg, J. Bradford Jensen, David Powell, Horst Raff, Thorsten Schank, Claus Schnabel, Yama Temouri, Vincenzo Verardi, Alexander Vogel, John P. Weche Gelübcke and all members of International Study Group on Exports and Productivity (ISGEP).

# Introduction: The Microeconometrics of International Trade — A Personal Review

When at the beginning of the 1990s some empirical trade economists started to realize that firms — and not nations or industries — engage in international economic activities,[1] I happened to be among these happy few. In my habilitation thesis that was published (in German) in Wagner (1990), I used firm level data from three manufacturing industries in the German federal state of Lower Saxony to investigate, among others, the determinants of the share of exports in total sales. While the samples were small and the data were cross-section data only, the results were interesting enough (at least, for me) to make me look for larger, more representative and longitudinal firm level data.

Accidently, at a workshop in the summer of 1990 a staff member[2] of the Statistical Office of Lower Saxony mentioned that such firm level data are readily available, because all manufacturing establishments with more than 20 employees have to report their exports in the monthly survey to the Statistical Office. Given that the firm has a unique identification number that is fixed over time and identical in all surveys performed by the Statistical Office

[1]Obviously, this was well known among scholars in International Management for decades; see the 95 papers reprinted in the five volumes edited by McNaughton and Bell (2009).

[2]This was Eckart Methner — who later became president of the Statistical Office of Lower Saxony.

these data can easily be linked over time to form a panel data set. It turned out that these data had never been used for empirical investigations at the micro-level before. I started to do exactly this immediately. From this project, a number of reports and papers in German emerged that are summarized in Wagner (1995). This paper presents facts on exports and firm size, showing that the probability that a firm is an exporter increases with firm size. There are many successful exporters among small firms, and non-exporters among larger firms, too, while most of the exports are from the top size groups of firms. Firm growth and export performance are positively related, as is expected from a model of a price-discriminating monopolist.

While the data from Official Statistics were extremely valuable then, in future research these data were limited in several ways. Among others, no information about the qualification of the employees in a firm or on innovation activities of the firms was available. To fill these and other gaps, together with colleagues from the Institute for Quantitative Economic Research at Hannover University, I started a project to build a tailor-made longitudinal establishment level data set for a representative sample of firms from manufacturing industries in Lower Saxony, *The Hannover Firm Panel* (Gerlach *et al.* 2003). I used these data to show that human capital intensity (measured by the proportion of jobs in the firm for which a degree from a polytech or university is needed) and product innovations are positively related to the share of exports in total sales (Wagner 1996).

Until the mid-1990s, the main focus of my own empirical research on exports was on the determinants of export activities of firms. This focus changed when Andy Bernard (then at MIT) came to visit me in Lüneburg soon after the publication of his now famous Brookings Paper along with Brad Jensen (Bernard and Jensen 1995). Bernard and Jensen (1995) focus on the differences between exporting and non-exporting firms in the United States and document the existence of an exporter premium (a positive difference between both groups of firms in favor of exporters) for various firm characteristics (including size, productivity, and wage per employee). Furthermore, they investigate whether these exporter premia are due to the fact that exporting improves firms or due to self-selection of more productive firms into exporting. We used the longitudinal data from official statistics for manufacturing establishments in Lower Saxony to replicate this study (Bernard and Wagner 1997). Results are rather similar for both countries, as is detailed in the first cross-country study in this literature (Bernard *et al.* 1997), and they point out that good firms are much more likely to become exporters — success leads to exporting rather than exporting to success (see also Bernard and Wagner 2001).

The Bernard and Jensen (1995) paper started a literature. Over the next ten years many studies from all over the world used firm level data and the standard methodology introduced by Bernard and Jensen (1995, 1999) to investigate the link between exports and firm performance with a focus on productivity. Furthermore, this standard approach has been augmented in three ways. First, starting with Wagner (2002) the propensity score matching method was applied in attempts to uncover causal relations between exporting and performance. Second, Delgado *et al.* (2002) looked not only at the difference in mean performance of exporters and non-exporters, but investigated differences in the whole distribution of productivity between firms from the two groups using the non-parametric Kolmogorov–Smirnov Test (for an application to German firms see Wagner (2006a)). Third, Yasar *et al.* (2006) applied quantile regression to uncover the productivity effect of exporting at different points of the conditional output distribution (see Wagner (2006b) for an application to German firms).

This first-generation literature has a focus on the empirical investigation of the strength and the direction of the links between export activity of a firm and its productivity. Wagner (2007) is a comprehensive survey of the evidence reported in 45 studies with data from 33 countries. This survey, that is included in this book in Chapter 1, concludes that exporters are more productive than non-exporters, and that the more productive firms self-select into export markets, while exporting does not necessarily improve productivity.

Over the following years, the microeconometric literature on international firm activities and firm performance grew exponentially and covered many new topics, including the role of export destination for trade and productivity; the link between imports and productivity; international trade and productivity in services firms; and international trade and other dimensions of firm performance beyond productivity, including wages, profits, and firm survival. This literature is surveyed in Wagner (2012a) which is included in this book in Chapter 2.

I contributed to several of these new developments in the microeconometrics of international trade. The chapters in this book are a selection of my papers that report findings for Germany, one of the biggest players on the world markets for goods and services, and that often investigate topics that have not been looked at before, applying newly available tools of analysis.

## Characteristics of Exporting and Importing Firms in Germany

Germany is one of the leading actors in the world market for manufactured goods but not every firm from a manufacturing industry in Germany is an exporter. Reliable information on the characteristics of exporting and non-exporting firms is important to guide theorists and policy makers in an evidence based way. In Wagner (2011a) which is reprinted in this book as Chapter 3 I use rich high quality data of a large representative panel of enterprises from German manufacturing industries to investigate the links between firm characteristics and export activities, demonstrating the decisive role of human capital intensity for exporting. It is shown that productivity *is* important for exporting as is hypothesized in formal theoretical models, but that contrary to the assumption made in these models productivity is not (only) the result of a random draw from the productivity distribution — it is strongly and positively related to human capital intensity.

Besides these aspects, the chapter discusses two points that are relevant for other papers included in this book, and for the microeconometrics of international trade in general. The first one deals with the correct estimation of an empirical model that has the share of exports in total sales as the dependent variable. This is a fractional variable that can only take values between zero and one (or between zero and 100 percent) and that has a probability mass at zero due to the large share of firms that do not export at all. Therefore, a fractional logit estimator (developed by Papke and Wooldridge (1996) and introduced to the literature on the microeconometrics of international trade in Wagner (2001)) has to be applied to estimate this type of empirical model with cross-section data. For (balanced) panel data, the approach suggested in Papke and Wooldridge (2008) and used for the first time in this literature in Wagner (2010a) should be used (see also Wagner (2003) for the case when the universality of all firms is observed and an unconditional fixed effects fractional logit model can be used).

The second more generally relevant point discussed in this chapter is the use of panel data and the application of fixed-effects models to control for unobserved heterogeneity in any study of the links between international trade and firm performance. One crucial problem in any application of the fixed effects strategy is that in the estimation of the coefficients only the within variation of variables over time is used. Therefore, an empirical model for export participation that includes fixed firm effects is estimated using only observations on firms that changed their exporter status over the sampling period at least once. Usually, this is a small group of firms only. Furthermore, firms that start or stop exporting are known to differ from firms that continue (not) to export. This means that an empirical model for export participation with fixed firm effects is estimated using a sample of firms that is different from the population of firms (or a representative random sample of this population).

Another problem related to using only the variation over time within observations in fixed effects models for firm level data is the high ratio of between to within variation that is often observed, at least over short periods of time. While enterprises tend to differ widely from each other in many characteristics at a point in time, differences from year-to-year tend to be much smaller. Evidently, there are firms that jump up and down with regard to the share of exports in total sales, or the number of employees, or other firm characteristics. But usually year-to-year changes in firm characteristics tend to be small on average.

That said, fixed effects models using panel data should not be considered as a panacea when it comes to deal with the problem of unobserved heterogeneity in the microeconometrics of international trade.

The next topic to deal with is imports. In a paper that is reprinted in this book as Chapter 4 Vogel and Wagner (2010a) use a comprehensive panel data set for German manufacturing enterprises to document the first empirical results on the relationship between imports and productivity for Germany. Furthermore, for the first time the direction of causality in this relationship is investigated systematically by testing for self-selection of more productive firms into importing, and for productivity-enhancing effects of imports ('learning-by-importing'). We find a positive link between importing and productivity. Compared to firms that do not trade at all two-way traders do have the highest premia, followed by firms that only export, while firms that only import have the smallest estimated premia. We find evidence of a positive impact of productivity on importing, pointing to self-selection of more productive enterprises into imports, but no clear evidence of the effect of importing on productivity due to learning-by-importing.

## Exports and Wages

One of the new and exciting findings reported in the pioneering paper by Bernard and Jensen (1995) is that exporters tend to pay higher wages and benefits: average wages and benefits (per worker, per production worker, and per non-production worker) are higher in exporting plants than in non-exporting plants of all sizes and classes. Exporter wage premia are statistically significant for all categories of wages and benefits after controlling for capital per worker, size of plant, multi-plant dummy, industry, year, plant age, and region. Coefficients of exporter status dummies are statistically significant in fixed effects regressions controlling for capital per worker, hours per worker, size of plant and year. Results from several other studies that use the same estimation strategy and data from different countries are broadly consistent with these findings.

An open question not dealt with in this literature is whether these exporter wage premia do indeed indicate that exporting plants pay higher wages in the sense that comparable workers are better paid when working on a comparable work place for an exporter, i.e. *ceteris paribus*. Given that all these studies use average data at the plant or firm level, individual characteristics of the workers that might influence their productivity (and therefore, their wages) cannot be taken into account, and certain characteristics of the work place that might call for compensating wage differentials are not represented adequately. In a paper reprinted in this book in Chapter 5 Schank, Schnabel and Wagner (2007) for the first time use a large set of linked employer-employee data from Germany to analyze this exporter wage premium appropriately. We show that the wage differential becomes smaller but does not completely vanish when observable and unobservable characteristics of the employees and of the work place are controlled for. For example, blue-collar (white-collar) employees working in a plant with an export–sales ratio of 60 percent earn about 1.8 (0.9) percent more than similar employees in otherwise identical non-exporting plants.

While it qualifies as a stylized fact that exporting firms pay higher wages than non-exporting firms, the direction of the link between exporting and wages is less clear. In a paper that is reprinted in this book in Chapter 6 Schank, Schnabel and Wagner (2010) investigate for the first time empirically with linked employer-employee data the sequencing behind the correlation of export activities and higher wages at the firm level. Does exporting lead to a wage premium? Or did exporting firms pay a wage premium even before they started to export? Using a rich set of German linked employer-employee panel data, we follow over time plants that start to export. We show that the exporter wage premium does already exist in the years before firms start to export, and that it does not increase in the following years. Higher wages in exporting firms are thus due to self-selection of more productive, better paying firms into export markets; they are not caused by export activities.

## International Trade and Profits

Exporting firms have to bear extra costs due to, among others, market research, adaptation of products to local regulations, or transport costs. As discussed above, these extra costs are one reason for a self-selection of the more productive firms on international markets. Furthermore, the papers reprinted in Chapters 5 and 6 report that exporting firms tend to pay higher wages than non-exporting firms. A question that is investigated for the first time in a paper by Fryges and Wagner (2010) that is reprinted in this book in Chapter 7 is whether the productivity advantage of exporting firms does lead to a profitability advantage of exporters compared to otherwise identical non-exporters even when exporters are facing extra costs and pay higher wages.

We document a positive profitability differential of exporters compared to non-exporters that is statistically significant, though rather small, when observed firm characteristics and unobserved firm specific effects are controlled for. In contrast to nearly all empirical studies on the relationship between productivity and exports we do not find any evidence for self-selection of more profitable firms into export markets. Due to the sampling frame of the data used we cannot test the hypothesis that firms which start exporting perform better in the years after the start than their counterparts which do not start. Instead, we use a newly developed continuous treatment approach (that was used in the literature on the micro-econometrics of international trade for the first time in Fryges (2009) and Fryges and Wagner (2008)) and show that exporting improves the profitability almost over the whole range of the export–sales ratio. This means that the usually observed higher productivity of exporters is not completely absorbed by the extra costs of exporting or by higher wages paid by internationally active firms.

In Wagner (2014d), I investigated for the first time the link between firm profitability and diversification of exports over goods and destination markets. I find that profits tend to be larger in firms with less diversified export sales over goods and in firms with more diversified export sales over destination countries.

In a paper that is reprinted here in Chapter 8 Vogel and Wagner (2010b) use the German business services statistics panel to conduct the first comprehensive empirical study on the relationship between exports and profitability for the business services sector. We document a negative profitability differential of services exporters compared to non-exporters that is statistically significant, though rather small, when observed firm characteristics and unobserved firm specific effects are controlled for. We find that export-starters in services are less profitable than non-starters, even two years before they begin to export, pointing to self-selection of less profitable firms into export markets. We use a recently developed continuous treatment approach to investigate the causal impact of exports on profits. The estimated dose-response function shows an s-shaped relationship between profitability in 2005 and firms' export–sales ratio in 2004. Enterprises with a very small share of exports in total sales have a lower rate of profit than non-exporting firms. Then, with an increase in export intensity the rate of profit increases, too. However, even at the maximum, the average profitability of the exporters is not, or only slightly, higher than the average rate of profit of the non-exporting firms.

While the papers in Chapters 7 and 8 focus on the link between exports and profits, the paper by Wagner (2012b), reprinted here in Chapter 9, documents for the first time the relationship between profitability and three types of international trade activities — exports, imports and two-way trade. Descriptive statistics and regression analysis (with and without controlling for unobserved firm heterogeneity and the role of outliers) point to the absence of any statistically significant and economically large effects of trade activities on profits. This demonstrates that any productivity advantages of trading firms are eaten up by extra costs related to selling and buying on foreign markets.

However, several caveats should be pointed out that might help to put these results into perspective. First of all, the data used do not contain any information on the amount of imports from beyond the European Union. Therefore, the role of the difference in the exports-to-sales ratio and the imports-to-sales ratio between trading firms cannot be investigated; especially, it is not possible to investigate the causal effects of trading on profits with a dose-response approach (see Fryges and Wagner (2010)). Furthermore, there is no information on the type of goods imported. Imports of different kinds can be expected to be linked to profitability in different ways. While there might be no link between imports of raw materials that cannot be produced in Germany at all (like oil or iron ore) and profits, imports of intermediate products that are cheaper than similar goods produced in Germany or imports of capital goods that incorporate advanced technologies not available in machines produced in Germany might well have a positive effect on price and non-price competitiveness of firms and, therefore, on profits. Due to other limitations in the data, further open questions include the role played by different export destinations and by the characteristics of these export-markets, and the importance of the number and the quality of products exported, for the relationship between exports and profitability. Given these (data driven) limitations of the study the results cannot be considered as pointing to stylized facts — they should be taken as a first step and as stimulation for replication and extensions with (richer) data from other countries.

## International Trade and Firm Survival

While the early papers in the literature on the microeconometrics of international trade had a focus on productivity, more recent papers realized that stakeholders in firms care for other dimensions of firm performance, too. Workers care for working conditions in general and especially for wages. Shareholders are interested in stock prices, dividends and profits. These dimensions of firm performance and their relation with international trade are discussed in Chapters 5–9. All stakeholders, however, care for the long-run development of the firm and for firm survival as the ultimate goal. The links between firm survival and three types of international trade activities — exports, imports and two-way trade — are investigated for the first time for a highly developed country in Wagner (2013a), reprinted here as Chapter 10. This paper uses unique new representative data for manufacturing enterprises from Germany. The results indicate a strong positive link between firm survival on the one hand and imports and two-way trading on the other hand, while exporting alone does not play a role for exiting the market or not.

In a companion paper that is reprinted here as Chapter 11 Wagner and Weche Gelübcke (2014) look at the link between internationalization and firm survival during the 2008/2009 crisis in Germany, a country which was hit relatively lightly compared to other countries. This is the first study which looks at the role of importing, exporting and foreign direct investment (FDI) simultaneously in the context of a global economic recession. Our most striking result is to demonstrate the disadvantages of exporting for the chances of survival of a firm during the crisis in western Germany. Importing instead reveals a positive correlation with survival and firms that both export and import do not show a different exit risk relative to non-traders. A plausible explanation is that in a global recession, deteriorating markets abroad cause demand losses for exporters and improved conditions on factor markets which result in an advantage for firms sourcing from factor markets abroad. Two-way traders do not show a link with exit risk, supporting the idea that they were able to outweigh their losses from exporting with their gains from importing, in what could be called an export–import hedge. Furthermore, we cannot support the hypothesis that foreign multinationals are more volatile during times of economic crisis.

## Credit Constraints and International Trade

Business managers are well aware of the fact that credit constraints can hamper or even prevent exporting. Economists only recently started to incorporate these arguments in theoretical models of heterogeneous firms and to test the implications of these models econometrically with firm-level data. Starting with the pioneering study by Greenaway *et al.* (2007) a growing number of empirical papers looked at the links between financial constraints and export activities using data at the level of the firm. My paper (Wagner 2014a) that is reprinted here as Chapter 12 presents a tabular survey of 32 empirical studies that covers 14 different countries plus five multi-country studies. The big picture can be summarized as follows: financial constraints are important for the export decisions of firms — exporting firms are less financially constrained than non-exporting firms. Studies that look at the direction of this link usually report that less constrained firms self-select into exporting, but that exporting does not improve financial health of firms. Evidence for Germany reported in Wagner (2014b) is in line with this big picture. Furthermore, Wagner (2015f) shows a negative impact of credit constraints on both the number of goods exported and the number of export destination countries that is both statistically highly significant and large from an economic point of view.

A companion paper (Wagner 2015a) that is reprinted in Chapter 13 looks at the links between credit constraints and importing in Germany. I find empirical evidence that a better credit rating score is positively related to extensive margins of import — firms with a better score have a higher probability to import, they import more goods and they source from more countries of origin. The intensive margin of imports — the share of imports in total sales — is found not to be related to credit constraints.

## Extensive Margins of Exports and Imports

The focus of the early papers in the literature on the microeconometrics of international trade has been on "Who exports?

What distinguishes exporters and non-exporters? How are exports linked to firm performance?" — with a special view on the links between exports and productivity. Later the scope of studies on trade that use firm-level data widened to ask "Who imports? What distinguishes importers and non-importers? How are imports linked to firm performance?" and the links between trade and other dimensions of firm performance besides productivity (including profitability, wages, and firm survival) were investigated. In this literature (that is covered in the surveys reprinted here in Chapters 1 and 2) a typical data set used is based on either census-type data collected regularly by official statistics or on large comprehensive surveys of firms from other sources.

A new generation of empirical studies on foreign trade goes one step further by asking not only "Who trades how much?" but "Who trades how much of which goods (or services) with whom?" The data used in these studies are based on records of (legal) cross-border transactions regularly collected by the customs. The unit of observation in these data is a single transaction between economic agents located in two countries, e.g. the export of 15.234 kilo of good A with a value of 124,756 Euro from Germany to China. The record of the transaction usually includes a firm identifier (tax registration number) of the exporting (or importing) firm. Using this identifier information at the transaction level can be aggregated at the level of the trading firm to generate period-firm-product-value-weight-destination (or –origin) data. These data show who trades how much of which good with customers (or suppliers) from which country in a given period (a year, or a month). Products are distinguished according to very detailed classifications, and the recording of value and weight allows the easy calculation of unit values that act as proxy variables for prices or indicators of quality. These transaction data can be linked over time to form panel data. Furthermore, the data can be linked to firm level data that has information on firm characteristics that is not included in the customs data, e.g. balance sheet data and data from regular surveys of the statistical offices.

Compared with the census-type data used in the earlier literature these transaction-level based data allow the researcher to look not only at one extensive margin of trade (participation in exporting, or importing), but at two more extensive margins, the number of goods traded and the number of countries traded with. These margins, and their links with characteristics of the firm and dimensions of firm performance, are investigated in a new and rapidly emerging literature. Wagner (2016) is a survey of 147 empirical studies for 39 countries, plus 8 studies that cover multiple countries that use transaction level data on exports or imports of firms.

In Germany, for the reporting year 2009, transaction-level data on exports and imports of goods have been aggregated at the level of the exporting or importing firm for the first time. In these data the number of goods exported and imported and the number of countries exported to and imported from is reported, together with the values of these cross-border transactions. Wagner (2012c), reprinted here in Chapter 14, uses these newly available data for firms from manufacturing industries to uncover new facts and to test theoretical hypotheses of the relationship between a core dimension of firm performance, namely productivity, and the number of goods traded and countries traded with. It documents that foreign trade is dominated by firms that trade multiple goods with multiple countries, and that a small number of very large multiple goods, multiple country exporters and importers play a decisive role in shaping exports and imports of one of the most important actors on the world market for goods. Firms that trade many goods or that trade with many countries are much more productive than firms of the same size from the same industry that trade some goods or trade with some countries only.

## Methods of Empirical Analysis of Heterogeneous Exporters and Importers

One important aim of microeconometric studies is to uncover stylized facts that hold over space and time, and that can both inspire theoretical models that are based on "realistic" assumptions and inform policy debates in an evidence-based way. Which results from the thousands of empirical estimates reported in the literature on the microeconometrics of international trade do we consider as convincing? Based on my own experience, I make twelve recommendations that, hopefully, will help to find the right way on the thorny road from estimation results to stylized facts in Wagner (2011b), reprinted here in Chapter 15. I deal with the following topics: comparisons of means vs. comparisons of distributions; extremely different firms, or outliers; unobserved heterogeneity; simultaneous occurrence of differences across quantiles and unobserved heterogeneity; heterogeneous effects of international firm activities on firm performance; replication; within-study replication by international research teams; meta-analysis and talking to practitioners. A practitioner's guide to new econometric methods for the analysis of links between international trade and firm performance with hints to papers that apply these methods is presented in Wagner (2015b).

## Concluding Remarks

Since the beginning of the 1990s, the mushrooming literature on the microeconometrics of international trade (and on the microeconometrics of international firm activities in a broader sense that include FDI and offshoring, among others) produced a lot of results that helped empirical trade economists to understand much better what drives exports and imports, and what the consequences of international firm activities are for various dimensions of firm performance.

Some of my contributions to this literature that cover the case of Germany, one of the leading actors on the world markets for goods and services, are reprinted in this volume. Due to space limitations papers on several topics I investigated could not be included here. Among these topics are the entry and exit of firms into exporting, and the post-entry performance of cohorts of new exporters (Wagner 2008a, 2012d); the links between innovative activities and international trade in manufacturing firms (Wagner 2008b, 2012e, 2014c) and in services firms (Vogel and Wagner 2013, 2014; Fryges, Vogel and Wagner 2015); the role of the extensive and intensive margins of trade in the dynamics of exports and imports over the short run (Wagner 2004, 2013b, 2013c, 2013d, 2013e); and the links between firm age, exports and imports (Wagner 2015c, 2015d, 2015e).[3]

Next time, my work in the field of microeconometrics of international trade will focus on studies that use the newly available transaction level data for German exports and imports. With tens of millions of transactions per year these data come close to what constitute *Big Data*, at least from the perspective of an empirical trade economist who started his work in this field with estimating models using data from small cross-section samples of firms and turned to panel data for larger representative samples of firms later. Hopefully, these newly available data will help us to understand even better what drives international activities of firms and how these activities are linked to the various dimensions of firm performance.

## References

Bernard, Andrew B. and J. Bradford Jensen (1995). Exporters, Jobs and Wages in U.S. Manufacturing, 1976–1987. *Brookings Papers on Economic Activity, Microeconomics* 67–119.

Bernard, Andrew B. and J. Bradford Jensen (1999). Exceptional Exporter Performance: Cause, Effect, or Both? *Journal of International Economics* 47(1), 1–25.

Bernard, Andrew B., J. Bradford Jensen and Joachim Wagner (1997). The Good Go Abroad: Evidence from Longitudinal Micro Data on German and U.S. Exporters. In: Seppo Laaksonen (Ed.), The Evolution of Firms and Industries. International Perspectives. Helsinki: Statistics Finland, pp. 489–500.

Bernard, Andrew B. and Joachim Wagner (1997). Exports and Success in German Manufacturing. *Weltwirtschaftliches Archiv/Review of World Economics* 133(1), 134–157.

Bernard, Andrew B. and Joachim Wagner (2001). Export Entry and Exit by German Firms. *Weltwirtschaftliches Archiv/Review of World Economics* 137(1), 105–123.

[3]For a complete list of my publications see http://www.leuphana.de/joachim-wagner.html.

Delgado, Miguel A., Jose Carlos Farinas and Sonia Ruano (2002). Firm productivity and Export Markets: A Non-parametric Approach. *Journal of International Economics* 57(2), 397–422.

Fryges, Helmut (2009). The Export-Growth Relationship: Estimating a Dose-Response Function. *Applied Economics Letters* 16 (18), 1855–59.

Fryges, Helmut, Alexander Vogel and Joachim Wagner (2015). The Impact of R&D Activities on Exports of German Business Services Enterprises: First Evidence from a Continuous Treatment Approach. *The World Economy* 38(4), 716–729.

Fryges, Helmut and Joachim Wagner (2008). Exports and Productivity Growth: First Evidence from a Continuous Treatment Approach. *Review of World Economics* 144(4), 695–722.

Fryges, Helmut and Joachim Wagner (2010). Exports and Profitability: First Evidence for German Manufacturing Firms. *The World Economy* 33(3), 399–423.

Gerlach, Knut, Olaf Hübler and Wolfgang Meyer (2003). The Hannover Firm Panel (HFP). *Schmollers Jahrbuch/Journal of Applied Social Science Studies* 123(3), 463–470.

Greenaway, David, Alessandra Guariglia, and Richard Kneller (2007). Financial factors and exporting decisions. *Journal of International Economics* 73(2), 377–395.

McNaughton, Rod B. and Jim Bell (Eds.) (2009). Entrepreneurship and Globalization, Vol. 1–5. Los Angeles etc., Sage.

Papke, Leslie E. and Jeffrey M. Wooldridge (1996). Econometric Methods for Fractional Response Variables with an Application to 401(k) Plan Participation Rates. *Journal of Applied Econometrics* 11(6), 619–632.

Papke, Leslie E. and Jeffrey M. Wooldridge (2008). Panel Data Methods for Fractional Response Variables with an Application to Test Pass Rates. *Journal of Econometrics* 145(1/2), 121–133.

Schank, Thorsten, Claus Schnabel and Joachim Wagner (2007). Do Exporters Really Pay Higher Wages? First Evidence from German Linked Employer–employee Data. *Journal of International Economics* 72(1), 52–74.

Schank, Thorsten, Claus Schnabel and Joachim Wagner (2010). Higher Wages in Exporting firms: Self-selection, Export Effect or Both? First Evidence from Linked Employer-employee Data. *Review of World Economics* 146(2), 302–322.

Vogel, Alexander and Joachim Wagner (2010a). Higher Productivity in Importing German Manufacturing Firms: Self-selection, Learning from Importing, or Both? *Review of World Economics* 145(4), 641–665.

Vogel, Alexander and Joachim Wagner (2010b). Exports and Profitability — First Evidence for German Business Services Enterprises. *Applied Economics Quarterly* 56(1), 7–30.

Vogel, Alexander and Joachim Wagner (2013). Exports, R&D and Productivity in German Business Services Firms: A Test of the Bustos-Model. *Empirical Economics Letters* 12(1), 1–6.

Vogel, Alexander and Joachim Wagner (2014). Innovation and exports of German business services enterprises. In: Anna Maria Ferragina, Erol Taymaz and Kamil Yilmaz (Eds.), Innovation, Globalization and Firm Dynamics.

Lessons for enterprise policy. Milton Park and New York: Routledge, pp. 137–160.

Wagner, Joachim (1990). Die bundesrepublikanische Industrie auf dem Weltmarkt. Ökonometrische Untersuchungen zu Bestimmungsgründen von Außenhandel und internationaler Produktion. Berlin: Duncker & Humblot.

Wagner, Joachim (1995). Exports, Firm Size and Firm Dynamics. *Small Business Economics* 7(1), 29–39.

Wagner, Joachim (1996). Export Performance, Human Capital and Product Innovation in Germany: A Micro View. *Jahrbuch für Wirtschaftswissenschaften/Review of Economics* 47(1), 40–45.

Wagner, Joachim (2001). A Note on the Firm Size — Export Relationship. *Small Business Economics* 17(4), 229–237.

Wagner, Joachim (2002). The Causal Effect of Exports on Firm Size and Labor Productivity: First Evidence from a Matching Approach. *Economics Letters* 77(2), 287–292.

Wagner, Joachim (2003). Unobserved Firm Heterogeneity and the Size-Exports Nexus: Evidence from German Panel Data. *Review of World Economics* 139(1), 161–172.

Wagner, Joachim (2004). On the Microstructure of the German Export Boom: Evidence from Establishment Panel Data, 1995–2002. *Review of World Economics* 140(3), 496–509.

Wagner, Joachim (2006a). Exports, Foreign Direct Investment and Productivity: Evidence from German Firm Level Data. *Applied Economics Letters* 13(6), 347–349.

Wagner, Joachim (2006b). Export Intensity and Plant Characteristics: What Can we learn from Quantile Regression? *Review of World Economics* 142(1), 195–203.

Wagner, Joachim (2007). Exports and Productivity: A Survey of the Evidence from Firm-level Data. *The World Economy* 30(1), 60–82.

Wagner, Joachim (2008a). Export Entry, Export Exit, and Productivity in German Manufacturing Industries. *International Journal of the Economics of Business* 15(2), 169–180.

Wagner, Joachim (2008b). International Firm Activities and Innovation: Evidence from Knowledge Production Functions for German Firms. *Icfai Journal of Knowledge Management* VI(2), 47–62.

Wagner, Joachim (2010a). Exports and Firm Characteristics — First Evidence from Fractional Probit Panel Estimates. *Empirical Economics Letters* 9(10), 935–940.

Wagner, Joachim (2011a). Exports and Firm Characteristics in German Manufacturing Industries: New Evidence from Representative Panel Data. *Applied Economics Quarterly* 57(2), 107–143.

Wagner, Joachim (2011b). From Estimation Results to Stylized Facts. Twelve Recommendations for Empirical Research in International Activities of Heterogeneous Firms. *De Economist* 159(4), 389–412.

Wagner, Joachim (2012a). International Trade and Firm Performance: A Survey of Empirical Studies Since 2006. *Review of World Economics* 148(2), 235–267.

Wagner, Joachim (2012b). Exports, Imports and Profitability: First Evidence for Manufacturing Enterprises. *Open Economies Review* 23(5), 747–765.

Wagner, Joachim (2012c). Trading Many Goods with Many Countries: Exporters and Importers from German Manufacturing Industries. *Jahrbuch für Wirtschaftswissenschaften/Review of Economics* 63(2), 170–186.

Wagner, Joachim (2012d). The Post-entry Performance of Cohorts of Export Starters in German Manufacturing Industries. *International journal of the Economics of Business* 19(2), 169–193.

Wagner, Joachim (2012e). Exports, R&D and Productivity: A Test of the Bustos-Model with German Enterprise Data. *Economics Bulletin* 32(3), 1942–1948.

Wagner, Joachim (2013a). Exports, Imports and Firm survival: First Evidence for Manufacturing Enterprises in Germany. *Review of World Economics* 149(1), 113–130.

Wagner, Joachim (2013b). The Granular Nature of the Great Export Collapse in German Manufacturing Industries, 2008/2009. *Economics — The Open-Access, Open-Assessment E-Journal* 7(5), 1–21.

Wagner, Joachim (2013c). Extensive Margins of Imports in the Great Import Recovery in Germany, 2009/2010. *Economics Bulletin* 33(4), 2732–2743.

Wagner, Joachim (2013d). The Great Export Recovery in German Manufacturing Industries, 2009/2010. *Review of Economics* 64(3), 325–339.

Wagner, Joachim (2013e). The Role of Extensive Margins of Exports in The Great Export Recovery in Germany, 2009/2010. *Jahrbücher für Nationalökonomie und Statistik/Journal of Economics and Statistics* 234(4), 518–526.

Wagner, Joachim (2014a). Credit Constraints and Exports: A Survey of Empirical Studies Using Firm-level Data. *Industrial and Corporate Change* 23(6), 1477–1492.

Wagner, Joachim (2014b). Credit Constraints and Exports: Evidence for German Manufacturing Enterprises. *Applied Economics* 46(3), 294–302.

Wagner, Joachim (2014c). Exports, R&D and Productivity: A Test of the Bustos-Model with Enterprise Data from France, Italy and Spain. *Economics Bulletin* 35(1), 716–719.

Wagner, Joachim (2014d). Is Export Diversification Good for Profitability? First Evidence for Manufacturing Enterprises in Germany. *Applied Economics* 46(33), 4083–4090.

Wagner, Joachim (2015a). Credit Constraints and Margins of Import: First Evidence for German Manufacturing Enterprises. *Applied Economics* 47(5), 415–430.

Wagner, Joachim (2015b). New Methods for the Analysis of Links between International Firm Activities and Firm Performance: A Practitioner's Guide. *The World Economy* 38(4), 704–715.

Wagner, Joachim (2015c). Firm Age and the Margins of International Trade: Comparable Evidence from Five European countries. *Economics Bulletin* 35(1), 145–158.

Wagner, Joachim (2015d). A Note on Firm Age and the Margins of Imports: First Evidence from Germany. *Applied Economics Letters* 22(9), 679–682.

Wagner, Joachim (2015e). A Note on Firm Age and the Margins of Exports: First Evidence from Germany. *The International Trade Journal* 29(2), 93–102.

Wagner, Joachim (2015f). Credit Constraints and the Extensive Margins of Exports: First Evidence for German Manufacturing. *Economics — The Open-Access Open-Assessment E-Journal* 9(18), 1–17.

Wagner, Joachim (2016). A Survey of Empirical Studies Using Transaction Level Data on Exports and Imports. *Review of World Economics* 152(1), 215–225.

Wagner, Joachim and John P. Weche Gelübcke (2014). Risk or Resilience? The Role of Trade Integration and Foreign Ownership for the Survival of German Enterprises During the Crisis 2008–2010. *Jahrbücher für Nationalökonomie und Statistik/Journal of Economics and Statistics* 234(6), 757–774.

Yasar, Mahmut, Carl H. Nelson and Roderick Rejesus (2006). Productivity and Exporting Status of Manufacturing Firms: Evidence from Quantile Regressions. *Review of World Economics* 142(4), 675–694.

# PART I
# Survey Papers

## Chapter 1

# Exports and Productivity: A Survey of the Evidence from Firm Level Data

Joachim Wagner

## 1. Introduction

Discussions on the role of exports in promoting growth in general and productivity in particular, have been ongoing for many years. Until some 10 years ago, empirical studies in this field used data at the country or industry level to test whether exports promote productivity growth or *vice versa* (see the surveys by Baldwin (2000), Giles and Williams (2000a, 2000b), and López (2005)). In 1995, Bernard and Jensen published the first of a number of papers that changed this research perspective (see Bernard and Jensen (1995, 1999, 2004a)). They used large comprehensive longitudinal data from surveys performed regularly by official statistics in the United States to look at differences between exporters and non-exporters in various dimensions of firm performance, including productivity. These papers started a literature. During the 10 years following the publication of Bernard and Jensen's Brookings Paper, researchers all over the world discovered the rich data sets collected by their statistical offices as a source to investigate the export activity of firms and its causes and consequences.[1] The extent and cause of productivity differentials between exporters and their counterparts

[1] Earlier research using longitudinal microdata from official statistics in Germany to investigate causes and consequences of exporting is summarised in Wagner (1995).

which sell on the domestic market only is one of the core topics in this literature.

There are two alternative but not mutually exclusive hypotheses on why exporters can be expected to be more productive than non-exporting firms (see Bernard and Jensen (1999) and Bernard and Wagner (1997)):

The first hypothesis points to self-selection of the more productive firms into export markets. The reason for this is that there exist additional costs of selling goods in foreign countries. The range of extra costs include transportation costs, distribution or marketing costs, personnel with skill to manage foreign networks or production costs in modifying current domestic products for foreign consumption. These costs provide an entry barrier that less successful firms cannot overcome. Furthermore, the behavior of firms might be forward-looking in the sense that the desire to export tomorrow leads a firm to improve performance today to be competitive in the foreign market too. Cross-section differences between exporters and non-exporters, therefore, may in part be explained by *ex-ante* differences between firms: the more productive firms become exporters.

The second hypothesis points to the role of learning-by-exporting. Knowledge flows from international buyers and competitors help to improve the post-entry performance of export starters. Furthermore, firms participating in international markets are exposed to more intense competition and must improve faster than firms who sell their products domestically only. Exporting makes firms more productive.

These two hypotheses are by no means mutually exclusive. This paper reviews the findings of studies that use microdata at the level of firms (i.e. plants, establishments, local production units) to investigate the relationship between export activities and productivity empirically.[2] The rest of the paper is organized as follows: Section 2 describes the various empirical approaches used

[2]For contemporaneous but less comprehensive surveys of this literature with a partly different focus, see López (2005) and Greenaway and Kneller (2005).

in the post-1995 literature to identify the extent and direction of the relationship between exports and productivity using microdata at the firm level. Section 3 reviews 45 studies with data from 33 countries and summarizes the core results. Section 4 concludes.

## 2. Investigating the Exports/Productivity Relationship: Empirical Strategies

### 2.1. *A standard approach*

A common approach to investigate differences in productivity between exporters and non-exporters is to follow (sometimes only in part and sometimes with modifications and extension) the methodology introduced by Bernard and Jensen (1995, 1999). Studies of this type use longitudinal data for plants (usually from the regular surveys conducted by official statistics) to document differences in levels and growth rates of productivity between exporters and non-exporters in a first step. Here one starts by looking at differences in average labour productivity (total value of shipments per worker or value added per worker) or average total factor productivity[3] between exporters and non-exporters. The result is an unconditional productivity differential.

The next step is the computation of so-called exporter premia, defined as the *ceteris paribus* percentage difference of labor productivity between exporters and non exporters. These premia are computed from a regression of log labor productivity on the current export status dummy and a set of control variables (usually including industry, region, firm size measured by the number of employees and year):

$$\ln \mathrm{LP}_{it} = a + ß\ \mathrm{Export}_{it} + c\ \mathrm{Control}_{it} + e_{it}, \qquad (1)$$

where $i$ is the index of the firm, $t$ is the index of the year, LP is labour productivity, Export is a dummy variable for current export status (1 if the firm exports in year t, 0 else), Control is a vector of control

[3]To simplify the exposition, we will refer to labor productivity only from now on.

variables (like four-digit industry dummies, dummies for regions, firm size, and year dummies), and $e$ is an error term. The export premium, computed from the estimated coefficient ß as $100(\exp(ß) - 1)$, shows the average percentage difference between exporters and non-exporters controlling for the characteristics included in the vector control. To control for unobserved plant heterogeneity due to time-invariant firm characteristics which might be correlated with the variables included in the empirical model and which might lead to a biased estimate of the exporter premia, a variant of (1) is often estimated with fixed plant effects too.

Next, differences in productivity growth between exporters and non-exporters are investigated based on an empirical model that can be written as:

$$\begin{aligned} \ln \mathrm{LP}_{it} - \ln \mathrm{LP}_{i0} = a &+ ß_1\ \mathrm{Start}_{it} + ß_2\ \mathrm{Both}_{it} \\ &+ ß_3\ \mathrm{Stop}_{it} + c\ \mathrm{Control}_{i0} + e_{it}, \end{aligned} \tag{2}$$

where Control is a vector of plant characteristics in year 0, and the dummies for export status are defined as follows:

$$\begin{aligned} \mathrm{Start}_{it} &= 1 \text{ if } (\mathrm{Export}_{i0} = 0) \text{ and } (\mathrm{Export}_{it} = 1), \\ \mathrm{Both}_{it} &= 1 \text{ if } (\mathrm{Export}_{i0} = 1) \text{ and } (\mathrm{Export}_{it} = 1), \\ \mathrm{Stop}_{it} &= 1 \text{ if } (\mathrm{Export}_{i0} = 1) \text{ and } (\mathrm{Export}_{it} = 0), \end{aligned}$$

where non-exporting in both years is the reference category. The regression coefficients $ß_1, ß_2$ and $ß_3$ are estimates for the increase in growth rates of labor productivity for export starters, exporters in both years, and export stoppers relative to non-exporters in both years, controlling for firm characteristics included in the vector Control. Here we look at $ß_2$ to compare exporters and non-exporters.

To shed light on the empirical validity of the first hypothesis mentioned — namely, that the more productive firms go abroad — the pre-entry differences in productivity between export starters and non-exporters are investigated next. If good firms become exporters then we should expect to find significant differences in performance measures between future export starters and future non-starters several years before some of them begin to export.

To test whether today's export starters were more productive than today's non-exporters several years back when all of them did not export, select all firms that did not export between year $t-3$ and $t-1$, and compute the average difference in labour productivity in year $t-3$ between those firms who did export in year $t$ and those who did not. More formally, estimate the empirical model

$$\ln \mathrm{LP}_{it\text{-}3} = a + ß\ \mathrm{Export}_{it} + c\,\mathrm{Control}_{it\text{-}3} + e_{it}, \qquad (3)$$

where $i$ is the index of the firm, $t$ is the index of the year, LP is labor productivity in year $t-3$, Export is a dummy variable for current export status (1 if the firm exports in year $t$, 0 else), Control is a vector of control variables (like four-digit industry dummies, dummies for regions, firm size and year dummies), and $e$ is an error term. The pre-entry premium, computed from the estimated coefficient ß as $100(\exp(ß) - 1)$, shows the average percentage difference between today's exporters and today's non-exporters three years before starting to export, controlling for the characteristics included in the vector Control. To investigate the related question whether productivity increased more in export starters in the years before the start than in firms that continue not to export, the empirical model

$$\ln \mathrm{LP}_{it\text{-}1} - \ln \mathrm{LP}_{it\text{-}3} = a + ß\,\mathrm{Export}_{it} + c\,\mathrm{Control}_{i0} + e_{it}, \qquad (4)$$

is used. The estimated regression coefficient ß shows the extent in which future exporters outperformed the non-exporting firms in the years prior to entry.

To test for the second hypothesis mentioned — namely, that exporting fosters productivity — the post-entry differences in productivity growth between export starters and non-exporters are investigated. This is done by looking at $ß_1$ from (2) to compare the productivity growth performance of export starters and non-exporters.

Finally, to find out whether stopping to export is negatively related with productivity performance, post-exit differences in productivity growth between export stoppers and non-exporters are investigated by looking at $ß_3$ from (2) to compare the productivity growth performance of export stoppers and non-exporters.

While most of the empirical studies that use (variants of) the now standard approach outlined in this section compare exporters and non-exporters across all (manufacturing) industries, some focus on firms from selected industries only and document similarities and differences (see e.g. Alvarez and López (2005), Blalock and Gertler (2004), De Loecker (2004), and Greenaway and Kneller (2004b)). Damijan, Polanec and Prasnikar (2004) recently looked at differences by foreign markets served and found that it matters whether firms exported to advanced countries or developing countries. Furthermore, Fernandes and Isgut (2005) look at young and old firms separately when testing for learning-by-exporting.

## 2.2. *Extensions*

The standard approach outlined in the last section has been augmented by extension and alternative approaches that deal with some of its weaknesses and problems. Here we will discuss two of these recent developments that are used more and more in empirical investigations, namely the comparison of productivity between matched firms, and differences in the distribution of productivity as a whole between exporters and non-exporters.[4]

To motivate the first approach mentioned, consider the following situation: assume that a study reports that plants entering the export market have substantially faster productivity growth in the following years than firms that keep selling their products on the domestic market only. Does this point to a causal effect of starting to export on productivity? The answer is, obviously, no: if better firms self-select into export-starting, and if, therefore, today's export starters are 'better' than today's non-exporters (and have been so in the recent past), we would expect that they should, on average, perform better in the future even if they do not start to export today. However, we cannot observe whether they would really do so because they do start to export today; we simply have

[4]An important extension not dealt with here is the application of (a variant of) the standard approach to the relationship between productivity and both foreign direct investment (FDI) and exports; see the study by Kimura and Kiyota (2004) using Japanese firm level data.

no data for the counterfactual situation. So how can we be sure that the better performance of starters compared to non-exporters is caused by exporting (or not)? This closely resembles a situation familiar from the evaluation of active labor market programs (or any other form of treatment of units): if participants, or treated units, are not selected randomly from a population but are selected or self-select according to certain criteria, the effect of a treatment cannot be evaluated by comparing the average performance of the treated and the non-treated. However, given that each unit (plant, or person, etc.) either participated or not, we have no information about its performance in the counterfactual situation. A way out is to construct a control group in such a way that every treated unit is matched to an untreated unit that has been as similar as possible (ideally, identical) at the time before the treatment. Differences between the two groups (the treated, and the matched non-treated) after the treatment can then be attributed to the treatment (for a comprehensive discussion, see Heckman, LaLonde and Smith (1999)).

The use of a matching approach to search for causal effects of starting or stopping to export on productivity (and other dimensions of firm performance) has been pioneered by Wagner (2002) and Girma, Greenaway and Kneller (2003, 2004), and it has been used in a growing number of empirical studies ever since (including De Loecker (2004), Arnold and Hussinger (2005a), Yasar and Rejesus (2005), Alvarez and López (2005), Fernandes and Isgut (2005), Wagner (2005b), and Kostevc (2005)).

As regards the second recent methodological innovation in this literature, consider the comparison of productivity (or productivity growth) between exporters and non-exporters. If one looks at differences in the mean value for both groups only, one focuses on just one moment of the productivity distribution. A stricter test that considers all moments is a test for stochastic dominance of the productivity distribution for exporters over the productivity distribution for non-exporters. More formally, let $F$ and $G$ denote the cumulative distribution functions of productivity for exporters and non-exporters. Then first order stochastic dominance of $F$

relative to $G$ means that $F(z) - G(z)$ must be less or equal zero for all values of $z$, with strict inequality for some $z$. Whether this holds or not is tested non-parametrically by adopting the Kolmogorov–Smirnov test. This method has been used to discuss the issue of exports and productivity for the first time by Delgado, Farinas and Ruano (2002); recent applications comparing firms that produce for the local market only, that export, and that are foreign direct investors are Girma, Görg and Strobl (2004), Girma, Kneller and Pisu (2005), Wagner (2005a), and Arnold and Hussinger (2005b).

A related extension of the standard approach used in the investigation of the relationship between exports and productivity is the application of quantile regression, introduced to this field of analysis by Yasar, Nelson and Rejesus (2003) and used to investigate the determinants of export activities for the first time by Wagner (2004). By construction this method examines the productivity effect of exporting at different points of the conditional output distribution. To state it differently, quantile regression allows to test for differences in the effects of exporting on plant productivity as one moves from the lower to the upper tail of the conditional productivity distribution, and to identify the regions where these effects are especially weak, or strong, or not significantly different from zero at all.

## 3. A Survey of the Evidence, 1995–2005

During the 10 years following the publication of the pathbreaking Brookings paper by Bernard and Jensen (1995), researchers all over the world used firm level data to investigate the relationship between exporting and productivity in microeconometric studies. Table 1 gives a synopsis of findings from 54 empirical studies covering 34 countries. Among the countries covered are highly industrialized countries (e.g., United States, United Kingdom, Canada, Germany); countries from Latin America (Chile, Colombia, Mexico); Asian countries (China, Korea, Indonesia, Taiwan); transition countries (Estonia, Slovenia); and least developed countries from sub-Saharan Africa.

Given this wide range of countries the big picture emerging from column two of Table 1 that summarizes findings on differences in levels and growth rates between exporters and non-exporters is amazingly clear-cut: with only a few exceptions exporters are found to have higher productivity and often higher productivity growth and this tends to hold after controlling for observed plant characteristics (like industry and size), too. Exporters are better.

The findings for pre-entry differences surveyed in column three often present evidence in favor of the self-selection hypothesis: future export starters tend to be more productive than future non-exporters years before they enter the export market, and often have higher *ex-ante* growth rates of productivity. The good firms go abroad.

Evidence regarding the learning-by-exporting hypothesis is somewhat more mixed: Results for post-entry differences in performance between export starters and non-exporters collected in column four point to faster productivity growth for the former group in some studies only (see also the selective review in Table 1 in Fernandes and Isgut (2005)). If matched firms are compared, often no statistically significant exporter premia are found. Furthermore, Kostevc (2005, p. 31) finds evidence for his thesis that "the initially experienced productivity hike may be a result of a simple scale effect caused by the firm market expansion allowing firms to utilize excess capacity rather than actual permanent productivity improvements." Exporting does not necessarily improve firms.

Finally, a look at the results for post-exit differences collected in the last column reveals that stopping to export tends to be accompanied by a decrease in productivity in most cases. Girma, Greenaway and Kneller (2003) in the only study using matched firms, however, find only weak negative effects in the year of exit, and no effect for later years.

Obviously the big picture sketched here — exporters are more productive than non-exporters, and the more productive firms self-select into export markets, while exporting does not necessarily improve productivity — hides a lot of cross-country heterogeneity which is documented in some detail in Table 1, and in even more detail in the studies surveyed. Cross-country comparisons, and even cross-study comparisons for one country, are difficult because the studies differ in details of the approach used. Therefore, the jury is still out on many of the issues regarding the relationship between exporting and productivity. One promising approach to generate stylized facts in a more convincing way is to coordinate microeconometric studies for many countries *ex-ante*, and to agree on a common approach and on the specification of the empirical models estimated. The outcome of such a joint effort would be a set of results that could be compared not only qualitatively (i.e. with regard to the signs and the statistical significance of the estimated coefficients) but with a view on the magnitude of the estimated effects too.[5]

## 4. Concluding Remarks

Details aside, the big picture that emerges after 10 years of microeconometric research in the relationship between exporting and productivity is that exporters are more productive than non-exporters, and that the more productive firms self-select into export markets, while exporting does not necessarily improve productivity. However, given all the difficulties (mentioned above) to compare the results from the vast numbers of studies in detail, it still seems to be too early to speak of these findings as stylized facts and to discuss any policy conclusions to be based thereon. Furthermore, there are a number of important issues that have only been touched upon recently in some studies and that deserve future research efforts that cover more countries:

— If high-productivity firms self-select into export markets, is their high productivity due to an exogeneous random shock or is it the result of a planned strategy to prepare for entering export markets? Hallward–Driemeier, Iarossi and Sokoloff

[5]See Bernard, Jensen and Wagner (1997) for this type of study using data for the United States and Germany. Volunteers willing to participate in an international study of this kind are asked to contact me!

(2002), López (2003), and Alvarez and López (2005) present evidence for the latter view based on data from five East Asian countries and Chile. López (2005, p. 624) argues that, "at least in developing countries, the self-selection process may well be a conscious decision by which firms purposefully increase their productivity with the clear intention of becoming exporters. Therefore, the macroeconomic evidence showing that more open economies grow faster can be reconciled with the recent microeconomic findings."[6]

— If exporting improves productivity via technology transfer from international buyers, what are the mechanisms by which this learning from exporting occurs? Blalock and Gertler (2004) report some anecdotal evidence from interviews with Indonesian exporting factory managers on this; López (2005, p. 629f.) surveys evidence from case studies.

— Which role is played by different target countries of exports for higher productivity as a precondition or result of exporting? Damijan, Polanec and Prasnikar (2004) report that in Slovenia the productivity difference between future export starters and non-exporters is higher for firms that start to export to more advanced markets.

To answer these questions, microeconometric research based on large sets of longitudinal plant level data has to be supplemented by field research in firms, following Susan Helper's (2000) credo that "you can observe a lot just by watching." Case studies of this kind cannot only produce the anecdotal evidence that helps us to understand what is behind the estimated coefficients that we produce with our PCs, they can point to the tailor-made questions to be included in future surveys that are aimed to collect data for a new generation of microeconometric studies too.

Furthermore, there is a different area of future research that is driven by an emerging theoretical literature. While at the dawn of

[6]Note further that Falvey *et al.* (2004), using data for Sweden, found a clear, causal link between exporting and industry productivity which is independent of the link between exporting and firm productivity.

the empirical literature surveyed here Leamer and Levinson (1994, p. 1) stated that "(i)nternational microeconomics is primarily a theoretical enterprise that seems little affected by empirical results," this is no longer true for some years now. A number of theoretical papers, including Bernard, Eaton, Jensen and Kortum (2003), Melitz (2003), Helpman, Melitz and Yeaple (2004), and Yeaple (2005), take the results from the empirical literature on firms and exports as a starting point and develop models of international trade with heterogeneous firms which focus on the relationship between productivity and exports or firm level globalisation in general. These theoretical models in turn generate testable hypotheses and serve as catalysts for future microeconometric studies (see Greenaway and Kneller (2005) for a survey and evaluation of this theoretical literature and the relations to the microeconometric studies surveyed here).

## References

Alvarez, Roberto and Ricardo A. López (2005), Exporting and Performance: Evidence from Chilean Plants. *Canadian Journal of Economics* 38, 1384–1400.

Arnold, Jens Martin and Katrin Hussinger (2005a), Export Behavior and Firm Productivity in German Manufacturing. A Firm-level Analysis. *Review of World Economics* 141, 219–243.

Arnold, Jens Martin and Katrin Hussinger (2005b), Export versus FDI in German Manufacturing: Firm Performance and Participation in International Markets. Centre for European Economic Research Discussion Paper No. 05-73, October.

Aw, Bee Yan, Xiaomin Chen and Mark J. Roberts (1997), Firm-level Evidence on Productivity Differentials, Turnover, and Exports in Taiwanese Manufacturing. Pennsylvania State University mimeo, June.

Aw, Bee Yan, Sukkyun Chung and Mark J. Roberts (2000), Productivity and Turnover in the Export Market: Micro-level Evidence from the Republic of Korea and Taiwan (China). *The World Bank Economic Review* 14, 65–90.

Aw, Bee Yan and A. R. Hwang (1995), Productivity and the export market: A firm-level analysis. *Journal of Development Economics* 47, 313–332.

Aw, Bee Yan, Mark J. Roberts and Tor Winston (2005), The Complementary Role of Exports and R&D Investments As Sources of Productivity Growth. Pennsylvania State University. Mimeo, July.

Baldwin, John R. and Wulong Gu (2003), Export-market participation and productivity performance in Canadian manufacturing. *Canadian Journal of Economics* 36, 634–657.

Baldwin, Robert (2000), Trade and Growth: Still Disagreement about the Relationships. Organisation for Economic Co-operation and Development, Economics Department Working Paper ECO/WKP(2000)37, October.

Bernard, Andrew B (1995), Exporters and Trade Liberalization in Mexico: Production Structure and Performance. MIT mimeo, February.

Bernard, Andrew B., Jonathan Eaton, J. Bradford Jensen and Samuel Kortum (2003), Plants and Productivity in International Trade. *American Economic Review* 93, 1268–1290.

Bernard, Andrew B. and J. Bradford Jensen (1995), Exporters, Jobs, and Wages in United States Manufacturing: 1976–1987. *Brookings Papers on Economic Activity: Microeconomics*. 67–119.

Bernard, Andrew B. and J. Bradford Jensen (1999), Exceptional exporter performance: cause, effect, or both? *Journal of International Economics* 47, 1–25.

Bernard, Andrew B. and J. Bradford Jensen (2004a), Exporting and Productivity in the USA. *Oxford Review of Economic Policy* 20, 343–357.

Bernard, Andrew B. and J. Bradford Jensen (2004b), Why some firms export. *Review of Economics and Statistics* 86, 561–569.

Bernard, Andrew B., J. Bradford Jensen and Joachim Wagner (1997), The Good go Abroad: Evidence from Longitudinal Micro Data on German and United States Exporters. in Seppo Laaksonen (Ed.), *The Evolution of Firms and Industries — International Perspectives*. Helsinki: Statistics Finland, 489–500.

Bernard, Andrew B. and Joachim Wagner (1997), Exports and Success in German Manufacturing. *Weltwirtschaftliches Archiv/Review of World Economics* 133, 134–157.

Bernard, Andrew B. and Joachim Wagner. 2001, Export Entry and Exit by German Firms. *Weltwirtschaftliches Archiv/Review of World Economics* 137, 105–123.

Bigsten, Arne *et al.* (2000), Exports and Firm-level Efficiency in African Manufacturing. Centre for the Study of African Economies, Oxford University, WPS/2000-16, July.

Blalock, Garrick and Paul J. Gertler (2004), Learning from exporting revisited in a less developed setting. *Journal of Development Economics* 75, 397–416.

Castellani, Davide (2002), Export Behavior and Productivity Growth: Evidence from Italian Manufacturing Firms. *Weltwirtschaftliches Archiv/Review of World Economics* 138, 605–628.

Castellani, Davide and Antonello Zanfei (2004), Internationalisation, innovation and productivity: how do firms differ in Italy? Università di Urbino "Carlo Bo", mimeo, July.

Clerides, Sofronis K., Saul Lach and James R. Tybout (1998), Is Learning by Exporting Important? Micro-dynamic Evidence from Colombia, Mexico, and Morocco. *Quarterly Journal of Economics* CXIII, 903–947.

Damijan, Jose P., Saso Polanec and Janez Prasnikar (2004), Self-selection, Export Market Heterogeneity and Productivity Improvements: Firm Level Evidence from Slovenia. Katholieke Universiteit Leuven, LICOS Discussion Paper 148/2004, May.

De Loecker (2004), Do Exports Generate Higher Productivity? Evidence from Slovenia. Katholieke Universiteit Leuven, LICOS Discussion Paper 151/2004, July.

Delgado, Miguel A., Jose C. Farinas and Sonia Ruano (2002), Firm productivity and export markets: a non-parametric approach. *Journal of International Economics* 57, 397–422.

Falvey, Rod, David Greeneway, Zhihong Yu and Joakim Gullstrand (2004), Exports, Restructuring and Industry Productivity Growth. University of Nottingham, GEP Research Paper 2004/40.

Farinas, José C. and Ana Martin-Marcos (2003), Exporting and Economic Performance: Firm-Level Evidence for Spanish Manufacturing. Universidad Complutense and UNED, Madrid, mimeo, April.

Fernandes, Ana M. and Alberto E. Isgut (2005), Learning-by Doing, Learning-by-Exporting, and Productivity: Evidence from Colombia. World Bank Working Paper WPS3544.

Giles, Judith A. and Cara L. Williams (2000a), Export-led Growth: A Survey of the Empirical Literature and Some Non-causality Results. Part I. *Journal of International Trade & Economic Development* 9, 261–337.

Giles, Judith A. and Cara L. Williams (2000b), Export-led Growth: A Survey of the Empirical Literature and Some Non-causality Results. Part II. *Journal of International Trade & Economic Development* 9, 445–470.

Girma, Sourafel, Holger Görg and Eric Strobl (2004), Exports, International Investment, and Plant Performance: Evidence from a Non-parametric Test. *Economics Letters* 83, 317–324.

Girma, Sourafel, David Greenaway and Richard Kneller (2003), Export Market Exit and Performance Dynamics: A Causality Analysis of Matched Firms. *Economics Letters* 80, 181–187.

Girma, Sourafel, David Greenaway and Richard Kneller (2004), Does Exporting Increase Productivity? A Microeconometric Analysis of Matched Firms. *Review of International Economics* 12, 855–866.

Girma, Sourafel, Richard Kneller and Mauro Pisu (2005), Exports versus FDI: An Empirical Test. *Review of World Economics* 141, 193–218.

Greenaway, David, Joakim Gullstrand and Richard Kneller (2005), Exporting May Not Always Boost Firm Level Productivity. *Review of World Economic* 141, 561–582.

Greenaway, David and Richard Kneller (2003), Exporting, Productivity and Agglomeration: A Difference in Difference Analysis of Matched Firms. University of Nottingham, GEP Research Paper 03/45.

Greenaway, David and Richard Kneller (2004a), Exporting and Productivity in the United Kingdom. *Oxford Review of Economic Policy* 20, 358–371.

Greenaway, David and Richard Kneller (2004b), Industry Differences in the Effect of Export Market Entry: Learning by Exporting? University of Nottingham, GEP Research Paper 04/33.

Greenaway, David and Richard Kneller (2005), Firm Heterogeneity, Exporting and Foreign Direct Investment: A Survey. University of Nottingham, GEP Research Paper 2005/32.

Greenaway, David and Zhihong Yu (2004), Firm-Level Interactions between Exporting and Productivity: Industry-Specific Evidence. *Review of World Economics/Weltwirtschaftliches Archiv* 140, 376–392.

Hahn, Chin Hee (2004), Exporting and Performance of Plants: Evidence from Korean Manufacturing. NBER Working Paper 10208, January.

Hallward-Driemeier, Mary, Giuseppe Iarossi and Kenneth L. Sokoloff (2002), Exports and Manufacturing Productivity in East Asia: A Comparative Analysis with Firm-level Data. NBER Working Paper 8894, April.

Hansson, Pär and Nan Nan Lundin (2004), Exports as an Indicator on or Promoter of Successful Swedish Manufacturing Firms in the 1990s. *Review of World Economics/Weltwirtschaftliches Archiv* 140, 415–445.

Heckman, James J., R. J. LaLonde and J. A. Smith (1999), The economics and econometrics of active labor market programs. In: Ashenfelter, O. C. and David Card (Eds.), *Handbook of Labor Economics, Vol. 3A*, Amsterdam: North-Holland, 1865–2097.

Helper, Susan (2000), Economists and Field Research: You Can Observe a Lot Just by Watching. *American Economic Review Papers and Proceedings* 90, 228–232.

Helpman, Elhanan, Marc J. Melitz and Stephen R. Yeaple (2004), Export Versus FDI with Heterogeneous Firms. *American Economic Review* 94, 300–316.

Isgut, Alberto E (2001), What's Different about Exporters? Evidence from Colombian Manufacturing. *Journal of Development Studies* 37, 57–82.

Jensen, J. Bradford and Nathan Musick (1996), Trade, Technology, and Plant Performance. Economics and Statistics Administration, Office of Policy Development, ESA/OPD 96-4, April.

Kimura, Fukunari and Kozo Kiyota (2004), Exports, FDI, and Productivity of Firm: Cause and Effect. Yokohama National University, Faculty of Business Administration, Working Paper Series No. 216, November.

Kostevc, Crt (2005), Performance of Exporters: Scale Effects of Continuous Productivity Improvements. Katholieke Universiteit Leuven, LICOS Discussion Paper 159/2005, July.

Kraay, Aart (2002), Exports and economic performance: evidence from a panel of Chinese enterprises. In Mary-Francoise Renard (Ed.), *China and its Regions. Economic Growth and Reform in Chinese Provinces*. Cheltenham etc.: Elgar, 278–299. (Originally published in Revue d'Economie du Développement, no. 1–2, 1999)

Leamer, Edward E. and James Levinsohn (1994), International Trade Theory: The Evidence. NBER Working Paper 4940.

Liu, Jin-Tan, Meng-Wen Tsou and James K. Hammitt (1999), Export Activity and Productivity: Evidence from the Taiwan Electronics Industry. *Weltwirtschaftliches Archiv/Review of World Economics* 135, 675–691.

López, Ricardo A (2003), Entry to Export Markets and Firm-Level Productivity in Developing Countries. University of California, Los Angeles, mimeo, February.

López, Ricardo A (2005), Trade and Growth: Reconciling the Macroeconomic and Microeconomic Evidence. *Journal of Economic Surveys* 19, 623–648.

Melitz, Marc J, The Impact of Trade on Intra-Industry Reallocations and Aggregate Industry Productivity. *Econometrica* 71, 1695–1725.

Meller, Patricio (1995), Chilean Export Growth, 1970–90: An Assessment. In G. K. Helleiner (Ed.), *Manufacturing for Export in the Developing World. Problems and Possibilities.* London and New York: Routledge, 21–53.

Mengistae, Taye and Catherine Pattillo (2004), Export Orientation and Productivity in Sub-saharan Africa. *IMF Staff Papers* 51, 327–353.

Requena Silvente, Francisco (2005), Changing Export Status and Firm Performance: Evidence from UK Small Firms. *Applied Economics Letters* 12, 567–571.

Sinani, Evis (2003), Export Market Participation: The Importance of Sunk Costs and Spillovers. Center for East European Studies, Copenhagen Business School, mimeo, March.

Sjöholm, Frederic (1999), Exports, Imports and Productivity: Results from Indonesian Establishment Data. *World Development* 27, 705–715.

Tsou, Meng-Wen, Jin-Tan Liu and James Hammitt (2002), Exporting and Productivity. Harvard School of Public Health mimeo, December.

van Biesebroeck, Johannes (2003), Exporting Raises Productivity in Sub-Saharan African Manufacturing Plants. NBER Working Paper 10020, October.

Wagner, Joachim (1995), Exports, Firm Size, and Firm Dynamics. *Small Business Economics* 7, 29–39.

Wagner, Joachim (2002), The Causal Effect of Exports on Firm Size and Labor Productivity: First Evidence from a Matching Approach. *Economics Letters* 77, 287–292.

Wagner, Joachim (2004), Export Intensity and Plant Characteristics: What can we learn from Quantile Regression? Hamburg Institute of International Economics Discussion Paper 304, November. (forthcoming *Review of World Economics*).

Wagner, Joachim (2005a), Exports, foreign direct investment, and productivity: Evidence from German firm level data. Hamburg Institute of International Economics Discussion Paper 318, May. (forthcoming *Applied Economics Letters*).

Wagner, Joachim (2005b), Exporte und Produktivität in mittelständischen Betrieben. Befunde aus der niedersächsischen Industrie (1995–2004). University of Lueneburg, Institute of Economics, Working Paper Series in Economics No. 11, June.

Yasar, Mahmut, Carl H. Nelson and Roderick M. Rejesus (2003), Productivity and Exporting Status of Manufacturing Firms: Evidence from Quantile Regression. Emory University Department of Economics Working Paper 03-23, October.

Yasar, Mahmut and Roderick M. Rejesus (2005), Exporting Status and Firm Performance: Evidence from a Matched Sample. *Economics Letters* 88, 397–402.

Yeaple, Stephen Ross (2005), A Simple Model of Firm Heterogeneity, International Trade, and Wages. *Journal of International Economics* 65, 1–20.

## Appendix

Table 1. Synopsis of findings from empirical studies on exports and productivity using firm level data

| | Core findings | | | |
|---|---|---|---|---|
| Study (published) Country (period covered) | Differences in levels and growth rates between exporters and non-exporters | Pre-entry differences | Post-entry differences | Post-exit differences |
| Baldwin and Gu (2003) Canada (1974–1996) | LP and TFP higher for exporters than for non-exporters; difference increased over time. EP for LP increased from 19–83 percentage points between 1974 and 1996. | LP and growth of LP higher for starters than for non-exporters | Entrants had faster LP growth than non-entrants. | Exiters 13 percent less productive than continuers; exiters had slower growth of LP than continuers. |
| Meller (1995) Chile (1986–1989) | LP significantly higher in small and large export firms than in non-export firms; productivity differential differs between industries. | | | |
| Alvarez and López (2005) Chile (1990–1996) | EP positive and significant for LP and TFP. Productivity differentials differ considerably by industry. | Firms that enter export have higher LP and TFP than non-exporters. Firms make conscious efforts to increase productivity before starting to export. | Differences in LP and TFP growth insignificant or negative for export starters compared to non-exporters. Same result for all industry but wood Products. For matched firms no effect on TFP growth, weak positive for LP growth. | |

*(Continued)*

Table 1. (*Continued*)

| | Core findings | | | |
|---|---|---|---|---|
| Study (published) Country (period covered) | Differences in levels and growth rates between exporters and non-exporters | Pre-entry differences | Post-entry differences | Post-exit differences |
| Kraay (2002) China (1988–1992) | LP and TFP significantly higher in exporters than in non-exporters. EP positive and significant for LP and TFP. For established exporters, past exports are positively related to LP and TFP today, controlling for past firm performance and unobserved firm characteristics. | | For new entrants to export markets learning effects are insignificant and occasionally negative. | |
| Clerides, Lach and Tybout (1998) Colombia (1981–1991) | LP higher for exporting firms than for non-exporters. | LP higher for export starters than for other groups of firms (ongoing exporters, non-exporters and export stoppers). | LP improves after starting to export. | LP shows worst performance compared to other groups, particularly around time of exit. |

| | | | | |
|---|---|---|---|---|
| Isgut (2001) Colombia (1981–1991) | LP higher for exporting firms than for non-exporters, 80–100 percent for plants up to 100 employees and 27–32 percent for larger plants. EP ca. 45 percent. Growth of LP not significantly different for exporters and non-exporters over five year horizon. | Pre-entry premia 20–24 percent. Pre-entry growth 3–4 percent higher in future starters. | LP growth rate differences between export starters and non-exporters not significant for one year horizon; LP grows 1.5 percent faster for starters over horizon five years after entry. | Growth of LP not significantly lower for stoppers compared to non-exporters over five year horizon. |
| Fernandes and Isgut (2005) Colombia (1981–1991) | | Young plants that enter export markets have 3–4 percent higher annual growth rates of TFP than young plants that never export. Results robust to use of matching. Effects much smaller for old firms. Same for TFP-effects of additional years of export experience. | | |

*(Continued)*

Table 1. (*Continued*)

| | Core findings | | | |
|---|---|---|---|---|
| Study (published) Country (period covered) | Differences in levels and growth rates between exporters and non-exporters | Pre-entry differences | Post-entry differences | Post-exit differences |
| Sinani (2003) Estonia (1994–1999) | LP higher for exporting firms than for non-exporters; growth of LP much higher for exporters than for non-exporters. | | | |
| Bernard and Wagner (1997) Germany (1978–1992) | LP 3–4 percent lower in smaller export firms, but 30–50 percent higher in larger export firms. EP about 20 percent on average, increasing with share of exports in total sales. Growth of LP slower in exporting than in non-exporting firms. | Pre-entry premia 2–5 percent but insign. Pre-entry growth 1.0–1.6 percent higher in future starters, but difference insignificant. | Growth of LP significantly higher for export starters than for non-exporters in the year after exporting starts (4.8–6.7 percent). | Growth of LP significantly lower for export stoppers than for non-exporters in the year after exportingstops (3.6–8.4 percent). |

| | | | |
|---|---|---|---|
| Bernard and Wagner (2001) Germany (1978–1992) | | Higher productivity strongly positively correlated with future export entry, controlling for unobserved firm effects. | |
| Wagner (2002) Germany (1978–1989) | | EP in year before start positive but insignificant. | Growth of LP in export starters higher than in matched non-starters but difference between both groups not statistically significant. |
| Wagner (2005a) Germany (1995) | Productivity distribution of exporters dominates that of non-exporters | | |
| Wagner (2005b) Germany (1995–2004) | Productivity distribution of exporters dominates that of non-exporters. Same holds for growth rates in some periods. EP positive and significant in fixed-effects model (6.7 percent). | Three years before entry future exporters had significantly higher productivity in two out of seven years. Growth rates of LP did not differ between starters and non-starters in years before start. | LP growth higher for three out of four cohorts of starters compared to matched non-starters in three years following start but effect not statistically significant. |

*(Continued)*

Table 1. (*Continued*)

| | Core findings | | | |
|---|---|---|---|---|
| Study (published) Country (period covered) | Differences in levels and growth rates between exporters and non-exporters | Pre-entry differences | Post-entry differences | Post-exit differences |
| Arnold and Hussinger (2005a) Germany (1992–2004) | TFP higher for exporters than for non-exporters; high-productivity firms significantly more likely to be exporters, ceteris paribus. | In the two periods preceding entry future exporters experience signific. increase in TFP. Productivity Granger-causes exporting. | Productivity gap between exporters and non-exporters does not widen in years after entry. Exporting does not Granger-cause productivity. For matched firms there are no differences in levels or growth of TFP between exporters and non-exporters in years after entry. | |
| Arnold and Hussinger (2005b) Germany (1996–2002) | Productivity distribution of exporters dominates that of non-exporters | | | |
| Sjöholm (1999) Indonesia (1980–1991) | LP higher for exporting firms than for non-exporters; growth of LP higher for exporters and increasing with share of exports in output. | | | |

| | | | | |
|---|---|---|---|---|
| Blalock and Gertler (2004) Indonesia (1990–1996) | LP higher for exporting firms than for non-exporters. | Productivity does not rise prior to exporting. | Firms experience a jump in productivity of about 2–5 percent following the initiation of exporting. Effect of exporting is positive in all 10 industries, significant in 7. | No reduction in productivity after stopping to export. |
| Castellani (2002) Italy (1989–1994) | LP higher for exporting firms than for non-exporters; growth of LP not significantly different. Productivity growth higher in firms with a higher share of exports in total sales. | LP higher in future export starters than in non-starters three years before entry; growth of LP not different for the two groups of firms. LP and growth of LP have no impact on the probability to start to export, ceteris. paribus. | | |
| Castellani and Zanfei (2004) Italy (1996) | LP and TFP higher for exporters than for non-exporters (means); no difference when controlling for other variables, but this might reflect bias in favour of large firms. | | | |

(Continued)

Table 1. (*Continued*)

| | Core findings | | | |
|---|---|---|---|---|
| Study (published) Country (period covered) | Differences in levels and growth rates between exporters and non-exporters | Pre-entry differences | Post-entry differences | Post-exit differences |
| Girma, Görg and Strobl (2004) Ireland (2000) | LP on average higher for exporters than non-exporters, but the hypothesis of identical distribution of productivity cannot be rejected for exporters relative to non-exporters. | | | |
| Kimura and Kiyota (2004) Japan (1994–2000) | EP 3.4 percent in a fixed-effects model controlling for year, industry and firm characteristics | Firms with higher TFP have higher probability to enter export markets (based on random effects probit model). | Exporters have 2.4 percent higher TFP growth than non-exporters if initial TFP level is controlled for. | |
| Aw, Chung and Roberts (2000) Korea (Republic of) (1983–1993) | Total factor productivity (TFP) between 3.9 percent and 31.1 percent higher in five industries. TFP growth not different between exporters and non-exporters. | Higher TFP levels and growth rates for entrants prior to entry not significant. | Entrants have higher TFP than non-exporters. | Exiting plants have higher TFP than non-exporters in two industries; no difference in three industries. |

| | | | | |
|---|---|---|---|---|
| Hahn (2004) Korea | LP and TFP higher for exporters than for non-exporters. EP about 50–20 percent for LP, 2.5–7.5 percent for TFP. | LP higher for entrants prior to entry than for non-entrants, but no difference for TFP. No strong evidence for difference in growth rates of productivity ex ante. | Starters widen TFP gap with never exporters and close gap with ever exporters. Effect pronounced in period after entry. | Stoppers show decrease in TFP, absolute and relative to ever exporters, starter and never exporters, before and after exit. |
| Bernard (1995) Mexico (1986–1990) | LP almost 30 percent (shipments) or more than 50 percent (value added) greater for exporters. EP 34 percent (value added). Growth of LP not significantly different for exporters and non-exporters. | | Growth of LP not significantly different for export-starters and non-exporters. | Growth of LP not significantly different for export stoppers and non-exporters. |
| Clerides, Lach and Tybout (1998) Mexico (1986–1990) | LP higher for exporting firms than for non-exporters, export starters and export stoppers. | LP not higher for export starters than for non-exporters and lower than for exporters. | No suggestion of a learning effect from exporting. | LP shows worst performance compared to other groups. |

(*Continued*)

Table 1. (*Continued*)

| | Core findings | | | |
|---|---|---|---|---|
| Study (published) Country (period covered) | Differences in levels and growth rates between exporters and non-exporters | Pre-entry differences | Post-entry differences | Post-exit differences |
| Clerides, Lach and Tybout (1998) Morocco (1984–1991) | LP higher for exporting firms than for non-exporters. | LP higher for export starters than for non-exporters. | LP improves after starting to export. | LP sinks after stopping to export |
| Damijan, Polanec and Prasnikar (2004) Slovenia (1994–2002) | Productivity of exporters higher than of non-exporters; firms that export to more markets are on average more labor productive. | Productivity in starters higher than in non-starters in years before starting. Productivity difference higher for firms that start to export to more advanced markets. | No continuous productivity improvement from exporting but short run gains, only from serving advanced, high-wage foreign markets. | Firms ceasing exporting exhibit lower productivity levels than old exporters up to 20%. |
| De Loecker (2004) Slovenia (1994–2000) | EP about 30 percent for value added per worker. | | For matched firms starting to export raises productivity instantly and also in the years following. Analyses by industry find positive effects for most sectors, but these are significant in about half of them only. | |

| | | | |
|---|---|---|---|
| Kostevc (2005) Slovenia (1994–2002) | Exporters are more productive than non-exporting firms. Productivity distribution of exporters stochastically dominance that of firms selling on the domestic market only. | | Using matching and a difference-in-differences approach reveals relative productivity improvements innewly exporting firms, but these tend to dissipate shortly after initial entry. |
| Delgado, Farinas and Ruano (2002) Spain (1991–1996) | TFP distribution for exporters stochastically dominates the distribution for non-exporters. | TFP distribution for export starters stochastically dominates the distribution for non-exporters prior to entry. | No evidence of divergence of distribution of TFP growth between new exporters and non-exporters; but post-entry growth greater for young entering exporters compared to young non-exporters. |

*(Continued)*

Table 1. *(Continued)*

| | Core findings | | | |
|---|---|---|---|---|
| Study (published) Country (period covered) | Differences in levels and growth rates between exporters and non-exporters | Pre-entry differences | Post-entry differences | Post-exit differences |
| Farinas and Martin-Marcos (2003) Spain (1990–1999) | LP and TFP higher for exporters than for non-exporters. EP 17 percent. | LP ex-ante higher for entering exporters than for continuing non-exporters. | LP of entering exporters significantly higher than LP of non-exporters. Growth of LP and TFP not different between entering exporters and continuing non-exporters. | LP of exiting exporters not different from non-exporters; dito for rate of growth of LP and TFP. |
| Hansson and Lundin (2004) Sweden (1990–1999) | Productivity higher for exporters than for non-exporters: EP 6.3 percent for TFP. | LP and TFP higher for future starters two years before entry, but lower (not significant) three years before. Differences in growth of TFP and LP not significant. | No significant differences in TFP growth between various export groups and non-exporters. Starters LP growth higher than non-exporters'. | |
| Greenaway, Gullstrand and Kneller (2005) Sweden (1980–1997) | LP higher for exporters than for non-exporters; TFP lower for exporters, but around 10 percent higher after controlling for industry fixed effects. | TFP lower for starters in the year of entry than for never-exporters. | For matched firms first time entry into export markets is not associated with faster TFP growth compared to non-exporters. | |

| | | | | |
|---|---|---|---|---|
| Aw/Hwang (1995) Taiwan (1986) | LP 36 percent greater for export-oriented than domestic-market-oriented firms in electronics industry; differences vary between products examined. | | | |
| Aw, Chen and Roberts (1997) Taiwan (1981–1991) | Higher total factor productivity for exporting firms relative to non-exporters from 11 percent in basic metals to 24 percent in textiles. | Firms that eventually entered the export market were more productive than their non-entering counterparts in the years prior to their entry. | There may be some productivity improvement associated with exporting. | Firms exiting the export market have higher productivity than non-exporters. |
| Liu, Tsou and Hammitt (1999) Taiwan (1989–1993) | LP higher for exporters than non-exporters in electronics industry. EP about 15 percent, and increasing with export share. LP growth not different for exporters and non-exporters. | Pre-entry growth ca. 8–12 percent higher in future starters. | Growth of LP substantially higher for export starters than for non-exporters (6.9–8.7 percent). | Growth of LP slower in export-stoppers than in non-exporters, but coefficients not significant. |

(Continued)

Table 1. (*Continued*)

| | Core findings | | | |
|---|---|---|---|---|
| Study (published) Country (period covered) | Differences in levels and growth rates between exporters and non-exporters | Pre-entry differences | Post-entry differences | Post-exit differences |
| Aw, Chung and Roberts (2000) Taiwan (1981–1991) | Total factor productivity (TFP) between 11.8 percent and 27.6 percent higher for exporters than non-exporters in five industries. TFP growth in three industries not different for exporters and non-exporters, lower in two industries. | Entrants have higher TFP prior to entry than non-exporters. Initial difference widens after entry in three industries. | Entrants are 13.3% to 18.9% more productive than non-exporters. | Exiting plants have average TFP levels 4.4–10.3 percent higher than non-exporters. Plants that exit fall further behind exporting plants in the years following exit (significant in three industries). |
| Tsou, Liu and Hammitt (2002) Taiwan (1986–1996) | Growth of LP significantly higher for plants that export across all three census periods compared to non-exporters, but result sensitive to cyclical patterns: little difference in downturn; exporters outperform non-exporters in upturn period. | | Growth of TFP substantially higher for export starters than for non-exporters. | Growth of TFP not different between stoppers and non-exporters. |

| | | | |
|---|---|---|---|
| Aw, Roberts and Winston (2005) Taiwan (1986–1996) | | | Firms that export and invest in R&D and/or worker training have signific. higher future productivity than firms that only export. Export experience is an important source of productivity growth for firms from electronics. |
| Yasar, Nelson and Rejesus (2003) Turkey (1990–1996) | EP around 19 percent (OLS regression). EP vary significantly from 9 percent to 21 percent from lower quantile to higher quantile (quantile regression). | Productivity about 23 percent higher for entrants compared to non-exporters (OLS). Difference varies from 11–21 percent between lowest and highest quantile (quantile regression). | Productivity about 17 percent higher in stoppers compared to non-exporters (OLS). Difference varies from 7–21 percent between lowest and highest quantile. |

(*Continued*)

Table 1. (*Continued*)

| | Core findings | | | |
|---|---|---|---|---|
| Study (published) Country (period covered) | Differences in levels and growth rates between exporters and non-exporters | Pre-entry differences | Post-entry differences | Post-exit differences |
| Yasar and Rejesus (2005) Turkey (1990–1996) | | | For matched firms entrants have higher TFP and labor productivity growth than non-entrants. | For matched firms the productivity growth of continuous exporters is higher than that of firms leaving the export market. |
| Girma, Greenaway and Kneller (2003) United Kingdom (1991–1997) | | | | For matched firm exit has negative albeit weak effect on TFP in the year of exit; no effect detected for later years. |

| | | | |
|---|---|---|---|
| Greenaway and Kneller (2003) United Kingdom (1989–2002) | Productivity of exporters 5.4 percent above industry mean, of non-exporters 4.6 percent below the mean. | | For matched firms entry is associated with significant increase in LP. No robust evidence of productivity effects beyond the first few years for all firms, but for firms more exposed to export markets. |
| Girma, Greenaway and Kneller (2004) United Kingdom (1988–1999) | Productivity higher for exporters than for non-exporters. | Entrants more productive before entry than non-entrants. | For matched firms: On entry year, exporters experience TFP growth rate about 1.6 percentage points higher than non-starters. TFP continues to grow by an extra percentage point in the following year. Increase in share of exports raises rate at which TFP grows after entry. |

*(Continued)*

Table 1. (*Continued*)

| | Core findings | | | |
|---|---|---|---|---|
| Study (published) Country (period covered) | Differences in levels and growth rates between exporters and non-exporters | Pre-entry differences | Post-entry differences | Post-exit differences |
| Greenaway and Kneller (2004a) | LP 2.2 percent, TFP 9.7 percent higher for exporters compared to non-exporters; EP 11.4 percent for LP and 8.3 percent for TFP. | Past TFP positive effect on entry. Past productivity growth of future entrants higher compared to non-entrants. | For unmatched firms, TFP growth faster in years of and after entry than for continuing non-exporters. For matched firms differences are lower and only significant in entry year. | |
| Greenaway and Kneller (2004b) United Kingdom (1990–1998) | | Ceteris paribus the probability of export entry is increasing in the level of FTP. | For matched firms productivity growth in new export firms is on average 2.9 percent faster than in non-export firms. Effect is consistently lower in industries in which existing exposure to foreign firms is greater. | |
| Greenaway and Yu (2004) United Kingdom (Chemical Industry) (1989–1999) | Exporters more productive than non-exporters; EP 10.4 percent (output per worker) and 9.1 percent (TFP). | Higher TFP leads to higher exporting probability. | Learning-by-exporting effect strongest among new entrants, weaker for firms with more past export experience and negative for established exporters. | |

| | | | | |
|---|---|---|---|---|
| Girma, Kneller and Pisu (2005) United Kingdom (1990–1996) | Productivity distribution of exporters dominates that of non-exporters | | | |
| Requena Silvente (2005) United Kingdom (small firms) (1994–2000) | Regular exporters, irregular exporters, and new exporters have higher sales per worker than non-exporters | | Small firms experience substantial improvement of productivity the year they switch from being non-exporters to become exporting. | Small firms experience substantial deterioration of productivity the year they switch from being exporters to to stop exporting. |
| Bernard and Jensen (1995) United States (1976–1987) | LP approx. a third greater for exporters across all plant sizes. EP about 15 percent. | | | |
| Jensen and Musick (1996) United States (1987–1992) | EP 13 percent in 1987 and 14 percent in 1992 Growth of LP not significantly different for exporters and non-exporters. | | Growth of LP not significantly different for export-starters and non-exporters. | Growth of LP not significantly different for export-stoppers and non-exporters. |

(Continued)

Table 1. (*Continued*)

| | Core findings | | | |
|---|---|---|---|---|
| Study (published) Country (period covered) | Differences in levels and growth rates between exporters and non-exporters | Pre-entry differences | Post-entry differences | Post-exit differences |
| Bernard and Jensen (1999) United States (1984–1992) | EP ca. 20 percent (1984), ca. 16 percent (1987), ca. 18 percent (1992). Short run: Higher growth rate of LP in exporters than in non-exporters; long run: no difference. | Pre-entry premia 7–8 percent. Pre-entry growth in future starters generally not statistically signif. different compared to non-starters. | Growth of LP significantly higher for export starters than non-exporters in the short, medium and long run. | Growth of LP significantly lower in export stoppers than in non-exporters in the short, medium and long run. |
| Bernard and Jensen (2004a) United States (1983–1992) | Plants that always export 8–9 percent more productive than plants that never export. Exporters have 0.72 percent lower productivity growth rates per year than similar plants producing solely for domestic market. | Two years before starting entrants have productivity levels significantly above continuing non-exporters, but significantly below continuing exporters. | In the year that they enter starters have significantly faster productivity growth rates than other firms. | Plants that exit the export market have productivity growth rates 0.2–0.9 percent lower than continuing non-exporters. |

| | | | |
|---|---|---|---|
| Bernard and Jensen (2004b) United States (1984–1992) | | More productive plants have higher probability of starting to export, but controlling for plant fixed effects soaks the effect. Productivity effect is even negative (though insignificant) in GMM-first difference specification. | |
| Bigsten *et al.* (2000) Cameroon (1992–1995) Ghana (1991–1993) Kenya (1992–1994) Zimbabwe (1992–1994) | Exporters exhibit higher average efficiency levels than non-exporters. | Initial exporters tend to exhibit significantly higher levels of efficiency than other firms. | Exporting in one period raises efficiency in the next period; the first year of exporting raises efficiency by 14 percent. |

(*Continued*)

Table 1. (*Continued*)

| | Core findings | | | |
|---|---|---|---|---|
| Study (published) Country (period covered) | Differences in levels and growth rates between exporters and non-exporters | Pre-entry differences | Post-entry differences | Post-exit differences |
| Hallward-Driemeier, Iarossi and Sokoloff (2002) Indonesia, Korea, Malaysia, Phillipines, Thailand (1996–1998) | TFP larger for exporters than non-exporters; gap is larger the less developed is the local market. Firms that export from the beginning have higher levels of TFP years later, due to different firm policy (investment in fixed and human capital etc.). | | | |
| Van Biesebroeck (2003) Nine sub-Saharan African countries (1992–1996) | EP for LP about 50 percent. Growth of LP higher for exporters than for non-exporters. | LP higher for export starters than for non-exporters prior to entry. | LP not different between newly entered and continuous exporters, but higher compared to non-exporters. | LP lower in export-stoppers than in continuous exporters, but higher than in non-exporting firms. |

| | |
|---|---|
| Mengistae and Pattillo (2004) Three sub-Saharan African countries (1992–1995) | TFP 17.4 percent higher on average, 13.6 percent for Kenya. Difference higher for direct exporters, insignificant for indirect exporters. TFP growth on average 10 percent higher for exporters. Difference again higher for direct exporters, insign. for indirect exporters. |

*Note*: Studies are listed in alphabetical order for the countries covered and chronologically for each country (using the most recent version of the study). Studies covering up to three countries are listed separately for each country (if information on each country is available); multi-country studies covering more than three countries are listed at the end of the table.
LP = labour productivity (total value of shipments per worker or value-added per worker.
TFP = Total factor productivity, usually calculated as the residual from an estimated Cobb-Douglas-type production function.
EP = exporter premia: ceteris paribus percentage difference of LP between exporters and non-exporters, usually based on OLS regressions controlling for industries, regions, firm size (number of employees) and year.

## Chapter 2

# International Trade and Firm Performance: A Survey of Empirical Studies since 2006

Joachim Wagner

**Abstract**

The literature on international trade and firm performance grows exponentially. This chapter attempts to summarize what we learn from this literature to guide future empirical and theoretical work in this area. The focus is on the empirical part of the literature that consists of recently published papers using data for firms from manufacturing or services industries to study the links between international trade (exports and imports) and dimensions of firm performance (productivity, wages, profitability and survival).

*Keywords*: International trade, firm performance, empirical studies, survey

**JEL Classification:** F14

## 1. Introduction

During the recent past, the literature on international firm activities and firm performance grew exponentially The purpose of this survey is to summarize major new insights from these studies and to identify topics for future research.

Any attempt to summarize what we learn from this literature, however, has to be selective and has to focus on a subset of topics to keep the project tractable. The present survey

— is restricted to the economics literature,[1]
— focuses on the empirical part of that literature and does not deal with theoretical models,[2]
— looks at studies using micro-data at the level of the firm (establishment or enterprise) only and does not deal with studies that use aggregate data at the industry or country level,[3]
— covers only more recent papers published since 2006[4]
— and has a focus on international trade.[5]

This survey is aimed at readers who are basically familiar with the topics dealt with and the concepts, terms and methods used in the literature on international firm activities and firm performance (maybe from the earlier surveys by Greenaway and Kneller (2007) or Wagner (2007a)) but who did not follow all the new topics discussed in the recent literature.

The survey is organized as follows. Section 2 reviews recent studies on international trade and productivity. Going beyond earlier surveys that focused on the relation between manufacturing exports and productivity, this survey pays special attention to studies on export destination and productivity, imports and productivity, and trade and productivity in the service sector. Section 3 looks beyond productivity and reviews findings on international trade and further dimensions of firm performance, i.e. wages (Section 3.1), profits (Section 3.2) and firm survival (Section 3.3). Section 4 concludes with suggestions for further research.

[1]For a survey and meta-analysis of studies on the relation between internationalization and firm performance from the international management literature, see Bausch, Fritz and Boeseke (2007) and Bausch and Krist (2007).

[2]The recent theoretical literature on heterogeneous firms and trade is reviewed by Redding (2010).

[3]A comprehensive survey of studies on the effects of international trade on productivity and economic growth based on macro data is provided by Singh (2010).

[4]The earlier literature is surveyed in Greenaway and Kneller (2007) and Wagner (2007a).

[5]For a review of the literature on foreign direct investment and productivity, see Hayakawa, Machikita and Kimura (2011). For inward foreign direct investment and a survey of empirical studies on productivity differentials between foreign-owned firms and domestic firms, see Barba Navaretti and Venables (2004, pp. 155–162); for offshoring and productivity, see Wagner (2011a).

## 2. New Evidence on International Trade and Productivity

The big picture that emerged from the previous survey by Wagner (2007a) is remarkably clear-cut:

— The findings for pre-entry differences present substantial evidence in favor of the self-selection hypothesis: Future export starters tend to be more productive than future non-exporters years before they enter the export market, and often have higher *ex-ante* growth rates of productivity.
— Evidence regarding the learning-by-exporting hypothesis is somewhat more mixed: Results for post-entry differences in performance between export starters and non-exporters point to faster productivity growth for the former group in some studies only. This picture was largely confirmed in a recent survey by Singh (2010) which includes papers published between 2006 and 2008, and by a publication of the ISGEP (2008) that uses comparable micro-level panel data for 14 countries to look at the relationships between exports and productivity on the basis of identically specified empirical models. The ISGEP study finds that exporter premia vary substantially among countries and that on average productivity premia are larger for countries with lower export participation rates, with more restrictive trade policies, lower per capita GDP, less effective government and worse regulatory quality, and for countries exporting to relatively more distant markets.[6]

The authors of the ISGEP study also point out that the paucity of evidence on learning-by-exporting should be qualified, as it might be dependent on the specific methodology utilized (ISGEP (2008), p. 631). De Loecker (2010) shows that current methods that are used to test for learning-by-exporting are biased towards rejecting the hypothesis of positive effects of exports on productivity. For

[6]As has recently been shown by Powell and Wagner (2011), exporter premia may also vary substantially within the productivity distribution of firms within a country. In their study for Germany they find that the exporter premium is larger at the bottom end of the productivity distribution.

a recent survey of the learning-by-exporting literature, see Silva, Afonso and Africano (2010d) and the meta-study by Martins and Yang (2009).

In this section, we will go beyond the scope of earlier surveys and focus on three issues that have emerged only more recently: Export destination and productivity, imports and productivity and international trade and productivity of firms in the service sector.

## 2.1. *Export destination and productivity in manufacturing firms*

The findings from the literature on exports and productivity imply that plants that export to a larger number of foreign markets have to be more productive than plants that serve a smaller number of foreign markets only, because at least some of the extra costs mentioned recur for each market (e.g. preparing a user's manual in another language, or checking the relevant national laws). Lawless (2009) presents a simple theoretical model that is based on the seminal contributions by Melitz (2003) and Chaney (2008) and that comprises this testable prediction.

Positive productivity effects of exporting (learning-by-exporting) can be expected to differ between (groups of) destination countries. Productivity improvements due to learning will be higher if the destination countries are highly developed and exporting firms have to compete with or supply to firms that operate next to the technological frontier and use the latest vintage of capital goods and best practices in management to produce innovative products (see, e.g. De Loecker (2007)).

Only recently, empirical studies started to look at exports by a firm broken down by destination regions or countries. These studies apply the standard approach used in empirical studies on the exporter productivity premium when investigating the relationship between exports and productivity by destination country or region. They reveal new insights and shed light on hitherto unknown facts.

Table 1 summarizes[7] 25 microeconometric studies on export destination and productivity for firms from 11 different countries, most of which are highly industrialized western countries and include also two studies that were published before 2006.

Most of the studies focus on the different (groups of) destination countries. The number of countries exported to per se is only investigated in Muuls and Pisu (2009), Castellani, Serti and Tomasi (2010), Andersson, Lööf and Johansson (2008) and Eliasson, Hansson and Lindvert (2009).

While 5 studies use cross-section data only, 20 are based on panel data that allow to control for unobserved heterogeneity via fixed effects and that offer the opportunity to look at the direction of the relationship between productivity and destination of exports by testing for the presence of *ex-ante* differences (that existed before exporting to a destination started) and positive effects of exporting to a destination on firm performance (learning-by-exporting to a destination).

Although results are not strictly comparable between the studies due to differences in, among others, the number and type of destinations looked at (e.g. EU vs. non-EU; areas defined according to per capita income; or a large number of destination countries), the definition of the sample used (establishments or enterprises; cut-off point of number of employees), the period under investigation, and the statistical methods applied, a big picture emerges that can be sketched as follows:

(1) *The number of export markets served increases with productivity* (Belgium — Muuls and Pisu (2009); Germany — Wagner

[7]Here (and in all other tables in this literature survey), important results from empirical studies are summarized qualitatively only. Any attempt to reproduce the quantitative results by stating the size of the estimated coefficients and effects would suggest a high degree of comparability across the studies. This, however, is not given due to differences in the unit of analysis (establishment vs. enterprise), the sampling frame (all firms vs. firm with a number of employees above a certain threshold only), the specification of the empirical models estimated and the econometric methods applied. This point is discussed in the concluding Section 4.

Table 1. Microeconometric studies on export destination and productivity

| Country Author(s) (year of publication) | Period covered Areas covered | Topics investigated | Methods used | Important findings |
|---|---|---|---|---|
| Belgium Pisu (2008) | 1998–2005 Four groups of countries by per capita income | Exports and productivity by destination | Regression; matching approaches; diff-in-diff | Exporters to more developed economies have superior *ex-ante* productivity levels than non-exporters and firms exporting to less developed countries. No causal effect of export on productivity irrespective of development level of destination countries. |
| Belgium Muuls and Pisu (2009) | 1996–2004 Country of destination | Facts about Belgium firms | Descriptive statistics; regressions | Firms tend to serve only few foreign markets. Negative relation between number of exporting firms and number of export destinations served. Number of export markets served increase with productivity. |
| France Bellone, Guillou and Nesta (2010) | 2005 Europe vs. rest of the world | TFP differences between non-exporters, exporters to Europe, and global exporters | *t*-test; Kolmogorov–Smirnov test; OLS; Quantile regression | Global exporters have higher productivity than intra-Europe exporters while the TFP distribution of intra-Europe exporters is not significantly different from the one of non-exporters. No exporter premium for only intra-Europe exporters, but high and significant for global exporters. Export premia are very stable over the different quintiles, but tend to be higher for highest quintiles. |

| | | | | |
|---|---|---|---|---|
| Germany (West/East) Wagner (2007b) | 2004 eurozone vs. non-euro zone | Productivity differences | *t*-test; Kolmogorov–Smirnov test; with and without top/bottom one percent of the productivity distribution | Exporters inside eurozone more productive than firms selling in Germany only, but less productive than firms selling outside the eurozone too |
| Germany Verardi and Wagner (2010) | 2003–2006 Eurozone vs. Non-eurozone | Productivity premia for exporters to eurozone and beyond; test for self-selection | Fixed effects linear panel data model — standard and robust version | Exporters beyond eurozone are more productive than exporters to eurozone only; self-selection for exporters beyond eurozone only. Robust estimation methods point to tiny exporter premia only. |
| Ireland Ruane and Sutherland (2005) | 1991–1998 Exports to UK vs. global exports | Exports and performance by destination | Regression | Non-UK exporters are larger than UK exporters in terms of turnover, pay increasingly higher wages, employ a higher proportion of skilled labor and are more productive. |
| Ireland Lawless (2009) | 2000–2004 >50 countries of destination | Productivity and destinations | Descriptive statistics; OLS | Firms with greater market coverage tend to be more productive. No rigid ordering of destinations found. Firm-level export growth largely driven by existing markets; most growth due to continuing exporters. Changes in market portfolios of exporters are relatively common occurrence. |

(*Continued*)

Table 1. (*Continued*)

| Country Author(s) (year of publication) | Period covered Areas covered | Topics investigated | Methods used | Important findings |
|---|---|---|---|---|
| Italy Serti and Tomasi (2009) | 1993–1997 Geographical areas | Firm performance and export destinations | Regression | Productivity levels higher for firms exporting to high medium income countries compared to firms exporting to European and low income countries. Results more mixed in terms of size and workforce composition. *Ex-ante* trade premia higher for those firms that start investing in more advanced countries. |
| Italy Crinò and Epifani (2009) | 2003 EU-15; new EU members; other European countries; North America; Latin America; China; other Asian countries; Africa; Oceania | Export intensity and productivity | Descriptive statistics; regression | TFP strongly negatively correlated with export intensity to low income destinations and uncorrelated with export intensity to high income destinations, conditional on exporting. |
| Italy Castellani, Serti and Tomasi (2010) | 1993–1997 Countries of destination | Differences between firms with different numbers of countries of destination | Descriptive statistics; non-parametric kernel regressions; pooled OLS and fixed effects | Bulk of firms trade only with a few countries, but a handful of diversified traders account for the majority of exports. Firms that export to larger number of countries are larger, more productive, and more capital intensive. |
| Italy Conti, Turco and Maggioni (2010) | 2003 EU-25; EU-15; non-EU; industrial markets outside Europe | Exporters in services and productivity | Descriptive statistics; regression | Only more productive and skilled labor endowed firms have a higher probability to export to industrial countries outside Europe. |

| | | | | |
|---|---|---|---|---|
| Japan Wakasugi and Tanaka (2009) | 2005 Asia, North America, Europe | Productivity and exports by destination area | Regression | Productivity of firms simultaneously internationalized in multiple regions higher than in firms exporting in a single region. |
| Japan Yashiro and Hirano (2009) | 2002–2005 Asia, Western countries, other regions | Productivity effects of export boom | Diff-in-diff | Only exporters serving worldwide enjoyed significant advantage in productivity growth. |
| Portugal Silva, Afonso and Africano (2010a) | 1996–2003 All destination countries of exporters | Self-selection into exporting | Random-effects probit OLS regression | Firms that start exporting only to developed countries most productive in pre-entry period, together with firms that export to multiple countries. Self-selection varies over markets, suggesting different productivity thresholds. |
| Portugal Silva, Afonso and Africano (2010b) | 1996–2003 All destination countries of exporters | Learning-by-exporting | Propensity score matching, diff-in-diff estimator | No learning effect for exporters only to non-developed countries; fast effect for exporters only to EU countries; firms that mix several types of destinations get moderately positive effects. |
| Russia Wilhelmsson and Kozlov (2007) | 1996–2002 OECD vs. former Soviet Union (CIS) and other countries | Self-selection vs. learning-by-exporting | Fixed effects, pooled OLS, GMM | Firms that export mainly to OECD more productive than firms that exporter mainly to CIS or other countries; evidence for learning-by-exporting inconclusive. |

(*Continued*)

Table 1. (*Continued*)

| Country Author(s) (year of publication) | Period covered Areas covered | Topics investigated | Methods used | Important findings |
|---|---|---|---|---|
| Slovenia Damijan, Polanec and Prasnikar (2004) | 1994–2002 Countries of destination | Productivity and different export markets | Descriptive statistics; OLS, fixed effects, system GMM | Firms that export to more markets are on average more labor productive. Only high productivity firms can afford to export to advanced markets. Exporters can benefit from exporting through learning and competition effects only when serving more demanding advanced markets. |
| Slovenia Damijan and Kostevc (2006) | 1994–2002 ex-Yugoslavia vs. EU | Learning-by-exporting | Correlations; matching, diff-in-diff | Both firms exporting to EU markets as well as those exporting to former Yugoslav countries experience only a one-time increase in their productivity the year after they start exporting. |
| Slovenia De Loecker (2007) | 1994–2000 8 groups of countries | Productivity and different export markets | Propensity score matching; regression | Positive correlation between number of destinations and productivity. Productivity premia considerably higher for firms shipping products to more developed regions. Firms exporting only to low income regions get additional productivity gains, however, lower than their counterparts exporting to high income countries. |
| Slovenia Kostevc (2009) | 1994–2002 EU, Eastern and Central Europe, ex-Yugoslavia | Productivity differences *ex-ante* and learning-by-exporting | OLS; System GMM | More efficient exporters choose to serve more demanding markets; evidence of the learning process not conclusive. |

| | | | | |
|---|---|---|---|---|
| Spain Blanes-Cristóbal *et al.* (2008) | 1990–2002 EU, OECD, rest of the world | Sunk exporting cost differences between export destination markets | Descriptive statistics | Share of exports, advertisement, R&D on sales and presence of foreign capital larger for firms that export to the EU non-exclusively and to OECD. Exporters to EU more productive than other exporters and than non-exporters. |
| | | | Panel probit | Sunk costs differ among markets, higher in developed markets than in rest of the world. |
| Spain Mánez-Castillejo, Rochina-Barrachina and Sanchis-Llopis (2010) | 1990–2002 EU; rest OECD; rest of the world | Learning-by-exporting, firm size, and area of export destination | Descriptive statistics | Level of diversification across areas substantially higher for large firms than for small firms, and higher diversification in destination markets is expected to be associated with higher learning opportunities. |
| Spain Esteve-Pérez, Pallardó-López and Requena-Silvente (2011) | 1997–2006 Full portfolio of destinations (max. 122 countries) | Duration of firm-destination export relationships | Survival analysis | Firm productivity enhances duration of trade with low-risk countries but has no effect on trade survival with high-risk countries. |
| Sweden Andersson, Lööf and Johansson (2008) | 1997–2004 Number of countries of destination | Productivity differences | GLS random effects; two-step GMM | Exporter premium for labor productivity increases with the number of countries which firms export to. |
| Sweden Eliasson, Hansson and Lindvert (2009) | 1997–2006 Number of countries of destination | Productivity differences matching | OLS; propensity score | Larger firms tend to export to more destination countries. Information on destination of exports not used in investigation of learning-by-exporting vs. learning-to-export. |

(2007b), Verardi and Wagner (2010); Ireland — Ruane and Sutherland (2005), Lawless (2009); Italy — Castellani, Serti and Tomasi (2010), Conti, Turco and Maggioni (2010); Japan — Wakasugi and Tanaka (2009); Slovenia — Damijan, Polanec and Prasnikar (2004), De Loecker (2007); Spain — Blanes-Cristóbal *et al.* (2007), Mánez-Castillejo, Rochina-Barrachina and Sanchis-Llopis (2010); Sweden — Andersson, Lööf and Johansson (2008), Eliasson, Hansson and Lindvert (2009)).

(2) *Exporters to more developed economies have superior ex-ante productivity levels than non-exporters and firms exporting to less developed countries* (Belgium — Pisu (2008); Italy — Serti and Tomasi (2009); Slovenia — Damijan, Polanec and Prasnikar (2004), Damijan and Kostevc (2006), De Loecker (2007), Kostevc (2008); Portugal — Silva, Afonso and Africano (2010a); Russia — Wilhelmsson and Kozlov (2007); Spain — Blanes-Cristóbal *et al.* (2007)). This is interpreted as evidence for country-specific sunk costs of exports that are higher in advanced and more sophisticated markets (Pisu 2008).

(3) *Evidence for different effects of exporting on productivity by destination of exports is rare and not conclusive; where evidence of learning effects is found, they tend to be present for firms exporting to high income/advanced countries* (Belgium — Pisu (2008) reports no effect irrespective of development level of destination countries; Japan — Yashiro and Hirano (2009) find only exporters serving worldwide enjoyed significant advantage in productivity growth; Portugal — Silva, Afonso and Africano (2010b) report no learning effects for firms that export to non-developed countries only but fast effects for exporters only to EU countries; Russia — Wilhelmsson and Kozlov (2007) find inconclusive evidence for learning-by-exporting; Slovenia — Damijan, Polanec and Prasnikar (2004) state that exporters can benefit from exporting through learning and competition effects only when serving more demanding advanced markets; De Loecker (2007) finds that firms exporting only to low income regions get additional productivity gains that are lower than in firms exporting to high income countries; and

Kostevc (2009) states that evidence of the learning process is not conclusive).

What can we learn from the microeconometric studies surveyed here about the relationship between export destinations and productivity? Even if the evidence we have so far might not qualify as a stylized fact due to restrictions in the comparability of the studies it seems fair to state that we know that the number of export destinations is positively related to productivity and that we have evidence for self-selection of more productive firms into more demanding markets while the jury is still out regarding the issue of different learning-by-exporting effects by different export destinations.[8]

## 2.2. *Imports and productivity in manufacturing firms*

While the causes and consequences of export and its mutual relationships with productivity are prominent topics in the recent literature on internationally active firms, imports are seldom dealt with. A case in point is the Bruegel study on the internationalisation of European firms by Mayer and Ottaviano (2007) where imports are not addressed at all. As Bernard *et al.* (2007, p. 123) recently put it, "(t)he empirical literature on firms in international trade has been concerned almost exclusively with exporting, largely due to limitations in data sets.... As a result, the new theories of heterogeneous firms and trade were developed to explain facts about firm export behavior and yield few predictions (if any) for firm import behavior".

[8]Recently, a new literature started that looks at an alternative measure of the extensive margin of exports besides the number of destination markets, namely the number of products exported, and its relationship to firm performance. Muuls and Pisu (2009) find for Belgium that productivity is also increasing as the number of products exported (or imported) rises. Similarly, Silva, Afonso and Africano (2010c) show that Portuguese firms that export (or import) a larger number of products are more productive. These relationships are interpreted to be suggestive that fixed costs of trade are incurred for each new product a firm starts to trade internationally. Note that the direction of causality between the number of traded products and productivity is not investigated in these studies. The relation between the number of goods traded and firm performance is an important area of future research.

In the literature, arguments for both a positive impact of productivity on importing (which is in accordance with self-selection of more productive firms into import markets) and for a positive impact of importing on productivity (learning-by-importing) are discussed.

To start with the arguments in favor of self-selection of more productive firms into importing, it is pointed out that the use of foreign intermediates increases a firm's productivity but, due to fixed costs of importing, only inherently highly productive firms import intermediates. Importing is associated with fixed costs that are sunk costs, because the import agreement is preceded by a search process for potential foreign suppliers, inspection of goods, negotiation, contract formulation, etc. Furthermore, there are sunk costs of importing due to the learning and acquisition of customs procedures (see Kasahara and Lapham (2008), Andersson, Lööf and Johansson (2008), Castellani, Serti and Tomasi (2010)).

As regards learning-by-importing, it is stated that there are strong arguments in favor of a causal effect of imports on productivity, because by importing a firm can exploit global specialization and use inputs from the forefront of knowledge and technology. Proponents of this view point to the literature on international technology diffusion that advances imports as an important vehicle for knowledge and technology transfer. Furthermore, importing intermediate products allows a firm to focus resources and to specialize on activities where it has particular strengths. Importers may improve productivity by using higher quality foreign inputs or by extracting technology embodied in imported intermediates and capital goods. Furthermore, a variety effect is mentioned (in which the broader range of available intermediates contributes to production efficiency) and a quality effect caused by imported intermediates that might be of better quality than local ones. If importing increases productivity, this might lead firms to self-select into export markets and help to improve their success in these markets, which might contribute to an explanation why two-way traders are the most productive firms on average (see Andersson, Lööf and Johansson (2008), Castellani, Serti and Tomasi (2010),

Altomonte and Békés (2010), Halpern, Miklós and Szeidl (2005) and Muuls and Pisu (2009)).

From a theoretical point of view, therefore, the direction of causality between productivity and importing can run from one of the two sides or from both sides simultaneously. With new data sets that include information on imports at the firm level becoming available for more and more countries a new literature is emerging that has a focus on the links between productivity and imports. A number of recently published empirical studies based on data from a wide range of countries document the shares of firms that are exporters, importers and two-way traders (that both export and import), or that sell or buy in the national market only, and they look at differences between these four types of firms. Differences in productivity and their relationship with different degrees of involvement in international trade are at the centre of these studies. Table 2 summarizes the findings from 20 microeconometric studies on imports and productivity based on firm data from 12 countries.

Details aside, the big picture that emerges from this literature can be sketched as follows: There is a positive link between importing and productivity at the firm level, documented by a significant productivity differential between firms that import and firms that do not trade internationally; the same holds for exporting. Two-way traders are more productive than firms that either only import, or only export, or do not trade at all. Often, two-way traders are the most productive group of firms, followed by importers and then exporters, while firms selling or buying in the national market only come last. We have evidence for self-selection of more productive firms into exporting from most of the studies that look at this issue; the evidence on learning-by-importing, however, is still rare and inconclusive.

### 2.3. *Beyond manufacturing: International trade and productivity in services firms*

While we have evidence on the links between international trade and productivity in manufacturing firms from a large number of

Table 2. Microeconometric studies on imports and productivity

| Country Author(s) (year of publication) | Period covered | Topics investigated | Methods used | Important findings |
|---|---|---|---|---|
| Belgium Muuls and Pisu (2009) | 1996–2004 | International trading activities of firms | Regression analysis, dynamic panel probit | Two-way traders are most productive, followed by importing-only firms, exporting-only firms and non-traders. Number of import origins and number of products imported rise with increasing productivity. High degree of hysteresis in imports. |
| Chile Kasahara and Lapham (2008) | 1990–1996 | Productivity, exports and imports | Regression analysis, ML estimation of structural model | Two-way traders more productive than one-way traders; self-selection of more productive firms in import activities. |
| Chile Kasahara and Rodrigue (2008) | 1979–1996 | Imports of intermediate goods and plant performance | Fixed Effects, System GMM, TFP using Olley–Pakes and Levinsohn–Petrin estimators | Becoming an importer of foreign intermediates improves productivity. |
| Denmark Eriksson, Smeets and Warzynski (2009) | 1993–2003 | Key elements in characterizing Danish firms in international trade | Regression analysis | Entry into importing associated with higher productivity in the past. |
| Denmark Smeets and Warzynski (2010) | 1998–2005 | Learning-by-exporting and/or importing | Regression analysis | Exporting and importing positively related with firm productivity, two-way traders most productive. Evidence of self-selection into importing; no learning effect. |

| | | | | |
|---|---|---|---|---|
| France Bas and Strauss-Kahn (2010) | 1995–2005 | Link between imported intermediate inputs and firms' exports | Olley–Pakes and ACF estimates of TFP | Positive impact of higher diversification and increased number of imported inputs varieties on firms' TFP. |
| Germany Vogel and Wagner (2010a) | 2001–2005 | Productivity differences between firms that do not trade, exporters, importers and two-way traders; test for self-selection into importing and for learning-by — importing | Kolmogorov–Smirnov test; OLS and fixed effects; propensity score matching | Compared to firms that do not trade at all two-way traders have the highest productivity premium, followed by firms that only export, while firms that only import have smallest premium. Evidence for self-selection of more productive firms into imports. No clear evidence for learning-by-importing. |
| Hungary Békés, Harasztosi and Muraközy (2011) | 1992–2003 | Description of Hungarian trade data and key patterns at firm and product level | Regression analysis | Both exporters and importers show better performance than non-traders. |
| Hungary Altomonte and Békés (2010) | 1992–2003 | Relation between firms' trading activity and productivity | Regression analysis | Evidence of self-selection of the most productive firms into both importing and exporting; when taking importing status of exporters into account the productivity premium of exporters is greatly reduced. |

(Continued)

Table 2. *(Continued)*

| Country Author(s) (year of publication) | Period covered | Topics investigated | Methods used | Important findings |
|---|---|---|---|---|
| Ireland Forlani (2010) | 2000–2006 | Firms' productivity and imported inputs | OLS and fixed effects, GMM | Increase in the intensive margin of imports raises efficiency of domestic firms. No evidence for self-selection of more productive firms into importing, evidence for learning-by-importing. |
| Ireland Haller (2010) | 1996–2005 | Detailed analysis of Irish manufacturing firms engaged in international trade | OLS and fixed effects, quantile regression | On average firms can be ranked in terms of productivity from low to high as follows: no trade, export only, import only, two-way traders, firms engaged in intra-firm trade; within-group heterogeneity in some cases exceeds differences between groups of traders. |
| Italy Serti and Tomasi (2009) | 1993–1997 | Firm performance and different characteristics of markets where exports are directed and imports originate from | Descriptive statistics, OLS regression, quintile regression | Positive correlation between import and firm's productivity, two-way traders have highest productivity. Firms sourcing from more than one group of countries are by far the most productive. Importers sourcing from developed countries more productive than firms buying only from low income countries. Evidence for self-selection of more productive firms into importing; importers from high income countries have higher productivity premium. |

| | | | | |
|---|---|---|---|---|
| Italy Castellani, Serti and Tomasi (2010) | 1993–1997 | Firms' heterogeneity on the import and the export side | OLS and fixed effects | Firms engaged in international activities are more productive; results point to self-selection but some post-entry effects cannot be ruled out. Two-way traders outperform one-way traders. |
| Portugal Silva, Afonso and Africano (2010c) | 1996–2003 | Relationship between international trade engagement (exports and imports) and firms' performance | Descriptive statistics, OLS and Fixed Effects regression, dynamic panel data model | Two-way traders outperform only importers, only exporters and above all domestic firms. Greater diversification of imported goods and source markets related to higher productivity. Origin markets of imports important for performance. |
| Portugal Silva, Afonso and Africano (2010b) | 1996–2003 | Learning-by-exporting | Propensity score matching; differences-in-differences | Learning effects higher for new exporters that are also importers or start importing at the same time. |
| Spain Dovis and Milgram-Baleix (2009) | 1991–2002 | Effects of tariffs and foreign competition on TFP | Olley-Pakes TFP estimation, system GMM estimation | Evidence of additional productivity gains for importing firms. |
| Spain Augier, Cadot and Dovis (2010) | 1991–2002 | Effect of imported intermediate inputs and capital goods on TFP | Porpensity score matching and diff-in-diff; Olley–Pakes and ACF estimates | Starting to import raises productivity when proportion of skilled labor is controlled for; effect greatest for skill-intensive firms. |
| Spain Damijan and Kostevc (2010) | 1991–1999 | Learning from trade | Propensity score matching | Sequencing between imports, exports and innovation Firms learn primarily from import links, which enable them to innovate products and processes and to dress up for starting to export in small and partially medium firms. |

(*Continued*)

Table 2. (*Continued*)

| Country Author(s) (year of publication) | Period covered | Topics investigated | Methods used | Important findings |
|---|---|---|---|---|
| Sweden Lööf and Andersson (2010) | 1997–2004 | Imports from various groups of countries and productivity | OLS and fixed effects, dynamic GMM estimator | Instantaneous causality from import to productivity; productivity is an increasing function of the G-7 fraction in total imports. |
| United States Bernard *et al.* (2007) | 1997 | Evidence on firm imports from transaction data | OLS regression | Firm importing relative rarer than firm exporting; 41 (79) percent of exporting (importing) firms also import (export). Productivity premium positive for exporters and importers compared to firms that do not trade. |

empirical studies published during the past 15 years comparable information for firms from services industries is scarce and of a recent vintage. Given the high and increasing importance of the services sector it is interesting to review the empirical evidence from studies using micro data on trade and productivity in services firms.[9] Table 3 summarizes the findings from seven microeconometric studies on trade and productivity based on services firm data from six countries. All papers are published in 2010 or 2011, and only Breinlich and Criscuolo (2011) look beyond exports by investigating imports, too.

The big picture is similar to the one sketched above for trade in manufactured goods. Exporters are more productive than non-exporters and we have evidence for self-selection of more productive firms into services exports but no evidence for learning-by-exporting effects on productivity growth. Note, however, that Vogel and Wagner (2011) in a study for Germany find an estimated exporter productivity premium that is statistically significant and relevant from an economic point of view only when a standard fixed effects estimator is used. When a robust estimator that takes care of the presence of extreme observations, or outliers, is applied, this premium drops to zero. It would be interesting to see comparable results from similar empirical investigations for services industries in other countries.

## 3. Beyond Productivity: International Trade and Further Dimensions of Firm Performance

The prominent position of productivity as a topic in the empirical literature on international trade and firm performance is due to the central role played by productivity in the Melitz-type models from the *new new international trade theory*. Stakeholders in firms care for

[9]For a comprehensive survey of the literature on services trade with a focus on investigations of the determinants of international trade and investment in services, the potential gains from greater trade and efforts to achieve trade liberalization through agreements, see Francois and Hoekman (2010).

Table 3. Microeconometric studies on trade and productivity in services firms

| Country Author(s) (year of publication) | Period covered | Topics investigated | Methods used | Important findings |
|---|---|---|---|---|
| France Temouri, Vogel and Wagner (2011) | 2003–2007 | Comparison of business services exporters and non-exporters | Descriptive statistics, pooled OLS and fixed effects, propensity score matching | Exporters are more productive than non-exporters. Self-selection of more productive firms into exports, no empirical evidence for positive effects of exporting on productivity growth. |
| Germany Vogel (2011) | 2003–2005 | Exports and enterprise characteristics in German business services firms | Descriptive statistics, probit and pooled OLS/fixed effects, | Exporters are more productive than non-exporters; evidence for self-selection of more productive firms into exports. |
| Germany Temouri, Vogel and Wagner (2011) | 2003–2007 | Comparison of business services exporters and non-exporters | Descriptive statistics, pooled OLS and fixed effects, propensity score matching | Exporters are more productive than non-exporters. Self-selection of more productive firms into exports, no empirical evidence for positive effects of exporting on productivity growth. |
| Germany Vogel and Wagner (2011) | 2003–2007 | Role of outliers in shaping the relation between exports and productivity | Descriptive statistics, pooled OLS and fixed effects, robust fixed effects regression | Estimated exporter premium drops to zero when a robust estimator that controls for outliers is applied. |
| Italy Conti, Lo Turco and Maggioni (2010) | 2003 | Determinants of export performance of firms in services | Descriptive statistics, regression analysis | Exporters are more productive than non-exporters; more productive firms have higher probability to export to more distant and costly markets in terms of trade and transport costs. |

| | | | | |
|---|---|---|---|---|
| Netherlands Kox and Rojas-Romagosa (2010) | 1997–2005 | Determinants of export patterns of Dutch firms and plants in manufacturing and | Descriptive statistics, probit, pooled OLS and fixed effects | Exporter productivity premium of services firms positive but smaller than for manufacturing firms. Evidence for self-selection of more productive firms services into exports, but not for learning-by-exporting. |
| Sweden Lööf (2010) | 1997–2006 | Exports of services firms | Pooled OLS, random effects, fixed effects, dynamic GMM, propensity score matching | Exporter productivity premium larger for services firms than for manufacturing firms; self-selection of more productive firms into exporting, no evidence for positive effects of exporting on productivity growth. |
| UK Breinlich and Criscuolo (2011) | 2000–2005 | Stylized facts on firms engaging in service trade (exports and imports) | Descriptive statistics, regression analysis | Service traders are more productive, but export premia smaller for service traders than for goods traders. Service exporters are more productive than service importers. |
| UK Temouri, Vogel and Wagner (2011) | 2003–2007 | Comparison of business services exporters and non-exporters | Descriptive statistics, pooled OLS and fixed effects, propensity score matching | Exporters are more productive than non-exporters. Self-selection of more productive firms into exports, no empirical evidence for positive effects of exporting on productivity growth. |

other dimensions of firm performance, too — workers for working conditions in general and especially for wages, shareholders for stock prices, dividends and profits and all of them for the long-run development of the firm including survival as an ultimate goal. Empirical evidence on the links between international trade and further dimensions of firm performance beyond productivity will be surveyed next, starting with wages (in Section 3.1) and profitability (in Section 3.2) and concluding with survival (in Section 3.3).

### 3.1. *International trade and wages*

One of the important findings documented in the Brookings paper by Bernard and Jensen (1995) is that exporters tend to pay higher wages and benefits. Average wages and benefits (per worker, per production worker and per non-production worker) are higher in exporting plants than in non-exporting plants of all size classes. Exporter wage premia are statistically significant for all categories of wages and benefits after controlling for capital per worker, size of plant, multi-plant dummy, industry, year, plant age and region. Coefficients of exporter status dummies are statistically significant in fixed effects regressions controlling for capital per worker, hours per worker, size of plant and year. Schank, Schnabel and Wagner (2007) provide a synopsis of 21 studies published between 1995 and 2005 covering 22 different countries from highly developed economies like the United States, Germany and Sweden, and emerging economies like Taiwan, Korea and Mexico, to transition countries (Estonia, Slovenia) and least developed Sub-Saharan African economies like Burundi or Ethiopia. The empirical strategies used in these papers replicate (sometimes only partly) the approach introduced by Bernard and Jensen (1995), and the results regarding the exporter wage premia are broadly consistent with the findings from the pioneering study.

An open question not dealt with in this literature is whether these exporter wage premia do indeed indicate that exporting plants pay higher wages in the sense that comparable workers are better paid when working on a comparable work place for an exporter, i.e. *Ceteris paribus*. Given that all these empirical studies use average data at the plant or firm level, individual characteristics of the workers that might influence their productivity (and, therefore, their wages) cannot be taken into account, and certain characteristics of the work place that might call for compensating wage differentials are not represented adequately. This shortcoming has been recognized from the outset: Commenting on the presentation of the paper by Bernard and Jensen, Robert Z. Lawrence argued that "the impact of exports, while positive and statistically significant, is considerably reduced once the effects of capital intensity, industry, plant scale, and location are controlled for. One suspects, moreover, that the premiums would be even further reduced if the authors were able to control for worker characteristics. Thus the wage benefits that are attributable solely to exporting appear to be rather small". (Bernard and Jensen 1995, p. 113f.)

Starting with the pioneering study by Schank, Schnabel and Wagner (2007) a number of recent empirical papers test for the existence of these premia when observable and unobservable individual characteristics of the employees and the work place are controlled for using linked employer–employee panel data set. They are summarized in Table 4.[10] The number of these "second generation" studies on trade and wages based on linked employer–employee data is still small (and the number of countries covered is even smaller) and some studies only use cross-section data that do not allow to control for unobserved firm or worker heterogeneity. Therefore, a clear big picture has not emerged until today. One consensus, however, has been reached: Compared to the empirical evidence based on average information at the firm level the exporter wage premium is much smaller when (observed or unobserved) individual worker characteristics are controlled for; in some studies based on linked employer–employee data there is

[10]In Table 4, only studies based on linked employer–employee panel data are included. Recent studies on the relation between trade and wages using average data at the firm level include Serti, Tomasi and Zanfei (2010) for exports and imports in Italy; Tsou, Liu and Huang (2006) for Taiwan; Kandilov (2009) for Chile; Brambilla, Lederman and Porto (2010) for Brazil and Amiti and Davis (2008) for Indonesia.

Table 4. Microeconometric studies on trade and wages using linked employer–employee data

| Country Author(s) (year of publication) | Period covered | Topics investigated | Methods used | Important findings |
|---|---|---|---|---|
| Denmark Munch and Skaksen (2008) | 1995–2002 | Human capital and wages in exporting firms | Linked employer–employee panel data; individual-level wage regressions using spell-fixed effects | Inclusion of an interaction term between export intensity and the proportion of educated workers at the firm level enters the wage equation with a significant positive effect. Exporting *per se* does not matter for wages. |
| Germany Schank, Schnabel and Wagner (2007) | 1993–1997 | Do exporters Pay higher wages, *ceteris paribus*? | Linked employer–employee panel data; individual-level wage regressions using spell-fixed effects to control for unobserved firm and worker heterogeneity | Exporting *per se* hardly matters for wages, but wages increase with share of exports in total sales *ceteris paribus*. |
| Germany Schank, Schnabel and Wagner (2010) | 1994–2006 | Direction of causality between exports and wages | Linked employer–employee panel data; individual-level wage regressions and propensity score matching | Exporter wage premium already exists in the years before firms start to export (self-selection), but does not increase in the years after exporting started (no causal effect of exports on wages). |
| Germany Klein, Moser and Urban (2010) | 1993–2007 | Skill structure of the wage premia in exporting firms | Linked employer–employee panel data; individual-level wage regressions with worker-firm spell effects | Significant export wage premium for workers in the two highest skill categories, evidence of an export wage discount for lower-skilled workers. |
| Germany Baumgarten (2010) | 1996–2007 | Role of exporting firms in explaining rising wage dispersion | Linked employer–employee panel data; individual-level wage regressions; decomposition of change wage dispersion | Wage differential between exporters and non-exporters increased substantially; changes in skill compositions and skill prices can only account for a small fraction of this increase. Rising exporter wage gap contributed to growth in wage dispersion. |

| | | | | |
|---|---|---|---|---|
| Mexico Frías, Kaplan and Verhoogen (2009) | 1993–2001 | Relationship between exports and wage premia | Linked employer–employee panel data; dynamic panel approach. | Approximately two thirds of the correlation between plant level average wages and plant size can be explained by exporter wage premia and one third by workforce composition (*levels*); nearly all of the differential within-industry wage change due to the export shock (peso devaluation of late 1994) is explained by changes in wage premia (*changes*). |
| Morocco Fafchamps (2009) | 2000 | Education wage premium in exporting and non-exporting firms | Linked employer–employee data (10 workers per firm); firm fixed effects | No evidence that exporters pay higher premium to educated workers; no evidence that firms that start to export or increase exports increase wages as well; no evidence that workers who switch jobs enjoy larger pay increase if start to work for an exporter. |
| Portugal Martins and Opromolla (2009) | 1995–2005 | Relation of exports, imports types of goods traded with wages | Linked employer–employee panel data combined with firm-transaction panel data; job-spell fixed effects | Firms that increase their exports (imports) of high-(intermediate-) technology products tend to increase their salaries. |
| Spain Alcalá and Hernández (2010) | 2002 | Destination market effect in exporter wage premium | Linked employer–employee data; individual-level regressions with worker and firm characteristics | Output-market exporter wage premia are increasing in market remoteness and employer education. |
| United States (Los Angeles) Breau and Rigby (2006) | 1990, 2000 | Wage premium in exporting firms | Linked employer–employee data; individual-level wage regressions | After controlling for worker characteristics the export wage premium vanishes. |

no such thing as a wage premium for exporting *per se*. This points out that the use of linked employer–employee panel data is much more appropriate to investigate the existence and the size of the exporter wage premium.

Other findings vary between studies and some interesting aspects (like the role of imports, or destination markets or skill categories; the existence or not of self-selection and of causal effects of exporting on wages paid) are only dealt with in single studies. Internationally comparable studies are urgently needed here before results can be taken as a basis for any sound (policy) conclusions.

## 3.2. *Exports and profitability*

A question that has been investigated in the literature on the microeconometrics of international trade only recently is whether the productivity advantage of exporting firms does lead to a profitability advantage of exporters compared to otherwise identical non-exporters even when exporters are facing extra costs and pay higher wages.

This apparent gap in the literature on the microeconometrics of international trade comes as a surprise because maximization of profits (and not of productivity) is usually considered as a central goal for firms. Furthermore, looking at profitability instead of productivity is more appropriate from a theoretical point of view, too. Even if productivity and profitability are positively correlated (which tends to be the case) productivity is, as was recently pointed out by Foster, Haltiwanger and Syverson (2008, p. 395), only one of the several possible idiosyncratic factors that determine profits. Success of firms in general, and especially survival, depends on profitability. Often profitability is viewed both in theoretical models of market selection and in empirical studies on firm entry and exits as a positive monotonic function of productivity, and selection on profits then is equivalent to selection on productivity. In empirical studies, the use of productivity instead of profitability is usually due to the fact that productivity is easily observed in the data sets at hand while profitability is not. Fortunately, there are data sets that are rich enough to allow to measure profitability. Table 5 summarizes the findings from recent studies on trade and profits.

The number of studies on exports and profits is still small and the number of countries covered (all of which are member states of the EU) is even smaller. Results differ widely across the studies — from positive to negative profitability differences between exporters and non-exporters; from evidence for self-selection of more or less profitable firms into exporting to no evidence for self-selection at all; from no positive effects of exports on profits to positive effects. As of today, a big picture has not emerged. Open questions include the role played by different export destinations and by the characteristics of these export markets, and the importance of the number and the quality of products exported. Only one study listed in Table 5 looks at imports and profitability (Wagner 2011b). It documents the relationship between profitability and three types of international trade activities — exports, imports and two-way trade for manufacturing enterprises from Germany. Descriptive statistics and regression analysis (with and without controlling for unobserved firm heterogeneity and the role of outliers) point to the absence of any statistically significant and economically large effects of trade activities on profits. This demonstrates that in German manufacturing firms any productivity advantages of trading firms are eaten up by extra costs related to selling and buying on foreign markets. Whether this holds for firms from other countries, too, is an important topic for future research.

### 3.3. *International trade and firm survival*

Why should we expect that international trade activities and firm survival are linked, and in which direction should we expect these links to work? Following Wagner (2011c), exporting can be considered as a form of risk diversification through spread of sales over different markets with different business cycle conditions or in a different phase of the product cycle. Therefore, exports might provide a chance to substitute sales at home by sales abroad when

Table 5. Microeconometric studies on exports and profits

| Country Author(s) (year of publication) | Period covered | Topics investigated | Methods used | Important findings |
|---|---|---|---|---|
| France Temouri, Vogel and Wagner (2011) | 2003–2007 | Exports and profitability in business services enterprises | Descriptive analysis; regression analysis; propensity score matching | Services exporters are more profitable than non-exporters. No evidence for self-selection of more profitable firms into exporting. No evidence for positive effects of exports on profitability. |
| Germany Fryges and Wagner (2010) | 1999–2004 | Exports and profitability in manufacturing enterprises | Descriptive analysis; regression analysis; generalized propensity score methodology | Exporters are more profitable than non-exporters, but difference is small; rate of profit tends to increase with export–sales ratio. No evidence for self-selection of more profitable firms into exports. Positive causal effect of exporting on profitability almost over the whole domain of the export–sales ratio. |
| Germany Vogel and Wagner (2010b) | 2003–2005 | Exports and profitability in business services enterprises | Descriptive analysis; regression analysis; generalized propensity score methodology | Services exporters are less profitable compared to non-exporters, though difference is small. Evidence for self-selection of less profitable services firms into exports. No positive causal effect of exports on profits. |
| Germany Temouri, Vogel and Wagner (2011) | 2003–2007 | Exports and profitability in business services enterprises | Descriptive analysis; regression analysis; propensity score matching | Services exporters less profitable than non-exporters. Self-selection of less profitable firms into exports. No evidence for positive effects of exporting on profits. |

| | | | | |
|---|---|---|---|---|
| Germany Wagner (2011b) | 2003–2006 | Exports, imports and profits in manufacturing enterprises | Descriptive analysis; non-parametric tests; pooled OLS and fixedeffects regressions; robust pooled and fixed effects regressions | No statistically significant and economically large effects of trade on profits. |
| Italy Amendolagine, Capolupo and Petragallo (2008) | 1995–2003 | Exports and performance in manufacturing firms | Regression analysis; propensity score matching | Profitability difference between exporters and non-exporters not reported. No evidence for self-selection of more profitable firms into exporting. Evidence for positive effects of exports on profits. |
| Italy Grazzi (2011) | 1989–2004 | Trade and profitability | Descriptive analysis; non-parametric comparison of distributions; regression analysis | No evidence for profitability differential between exporters and non-exporters over all; positive relation for some sectors, negative for others. |
| Netherlands Kox and Rojas-Romagosa (2010) | 1997–2005 | Exports and performance of manufacturing and services firms | Descriptive analysis; OLS and probit regression | Profitability higher in exporting firms. Evidence for self-selection of more profitable firms into exporting. No positive effects of exporting on profitability. |
| United Kingdom Temouri, Vogel and Wagner (2011) | 2003–2007 | Exports and profitability in business services enterprises | Descriptive analysis; regression analysis; propensity score matching | Services exporters do not differ in profitability compared to non-exporters. No evidence for self-selection of more profitable firms into exports. No evidence for positive effects of exporting on profits. |

a negative demand shock hits the home market and would force a firm to close down otherwise. Furthermore, Baldwin and Yan (2011, p. 135) argue that non-exporters are in general less efficient than exporters (younger, smaller and less productive) and that, as a result, one expects that non-exporters are more likely to fail than exporters.

As regards imports, imported intermediate inputs or capital goods might be cheaper and/or technically more advanced than inputs bought in the national market. Gibson and Graciano (2011) argue that the benefit of using imported inputs lies in a combination of the relative price and the technology embodied in the inputs. Imports, therefore, lead to an increase in price competitiveness and non-price competitiveness of importers compared to firms that do not import. Furthermore, there is empirical evidence for a positive link of imports and productivity (discussed in Vogel and Wagner 2010a), documented by a significant productivity differential between firms that import and firms that do not trade internationally. Therefore, the probability to survive can be expected to be higher for importers than for non-importers, *ceteris paribus*.

Firms that both export and import can be expected to benefit from the positive effects of both forms of international trade on firm survival. Furthermore, two-way traders tend to be more productive than firms that either only import, or only export, or do not trade at all (see Vogel and Wagner 2010a). Therefore, we expect the probability of firm exit to be smaller for two-way traders than for firms that only export or only import.

A small number of recent empirical studies look at the role of international trade activities in shaping the chances for survival of firms; Table 6 summarizes this literature.[11] As a rule, the estimated chance of survival is higher for exporters, and this holds after controlling for firm characteristics that are positively associated with both exports and survival (like size, age, productivity). This might point to a direct positive effect of exporting on survival.

[11]This literature looks at the survival of exporting and non-exporting firms in the home market; studies that investigate the determinants of surviving as an exporter in the export market include Ilmakunnas and Nurmi (2010) and Wagner (2008, 2010).

Table 6. Microeconometric studies on international trade and firm survival

| Country Author(s) (year of publication) | Period covered | Topics investigated | Methods used | Important findings |
|---|---|---|---|---|
| Canada Baldwin and Yan (2011) | 1979–1996 | Effects of changes in tariffs and real exchange rates on plant death | Probit estimates for exit | Exporters have much lower failure rates than non-exporters but their survival is more sensitive to changes in tariffs and real exchange rates. |
| Chile López (2006) | 1990–1999 | Imports of intermediate inputs and plant survival | Probit estimates for exit | Importers are more likely to survive. Exporters are more likely to survive but only if they import intermediate inputs. Exporting itself does not seem to decrease probability of exit. |
| Chile Gibson and Graciano (2011) | 2001–2006 | Costs of starting to trade and costs of continuing to trade | Transition probabilities to exit | Importers are less likely to exit than non-importers. |
| Chile Namini, Facchini and López (2011) | 1990–1999 | Export growth and factor market competition | Probit and IV-probit estimates for 3-year survival | Importers of intermediate inputs are more likely to survive than non-importers. Exporting firms are more likely to survive than non-exporting firms, but probability of survival decreases with sector-wide export volumes. |
| Denmark Eriksson, Smeets and Warzynski (2009) | 1993–2003 | Evidence on exports and imports by product and origin/destination | Probit estimate for exit | Exporters are less likely to exit than non-exporters. |

(*Continued*)

Table 6. (*Continued*)

| Country Author(s) (year of publication) | Period covered | Topics investigated | Methods used | Important findings |
|---|---|---|---|---|
| France Görg and Spaliara (2010) | 1998–2005 | Financial constraints, exports and firm survival | Probit estimate for exit | Continuous exporters face a higher probability of survival compared to starters, continuous non-exporters and firms exiting the exporting market. |
| Germany Wagner (2011c) | 2001–2007 | Likelihood of survival of firms that do not trade, only export, only import, or export and import | Probit; rare events logit | Strong positive link between firm survival and imports and two-way trade; exporting only does not play a role for probability to exit the market. |
| Italy Amendola *et al.* (2010) | 2002–2008 | Differential effects of firm and industry-level variables on likelihood of survival | Probit estimates for exit | Exporting has a very high negative marginal impact on firm exit. |
| Japan Kimura and Kiyota (2006) | 1994–2000 | Export, FDI and productivity | Cox proportional hazard model | Exports have positive impacts on firm survival. Exporters face hazard rate that is lower than non-exporters. |

| | | | | |
|---|---|---|---|---|
| Spain Esteve-Pérez, Mánez-Castillejo and Sanchis-Llopis (2008) | 1990–2002 | "Survial-by-exporting" effect for small and medium sized enterprises (SME) | Discrete time proportional hazard models | Exporting SMEs face a significantly lower probability of failure than non-exporters. |
| Sweden Greenaway, Gullstrand and Kneller (2008) | 1980–1996 | Effects of international trade on firms' strategies for industry exit | Descriptive statistics; multinomial logit | Firms which export are less likely to close down. |
| Sweden Greenaway, Gullstrand and Kneller (2009) | 1980–1996 | Role of firm and industry characteristics for exit decision of firms | Descriptive statistics; multinomial logit | Firms which export are less likely to close down. |
| United Kingdom Görg and Spaliara (2010) | 1998–2005 | Financial constraints, exports and firm survival | Probit estimate for exit | Continuous exporters face a higher probability of survival compared to starters, continuous non-exporters and firms exiting the exporting market. |
| United States Bernard and Jensen (2007) | 1992–1997 | Determinants of plant closures | Probit estimates for plant death | Exporting is associated with large reduction in probability of closedown. |

López (2006); Gibson and Graciano (2011); Namini, Facchini and López (2011) and Wagner (2011c) present empirical studies on imports and survival. The first three studies use data for Chile. These studies find that importers are less likely to exit than non-importers. However, López (2006) reports that exporters are more likely to survive only if they import intermediate inputs — exporting *per se*, therefore, does not seem to decrease the probability of plant failure. In the light of the empirical evidence for a positive link of imports and productivity, the positive link between imports and firm survival does not come as a surprise. The same holds for the positive link between two-way trading (i.e. importing and exporting) and survival. Wagner (2011c) provides evidence on the role of exports, imports and two-way trade for firm survival in a highly developed country, Germany. Descriptive statistics and regression analysis (with and without explicitly taking the rare events nature of firm exit into account) point to a strong positive link between firm survival on the one hand and imports and two-way trading on the other hand, while exporting alone does not play a role for exiting the market or not. It would be interesting to see whether this pattern revealed for Germany is the same in other countries (and if not, why there is a difference).

## 4. Conclusion

The numerous empirical studies on international trade and firm performance that were published in recent years all added pieces of evidence to the state of our knowledge. One important aim of empirical studies in this field of economics (like in other fields, too) is to uncover stylized facts that hold over space and time, and that can both inspire theoretical models that are based on reasonable assumptions and inform policy debates in an evidence-based way. Can the accumulated evidence on international trade and firm performance qualify as stylized facts in this sense? I doubt.

On some topics, we have a large enough number of empirical studies using data from different countries reporting results that point in the same direction so that we can paint a big picture —

exporters and importers are more productive than non-exporters and non-importers and they were more productive in the years before they started to export or import (self-selection); the number of export markets served increases with firm productivity, and exporters to more developed economies have superior *ex-ante* productivity levels than non-exporters and firms exporting to less developed countries.

However, this big picture summarizes the results from the studies in a qualitative way only. Any attempt to extract information on the size of the effects — the economic relevance, not the statistical significance — is hindered by the absence of a reasonably high degree of comparability across the studies. This lack of comparability is due to differences in the unit of analysis (establishment vs. enterprise), the sampling frame (all firms vs. firm with a number of employees above a certain threshold only), the specification of the empirical models estimated and the econometric methods applied. The approach of the ISGEP (2008) to agree on the use of identically specified empirical model and identical econometric methods in the analysis of comparable samples of comparable data for a number of countries to compute estimates for each country and to use a meta-analysis in the second stage to explain cross-country differences is a promising way to make progress here. The use of this approach in investigations of other topics and for a larger group of countries, therefore, is highly recommended.

Besides topics where we have a big picture already there are others where the jury is still out. The most important of these topics is the presence or not of learning-by-exporting (and learning-by-importing) effects. Here, results differ widely across studies (see Silva, Afonso and Africano (2010d) for a comprehensive discussion). In other sub-fields the number of studies is still too small to argue that we have sound empirical evidence on the direction (not to talk about the size) of the link between trade and the respective dimension of firm performance. Topics here include the relation between firm performance and the number of goods traded, trade in services and productivity, trade and wages (after controlling for observed and unobserved heterogeneity in employers and employees), trade and profits and trade and firm survival. The marginal return to further microeconometric studies on these topics, therefore, is large.

Furthermore, even in sub-fields of the empirical literature on firm performance and trade that lead to a kind of consensus based on results of a large number of studies, recent research casts doubts that the standard approach applied in these studies deal with firm heterogeneity in an adequate way. Cases in point are the studies for Germany by Verardi and Wagner (2011) and by Vogel and Wagner (2011) that apply robust methods to deal with extreme observations (outliers) in an adequate way and that find a dramatic reduction in the estimated exporter productivity premium, and the paper by Powell and Wagner (2011) — also for Germany — that points to different exporter productivity premia at different parts of the productivity distribution. The lack of replication studies with data from other countries, however, makes it impossible to judge whether these results are specific for firms from manufacturing in Germany only or whether they are of a wider relevance. The marginal return to replication studies, therefore, is large in this case, too.

The bottom line, then, is that we made remarkable progress on the way to understand the links between international trade and firm performance over the recent past — but substantial further research is still needed.

**Acknowledgment**

I thank my co-authors of contributions to this literature from the past six years — Nils Braakmann, Helmut Fryges, Sourafel Girma, Holger Görg, David Powell, Horst Raff, Thorsten Schank, Claus Schnabel, Yama Temouri, Vincenzo Verardi, Alexander Vogel and all members of the International Study Group on Exports and Productivity (ISGEP) — for many insightful discussions and a lot of ideas that made the preparation of this literature survey possible. Suggestions from Harmen Lehment, the editor, and comments from two anonymous reviewers that helped to improve the chapter are gratefully acknowledged. Evidently, none of them is responsible for my summary and interpretation of the literature presented here.

## References

Alcalá, Francisco and Pedro J. Hernández (2010). Firms' Main Market, Human Capital, and Wages. *SERIEs* 1(4), 433–458.

Altomonte, Carlo and Gabor Békés (2010). Trade Complexity and Productivity. CeFiG Working Papers 12. Budapest: Center for Firms in the Global Economy.

Amendola, Adalgiso, Anna Ferragina, Rosanna Pittiglio and Filippo Reganati (2010). How is the 2007 Crisis Affecting Firms' Survival? Evidence from Italy, Paper presented at ETSG 2010 Lausanne, 9–11 September.

Amendolagine, Vito, Rosa Capolupo and Nadia Petragallo (2008). Export Status and Performance in a Panel of Italian Manufacturing Firms. S.E.R.I.E.S Working Paper No. 27. Dipartomento di Scienze Economiche, Università degli Studi Bari.

Amiti, Mary and Donald R. Davis (2008). Trade, Firms, and Wages: Theory and Evidence. NBER Working Paper 14106. Cambridge, MA: National Bureau of Economic Research.

Andersson, Martin, Hans Lööf and Sara Johansson (2008). Productivity and International Trade: Firm Level Evidence from a Small Open Economy. *Review of World Economics/Weltwirtschaftliches Archiv* 144(4), 774–801.

Augier, Patricia, Olivier Cadot and Marion Dovis (2010). Imports and TFP at the Firm Level: The Role of Absorptive Capacity. DEFI, University of Aix-Marseilles, mimeo, March.

Baldwin, John and Beiling Yan (2011). The Death of Canadian Manufacturing Plants: Heterogeneous Responses to Changes in Tariffs and Real Exchange Rates. *Review of World Economics/Weltwirtschaftliches Archiv* 147(1), 131–167.

Barba Navaretti, Giorgio and Anthony J. Venables (2004). *Multinational Firms in the World Economy*. Princeton and Oxford: Princeton University Press.

Bas, Maria and Vanessa Strauss-Kahn (2010). Does Importing more Inputs Raise Exports? Firm Level Evidence from France. MPRA Paper No. 27315. University Library of Munich: Munich Personal RePEc Archive.

Baumgarten, Daniel (2010). Exporters and the Rise in Wage Inequality. Evidence from German Linked Employer–Employee Data. Ruhr Economic Papers 217. Bochum, Dortmund, Duisburg, Essen: Ruhr Graduate School in Economics.

Bausch, Andreas, Thomas Fritz and Kathrin Boeseke (2007). Performance Effects of Internationalization Strategies: A Meta-Analysis. *Research in Global Strategic Management* 13, 143–176.

Bausch, Andreas and Mario Krist (2007). The Effect of Context-Related Moderators on the Internationalization-Performance Relationship: Evidence from Meta-Analysis. *Management International Review* 47(3), 319–347.

Békés, Gabor, Péter Harasztosi and Balázs Muraközy (2011). Firms and Products in International Trade: Evidence from Hungary. *Economic Systems*, 35(1), 4–24.

Bellone, Flora, Sarah Guillou and Lionel Nesta (2010). To What Extent Innovation Accounts for Firm Export Premia? University of Nice — Sophia Antipolis, mimeo, February 2010.

Bernard, Andrew B. and J. Bradford Jensen (1995). Exporters, Jobs, and Wages in U.S. Manufacturing: 1976–1987. *Brookings Papers on Economic Activity, Microeconomics* 1, 67–119.

Bernard, Andrew B. and J. Bradford Jensen (2007). Firm Structure, Multinationals, and Manufacturing Plant Deaths. *Review of Economics and Statistics* 89(2), 193–204.

Bernard, Andrew B., J. Bradford Jensen, Stephen J. Redding and Peter K. Schott (2007). Firms in International Trade. *Journal of Economic Perspectives* 21(3), 105–130.

Blanes-Cristóbal, José Vicente, Marion Dovis, Juliette Milgram-Baleix and Ana I. Moro-Egido (2008), Do Sunk Exporting Costs Differ Among Markets? Evidence from Spanish Manufacturing firms. *Economics Letters* 101(2), 110–112.

Brambilla, Irene, Daniel Lederman and Guido Porto (2010). Exports, Export Destinations, and Skills. NBER Working Paper 15995. Cambridge, MA: National Bureau of Economic Research.

Breau, Sébastian and David L. Rigby (2006). Is there Really an Export Wage Premium? A Case Study of Los Angeles using Matched Employer–Employee Data. CES Discussion Paper 06-06. Center for European Studies at Harvard University.

Breinlich, Holger and Chiara Criscuolo (2011). International Trade in Services: A Portrait of Importers and Exporters. *Journal of International Economics* 84(2), 188–206.

Castellani, Davide, Francesco Serti and Chiara Tomasi (2010). Firms in International Trade: Importers' and Exporters' Heterogeneity in the Italian Manufacturing Industry. *The World Economy* 33(3), 424-457.

Chaney, Thomas (2008). Distorted Gravity: The Intensive and Extensive Margins of International Trade. *American Economic Review* 98(4), 1707–1721.

Conti, Giuliano, Alessia Lo Turco and Daniela Maggioni (2010). Exporters in Services: New Evidence from Italian Firms. *Applied Economics Quarterly* 56(1), 73–98.

Crinò, Rosario and Paolo Epifani (2009). Export intensity and productivity. IAE-CSIC and Bocconi University, mimeo, April.

Damijan, Joze P. and Crt Kostevc (2006). Learning-by-Exporting: Continuous Productivity Improvements or Capacity Utilization Effects? Evidence from Slovenian Firms. *Review of World Economics/Weltwirtschaftliches Archiv* 142(3), 599–614.

Damijan, Joze P. and Crt Kostevc (2010). Learning from Trade through Innovation: Causal Link between Imports, Exports and Innovation in Spanish Microdata.

LICOS Discussion Papers 26410. Centre for Institutions and Economic Performance, K.U. Leuven.

Damijan, Joze P., Saso Polanec and Janez Prasnikar (2004). Self-selection, Export Market Heterogeneity and Productivity Improvements: Firm Level Evidence from Slovenia. LICOS Discussion Papers 14804. Centre for Institutions and Economic Performance, K.U. Leuven.

De Loecker, Jan (2007). Do Exports Generate Higher Productivity? Evidence from Slovenia. *Journal of International Economics* 73(1), 69–98.

De Loecker, Jan (2010), A Note on Detecting Learning by Exporting. NBER Working Paper 16548. Cambridge, MA: National Bureau of Economic Research.

Dovis, Marion and Juliette Milgram-Baleix (2009). Trade, Tariffs and Total Factor Productivity: The Case of Spanish Firms. *The World Economy* 32(4), 575–605.

Eliasson, Kent, Pär Hansson and Markus Lindvert (2009). Do Firms Learn by Exporting or Learn to Export? Evidence from Small and Medium-Sized Enterprises (SMEs) in Swedish Manufacturing. Working Paper No. 15. Swedish Business School, Örebro University.

Eriksson, Tor, Valérie Smeets and Frédéric Warzynski (2009). Small Open Economy Firms in International Trade: Evidence from Danish Transaction-Level Data. Working Papers 09-7. Aarhus School of Business, Department of Economics, University of Arhus.

Esteve-Pérez, Silviano, Juan A. Mánez-Castillejo and Juan A. Sanchis-Llopis (2008). Does a "Survival-by-Exporting" Effect for SMEs Exist? *Empirica* 35(1), 81–104.

Esteve-Pérez, Silviano, Vicente Pallardó-López and Francisco Requena-Silvente (2011). The Duration of Firm-Destination Export Relationships: Evidence from Spain, 1997–2006. Working Papers 1102. Department of Applied Economics II, Universidad de Valencia.

Fafchamps, Marcel (2009). Human Capital, Exports, and Earnings. *Economic Development and Cultural Change* 58(1), 111–141.

Forlani, Emanuele (2010). Irish Firms' Productivity and Imported Inputs. CORE Discussion Paper 2010015. Center for Operations Research and Econometrics, Université catholique de Louvain.

Foster, Lucia, John Haltiwanger and Chad Syverson (2008). Reallocation, Firm Turnover, and Efficiency: Selection on Productivity or Profitability? *American Economic Review* 98(1), 394–425.

Francois, Joseph and Bernard Hoekman (2010). Services Trade and Policy. *Journal of Economic Literature* 48(3), 642–692.

Frías, Judith A., David S. Kaplan and Eric A. Verhoogen (2009). Exports and Wage Premia: Evidence from Mexican Employer–Employee Data. Columbia University, mimeo, August.

Fryges, Helmut and Joachim Wagner (2010). Exports and Profitability: First Evidence for German Manufacturing Firms. *The World Economy* 33(3), 399–423.

Gibson, Mark J. and Tim A. Graciano (2011). Costs of Starting to Trade and Costs of Continuing to Trade. Washington State University, mimeo, January.

Görg, Holger and Marina-Eliza Spaliara (2010). Financial Health, Exports, and Firm Survival: A Comparison of British and French Firms. Kiel Working Paper 1568. Kiel: Kiel Institute for the World Economy.

Grazzi, Marco (2011). Export and Firm Performance: Evidence on Productivity and Profitability of Italian Companies. *Journal of Industry, Competition and Trade* (in press).

Greenaway, David, Joakim Gullstrand and Richard Kneller (2008). Surviving Globalization. *Journal of International Economics* 74(2), 264–277.

Greenaway, David, Joakim Gullstrand and Richard Kneller (2009). Live or Let Die? Alternative Routes to Industry Exit. *Open Economies Review* 20(3), 317–337.

Greenaway, David and Richard Kneller (2007). Firm Heterogeneity, Exporting and Foreign Direct Investment. *Economic Journal* 117, F134–F161.

Haller, Stefanie A. (2010). Exporting, Importing, Intra-Firm Trade and Firm Performance. Economic and Social Research Institute, mimeo, March.

Halpern, László, Koren Miklós and Ádám Szeidl (2005). Imports and Productivity. CEPR Discussion Papers 5139. London: Centre for Economic Policy Research.

Hayakawa, Kazunobu, Tomohiro Machikita and Fukunari Kimura (2011). Globalization and Productivity: A Survey of Firm-Level Analysis. *Journal of Economic Surveys* 25(1), 19–68.

Ilmakunnas, Pekka and Satu Nurmi (2010). Dynamics of Export Market Entry and Exit. *Scandinavian Journal of Economics* 112(1), 101–126.

International Study Group on Exports and Productivity (ISGEP) (2008). Understanding Cross-Country Differences in Exporter Premia: Comparable Evidence for 14 Countries. *Review of World Economics/Weltwirtschaftliches Archiv*, 144(4), 596–635.

Kandilov, Ivan T (2009). Do Exporters Pay Higher Wages? Plant-level Evidence from an Export Refund Policy in Chile. *World Bank Economic Review* 23(2), 269–294.

Kasahara, Hiroyuki and Beverly Lapham (2008). Productivity and the Decision to Import and Export: Theory and Evidence. CESifo Working Papers 2240. Ifo Institute for Economic Research, Munich.

Kasahara, Hiroyuki and Joel Rodrigue (2008). Does the Use of Imported Intermediates Increase Productivity? Plant Level Evidence. *Journal of Development Economics* 87(1), 106–118.

Kimura, Fukunari and Kozo Kiyota (2006). Exports, FDI, and Productivity: Dynamic Evidence from Japanes Firms. *Review of World Economics/Weltwirtschaftliches Archiv* 142(4), 695–719.

Klein, Michael W., Christoph Moser and Dieter M. Urban (2010). The Contribution of Trade to Wage Inequality: The Role of Skill, Gender and Nationality. NBER Working Paper 15985. Cambridge, MA: National Bureau of Economic Research.

Kostevc, Crt (2009). Foreign Market Competition as a Determinant of Exporter Performance. Evidence from Slovenian Manufacturing Firms. *The World Economy* 32(6), 888–913.

Kox, Henk L. M. and Hugo Rojas-Romagosa (2010). Exports and Productivity Selection Effects for Dutch Firms. *De Economist* 158(3), 295–322.

Lawless, Martina (2009). Firm Export Dynamics and the Geography of Trade. *Journal of International Economics* 77(2), 245–254.

Lööf, Hans (2010). Are Services Different Exporters? *Applied Economics Quarterly* 56(1), 99–117.

Lööf, Hans and Martin Andersson (2010). Imports, Productivity and Origin Markets: The Role of Knowledge-intensive Economies. *The World Economy* 33(3), 458–481.

López Ricardo A. (2006). Imports of Intermediate Inputs and Plant Survival. *Economics Letters* 92(1), 58–62.

Mánez-Castillejo, Juan A., Mariá E. Rochina-Barrachina and Juan A. Sanchis-Llopis (2010). Does Firm Size Affect Self-Selction and Learning-by-Exporting? *The World Economy* 33(3), 315–346.

Martins, Pedro S. and Luca David Opromolla (2009). Exports, Imports and Wages: Evidence from Matched Firm-Worker-Product Panels. IZA Discussion Papers 4646. Bonn: Institute for the Study of Labor.

Martins, Pedro S. and Yong Yang (2009). The Impact of Exporting on Firm Productivity: A Meta-Analysis of the Learning-by-Exporting Hypothesis. *Review of World Economics/Weltwirtschaftliches Archiv* 145(3), 431–445.

Mayer, Thierry and Gianmarco I. P. Ottaviano (2007). The Happy Few: The Internationalisation of European Firms. New Facts based on Firm-level Evidence. Bruegel Blueprint Series Vol. III, November.

Melitz, Mark J. (2003). The Impact of Trade on Intra-Industry Reallocations and Aggregate Industry Productivity. *Econometrica* 71(6), 1695–1725.

Munch, Jacob Roland and Jan Rose Skaksen (2008). Human Capital and Wages in Exporting Firms. *Journal of International Economics* 75(2), 363–372.

Muuls, Mirabelle and Mauro Pisu (2009). Imports and Exports at the Level of the Firm: Evidence from Belgium. *The World Economy* 32(5), 692–734.

Namini, Julian Emami, Giovanni Facchini and Ricardo López (2011). Export Growth and Factor Market Competition: Theory and Evidence. CEPR Discussion Papers 8256. London: Centre for Economic Policy Research.

Pisu, Mauro (2008). Export Destination and Learning-by-Exporting: Evidence from Belgium. Working Paper Research 140. Brussels: National Bank of Belgium.

Powell, David and Joachim Wagner (2011). The Exporter Productivity Premium along the Productivity Distribution: Evidence from Unconditional Quantile Regression with Firm Fixed Effects. RAND Working Paper 837. Santa Monica: RAND Corporation Publications Department.

Redding, Stephen J. (2010). Theories of Heterogeneous Firms and Trade. NBER Working Paper 16562. Cambridge, MA: National Bureau of Economic Research.

Ruane, Frances and Julie Sutherland (2005). Export Performance and Destination Characteristics of Irish Manufacturing Industry. *Review of World Economics/Weltwirtschaftliches Archiv* 141(3), 442–459.

Schank, Thorsten, Claus Schnabel and Joachim Wagner (2007). Do Exporters Really Pay Higher Wages? First Evidence from German Linked Employer–Employee Data. *Journal of International Economics* 72(1), 52–74.

Schank, Thorsten, Claus Schnabel and Joachim Wagner (2010). Higher Wages in Exporting Firms: Self-Selection, Export Effect, or Both? First Evidence from Linked Employer–Employee Data. *Review of World Economics/ Weltwirtschaftliches Archiv* 146(2), 303–322.

Serti, Francesco and Chiara Tomasi (2009). Self-Selection Along Different Export and Import Markets. LEM Papers Series 2009/18. Pisa: Laboratory of Economics and Management, Sant'Anna School of Advanced Studies.

Serti, Francesco, Chiara Tomasi and Antonello Zanfei (2010). Who Trades with Whom? Exploring the Links between Firms' International Activities, Skills, and Wages. *Review of International Economics* 18(5), 951–971.

Silva, Armando, Óscar Afonso and Ana Paula Africano (2010a). Do Portugese Manufacturing Firms Self Select to Exports? FEP Working Papers 371. Universidade de Porto, Faculdade de Economia do Porto.

Silva, Armando, Óscar Afonso and Ana Paula Africano (2010b). International Trade Involvement and Performance of Portuguese Manufacturing Firms: Causal Links. Instituto Politécnico do Porto — ESEIG, mimeo, July.

Silva, Armando, Óscar Afonso and Ana Paula Africano (2010c). Economic Performance and International Trade Engagement: The Case of Portuguese Manufacturing Firms. FEP Working Papers 369. Universidade de Porto, Faculdade de Economia do Porto.

Silva, Armando, Ana Paula Africano and Óscar Afonso (2010d). Learning-by-Exporting: What We Know and What We Would Like to Know. FEP Working Papers 364. Universidade de Porto, Faculdade de Economia do Porto.

Singh, Tarlok (2010), Does International Trade Cause Economic Growth? A Survey. *The World Economy* 33(11), 1517–1564.

Smeets, Valérie and Frédéric Warzynski (2010). Learning by Exporting, Importing or Both? Estimating Productivity with Multi-Product Firms, Pricing Heterogeneity and the Role of International Trade. Working Papers 10-13. University of Aarhus: Aarhus School of Business, Department of Economics.

Temouri, Yama, Alexander Vogel and Joachim Wagner (2011). Self-Selection into Export Markets by Business Services Firms — Evidence from France, Germany and the United Kingdom. Working Paper Series in Economics 183. University of Lueneburg: Institute of Economics.

Tsou, Meng-Wen, Jin-Tan Liu and Cliff J. Huang (2006). Export Acitivity, Firm Size and Wage Structure: Evidence from Taiwanese Manufacturing Firms. *Asian Economic Journal* 20(4), 333–354.

Verardi, Vincenzo and Joachim Wagner (2010). Productivity Premia for German Manufacturing Firms Exporting to the Euro-Area and Beyond: First Evidence from Robust Fixed Effects Estimations. Working Paper Series in Economics 172. University of Lueneburg: Institute of Economics.

Verardi, Vincenzo and Joachim Wagner (2011). Robust Estimation of Linear Fixed Effects Panel Data Models with an Application to the Exporter Productivity Premium. *Jahrbücher für Nationalökonomie und Statistik* 231(4), 546–557.

Vogel, Alexander (2011). Exporter Performance in the German Business Services Sector. *The Services Industries Journal* 31(7), 1015–1031.

Vogel, Alexander and Joachim Wagner (2010a). Higher Productivity in Importing German Manufacturing Firms: Self-Selection, Learning from Importing, or Both? *Review of World Economics/Weltwirtschaftliches Archiv* 145(4), 641–665.

Vogel, Alexander and Joachim Wagner (2010b). Exports and Profitability — First Evidence for German Business Services Enterprises. *Applied Economics Quarterly* 56(1), 7–30.

Vogel, Alexander and Joachim Wagner (2011). Robust estimates of exporter productivity premia in German business services enterprises. Working Paper Series in Economics 207. University of Lueneburg: Institute of Economics.

Wagner, Joachim (2007a). Exports and Productivity: A Survey of the Evidence from Firm-Level Data. *The World Economy* 30(1), 60–82.

Wagner, Joachim (2007b). Productivity and Size of the Export Market — Evidence for West and East German plants 2004. *Jahrbücher für Nationalökonomie und Statistik/Journal of Economics and Statistics* 227(4), 403–408.

Wagner, Joachim (2008). Export Entry, Export Exit and Productivity in German Manufacturing Industries. *International Journal of the Economics of Business* 15(2), 169–180.

Wagner, Joachim (2010). The post-entry performance of cohorts of export starters in German manufacturing industries. Working Paper Series in Economics 187. University of Lueneburg: Institute of Economics.

Wagner, Joachim (2011a). Offshoring and Firm Performance: Self-Selection, Effects on Performance, or Both? *Review of World Economics/Weltwirtschaftliches Archiv* 147(2), 217–247.

Wagner, Joachim (2011b). Exports, Imports and Profitability: First Evidence for Manufacturing Enterprises. Working Paper Series in Economics 206. University of Lueneburg: Institute of Economics.

Wagner, Joachim (2011c). Exports, Imports and Firm Survival: First Evidence for Manufacturing Enterprises in Germany. Working Paper Series in Economics 211. University of Lueneburg: Institute of Economics.

Wakasugi, Ryuhei and Ayumu Tanaka (2009). Firm Heterogeneity and Different Modes of Internationalization: Evidence from Japanese Firms. KIER Working Paper 681. Kyoto University: Institute of Economic Research.

Wilhelmsson, Frederik and Konstantin Kozlov (2007). Exports and Productivity of Russian Firms: In Search of Causality. *Economic Change and Restructuring* 40(4), 361–385.

Yashiro, Naomitsu and Daisuke Hirano (2009). Do All Exporters Benefit from Export Boom? Evidence from Japan. KIER Working Paper 689. Kyoto University: Institute of Economic Research.

# PART II

# Characteristics of Exporting and Importing Firms in Germany

## Chapter 3

# Exports and Firm Characteristics in German Manufacturing Industries: New Evidence from Representative Panel Data

Joachim Wagner

**Abstract**

Germany is one of the leading actors in the world market for manufactured goods but not every firm from a manufacturing industry in Germany is an exporter. In 2006, the share of exporters in all enterprises was 69 percent in West Germany and 52 percent in East Germany. Reliable information on the characteristics of exporting and non-exporting firms is important to guide theorists and policy makers in an evidence-based way. This chapter uses recently released rich high quality data for a large representative panel of enterprises from German manufacturing industries to investigate the links between firm characteristics and export activities, demonstrating the decisive role of human capital intensity for exporting. It links these findings to the recent literature from the *new new trade theory* on international activities of heterogeneous firms that emphasizes the role of productivity for exporting. It shows that productivity *is* important for exporting as is hypothesized in the formal theoretical models, but that contrary to the assumption made in these models productivity is not (only) the result from a random draw from the productivity distribution — it is strongly positively related to human capital intensity.

*Keywords*: Exports, firm characteristics, Germany

**JEL Classification:** F14

## 1. Motivation

Germany is one of the leading actors in the world market for manufactured goods, and exports play a key role in shaping the development of the economy. Contrary to what many people (especially people from other countries) think, however, not every firm from a manufacturing industry in Germany is an exporter. In 2006, the share of exporters in all enterprises with at least 20 employees was 69 percent in West Germany and 52 percent in East Germany.[1]

How do these exporting firms differ from firms that sell their products in the national market only? What makes a successful exporter? Are there easily observable characteristics of a firm that are closely related to success in international markets? If this is the case, policy measures might be designed that either target firms with these characteristics to foster export activities, or that help firms that do not yet have these characteristics to build them up and to become the successful exporters of the future. If there are no such characteristics, this casts doubts on the adequacy of specially targeted export promotion programs with a focus on selected groups of firms.

Characteristics of exporting firms from Germany have been investigated before in a number of studies using micro data at the establishment or enterprise level. Wagner (2011) summarizes important aspects of 51 studies published between 1991 and 2011. This synopsis shows that many studies use data for a part of Germany only. These data may or may not be representative for the German economy as a whole. Furthermore, many studies are based on small samples, and often only cross section data are investigated. Most of the studies use data at the level of the local production unit (establishment, plant), and this is problematic when the link between firm characteristics and export activities is investigated and when the local production unit is part of a multi-plant enterprise (which is often the case), because in a multi-plant

[1]All figures are based on the author's own computations; a detailed descriptive table is available on request.

enterprise plants may have different roles, and exports might be concentrated in one unit (or a small number of units) while other units deliver their products to these units and do not report any export activities. The usual approach to include a dummy variable for plants that are part of a multi-plant enterprise cannot take care of this appropriately. The studies that are based on nationally representative and large panel data sets for enterprises usually suffer from lack of information on important firm characteristics — physical capital is not reported in the surveys, and information on activities related to innovation is lacking. Furthermore, only a small number of studies use an econometric method that is suited to model empirically the share of exports in total sales which is a proportion variable with a probability mass at zero due to a large share of non-exporting firms,[2] and among these studies only two attempt to control for unobserved heterogeneity by using a fixed effects model for panel data.

That said, the 51 empirical studies summarized in Wagner (2011) cannot be considered to form a solid basis to extract stylized facts that can be used to inform researchers and policy makers in an evidence-based way. This chapter contributes to the literature by using recently released rich high quality data for a large representative panel of enterprises from German manufacturing industries to investigate the links between firm characteristics and export activities.

The rest of the chapter is organized as follows. Section 2 briefly discusses theoretical considerations and introduces the hypotheses to be tested in the econometric investigations. In Section 3, the data and the definition of the variables used are discussed. Section 4 documents the links between observed firm characteristics and exports. Section 5 investigates the role of unobserved characteristics of the enterprises for the decision to export or not and for the share of exports in total sales. Section 6 links these findings to the recent literature from the *new new trade theory* on international activities

[2]See Wagner (2001) for a discussion of this point and Section 3.3.

of heterogeneous firms that emphasizes the role of productivity for exporting. Section 7 concludes.

## 2. Theoretical Considerations and Hypothesis

A comprehensive theoretical model for the export decision of a firm that discriminates between exporters and non-exporters and that explains the share of exports in total sales is lacking. Therefore, the empirical models used in this study are based on elements of a theory of the exporting firm.[3]

A starting point is the stylized fact that firm size and exports are positively related. This positive link between exports and firm size is due to fixed costs of exporting and efficiency advantages of larger firms due to scale economies, advantages of specialization in management and better conditions in the markets for inputs. Large firms can be expected to have cost advantages on credit markets while small firms often face higher restrictions in the capital market leading to a higher risk of insolvency and illiquidity. Furthermore, there might be disadvantages of small firms in the competition for highly qualified employees. There are limits to the advantage of size, because coordination costs mount as the scale of operations increases, and at some point any further expansion might cease to be profitable. Therefore, a positive relationship between firm size and exports, at least up to a point, is expected.

Further elements of an empirical model to explain the export performance of firms can be taken from the theory of international trade. Countries have a comparative advantage in the production of goods that use the relative abundant factors of production relatively intensively. Given that Germany is relatively rich in physical and human capital and one of the technologically leading countries, firms that use physical and human capital intensively and that are

[3]The theoretical arguments are standard in the literature on the microeconometrics of exports. Therefore, the discussion can be brief here; see Wagner (1995) for a more complete statement.

active in R&D can be expected to have a comparative advantage in the international market.

While the links between exporting on the one hand and firm size, physical and human capital intensity, and R&D activity on the other hand have been explored empirically for quite a long time,[4] the more recent literature dealing with the export activity of firms focuses on the role of productivity. The reason for this switch in emphasis is the central role played by productivity in the literature that is labeled the *new new trade theory*. Canonical theoretical papers in this literature include Melitz (2003) and Helpman, Melitz and Yeaple (2005). In this theoretical literature that was motivated by earlier empirical studies on exports and productivity (including the seminal Brookings paper by Bernard and Jensen (1995) for the United States and the paper by Bernard and Wagner (1997) for Germany), it is argued that only firms with a productivity that lies above a critical point in the productivity distribution can cover the extra (fixed) costs of exporting and make profits simultaneously.

These theoretical papers kicked off a large empirical literature that deals with the existence, statistical significance, and size of productivity differentials between exporters and non-exporters, and with the direction of causality between exports and productivity. A recent review of 45 empirical studies (published between 1995 and 2006) using firm-level panel data from 33 countries concludes that exporters are indeed more productive than non-exporters of the same size from the same narrowly defined industry, and that the more productive firms self-select into export markets, while exporting does not necessarily improve productivity (see Wagner (2007a)).[5] We therefore expect that productivity and exports are positively related.

---

[4]For Germany, see the synopsis in Wagner (2011).

[5]Recent evidence for Germany on productivity and exports is reported in Wagner (2007b) and Vogel and Wagner (2009); for comparable evidence from 14 countries see International Study Group on Exports and Productivity (2008).

## 3. Data and Definition of Variables

The data used in this study are merged from two surveys conducted by the German statistical offices. One source is the monthly report for establishments in manufacturing industries described in Konold (2007). This survey covers all establishments from manufacturing industries that employ at least 20 persons in the local production unit or in the company that owns the unit. Participation of firms in the survey is mandated in official statistics law. For this project, the information collected at the establishment level has been aggregated at the enterprise level to match the unit of observation from the second source of data used here.

This survey is the source for information on the location of the firm in West Germany or East Germany, the industry affiliation, the number of employees (used to measure firm size), the export activities and the average wage per employee (used as a proxy for human capital intensity).

In this data set, export refers to the amount of sales to a customer in a foreign country plus sales to a German export trading company; indirect exports (for example, tires produced in a plant in Germany that are delivered to a German manufacturer of cars who exports some of his products) are not covered by this definition.

Unfortunately, there is no better proxy for human capital intensity than the average wage per employee in a firm. For example, the data has no information on the share of employees with a university degree or the share of employees that successfully passed the exams following apprenticeship. The distinction between blue collar workers and white collar workers that is often used in the literature is no way to proxy human capital intensity for two reasons. First, often blue collar workers are highly qualified skilled employees with apprenticeship (so-called *Facharbeiter*) while white collar workers include many unskilled employees. Second, the distinction between blue collar workers (*Arbeiter*) and white collar workers (*Angestellte*) is no longer used in Germany after a reform of the pension system; in the data from official statistics, for example, there is no separate information on wages (for blue collar workers) and salaries (for white collar employees) from the reporting year 2006 onwards. Obviously, qualification of the work force is not the only determinant of the average wage in a firm, but it can be expected to be highly positively correlated with it. Furthermore, in the empirical model linking wage per employee to exporting both firm size and industry affiliation are included, and therefore, both firm- size wage differentials and inter-industry wage differentials are controlled for.

The second source of data is the cost structure survey for enterprises in the manufacturing sector. This survey is carried out annually as a representative random sample survey (stratified according to the number of employees and the industries) of around 18.000 enterprises (see Fritsch *et al.* 2004). While firms with 500 and more employees are covered by the cost structure survey in each year, the sample of smaller firms is part of the survey for four years in a row only. In this study, we use the data from the most recent complete sample period available that cover the years from 2003 to 2006.

This survey is the source for information on the R&D intensity of the firm (measured as the relation of spending for research and development activities to total sales) and the share of employees working in R&D. Data on the stock of physical capital is neither available from the monthly report for establishments in manufacturing industries nor from the cost structure survey for enterprises in the manufacturing sector.[6] The cost structure survey, however, has information on the amount of depreciation in an enterprise. Together with information on the average life span of capital goods (for equipments, and for buildings) and information in the composition of the capital stock at the level of 2-digit industries,

[6]Annual data for investments are available from a separate survey on investments (*Investitionserhebung*) that can be linked to the data used here. A careful inspection of these investment data revealed that they should not be used to construct estimates of the capital stock of the firm by using the perpetual inventory method. The crucial problem here lies in the fact that investment at the firm level tends to be highly volatile. Often very high values in some year and very low values (or no investments at all) in some other year are reported, and this leads to rather different values for the capital stock proxy variable depending on the year(s) used.

these figures for depreciation can be used to estimate the capital stock in an enterprise (see Wagner (2010a) for details).[7] The capital stock per employee is used as a measure for the physical capital intensity in the enterprise.

Productivity is measured by labor productivity defined as value added per employee. Bartelsman and Doms (2000, p. 575) point to the fact that heterogeneity in labor productivity has been found to be accompanied by similar heterogeneity in total factor productivity in the reviewed research where both concepts are measured. In a recent comprehensive survey, Chad Syverson (2011) argues that high-productivity producers will tend to look efficient regardless of the specific way that their productivity is measured.[8] Furthermore, Foster, Haltiwanger and Syverson (2008) show that productivity measures that use sales (i.e. quantities multiplied by prices) and measures that use quantities only are highly positively correlated.

Data from the two surveys are matched using the enterprise identifier available in both surveys.[9] These data are confidential but not exclusive; they can be used for empirical investigations inside the research data centers of the statistical offices in Germany (see Zühlke *et al.* (2004) for details). The balanced panels[10] used cover 10,038 enterprises in West Germany and 1,852 enterprises in East Germany. Given that there are large differences between enterprises from West Germany and East Germany even more than 10 years after re-unification in 1990 especially with regard to export

[7]Physical capital is constructed here based on reported depreciation. Depreciation, however, is governed by accounting rules, i.e. it is not necessarily representative for the true economic loss of value of investment goods. Results reported below may be driven by the way capital intensity is proxied. However, with the data at hand this cannot be tested.

[8]See ISGEP (2008) for a comparison of results for productivity differentials between exporting and non-exporting firms based on sales per employee, value added per employee and total factor productivity. Results proved remarkably robust.

[9]For a description of the matched data from various surveys from official statistics see Malchin and Voshage (2009).

[10]Note that by construction there are no entries into the sample covered by the cost structure survey during a four year period. Enterprises exit the survey if they close down, relocate to services industries or agriculture, or to another country, or shrink below the threshold of 20 employees. Given that one estimator for panel data models used in Section 4 is only available for balanced panels all computations use the data from the balanced panel to facilitate comparisons between analyses based on cross section data and on panel data.

activities,[11] all computations are performed for the two parts of Germany separately.

## 4. Observed Firm Characteristics and Export Activity

In the balanced panels used in this study, the share of exporting firms increased slightly over the years covered. In West Germany, this share was 80.4 percent in 2003, 80.6 percent in 2004, 80.9 percent in 2005 and 81.4 percent in 2006. The corresponding figures for East Germany were 62.5 percent (2003), 62.8 percent (2004), 63.7 percent (2005) and 65.1 percent (2006), considerably lower than in West Germany.[12] The export participation patterns reported in Table 1 demonstrate that this overall net increase in export participation is not only the result of entry of firms into exporting — from year to year, firms enter and exit the export market, some of them more than once. The share of permanent exporters in all firms, therefore, is lower than the share of firms that exported in a single year.

### 4.1. *Unconditional differences between exporters and non-exporters*

Exporting and non-exporting firms are different in a number of ways. Table 2 shows that on average exporters are larger (measured by the number of employees), employ more physical capital per employee, pay higher wages per employee (and, therefore, can be viewed as more human capital intensive), are more intensively engaged in research and development activities and are more

[11] See Wagner (2008a) for a discussion of the difference in exporting between firms from West Germany and East Germany.

[12] The share of exporters in all firms in the balanced panel is larger than the share of exporters in all manufacturing firms reported at the beginning of section 1. This difference is due to the fact that in the cost structure survey all firms with 500 and more employees are included while only a sample of smaller firms (stratified by industry and size class) has to report to this survey. Larger firms, therefore, are oversampled. Given that larger firms have a higher propensity to export than smaller firms the share of exporters in the balanced panel is higher than in the population of firms. In the econometric analysis the inclusion of firm size and industry as control variables takes care of this sampling frame.

Table 1. Export participation patterns 2003–2006

| Pattern | Frequency | Percent | Cumulated |
|---|---|---|---|
| *West Germany* | | | |
| 0000 | 1,658 | 16.52 | 16.52 |
| 0001 | 99 | 0.99 | 17.50 |
| 0010 | 23 | 0.23 | 17.73 |
| 0011 | 56 | 0.56 | 18.29 |
| 0100 | 25 | 0.25 | 18.54 |
| 0101 | 10 | 0.10 | 18.64 |
| 0110 | 12 | 0.12 | 18.76 |
| 0111 | 80 | 0.80 | 19.56 |
| 1000 | 74 | 0.74 | 20.29 |
| 1001 | 11 | 0.11 | 20.40 |
| 1010 | 7 | 0.07 | 20.47 |
| 1011 | 19 | 0.19 | 20.66 |
| 1100 | 31 | 0.31 | 20.97 |
| 1101 | 12 | 0.12 | 21.09 |
| 1110 | 41 | 0.41 | 21.50 |
| 1111 | 7,880 | 78.50 | 100.00 |
| Total | 10,038 | 100.00 | |
| *East Germany* | | | |
| 0000 | 565 | 30.51 | 30.51 |
| 0001 | 45 | 2.43 | 32.94 |
| 0010 | 8 | 0.43 | 33.37 |
| 0011 | 26 | 1.40 | 34.77 |
| 0100 | 8 | 0.43 | 35.21 |
| 0101 | 7 | 0.38 | 35.58 |
| 0110 | 8 | 0.43 | 36.02 |
| 0111 | 28 | 1.51 | 37.53 |
| 1000 | 25 | 1.35 | 38.88 |
| 1001 | 5 | 0.27 | 39.15 |
| 1010 | 3 | 0.16 | 39.31 |
| 1011 | 12 | 0.65 | 39.96 |
| 1100 | 12 | 0.65 | 40.60 |
| 1101 | 6 | 0.32 | 40.93 |
| 1110 | 17 | 0.92 | 41.85 |
| 1111 | 1,077 | 58.15 | 100.00 |
| Total | 1,852 | 100.00 | |

*Note*: Frequency is the number of enterprises with a pattern. A zero indicates that an enterprise did not export in a year, a one indicates that it did export. A firm with the pattern 0000 did never export between 2003 and 2006, a firm with the pattern 0001 exported only in the last year (2006), etc.

Table 2. Differences between exporters and non-exporters: Mean values of variables

| | | | Number of employees | Physical capital per employee (€) | Wage per employee per year (€) | Share of R&D expend in total sales (percent) | Share of employees in R&D (percent) | Value added per employee (€) |
|---|---|---|---|---|---|---|---|---|
| *West Germany* | | | | | | | | |
| 2003 | Exporter | mean | 398.1 | 91,666.3 | 33,783.9 | 1.25 | 2.60 | 56,690 |
| | | sd | 2,725.2 | 109,625.3 | 9,246.3 | 2.97 | 5.68 | 29,988 |
| | Non-export. | mean | 116.0 | 82,553.9 | 28,436.2 | 0.18 | 0.41 | 45,165 |
| | | sd | 212.0 | 120,346.5 | 10,117.7 | 1.22 | 2.47 | 25,038 |
| | *t*-test | (*p*-value) | 0.000 | 0.002 | 0.000 | 0.000 | 0.000 | 0.000 |
| 2004 | Exporter | mean | 395.2 | 88,966.3 | 34,612.7 | 1.23 | 2.61 | 59,307 |
| | | sd | 2,720.2 | 107,519.2 | 9,570.1 | 3.06 | 5.70 | 31,988 |
| | Non-export. | mean | 109.7 | 81,768.8 | 28,654.8 | 0.20 | 0.41 | 46,263 |
| | | sd | 182.2 | 124,986.2 | 9,570.1 | 1.34 | 2.36 | 26,745 |
| | *t*-test | (*p*-value) | 0.000 | 0.019 | 0.000 | 0.000 | 0.000 | 0.000 |
| 2005 | Exporter | mean | 388.2 | 88,100.9 | 35,035.7 | 1.26 | 2.67 | 60,032 |
| | | Sd | 2,705.1 | 104,426.4 | 9,944.6 | 3.26 | 5.72 | 35,683 |
| | Non-export. | mean | 114.2 | 81,202.9 | 28,607.0 | 0.21 | 0.44 | 46,533 |
| | | Sd | 217.1 | 119,153.2 | 10,356.5 | 1.57 | 2.75 | 28,863 |
| | *t*-test | (*p*-value) | 0.000 | 0.020 | 0.000 | 0.000 | 0.000 | 0.000 |
| 2006 | Exporter | mean | 385.2 | 92,477.0 | 35,631.0 | 1.19 | 2.69 | 62,689 |
| | | Sd | 2,733.9 | 209,687.0 | 10,484.8 | 2.81 | 5.73 | 45,195 |
| | Non-export. | mean | 114.2 | 84,441.1 | 28,871.3 | 0.18 | 0.38 | 47,834 |
| | | Sd | 215.5 | 125,666.2 | 10,684.9 | 1.34 | 2.57 | 29,917 |
| | *t*-test | (*p*-value) | 0.000 | 0.031 | 0.000 | 0.000 | 0.000 | 0.000 |

(*Continued*)

Table 2. *(Continued)*

| | | | Number of employees | Physical capital per employee (€) | Wage per employee per year (€) | Share of R&D expend in total sales (percent) | Share of employees in R&D (percent) | Value added per employee (€) |
|---|---|---|---|---|---|---|---|---|
| *East Germany* | | | | | | | | |
| 2003 | Exporter | mean | 196.5 | 150,654.3 | 24,816.2 | 1.63 | 3.75 | 47,237 |
| | | Sd | 542.2 | 248,688.2 | 8,073.6 | 4.74 | 8.07 | 33,255 |
| | Non-export. | mean | 115.0 | 129,388.6 | 21,437.8 | 0.28 | 0.79 | 40,644 |
| | | Sd | 277.7 | 417,982.4 | 7,841.4 | 1.26 | 3.54 | 35,027 |
| | *t*-test | (*p*-value) | 0.000 | 0.224 | 0.000 | 0.000 | 0.000 | 0.000 |
| 2004 | Exporter | mean | 196.5 | 150,553.5 | 25,687.0 | 1.58 | 3.41 | 49,616 |
| | | Sd | 532.8 | 279,337.0 | 8,212.2 | 4.45 | 7.99 | 47,473 |
| | Non-export. | mean | 115.1 | 113,970.4 | 22,117.7 | 0.34 | 0.76 | 40,578 |
| | | Sd | 272.3 | 164,268.3 | 7,796.2 | 1.59 | 3.22 | 30,347 |
| | *t*-test | (*p*-value) | 0.000 | 0.000 | 0.000 | 0.000 | 0.000 | 0.000 |
| 2005 | Exporter | mean | 194.9 | 151,016.2 | 25,964.2 | 1.61 | 3.41 | 50,933 |
| | | Sd | 513.8 | 274,276.4 | 8,340.7 | 4.48 | 7.92 | 47,243 |
| | Non-export. | mean | 114.0 | 111,159.0 | 22,289.2 | 0.27 | 0.71 | 40,719 |
| | | Sd | 240.4 | 156,757.1 | 8,154.4 | 1.29 | 3.24 | 28,884 |
| | *t*-test | (*p*-value) | 0.000 | 0.000 | 0.000 | 0.000 | 0.000 | 0.000 |
| 2006 | Exporter | mean | 194.2 | 147,077.9 | 26,465.8 | 1.46 | 3.36 | 52,845 |
| | | Sd | 497.4 | 233,062.8 | 8,928.9 | 3.81 | 7.74 | 41,529 |
| | Non-export. | mean | 111.7 | 107,526.3 | 22,400.6 | 0.25 | 0.77 | 41,289 |
| | | Sd | 240.2 | 233,062.8 | 8,117.3 | 1.16 | 3.10 | 37,626 |
| | *t*-test | (*p*-value) | 0.000 | 0.000 | 0.000 | 0.000 | 0.000 | 0.000 |

*Note*: sd is the standard deviation. The *t*-test is for $H_0$: equality of mean values, assuming unequal variances for the two groups.

productive. These differences in the means are statistically highly significant with the exception of physical capital intensity in some years. Furthermore, the differences are very large from an economic point of view for R&D activities, and rather high for firm size, wage per employee and productivity.

These findings are in line with evidence from earlier empirical studies summarized in Wagner (2011). Furthermore, given that Germany is one of the most highly developed countries, we expect that firms using human capital and new technology intensively to produce new products have a comparative advantage and, therefore, are the more successful exporters.

Everybody who is familiar with firm-level data knows that firms tend to be heterogeneous. Some exporters are very large and well known firms like Volkswagen, Daimler or Siemens. In 2006, the share of the largest 50 exporters in total exports as 43.0 percent in West Germany and 51.6 percent in East Germany.[13] Many exporting firms, however, were small firms, and each of them contributed only a tiny share to total exports. This heterogeneity of exporting firms with regard to size is illustrated in column two of Table 3. In 2003,[14] the smallest exporters in West Germany had less than 20 employees, the median size was 115 employees (far below the average value of 398 employees), and the three largest exporting firms had on average more than 100,000 employees.

Heterogeneity of exporting firms is not limited to size. As shown in Table 3 successful exporters can be found among firms that produce goods with a very high capital to labor ratio, but there are exporters who manufacture goods with nearly no physical capital. Many exporters have a high share of highly qualified employees, while human capital intensity is rather low in other firms. Some exporters are very active in research and development, others not

[13]These figures refer to all enterprises (legal units) with at least 20 employees and not to the samples used in this study. They are based on the author's own computations; a detailed descriptive table is available on request. Note that the names of these large exporters are confidential like all information from official statistics that relates to a single firm.

[14]Results for the other years show an identical picture and are not reported to economize on space.

Table 3. Distribution of characteristics of exporters and non-exporters in 2003

| | | Share of exports in total sales (percent) | Number of employees | Physical capital per employee (€) | Wage per employee per year (€) | Share of R&D expend in total sales (percent) | Share of employees in R&D (percent) | Value added per employee (€) |
|---|---|---|---|---|---|---|---|---|
| *West Germany* | | | | | | | | |
| Exporters | mean | 31.62 | 398.1 | 91,666.3 | 33,783.9 | 1.25 | 2.60 | 56,699 |
| ($N = 8075$) | sd | 24.79 | 2725.2 | 109,625.3 | 9,246.3 | 2.97 | 5.68 | 29,888 |
| | average of 3 smallest | 0.003 | 18.37 | 53.33 | 5,266.8 | 0 | 0 | −120,821 |
| | p1 | 0.11 | 22.1 | 1,766.4 | 13,023.8 | 0 | 0 | 12,956 |
| | p5 | 0.97 | 26.8 | 10,462.5 | 19,456.5 | 0 | 0 | 25,259 |
| | p25 | 10.39 | 53.7 | 35,994.9 | 27,742.4 | 0 | 0 | 40,686 |
| | p50 | 26.89 | 114.8 | 65,327.0 | 33,486.6 | 0 | 0 | 52,054 |
| | p75 | 49.54 | 293.1 | 112,178.7 | 39,255.3 | 1.20 | 2.83 | 65,789 |
| | p95 | 78.98 | 1,214.4 | 247,795.2 | 49,028.8 | 6.45 | 13.02 | 102,111 |
| | p99 | 93.46 | 3,599.0 | 474,227.8 | 60,201.5 | 13.81 | 26.91 | 155,097 |
| | average of 3 largest | 100.00 | 117,365.5 | 2,430,620 | 94,453.1 | 48.09 | 74.3 | 616,678 |

| | | | | | | | | |
|---|---|---|---|---|---|---|---|---|
| *East Germany* | | | | | | | | |
| Non-exporters | mean | 0 | 116.0 | 82,553.9 | 28,436.2 | 0.18 | 0.41 | 45,165 |
| ($N = 1963$) | sd | 0 | 212.0 | 120,346.5 | 10,117.7 | 1.22 | 2.47 | 25,038 |
| | average of 3 smallest | 0 | 9.3 | 100.6 | 1,780.1 | 0 | 0 | −15,413 |
| | p1 | 0 | 18.6 | 870.6 | 6,510.9 | 0 | 0 | 7,930 |
| | p5 | 0 | 22.5 | 5,384.0 | 12,447.4 | 0 | 0 | 15,925 |
| | p25 | 0 | 32.8 | 22,804.9 | 21,823.5 | 0 | 0 | 28,937 |
| | p50 | 0 | 53.7 | 47,360.5 | 28,334.2 | 0 | 0 | 41,791 |
| | p75 | 0 | 108.8 | 100,118.6 | 34,314.9 | 0 | 0 | 55,623 |
| | p95 | 0 | 442.0 | 252,575.8 | 45,433.1 | 0.43 | 1.49 | 87,770 |
| | p99 | 0 | 1,081.3 | 570,090.8 | 55,445.1 | 5.76 | 13.79 | 122,148 |
| | average of 3 largest | 0 | 2,959.2 | 1,590,138 | 79,413.2 | 19.1 | 36.8 | 289,533 |

(*Continued*)

Table 3. (*Continued*)

| | | Share of exports in total sales (percent) | Number of employees | Physical capital per employee (€) | Wage per employee per year (€) | Share of R&D expend in total sales (percent) | Share of employees in R&D (percent) | Value added per employee (€) |
|---|---|---|---|---|---|---|---|---|
| *East Germany* | | | | | | | | |
| Exporters | mean | 25.78 | 196.5 | 150,654.3 | 24,816.2 | 1.63 | 3.75 | 49,616 |
| ($N = 1,157$) | sd | 24.87 | 542.2 | 248,688.2 | 8,073.6 | 4.74 | 8.07 | 47,473 |
| | average of 3 smallest | 0.009 | 19.9 | 421.5 | 3,913.6 | 0 | 0 | −14,665 |
| | p1 | 0.03 | 21.6 | 2,596.9 | 9,680.9 | 0 | 0 | 6,358 |
| | p5 | 0.35 | 25.0 | 14,230.4 | 13,637.4 | 0 | 0 | 18,255 |
| | p25 | 5.04 | 42.7 | 46,213.8 | 19,587.9 | 0 | 0 | 30,435 |
| | p50 | 17.83 | 82.6 | 92,230.0 | 23,788.6 | 0 | 0 | 41,627 |
| | p75 | 40.43 | 165.3 | 160,483.1 | 29,179.4 | 1.04 | 3.45 | 57,331 |
| | p95 | 77.43 | 613.3 | 466,558.1 | 39,957.3 | 9.35 | 22.04 | 97,904 |
| | p99 | 96.51 | 2,073.7 | 981,023.6 | 49,785.8 | 21.08 | 36.84 | 172,254 |
| | average of 3 largest | 100.00 | 7,753.1 | 3,333,004 | 65,104.0 | 58.74 | 57.46 | 405,536 |

| | | | | | | | | |
|---|---|---|---|---|---|---|---|---|
| Non-exporters ($N = 695$) | mean | 0 | 115.0 | 129,388.6 | 21,437.8 | 0.28 | 0.79 | 40,578 |
| | sd | 0 | 277.7 | 417,982.4 | 7,841.4 | 1.26 | 3.54 | 30,347 |
| | average of 3 smallest | 0 | 16.6 | 497.6 | 2,731.6 | 0 | 0 | −3,378 |
| | p1 | 0 | 19.3 | 1,765.0 | 7,885.9 | 0 | 0 | 9,172 |
| | p5 | 0 | 23.2 | 8,934.4 | 11,235.2 | 0 | 0 | 16,145 |
| | p25 | 0 | 32.8 | 29,930.2 | 16,128.5 | 0 | 0 | 24,613 |
| | p50 | 0 | 54.8 | 60,471.3 | 20,434.8 | 0 | 0 | 33,560 |
| | p75 | 0 | 101.9 | 135,825.8 | 25,030.7 | 0 | 0 | 46,354 |
| | p95 | 0 | 367.1 | 408,884.1 | 37,297.0 | 1.48 | 5.00 | 86,132 |
| | p99 | 0 | 1,372.3 | 863,976.2 | 46,042.3 | 7.37 | 18.18 | 171,095 |
| | average of 3 largest | 0 | 3,126.6 | 4,353,952 | 53,759.8 | 11.15 | 33.90 | 376,785 |

*Note*: sd is the standard deviation; p1 is the first percentile, etc. The mimima and maxima are confidential because they are information for single enterprises; therefore, the average values of the three smallest and the three largest values are reported.

at all. Some exporters have a negative value for value added, others have a high productivity. And heterogeneity is not limited to exporting firms, it is found in non-exporting firms too. This illustrates what James Heckman (2001, p. 674) pointed out in his Nobel-lecture, namely that "(t)he most important discovery [from micro-econometric investigations, *J.W.*] was the evidence on the pervasiveness of heterogeneity and diversity in economic life."

A test for differences in the mean values, therefore, can only be a first step in a comparison of exporters and non-exporters. As Moshe Buchinsky (1994, p. 453) put it: "On the average' has never been a satisfactory statement with which to conclude a study on heterogeneous populations." An empirical study of heterogeneous firms should look at differences in the whole distribution of the variables under investigation between groups of firms, not only in differences at the means.

The hypothesis that the distribution of firm size, physical capital intensity, human capital intensity and R&D intensity for exporters stochastically dominates the respective distribution of non-exporters can be tested by the Kolmogorov–Smirnov test. This non-parametric test for first order stochastic dominance of one distribution over another was introduced into the empirical literature on exports by Delgado, Farinas and Ruano (2002). Let $F$ and $G$ denote the cumulative distribution functions of a variable for two groups of firms, exporters and non-exporters. First order stochastic dominance of $F$ relative to $G$ is given if $F(z) - G(z)$ is less or equal zero for all $z$ with strict inequality for some $z$. Given two independent random samples of firms from each group, the hypothesis that $F$ is to the right of $G$ can be tested by the Kolmogorov–Smirnov test based on the empirical distribution functions for $F$ and $G$ in the samples (for details, see Conover (1999), p. 456ff.).

The results for the Kolmogorov–Smirnov test indicate that the distributions of all variables differ between exporters and non-exporters in each year in West Germany and in East Germany, and that the difference is in favor of the exporters in all cases considered.[15] These results are highly significant statistically. The bottom line, then, is that exporters are larger (measured by the number of employees), employ more physical capital per employee, pay higher wages per employee (and, therefore, can be viewed as more human capital intensive) and are more intensively engaged in research and development activities not only on average but over the whole distribution of these characteristics.

### 4.2. *Conditional differences between exporters and non-exporters*

So far, only the unconditional differences between one observed characteristic of exporters and non-exporters at a time have been investigated. Next, the link between a characteristic and the export activity will be looked at conditional on the industry of the firm and on the effects of the other characteristics. To do so, we proceed in two steps: In step one in Sections 4 and 5, the empirical models include as firm characteristics the number of employees, physical capital per employee, wage per employee and R&D intensity plus a full set of 4digit industry dummy variables as exogenous variables.[16] This step one, therefore, is related to the older literature

[15]The $p$-values for the hypotheses that the distributions do not differ and that the differences are in favor of non-exporters are 0.000 throughout; the $p$-values for the hypothesis that the differences are in favor of the exporters are always higher than 0.580 and next to 1.000 in most cases. Tables with detailed results are available from the author on request.

[16]It might be argued that these firm characteristics should not be treated as exogenous because exporting might cause firms to grow, to invest in physical or human capital or to increase the level of R&D activities. To justify the approach taken here, it should be pointed out that a large literature finds support for the hypothesis that "better" (larger, more productive, more innovative, etc.) firms tend to self-select into exporting, while positive effects of exports on firm characteristics are only rarely found (see Wagner (2007a) for a survey of this literature). For empirical evidence that higher wages in exporting firms already exist in the years before firms start to export, and that the exporter wage premium does not increase in the following years, see Schank, Schnabel and Wagner (2010). Higher wages in exporting firms are thus not caused by export activities. Note that the use of lagged value of firm characteristics in the empirical models is no convincing strategy to deal with a potential endogeneity problem here because the firm characteristics are highly positively correlated over time (the correlation coefficients in the sample used in this study are around 0.9 for two adjacent years).

on determinants of exports while step two links the findings from step one to the more recent literature from the *new new trade theory* and the related micro-econometric studies on exports and productivity.

The endogenous variable in the empirical model is a dummy variable that takes the value one if the firm is an exporter (and zero otherwise). Results are reported in Table 4. For each year from 2003 to 2006, results for two empirical models are given. Model 1 measures R&D activity by the share of R&D expenditures in total sales, model 2 uses the share of employees in R&D. Both R&D measures are highly positively correlated (the correlation coefficient lies between 0.75 and 0.81 in the four years). Table 4 reports the estimated marginal effects from a probit regression.

*Ceteris paribus* the probability that a firm is an exporter is higher for larger firms,[17] firms that pay higher wages per employee (and that can be considered to be more human capital intensive) and firms that are more actively engaged in R&D both in West Germany and in East Germany. While these results are in line with the results reported above for unconditional differences in firm characteristics between exporters and non-exporters, the result for physical capital intensity is different. Controlling for industry affiliation and the other firm characteristics included in the empirical model physical capital intensity and exporting are not positively related. For all but one year and one part of Germany the estimated regression coefficient is not statistically significant at the usual error level of 5 percent — and the results indicate a negative relation for this case (West Germany in 2004).

[17]Note that the sign pattern of the estimated coefficients for the number of employees and the squared value of the number of employees points to an inversely u-shaped relation between firm size and the probability of exporting. From the estimated coefficients (not reported here to economize on space) the estimated maximum value of this inversely u-shaped relation can be computed. This value is very large. The maximum value from the estimated coefficients for model 1 in 2003 in West Germany is 55,488 — this is much larger than the 99$^{th}$ percentile of the distribution of the number of employees for both exporters and non-exporters (see Table 3). The same holds for East Germany where the estimated maximum value is 3,950. Therefore, the estimated coefficients indicate that the probability to export increases with the number of employees in a firm, but at a decreasing rate.

Table 4. Determinants of export participation: Probit-estimates

| | | 2003 | | 2004 | | 2005 | | 2006 | |
|---|---|---|---|---|---|---|---|---|---|
| | | Model 1 | Model 2 | Model 1 | Model 2 | Model 1 | Model 2 | Model 1 | Model 2 |
| *West Germany* | | | | | | | | | |
| Number of | $\beta$ | 0.000193 | 0.000198 | 0.000228 | 0.000229 | 0.000171 | 0.000172 | 0.000161 | 0.000161 |
| employees | $p$ | 0.000 | 0.000 | 0.000 | 0.000 | 0.000 | 0.000 | 0.000 | 0.000 |
| Number of | $\beta$ | −1.74e-9 | −1.78e-9 | −1.63e-9 | −1.63e-9 | −1.22e-9 | −1.23e-9 | −1.21e-9 | −1.21e-9 |
| employees (squared) | $p$ | 0.000 | 0.000 | 0.000 | 0.000 | 0.000 | 0.000 | 0.000 | 0.000 |
| Physical capital per | $\beta$ | −3.73e-8 | −3.74e-8 | −7.89e-8 | −7.777e-8 | −7.10e-8 | −7.22e-8 | −4.92 | −6.55e-9 |
| employee (€) | $p$ | 0.403 | 0.399 | 0.033 | 0.034 | 0.106 | 0.097 | 0.789 | 0.715 |
| Wage per employee | $\beta$ | 5.21e-6 | 5.08e-6 | 5.37e-6 | 5.15e-6 | 5.78e-6 | 5.60e-6 | 5.18e-6 | 4.96e-6 |
| per year (€) | $p$ | 0.000 | 0.000 | 0.000 | 0.000 | 0.000 | 0.000 | 0.000 | 0.000 |
| Share of R&D expend. | $\beta$ | 0.019979 | | 0.01461 | | 0.01212 | | 0.01532 | |
| in total sales (percent) | $p$ | 0.000 | | 0.000 | | 0.010 | | 0.001 | |
| Share of employees | $\beta$ | | 0.01014 | | 0.00879 | | 0.00722 | | 0.00847 |
| in R&D (percent) | $p$ | | 0.000 | | 0.000 | | 0.001 | | 0.002 |
| Number of cases | | 9,357 | 9,357 | 9,424 | 9,424 | 9,410 | 9,410 | 9,353 | 9,353 |

(*Continued*)

Table 4. (*Continued*)

| | | 2003 | | 2004 | | 2005 | | 2006 | |
|---|---|---|---|---|---|---|---|---|---|
| | | Model 1 | Model 2 | Model 1 | Model 2 | Model 1 | Model 2 | Model 1 | Model 2 |
| *East Germany* | | | | | | | | | |
| Number of | $\beta$ | 0.000287 | 0.000298 | 0.000307 | 0.000304 | 0.000369 | 0.000370 | 0.000334 | 0.000338 |
| employees | $p$ | 0.009 | 0.007 | 0.006 | 0.007 | 0.002 | 0.002 | 0.005 | 0.005 |
| Number of | $\beta$ | −3.75e-8 | −3.79e-8 | −3.87e-8 | −3.79e-8 | −4.43e-8 | −4.40e-8 | −4.17e-8 | −4.18e-8 |
| employees (squared) | $p$ | 0.014 | 0.009 | 0.011 | 0.014 | 0.006 | 0.007 | 0.010 | 0.011 |
| Physical capital per | $\beta$ | −7.09e-8 | −6.87e-8 | −2.89e-8 | −2.35e-8 | 7.80e-9 | 1.15e-8 | 1.21e-8 | 1.47e-8 |
| employee (€) | $p$ | 0.079 | 0.087 | 0.650 | 0.711 | 0.903 | 0.857 | 0.870 | 0.844 |
| Wage per employee | $\beta$ | 0.000011 | 0.000011 | 0.000012 | 0.000012 | 9.10e-6 | 9.38e-6 | 0.000011 | 0.000011 |
| per year (€) | $p$ | 0.000 | 0.000 | 0.000 | 0.000 | 0.000 | 0.000 | 0.000 | 0.000 |
| Share of R&D expend. | $\beta$ | 0.03668 | | 0.02491 | | 0.0378 | | 0.0446 | |
| in total sales (percent) | $p$ | 0.000 | | 0.002 | | 0.000 | | 0.000 | |
| Share of employees | $\beta$ | | 0.01527 | | 0.01524 | | 0.01601 | | 0.01699 |
| in R&D (percent) | $p$ | | 0.000 | | 0.000 | | 0.000 | | 0.000 |
| Number of cases | | 1,624 | 1,624 | 1,610 | 1,610 | 1,597 | 1,597 | 1,609 | 1,609 |

*Note*: $\beta$ is the estimated marginal effect at the mean of the independent variable; $p$ is the prob-value. All models include a full set of 4 digit industry-dummies plus a constant. The number of cases differs between years because firms from industries were all or no firms exported were dropped before the probit estimates were computed.

While the statistical significance and the direction of the relationship between the firm characteristics included in the model and the probability that a firm is an exporter can be seen from Table 4 at a glance, the relevance of a specific firm characteristic for the probability of being an exporter — the significance from an economic point of view — cannot be seen here. Table 4 reports the marginal effects, that is, the change in the probability of being an exporter for an infinitesimal change in the firm characteristic, measured at the mean of the variable. While marginal effects can in a sense be more easily interpreted than the estimated coefficients from the probit regression (that are not reported here to economize on space), it is still difficult to see which of the statistically significant effects can be considered to be important. If, for example, an increase in the annual wage per employee by 10.000 Euro would increase the probability that a firm is an exporter by 0.01 percent, we would consider this effect as negligible and we would argue that human capital intensity does not matter for the probability that a firm is an exporter, regardless of the prob-value of the estimated coefficient.

To elaborate on this, let us look at model 1 for West Germany in 2003.[18] From the reported marginal effect for wage per employee per year, we see that an increase of this measure for human capital intensity (evaluated at the sample mean of this variable) by 10.000 € has an estimated effect of +0.0521 — the estimated probability that a firm is an exporter is 5.21 percent higher than before *ceteris paribus*. This indicates an important link between human capital intensity and export participation. The same holds for the R&D variables. An increase in the share of R&D expenditures in total sales by 2 percentage points (again evaluated at the sample mean of this variable) has an estimated effect of 4 percentage points on the probability that a firm is an exporter. Firm size is important, too. An increase in the number of employees (again evaluated at the sample mean of this variable) by 100 persons has an estimated effect of 1.9 percent.

[18]Given that the estimated results are very similar for the various models the conclusions from looking at this particular model hold for the other models, too.

Table 5. Firm characteristics and export participation: Simulations[1]

| Case Number | Number of employees | Number of employees (squared) | Physical capital per employee (€) | Wage per employee per year (€) | Share of R&D expenditures in total sales (percent) | Estimated probability for being an exporter |
|---|---|---|---|---|---|---|
| *West Germany* | | | | | | |
| 1 | 20 | 400 | 2,000 | 15,000 | 0 | 0.730 |
| 2 | 100 | 10,000 | 2,000 | 15,000 | 0 | 0.751 |
| 3 | 100 | 10,000 | 55,000 | 15,000 | 0 | 0.745 |
| 4 | 100 | 10,000 | 55,000 | 30,000 | 0 | 0.857 |
| 5 | 100 | 10,000 | 55,000 | 30,000 | 1.0 | 0.870 |
| 6 | 500 | 250,000 | 55,000 | 30,000 | 1.0 | 0.926 |
| 7 | 500 | 250,000 | 400,000 | 30,000 | 1.0 | 0.908 |
| 8 | 500 | 250,000 | 400,000 | 60,000 | 1.0 | 0.984 |
| 9 | 500 | 250,000 | 400,000 | 60,000 | 10.0 | 0.996 |
| *East Germany* | | | | | | |
| 1 | 20 | 400 | 2,000 | 15,000 | 0 | 0.474 |
| 2 | 100 | 10,000 | 2,000 | 15,000 | 0 | 0.505 |
| 3 | 100 | 10,000 | 55,000 | 15,000 | 0 | 0.505 |
| 4 | 100 | 10,000 | 55,000 | 30,000 | 0 | 0.645 |
| 5 | 100 | 10,000 | 55,000 | 30,000 | 1.0 | 0.681 |
| 6 | 500 | 250,000 | 55,000 | 30,000 | 1.0 | 0.797 |
| 7 | 500 | 250,000 | 400,000 | 30,000 | 1.0 | 0.799 |
| 8 | 500 | 250,000 | 400,000 | 60,000 | 1.0 | 0.940 |
| 9 | 500 | 250,000 | 400,000 | 60,000 | 10.0 | 0.993 |

[1]The simulations are based on the estimated model 1 for 2005.

Another way to understand which firm characteristics are important for becoming an exporter uses the estimated results from the probit models to perform simulation exercises by looking at hypothetical firms and computing the estimated probability that these firms are exporters. Results for such exercises are reported in Table 5.

Based on the estimation results for model 1 in 2005,[19] the probability to be an exporter is estimated for nine hypothetical

[19]This model is used because it is the only model for which results using a full set of 4-digit industry dummy variables could be computed for the share of exports in total sales (see Table 6).

firms from an arbitrarily chosen manufacturing industry[20] in either West Germany or East Germany. Firm 1 is a very small firm with low physical and human capital intensity and no R&D activity. For West Germany, the estimated probability of being an exporter is 73 percent — well below the share of exporters in the sample (80.9 percent). A *ceteris paribus* increase in employment from 20 to 100 increases the export probability only slightly to 75.1 percent (firm 2), and a ceteris paribus increase in physical capital intensity decreases it slightly to 74.5 percent (firm 3). Doubling the human capital intensity leads to a large increase in the probability of exporting to 85.7 percent (firm 4). If a firm that is identical to firm 4 is active in R&D and spends 1 percent of its total sales for R&D, we see a small increase in the export probability of 1 percentage point (firm 5). A *ceteris paribus* increase in the number of employees by 400 increases the probability to export by nearly 6 percentage points (firm 6). While a huge *ceteris paribus* increase in physical capital intensity lowers this probability by 2 percentage points (firm 7), a huge increase in human capital intensity increases it by 8 percentage points (firm 8). The large firm that uses physical capital and human capital intensively and that spends a large share of total sales for R&D 8 (firm 9) is for sure an exporter.

For East Germany, the pattern is rather similar, though at a lower level. Firm 1, firm 2 and firm 3 have estimated export participation probabilities that are below the share of exporters in the sample (which is 63.7 percent in 2005). Firm size and human capital intensity turn out to be important again, while R&D activity increases the probability to export only slightly. Like in West Germany, in East Germany the large firm that uses physical capital and human capital intensively and that spends a large share of total sales for R&D 8 (firm 9) is for sure an exporter.

[20]This industry is the industry of the first observation in the data set for West Germany and East Germany, respectively. Note that due to strict data protection rules neither this industry nor the industry used as a reference group in the estimation of the probit model can be revealed.

### 4.3. *Firm characteristics and the share of exports in total sales*

The share of exports in total sales varies widely among exporting firms (see the evidence reported in Table 3 for 2003 and the sample of firms used in this study). The next step in the investigation of the links between firm characteristics and export activities, therefore, looks at the role of firm characteristic for the relative importance of exports. To do so, empirical models are estimated that include the firm characteristics (number of employees, physical capital per employee, wage per employee and R&D intensity) plus a full set of 4-digit industry dummy variables as exogenous variables. The endogenous variable is the share of exports in total sales. This share of exports in total sales is a percentage variable that is by definition limited between zero and 100 percent, and that has a lot of observations at the lower bound because many firms do not export at all (see Table 1 for the sample used in this study). Papke and Wooldridge (1996) showed that for a fractional response variable of this type, and using cross section data, a fractional logit estimator is appropriate.[21]

The estimated coefficients from fractional logit regressions are reported in Table 7.[22] In West Germany, all estimated coefficients are statistically highly significant and all firm characteristics included in the empirical models are positively related to the share of exports in total sales. Export intensity tends to increase with the number of employees[23] and the intensity of physical capital, human capital

[21] Wagner (2001) introduced this estimation strategy into the literature on the determinants of exporting activities of firms, and discussed the flaws related to alternative approaches like Tobit or two-step estimators. For a comprehensive recent discussion of estimation strategies for fractional response variables with a non-ignorable probability mass at zero, see Ramalho, Ramalho and Murteira (2010).

[22] Computations were done with Stata 11 using the glm routine with a logit link. Like in the case of the determinants of export participation for each year from 2003 to 2006 results for two empirical models are given. Model 1 measures R&D activity by the share of R&D expenditures in total sales, model 2 uses the share of employees in R&D.

[23] The sign pattern of the estimated coefficients for the number of employees and the squared value of the number of employees points to an inversely u-shaped relation between firm size and the share of exports in total sales. From the estimated coefficients, the estimated maximum value of this inversely u-shaped relation can be computed. This value is very large;

and R&D. The big picture is broadly the same in East Germany.[24] Larger firms with a higher intensity of human capital and R&D are more export intensive here, too. However, physical capital intensity does not play a role in three out of four years.

While the statistical significance and the direction of the relationship between the firm characteristics included in the model and the share of exports in total sales can be seen from Table 6 at a glance, like in the case of the results from the probit regressions for the probability of being an exporter, the relevance of a specific firm characteristic for export intensity — the significance from an economic point of view — cannot be seen here. The estimated coefficients form the fractional logit model reported in Table 6 cannot be interpreted directly in a straightforward way. To understand which firm characteristics are important for the share of exports in total sales, the estimated results from the fractional logit models are used to perform simulation exercises by looking at hypothetical firms and computing their estimated share of exports in total sales. Results for such exercises are reported in Table 7.

Like in the case of the empirical models for the participation in exporting discussed above, we use the estimation results for model 1 in 2005 to estimate the share of exports in total sales for nine hypothetical firms from an arbitrarily chosen manufacturing industry in either West Germany or East Germany. Firm 1 is a very small firm with low physical and human capital intensity and no R&D activity. For West Germany, the estimated share of exports in total sales is only 11.1 percent. A *ceteris paribus* increase in employment from 20 to 100 does not increase the estimated export

---

in model 1 and for 2003 it is 63.172. This value is much larger than the number of employees in the exporting firm at the 99$^{th}$ percentile (see Table 3). Therefore, the estimated coefficients indicate that the share of exports in total sales increases with the number of employees in a firm, but at a decreasing rate.

[24]Note that model 1 for 2005 was the only model that could be estimated with a full set of 4-digit industry dummy variables for East Germany; in all other cases Stata reported that the variance matrix is non-symmetric or highly singular. All other models for East Germany were estimated with a full set of 2-digit industry dummy variables. The results for model 1 for 2005 do not differ qualitatively between the two variants for all estimated coefficients but the number of employees that has a $p$-value of 0.043 in the model with 2-digit industry dummy variables.

Table 6. Determinants of the share of exports in total sales: Fractional logit estimates

| | | 2003 | | 2004 | | 2005 | | 2006 | |
|---|---|---|---|---|---|---|---|---|---|
| | | Model 1 | Model 2 | Model 1 | Model 2 | Model 1 | Model 2 | Model 1 | Model 2 |
| *West Germany* | | | | | | | | | |
| Number of | $\beta$ | 0.000094 | 0.000107 | 0.000092 | 0.000098 | 0.000098 | 0.000095 | 0.000105 | 0.000109 |
| employees | $p$ | 0.000 | 0.000 | 0.000 | 0.000 | 0.000 | 0.000 | 0.000 | 0.000 |
| Number of | $\beta$ | −7.44e-10 | −8.38e-10 | −7.24e-10 | −7.60e-10 | −7.39e-10 | −7.44e-10 | −8.27e-10 | −8.53e-10 |
| employees (squared) | $p$ | 0.000 | 0.000 | 0.000 | 0.000 | 0.000 | 0.000 | 0.000 | 0.000 |
| Physical capital per | $\beta$ | 4.65e-7 | 4.69e-7 | 5.92e-7 | 5.89e-7 | 6.26e-7 | 6.16e-7 | 2.34e-7 | 2.26e-7 |
| employee (€) | $p$ | 0.004 | 0.004 | 0.000 | 0.000 | 0.0.00 | 0.000 | 0.002 | 0.003 |
| Wage per employee | $\beta$ | 0.000034 | 0.000033 | 0.000035 | 0.000033 | 0.000035 | 0.000033 | 0.000034 | 0.000033 |
| per year (€) | $p$ | 0.000 | 0.000 | 0.000 | 0.000 | 0.000 | 0.000 | 0.000 | 0.000 |
| Share of R&D expend. | $\beta$ | 0.05553 | | 0.05039 | | 0.04783 | | 0.05439 | |
| in total sales (percent) | $p$ | 0.000 | | 0.000 | | 0.000 | | 0.000 | |
| Share of employees | $\beta$ | | 0.02888 | | 0.02953 | | 0.02835 | | 0.02913 |
| in R&D (percent) | $p$ | | 0.000 | | 0.000 | | 0.000 | | 0.000 |
| Number of cases | | 10,038 | 10,038 | 10,038 | 10,038 | 10,038 | 10,038 | 10,038 | 10,038 |

| | | | | | | | | | |
|---|---|---|---|---|---|---|---|---|---|
| *East Germany*[1] | | | | | | | | | |
| Number of | $\beta$ | 0.00057 | 0.00062 | 0.00044 | 0.00046 | 0.00034 | 0.00038 | 0.00047 | 0.00047 |
| employees | $p$ | 0.003 | 0.001 | 0.015 | 0.011 | 0.090 | 0.039 | 0.014 | 0.015 |
| Number of | $\beta$ | −5.05e-8 | −5.58e-8 | −3.63e-8 | −3.83e-8 | −3.82e-9 | −3.03e-8 | −4.45e-8 | −4.38e-8 |
| employees (squared) | $p$ | 0.050 | 0.032 | 0.145 | 0.124 | 0.890 | 0.243 | 0.105 | 0.112 |
| Physical capital per | $\beta$ | 1.80e-8 | 3.22e-8 | 2.16e-7 | 2.31e-7 | 1.08e-7 | 3.30e-7 | 5.67e-7 | 5.70e-7 |
| employee (€) | $p$ | 0.887 | 0.803 | 0.309 | 0.286 | 0.537 | 0.220 | 0.033 | 0.032 |
| Wage per employee | $\beta$ | 0.000039 | 0.000035 | 0.000044 | 0.000041 | 0.000045 | 0.000038 | 0.000041 | 0.000040 |
| per year (€) | $p$ | 0.000 | 0.000 | 0.000 | 0.000 | 0.000 | 0.000 | 0.000 | 0.000 |
| Share of R&D expend. | $\beta$ | 0.0278 | | 0.0325 | | 0.0203 | | 0.0530 | |
| in total sales (percent) | $p$ | 0.025 | | 0.000 | | 0.022 | | 0.000 | |
| Share of employees | $\beta$ | | 0.0274 | | 0.0261 | | 0.0255 | | 0.0274 |
| in R&D (percent) | $p$ | | 0.000 | | 0.000 | | 0.000 | | 0.000 |
| Number of cases | | 1,852 | 1,852 | 1,852 | 1,852 | 1,852 | 1,852 | 1,852 | 1,852 |

*Note*: $\beta$ is the estimated regression coefficient: $p$ is the prob-value. All models include a full set of 4digit industry-dummy variables plus a constant.

[1]Model 1 for 2005 was the only model that could be estimated with a full set of 4digit industry dummy variables for East Germany; in all other cases Stata reported that the variance matrix is non-symmetric or highly singular. All other models for East Germany were estimated with a full set of 2digit industry dummy variables. The results for model 1 for 2005 do not differ qualitatively between the two variants for all estimated coefficients but the number of employees that has a $p$-value of 0.043 in the 2digit dummies model.

Table 7. Firm characteristics and share of exports in total sales: Simulations[1]

| Case Number | Number of employees | Number of employees (squared) | Physical capital per employee (€) | Wage per employee per year (€) | Share of R&D expenditures in total sales (percent) | Estimated share of exports in total sales (percent) |
|---|---|---|---|---|---|---|
| *West Germany* | | | | | | |
| 1 | 20 | 400 | 2,000 | 15,000 | 0 | 0.111 |
| 2 | 100 | 10,000 | 2,000 | 15,000 | 0 | 0.111 |
| 3 | 100 | 10,000 | 55,000 | 15,000 | 0 | 0.115 |
| 4 | 100 | 10,000 | 55,000 | 30,000 | 0 | 0.179 |
| 5 | 100 | 10,000 | 55,000 | 30,000 | 1.0 | 0.186 |
| 6 | 500 | 250,000 | 55,000 | 30,000 | 1.0 | 0.192 |
| 7 | 500 | 250,000 | 400,000 | 30,000 | 1.0 | 0.228 |
| 8 | 500 | 250,000 | 400,000 | 60,000 | 1.0 | 0.456 |
| 9 | 500 | 250,000 | 400,000 | 60,000 | 10.0 | 0.563 |
| *East Germany* | | | | | | |
| 1 | 20 | 400 | 2,000 | 15,000 | 0 | 0.223 |
| 2 | 100 | 10,000 | 2,000 | 15,000 | 0 | 0.228 |
| 3 | 100 | 10,000 | 55,000 | 15,000 | 0 | 0.229 |
| 4 | 100 | 10,000 | 55,000 | 30,000 | 0 | 0.370 |
| 5 | 100 | 10,000 | 55,000 | 30,000 | 1.0 | 0.374 |
| 6 | 500 | 250,000 | 55,000 | 30,000 | 1.0 | 0.406 |
| 7 | 500 | 250,000 | 400,000 | 30,000 | 1.0 | 0.415 |
| 8 | 500 | 250,000 | 400,000 | 60,000 | 1.0 | 0.734 |
| 9 | 500 | 250,000 | 400,000 | 60,000 | 10.0 | 0.768 |

[1]The simulations are based on the estimated model 1 for 2005.

share (firm 2), and a large *ceteris paribus* increase in physical capital intensity has no effect, too (firm 3). Doubling the human capital intensity leads to an increase in the share of exports in total sales by 6.5 percentage points (firm 4). If a firm that is identical to firm 4 is active in R&D and spends 1 percent of its total sales for R&D we see a small increase in the export share of less than 1 percentage point. A *ceteris paribus* increase in the number of employees by 400 increases the share of exports in total sales only marginally (firm 6). While a huge *ceteris paribus* increase in physical capital intensity leads to an increase of the export share by more than 3 percentage points (firm 7), a huge increase in human capital intensity increases it by 23 percentage points (firm 8). The large firm that uses physical capital and human capital intensively and that spends a large share of total sales for R&D 8 (firm 9) has an estimated share of exports in total sales of 56.3 percent.

For East Germany, the estimation results reported for model 1 in 2005 indicate that firm size is only weakly significant, and physical capital intensity does not play a role. Firms with a higher intensity of human capital and R&D, however, are more export intensive in East Germany, too. Simulation results for East Germany that use the same hypothetical firms as for West Germany are reported in the lower panel of Table 8. Given that only the estimated coefficients for human capital intensity and R&D are statistically significantly different from zero at a usual error level, we focus on the role of these two firm characteristics. A *ceteris paribus* increase in human capital intensity turns out to have a large effect — see firm 3 compared to firm 4 and the increase from 23 percent to 37 percent, and firm 7 compared to firm 8 and the increase from 41.5 percent to 73.4 percent. The estimated effect of R&D spending, on the other hand, is tiny according to a comparison of firm 4 and firm 5, and firm 8 and firm 9.

The bottom line, then, is that according to the empirical models estimated so far in this chapter human capital intensity is the most important firm characteristic in both parts of Germany for the probability to be an exporter and for the share of exports in total sales.

## 5. Unobserved Firm Characteristics and Export Activity

The proof that certain characteristics of a firm are closely related to its export activity is all but easily delivered. In Section 4, exporters and non-exporters (or firms that export different shares of their total product) are compared with respect to firm size, physical capital intensity, human capital intensity, or R&D activities. Such comparisons, however, are only based on observed firm characteristics. They cannot deal with the role of unobserved (and sometimes unobservable) characteristics — like a unique product, or superior

Table 8. Decomposition of overall variation into between and within variation

| Variable | West Germany | | East Germany | |
|---|---|---|---|---|
| | Standard | deviation | Standard | deviation |
| Exporter | overall | 0.39 | overall | 0.48 |
| (Dummy; 1 = yes) | between | 0.38 | between | 0.46 |
| | within | 0.10 | within | 0.15 |
| Share of exports | overall | 26.10 | overall | 23.87 |
| in total sales | between | 25.67 | between | 23.18 |
| | within | 4.72 | within | 5.71 |
| Number of employees | overall | 2450.34 | overall | 445.60 |
| | between | 2447.71 | between | 443.66 |
| | within | 115.59 | within | 42.54 |
| Physical capital per | overall | 137,056 | overall | 257,072 |
| employee (€) | between | 112,443 | between | 246,653 |
| | within | 78,369 | within | 72,615 |
| Wage per employee | overall | 10,224 | overall | 8,450 |
| per year (€) | between | 9,932 | between | 8,226 |
| | within | 2,427 | within | 1,940 |
| Share of R&D expend. | overall | 2.82 | overall | 3.63 |
| in total sales (percent) | between | 2.60 | between | 3.33 |
| | within | 1.08 | within | 1.44 |
| Share of employees | overall | 5.32 | overall | 6.75 |
| in R&D (percent) | between | 5.06 | between | 6.37 |
| | within | 1.66 | within | 2.24 |
| 4-digit industry | overall | 591.3 | overall | 634.0 |
| Identifier | between | 590.5 | between | 633.4 |
| | within | 31.1 | within | 30.2 |
| Number of observations | 40,152 | | 7,408 | |
| Number of firms | 10,038 | | 1,852 | |
| Number of years | 4 | | 4 | |

quality of the management of a firm — that might be correlated with the observed characteristics. If these unobserved characteristics are correlated with the observed characteristics included in the empirical model, the estimates for the coefficients of these observed firm characteristics are biased. The workhorse in empirical studies faced with this problem is an empirical model estimated with panel data that includes fixed effects to control for time invariant unobserved firm characteristics that might be correlated with the variables in that empirical model.

One crucial problem in any application of the fixed effects strategy is that in the estimation of the coefficients only the within variation of variables over time is used. Therefore, the empirical model for export participation that includes fixed firm effects is estimated using only observations on firms that changed their exporter status between 2003 and 2006 at least once. We know from Table 1 that this is a small group of firms only — in West Germany, 95 percent of all enterprises had a stable exporter status over the years, and in East Germany 89 percent of the firms did not switch into or out of exporting. Firms that start or stop exporting are known to differ from firms that continue (not) to export.[25] This means that an empirical model for export participation with fixed firm effects is estimated using a sample of firms that is different from the population of firms (or a representative random sample of this population).

Another problem related to using only the variation over time within observations in fixed effects models for firm-level data is the high ratio of between to within variation that is often observed, at least over short periods of time (like four years in our case). While enterprises differ widely from each other in all characteristics considered in this study at a point in time (as is demonstrated in Table 3), differences from year to year tend to be much smaller. Evidently, there are firms that jump up and down with regard to the share of exports in total sales, or the number of employees, or other firm characteristics. But usually year-to-year changes in firm characteristics tend to be small on average.

For the sample of firms investigated in this study, this point is illustrated in Table 8. The total variation of the variables is decomposed into variation over time for a given firm (within variation) and variation across firms (between variation).[26] For all variables,

---

[25]See Wagner (2008b) for evidence on this for Germany.

[26]See Cameron and Trivedi ((2010), p. 244f.) for a discussion and formulas.

the within variation is much smaller than the between variation (especially for the share of exports in total sales, the number of employees and the wage per employee). This is important to see because in an empirical model with fixed effects the coefficient of a regressor with little within variation will be imprecisely estimated.

Usually, the within variation that is needed to identify the coefficient of a regressor in a fixed effects model tends to increase with the length of the panel used in the estimation. A long panel covering many years, therefore, might be considered to be a better basis for empirical investigations than a short panel for only some years. However, the fixed effects that control for unobserved firm heterogeneity are by assumption time invariant, and this assumption seems more appropriate in shorter than in longer panels. A case in point is the quality of the management of a firm mentioned to motivate the application of fixed effects regression methods in this study. The assumption that management quality does not vary over time seems more convincing in the short run than in the long run (if only because bad management quality can be expected to lead to either market exit or to a new and better, or at least, different group of management in the longer run). The empirical researcher, therefore, is facing a trade-off — usually, the longer the panel, the larger is the within variation in the regressors, but the less appropriate is the assumption of time invariant unobserved heterogeneity.

The panel used in this study seems to be short enough to justify the assumption that important unobserved firm characteristics can indeed be considered as time-invariant. But as demonstrated in Table 8, the within variation of the regressors might well be too small over this short time period to estimate their effect precisely.

Furthermore, any attempt to apply a fixed effects strategy to the estimation of a model for the share of exports in total sales is confronted with a problem that is due to the nature of the variable to be explained. If the number of panels (i.e. firms) in a population (an industry, or a country) is finite and each panel is represented in the data set, an unconditional fixed effects fractional logit model can be used which simply includes an indicator variable for each firm (see Hardin and Hilbe (2001), p. 195).[27] This unconditional fixed effects approach, however, can only be used when information for the population of firms is available for a number of periods, and that is rarely the case.

In a recent paper, Papke and Wooldridge (2008) introduce a method that can be applied to estimate fractional response models for panel data with a large cross-sectional dimension and relatively few time periods while explicitly allowing for time-constant unobserved effects that can be correlated with explanatory variables. The data need not cover the whole population, but they must form a balanced panel data set with complete information on all variables in each year for each firm. Papke and Wooldridge prove that time-constant unobserved effects that can be correlated with explanatory variables are controlled for by adding the time averages of the explanatory variables to an empirical model.

That said, empirical models for the export participation of firms and for the share of exports in total sales that use the same specification as the empirical models for cross section data used in Section 4[28] and that include firm fixed effects were estimated for pooled data from 2003 to 2006, using fixed effects logit and the fractional probit panel estimator introduced by Papke and Wooldrige (2008). Results are reported in Table 9.

The big picture from the models with fixed firm effects differs completely from the results reported for models without fixed effects in Tables 4 and 6. The decision to participate in the export market that is strongly positively influenced by a higher human capital intensity and a more intensive engagement in R&D according to the empirical models based on cross section data in both West Germany and East Germany is no longer related to these firm characteristics in the empirical models with fixed firm effects.

---

[27]Wagner (2003) applied this modelling strategy using information on all firms in three manufacturing industries from one German federal state.

[28]The models with fixed firm effects do not include 4-digit industry dummy variables. Changes between industries are rare (see Table 8), and any industry specific effects are included in the firm fixed effects. All models include time dummy variables for the years 2004 to 2006.

Table 9. Determinants of export participation and the share of exports in total sales: Fixed effects panel estimates

| | | Export participation (Fixed effects logit) | | Share of exports in total sales (Fractional probit panel) | |
|---|---|---|---|---|---|
| | | Model 1 | Model 2 | Model 1 | Model 2 |
| *West Germany* | | | | | |
| Number of employees | $\beta$ | 0.010 | 0.010 | 0.00002 | 0.00002 |
| | $p$ | 0.000 | 0.000 | 0.304 | 0.303 |
| Number of employees (squared) | $\beta$ | −1.55e-6 | −1.49e-6 | −7.90e-11 | −7.69e-11 |
| | $p$ | 0.000 | 0.001 | 0.213 | 0.217 |
| Physical capital per employee (€) | $\beta$ | −3.75e-6 | −3.76e-6 | 1.29e-8 | 1.27e-8 |
| | $p$ | 0.004 | 0.004 | 0.169 | 0.171 |
| Wage per employee per year (€) | $\beta$ | −0.00002 | −0.00002 | 1.23e-6 | 1.25e-6 |
| | $p$ | 0.234 | 0.279 | 0.006 | 0.006 |
| Share of R&D expend. in total sales (percent) | $\beta$ | −0.006 | | −0.0005 | |
| | $p$ | 0.913 | | 0.799 | |
| Share of employees in R&D (percent) | $\beta$ | | −0.076 | | −0.001 |
| | $p$ | | 0.115 | | 0.137 |
| Number of observations | | 2,000 | 2,000 | 40,152 | 40,152 |
| Number of firms | | 500 | 500 | 10,038 | 10,038 |
| *East Germany* | | | | | |
| Number of employees | $\beta$ | 0.035 | 0.035 | 0.0005 | 0.0006 |
| | $p$ | 0.000 | 0.000 | 0.001 | 0.001 |
| Number of employees (squared) | $\beta$ | −0.00002 | −0.00002 | −3.29e-8 | −3.32e-8 |
| | $p$ | 0.001 | 0.001 | 0.083 | 0.078 |
| Physical capital per employee (€) | $\beta$ | −2.09e-7 | −2.07e-7 | −8.12e-8 | −8.21e-8 |
| | $p$ | 0.569 | 0.572 | 0.233 | 0.223 |
| Wage per employee per year (€) | $\beta$ | −3.51e-6 | −2.64e-6 | 4.54e-6 | 4.39e-6 |
| | $p$ | 0.915 | 0.936 | 0.047 | 0.060 |
| Share of R&D expend. in total sales (percent) | $\beta$ | −0.005 | | −0.004 | |
| | $p$ | 0.950 | | 0.046 | |
| Share of employees in R&D (percent) | $\beta$ | | −0.016 | | −0.0002 |
| | $p$ | | 0.527 | | 0.867 |
| Number of observations | | 840 | 840 | 7,408 | 7,408 |
| Number of firms | | 210 | 210 | 1,852 | 1,852 |

*Note*: $\beta$ is the estimated regression coefficient; $p$ is the prob-value. All models include a full set of year-dummies; the fractional probit panel models include a full set of mean values of the exogenous variables plus a constant, too.

Contrary to results reported in Table 6 for models without fixed effects, results in Table 9 show that neither firm size, nor physical capital, nor R&D intensity matter for the share of exports in total sales in West Germany, and that R&D intensity is (if anything) negatively related to export intensity in East Germany.

Does this really indicate that in German manufacturing industries human capital intensity and R&D intensity are irrelevant for the decision to export, and that a higher R&D intensity *per se* does not make a successful exporter, but that unobserved time-invariant characteristics that are correlated with these observed characteristics matter a lot and shape the results of empirical models estimated with cross section data that ignore these unobserved characteristics?[29] The results reported in Table 8 on relatively low within variation over the four years under investigation cast doubts on this conclusion, because in an empirical model with fixed effects the coefficient of a regressor with little within variation will be imprecisely estimated. This might well be the reason for the somewhat strange results reported in Table 9 that contradict the findings from empirical models estimated with cross section data.

This does not mean to deny the role of unobserved firm characteristics like quality of management. These factors matter for export activities. A recent study by Bloom and Van Reenen (2010) that relates management practices to productivity shows, among others, that firms that export are better-managed than domestic non-exporters. Syverson (2011) points out that economists have long proposed that managers drive differences between firms, and cites a paper by Walker (1887) published more than 120 years ago. But in the data used in this study (and in many other empirical studies using comparable firm-level data for Germany or other countries as well) there is simply not enough variation in the observed firm characteristics to control for unobserved time invariant firm characteristics like management quality in empirical models for export activity with fixed firm effects.

---

[29]See Wagner ((2003), (2010b)) for papers arguing in this direction.

## 6. Productivity and Exports

While the links between exporting on the one hand and firm size, physical and human capital intensity and R&D activity on the other hand have been explored empirically for quite a long time (although not comprehensively and with large, rich sets of longitudinal data for representative samples of firms for Germany), the more recent theoretical and empirical literature dealing with the export activity of firms focuses on the role of productivity. In the next step of the empirical analyses of exporter characteristics, therefore, productivity is included in the set of firm characteristics considered.

To start, empirical models are estimated that include value added per employee and a full set of 4-digit industry dummy variables as exogenous variables.[30] The endogenous variable is a dummy variable that takes the value one if the firm is an exporter (and zero otherwise). Results for these empirical models for export participation are reported in Table 10.

The results indicate that more productive firms do have a higher probability to participate in exporting when the detailed industry affiliation of the enterprise is controlled for. The reported marginal effect at the mean of productivity is always positive and it is statistically significantly different from zero in all cases with the exception of East Germany in the first year investigated.

These empirical findings of a positive link between exporting and productivity are in line with the predictions of the theoretical models from the *new new trade theory*. In these theoretical models, productivity of a firm is modeled as a random draw from a given distribution of productivity. While this is for sure an appropriate approach to build a theoretical model for trade with heterogeneous

---

[30]From the literature on exports and productivity we have ample empirical evidence that firms with a higher productivity self-select into exporting and that exporting does not tend to increase productivity; see Wagner (2007a) for a survey and Wagner (2007b) and Vogel and Wagner (2009) for Germany. Therefore, productivity can be regarded to be exogenous with respect to the decision to export. Note that the data at hand cover only four years due to the sampling frame used (detailed in Section 3). Therefore, an empirical test of the self-selection and learning-by-exporting hypotheses is not possible with these data.

Table 10. Productivity and export participation: Probit-estimates

| | | 2003 | 2004 | 2005 | 2006 |
|---|---|---|---|---|---|
| *West Germany* | | | | | |
| Value added per | $\beta$ | 2.30e-6 | 1.99e-6 | 1.37e-6 | 7.33e-7 |
| Employee (€) | p | 0.000 | 0.000 | 0.000 | 0.029 |
| Number of cases | | 9,357 | 9,424 | 9,410 | 9,353 |
| *East Germany* | | | | | |
| Value added per | $\beta$ | 1.11e-6 | 1.47e-6 | 2.06e-6 | 1.76e-6 |
| Employee (€) | p | 0.116 | 0.039 | 0.003 | 0.012 |
| Number of cases | | 1,624 | 1,610 | 1,597 | 1,609 |

*Note*: $\beta$ is the estimated marginal effect at the mean of the independent variable; $p$ is the prob-value. All models include a full set of 4-digit industry-dummies plus a constant. The number of cases differs between years because firms from industries were all or no firms exported were dropped before the probit estimates were computed.

firms, it is far from satisfactory from an empirical point of view. Obviously, there is a role for random shocks, or good or bad luck, in shaping the productivity level of a firm, but we have good reasons to believe that a high or low level of productivity is not a matter of luck alone. Productivity can be expected to be related to the amount and the quality of inputs used in the production process, and to the way these production factors are combined.

How are the characteristics of a firm that are investigated in Sections 4 and 5 related to labor productivity (measured as value added per employee) in our sample? To investigate this question, empirical models are estimated with value added per employee as the endogenous variable and firm size, physical capital per employee, human capital intensity and R&D activities plus a full set of detailed dummy variables for the industry a firm is active in as exogenous variables. Results are reported in Table 11.[31]

[31]Note that these regression equations are not meant to be an empirical model to explain labor productivity at the enterprise level; the data set at hand here is not rich enough for such an exercise. They are just a vehicle to test for, and estimate the size of, the relation between one firm characteristic and labor productivity controlling for other plant characteristics. Furthermore, note that productivity differences at the firm level are notoriously difficult to explain empirically. "At the micro level, productivity remains very much a measure of our

Table 11. Labor productivity and firm characteristics: OLS estimates for value added per employee

| | | 2003 | | 2004 | | 2005 | | 2006 | |
|---|---|---|---|---|---|---|---|---|---|
| | | Model 1 | Model 2 | Model 1 | Model 2 | Model 1 | Model 2 | Model 1 | Model 2 |
| *West Germany* | | | | | | | | | |
| Number of | $\beta$ | 0.322 | 0.017 | 0.295 | 0.046 | 0.609 | 0.354 | 2.691 | 2.285 |
| employees | $p$ | 0.275 | 0.953 | 0.349 | 0.886 | 0.296 | 0.529 | 0.142 | 0.190 |
| Number of | $\beta$ | −3.05e-6 | −6.61e-7 | −3.26e-6 | −1.28e-6 | −5.30e-6 | −3.33e-6 | −0.00002 | −0.00002 |
| employees (squared) | $p$ | 0.157 | 0.747 | 0.133 | 0.558 | 0.127 | 0.317 | 0.091 | 0.133 |
| Physical capital per | $\beta$ | 0.075 | 0.075 | 0.098 | 0.098 | 0.086 | 0.085 | 0.004 | 0.004 |
| employee (€) | $p$ | 0.000 | 0.000 | 0.000 | 0.000 | 0.000 | 0.000 | 0.845 | 0.855 |
| Wage per employee | $\beta$ | 1.250 | 1.207 | 1.314 | 1.276 | 1.384 | 1.348 | 1.463 | 1.420 |
| per year (€) | $p$ | 0.000 | 0.000 | 0.000 | 0.000 | 0.000 | 0.000 | 0.000 | 0.000 |
| Share of R&D expend. | $\beta$ | −497.86 | | −649.83 | | −735.03 | | −1103.42 | |
| in total sales (percent) | $p$ | 0.001 | | 0.000 | | 0.019 | | 0.165 | |
| Share of employees | $\beta$ | | 137.72 | | −5.547 | | −45.627 | | −93.910 |
| in R&D (percent) | $p$ | | 0.175 | | 0.960 | | 0.788 | | 0.795 |
| $R^2$ | | 0.395 | 0.394 | 0.445 | 0.442 | 0.373 | 0.370 | 0.228 | 0.225 |
| Number of cases | | 10,038 | 10,038 | 10,038 | 10,038 | 10,038 | 10,038 | 10,038 | 10,038 |

| | | | | | | | | | |
|---|---|---|---|---|---|---|---|---|---|
| *East Germany* | | | | | | | | | |
| Number of | $\beta$ | 8.912 | 9.419 | 4.529 | 4.931 | 1.049 | 1.325 | −1.393 | −0.977 |
| employees | $p$ | 0.052 | 0.041 | 0.439 | 0.399 | 0.852 | 0.814 | 0.801 | 0.860 |
| Number of | $\beta$ | −0.00095 | −0.0011 | −0.00065 | −0.00074 | −0.000095 | −0.00016 | 0.00028 | 0.00019 |
| employees (squared) | $p$ | 0.135 | 0.094 | 0.478 | 0.407 | 0.913 | 0.848 | 0.701 | 0.793 |
| Physical capital per | $\beta$ | 0.065 | 0.065 | 0.128 | 0.128 | 0.121 | 0.121 | 0.103 | 0.103 |
| employee (€) | $p$ | 0.000 | 0.000 | 0.000 | 0.000 | 0.000 | 0.000 | 0.000 | 0.000 |
| Wage per employee | $\beta$ | 1.350 | 1.311 | 1.314 | 1.286 | 1.442 | 1.411 | 1.794 | 1.771 |
| per year (€) | $p$ | 0.000 | 0.000 | 0.000 | 0.000 | 0.000 | 0.000 | 0.000 | 0.000 |
| Share of R&D expend. | $\beta$ | −414.81 | | −531.09 | | −249.51 | | −532.62 | |
| in total sales (percent) | $p$ | 0.005 | | 0.031 | | 0.247 | | 0.032 | |
| Share of employees | $\beta$ | | 33.694 | | −97.540 | | 61.239 | | −92.567 |
| in R&D (percent) | $p$ | | 0.701 | | 0.459 | | 0.666 | | 0.466 |
| $R^2$ | | 0.715 | 0.713 | 0.764 | 0.763 | 0.726 | 0.726 | 0.616 | 0.615 |
| Number of cases | | 1,852 | 1,852 | 1,852 | 1,852 | 1,852 | 1,852 | 1,852 | 1,852 |

*Note*: $\beta$ is the estimated regression coefficient; $p$ is the prob-value. All models include a full set of 4digit industry-dummy variables plus a constant.

The big picture that arises from the regression results reported in Table 11 can be sketched as follows:

— *Firm size is unrelated to productivity*. This finding fits with the evidence available from numerous reports on very small German firms that are highly successful in exporting.[32]
— Both physical capital intensity and human capital intensity are positively related to labor productivity, and the estimated regression coefficients are highly significant. Human capital intensity, however, is much more important for value added per employee than physical capital intensity. To see this, consider the case of West Germany in 2003.[33] The mean value of physical capital per employee was about 92.000 € and the mean value added per employee was about 57.000 € (see Table 2). Using the regression results reported for model 1 in Table 11, a 10 percent increase in the physical capital intensity leads to an estimated increase in labor productivity by 690 € (9.200 ∗ 0.075), a tiny amount. If physical capital increases by 50 percent, the related estimated increase in value added per employee is still small — 3.450 €, or 6 percent. Results for human capital intensity are much different. The mean value of wages per employee was about 34.000 € and the mean value added per employee was about 57.000 € in West Germany in 2003 (see Table 2). Using again the regression results reported for model 1 in Table 16, a 10 percent increase in human capital intensity leads to an increase in labor productivity by 4.250 € (3.400 ∗ 1.250) or 7.5 percent. If the human capital intensity increases by 50 percent, the related estimated increase in value added per employee is 21.250 €, or 37.3 percent. The bottom line then is: *Human capital intensity is*

ignorance." (Bartelsman and Doms 2000, p. 586) Syverson (2011) surveys the recent literature on determinants of productivity at the firm level. *Inter alia*, he mentions effects of competition, organizational structures within firms, payment systems, other human resources practices, managerial talent, human capital, higher-quality capital inputs, information technology (IT) and R&D. Only some of these determinants of productivity can be looked at here with the data at hand. These limitations should be kept in mind when putting the results into perspective.

[32]See the examples mentioned in Wagner (2003).

[33]Results for other years and for East Germany are of a similar order of magnitude.

*strongly positively related to labor productivity, while physical capital intensity matters only marginally.*

— *R&D activity is not related to labor productivity.* The estimated regression coefficient for one measure of R&D activity, the share of employees in a firm that is active in R&D, is never statistically significantly different from zero. As regards the other measure of R&D activity, the share of R&D expenditures in total sales, the estimated regression coefficient points to a negative and statistically significant relation in three out of four years in West Germany and in East Germany. The estimated effect, however, is tiny. From Table 3, it can be seen that in West Germany the median firm has no R&D at all. The share of R&D expenditures in total sales is 1.20 for the exporting firm at the $75^{th}$ percentile of the distribution of R&D intensity. According to the results for model 1 in 2003, this switch from no R&D expenditure to an R&D expenditure of 1.20 percent of total sales is related to a decrease in value added per employee by 597.43 € ($-497.86 * 1.2$) — a tiny amount compared to the average amount of value added in exporting firms that was 56,699 € in 2003 according to Table 2. Results for East Germany are of the same order of magnitude.

The bottom line, then, is that productivity *is* important for exporting as is expected from the formal models from the *new new trade theory*, but contrary to the assumption made in these theoretical models productivity is not only the result from a random draw — it is strongly positively related to human capital intensity.

## 7. Concluding Remarks

Reliable information on the characteristics of exporting and non-exporting firms is important to guide theorists and policy makers in an evidence-based way. This holds true especially for Germany, a leading actor in the world markets for goods and services. This chapter makes two contributions towards this aim:

— Recently released rich high quality data for a large representative panel of enterprises from German manufacturing industries are used to investigate the links between firm characteristics (firm size, physical and human capital intensity, and R&D activities) and export activities, and the decisive role of human capital intensity for exporting is documented.

— The findings are linked to the recent literature from the *new new trade theory* on international activities of heterogeneous firms that emphasizes the role of productivity for exporting. It is shown that productivity *is* important for exporting as is hypothesized in the formal theoretical models, but that contrary to the assumption made in these models productivity is not (only) the result from a random draw from the productivity distribution — it is strongly positively related to human capital intensity.

The bottom line, then, is that human capital plays a central role for the (international) competitiveness of firms. Therefore, human capital intensity is important for the (international) competitiveness and the growth of industries and regions, and of the economy as a whole. This points out the decisive role of policy measures that focus on improvements in the qualification of employees, both young and old, and to an immigration policy that can help to overcome a shortage of skilled labor as a consequence of an ageing population and demographic change. However, only some of the determinants of productivity at the firm level can be looked at here with the data at hand. The limitations due to this shortcoming should be kept in mind when putting the results into perspective — stressing just one factor (human capital) here should not be interpreted as a recommendation that policy measures that intend to foster productivity growth should focus on human capital alone.

## Acknowledgment

I thank Jeff Wooldridge and Leslie Papke for sharing their Stata code to estimate fractional probit panel models, and Nils Braakmann and Alexander Vogel for extremely helpful discussions. Comments from the editor (Uwe Sunde) and two anonymous referees on an earlier version helped to improve the paper considerably.

The data used are confidential but not exclusive; see Zühlke *et al.* (2004) for a description of how to access the data. All computations were done inside the Research Data Centre of the Statistical Office of Berlin. To facilitate replication the Stata do-files are available from the author on request.

## References


Bartelsman, Eric J. and Mark Doms (2000). Understanding Productivity: Lessons from Longitudinal Micro Data. *Journal of Economic Literature* XXXVIII (3), 569–594.

Bernard, Andrew B. and J. Bradford Jensen (1995). Exporters, Jobs, and Wages in U.S. Manufacturing: 1976–1987. *Brookings Papers on Economic Activity, Microeconomics* 1, 67–119.

Bernard, Andrew B. and Joachim Wagner (1997). Exports and Success in German Manufacturing. *Weltwirtschaftliches Archiv/Review of World Economics* 133 (1), 134–157.

Bloom, Nicholas and Van J. Reenen (2010). Why Do Management Practices Differ across Firms and Countries? *Journal of Economic Perspectives* 24(1), 203–224.

Buchinsky, Moshe (1994). Changes in the U.S. Wage Structure 1963–1987: Application of Quantile Regression. *Econometrica* 62(2), 405–458.

Cameron, A. Colin and Pravin K. Trivedi (2010). *Microeconometrics Using Stata*, Revised Edition. College Station, TX: Stata Press.

Conover, W. J. (1999). *Practical Nonparametric Statistics*. Third edition. New York: John Wiley.

Delgado, Miguel A., Jose C. Farinas and Sonia Ruano (2002). Firm Productivity and Export Markets: A Non-Parametric Approach. *Journal on International Economics* 57(2), 397–422.

Foster, Lucia, John Haltiwanger and Chad Syverson (2008). Reallocation, Firm Turnover, and Efficiency: Selection on Productivity or Profitability? *American Economic Review* 98(1), 394–425.

Fritsch, Michael, Bernd Görzig, Ottmar Hennchen and Andreas Stephan (2004), Cost Structure Surveys for Germany. *Journal of Applied Social Science Studies* 124(4), 557–566.

Hardin, James and Joseph Hilbe (2001). *Generalized Linear Models and Extensions*, College Station, TX: Stata Press.

Heckman, James. J. (2001). Micro Data, Heterogeneity, and the Evaluation of Public Policy: Nobel Lecture. *Journal of Political Economy* 109(4), 673–748.

Helpman, Elhanan, Marc J. Melitz and Stephen R. Yeaple (2004). Export versus FDI with Heterogeneous Firms. *American Economic Review* 94(1), 300–316.

International Study Group on Exports and Productivity (ISGEP) (2008). Understanding Cross-Country Differences in Exporter Premia: Comparable Evidence for 14 Countries. *Review of World Economics* 144(4), 596–635.

Konold, Michael (2007). New Possibilities for Economic Research through Integration of Establishment-Level Panel Data of German Official Statistics. *Journal of Applied Social Science Studies* 127(2), 321–334.

Malchin, Anja and Ramona Voshage (2009). Official Firm Data for Germany. *Journal of Applied Social Science Studies* 129(3), 501–513.

Melitz, Mark J. (2003). The Impact of Trade on Intra-Industry Reallocations and Aggregate Industry Productivity. *Econometrica* 71(6), 1695–1725.

Papke, Leslie E. and Jeffrey M. Wooldridge (1996). Econometric Methods for Fractional Response Variables with an Application to 401(k) Plan Participation Rates. *Journal of Applied Econometrics* 11(6), 619–632.

Papke, Leslie E. and Jeffrey M. Wooldridge (2008). Panel Data Methods for Fractional Response Variables with an Application to Test Pass Rates. *Journal of Econometrics* 145(1/2), 121–133.

Ramalho, Esmeralda A., Joaquim J. S. Ramalho and José M. R. Murteira (2010). Alternative Estimating and Testing Empirical Strategies for Fractional Regression Models. *Journal of Economic Surveys* 25(1), 19–68.

Schank, Thorsten, Claus Schnabel and Joachim Wagner (2010). Higher Wages in Exporting Firms: Self-Selection, Export Effect, or Both? First Evidence from Linked Employer–Employee Data. *Review of World Economics* 146(2), 303–322.

Syverson, Chad (2011). What Determines Productivity? *Journal of Economic Literature* 49(2), 326–365.

Vogel, Alexander and Joachim Wagner (2009). Higher Productivity in Importing German Manufacturing Firms: Self-Selection, Learning from Importing, or Both? *Review of World Economics* 145(4), 641–665.

Wagner, Joachim (1995). Exports, Firm Size, and Firm Dynamics. *Small Business Economics* 7(1), 29–39.

Wagner, Joachim (2001). A Note on the Firm Size — Export Relationship. *Small Business Economics* 17(4), 229–237.

Wagner, Joachim (2003). Unobserved Firm Heterogeneity and the Size-Exports Nexus: Evidence from German Panel Data. *Review of World Economics* 139(1), 161–172.

Wagner, Joachim (2007a). Exports and Productivity: A Survey of the Evidence from Firm-Level Data. *The World Economy* 30(1), 60–82.

Wagner, Joachim (2007b). Exports and Productivity in Germany. *Applied Economics Quarterly* 55(4), 353–373.

Wagner, Joachim (2008a). Why More West Than East German Firms Export. *International Economics and Economic Policy* 5(4), 363–370.

Wagner, Joachim (2008b). Export Entry, Export Exit and Productivity in German Manufacturing Industries. *International Journal of the Economics of Business* 15(2), 169–180.

Wagner, Joachim (2010a). Estimated Capital Stock Values for German Manufacturing Enterprises Covered by the Cost Structure Surveys. *Journal of Applied Social Science Studies* 130(3), 403–408.

Wagner, Joachim (2010b). Exports and Firm Characteristics — First Evidence from Fractional Probit Panel Estimates. *Applied Economics Letters* 9(10), 935–940.
Wagner, Joachim (2011). Exports and Firm Characteristics in Germany: A Survey of Empirical Studies (1991 to 2011), mimeo, August.
Walker, Francis A. (1887). The Source of Business Profits. *Quarterly Journal of Economcis* 1(3), 265–288.
Zühlke, Sylvia, Markus Zwick, Sebastian Scharnhorst and Thomas Wende (2004). The Research Data Centres of the Federal Statistical Office and the Statistical Offices of the *Länder*. *Journal of Applied Social Science Studies* 124(4), 567–578.

Chapter 4

# Higher Productivity in Importing German Manufacturing Firms: Self-selection, Learning from Importing or Both?

Alexander Vogel and Joachim Wagner

**Abstract**

This chapter uses a newly available comprehensive panel data set for manufacturing enterprises from 2001 to 2005 to document the first empirical results on the relationship between imports and productivity for Germany, a leading actor in the world market for goods. Furthermore, for the first time, the direction of causality in this relationship is investigated systematically by testing for self-selection of more productive firms into importing, and for productivity-enhancing effects of imports ("learning-by-importing"). We find a positive link between importing and productivity. From an empirical model with fixed enterprise effects that controls for firm size, industry and unobservable firm heterogeneity, we see that the premia for trading internationally are about the same in West and East Germany. Compared to firms that do not trade at all, two-way traders do have the highest premia, followed by firms that only export, while firms that only import have the smallest estimated premia. We find evidence for a positive impact of productivity on importing, pointing to self-selection of more productive enterprises into imports, but no clear evidence for the effect of importing on productivity due to learning-by-importing.

*Keywords*: Imports, exports, productivity, enterprise panel data, Germany

**JEL Classification:** F14, D21

## 1. Motivation

Since the mid-1990s, economists used micro-data at the firm-level from many countries to uncover the role that firms play in international trade. These micro-econometric studies revealed a number of stylized facts regarding differences between exporting and non-exporting firms (summarized in Bernard *et al.* (2007)) that in turn inspired theoretical models with heterogeneous firms in open economies (see the influential contributions by Melitz (2003) and Bernard *et al.* (2003)) instead of the representative firm models from the older literature on international economics with a focus on industries or countries. Productivity differences between exporting and non-exporting firms from the same industry play a central role in both the empirical investigations and the new theoretical models. Numerous empirical studies show that exporting firms are more productive than non-exporting firms even if observed and unobserved firm characteristics are controlled for, and that there is self-selection of the more productive firms into exporting, while empirical evidence for positive effects of exporting on productivity is scarce (for a survey of the empirical literature, see Wagner (2007a)).

While the causes and consequences of export and its mutual relationships with productivity (and with other firm characteristics, including firm size and growth, and wages paid) are prominent topics in the recent literature on internationally active firms, imports are seldom dealt with. A case in point is the recently published Bruegel study on the internationalization of European firms (Mayer and Ottaviano 2007) where imports are not dealt with at all. As Bernard *et al.* (2007, p. 123) recently put it, "(t)he empirical literature on firms in international trade has been concerned almost exclusively with exporting, largely due to limitations in datasets· · · . As a result, the new theories of heterogeneous firms and trade were developed to explain facts about firm export behavior and yield few predictions (if any) for firm import behavior."

This situation, however, is changing rapidly. With new data sets that include information on imports at the firm level becoming available for more and more countries a new literature (reviewed in Section 2 below) is emerging since 2005 that has a focus on the links between productivity and imports. This chapter contributes to the literature by presenting the first empirical results on the relationships between imports and productivity for Germany, a leading actor in the world market for goods.[1] Furthermore, we look for the first time systematically at the direction of causality in this relationship by testing for self-selection of more productive firms into importing, and for productivity-enhancing effects of imports ("learning-by-importing").

The rest of the chapter is organized as follows: Section 2 reviews the recent literature on imports and productivity. Section 3 introduces the newly available firm level panel data for Germany used in our empirical investigation. Section 4 reports productivity premia for firms active in international trade. Section 5 investigates whether more productive firms self-select into import activities. Section 6 reports findings on productivity-enhancing effects of imports. Section 7 provides the conclusion.

## 2. Literature Review

In their comprehensive empirical study of firms in the U.S. that trade goods, Bernard, Jensen and Schott (2005: 5) noted "that there is virtually no research documenting and analyzing importing firms." This is no longer the case. A number of recently published empirical studies based on data from a wide range of countries document the shares of firms that are exporters, importers and two-way traders (that both export and import), or that sell or buy in the national market only, and they look at differences between these four types of firms. Differences in productivity and their relationship with different degrees of involvement in international trade are at the center of these studies. As of today,[2] we have evidence on

[1] The relationship between exports and productivity in Germany is investigated in Bernard and Wagner (1997) and in Wagner (2002, 2007b).

[2] The literature on the microeconometrics of imports is growing rapidly. We are grateful for any hints to empirical studies not listed here.

this issue for Belgium (Muuls and Pisu 2007), Chile (Kasahara and Rodrigue 2005; Kasahara and Lapham 2008), Hungary (Halpern, Miklós and Szeidl 2005; Altomonte and Békés 2008), India (Tucci 2005), Indonesia (Sjöholm 1999), Italy (Castellani, Serti and Tomasi 2008), Poland (Hagemejer and Kolasa 2008), Sweden (Andersson, Lööf and Johansson 2008), and the U.S. (Bernard *et al.* 2007).[3]

Details aside, the big picture that emerges from this literature can be sketched as follows: There is a positive link between importing and productivity at the firm level, documented by a significant productivity differential between firms that import and firms that do not trade internationally; the same holds for exporting. Two-way traders are more productive than firms that either only import, or only export or do not trade at all. Often, two-way traders are the most productive group of firms, followed by importers and then exporters, while firms selling or buying in the national market come last.

How can this empirical regularity of a positive relationship between importing and productivity at the firm level be explained theoretically? In the literature, arguments for both a positive impact of productivity on importing (henceforth, Hypothesis H1) and for a positive impact of importing on productivity (henceforth, Hypothesis H2) are discussed. While H1 is in accordance with self-selection of more productive firms into import markets, H2 points to productivity-enhancing effects of imports ("learning-by-importing"). Let us consider the arguments in turn.

To start with H1, Kasahara and Lapham (2008) extend the Melitz (2003) model to incorporate imported intermediate goods. In their model, the use of foreign intermediates increases a firm's productivity but, due to fixed costs of importing, only inherently

[3]Related papers include Tomiura (2007) who looks at productivity differentials between Japanese firms that export, invest abroad and contract out manufacturing or processing tasks to other firms overseas; Amiti and Konings (2007) who investigate the productivity effects of tariff reductions on final goods and on imported intermediate inputs in Indonesia; and MacGarvie (2006) who, in a study on patent citations, report differences in labor productivity between exporters and non-exporters, and non-importers and importers, for a sample of French firms.

highly productive firms import intermediates. Andersson, Lööf and Johansson (2008) point out that importing is associated with fixed costs that are sunk costs, because the import agreement is preceded by a search process for potential foreign suppliers, inspection of goods, negotiation, contract formulation, etc. Castellani, Serti and Tomasi (2008) argue in a similar way, adding that there are sunk costs of importing due to the learning and acquisition of customs procedures.

As regards H2, Andersson, Lööf and Johansson (2008) argue that there are strong arguments in favor of causal effect of imports on productivity, because by importing a firm can exploit global specialization and use inputs from the forefront of knowledge and technology. They point to the literature on international technology diffusion that advances imports as an important vehicle for knowledge and technology transfer. Furthermore, importing intermediate products allows a firm to focus resources and to specialize on activities where it has particular strengths. Similarly, Castellani, Serti and Tomasi (2008) argue that importers may improve productivity by using higher quality foreign inputs or by extracting technology embodied in imported intermediates and capital goods. Altomonte and Békés (2008) point to this "learning" effect, in which importing firms acquire part of the technology incorporated in the imported goods; furthermore, they mention a variety effect (in which the broader range of available intermediates contributes to production efficiency) and a quality effect caused by imported intermediates that might be of better quality than local ones (see also Halpern, Miklós and Szeidl (2005), and Muuls and Pisu (2007). If importing increases productivity, this might lead firms to self-select into export markets and help to improve their success in these markets, which might contribute to an explanation of the empirical regularity that two-way traders are the most productive firms on average (see Andersson, Lööf and Johansson (2008)).

From a theoretical point of view, therefore, the direction of causality between productivity and importing can run from either sides, or from both sides simultaneously. Only some of the studies mentioned above tackle this issue (or at least a part of it) empirically. In the earliest contribution to this literature, Sjöholm (1999) reports some indications of a positive growth effect from imports for his sample of Indonesian firms, but he adds as a caveat that this result is sensitive to changes in the specification of the variables and the test equation. Altomonte and Békés (2008) find that adding a new trade activity — for example, starting to import — has a positive impact on the performance of Hungarian firms. Similarly, Kasahara and Rodrigue (2005) document that switching from being a non-importer to being an importer of foreign intermediates improves productivity in Chilean manufacturing plants, while the inherently more productive plants tend to use imported intermediates. They argue that their findings indicate that the direction of causality between productivity and import status goes both ways.

The bottom line, then, is that we have convincing empirical evidence on a positive relationship between importing and productivity at the level of the firm for a large and growing number of developed and developing countries, while research on the direction of causality between productivity and import status is still in its infancy. Furthermore, none of the very few papers tackling the issue of direction of causality does so by applying the now standard approach used to uncover the direction of causality between productivity and exporting (detailed e.g. in the survey by Wagner (2007a)).

## 3. Data

In our empirical investigation, we use data from the German Turnover Tax Statistics Panel (described in detail in Vogel and Dittrich (2008)). This data set is based on the yearly turnover tax statistics and includes information on more than 4.3 million enterprises from all economic sectors over the time period from 2001 to 2005. All enterprises with a turnover that exceeds a rather low threshold (17,500€ since 2003) are covered in the data.

For our study, we focus on enterprises from manufacturing because import and export activities can only be identified for firms from this part of the economy.[4] However, neither exports nor imports are directly recorded in the data set. Regarding exports, the information about "tax free turnover with input tax deduction" can be used as a proxy. This item contains mainly the exports of goods and some activities of minor importance like gold deliveries to central banks. In addition, exports of goods within the EU (intra-Community deliveries and other performances) are directly included in the data set. Concerning import activities, imports from EU member states are reported under the item of "intra-Community acquisitions". The amount of imports from states beyond the EU is not included in the turnover tax statistics. In this case, an import turnover tax is charged by the customs authorities. Nonetheless, this import turnover tax is deductible as input tax and therefore reported in the data set. With this information, a dummy variable which shows whether the enterprise imports from non-EU states or not can be generated (taking the value 1 if the import turnover tax is greater than 0, and 0 if no import turnover tax is deducted as input tax). Therefore, it is possible to distinguish between four types of enterprises, namely, enterprises that both import and export, that only export, that only import and that neither export nor import.

Productivity is defined as labor productivity, computed as turnover per employee covered by social insurance, because information on the number of employees was matched to the data from the turnover statistics from the German business register, and these figures refer to employees covered by social insurance only. Therefore, we had to drop all enterprises without employees that were liable to pay social insurance. Note that we cannot use more appropriate measures of productivity like value added per employee, or total factor productivity, because the information needed to compute these measures are lacking in the data. In our empirical investigation, we will control for the industry an enterprise is active in by using information at the detailed 3-digit industry level to take care of inter-industry variation in capital intensity and the degree of

[4]For further details, see Vogel and Dittrich (2008).

vertical integration. Furthermore, some enterprises reported either tiny or very huge amounts of turnover in some years, leading to tiny or very huge values of labor productivity. Due to data protection rules, it is impossible for us to investigate the reasons for these implausible figures, and to discriminate between reporting errors, idiosyncratic events or other causes. Given that outliers of this kind might influence findings from both descriptive statistics and econometric investigations, enterprises from the bottom and top 1 percent of the labor productivity distribution were excluded from all computations.

Our empirical study, therefore, is based on information for all German enterprises from the manufacturing sector in the period 2001–2005 that had a turnover that exceeded the (small) tax threshold and that had at least one employee covered by social insurance, excluding very small enterprises that are mostly sole proprietorships. Table 1 reports the share of enterprises that both import and export, that only export, that only import and that neither export nor import in each year. Given that there are large differences in the participation in international trade between manufacturing firms from West and East Germany,[5] results are reported for both parts of Germany separately.

In West Germany, about half of all enterprises participated in international trade. Among the trading enterprises, about 50 percent are two-way traders that both export and import, while the share of firms that only import is somewhat larger than the share of firms that only export. The share of firms that are active in the German market only declined between 2001 and 2005, while both the share of two-way traders and firms that only import increased, and the share of firms that only export remained the same. The picture for East Germany is different. The share of firms that do not participate in international trade is more than 10 percentage points higher than in West Germany, and the share of both two-way traders and firms that only export is much lower in East Germany,

[5]For a discussion of the difference in export participation see Wagner (2008).

Table 1. Import and export participation of manufacturing enterprises in west and east germany

| | Share of enterprises (in percent) that... | | | | |
|---|---|---|---|---|---|
| | Neither export nor import | Only export | Only import | Both export and import (two-way traders) | Number of total observations |
| | | | West Germany | | |
| 2001 | 54.35 | 10.08 | 11.26 | 24.31 | 135,827 |
| 2002 | 54.07 | 10.10 | 11.19 | 24.64 | 131,941 |
| 2003 | 52.73 | 10.18 | 11.48 | 25.62 | 134,288 |
| 2004 | 51.08 | 10.17 | 11.91 | 26.84 | 132,305 |
| 2005 | 49.97 | 10.07 | 12.47 | 27.49 | 131,170 |
| | | | East Germany | | |
| 2001 | 68.37 | 5.75 | 13.03 | 12.85 | 30,630 |
| 2002 | 67.43 | 6.02 | 13.05 | 13.51 | 29,490 |
| 2003 | 66.14 | 6.00 | 13.43 | 14.43 | 28,718 |
| 2004 | 63.25 | 6.64 | 14.12 | 15.99 | 27,894 |
| 2005 | 61.89 | 7.03 | 14.17 | 16.91 | 27,451 |

*Note*: Only enterprises with one or more employees liable for paying social insurance and a turnover higher than 17,081 € in 2001 prices are considered. Tax groups and enterprises with a foreign legal form are excluded from all computations.
*Data source*: German turnover tax statistics panel 2001–2005.

while the share of firms that only import is even larger. Over time, the share of all kinds of trading firms increased in East Germany.

Tables 2A and 2B report how many enterprises changed their status (neither export nor import; only export; only import; both export and import) between the first and the last year covered by our empirical investigation in West and East Germany, respectively. Among the firms that were active in both years, the largest group in both parts of Germany is made of firms that did not change their status. This type of stability is most often found among two-way traders. Enterprises that were active in 2001 but not in 2005 are found among all four types. Status changes in and out of one of the four categories can be found in both parts of Germany, but note that switching from no trade to two-way trade (and vice versa) is a rare event. Interestingly, about half of all firms that were not active

Table 2. Panel A: Transition matrix of manufacturing enterprises in West Germany 2001/2005

| | | Enterprise status in 2005 | | | | | |
|---|---|---|---|---|---|---|---|
| | | Not active in 2005 | Neither export nor import | Only export | Only import | Both export and import (two-way traders) | Total |
| | Not active in 2001 | — | 19,826 (30.2) [51.5] | 3,749 (28.4) [9.7] | 4,958 (30.3) [12.9] | 9,941 (27.6) [25.8] | 38,474 (22.1) [100.0] |
| | Neither export nor import | 25,289 (58.6) [34.3] | 39,918 (60.9) [54.1] | 2,909 (22.0) [3.9] | 4,375 (26.8) [5.9] | 1,333 (3.7) [1.8] | 73,824 (42.4) [100.0] |
| Enterprise status in 2001 | Only export | 4,284 (9.9) [31.3] | 2,128 (3.2) [15.5] | 4,411 (33.4) [32.2] | 493 (3.0) [3.6] | 2,377 (6.6) [17.4] | 13,693 (7.9) [100.0] |
| | Only import | 4,650 (10.8) [30.4] | 3,048 (4.7) [19.9] | 492 (3.7) [3.2] | 5,134 (31.4) [33.6] | 1,965 (5.4) [12.9] | 15,289 (8.8) [100.0] |
| | Both export and import (two-way trader) | 8,908 (20.7) [27.0] | 626 (1.0) [1.9] | 1,651 (12.5) [5.0] | 1,394 (8.5) [4.2] | 20,442 (56.7) [61.9] | 33,021 (18.9) [100.0] |
| | Total | 43,131 (100.0) [24.7] | 65,546 (100.0) [37.6] | 13,212 (100.0) [7.6] | 16,354 (100.0) [9.4] | 36,058 (100.0) [20.7] | 174,301 (100.0) [100.0] |

in 2001 in West Germany, and some 40 percent of these firms in East Germany, were trading in 2005, with 25.8 percent and 17.4 percent of these new firms being two-way traders that might be considered to be "born globals".

## 4. Productivity Premia for Firms in International Trade

As a first step in our empirical investigation, we compare the four types of enterprises with respect to labor productivity. Results are fully in line with the big picture that emerges from the literature reviewed in Section 2. For 2005, figures reported in Table 3 for the mean value of labor productivity show a positive link between importing and productivity at the firm level, documented by an unconditional productivity differential between firms that import and firms that do not trade internationally; and the same holds for

Table 2. Panel B: Transition matrix of manufacturing enterprises in East Germany 2001/2005

| | | Enterprise status in 2005 | | | | | |
|---|---|---|---|---|---|---|---|
| | | Not active in 2005 | Neither export nor import | Only export | Only import | Both export and import (two-way traders) | Total |
| Enterprise status in 2001 | Not active in 2001 | — | 4,859<br>(28.6)<br>[61.4] | 557<br>(28.9)<br>[7.0] | 1,127<br>(29.0)<br>[14.2] | 1,377<br>(29.7)<br>[17.4] | 7,920<br>(20.5)<br>[100.0] |
| | Neither export nor import | 7,991<br>(72.0)<br>[38.2] | 10,880<br>(64.0)<br>[52.0] | 586<br>(30.4)<br>[2.8] | 1,185<br>(30.5)<br>[5.7] | 300<br>(6.5)<br>[1.4] | 20,942<br>(54.3)<br>[100.0] |
| | Only export | 572<br>(5.2)<br>[32.5] | 335<br>(2.0)<br>[19.0] | 480<br>(24.9)<br>[27.3] | 88<br>(2.3)<br>[5.0] | 286<br>(6.2)<br>[16.2] | 1,761<br>(4.6)<br>[100.0] |
| | Only import | 1,328<br>(12.0)<br>[33.3] | 811<br>(4.8)<br>[20.3] | 97<br>(5.0)<br>[2.4] | 1,261<br>(32.4)<br>[31.6] | 493<br>(10.6)<br>[12.4] | 3,990<br>(10.4)<br>[100.0] |
| | Both export and import (two-way trader) | 1,208<br>(10.9)<br>[30.7] | 104<br>(0.6)<br>[2.6] | 209<br>(10.8)<br>[5.3] | 229<br>(5.9)<br>[5.8] | 2,187<br>(47.1)<br>[55.5] | 3,937<br>(10.2)<br>[100.0] |
| | Total | 11,099<br>(100.0)<br>[28.8] | 16,989<br>(100.0)<br>[44.1] | 1,929<br>(100.0)<br>[5.0] | 3,890<br>(100.0)<br>[10.1] | 4,643<br>(100.0)<br>[12.0] | 38,550<br>(100.0)<br>[100.0] |

*Note*: Reported are the number of cases, the column percentages in parenthesis ( ), and the row percentages in brackets [ ]. Only enterprises with one or more employees liable for paying social insurance and a turnover higher than 17,081 € in 2001 prices are considered. Tax groups and enterprises with a foreign legal form are excluded from all computations.
*Data source*: German turnover tax statistics panel 2001–2005.

exporting. Two-way traders are more productive than firms that either only import, or only export, or do not trade at all. In both parts of Germany, two-way traders are the most productive group of firms, followed by importers and then exporters, while firms selling in the national market only come last. All these results hold for 2001, too, and *t*-tests show that all these differences in means are statistically different from 0 at an error level of 0.01 or better.[6]

[6]To economize on space, results for statistical tests of differences in means (or distributions — see below) are not reported in detailed tables but summarized in the text. Detailed results are available on request.

Table 3. Comparison of internationally active and non-active manufacturing enterprises in West and East Germany in 2005

| | Labour productivity | | Number of employees liable to pay social insurance | |
|---|---|---|---|---|
| | Mean (in 1,000 €) | Index (in percent) | Mean | Index (in percent) |
| | West Germany | | | |
| All enterprises | 143.1 | 100.0 | 25.5 | 100.0 |
| Enterprises that... | | | | |
| neither export nor import | 110.7 | 85.8 | 6.2 | 41.7 |
| only export | 141.0 | 98.4 | 11.1 | 59.6 |
| only import | 145.5 | 101.5 | 12.7 | 77.6 |
| both export and import | 199.8 | 125.9 | 72.0 | 232.2 |
| | East Germany | | | |
| All enterprises | 91.4 | 100.0 | 16.3 | 100.0 |
| Enterprises that... | | | | |
| neither export nor import | 76.6 | 90.5 | 6.9 | 53.5 |
| only export | 99.7 | 99.2 | 14.4 | 96.0 |
| only import | 105.1 | 109.3 | 15.2 | 107.5 |
| both export and import | 131.1 | 127.9 | 52.9 | 268.8 |

*Note*: The index is computed as the percentage difference of the respective variable in an enterprise compared to the average value of all enterprises from the same 3-digit industry. Only enterprises with one or more employees liable for paying social insurance and a turnover higher than 17,081€ in 2001 prices are considered. Tax groups, enterprises with a foreign legal form and the 1st and the 99th percentiles of the labor productivity distribution are excluded from all computations.
*Data source*: German turnover tax statistics panel 2001–2005.

Note that these statistically significant differences in mean labor productivity are of an economically relevant size if two-way traders or one-way traders are compared to firms that do not trade, and if two-way traders are compared to firms that either only import or only export.[7]

[7]Note that the levels of labor productivity differ considerably if firms from West and East Germany are compared. This is one reason why all empirical investigations are carried out for the two parts of Germany separately.

If one looks at differences in the mean value for both groups only, one focuses on just one moment of the productivity distribution. A stricter test that considers all moments is a test for stochastic dominance of the productivity distribution for one group over the productivity distribution for another group. More formally, let $F$ and $G$ denote the cumulative distribution functions of productivity e.g. for importers and non-traders. If $F(x) - G(x) = 0$ means that the two distributions do not differ, and first order stochastic dominance of $F$ relative to $G$ means that $F(z) - G(z)$ must be less than or equal to 0 for all values of $z$, with strict inequality for some $z$. Whether this holds or not is tested non-parametrically by adopting the Kolmogorov–Smirnov test.[8] Here six Kolmogorov–Smirnov tests were performed, comparing the productivity distribution of neither exporting nor importing enterprises vs. only exporters, neither exporting nor importing enterprises vs. only importers, neither exporting nor importing enterprises vs. two-way traders, only exporters vs. two-way traders, only exporters vs. only importers and only importers vs. two-way traders.

Given that enterprises from the four groups compared are from different industries with different values of average labor productivity (due to, for example, differences in capital intensity), and that trading and non-trading, exporting and importing enterprises are not evenly distributed among the different industries, we control for these inter-industry differences by not using the unconditional labor productivity. Instead, we use an index that is computed as the percentage difference of labor productivity in an enterprise compared to the average value of all enterprises from the same 3-digit industry. For both West Germany and East Germany, and for both years, the Kolmogorov–Smirnov test indicates (at an error level of 0.01 or smaller) that the distributions do differ, and that the distribution for firms that participate in international trade first-order stochastically dominates the distribution for non-traders.

[8]This method has been used to discuss the issue of exports and productivity for the first time by Delgado, Farinas and Ruano (2002).

The hierarchy of distributions is the same as the one found for the mean values of the unconditional labor productivity.

Table 3 shows that the firms from the four groups differ in size (measured by the number of employees covered by social insurance), too. In both West and East Germany, enterprises that do not participate in international trade at all are on average smaller than firms that trade. Among the trading firms, those that only export are smaller than those that only import, while the two-way traders are much larger on average than enterprises from both other groups of trading firms. $T$-tests and $K-S$ tests again show that all these differences are statistically different from 0 at an error level of 0.01 or smaller for the unconditional mean values of firm size and the whole distributions of the number of employees are conditional on the 3-digit industries.

These descriptive findings for Germany fit into the big picture that emerges from the literature reviewed in Section 2. The next step in our empirical investigation is a test for the existence or not of the so-called trader premia, defined as the *ceteris paribus* percentage difference of labor productivity between enterprises from the four groups. This is motivated by the fact that firms with different forms of participation in international trade tend to differ in size (as demonstrated above) and might be concentrated in different industries. Therefore, for example, a positive unconditional productivity differential in favor of two-way traders compared to firms that do not trade at all comes at no (or only a small) surprise. The question is whether or not this differential exists if other factors related to productivity are controlled for. To test for these trader productivity premia, log labor productivity is regressed on three dummy variables indicating whether or not an enterprise only exports, only imports, or is a two-way trader (using the enterprises that do not trade at all as the reference group). The empirical model is estimated using pooled data from the years 2001 to 2005. As control variables, the number of employees and its squared value and a full set of interaction terms of dummies for each year and each 3-digit industry are included in the model. The year–industry interaction terms control for time and industry specific effects like variations in output prices and labor costs (see Lichtenberg (1988), p. 425). The empirical model is specified as follows:

$$\begin{aligned}\ln \mathrm{LP}_{it} &= a + ß_1 Ex\text{-only}_{it} + ß_2 Im\text{-only}_{it} \\ &\quad + ß_3 Im\text{-and-}Ex_{it} + c\,\mathrm{Control}_{it} + e_{it}, \qquad (1)\end{aligned}$$

where $i$ is the index of the enterprise, $t$ it the index of the year, LP is labour productivity, *Ex*-only and *Im*-only are dummy variables for enterprises that only export and only import in year $t$, and *Im*-and-*Ex* is a dummy variable for two-way traders in $t$. Control is the vector of control variables, and $e$ is an error term. The trader premium, computed from the estimated coefficient ß as $100(\exp(ß)-1)$, shows the average percentage difference in labor productivity between an enterprise from the respective group of trading firms and the non-trading enterprises, controlling for the characteristics included in the vector Control.[9]

To demonstrate the importance of distinguishing four different groups of firms according to their involvement in international trade instead of only looking at exporting vs. non-exporting firms when productivity differences between internationally active and non-active firms are investigated, a variant of the Model 1 is estimated that includes a dummy variable that takes the value 1 if a firm is an exporter (and 0 otherwise), completely ignoring any import activities. This is a model that is a workhorse in the empirical literature on exports and productivity (surveyed in Wagner (2007a)).

To control for unobserved plant heterogeneity due to time-invariant firm characteristics which might be correlated with the variables included in the empirical model and which might lead to a biased estimate of the trader premia, (1) is estimated using

[9]Note that the regression equation specified in (1) is not meant to be an empirical model to explain labor productivity at the firm level; the data set at hand here is not rich enough for such an exercise. Equation (1) is just a vehicle to test for, and estimate the size of, trader premia controlling for other firm characteristics that are in the data set. Furthermore, note that productivity differences at the firm level are notoriously difficult to explain empirically. "At the micro-level, productivity remains very much a measure of our ignorance." (Bartelsman and Doms 2000, p. 586)

pooled data for the years 2001–2005 and including fixed enterprise effects, too.

Results are reported in Table 4. All estimated productivity premia for firms that engage in international trade are highly statistically significant and often large from an economic point of view. Controlling for fixed enterprise effects[10] reduces the estimated premia considerably, pointing to the role of unobserved heterogeneity and the importance of enterprise specific factors that are both important for productivity and correlated with international activities of firms, and that lead to biased estimates of trade premia in the pooled regressions. From the results for Model 1 with fixed enterprise effects, we see that the premia are about the same in West and East Germany. Two-way traders do have the highest premia, followed by firms that only export, while firms that only import have the smallest estimated premia. This hierarchy differs from the picture painted by the descriptive evidence reported in Section 3 where it was found that firms that only import are more productive than firms that only export. A comparison of the exporter premia estimated in Model 2 with the premia for firms that export only and firms that both export and import estimated in Model 1 demonstrates that it is important to consider import activities, too, even if one is interested in the relationship between exports and productivity only. In part, the exporter premium estimated in Model 2 here is an importer premium.

## 5. Do More Productive Firms Self-Select Into Importing?

Descriptive evidence reported in Section 3 and evidence from a panel-econometric study presented in Section 4 show a positive relationship between importing and productivity at the firm level for West and East German manufacturing enterprises. This finding

[10]Due to limitations concerning the size of main memory available on the computers in the research data centre, it was not possible to estimate the fixed effects model with all West German enterprises. Therefore, the mean number of observations, the mean coefficients and the mean $p$-values of five 30 percent random samples are reported. A documentation of the results for the five random samples can be found in Table A.1 in the Appendix.

Table 4. Export and import productivity premia in manufacturing enterprises in West and East Germany (2001–2005)

| | Estimation of the log labor productivity in *t* | | | | | | | |
|---|---|---|---|---|---|---|---|---|
| | West Germany | | | | East Germany | | | |
| | Pooled regression | | Fixed effects* | | Pooled regression | | Fixed effects | |
| | 1 | 2 | 1 | 2 | 1 | 2 | 1 | 2 |
| Exporter | — | 36.7 | — | 5.25 | — | 26.8 | — | 5.7 |
| dummy$_t$ | — | (0.00) | — | (0.00) | — | (0.00) | — | (0.00) |
| Only export | 18.9 | — | 4.17 | — | 12.3 | — | 4.6 | — |
| dummy$_t$ (ß1) | (0.00) | — | (0.00) | — | (0.00) | — | (0.00) | — |
| Only import | 22.3 | — | 2.31 | — | 25.6 | — | 3.8 | — |
| dummy$_t$ (ß2) | (0.00) | — | (0.00) | — | (0.00) | — | (0.00) | — |
| Two-way trader | 55.8 | — | 8.79 | — | 47.8 | — | 10.4 | — |
| dummy$_t$ (ß3) | (0.00) | — | (0.00) | — | (0.00) | — | (0.00) | — |
| Number of observations | 652,219 | | 195,623 | | 141,299 | | 141,299 | |

*Note:* Reported are the estimated regression coefficients and the *p*-values (in parentheses) from two estimations of the log labor productivity at *t*. Model 1 contains an only export, an only import and a two-way trader dummy. ß1 is the average percentage productivity difference between exporters and non-exporters among enterprises that do not import. ß2 is the average percentage difference between importers and non-importers among non-exporters. ß3 is the average percentage difference between importer-exporters and enterprises that do neither export nor import. Model 2 contains an exporter dummy that shows the average percentage productivity difference between exporters and non-exporters. To facilitate the interpretation, the estimated coefficients of the dummy variables are transformed by 100(exp(ß)−1). Both models include the number of employees and its squared value, and a full set of interaction terms of year dummy variables and dummy variables for 3-digit level industries. Only enterprises with one or more employees liable for paying social insurance and a turnover higher than 17,081 € in 2001 prices are considered. Tax groups, enterprises with a foreign legal form and from the 1st and the 99th percentiles of the labor productivity distribution are excluded from all computations.
*Data source*: German turnover tax statistics panel 2001–2005.

*Due to limitations concerning the size of main memory available on the computers in the research data centre, it was not possible to estimate the fixed effects model with all West German enterprises. Therefore, the mean number of observations, the mean coefficients, and the mean *p*-values of five 30 percent random samples are reported. A documentation of the results for the five samples can be found in Table A.1 in the Appendix.

is in accordance with the results for other countries reviewed above. As discussed in the literature survey in Section 2, one hypothesis to explain this stylized fact is that causality runs from productivity to imports, and that more productive firms self-select into import activities. To shed light on the empirical validity of the hypothesis that the more productive firms go abroad and import, the pre-entry differences in productivity between import starters and non-importers are investigated next.

If more productive firms become importers then we should expect to find significant differences in productivity between future import starters and future non-starters several years before some of them begin to import. A way to test whether today's import starters were more productive than today's non-importers several years back when all of them did not import is to select all firms that did not import between years $t-3$ and $t-1$, and compute the average difference in labor productivity in year $t-3$ between those firms who did import in year $t$ and those who did not. Note that some of the firms labeled "import starters" might have imported several years earlier, stopped to import then and started again at time $t$. Unfortunately, the panel used here is not long enough to identify these "re-starters." The data set we use in this empirical investigation covers the years 2001–2005. Therefore, we can look at two cohorts of import starters — firms that start to import in 2005 (where $t-3$ corresponds to 2002, and $t$ to 2005) and firms that start to import in 2004 (where $t-3$ is equal to 2001 and $t$ to 2004). Furthermore, we can on the one hand compare firms that did not trade internationally at all between $t-3$ and $t-1$ and that start to import in $t$ with firms that did not trade at all between $t-3$ and $t$, and on the other hand firms that exported but not imported between $t-3$ and $t-1$ and start to import in $t$ with firms that exported but not imported between $t-3$ and $t$.

If one looks at differences in the mean value for both groups only, one focuses on just one moment of the productivity distribution. A stricter way that considers all moments is to test for a difference in the distribution, and for stochastic dominance of the productivity distribution for future importers over the productivity distribution for future non-importers, and to apply the Kolmogorov–Smirnov test (discussed in more detail in Section 4) to the data for year $t - 3$ (using, like in Section 4, an index that is computed as the percentage difference of labor productivity in an enterprise compared to the average value of all enterprises from the same 3-digit industry).

Results reported in Table 5 panel A (for import starters in 2005) and Table 5 panel B (for import starters in 2004) indicate self-selection of more productive (and larger) enterprises into import

Table 5. Panel A: Import starters vs. non-starters in West and East Germany in 2005

| | Labor productivity in 2002 | | Number of employees liable to pay social insurance in 2002 | | |
|---|---|---|---|---|---|
| | Mean (in 1,000 €) | Index (in percent) | Mean | Index (in percent) | Number of cases |
| | West Germany | | | | |
| Non-trading enterprises that start to import in 2005 | 112.0 | 103.8 | 9.6 | 149.3 | 2,122 |
| Enterprises that neither export nor import between 2002 and 2005 | 102.6 | 99.8 | 6.2 | 97.7 | 44,566 |
| Exporters that start to import in 2005 | 151.9 | 103.1 | 15.2 | 118.2 | 666 |
| Enterprises that only export between 2002 and 2005 | 150.2 | 99.4 | 13.2 | 96.7 | 3,702 |
| | East Germany | | | | |
| Non-trading enterprises that start to import in 2005 | 88.5 | 111.4 | 10.0 | 155.0 | 606 |
| Enterprises that neither export nor import between 2002 and 2005 | 71.2 | 99.5 | 6.7 | 97.4 | 12,614 |
| Exporters that start to import in 2005 | 112.9 | 105.8 | 21.2 | 112.2 | 87 |
| Enterprises that only export between 2002 and 2005 | 94.5 | 98.7 | 15.0 | 97.2 | 380 |

Table 5. Panel B: Import starters vs. non-starters in West and East Germany in 2004

| | Labor productivity in 2002 | | Number of employees liable to pay social insurance in 2001 | | |
|---|---|---|---|---|---|
| | Mean (in 1,000 €) | Index (in percent) | Mean | Index (in percent) | Number of cases |
| | | West Germany | | | |
| Non trading enterprises that start to import in 2004 | 118.9 | 106.5 | 8.5 | 140.9 | 2,033 |
| Enterprises that neither export nor import between 2001 and 2004 | 106.7 | 99.7 | 6.4 | 98.2 | 46,932 |
| Exporters that start to import in 2004 | 154.1 | 101.6 | 17.0 | 125.4 | 673 |
| Enterprises that only export between 2001 and 2004 | 152.3 | 99.7 | 13.6 | 95.7 | 3,945 |
| | | East Germany | | | |
| Non trading enterprises that start to import in 2004 | 85.6 | 108.8 | 11.9 | 165.7 | 629 |
| Enterprises that neither export nor import between 2001 and 2004 | 73.6 | 99.6 | 6.9 | 96.9 | 13,483 |
| Exporters that start to import in 2004 | 116.5 | 106.0 | 17.1 | 113.0 | 65 |
| Enterprises that only export between 2001 and 2004 | 97.4 | 99.0 | 15.6 | 97.8 | 393 |

*Note*: The index is computed as the percentage difference of the respective variable in an enterprise compared to the average value of all enterprises from the same 3-digit industry. Only enterprises with one or more employees liable for paying social insurance and a turnover higher than 17,081 € in 2001 prices are considered. Tax groups, enterprises with a foreign legal form and the 1$^{st}$ and the 99$^{th}$ percentiles of the labor productivity distribution are excluded from all computations.
*Data source*: German turnover tax statistics panel 2001–2005.

activities. Regardless of the start year $t$, the part of Germany, and the definition of starters and the reference group, on average the future importers were more productive and had a larger number of employees than the future non-importers three years before starting to import. If firms that did not trade internationally at all between $t-3$ and $t-1$ and that start to import in t are compared with firms that did not trade at all between $t-3$ and $t$, at an error level of 0.01 or less these average differences are statistically significantly different from zero according to $t$-tests, and the distribution of import starters stochastically dominates the distribution of non-starters. If firms that exported but not imported between $t-3$ and $t-1$ and start to import in t are compared with firms that exported but not imported between $t-3$ and $t$, the picture is different — the differences in productivity are never statistically significant at the usual error level, and the same holds for differences in the number of employees in East Germany.

Furthermore, labor productivity premia of future importers compared to future non-importers were estimated, controlling for plant size and industry affiliation by estimating the empirical model

$$\ln \mathrm{LP}_{it-3} = a + ß\ \mathrm{Import}_{it} + c\ \mathrm{Control}_{it-3} + e_{it}, \tag{2}$$

where $i$ is the index of the firm, $t$ is the index of the year, LP is labor productivity in year $t-3$, Import is a dummy variable for current import status (1 if the firm imports in year $t$, 0 else), Control is a vector of control variables (the number of employees — also included in squares — and 3-digit industry dummies), and $e$ is an error term. The pre-entry premium, computed from the estimated coefficient ß as 100(exp(ß)−1), shows the average percentage difference between today's importers and today's non-importers three years before starting to import, controlling for the characteristics included in the vector Control.

Results are reported in Table 6. In Model 1, the coefficient shows the average percentage productivity difference at $t-3$ between import starters at $t$ and enterprises with no international activities over the whole period (year $t-3$ to $t$). In Model 2, the coefficient shows the average percentage productivity difference at $t-3$ between exporters that start to import at $t$ and exporters that do not start to import. All point estimates are positive, and larger for East than for West Germany. In both parts of Germany, the pre-entry

Table 6. Self-selection into import markets of manufacturing enterprises in West and East Germany

| | OLS estimation of the log labor productivity in $t-3$ | | | | | | | |
|---|---|---|---|---|---|---|---|---|
| | West Germany | | | | East Germany | | | |
| | $t = 2004$ | | $t = 2005$ | | $t = 2004$ | | $t = 2005$ | |
| | 1 | 2 | 1 | 2 | 1 | 2 | 1 | 2 |
| Non-trader that starts | 10.4 | — | 7.3 | — | 14.4 | — | 14.1 | — |
| to import in $t$ (dummy) | (0.00) | — | (0.00) | — | (0.00) | — | (0.00) | — |
| Exporter that starts | — | 4.7 | — | 8.4 | — | 9.3 | — | 11.0 |
| to import in $t$ (dummy) | — | (0.06) | — | (0.00) | — | (0.30) | — | (0.20) |
| Number of observations | 48,965 | 4,618 | 46,688 | 4,368 | 14,112 | 458 | 13,220 | 467 |

*Note*: Reported are the estimated regression coefficients and the $p$-values (in parentheses) from the OLS estimation of the log labor productivity at $t-3$. To facilitate the interpretation, the estimated coefficient for the export dummy has been transformed by 100(exp(ß)−1). In Model 1, the transformed coefficient shows the average percentage productivity difference at $t-3$ between import starters at $t$ and enterprises with no international activities over the whole period (year $t-3$ to $t$). In Model 2, the transformed coefficient shows the average percentage productivity difference at $t-3$ between exporters that start to import at $t$ and exporters that do not start to import. Both models include the number of employees and its squared value, and a full set of dummy variables for 3-digit level industries. Only enterprises with one or more employees liable for paying social insurance and a turnover higher than 17,081 € in 2001 prices are considered. Tax groups, enterprises with a foreign legal form and the 1st and the 99th percentiles of the labor productivity distribution are excluded from all computations.
*Data source*: German turnover tax statistics panel 2001–2005.

productivity premia of import starters are statistically different from zero at a usual error level, and large from an economic point of view, when non-traders that start to import in $t$ are compared to firms that do not trade at all over the whole period. For exporters that start to import in $t$ compared to exporters that do not import over the whole period, this is only the case in West Germany. Note, however, that the number of import starters from this group is small in East Germany (65 and 87 firms in the starter cohort 2004 and 2005, respectively; see Table 5A and 5B), and this may cause an imprecisely estimated regression coefficient.

The bottom line, then, is that for German manufacturing firms we find evidence in favor of H1 — a positive impact of productivity on importing.

## 6. Do Import Starters Become More Productive?

The second hypothesis why importers can be expected to be more productive than their counterparts that buy intermediate inputs on the domestic market only points to the role of learning-by-importing. As is argued in Section 2, an importing firm can exploit global specialization and use inputs from the forefront of knowledge and technology. Imports, therefore, can act as an important vehicle for knowledge and technology transfer. Furthermore, importing intermediate products allows a firm to focus resources and to specialize on activities where it has particular strengths.

The possible causal effect of imports on productivity can be divided in two effects: First, a continuous learning effect that improves the post-entry performance of import starters. This "dynamic" effect could be caused by, for example, knowledge flows from international sellers and competitors as well as continuous knowledge and technology transfer. Second, one could expect that starting to import immediately raises the productivity level of the firm. Such a static-level effect could be explained, for example, by inputs of better quality or cheaper inputs from abroad that are used immediately in the production process. Below, both effects are investigated empirically. Section 6.1 analyzes the dynamic and Section 6.2 the static effect of imports on productivity.

### 6.1. *Dynamic effect of imports on the pre-entry productivity growth*

If importing improves the post-entry productivity growth then we should expect to find significant differences in the rate of growth of labor productivity between import starters and firms that continue to buy intermediate inputs in the national market only during the years after the start. This hypothesis is tested by looking at the growth rate of labor productivity over the period 2004–2005 for a cohort of import starters in 2003 compared to the growth performance of non-importers over the same period. Furthermore, for the period 2004–2005 the performance of exporters that start to import in 2003 is compared to the performance of firms that only export between 2001 and 2005.

Results are reported in Table 7. On average, the productivity growth performance of import starters from both groups was better compared to non-importers in West Germany, and the same holds for the growth of the number of employees. The big picture is the same for East Germany except for productivity growth in import starters compared to non-trading firms. All these post-entry performance differences, however, are never statistically different from 0 at an error level of 5 percent using *t*-tests or Kolmogorov–Smirnov tests.

Furthermore, differences in productivity growth between import starters and non-importers are investigated based on the empirical model

$$\ln \mathrm{LP}_{it+2} - \ln \mathrm{LP}_{it+1} = a + ß\,\mathrm{Start}_{it} + c\,\mathrm{Control}_{it} + e_{it}, \qquad (3)$$

where $i$ is the index of the firm, $t$ is the index of the year, LP is labor productivity, Start is a dummy variable for import starters (1 if the firm starts to import in year $t$, 0 else), Control is a vector of control variables (the number of employees — also included in squares — and 3-digit industry dummies), and $e$ is an error term. Results are reported in Table 8. To facilitate interpretation, the estimated coefficient for the starter-dummy has been transformed by 100(exp(ß)−1). In Model 1, the transformed coefficient shows the average productivity growth premium of import starters in 2003 compared to enterprises with no international activities two years after starting to import. In Model 2, the transformed coefficient shows the average productivity growth premium of exporters that start to import in 2003 compared to enterprises that only export over the whole period two years after starting to import. While the point estimates of three out of four regression coefficients are positive, none is statistically different from zero at a conventional level of significance. Therefore, again we have no evidence for learning-by-importing. Note, however, that the number of import starters is small in East Germany (see Table 7), and this may cause imprecisely estimated regression coefficients.

Table 7. Growth rates of import starters and non-starters in West and East Germany

| | Growth rates of labor productivity between 2004 and 2005 | | Growth rates of employees liable to pay social insurance between 2004 and 2005 | | |
|---|---|---|---|---|---|
| | Mean (in percent) | Index (in percent) | Mean (in percent) | Index (in percent) | Number of cases |
| | | West Germany | | | |
| Non-trading enterprises that start to import in 2003 | 4.4 | 100.7 | 2.0 | 101.2 | 607 |
| Enterprises that neither export nor import between 2001 and 2005 | 3.9 | 99.9 | 0.4 | 100.0 | 36,255 |
| Exporters that start to import in 2003 | 4.7 | 101.2 | 1.7 | 101.2 | 385 |
| Enterprises that only export between 2001 and 2005 | 3.1 | 99.8 | −0.2 | 99.8 | 2,757 |
| | | East Germany | | | |
| Non-trading enterprises that start to import in 2003 | 7.3 | 98.5 | 1.9 | 102.2 | 116 |
| Enterprises that neither export nor import between 2001 and 2005 | 7.4 | 100.0 | −0.5 | 100.0 | 9,690 |
| Exporters that start to import in 2003 | 8.7 | 101.4 | 7.3 | 105.5 | 49 |
| Enterprises that only export between 2001 and 2005 | 2.4 | 99.7 | 1.5 | 99.0 | 266 |

*Note*: The index is computed as the percentage difference of the respective growth rate in an enterprise compared to the average growth rate of all enterprises from the same 3-digit industry. Only enterprises with one or more employees liable for paying social insurance and a turnover higher than 17,081 € in 2001 prices are considered. Tax groups, enterprises with a foreign legal form and the 1$^{st}$ and the 99$^{th}$ percentiles of the labor productivity distribution are excluded from all computations.

*Data source*: German turnover tax statistics panel 2001–2005.

Table 8. Learning-by-importing in manufacturing enterprises in West and East Germany

| | OLS estimation of growth of labor productivity (log labor productivity$_{t+2}$ — log labor productivity$_{t+1}$) | | | |
|---|---|---|---|---|
| | West Germany | | East Germany | |
| | 1 | 2 | 1 | 2 |
| | | $t = 2003$ | | |
| Non-trading enterprise that starts to import in $t$ (dummy) | 1.2<br>(0.33) | | −2.8<br>(0.40) | |
| Exporter that starts to import in $t$ (dummy) | | 1.9<br>(0.18) | | 3.0<br>(0.51) |
| Number of observations | 36,862 | 3,142 | 9,806 | 315 |

*Note*: Reported are the estimated regression coefficients and the $p$-values (in parentheses) from the OLS estimation of log labor productivity in 2005 minus log labor productivity in 2004. To facilitate interpretation the estimated coefficient for the starter-dummy has been transformed by 100(exp(ß)−1). In Model 1 the transformed coefficient shows the average productivity growth premium of import starters in 2003 compared to enterprises with no international activities two years after starting to import. In Model 2 the transformed coefficient shows the average productivity growth premium of exporters that start to import in 2003 compared to enterprises that only export over the whole period two years after starting to import. Both models include the number of employees and its squared value plus a full set of 3-digit industry dummy variables. Only enterprises with one or more employees liable for paying social insurance and a turnover higher than 17,081 € in 2001 prices are considered. Tax groups, enterprises with a foreign legal form and the 1st and the 99th percentiles of the labor productivity growth rate distribution are excluded from all computations.
*Data source*: German turnover tax statistics panel 2001–2005.

In line with a recent development in the literature on the impact of exporting on productivity, an alternative approach to test for productivity enhancing effects of starting to import is applied next. To motivate this approach, consider the following situation: Assume that a study reports that plants entering the import market have substantially faster productivity growth in the following years than firms that keep buying intermediate inputs in the domestic market only. Does this point to a causal effect of starting to import on productivity? The answer is, obviously, no: If better firms self-select into import-starting, and if, therefore, today's import starters are "better" than today's non-importers (and have been so in the recent past), we would expect that they should, on average, perform better in the future even if they do not start to import today. However, we cannot observe whether they would really do so because they do start to import today; we simply have no data for the counterfactual situation. So how can we be sure that the better performance of starters compared to non-importers is caused by importing (or not)? This closely resembles a situation familiar from the evaluation of active labor market programs (or any other form of treatment of units): If participants, or treated units, are not selected randomly from a population but are selected or self-select according to certain criteria, the effect of a treatment cannot be evaluated by comparing the average performance of the treated and the non-treated. However, given that each unit (plant, person, etc.) either participated or not, we have no information about its performance in the counterfactual situation. A way out is to construct a control group in such a way that every treated unit is matched to an untreated unit that has been as similar as possible (ideally, identical) at the time before the treatment. Differences between the two groups (the treated, and the matched non-treated) after the treatment can then be attributed to the treatment (for a comprehensive discussion, see Heckman, LaLonde and Smith 1999).

The use of a matching approach to search for effects of starting to export on productivity (and other dimensions of firm performance) has been pioneered by Wagner (2002), and it has been used in a growing number of empirical studies (surveyed in Wagner (2007a)) ever since. Here, import starters in 2003 were matched with "twins" from the large group on non-importers based on characteristics of the enterprises in 2002 (the year before the starters start),[11] and

[11]Matching was done by nearest neighbors propensity score matching. The propensity score was estimated from a probit regression of a dummy variable indicating whether or not a firm is an import starter in 2003 on the log of labor productivity, number of employees and 3-digit industry dummy variables (all measured in year 2002) plus the rate of growth of labor productivity in the years 2001–2002. The balancing property (that

the difference in the average rate of growth of labor productivity over the period 2004–2005 between import starters and matched non-importers is computed. This difference is the so-called average treatment effect (ATT) on the treated, or ATT, the estimated effect of import start on the growth of labor productivity (see Wagner (2002) for a discussion of this method).

Results are reported in Table 9. The big picture arising from comparing import starters with matched non-importers is the same as the one sketched above based on the comparison of import starters and all non-importers. The estimated ATT is positive for three out of four cases, but it is statistically significantly different from zero (and negative) for East Germany only when non-trading enterprises that start to import in 2003 are compared to matched enterprises that do not trade at all. Therefore, from the matching approach we have no evidence in favor of the learning-by-importing hypothesis for German manufacturing enterprises.

### 6.2. *Static effect of imports on the productivity level*

To capture the static effect of imports on the productivity level, we compare the productivity levels before and after the import start of two cohorts of import starters (start year $t$: 2003 and 2004). However, again, we would need information about the counterfactual situation to be sure that the level differences are due to the start of importing. Therefore, in line with Section 6.1, import starters in 2003 and 2004 were matched with "twins" from the group of non-importers based on characteristics of the firms in the year before the

requires an absence of statistically significant differences between the treatment group and the control group in the covariates after matching) is satisfied. The difference in means of the variables used to compute the propensity score were never statistically significant between the starters and the matched non-starters. The common support condition (that requires that the propensity score of a treated observation is neither higher than the maximum nor less than the minimum propensity score of the controls) was imposed by dropping import starters (treated observations) whose propensity score is higher than the maximum or lower than the minimum propensity score of the non-importers (the controls). Matching was done using Stata 10 and the psmatch2 command (version 3.0.0), see Leuven and Sianesi (2003). The results of the probit estimates used in the matching are available on request.

Table 9. Growth rates of matched import starters and non-starters in West and East Germany — dynamic effect of imports on productivity

| | Growth of labor productivity between 2004 and 2005 | | | |
|---|---|---|---|---|
| | Mean (in percent) | ATT | Bootstrapped $p$-value | Observations (treated) |
| | West Germany | | | |
| Non-trading enterprises that start to import in 2003 | 4.6 | 1.8 | 0.449 | |
| Matched Enterprises that neither export nor import between 2001 and 2005 | 2.7 | | | 517 |
| Exporters that start to import in 2003 | 4.7 | 3.1 | 0.224 | |
| Matched Enterprises that only export between 2001 and 2005 | 1.6 | | | 343 |
| | East Germany | | | |
| Non-trading enterprises that start to import in 2003 | 5.3 | −15.8 | 0.047 | |
| Matched Enterprises that neither export nor import between 2001 and 2005 | 21.1 | | | 102 |
| Exporters that start to import in 2003 | 13.0 | 12.2 | 0.096 | |
| Matched Enterprises that only export between 2001 and 2005 | 0.7 | | | 35 |

*Note*: Reported are the mean labor productivity growth rates of the treated and the matched control groups, the ATT as well as the bootstrapped (1,000 replications) $p$-values that indicate the statistical significance of the ATT. Matching was done by nearest neighbors propensity score matching. The propensity score was estimated from a probit regression of the import starter dummies on the log of labor productivity, number of employees and a set of 3-digit industry dummy variables (all measured in 2002) plus the rate of growth of labor productivity between 2001 and 2002. The common support condition was imposed by dropping import starters (treated observations) whose propensity score was higher than the maximum or lower than the minimum propensity score of the control group. Only enterprises with one or more employees liable for paying social insurance and a turnover higher than 17,081 € in 2001 prices are considered. Tax groups, enterprises with a foreign legal form and the 1$^{st}$ and the 99$^{th}$ percentiles of the labor productivity growth rate distribution are excluded from all computations.
*Data source*: German turnover tax statistics panel 2001–2005. The matching was done using Stata 10 and the psmatch2 command (version 3.0.0), see Leuven and Sianesi (2003).

Table 10. Panel A: Growth rates of matched import starters 2003 and non-starters in West and East Germany — static effect of imports on productivity

| | Growth of labor productivity between 2002 and 2003 | | | Growth of labor productivity between 2002 and 2004 | | | |
|---|---|---|---|---|---|---|---|
| | Mean (in percent) | ATT | *p*-value | Mean (in percent) | ATT | *p*-value | Number of cases (treated) |
| | | West Germany | | | | | |
| Non-trading enterprises that start to import in 2003 | 5.3 | 1.9 | 0.279 | 3.4 | −0.3 | 0.905 | |
| Matched Enterprises that neither export nor import between 2001 and 2004 | 3.4 | | | 3.7 | | | 798 |
| Exporters that start to import in 2003 | 5.6 | 3.2 | 0.126 | 11.6 | 5.4 | 0.068 | |
| Matched Enterprises that only export between 2001 and 2004 | 2.3 | | | 6.2 | | | 497 |
| | | East Germany | | | | | |
| Non-trading enterprises that start to import in 2003 | 10.2 | 3.0 | 0.449 | 9.6 | 7.5 | 0.127 | |
| Matched Enterprises that neither export nor import between 2001 and 2004 | 7.2 | | | 2.1 | | | 194 |
| Exporters that start to import in 2003 | 6.5 | 6.3 | 0.248 | 3.2 | −6.1 | 0.388 | |
| Matched Enterprises that only export between 2001 and 2004 | 0.2 | | | 9.4 | | | 61 |

starters start to import.[12] Then the level difference that is caused by the import start (ATT on the treated) is computed by comparing the

[12]The propensity score was estimated from a probit regression of a dummy variable indicating whether or not a firm is an import starter in $t$ (2003 or 2004 respectivly) on the log of labor productivity, number of employees and 3-digit industry dummy variables (all measured in year $t-1$) plus the rate of growth of labor productivity in the years $t-2$–$t-1$.

Table 10. Panel B: Growth rates of matched import starters 2004 and non-starters in West and East Germany — static effect of imports on productivity

| | Growth of labor productivity between 2003 and 2004 | | | Growth of labor productivity between 2003 and 2005 | | | |
|---|---|---|---|---|---|---|---|
| | Mean (in percent) | ATT | *p*-value | Mean (in percent) | ATT | *p*-value | Number of cases (treated) |
| | | | West Germany | | | | |
| Non-trading enterprises that start to import in 2004 | 3.4 | 2.1 | 0.223 | 4.9 | 5.3 | 0.011 | |
| Matched Enterprises that neither export nor import between 2002 and 2005 | 1.3 | | | −0.4 | | | 925 |
| Exporters that start to import in 2004 | 4.5 | −1.6 | 0.471 | 6.6 | 1.5 | 0.548 | |
| Matched Enterprises that only export between 2002 and 2005 | 6.1 | | | 5.1 | | | 548 |
| | | | East Germany | | | | |
| Non-trading enterprises that start to import in 2004 | 3.4 | 6.1 | 0.047 | 8.1 | 8.7 | 0.011 | |
| Matched Enterprises that neither export nor import between 2002 and 2005 | −2.8 | | | −0.6 | | | 314 |
| Exporters that start to import in 2004 | 4.0 | −2.1 | 0.748 | 10.7 | 3.9 | 0.668 | |
| Matched Enterprises that only export between 2002 and 2005 | 6.1 | | | 14.6 | | | 68 |

*Note*: Reported are the mean labor productivity growth rates of the treated and the matched control groups, the ATT as well as the bootstrapped (1,000 replications) *p*-values that indicate the statistical significance of the ATT. Matching was done by nearest neighbors propensity score matching. The propensity score was estimated from a probit regression of the import starter dummies on the log of labor productivity, number of employees and a set of 3-digit industry dummy variables (all measured in 2003) plus the rate of growth of labor productivity between 2003 and 2005. The common support condition was imposed by dropping import starters (treated observations) whose propensity score was higher than the maximum or lower than the minimum propensity score of the control group. Only enterprises with one or more employees liable for paying social insurance and a turnover higher than 17,081 € in 2001 prices are considered. Tax groups, enterprises with a foreign legal form and the 1st and the 99th percentiles of the labor productivity growth rate distribution are excluded from all computations.

*Data source*: German turnover tax statistics panel 2001–2005. The matching was done using Stata 10 and the psmatch2 command (version 3.0.0), see Leuven and Sianesi (2003).

average rate of growth of labor productivity over the period $t-1$ to $t$ as well as $t-1$ to $t+1$ between import starters and matched non-importers. Following the previous sections, we compare in addition the growth rates over the period $t-1$ to $t$ as well as $t-1$ to $t+1$ between exporters that start to import in $t$ with the growth rates of firms that only export in all periods.

Results for the cohort of import starters 2003 are reported in Table 10 (Panel A) and for the cohort of import starters 2004 in Table 10 (Panel B). Overall, the results are somewhat mixed: In 5 of the 16 cases, the estimated ATT is negative but not significant, in 7 cases the ATT is positive but not significant, and in 4 cases a significant positive (at least at a weak significance level) estimated ATT is found. Therefore, the evidence concerning a static effect of imports on productivity is not clear.[13]

## 7. Concluding Remarks

This chapter uses a newly available comprehensive panel data set for manufacturing enterprises from 2001 to 2005 to present the first empirical results on the relationship between imports and productivity for Germany, a leading actor in the world market for goods. Furthermore, for the first time, the direction of causality in this relationship is investigated systematically by testing for self-selection of more productive firms into importing, and for productivity-enhancing effects of imports ("learning-by-importing").

Descriptive statistics show a positive link between importing and productivity at the firm level, documented by an unconditional productivity differential between firms that import and firms that do not trade internationally; and the same holds for exporting. From an empirical model with fixed enterprise effects that controls for firm size, industry and unobservable firm heterogeneity, we see that the premia for trading internationally are about the same

[13]Descriptive mean comparisons as well as OLS estimations of the growth of labor productivity in the above-mentioned time periods on import starter dummies confirm the big picture of unclear evidence. The results are available on request.

in West and East Germany. Two-way traders do have the highest premia, followed by firms that only export, while firms that only import have the smallest estimated premia. We find evidence for a positive impact of productivity on importing, pointing to self-selection of more productive enterprises into imports, but no evidence for positive effects of importing on productivity due to learning-by-importing.

The empirical evidence on a positive relationship between importing and productivity at the level of the firm is in accordance with findings for a large and growing number of developed and developing countries. Research on the direction of causality between productivity and import status, however, is still in its infancy. No other of the very few papers tackling the issue of direction of causality known to us does so by applying the approach used here. Future research will hopefully show whether the lack of evidence for learning-by-importing (that is matched by a similar lack of evidence regarding learning-by-exporting, see Wagner (2007b)) found for Germany is special, or whether it can be found in other developed and developing countries, too. Stylized facts based on comparable studies using data from many countries can then be used as an input for both appropriate theoretical models of heterogeneous firms that trade, and the discussion of policy conclusions based thereon.

## Acknowledgment

All computations were performed inside the Research Data Centre of the German Federal Statistical Office (Destatis). We thank Tim Hochgürtel for running our Stata do-files and checking the voluminous outputs for any violations of privacy, Stefan Dittrich from Destatis for his invaluable help with the data from the German Turnover Tax Statistics Panel, and an anonymous referee for helpful comments. The enterprise data used in this study are confidential but not exclusive; see Vogel and Dittrich (2008) for details on how to access these data via the Research Data Centre. To facilitate replication and extensions the do-files used in this study are available from the first author on request.

## References

Altomonte, Carlo and Gabor Békés (2008). Trading Activities, Firms and Productivity. Bocconi University, Milan, and Hungarian Academy of Science, Budapest, mimeo, June.

Amiti, Mary and Jozef Konings (2007). Trade Liberalization, Intermediate Inputs, and Productivity: Evidence from Indonesia. *American Economic Review*, 97(5), 1611–1638.

Andersson, Martin, Hans Lööf and Sara Johansson (2008). Productivity and International Trade — Firm-level Evidence from a Small Open Economy, *Review of World Economics* 144(4), 774–801.

Bartelsman, Eric J. and Mark Doms (2000). Understanding Productivity: Lessons from Longitudinal Micro Data. *Journal of Economic Literature* XXXVIII(3), 569–594.

Bernard, Andrew B., Bradford J. Jensen and Peter K. Schott (2005). Importers, Exporters, and Multinationals: A Portrait of Firms in the U.S. That Trade Goods. NBER Working Paper Series No. 11404, June.

Bernard, Andrew B., Bradford J. Jensen, Stephen J. Redding and Peter K. Schott (2007). Firms in International Trade. *Journal of Economic Perspectives*, 21(3), 105–130.

Bernard, Andrew B. and Joachim Wagner (1997). Exports and Success in German Manufacturing. *Review of World Economics* 133(1), 134–157.

Bernard, Andrew B., Jonathan Eaton, Bradford J. Jensen and Samuel S. Kortum (2003). Plants and Productivity in International Trade. *American Economic Review*, 93(4), 1268–1290.

Castellani, Davide, Francesco Serti and Chiara Tomasi (2008). Firms in International Trade: Importers and Exporters Heterogeneity in the Italian Manufacturing Industry. University of Perugia, draft mimeo, January.

Delgado, Miguel A., Jose C. Farinas and Sonia Ruano (2002). Firm Productivity and Export Markets: A Non-Parametric Approach. *Journal of International Economics* 57(2), 397–422.

Hagemejer, Jan and Marcin Kolasa (2008). Internationalization and Economic Performance of Enterprises: Evidence from Firm-Level Data. Munich Personal RePEc Archive Paper No. 8720, May.

Halpern, László, Koren Miklós and Ádám Szeidl (2005). Imports and Productivity. Institute of Economics, Hungarian Academy of Sciences, mimeo, June.

Heckman, James J., R. J. LaLonde and J. A. Smith. (1999). The economics and econometrics of active labor market programs. In: Ashenfelter, Orley C and David Card (Eds.), *Handbook of Labor Economics*, Vol. 3A, Amsterdam: North-Holland, pp. 1865–2097.

Kasahara, Hiroyuki and Beverly Lapham (2008). Productivity and the Decision to Import and Export: Theory and Evidence. CESifo Working Paper No. 2240, March (forthcoming, *Journal of International Economics*).

Kasahara, Hiroyuki and Joel Rodrigue (2005). Does the Use of Imported Intermediates Increase Productivity? Plant-Level Evidence. University of Western Ontario EPRI Working Paper Series No. 2005-7, September.

Leuven, Edwin and Barbara Sianesi (2003). PSMATCH2: Stata Module to Perform Full Mahalanobis and Propensity Score Matching, Common Support Graphing, and Covariate Imbalance Testing. Available at http://ideas.repec.org/c/boc/bocode/s432001.html.

Lichtenberg, Frank R. (1988). Estimation of the Internal Adjustment Costs Model Using Longitudinal Establishment Data. *Review of Economics and Statistics* 70(3), 421–430.

MacGarvie, Megan (2006). Do Firms Learn From International Trade? *Review of Economics and Statistics*, 88(1), 46–60.

Mayer, Thierry and Gianmarco I. P. Ottaviano (2007). The Happy Few: The Internationalisation of European Firms. New Facts based on Firm-level Evidence. Bruegel Blueprint Series Volume III, November.

Melitz, Marc J. (2003). The Impact of Trade on Intra-Industry Reallocations and Aggregate Industry Productivity. *Econometrica*, 71(6), 1695–1725.

Muuls, Mirabelle and Mauro Pisu (2007). Imports and Exports at the Level of the Firm: Evidence from Belgium. London School of Economics and Political Science CEP Discussion Paper No. 801, June.

Sjöholm, Frederik (1999). Exports, Imports and Productivity: Results from Indonesian Establishment Data. *World Development* 27(4), 705–715.

Tomiura, Eiichi (2007). Foreign Outsourcing, exporting, and FDI: A Productivity Comparison at the Firm Level. *Journal of International Economics* 72(1), 113–127.

Tucci, Alessandra (2005). Trade, Foreign Networks and Performance: A Firm-level Analysis for India. Centro Studi Luca D'Agliano Development Studies Working Papers No. 199, March.

Vogel, Alexander and Stefan Dittrich (2008). The German Turnover Tax Statistics Panel. *Schmollers Jahrbuch/Journal of Applied Social Science Studies* 128(4), 661–670.

Wagner, Joachim (2002). The Causal Effects of Exports on Firm Size and Labor Productivity: First Evidence from a Matching Approach. *Economics Letters* 77(2), 287–292.

Wagner, Joachim (2007a). Exports and Productivity: A Survey of the Evidence from Firm Level Data. *The World Economy* 30(1), 60–82.

Wagner, Joachim (2007b). Exports and Productivity in Germany. *Applied Economics Quarterly* 53(4), 353–373.

Wagner, Joachim (2008). A Note on Why more West than East German Firms Export. *International Economics and Economic Policy* 5(4), in press.

## Appendix

Table A.1. Export and import productivity premia in manufacturing enterprises in West Germany (2001–2005) — results for the five 30 percent random samples

| | Estimation of the log labor productivity in $t$<br>Model with fixed effects, West Germany | | | | | | | | | |
|---|---|---|---|---|---|---|---|---|---|---|
| | Random sample 1 | | Random sample 2 | | Random sample 3 | | Random sample 4 | | Random sample 5 | |
| | 1 | 2 | 1 | 2 | 1 | 2 | 1 | 2 | 1 | 2 |
| Exporter | — | 4.98 | — | 5.00 | — | 5.23 | | 5.79 | — | 5.25 |
| dummy$_t$ | — | (0.00) | — | (0.00) | — | (0.00) | | (0.00) | — | (0.00) |
| Only export | 4.12 | — | 3.81 | — | 4.14 | — | 4.28 | — | 4.51 | — |
| dummy$_t$ (ß1) | (0.00) | — | (0.00) | — | (0.00) | — | (0.00) | — | (0.00) | — |
| Only import | 2.71 | — | 2.81 | — | 2.20 | — | 2.02 | — | 1.83 | — |
| dummy$_t$ (ß2) | (0.00) | — | (0.00) | — | (0.00) | — | (0.00) | — | (0.00) | — |
| Two-way trader | 8.60 | — | 9.12 | — | 8.73 | — | 9.57 | — | 7.90 | — |
| dummy$_t$ (ß3) | (0.00) | — | (0.00) | — | (0.00) | — | (0.00) | — | (0.00) | — |
| Number of observations | 195,591 | | 195,633 | | 195,777 | | 194,562 | | 196,553 | |

*Note*: Due to limitations concerning the size of the main memory available on the computers in the research data centre, it was not possible to estimate the fixed effects model with all West German enterprises. Therefore, the mean values of the estimated regression coefficients and the $p$-values of five 30 percent random samples taken from all firms are reported in Table 4. This table reports the results for each of these samples. Model 1 contains an only export, an only import and a two-way trader dummy. ß1 is the average percentage productivity difference between exporters and non-exporters among enterprises that do not import. ß2 is the average percentage difference between importers and non-importers among non-exporters. ß3 is the average percentage difference between importer-exporters and enterprises that do neither export nor import. Model 2 contains an exporter dummy that shows the average percentage productivity difference between exporters and non-exporters. To facilitate the interpretation, the estimated coefficients of the dummy variables are transformed by 100(exp(ß)−1). Both models include the number of employees and its squared value, and a full set of interaction terms of year dummy variables and dummy variables for 3-digit level industries. Only enterprises with one or more employees liable for paying social insurance and a turnover higher than 17,081 € in 2001 prices are considered. Tax groups, enterprises with a foreign legal form and the 1$^{st}$ and the 99$^{th}$ percentiles of the labor productivity distribution are excluded from all computations.
*Data source*: German turnover tax statistics panel 2001–2005.

# PART III

# Exports and Wages

# Chapter 5

# Do Exporters Really Pay Higher Wages? First Evidence from German Linked Employer–Employee Data

Thorsten Schank, Claus Schnabel and Joachim Wagner

**Abstract**

Many plant-level studies find that average wages in exporting firms are higher than in non-exporting firms from the same industry and region. This paper uses a large set of linked employer–employee data from Germany to analyze this exporter wage premium. We show that the wage differential becomes smaller but does not completely vanish when observable and unobservable characteristics of the employees and of the work place are controlled for. For example, blue-collar (white-collar) employees working in a plant with an export–sales ratio of 60 percent earn about 1.8 (0.9) percent more than similar employees in otherwise identical non-exporting plants.

*Keywords*: Exports, wages, exporter wage premium, linked employer–employee data, Germany

**JEL Classification:** F10, D21, L60

## 1. Motivation

About 10 years ago, Bernard and Jensen (1995) published a Brookings paper on "Exporters, Jobs and Wages in U.S. Manufacturing" that used hundreds of thousands of plant-level data to provide facts and figures on exporting plants compared to their non-exporting counterparts. One of the new and exciting findings documented in this paper is that exporters tend to pay higher wages and benefits:

Average wages and benefits (per worker, per production worker and per non-production worker) are higher in exporting plants than in non-exporting plants of all size classes. Exporter wage premia are statistically significant for all categories of wages and benefits after controlling for capital per worker, size of plant, multi-plant dummy, industry, year, plant age and region. Coefficients of exporter status dummies are statistically significant in fixed effects regressions controlling for capital per worker, hours per worker, size of plant and year.

The Bernard and Jensen (1995) paper started a literature. A synopsis of 21 studies covering 22 different countries from highly developed economies like United States, Germany and Sweden, and emerging economies like Taiwan, Korea and Mexico, to transition countries (Estonia, Slovenia) and least developed Sub-Saharan African economies like Burundi or Ethiopia is provided in Appendix 1. The empirical strategies used in these papers replicate (sometimes only partly) the approach introduced by Bernard and Jensen, and the results regarding the exporter wage premia are broadly consistent with the findings from the pioneering study.

An open question not dealt with in this literature is whether these exporter wage premia do indeed indicate that exporting plants pay higher wages in the sense that comparable workers are better paid when working on a comparable work place for an exporter, i.e. *ceteris paribus*. Given that all the empirical studies listed use average data at the plant- or firm-level, individual characteristics of the workers that might influence their productivity (and, therefore, their wages) cannot be taken into account, and certain characteristics of the work place that might call for compensating wage differentials are not represented adequately. This shortcoming has been recognized from the outset: Commenting on the presentation of the paper by Bernard and Jensen, Robert Z. Lawrence argued that "the impact of exports, while positive and statistically significant, is considerably reduced once the effects of capital intensity, industry, plant scale, and location are controlled for. One suspects, moreover, that the premiums would be even further reduced if the authors were able to control for worker characteristics. Thus the wage benefits that are attributable solely to exporting appear to be rather small." (Bernard and Jensen 1995, p. 113f)

Besides providing a synopsis of the literature on exporter wage premia, this paper contributes to the literature by testing for the existence of these premia when observable and unobservable individual characteristics of the employees and the work place are controlled for using a rich German linked employer–employee panel data set. The rest of the paper is organized as follows: Section 2 introduces the data set while Section 3 replicates the now standard approach using plant-level data. Section 4 provides results for exporter wage premia based on linked employer–employee data using information for both individual workers and the plants they are working in. Section 5 concludes.

## 2. The Linked Employer–Employee Data Set

The use of linked employer–employee data has recently become popular as it allows a more detailed analysis of economic relationships. In particular, various analyses of the labor market can benefit from the availability of employer–employee data.[1] In this paper, we use the LIAB, which combines the employment statistics of the German Federal Labor Services with plant-level data from the IAB Establishment Panel.

The employment statistics (*cf.* Bender, Haas and Klose 2000) cover all employees and trainees subject to social security. They exclude, among others, the self-employed, family workers, a subgroup of civil servants ("Beamte"), students enrolled in higher education and those in marginal employment. The employment statistics cover nearly 80 percent of all employed persons in Western Germany and about 85 percent in Eastern Germany. They are collected by the social insurance institutions for their purposes according to a procedure introduced in 1973 and are made available

[1] A survey of analyses using matched employer–employee data sets can be found in Abowd and Kramarz (1999).

to the Federal Employment Services. Notifications are prescribed at the beginning and at the end of a person's employment in a plant. In addition an annual report for each employee is compulsory at the end of a year. Misreporting is legally sanctioned. The employment statistics contain information on an employee's occupation, the occupational status, and gross earnings up to the contribution assessment ceiling, and on individual characteristics like sex, age, nationality, marital status and qualification. Each personnel record also contains the establishment identifier, the industry and the size of the plant.

Starting in 1993, the IAB Establishment Panel (*cf.* Kölling 2000) is drawn from a stratified sample of the plants included in the employment statistics, where the strata are defined over industries and plant sizes (large plants are oversampled), but the sampling within each cell is random. In 1993, the sample started with 4,265 plants, covering 0.27 percent of all plants in Western Germany (2 million) and 11 percent of total employment (29 million). In 1996, the Eastern German establishment panel started with 4,313 establishments representing 1.1 percent of all plants (391,000) and 11 percent of total employment (6 million). The IAB Establishment Panel has been set up for the needs of the Federal Labor Services to provide further information about the demand side of the labor market. Therefore, detailed information on the composition of the workforce and its development through time constitutes a major part of the questionnaire. Further questions include information on training and further education, wages, working time, business activities, establishment policies and general information about the plant. Other topics, for instance, questions on innovations or the flexibility of labor, are asked biannually or triannually.

The LIAB is created by linking the employment statistics and the IAB Establishment Panel through a plant identifier which is available in both data sets.[2] This matched employer–employee data

[2]The LIAB data are confidential but not exclusive. They are available for non-commercial research by visiting the data access center of the German Federal Labor Services at the IAB in Nuremberg, Germany. Researchers interested in replications or extensions of our work may

set is unique for Germany. The version we use comprises the years 1993–1997. Since precise information on the collective bargaining regime of plants (needed for the imputation of wage data) is not available before 1995 and since we employ lags of investment, we can only make use of the waves 1995–1997. We exclude establishments that are located in the eastern part of Germany since the economic situation (and the level of wages) in post-communist Eastern Germany still differs considerably from that in Western Germany. Also, we focus on the manufacturing sector since exports are only of minor importance in the service sector. Therefore, in the regressions we end up with a sample of 1,855,034 observations of 918,149 employees in 1,262 establishments. This is composed of 1,189,469 observations of 585,692 blue-collar workers and 601,250 observations of 306,229 white-collar employees.

The dependent variable in our investigation is the log of wages, taken from the IAB Establishment Panel and, alternatively, from the employment statistics. Whereas the IAB panel data just provide information on the total wage bill of an establishment, the information on individual earnings in the employment statistics is more detailed, but it refers only to the income subject to social security contributions (i.e. up to the contribution assessment ceiling of the social security system).

For blue-collar workers, this problem is of minor importance since only 1.7 percent of the observations are reported to be at the ceiling. For white-collar workers, however, one-third of the wage-observations is censored. As is well known, not taking account of the censoring and applying OLS (or standard fixed effects techniques) to either all observations or to the reduced sample without the values on the ceiling yields biased estimates. We treat the data problem as a missing data problem and multiply impute the censored wages of white-collar workers by draws of a random variable from a truncated distribution.[3] Details of the applied

contact the first author (e-mail: thorsten.schank@wiso.uni-erlangen.de) for a copy of the Stata do-files used to produce the results reported here.

[3]MI has been developed by Rubin (1978) and is explained in Rubin (1996), Schafer (1997) and Rässler, Rubin and Schenker (2004). The theoretical motivation for MIs is Bayesian,

Markov chain Monte Carlo technique can be found in Appendix 2. To obtain more precise imputed values, we have performed the procedure separately for each of the 14 manufacturing industries in our sample. We should also point out that the imputation takes account of plant-fixed effects, which seems important since the variable under examination in this paper (a plant's export behavior) is a plant-level variable.[4]

Provided that certain regularity conditions are satisfied, the stationary distribution of the Markov chain approaches the conditional distribution of the unobserved wages above the ceiling, given the observed uncensored wages (see Schafer (1997)). Making use of only a single imputation and then applying OLS would — in our context — yield parameter estimates equivalent to a Tobit regression with unimputed data. However, in subsequent analyses, we want to control for person or plant heterogeneity, which is less straightforward with a Tobit model. In addition, without special corrective measures, single-imputation inference tends to overstate precision because it omits the between-imputation component of variability (Schafer 1997). For this reason, we apply multiple imputation (MI).

All individual-level wage regressions reported in Sec. 4 are carried out separately for blue-collar and for white-collar workers. As mentioned above, the censoring problem is neglectable for the former group, such that we can use the unimputed data. For white-collar workers, we report both, results based on unimputed data (including the censored values) as well as on the data sets which also include imputed values. In the case of imputed data, we estimate a wage regression for a given specification for each of the five (imputed) data sets and obtain five parameter estimates. The

---

although the resulting MI inference is usually also valid from a frequentist point of view. In the context of censored wages MI has been proposed and applied by Gartner and Rässler (2005).

[4]Due to technical constraints, the imputation does not deal with person effects. However, we believe that this is of a lesser problem in our context. The results reported in Section 4 indicate that the unobserved individual heterogeneity correlated with exports (and wages) is more or less collinear with the unobserved plant heterogeneity correlated with exports (and wages).

Table 1. Incidence and coverage of exporting plants. Manufacturing, Western Germany (percentages)

| | Weighted[1] | Unweighted[2] |
|---|---|---|
| Share of exporting plants | 19.1 | 70.6 |
| Employment share of exporting plants | 64.8 | 92.7 |
| Proportion of exports within total sales of exporting plants | 18.9 | 33.8 |

*Source*: IAB Establishment Panel 1995–1997.
[1]Weights refer to the inverse sample selection probabilities.
[2]Plant level regression sample.

average of these five estimates yields the MI point estimate. The standard error of the MI point estimate is composed of a between component (the standard deviation of the five estimates) and a within component (the average of the five standard errors).[5]

The main focus of our analysis is on the influence of exports on wages. We can make use of two alternative indicators of exports: First, a dummy variable indicating whether or not a plant has any exports, and, second, the proportion of exports within total sales. Table 1 reports descriptive statistics for these variables in our sample. From the results using weighted data — population weights are constructed as the inverse of sample selection probabilities — it follows that one in five manufacturing plants was an exporter in the years covered. This is in line with results from official statistics reporting a share of exporters in all manufacturing plants of 23 percent for 1996 (Günterberg and Wolter 2002, p. 250). It is well known that both the propensity to export and the share of exports in total sales tend to increase with firm size in Germany (see, e.g. Wagner (2001)). Therefore, the share of employees working in exporting firms is much larger — about two-third in our sample (weighted data). Due to the oversampling of larger firms in the IAB panel (mentioned above), the unweighted figures are much higher for both the share of exporters in all plants (70 percent) and the share of employees in exporting plants (more than 90 percent).

[5]The formulas are presented in Schafer (1997).

Furthermore, the positive relationship between firm size and the share of exports in total sales, and the oversampling of larger firms in the IAB panel, leads to a proportion of exports in total sales of all exporting firms that is 34 percent in the unweighted data compared to 19 percent in the weighted data.

On average, exporting firms pay higher wages than non-exporters. According to the sample of establishments from the IAB panel used in our empirical investigation, the difference between the average monthly wage per employee working in a firm that does or does not export is 36.6 percent. This raw exporter wage premium is both statistically significant and large from an economic point of view. Descriptive information on the other variables employed in our analysis is reported in Appendix 3.

## 3. Traditional Approach

We start our econometric investigations with a specification which is very similar to that adopted by Bernard and Jensen (1995) in their seminal article. This should constitute a reasonable basis for comparison. Using aggregate plant data from the IAB Establishment Panel, we estimate the impact of exports on the monthly wage bill per employee, where we make use of two alternative indicators of exports: First, a dummy variable indicating whether or not a plant has any exports, and, second, the proportion of exports within total sales. We include as control variables the logarithm of the number of employees and its square, the logarithm of capital per worker,[6] average weekly standard hours and year dummies. Finally, a dummy variable for the existence of paid overtime work takes account of the fact that additional (paid) hours are typically compensated with an overtime premium.[7] The parameter estimates

[6]The capital stock in year $t$ is approximated by the average of a plant's investment in the years $t, t-1$ and $t-2$. If for the years $t$, $t-1$ and $t-2$ there was only investment information available for one year (and two missing values), the respective (plant-year) observation was dropped from the analysis.

[7]We cannot control for the actual number of overtime hours since a considerable part of the plants in the sample provided no information on this variable.

Table 2. Plant-level wage regressions. Manufacturing, Western Germany (Endogenous variable: logarithm of monthly wage bill per employee).

| Estimation method | OLS | OLS | Plant-fixed effects | OLS | OLS | Plant-fixed effects |
|---|---|---|---|---|---|---|
| Variables | | | | | | |
| Exporting | 0.017 | 0.005 | 0.024 | | | |
| plant (1 = yes) | [0.75] | [0.23] | [0.94] | | | |
| Exports (proportion | | | | 0.140 | 0.067 | 0.026 |
| of total sales) | | | | [4.50]*** | [2.14]** | [0.38] |
| Logarithm of | 0.213 | 0.239 | −0.236 | 0.211 | 0.238 | −0.235 |
| establishment size (number of employees) | [8.44]*** | [9.35]*** | [1.54] | [8.84]*** | [9.77]*** | [1.54] |
| Squared logarithm | −0.014 | −0.017 | 0.010 | −0.015 | −0.017 | 0.010 |
| of establishment size | [6.21]*** | [7.46]*** | [0.75] | [6.66]*** | [7.80]*** | [0.75] |
| Logarithm of | 0.035 | 0.037 | 0.012 | 0.035 | 0.037 | 0.012 |
| capital per worker | [4.74]*** | [5.16]*** | [1.13] | [4.69]*** | [5.11]*** | [1.12] |
| Weekly standard | −0.027 | −0.012 | −0.008 | −0.025 | −0.012 | −0.008 |
| hours | [4.83]*** | [1.90]* | [1.09] | [4.67]*** | [1.88]* | [1.10] |
| Paid overtime work | 0.098 | 0.076 | 0.019 | 0.097 | 0.076 | 0.019 |
| in establishment (1 = yes) | [5.17]*** | [4.24]*** | [1.19] | [5.13]*** | [4.25]*** | [1.18] |
| 13 industry dummies | no | yes*** | no | no | yes*** | no |
| 9 federal state dummies | no | yes*** | no | no | yes*** | no |
| Constant | 8.264 | 7.868 | 9.434 | 8.232 | 7.867 | 9.445 |
| Constant | [36.42]*** | [28.45]*** | [18.14]*** | [36.49]*** | [28.30]*** | [18.12]*** |
| $R^2$ | 0.337 | 0.414 | 0.888 | 0.343 | 0.415 | 0.888 |

*Source*: IAB Establishment Panel 1995–1997. 2,797 observations from 1,287 plants. Regressions include year dummies. Absolute values of *t*-statistics in brackets. Residuals within plants are allowed to be not independent. ***/**/* denote significance at the 1/5/10 percent level, respectively.

from an OLS regression are reported in the first (export dummy) and fourth (export proportion) column of Table 2. *Ceteris paribus* exporting plants do not pay higher wages than non-exporters. The statistically significant and economically large differential between the average wage paid by exporters and non-exporters mentioned above, therefore, is due to differences in the plant observables included in the empirical model. The export share, however, is positively related with wages. If the proportion of exports in total sales rises by 10 percentage points, say, the wage per employee will increase by 1.4 percent. We should also note that the parameters of the control variables show the expected sign and are statistically significant at the 1 percent level.

Columns two and five of Table 2 report the estimates of wage regressions which additionally include 13 industry and 9 federal state dummies. While the coefficient on the export dummy remains zero, the impact of the export proportion halves in size, but is still significant. Therefore, the positive relationship between the export share and wages is partly due to between-industry differences.[8] Next, we control for unobserved plant heterogeneity and include plant-fixed effects in the regression.[9] As can be seen from columns three and six of Table 2, both the coefficients on the export dummy and the export share are now totally insignificant, from which one might conclude that (omitted) plant heterogeneity had been responsible for the positive impact of the export share on wages reported above. However, the fixed effects estimates contain much more noise. The standard error for the coefficient on the export share is twice as large as the respective figure obtained by OLS, and all the control variables are also insignificant.

These results differ considerably from those reported by Bernard and Wagner (1997) in the only other study using German data and a comparable approach: Bernard and Wagner found that exporting or not does make a difference, while the share of exports in total sales does not matter. The coefficient of the exporter dummy variable is statistically significant whether fixed plant effects are controlled for or not. One reason for the different findings of Bernard and Wagner (1997) could be that they relied on census-type data from official statistics (where firms are obliged to report true data) over a

---

[8]Separate regressions which (are available upon request and) either include industry or federal state dummies show that the industry dummies are responsible for the reduction in the coefficient on the export share.

[9]The industry and federal state dummies are dropped again since plants do generally neither change industry nor location and it is impossible to distinguish between misreporting and genuine switchers for those (few) who report different affiliations.

longer and different time period (1978–1992) and, therefore, with considerable variation of export status and export share within plants.[10]

## 4. Individual Level Wage Regressions

Plant-level estimations may suffer from aggregation bias since we cannot control for observable and unobservable individual heterogeneity which influence wages. Furthermore, the wage information obtained from plant surveys is *per se* less detailed and any adjustments for part-time employment and apprentices, for example, can only be approximative. In this section, we present individual level wage regressions based on the linked employer–employee data described in Section 2. Throughout, the analysis will be carried out separately for blue-collar and white-collar workers. Besides the different degree of wage-censoring for both groups, there may also be varying exporter wage premia. Bernard and Wagner (1997) report in their study using plant-level data that the positive exporter wage differential is almost exclusively driven by higher wages of white-collar workers.

We first apply OLS to a model without establishment-level variables (except the information on exports), but with individual characteristics which are typically included in the empirical literature on wages. These comprise the following variables, all of which are available from the employment statistics: The age of the employee (and its square), a gender dummy, education dummies (without A-levels and apprenticeship (base category)), with apprenticeship but without A-levels, without apprenticeship but with A-levels, with apprenticeship and A-levels, technical college degree, university degree, unknown education), a dummy variable indicating that the professional status is a master craftsman or a foreman and a dummy variable for non-German nationality.[11]

[10]In our regression sample, only 90 out of 1,287 plants switch between exporting and non-exporting (or *vice versa*) during the sample period.

[11]The full results including the estimated coefficients of the control variables can be found in Schank, Schnabel and Wagner (2006). Available at http://www.uni-lueneburg.de/vwl/RePEc/28.pdf.

Note that both the data for the individual characteristics and the information on earnings are from official statistics, and, therefore, can be considered to be highly reliable.

As can be seen from the first column of Table 3, exporting plants do *ceteris paribus* pay higher wages of around 2 percent, but the difference is not statistically significant at conventional levels. In contrast, we find again a significant positive relationship between the export share and wages. Raising the proportion of exports in total sales by 10 percentage points increases the wage by 1.3 percent for blue-collar workers and by 0.6 percent for white-collar workers. Based on the export share variable, there are two results emerging from this first column which recur throughout. First, the export wage premia is (about two times) larger for blue-collar workers than for white-collar employees. Second (and as expected), for white-collar employees the parameter estimate on the export share rises somewhat when using the wage data including the imputed values instead of the original censored observations. Since the latter yields biased estimates, in what follows we will always refer to the coefficients from the imputed data.

As in the plant-level estimations, including industry and federal state dummies reduces the coefficient on the export variables (column 2 of Table 3), but (again) the impact of the export share on wages can only partly be attributed to differences between industries.

Next, we control for individual-level heterogeneity by including person-fixed effects. The parameter on the export share is now identified either (i) if a plant changes its export share or (ii) if an employee moves to a plant with a different export share than its previous employer (and analogously for the parameter on the export dummy). Note that 827 (or 64.3 percent) of the firms included in our sample exported in each year and 370 (or 28.7 percent) did not export at all, while 80 firms (6.2 percent) changed their exporter status once and 10 firms (0.8 percent) did so twice. 2,271 persons (0.2 percent) changed once between employers included in our sample, 20 persons (0.002 percent) did so twice. While the share of exporter status or employer changers in all firms or persons

Table 3. Estimates of exporter wage premium individual level regressions of manufacturing, Western Germany (Endogenous variable: Logarithm of daily wage; separate regression for each cell)

| | Estimation method | OLS | OLS | Person-fixed effects |
|---|---|---|---|---|
| Industry effects | | No | Yes | Yes |
| Regional effects | | No | Yes | Yes |
| Group of employees | Export variable | | | |
| Blue-collar, unimputed data | Exporting plant (1 = yes) | 0.022 | 0.014 | 0.008 |
| | | [1.24] | [1.23] | [1.47] |
| | $R^2$ | 0.349 | 0.479 | 0.968 |
| | Degress of freedom | 1,189,454 | 1,189,432 | 603,744 |
| | Exports (proportion of total sales) | 0.128 | 0.079 | 0.028 |
| | | [4.20]*** | [4.40]*** | [2.63]*** |
| | $R^2$ | 0.366 | 0.484 | 0.968 |
| | Degress of freedom | 1,189,454 | 1,189,432 | 603,744 |
| White-Collar, unimputed data | Exporting plant (1 = yes) | 0.018 | 0.013 | 0.004 |
| | Exporting plant (1 = yes) | [1.63] | [1.54] | [1.45] |
| | $R^2$ | 0.482 | 0.517 | 0.984 |
| | Degress of freedom | 601,236 | 601,214 | 294,989 |
| | Exports (proportion of total sales) | 0.046 | 0.024 | 0.011 |
| | | [2.70]*** | [2.36]** | [2.50]** |
| | $R^2$ | 0.484 | 0.517 | 0.984 |
| | Degress of freedom | 601,236 | 601,214 | 294,989 |
| White-collar, imputed data | Exporting plant (1 = yes) | 0.022 | 0.011 | 0.006 |
| | | [1.45] | [0.96] | [1.59] |
| | $R^2$ | 0.505 | 0.539 | 0.953 |
| | Degress of freedom | 601,236 | 601,214 | 294,989 |
| | Exports (proportion of total sales) | 0.059 | 0.036 | 0.013 |
| | | [2.45]** | [2.37]** | [1.86]* |
| | $R^2$ | 0.506 | 0.539 | 0.953 |
| | Degress of freedom | 601,236 | 601,214 | 294,989 |

*Source*: LIAB 1995–1997. 1,189,469 observations of 585,692 blue-collar workers; 601,250 observations of 306,229 white-collar workers. Absolute values of *t*-statistics in brackets. Residuals within plants are allowed to be not independent. ***/**/* denote significance at the 1/5/10 percent level, respectively. Regressions include as further independent variables: age of employee, age squared of employee, gender, six education dummies, a dummy variable for the professional status being a master craftsman or a foreman (blue-collar workers only), a dummy variable for Non-German nationality, two year dummies and (only in the second OLS and Person-Fixed Effects estimations) 13 industry and nine federal state dummies.

is rather small, the absolute numbers of cases are large enough to identify the parameters of the export variables included in our empirical models.

Column 3 of Table 3 reports the person-fixed effects regression estimates of the export variables. For both blue- and white-collar workers, the wage difference between exporting and non-exporting plants is effectively zero. Compared with column 2, the impact of the export share on wages reduces further, but is still (weakly) significant. The reduction of the coefficients (both for the exporting dummy as well as for the export share) when controlling for unobserved individual heterogeneity implies that unobserved worker characteristics are positively correlated with export behavior.

The coefficients on the export variables might still be biased because of the omission of observed and unobserved plant characteristics. As a next step, we therefore add the same variables which have been used in the plant-level regressions discussed in the previous section. We also include industry and federal state dummies. The OLS estimates which do not take account of unobserved heterogeneity are reported in the first column of Table 4. These are best compared to the second column of Table 3. It can be observed that the inclusion of the plant characteristics reduces the parameters on the export variables. As before, the effect of the export dummy is zero. While the export share has still a positive and significant impact on the wages of blue-collar workers, its estimate is now insignificant for white-collar employees. As above, we control next for unobserved personnel heterogeneity (column 2 of Table 4). Compared to conditioning on individual as well as on plant observables, the export share coefficient for wages of blue-collar workers falls from 4.0 percent to 2.7 percent, while the export dummy remains insignificant for this group. Both export variables are now significant for white-collar workers, which was not the case without controlling for unobserved personnel heterogeneity. The coefficient on the export share implies that a rise in the proportion of exports in total sales by ten percentage points increases the wage for white-collar workers by 0.15 percent.

Table 4. Estimates of exporter wage premium individual level wage regressions Including plant characteristics. Manufacturing, western Germany (Endogenous variable: Logarithm of daily wage; separate regression for each cell)

| | Estimation method | OLS | Fixed effects (FE) | | |
|---|---|---|---|---|---|
| | | | Person FE | Plant FE | Spell FE |
| Industry effects | | Yes | Yes | No | No |
| Regional effects | | Yes | Yes | No | No |
| Group of employees | Export variable | | | | |
| Blue-Collar, | Exporting plant (1 = yes) | −0.011 | 0.009 | 0.005 | 0.009 |
| unimputed data | Exporting plant (1 = yes) | [1.11] | [1.51] | [0.73] | [1.49] |
| | $R^2$ | 0.501 | 0.969 | 0.636 | 0.969 |
| | Degress of freedom | 1,189,427 | 603,739 | 1,188,188 | 602,637 |
| | Exports (proportion | 0.040 | 0.028 | 0.027 | 0.030 |
| | of total sales) | [2.05]** | [3.13]*** | [2.87]*** | [3.26]*** |
| | $R^2$ | 0.502 | 0.969 | 0.636 | 0.969 |
| | Degress of freedom | 1,189,427 | 603,739 | 1,188,188 | 602,637 |
| White-Collar, | Exporting plant (1 = yes) | −0.001 | 0.005 | 0.004 | 0.005 |
| unimputed data | | [0.07] | [2.17]** | [1.53] | [2.17]** |
| | $R^2$ | 0.528 | 0.984 | 0.588 | 0.984 |
| | Degress of freedom | 601,209 | 294,984 | 600,028 | 293,921 |
| | Exports (proportion | 0.006 | 0.012 | 0.011 | 0.012 |
| | of total sales) | [0.61] | [3.18]*** | [2.79]*** | [3.31]*** |
| | $R^2$ | 0.528 | 0.984 | 0.588 | 0.984 |
| | Degress of freedom | 601,209 | 294,984 | 600,028 | 293,921 |
| White-Collar, | Exporting plant (1 = yes) | −0.004 | 0.008 | 0.008 | 0.008 |
| imputed data | | [0.42] | [2.27]** | [1.74]* | [2.16]** |
| | $R^2$ | 0.547 | 0.953 | 0.609 | 0.954 |
| | Degress of freedom | 601,209 | 294,984 | 600,028 | 293,921 |
| | Exports (proportion | 0.012 | 0.015 | 0.014 | 0.015 |
| | of total sales) | [0.86] | [2.51]*** | [2.04]** | [2.44]** |
| | $R^2$ | 0.547 | 0.953 | 0.609 | 0.954 |
| | Degress of freedom | 601,209 | 294,984 | 600,028 | 293,921 |

*Source*: LIAB 1995–1997. 1,189,469 observations of 585,692 blue-collar workers working belonging to 1,262 plants (586,816 spells); 601,250 observations of 306,229 white-collar workers belonging to 1,204 plants (307,314 spells). Absolute values of t-statistics in brackets. Residuals within plants are allowed to be not independent. ***/**/* denote significance at the 1/5/10 percent level, respectively. In addition to the regressions reported in Table 3, the following plant-level variables are included: Logarithm of the number of employees, squared logarithm of the number of employees, logarithm of capital per worker, weekly standard hours, a dummy variable indicating that the plant works overtime.

In the next step, we control for unobserved plant characteristics, but not for unobserved personnel heterogeneity. The estimates of these plant fixed effects regressions, which are identified through variations of the variables within a plant, are reported in column 3 of Table 4. Interestingly, the coefficients on the export variables are almost identical for person and plant-fixed effects.

However, the coefficients for both person- and plant-fixed effects might still be biased — in this particular application by the same amount — because in each case we have controlled only for one side of the labor market. To investigate this, the two types of heterogeneity have to be taken account of at the same time in the regression. Unfortunately, because of movement between plants, there is no transformation which sweeps out both sets of fixed effects simultaneously. This means that person demeaned (or differenced) firm dummies need to be created and estimated.[12] If one is not interested in the estimates of the heterogeneity themselves, consistent estimates of the coefficients on the observables can be obtained in a computationally far more straightforward way (see Andrews, Schank and Upward 2006). One simply defines unique worker-firm combinations (or "spells"). By definition, neither the worker nor the firm unobserved (time-invariant) characteristics vary for a given spell. Therefore, we can sweep out both by applying spell-fixed effects. Effectively, this uses only the differences between two consecutive observations if the worker does not change his employer between two periods.[13]

Spell-fixed effects thus are our preferred specification, the results of which are reported in the last column of Table 4; the parameter

[12] Alternatively, one could also create and estimate firm demeaned person dummies, but the dimension of persons is usually much larger than the dimension of firms.

[13] Note that this applies to nearly all persons in our regression sample because only 2,271 persons changed between employers included here once, and 20 did so twice. Since the proportion of plant-movers is tiny, any selection bias due to ignoring wage changes of individuals moving between plants should be negligible. Moreover, it is often argued that mobility is not exogenous, which means that an individual's productivity may differ between firms because the quality of the match between an individual and a firm varies. To the extent that the (unobserved) quality of the match and a firm characteristic are correlated, the estimated firm coefficients will be biased (see Gibbons and Katz (1992) for a simple model in the context of industry wage differentials).

estimates of all the plant- and person-specific control variables are provided in Appendix 4. It appears that the parameter estimates on the export variables are more or less identical to person- or plant-fixed effects. Therefore, we can safely conclude that exporting *per se* does hardly matter, but that the export share has a statistically significant impact on wages. An increase in the proportion of exports by 10 percentage points increases the wage of a blue-collar (white-collar) worker by 0.3 (0.15) percent. This means that a blue-collar employee working in a plant that exports 40/60/80 percent of its production earns about 1.2/1.8/2.4 percent more than an employee in a non-exporting plant, *ceteris paribus*, i.e. after controlling for observable and unobservable individual and plant characteristics. For white-collar workers, the exporter wage premium is lower and amounts to exactly half of the respective values. As the synopsis in Appendix 1 demonstrates, similar results have been obtained in studies for other countries (see, e.g. Bernard and Jensen (1995, 1999, 2004); Isgut 2001), although the majority of studies find higher wage premia for white-collar workers.

## 5. Conclusions

The bottom line of our empirical study on the relationship between exporting and wages in Western German manufacturing plants is an affirmative answer to the question in the title — exporters really do pay higher wages. Using linked employer–employee data to control for observable and unobservable individual and plant characteristics in the most comprehensive way possible we observe that wages increase with the share of production firms sell on foreign markets. This *ceteris paribus* exporter wage premium is neither (unplausibly) large nor negligible — working in a plant with, e.g. an export/sales ratio of 60 percent means for a blue-collar (white-collar) employee earning about 1.8 (0.9) percent more compared to working in an otherwise identical plant that does not export at all.

The positive relationship between wages and the share of exports in total sales is in line with previous findings reported in the literature. Three of the studies for other countries using aggregate firm-level data (listed in the synopsis in Appendix 1) look at the role of export shares. Both Liu, Tsou and Hammitt (1999) for Taiwan and Isgut (2001) for Colombia report a positive impact of the export share on wages after controlling for unobservable plant heterogeneity, as do Hansson and Lundin (2004) for Sweden based on plant observables only. None of these studies, however, uses linked employer–employee data, so the results may be biased because neither observed nor unobserved individual characteristics are controlled for.[14]

An open question to be considered next is why according to our preferred specification with spell-fixed effects (reported in the last column of Table 4) wages tend to increase with the proportion of exports in total sales, *ceteris paribus*. By construction neither observed nor (time-invariant) unobserved characteristics of the workers or the workplace can matter here. Given that the exporter wage premia are paid voluntarily and that the higher wages paid by more export-intensive plants lead to higher costs, the answer must lie in a positive relationship between wage premia over and above the going wage paid in other firms on the one hand, and success on exports markets that leads to a higher surplus on the other hand.

This said, efficiency wage theories form a natural pool of candidates to answer the question under consideration here. Among the various variants of models (Yellen 1984), the "higher-wages-reduce-turnover" variant seems to be most relevant in the context of German firms and exporting. To see why, remember that Germany is a high-wage country. Labor costs per unit of output are higher in

[14]To the best of our knowledge there is only one contemporaneous study on exports and wages based on linked employer–employee data: Milner and Tandrayen (2004) use data for 1993–1995 from six African countries (Cameroon, Ghana, Kenya, Tanzania, Zambia and Zimbabwe). They find a positive and significant wage premium for workers in exporting firms, even after controlling for firm and individual characteristics. The positive effect is larger for skilled workers, but positive only for firms that sell inside Africa. The relation between the share of exports in total sales and wages is not investigated in this study, however. Two papers by Gustavsson, Heyman and Sjöholm (2004) and by Martins (2004) use linked employer–employee data to look at the related issue of wage differentials between local and foreign owned firms in Sweden and Portugal, respectively.

Germany than in other competing highly industrialized countries including United States, UK and Japan (Institut der deutschen Wirtschaft Köln 2004, p. 7). High unit labor costs and a strong currency mean that German exporters cannot base their success in international market on low-priced products. Instead, they have to rely on complex high-quality products. To successfully produce this kind of products, the tacit knowledge of the experienced workforce is a limiting factor of production. Managers often point to the non-transferable know-how incorporated in the firm's workforce when asked why they still produce in high-cost Germany instead of, say, China or India.[15] Labor turnover is rather costly in these cases, so firms will be interested to reduce quits. One way to achieve this is to pay a premium above the going wage that a worker could earn in another plant. The higher the export/sales ratio and the share of profits earned on the world market, the more important will an experienced workforce be to secure high quality of products and competitiveness of the firm as a whole, and the higher will be the wage premium paid.[16]

An alternative interpretation of our finding that wages tend to increase with the proportion of exports in total sales would be that firms with high export shares might have experienced relatively favorable foreign demand shocks, and have raised wages to attract a relatively large work force in response. Such an explanation for cross-firm wage heterogeneity when workers are homogeneous can be found in some search-theoretic models which assume that individuals work at different wages, so that the labor supply curve is upward-sloping from the point of view of an employer (see, e.g. Bontemps, Robin and van den Berg (2000)). While in equilibrium all firms have the same level of profits, this can be attained by paying a low wage (thus attracting few workers) as well as by

[15] For a recent example, see Bernhard Schreier of Heidelberger Druckmaschinen, the world market leader in the production of printing equipment, quoted in Handelsblatt, June 30, 2004, p. 13.

[16] Unfortunately with the data used here it is not possible to test for a difference in labor turnover due to quits between firms with different export shares and different wage premia paid.

paying a high wage (thus attracting many workers). Furthermore, if firms employ different production technologies so that workers are more productive in one firm than in another, more productive firms may offer higher wages. Since there is some theoretical support (see Helpman, Melitz and Yeaple (2004)) and empirical evidence (for Germany, see Wagner (2006)) for exporting firms being more productive, this could also explain the exporter wage premium. Unfortunately, with our data we are not able to adequately test and empirically discriminate between the alternative explanations sketched above.

A question not discussed here is the direction of causality: Do exporters pay higher wages because they are exporters? Did they pay higher wages before they started to export? Do wages increase faster in firms that started to export than in comparable non-exporting firms? To investigate this important topic in a convincing way, linked employer–employee data are needed for a panel that covers at least seven years, and that includes a large number of export starters which can be monitored (at least three years) before and (at least three years) after beginning to export, and which can be compared to (matched) firms that did not start to export (see Wagner (2002) for such a study using plant level panel data). The LIAB data used in our study are not (yet) suited for this kind of study, so the topic of causality is left for future research.

## Acknowledgements

We would like to thank two anonymous referees and a co-editor of this journal for extremely helpful comments that guided us in the revision of an earlier version which has been circulating as IZA Discussion Paper No. 1185 since June 2004. We are also grateful to comments of Mark Roberts and of participants at presentations at the European Trade Study Group conference (Nottingham) in September 2004, the *1. Nutzerkonferenz zu den Daten der BA und des IAB* (Nuremberg) in July 2005 and the Annual Congress of the *Verein für Socialpolitik* in September 2005 (Bonn). Many thanks also go to Susanne Rässler and Hermann Gartner for helpful discussions and for providing their (unpublished) multiple imputation algorithm, and to Manfred Antoni for technical assistance. The usual disclaimer applies.

## References

Abowd, J. and F. Kramarz, (1999). The analysis of labor markets using matched employer-employee data. In: O. Ashenfelter, D. Card (Eds.), *Handbook of Labor Economics*, Vol. 3B, Amsterdam: North-Holland, pp. 2629–2710.

Alvarez, R. and R. A. López, (2005). Exporting and performance: Evidence from Chilean Plants. *Canadian Journal of Economics* 38, 1384–1400.

Arnold, J.M. and K. Hussinger, (2005). Export Behavior and Firm Productivity in German Manufacturing. A firm-level analysis. *Review of World Economics/Weltwirtschaftliches Archiv* 141, 219–243.

Andrews, M., T. Schank and R. Upward, (2006). Practical Fixed Effects Estimation Methods for the Three-way Error Components Model. *The Stata Journal* (forthcoming).

Aw, B.Y. and G. Batra, (1999). Wages, firm size, and wage inequality: How much do exports matter? In: Audretsch, D.B., Thurik, A.R. (Eds.), *Innovation, Industry Evolution, and Employment*, Cambridge, UK: Cambridge University Press, pp. 13–56.

Bender, S., A. Haas and C. Klose, (2000). The IAB Employment Subsample 1975–1995. *Schmollers Jahrbuch/Journal of Applied Social Science Studies* 120, 649–662.

Bernard, A.B., (1995). *Exporters and Trade Liberalization in Mexico: Production Structure and Performance*. Boston: Mimeo MIT.

Bernard, A.B. and J.B. Jensen, (1995). Exporters, Jobs, and Wages in U.S. Manufacturing: 1976 1987. *Brookings Papers on Economic Activity, Microeconomics*, 67–119.

Bernard, A.B. and J.B. Jensen, (1999). Exceptional Exporter Performance: Cause, Effect, or Both? *Journal of International Economics* 47, 1–25.

Bernard, A.B. and J.B. Jensen, (2004). Why Some Firms Export. *Review of Economics and Statistics* 86, 561–569.

Bernard, A.B. and J. Wagner, (1997). Exports and Success in German Manufacturing. *Weltwirtschaftliches Archiv/Review of World Economics* 133, 134–157.

Bontemps, C., J.-M. Robin, and G.J. van den Berg, (2000). Equilibrium search with continuous productivity dispersion: Theory and nonparametric estimation. *International Economic Review* 41, 305–358.

De Loecker, J., (2004). Do Exports Generate Higher Productivity? Evidence from Slovenia. Katholieke Universiteit Leuven, LICOS Centre for Transition Economics, Discussion Paper 151/2004.

Farinas, J.C. and A. Martin-Marcos, (2003). Exporting and Economic Performance: Firm-Level Evidence for Spanish Manufacturing. Madrid: Mimeo, Universidad Complutense.

Gartner, H. and S. Rässler, (2005). Analyzing the Changing Gender Wage Gap based on Multiply Imputed Right Censored Wages. IAB Discussion Paper No. 05/2005, Nürnberg.

Gibbons, R. and L. Katz, (1992). Does Unmeasured Ability Explain Inter-Industry Wage Differentials? *Review of Economics and Statistics* 59, 515–535.

Greenaway, D. and Z. Yu, (2004). Firm-Level Interactions between Exporting and Productivity: Industry-Specific Evidence. *Review of World Economics/Weltwirtschaftliches Archiv* 140, 376–392.

Günterberg, B. and H.-J. Wolter, (2002). *Unternehmensgrößenstatistik 2001/2002 — Daten und Fakten*. Bonn: Institut für Mittelstandsforschung.

Gustavsson, P., F. Heyman and F. Sjöholm, (2004). Foreign Ownership and Wages: Results from Matched Worker — Firm Data. Paper presented at the European Trade Study Group (ETSG) conference in Nottingham, September 9–11.

Hahn, C.H., (2004). Exporting and Performance of Plants: Evidence from Korean Manufacturing. National Bureau of Economic Research, NBER Working Paper Series No. 10208.

Hansson, P. and N.N. Lundin, (2004). Exports as an Indicator on or Promoter of Successful Swedish Manufacturing Firms in the 1990s. *Review of World Economics/Weltwirtschaftliches Archiv* 140, 415–445.

Helpman, E., M.J. Melitz and S.R. Yeaple, (2004). Export versus FDI with Heterogeneous Firms. *American Economic Review* 94, 300–316.

Institut der deutschen Wirtschaft Köln, (2004). *Standort Deutschland — Ein internationaler Vergleich*. Köln: Deutscher Instituts-Verlag.

Isgut, A.E., (2001). What's Different about Exporters? Evidence from Colombian Manufacturing. *Journal of Development Studies* 37, 57–82.

Kölling, A., (2000). The IAB-Establishment Panel. *Schmollers Jahrbuch/Journal of Applied Social Science Studies* 120, 291–300.

Liu, J.-T., M.-W. Tsou and J.K. Hammitt, (1999). Export Activity and Productivity: Evidence from the Taiwan Electronics Industry. *Weltwirtschaftliches Archiv/Review of World Economics* 135, 675–691.

Martins, P.S., (2004). Do Foreign Firms Really Pay Higher Wages? Evidence from Different Estimators. Bonn: Institute for the Study of Labor IZA DP No. 1388, November.

Meller, P., (1995). Chilean Export Growth, 1970–1990: An Assessment. In: Helleiner, G. K. (Ed.), *Manufacturing for Export in the Developing World. Problems and Possibilities*. Routledge, London and New York, pp. 21–53.

Milner, C. and V. Tandrayen, (2004). The Impact of Exporting and Export Destination on Manufacturing Wages: Evidence for Sub-Saharan Africa. University of Nottingham, Centre for Research in Economic Development and International Trade, CREDIT Research Paper No. 04/01.

Rässler, S., D. B. Rubin and N. Schenker, (2004). Imputation. In: Lewis-Beck, M.S., Bryman, A., Liao, T.F. (Eds.), *The SAGE Encyclopedia of Social Science Research Methods*, Vol. 2, Sage, Thousand Oaks, pp. 477–481.

Rubin, D., (1978). Multiple imputation in sample surveys — A phenomenological bayesian approach to nonresponse. *Proceedings of the Survey Research Methods Sections of the American Statistical Association* 20–34.

Rubin, D., (1996). Multiple Imputation after 18 years. *Journal of the American Statistical Association* 91, 473–489.

Schafer, J., (1997). *Analysis of Incomplete Multivariate Data*. London: Chapman & Hall.

Schank, T., C. Schnabel and J. Wagner, (2006). Do Exporters Really Pay Higher Wages? First Evidence From German Linked Employer-Employee Data. Working Paper Series in Economics 28, University of Lüneburg, Institute of Economics.

Sinani, E., (2003). *Export Market Participation: The Importance of Sunk Costs and Spillovers*. Mimeo, Center for East European Studies, Copenhagen Business School.

Tsou, M.-W., J.-T. Liu and J.K. Hammitt, (2002). Exporting and Productivity. Boston: Mimeo, Harvard School of Public Health.

Van Biesebroeck, J., (2005). Exporting raises Productivity in Sub-Saharan African Manufacturing Plants. *Journal of International Economics* 67, 373–391.

Verhoogen, E., (2003). *Trade, Quality Upgrading and Wage Inequality in the Mexican Manufacturing Sector: Theory and Evidence from an Exchange-Rate Shock*. Berkeley: Mimeo, University of California.

Wagner, J., (2001). A Note on the Firm Size — Export Relationship. *Small Business Economics* 17, 229–237.

Wagner, J., (2002). The Causal Effects of Exports on Firm Size and Labor Productivity: First Evidence From A Matching Approach. *Economics Letters* 77, 287–292.

Wagner, J., (2006). Exports, Foreign Direct Investment, and Productivity: Evidence From German Firm Level Data. *Applied Economics Letters* 13, 347–349.

Yellen, J., (1984). Efficiency Wage Models of Unemployment. *American Economic Review Papers and Proceedings* 74, 200–205.

Zhou, L., (2003). Why do Exporting Firms Pay Higher Wages? Atlanta: Mimeo, Emory University.

## Appendix 1: Synopsis of Studies on Exporter Wage Differentials

| Study | Country (period) | Sample | Wage variable(s) | Important results |
|---|---|---|---|---|
| Meller (1995) | Chile (1986–1989) | Sample of 138 export firms and 436 non-export firms from five industries (food, wine, wood products, chemicals, basic metal) | Median value of average annual wage | The null hypothesis of equal means for wage levels among export and non-export firms (for small and large firms separately) is rejected at the 1 per cent level of significance. Workers of export firms have consistently higher wages than those from non-export firms in all industries. (Note that a firm was considered an exporter if at least 30 per cent of its production was destined for foreign markets; non-exporters sell only on the domestic market. Firms with less than 100 workers were classified as small firms.) |
| Alvarez and López (2005) | Chile (1990–1996) | 7,132 manufacturing plants (unbalanced panel) | Average wage, average wage for production workers and for non-production workers | Controlling for plant size, foreign ownership, three-digit sector, and year, exporter premia are 21 percent for average wages, 15 percent for production wages and 28 percent for non-production wages. |

*(Continued)*

*(Continued)*

| Study | Country (period) | Sample | Wage variable(s) | Important results |
|---|---|---|---|---|
| Isgut (2001) | Colombia (1981–1991) | 5,956–6,909 manufacturing plants (unbalanced panel) | Average annual wages for all workers, blue-collar workers, white-collar workers, technicians, and managers | Average annual wages are much higher in exporting plants than in non-exporting plants by all five measures of wages in all plants and in plants from three different size classes (less than 30, 30 to 100, more than 100 workers). Exporter wage premia are statistically significant for all wage measures after controlling for plant size, industry, region, year, export/sales ratio and capital per worker. Fixed effects regressions including the exports/sales ratio, plant size, capital per worker and year estimate exporter wage premia between 1.5 (white collar workers) and 3.3 percent (blue collar workers). |
| Sinani (2003) | Estonia (1994–1999) | 2,335 observations on manufacturing firms (unbalanced panel); with 420 firms in 1994 and 303 firms in 1999. | Average labor costs | Average labor costs for exporters equal about four times (1994) and three times (1999) the average labor costs for non-exporters. |

| | | | | |
|---|---|---|---|---|
| Bernard and Wagner (1997) | Germany [Federal State of Lower Saxony] (1978–1992) | 4,263 manufacturing plants in 1978; 4,270 manufacturing plants in 1992 | Average annual wage; average annual production wage; average annual non-production wage | Average annual wage, production wage and non-production wage is higher in all plants and in plants with less than 250 employees in 1978 and 1992, but not for plants with more than 250 or more than 500 employees. Wage differences are much more pronounced for white-collar workers. Exporter wage premia are in part statistically significant after controlling for plant size, capital per worker, production hours per worker, a multi-plant dummy and industry: The average wage premium in exporting plants is 2.6 percent, while blue-collar workers receive no premium and white-collar workers are paid 3.3 percent more. Results including export intensity are similar. In a fixed effects specification both the premia for average wages and for white-collar wages remain significant. |
| Arnold and Hussinger (2005) | Germany (1992–2000) | Unbalanced panel of 2,149 observations on the firm level taken from the Mannheim Innovation Panel covering the manufacturing sector | Wage per employee (exact definition not given) | The wage per employee for the 1,260 exporters is 24.7 percent higher than the wage paid by the 889 non-exporters. Note that firms are considered to be exporters only if they sell at least five percent of their turnover abroad. |

(*Continued*)

(*Continued*)

| Study | Country (period) | Sample | Wage variable(s) | Important results |
|---|---|---|---|---|
| Hahn (2004) | Korea (1990–1998) | ca. 69,000–97,000 manufacturing plants (unbalanced panel) | Average wage; average production worker wage; average non-production worker wage | Average wages are higher in exporting plants than in non-exporting plants by all three measures of wages in 1990, 1994 and 1998. Exporter wage premia are statistically significant and high controlling for industry, region and plant size (in 1998, 12.5 percent, 10.5 percent, and 12 percent for the three different measures of wages, respectively). |
| Bernard (1995) | Mexico (1986–1990) | 2,370 manufacturing plants (balanced panel) | Average annual wage and benefits; average annual production wage; average annual non-production wage; average hourly production wage; average hourly non-production wage; average annual benefits | Exporting plants pay higher average amounts than non-exporting plants for all measures of wages and benefits in 1986 and 1992. Exporter premia are statistically significant after controlling for capital per worker, hours per worker, size of plant, foreign ownership, white collar/total employment, industry, state and year. In a fixed effects model only the premia for benefits per employee is statistically significant. However, the number of plants changing from non-exporter to exporter or *vice versa* is rather small so the results from the fixed effects model rely on a very small sample. |

| | | | | |
|---|---|---|---|---|
| Zhou (2003) | Mexico (1986–1990) | 2,353 manufacturing plants | Average white-collar wages; average blue-collar wages; average earnings including non-wage benefits and social security contributions but excluding profit sharing; average earnings including everything | Average wages are much higher in exporting plants than in non-exporting plants by all four measures of wages. Exporter wage premia are statistically significant and high controlling for industry and state; and controlling for size of firm, capital–labor ratio, white-collar worker share in total employment, foreign equity participation dummy, imported machinery share, royalty payment share, total factor productivity growth, tariff rates on outputs and inputs, and license requirements on outputs and inputs. Exporter wage premia are statistically significant and high (between 7 percent and 9 percent) in fixed effects regressions. |
| Verhoogen (2003) | Mexico (1984–2001) (1993–2001) | 3,003 manufacturing plants for 1993–2001 in a balanced panel; 3,605 manufacturing plants for 1993–2001 in an unbalanced panel; 706 plants for 1984–2001 in a balanced panel | Average white-collar hourly wage; average blue-collar hourly wage; ratio of white-collar/ blue-collar wage | Average white-collar and blue-collar wages, and ratio of white-collar to blue-collar wage higher for exporters than for non-exporters in 1993, 1997 and 2001 (balanced panel 1993–2001); no results reported for the two other panels. |

(*Continued*)

(*Continued*)

| Study | Country (period) | Sample | Wage variable(s) | Important results |
|---|---|---|---|---|
| De Loecker (2004) | Slovenia (1994–2000) | 7,915 manufacturing establishments (unbalanced panel); 20,580 observations | Average wage | Controlling for the number of employees, exporters pay 16.14 percent higher wages than non-exporters. |
| Farinas and Martin-Marcos (2003) | Spain (1990–1999) | 10,145 observations on 1,403 manufacturing plants (unbalanced panel) | Average wage per hour | Average wages are higher in exporting firms than in non-exporting firms for all firms, small firms and large firms in 1990 and 1999; note that differences are small in large firms (0.3 € and 0.5 €, respectively). Exporter wage premium is statistically significant and positive (6 percent) controlling for firm size, industry, year, foreign ownership and firm age. |
| Hansson and Lundin (2004) | Sweden (1990–1999) | 3,275 manufacturing firms (between 1,565 and 1,820 each year) in an unbalanced panel. | Average annual labor costs (including social security) per employee; average earning per employee; average earnings of skilled employees; average earnings of less-skilled employees | Average wages are significantly higher for all four wage measures in exporting firms than in non-exporting firms in 1990; in 1999, this holds only for skilled employees (while exporting firms had on average lower labor costs per employee). Using pooled data for 1990 to 1999 (15,262 or 15,413 observations) exporter wage premia are computed controlling for export share, firm size, capital intensity, industry and year dummies; results are positive and statistically significant for average labor costs (wage premium: 1 percent), average earnings per employee (1.5 percent), and average earnings of skilled workers (7 percent), but not for average earnings of less-skilled workers. |

| | | | | |
|---|---|---|---|---|
| Aw and Batra (1999) | Taiwan (1986) | 80,584 firms in ten manufacturing industries from the 1986 census | Average annual wage of non-production labor and of production labor | For all ten industries exporters pay higher wages than non-exporters to both their non-production and production labor. The average cross-industry export wage premium (after controlling for firm size, foreign capital, firm age, multiplant status and technology investment) is almost 30 percent for non-production workers and 14 percent for production workers. |
| Liu, Tsou and Hammitt (1999) | Taiwan (1989–1993) | 875 plants from electronics industry (balanced panel); information on exports only available for 1990 and 1992 | Average annual wage | Average annual wage is much higher in exporting plants than in non-exporting plants in 1992. Exporter wage premium is statistically significant and positive (15.5 percent) in a random effects regression controlling for capital intensity, ratio of subcontracting revenues to total sales and ratio of R&D expenditure to total sales. |
| Tsou, Liu and Hammitt (2002) | Taiwan (1986–1996) | Plant level data from the electrical machinery and electronics industry; 5,923 plants in 1986, 8,346 plants | Average annual wage | Average annual wages were significantly higher for exporters than for non-exporters; the differentials were 23.8 percent in 1991 and 18.6 percent in 1996. |

(*Continued*)

(*Continued*)

| Study | Country (period) | Sample | Wage variable(s) | Important results |
|---|---|---|---|---|
| Greenaway and Yu (2004) | UK (1989–1999) | 461 firms (unbalanced panel) from the chemical industry; 2,383 observations. Some results for "other manufactures" are reported, too. | Average annual wage | Average annual wages are 1.5 percent higher for exporters from other manufacturing, and 7.6 percent higher for exporters from the chemical industry. Exporter premia (controlling for industry and time effects) are 4.5 percent and 6.4 percent, respectively. |
| Bernard and Jensen (1995) | U.S. (1976–1987) | 193,463 manufacturing plants (1987 Census of Manufactures) ca. 400,000 manufacturing plants (pooled data for 1976–1987). | Average annual wage per worker; average annual wage per production worker; average annual wage per non-production worker; average annual benefits per worker | All average wages and benefits are higher in exporting plants than in non-exporting plants of all size classes, and with less than 250 employees or with 250 and more employees in 1987. Exporter wage premia are statistically significant for all categories of wages and benefits after controlling for capital per worker, hours per worker, size of plant, multi-plant dummy, industry, year, plant age, and region, amounting to 4.4 percent for wage per worker and 7.6 percent for benefits. Coefficients of exporter status dummies are statistically significant in fixed effects regressions controlling for capital per worker, hours per worker, size of plant and year. |
| Bernard and Jensen (1999) | U.S. (1984–1992) | 56,257 manufacturing plants in 1984; 199,258 manufacturing plants in 1987; 224,009 manufacturing plants in 1992. | Annual average wage; annual average production wage; annual average non-production wage | Exporter wage premia are statistically significant after controlling for industry, state, and plant size. Estimates for 1992 are 9.3 percent for average wage, 6.6 percent for production wage, and 4.6 for non-production wage. |

| | | | | |
|---|---|---|---|---|
| Bernard and Jensen (2004) | U.S. (1984–1992) | 13,550 manufacturing plants (balanced panel). | Average annual wage; annual blue-collar wage; annual white-collar wage | Exporter wage premia are statistically significant after controlling for industry and state in 1984 and 1992; estimates for 1992 are 6.9 percent for average wage and blue-collar wage, and 3.7 percent for white-collar wage. |
| Van Biesebroeck (2005) | Sub-Saharan Africa: Burundi, Cameroon, Cote d'Ivoire, Ethiopia, Ghana, Kenya, Tanzania, Zambia, Zimbabwe (1992/1996) | approx. 200 firms and three consecutive years in each country except Cote d'Ivoir (two years) and Burundi and Ethiopia (one year); unbalanced panels. | Average wage; production wage; non-production wage | Exporter wage premia is statistically significant and high (about 40 percent) for average wage after controlling for country, year, industry, location, and plant size. The premia is statistically significant and high (about 33 percent) for non-production wage in a sub-sample with information on it, but not statistically significant for production wage. |

*Note*: The studies are listed in alphabetical order of the country considered; studies covering up to three countries are listed separately for each country, other multi-country studies are listed at the bottom of the table.

## Appendix 2: The Imputation Procedure

In MI, each value of the unknown missing data $Y_{\text{mis}}$ is replaced by $m$ simulated values $Y^1_{\text{mis}}, Y^2_{\text{mis}}, \ldots, Y^m_{\text{mis}}$. The $m$ (as opposed to one) sets of imputations reflect uncertainty about the true values of the data. After the MIs have been carried out, $m$ completed data sets (and plausible versions of the real data) exist, each of which can then be analyzed by standard complete-data methods.

We assume that the (logarithm of the) wage is given by

$$w^* = X'\beta + \varepsilon,$$

where $X$ is a vector of covariates and $\varepsilon \sim N(0, \sigma^2)$. Observed wages are uncensored and equal to actual wages ($w^{\text{obs}} = w^{\text{unc}} = w^*$) if the latter are on or below the ceiling. Otherwise observed wages are censored at the ceiling ($w^{\text{obs}} = w^{\text{cen}} = c$). We will multiply impute the censored wages by estimates of the unobserved wages above the ceiling, which follow a normal distribution truncated at $c$. The MI is based on a Markov chain Monte Carlo (MCMC) technique, where the $m$ simulated values are obtained through iterations of two steps[17]:

(1) In the first step, values for the missing information (i.e. for those observations where the wages are censored) are drawn from a truncated normal distribution[18]:

$$w^{imp} \sim N^c(X'\beta^{(t)}, \sigma^{2(t)}),$$

where the $c$ indicates that the distribution is truncated at the ceiling $c$ from above. Based on the uncensored and the imputed wage data ($w^{\text{unc}}, w^{\text{imp}}$), we then estimate a wage equation by OLS, where we include as $x$-variables the same covariates as in the individual-level wage regressions reported in Section 4. These comprise both individual- and plant-level information (see footnotes to Tables 3

---

[17]MIs based on Markov chain Monte Carlo techniques are discussed in Schafer (1997). We apply an algorithm of this technique proposed by Gartner and Rässler (2005) in the context of censored data. For a formal presentation, the reader is referred to Gartner and Rässler (2005).

[18]The starting values ($\beta^{(0)}, \sigma^{2(0)}$) for the truncated distribution are obtained from a tobit estimation.

and 4 for a complete list of variables in addition to the export share and the export dummy) and also include plant dummies, but no person effects.[19]

(2) In the second step, the data posterior distributions can be specified, based on the estimates from the OLS regression, and new parameters are drawn according to the following:

$$\sigma^{2(t+1)} = \text{RSS}/g,$$

where RSS is the residual sum of squares from the OLS regression and $g$ is drawn from a $\chi^2$-distribution (with degrees of freedom corresponding to those in the OLS regression).

$$\beta^{(t+1)} \sim N\left(\hat{\beta}, \sigma^{2(t+1)}(X'X)^{-1}\right),$$

where $\hat{\beta}$ is the estimated coefficient vector from the OLS regression.[20] With the new parameters $(\beta^{(t+1)}, \sigma^{2(t+1)})$, we can start again with Step (1).

In general, we will not be able to use successive iterates of the imputed data because the parameters tend to be correlated (Schafer 1997). Therefore, we repeat Steps (1) and (2) 5,000 times and keep the data draws (Step (1)) of every 1,000$^{\text{th}}$ iteration as a new-data set.[21] Hence, we end up with five complete data sets, each consisting of the same unimputed data below the ceiling ($w^{\text{obs}} = w^{\text{unc}}$) and different draws of imputed data if observed wages were censored ($w^{\text{imp}}$).

[19]For ease of exposition, we have combined individual and plant level observables as well as plant dummies into the vector X. This could be done without harm, since plant dummies are not treated differently from any other variable.

[20]Such random draws of $(\beta^{(t)}, \sigma^{2(t)})$ are considered to be the Bayesian stochastic counterpart of maximizing the complete-data likelihood.

[21]For our data, autocorrelation functions of the parameters estimated from 5,000 iterations show that the chain converges and that — for the chosen lag of 1,000 — autocorrelation does not cause problems.

## Appendix 3. Descriptive Statistics; Regression Sample (Individual Level), Manufacturing, Western Germany.

| | Blue-collar workers | | White-collar workers | |
|---|---|---|---|---|
| Variables | Mean | s.d. | Mean | s.d. |
| Logarithm of daily wage (in Pfennigen), | | | | |
| reported | 9.692 | 0.223 | 9.993 | 0.235 |
| imputed wages | | | 10.056 | 0.300 |
| Exporting plant (1 = yes) | 0.931 | 0.254 | 0.915 | 0.278 |
| Exports (proportion of total sales) | 0.391 | 0.230 | 0.403 | 0.248 |
| Age of employee (years) | 39.296 | 10.374 | 41.574 | 10.121 |
| Age of employee squared (divided by 100) | 16.518 | 8.418 | 18.308 | 8.573 |
| Gender (1 = female) | 0.141 | 0.348 | 0.240 | 0.427 |
| Educational dummies | | | | |
| without apprenticeship, without A-levels (reference group) | 0.306 | 0.461 | 0.041 | 0.197 |
| with apprenticeship, without A-levels | 0.652 | 0.476 | 0.586 | 0.493 |
| without apprenticeship, with A-levels | 0.003 | 0.052 | 0.012 | 0.109 |
| with apprenticeship, with A-levels | 0.004 | 0.065 | 0.064 | 0.244 |
| technical college degree | 0.001 | 0.033 | 0.164 | 0.371 |
| university degree | 0.000 | 0.020 | 0.127 | 0.333 |
| unknown education | 0.034 | 0.181 | 0.006 | 0.078 |
| Master craftsman, foreman (1 = yes) | 0.036 | 0.186 | 0.000 | 0.000 |
| Foreign employee (1 = yes) | 0.183 | 0.387 | 0.032 | 0.177 |
| Logarithm of establishment size | 7.489 | 1.294 | 7.499 | 1.262 |
| Logarithm of establishment size squared | 57.757 | 19.268 | 57.828 | 18.921 |
| Logarithm of capital per worker | 9.495 | 0.824 | 9.480 | 0.900 |
| Weekly standard hours | 36.005 | 1.479 | 36.151 | 1.397 |
| Paid overtime in establishment (1 = yes) | 0.905 | 0.293 | 0.914 | 0.280 |
| Year dummies (reference: Year = 1995) | | | | |
| 1996 | 0.301 | 0.459 | 0.316 | 0.465 |
| 1997 | 0.327 | 0.469 | 0.328 | 0.469 |
| Number of observations: | | | | |
| total | 1,189,469 | | 601,250 | |
| censored | (20,378) | | (203,850) | |

*Source*: LIAB 1995–1997.

## Appendix 4. Individual Level Wage Regressions; Manufacturing, Western Germany (Endogenous Variable: Logarithm of Daily Wage)

| | Spell-fixed effects | | | | | |
|---|---|---|---|---|---|---|
| | Blue-collar workers | | White-collar workers | | | |
| Estimation method | Unimputed Data | | Unimputed Data | | Imputed Data | |
| Variables | | | | | | |
| Exporting plant | 0.009 | | 0.005 | | 0.008 | |
| (1 = yes) | [1.49] | | [2.17]** | | [2.16]** | |
| Exports | | 0.030 | | 0.012 | | 0.015 |
| (proportion of total sales) | | [3.26]*** | | [3.31]*** | | [2.44]** |
| Age of employee | 0.043 | 0.043 | 0.078 | 0.078 | 0.092 | 0.091 |
| (years) | [11.72]*** | [11.71]*** | [35.69]*** | [35.33]*** | [37.35]*** | [36.88]*** |
| Age of employee squared | −0.030 | −0.030 | −0.055 | −0.055 | −0.070 | −0.070 |
| (divided by 100) | [11.00]*** | [11.08]*** | [27.48]*** | [27.57]*** | [30.68]*** | [30.81]*** |
| Gender (1 = female) | | | | | | |
| Educational dummies | | | | | | |
| with apprenticeship, | −0.003 | −0.002 | 0.013 | 0.013 | 0.022 | 0.022 |
| without A-levels | [0.33] | [0.28] | [1.83]* | [1.83]* | [2.07]** | [2.08]** |
| without apprenticeship, | 0.009 | 0.010 | −0.042 | −0.042 | −0.018 | −0.018 |
| with A-levels | [0.49] | [0.53] | [1.75]* | [1.74]* | [0.68] | [0.68] |
| with apprenticeship, | 0.012 | 0.014 | 0.008 | 0.008 | 0.025 | 0.026 |
| with A-levels | [0.60] | [0.70] | [0.57] | [0.59] | [1.47] | [1.49] |
| technical college degree | 0.047 | 0.048 | 0.023 | 0.023 | 0.074 | 0.074 |
| | [1.94]* | [1.96]* | [2.43]** | [2.46]** | [4.30]*** | [4.30]*** |
| university degree | 0.034 | 0.035 | 0.036 | 0.036 | 0.106 | 0.106 |
| | [1.24] | [1.26] | [3.29]*** | [3.28]*** | [6.47]*** | [6.47]*** |
| unknown education | −0.034 | −0.035 | 0.010 | 0.010 | 0.017 | 0.017 |
| unknown education | [2.18]** | [2.28]** | [1.63] | [1.51] | [1.26] | [1.22] |

*(Continued)*

*(Continued)*

| | Spell-fixed effects | | | | | |
|---|---|---|---|---|---|---|
| | Blue-collar workers | | White-collar workers | | | |
| Estimation method | Unimputed Data | | Unimputed Data | | Imputed Data | |
| Master craftsman, | 0.051 | 0.051 | | | | |
| foreman (1= yes) | [2.34]** | [2.37]** | | | | |
| Foreign employee (1 = yes) | | | | | | |
| Logarithm of establishment | −0.208 | −0.204 | −0.058 | −0.057 | −0.127 | −0.125 |
| size (number of employees) | [2.13]** | [2.16]** | [1.49] | [1.49] | [2.01]** | [2.01]** |
| Squared logarithm of | 0.019 | 0.019 | 0.005 | 0.005 | 0.010 | 0.010 |
| establishment size | [2.48]** | [2.52]** | [1.55] | [1.56] | [1.99]** | [1.99]** |
| Logarithm of capital | 0.005 | 0.005 | 0.004 | 0.004 | 0.004 | 0.004 |
| per worker | [1.77]* | [1.98]** | [3.77]*** | [3.83]*** | [2.86]*** | [2.77]*** |
| Weekly standard hours | 0.004 | 0.004 | 0.002 | 0.002 | 0.003 | 0.003 |
| | [1.78]* | [1.94]* | [1.73]* | [1.97]** | [2.48]** | [2.59]*** |
| Paid overtime work in | 0.010 | 0.010 | 0.006 | 0.006 | 0.009 | 0.009 |
| establishment (1 = yes) | [2.28]** | [2.35]** | [4.14]*** | [4.24]*** | [4.56]*** | [4.63]*** |
| Constant | 8.737 | 8.718 | 7.770 | 7.767 | 7.709 | 7.706 |
| | [25.38]*** | [26.06]*** | [54.35]*** | [55.30]*** | [35.07]*** | [35.37]*** |
| $R^2$ | 0.969 | 0.969 | 0.984 | 0.984 | 0.950 | 0.950 |
| No. of observations | 1,189,469 | | 601,250 | | | |
| No. of employees | 585,692 | | 306,229 | | | |
| No. of plants | 1,262 | | 1,204 | | | |
| No. of spells | 586,816 | | 307,314 | | | |
| Degress of freedom | 602,637 | | 293,921 | | | |

*Source*: LIAB 1995–1997. Regressions include also year dummies. Reference category of education dummies is without apprenticeship, without A-levels. Absolute values of *t*-statistics in brackets. Residuals within plants are allowed to be not independent. ***/**/* denote significance at the 1/5/10 percent level, respectively.

# Chapter 6

# Higher Wages in Exporting Firms: Self-selection, Export Effect, or Both? First Evidence from Linked Employer–Employee Data

Thorsten Schank, Claus Schnabel and Joachim Wagner

**Abstract**

While it is a stylized fact that exporting firms pay higher wages than non-exporting firms, the direction of the link between exporting and wages is less clear. Using a rich set of German linked employer–employee panel data, we follow over time plants that start to export. We show that the exporter wage premium does already exist in the years before firms start to export, and that it does not increase in the following years. Higher wages in exporting firms are thus due to self-selection of more productive, better paying firms into export markets; they are not caused by export activities.

*Keywords*: Exports, wages, exporter wage premium, Germany

**JEL Classification:** F10, D21, J31

## 1. Motivation

Exporting firms pay higher wages than firms that serve the national market only. This is one of the stylized facts from the emerging literature on the microeconometrics of international firm activities. It was pointed out by Bernard and Jensen (1995) in their pioneering Brookings Paper, and it has been confirmed in a large number of studies (surveyed in Schank, Schnabel and Wagner 2007) with firm level data from many different countries. Some recent studies using linked employer–employee data have demonstrated that this positive link between export activities and the level of wages paid by a firm can even be found after controlling for observed and unobserved characteristics of both the employers and the employees.[1]

An issue that, to the best of our knowledge, has not been investigated empirically with linked employer–employee data is the sequencing behind the correlation of export activities and higher wages at the firm level. Does exporting lead to a wage premium? Or did exporting firms pay a wage premium even before they started to export? Theoretical considerations point to possible links in both directions that are by no means mutually exclusive:

— *H1: The observed exporter wage premium reflects self-selection of more productive firms with higher wages into export markets.*

The recent literature on exporting by heterogeneous firms, pioneered by Melitz (2003) and surveyed by Greenaway and Kneller (2007), argues that only the more productive firms in an industry can bear the extra costs of entering foreign markets. In these models, exporters are more productive than non-exporters, and we observe self-selection of more productive firms into export activities, with the *ex-ante* more productive firms becoming exporters. If wages are higher in more productive firms — due to higher profits and rent-sharing, or because higher (efficiency) wages cause higher productivity (see Akerlof and Yellen (1986))[2] — and if more productive

[1]See Munch and Skaksen (2008) for Denmark, Alcalá and Hernández (2007) for Spain, and Schank, Schnabel and Wagner (2007) for Germany. Note, however, that Breau and Rigby (2006) find no wage difference between exporting and non-exporting plants after controlling for worker characteristics for the Los Angeles Consolidated Metropolitan Statistical Area.

[2]Egger and Kreikemeier (2009) develop a model that incorporates workers' fair wage preferences into a general equilibrium framework à la Melitz (2003). They modify the original Akerlof and Yellen (1990) fair-wage effort mechanism by introducing a rent-sharing motive as a determinant of workers' fair wage preferences, assuming that the wage considered to be fair depends, among others, on the productivity level and thus on the performance of the firm. Identical workers then earn different wages in equilibrium, and higher wages are paid to employees working in more productive firms. They refer to Fehr and Gächter (2000) who point out that the idea of gift exchange which is central to the fair-wage effort hypothesis implies exactly this. The theory of a positive correlation between productivity

firms self-select into export markets, we expect that these future exporters already paid a wage premium to the workers *ex-ante*, i.e. before they started to export.

— *H2: Exporting makes firms more productive and leads to higher wages.*

This hypothesis found in the literature on exports and productivity points to the role of learning-by-exporting (see Bernard and Jensen 1999, Bernard and Wagner 1997 and Baldwin and Gu 2003). Knowledge flows from international buyers and competitors help to improve the post-entry performance of export starters (see Crespi, Criscuolo and Haskel 2008). Furthermore, firms participating in international markets are exposed to more intense competition and must improve faster than firms which only sell their products domestically. Exporting thus makes firms more productive. If wages are higher in more productive firms due to higher profits and rent-sharing, we may expect that exporting leads to higher wages. More specifically, this hypothesis predicts that after a firm has started to export, the wages of its employees increase stronger than the wages of employees who work in firms that continue to produce for the national market only, leading to an *ex-post* exporter wage premium.[3]

levels, profits and wages is well in line with empirical findings on rent-sharing in firms, as pointed out by Egger and Kreikemeier (2009). A different approach of introducing efficiency wages into heterogeneous firms models of the Melitz (2003) type is followed by Davis and Harrigan (2007) who argue that heterogeneity in the ability of firms to monitor effort leads to different wages for identical workers in equilibrium, following the variant of the efficiency wage theory put forward by Shapiro and Stiglitz (1984). If export starters are larger than non-exporters in the years before the start, and if monitoring costs are systematically higher in larger firms, this might lead to *ex-ante* wage differentials for identical workers in future export starters and non-exporters. Furthermore, Amiti and Davis (2008) introduce a fair-wage effort model into the Melitz framework, and in addition, provide some evidence for their theoretical hypotheses using Indonesian data. Also notable in this respect is a recent paper by Helpman, Itskhoki and Redding (2008) which produces wage differentiation across firms in a variant of the Melitz model in which labor market imperfections arise due to search frictions. This model generates a pure exporter wage premium even though productivity stays constant when a firm starts exporting. A similar result can be derived from a recent paper by Egger and Kreickemeier (2008).

[3]Note that profits play a role in both H1 and H2. Profits, however, cannot be directly controlled for in the empirical analysis here due to lack of information in the data. Using German firm level data Fryges and Wagner (2010) find no evidence for self-selection of more

Mainly due to lack of suitable data at the level of individuals, these two hypotheses have not been convincingly investigated for wages.[4] Since empirical studies of exporter wage differentials must control for observed and unobserved characteristics of both employers and employees that might determine wages besides exporting, they have to use linked employer–employee (LEE) panel data. To investigate the relevance of both the self-selection hypothesis and the learning-by-exporting hypothesis in explaining exporter wage differentials, LEE data are needed which cover a period that is long enough to follow cohorts of firms over a couple of years before and after they start to export, and which can be used to test for *ex-ante* and *ex-post* wage differentials. Apparently, such LEE data were not available until recently.

Using suitable LEE data for Germany, a leading actor on the world market for goods, this chapter contributes to the literature by testing the two hypotheses mentioned above on the direction of the link between exporting and wages.[5] For the period 1994–2006, we show that the exporter wage premium does already exist in the years before firms start to export, and that it does not increase in the years after exporting started. According to our findings, higher wages in exporting firms are due to self-selection of more productive, better paying firms into export markets, but they are not caused by export activities.

The rest of the chapter is organized as follows: Section 2 describes the LEE data. Section 3 presents the results of our empirical investigation, and Section 4 concludes.

---

profitable enterprises into exporting and a positive but small causal effect of exporting on profits.

[4]In contrast to wages, there is ample empirical evidence on the relationship between productivity and exporting, showing substantial exporter productivity premia and many findings in favor of the self-selection hypothesis but much fewer results in favor of the learning-by-exporting hypothesis. See Wagner (2007) for a survey, and International Study Group on Exports and Productivity (2008) for recent comparable results for 14 countries.

[5]In contrast to Schank *et al.* (2007), where the size of the exporter wage premium is estimated using similar data (albeit for a shorter time period), we focus on export starters and the evolution of this wage premium before and after exports start. This allows us to explicitly investigate the direction of the link between exporting and wages and test two alternative hypotheses.

## 2. The German Linked Employer–Employee Data

The dataset used in the subsequent empirical analyses is the German LIAB, i.e. the linked employer–employee dataset of the Institute for Employment Research (*Institut für Arbeitsmarkt- und Berufsforschung, IAB*). The LIAB combines the Employment Statistics of the German Federal Employment Agency (*Bundesagentur für Arbeit*) with plant-level data from the IAB Establishment Panel. For detailed information on the LIAB, see Alda, Bender and Gartner (2005).

The employee side of our dataset is the Employment Statistics, covering all employees and trainees subject to social security. They exclude, among others, the self-employed, family workers, a subgroup of civil servants ("Beamte"), students enrolled in higher education, and those in marginal employment. The employment statistics cover nearly 80 percent of all employed persons in western Germany and about 85 percent of employees in Eastern Germany. They are collected by the social insurance institutions for their purposes according to a procedure introduced in 1973 and are made available to the Federal Employment Agency. Notifications are prescribed at the beginning and at the end of a person's employment in a plant. In addition, an annual report for each employee is compulsory at the end of a year. Misreporting is legally sanctioned. The employment statistics contain information on an employee's occupation, the occupational status, and gross earnings up to the contribution assessment ceiling,[6] as well as on individual characteristics like sex, age, nationality, marital status, and qualification. Each personnel record also contains the establishment identifier, the industry, and the size of the plant.

The employer side of our dataset is given by the IAB Establishment Panel, a random sample of establishments that is drawn

[6]For daily gross wages, the ceiling in 2000, for example, is at 143.92€ for Western and at 118.81€ for Eastern Germany. In our regression sample, 9.0 (4.5) percent of the wage observations in Western (Eastern) Germany are censored. In order to cope with a potential bias due to censoring, we also conducted analyses not reported here (but available on request) which show that restricting the sample to uncensored observations does not change our conclusions.

from a stratified sample of the plants included in the Employment Statistics, where the strata are defined over industries and plant sizes (large plants are oversampled). In 1993, the panel started with 4,265 plants, covering 0.27 percent of all plants in Western Germany (2 million) and 11 percent of total employment (29 million). In 1996, the establishment panel also started in Eastern Germany with 4,313 establishments representing 1.1 percent of all plants (391,000) and 11 percent of total employment (6 million). The IAB Establishment Panel has been set up for the needs of the Federal Employment Agency to provide further information about the demand side of the labor market. Therefore, detailed information on the composition of the workforce and its development through time constitutes a major part of the questionnaire. Further questions include information on training and further education, wages, working time, business activities, establishment policies, and general information about the plant.

The LIAB is created by linking the Employment Statistics and the IAB Establishment Panel through a plant identifier which is available in both data sets.[7] Because the Employment Statistics is spell-based (one record for each employment spell), the combined data is potentially complex. To simplify, we select all (full-time) workers in the employment statistics who are employed by the surveyed plants on June 30$^{th}$ in a year. This yields an unbalanced annual panel of workers together with detailed information on the plants in which they work, which is unique for Germany. We are able to use the years 1994–2006, and we focus on the private sector. Finally, in order to avoid that the individual-level estimates may be driven by a few very large plants we keep only plants which employ less than 1,000 workers in the first year they are observed.[8]

[7]The LIAB data are confidential but not exclusive. They are available for non-commercial research by visiting the research data center of the German Federal Employment Agency at the IAB in Nuremberg, Germany. Researchers interested in replications or extensions of our work may contact the first author (thorsten.schank@wiso.uni-erlangen.de) for a copy of the Stata do-files used to produce the results reported here.

[8]This reduced our regression sample by 4 export starters and 72 non-exporters. When we kept all plants as a robustness check in the sample, the overall picture did not change substantially, but matching became more difficult (results are available upon request).

## 3. Empirical Investigation

The core of our empirical strategy to test for the validity of the two hypotheses on export activities and higher wages consists in comparing over-time wages in plants that start to export with wages in plants that continue to produce for the national market only. We start at a point in time when both groups of plants did not export, and end at a point in time when some of these firms have exported for a while. Using observation periods of six years, we define *export starters* as plants that do not export in the first three years ($t = 1, 2, 3$), but start to export in year $t = 4$ and continue to export in the years $t = 5$ and $t = 6$; *non-exporters* are plants that do not export in any of the years $t = 1, \dots, 6$.

### 3.1. *Descriptive Statistics*

Using the LIAB data described in Section 2 above, the six-year-windows considered here are 1994 to 1999, 1995 to 2000,. . ., 2001 to 2006. Data for export starters and non-exporters were pooled over these eight cohorts, and wages and sales were deflated. Table 1 reports descriptive statistics for both groups of plants and each year $t = 1, \dots, 6$.

Since the design of our investigation requires establishments to be observed in six consecutive years and to show particular patterns of export behavior, the sample available for our empirical investigation reduces to 70 export starters and 3,517 non-exporters. A comparison of plants from both groups with regard to size (number of employees), labor productivity (sales per employee) and wages paid (average daily wage) reveals that export starters are on average larger, more productive, and better paying in each year. Compared to non-exporters, export starters have on average almost twice the number of employees, and pay wages that are more than 20 percent higher.

The descriptive statistics reported in Table 1 are in line with the first hypothesis (*H1*) according to which higher wages in exporting firms are due to self-selection of more productive and better paying

Table 1. Descriptive statistics for export starters and non-exporters, all plants

| | Export starters ($N = 70$) | Non-exporters ($N = 3,517$) | Prob-value for $H_0$: Diff. of means $= 0$ |
|---|---|---|---|
| | Mean | Mean | |
| Plant size (number of persons) | | | |
| $t = 1$ | 108.31 | 60.08 | 0.01 |
| $t = 2$ | 107.90 | 59.36 | 0.00 |
| $t = 3$ | 106.93 | 58.47 | 0.00 |
| $t = 4$ | 108.04 | 57.95 | 0.00 |
| $t = 5$ | 110.33 | 56.79 | 0.00 |
| $t = 6$ | 110.52 | 55.63 | 0.00 |
| Yearly sales per employee (in thousands of €) | | | |
| $t = 1$ | 144.66 | 117.56 | 0.27 |
| $t = 2$ | 151.58 | 122.03 | 0.28 |
| $t = 3$ | 129.22 | 119.07 | 0.56 |
| $t = 4$ | 124.29 | 121.13 | 0.83 |
| $t = 5$ | 114.30 | 118.44 | 0.76 |
| $t = 6$ | 136.58 | 124.50 | 0.63 |
| Average daily wage (in €) | | | |
| $t = 1$ | 73.73 | 60.39 | 0.00 |
| $t = 2$ | 73.83 | 60.54 | 0.00 |
| $t = 3$ | 75.42 | 61.22 | 0.00 |
| $t = 4$ | 75.26 | 61.36 | 0.00 |
| $t = 5$ | 74.30 | 60.82 | 0.00 |
| $t = 6$ | 74.24 | 59.85 | 0.00 |
| Growth rates between $t = 3$ and $t = 6$, in percent | | | |
| Plant size (number of persons) | 23.48 | −0.63 | 0.20 |
| Yearly sales per employee (in thousands of €) | −0.68 | 7.40 | 0.16 |
| Average daily wage (in €) | −1.77 | −1.52 | 0.84 |

Sample is lower for sales per employee due to missing values. Export starters are plants which do not export in the first three years ($t = 1, 2, 3$), but export in the last three years ($t = 4, 5, 6$). Non-exporters do not export in any year. Wages and sales are deflated by the aggregate consumer price index. $t = 1, \ldots, 6$ refers to a specific year in the 6-year-window a plant is observed. Start (end) years for these windows vary across plants between 1994 (1999) and 2001 (2006).

firms into export markets — labor productivity and daily wages are higher in future export starters compared to non-exporters even in the years before the start (although the difference in average productivity is not statistically significant at any conventional level). In contrast, we find no evidence to support the second hypothesis (*H2*) which argues that exporting increases productivity and thus wages due to learning-by-exporting. Changes in labor productivity and in the daily wage between $t = 3$ and $t = 6$ do not differ in a statistically significant way between export starters and non-exporters.

### 3.2. *Plant-Level Regressions*

While providing interesting information, the descriptive statistics reported in Table 1 cannot be considered as a basis for a convincing test of the two hypotheses *H1* and *H2*. Since an exporter wage premium is a positive difference between the wages paid to employees in exporting and non-exporting firms after controlling for differences in other variables than exporting that determine wages, the rest of the empirical investigation is concerned with controlling for these influences on wages.

As a first step, we look at the difference in the plant average of daily wages between export starters and non-exporters over time, controlling for plant characteristics that can be expected to be related to the average wage level of a plant (including plant size, the presence or not of a works council, the use of new production technology, location in Western or Eastern Germany, various measures for the average qualification of the workforce, and dummies for industries, regions, and years). Results based on data for 3,587 plants are reported in column 1 of Table 2.

The coefficient of the exporter starter dummy variable captures any time-invariant (unobserved) differences between export starters and non-exporters and reflects the selection effect into export activity. It shows that the average daily wage paid by export starters is 7.2 percent higher than in comparable non-exporting plants in $t = 1$, i.e. three years before exports start (see row 1 of Table 2). This difference is both statistically significant and of a

Table 2. Plant-level regressions of wages and labor productivity (OLS); Germany

| Dependent variable: | Logarithm of (plant average of) daily wage | | Logarithm of sales per employee | |
|---|---|---|---|---|
| Explanatory variables | Full sample | Matched sample | Full sample | Matched sample |
| Export starter (dummy: 1 = yes) | 0.072<br>[3.02]*** | 0.041<br>[1.30] | 0.204<br>[2.78]*** | 0.120<br>[1.12] |
| Dummy ($t = 2$) × export starter | 0.001<br>[0.12] | −0.005<br>[0.30] | 0.033<br>[0.65] | −0.023<br>[0.34] |
| Dummy ($t = 3$) × export starter | −0.001<br>[0.12] | −0.007<br>[0.34] | −0.009<br>[0.13] | 0.007<br>[0.07] |
| Dummy ($t = 4$) × export starter | 0.004<br>[0.33] | −0.021<br>[0.83] | −0.005<br>[0.08] | 0.007<br>[0.07] |
| Dummy ($t = 5$) × export starter | 0.006<br>[0.41] | −0.012<br>[0.49] | −0.022<br>[0.28] | −0.043<br>[0.41] |
| Dummy ($t = 6$) × export starter | 0.015<br>[0.98] | −0.002<br>[0.08] | 0.035<br>[0.35] | −0.041<br>[0.34] |
| Plant size dummies (number of employees; reference: 1–9) | | | | |
| 10–19 | 0.094<br>[10.48]*** | 0.015<br>[0.34] | 0.003<br>[0.10] | −0.249<br>[1.62] |
| 20–49 | 0.119<br>[12.08]*** | −0.012<br>[0.20] | 0.002<br>[0.07] | −0.254<br>[1.37] |
| 50–99 | 0.105<br>[8.78]*** | −0.022<br>[0.32] | −0.101<br>[2.54]** | −0.085<br>[0.43] |
| 100–199 | 0.115<br>[7.66]*** | −0.036<br>[0.51] | −0.146<br>[2.64]*** | −0.442<br>[2.28]** |
| 200–499 | 0.141<br>[8.89]*** | 0.006<br>[0.08] | −0.207<br>[3.13]*** | −0.139<br>[0.52] |
| 500–999 | 0.134<br>[6.22]*** | −0.145<br>[1.67]* | −0.263<br>[3.02]*** | −1.228<br>[3.22]*** |
| 1000 and more | 0.126<br>[1.69]* | | 0.135<br>[0.37] | |
| Works council (dummy: 1 = yes) | 0.098<br>[9.85]*** | 0.091<br>[2.65]*** | 0.252<br>[7.08]*** | 0.216<br>[1.55] |

*(Continued)*

Table 2. (*Continued*)

| Dependent variable: | Logarithm of (plant average of) daily wage | | Logarithm of sales per employee | |
|---|---|---|---|---|
| Explanatory variables | Full sample | Matched sample | Full sample | Matched sample |
| Collective agreement (reference: no collective agreement) | | | | |
| at sectoral level | 0.062 | 0.027 | 0.038 | 0.082 |
| (dummy: 1 = yes) | [8.70]*** | [0.98] | [1.75]* | [0.86] |
| at firm level | 0.054 | 0.055 | 0.040 | −0.016 |
| (dummy: 1 = yes) | [5.77]*** | [2.30]** | [1.17] | [0.18] |
| Plant belongs to a larger | 0.119 | 0.140 | 0.363 | 0.407 |
| unit (dummy: 1 = yes) | [10.15]*** | [4.10]*** | [8.49]*** | [2.87]*** |
| New production technology | 0.047 | 0.043 | 0.127 | 0.164 |
| (dummy: 1 = yes) | [8.57]*** | [2.54]** | [7.37]*** | [2.14]** |
| Eastern Germany | −0.257 | −0.265 | −0.175 | 0.353 |
| (dummy: 1 = yes) | [9.12]*** | [2.66]*** | [1.91]* | [1.07] |
| Average age of | 0.001 | 0.042 | 0.011 | 0.072 |
| employees (in years) | [0.16] | [1.11] | [0.71] | [0.86] |
| Average age squared | 0.001 | −0.043 | −0.019 | −0.082 |
| (divided by 100) | [0.19] | [0.93] | [0.96] | [0.76] |
| Average tenure | 0.025 | 0.026 | 0.058 | 0.092 |
| of employees | [7.86]*** | [1.87]* | [7.27]*** | [1.97]* |
| Average tenure squared | −0.098 | −0.141 | −0.236 | −0.527 |
| (divided by 100) | [5.07]*** | [2.04]** | [5.96]*** | [2.26]** |
| Proportion within total workforce of plant: | | | | |
| Female workers | −0.310 | −0.306 | −0.188 | −0.738 |
| | [16.62]*** | [3.59]*** | [3.63]*** | [3.24]*** |
| Non-German workers | −0.104 | −0.286 | −0.155 | 0.152 |
| | [2.41]** | [1.95]* | [2.02]** | [0.37] |
| Workers with | 0.100 | 0.090 | 0.139 | −0.046 |
| apprenticeship, no *Abitur* | [3.80]*** | [0.84] | [1.88]* | [0.11] |
| Workers without | 0.086 | 3.329 | 0.279 | 5.050 |
| apprenticeship, with | [0.66] | [4.05]*** | [1.69]* | [1.60] |
| *Abitur* Workers with | 0.323 | 0.302 | 0.325 | −1.038 |
| apprenticeship and | [5.70]*** | [1.39] | [2.18]** | [1.58] |
| *Abitur* Workers with | 0.592 | 0.406 | 0.825 | −0.780 |
| technical college degree | [10.69]*** | [2.27]** | [4.38]*** | [1.28] |

(*Continued*)

Table 2. (*Continued*)

| Dependent variable: | Logarithm of (plant average of) daily wage | | Logarithm of sales per employee | |
|---|---|---|---|---|
| Explanatory variables | Full sample | Matched sample | Full sample | Matched sample |
| Workers with university degree | 0.604 | 0.434 | 0.816 | 1.183 |
| | [12.28]*** | [1.95]* | [5.16]*** | [1.98]** |
| Workers with unreported education | 0.095 | 0.116 | 0.193 | 0.232 |
| | [3.40]*** | [1.18] | [2.48]** | [0.55] |
| Master craftsman | 0.131 | 0.658 | −0.032 | −0.237 |
| | [2.62]*** | [2.07]** | [0.20] | [0.24] |
| Constant | 3.685 | 2.969 | 11.143 | 9.703 |
| | [34.39]*** | [3.86]*** | [37.49]*** | [5.09]*** |
| Observations | 21,103 | 708 | 18,342 | 634 |
| Plants | 3,587 | 118 | 3,444 | 118 |
| $R^2$ | 0.63 | 0.85 | 0.45 | 0.75 |

Regressions also include 37 sectoral dummies, 9 urbanisation dummies, 15 regional dummies, 12 year dummies as well as 5 dummies for the respective periods $t$. $|t|$-statistics in parentheses, based on robust standard errors adjusted for clustering at the plant-level. *Full sample* refers to all observations with no missing values in the covariates. *Matched sample* refers to observations from plants which have been selected via nearest neighbor propensity score matching, where the propensity score has been obtained from a probit on export starting.

relevant order of magnitude from an economic point of view.[9] Results reported in column 3 of Table 2 show that the same holds for labor productivity. Controlling for all plant characteristics used in the wage regression, the estimated productivity premium for export starters three years before the start is 20.4 percent. The statistically insignificant coefficients of the interaction terms of the export starter dummy variable and the dummy variables for $t = 2$

[9]The control variables all have the expected signs, and most of them are statistically significant. Since the focus of this chapter is on the exporter wage premium, we do not comment on the results for the control variables here and in other regressions. As a robustness check, we also included average investment per employee as a proxy for the capital stock per head (which reduced the regression sample due to missing information). While the estimated coefficient indicated a positive relationship with wages, the export dummy and the interaction terms of the export starter dummy and the year dummies remained literally unchanged.

to $t = 6$ show that neither the difference in the average wage nor the difference in the average productivity changes over the years $t = 2$ to $t = 6$.

These results are in line with our hypothesis *H1* — plants with higher wages (and a higher productivity) self-select into export markets. Contrary to this, hypothesis *H2* — that wages (and productivity) increase after starting to export due to learning-by-exporting effects — is not supported. All point estimates of the interaction terms of the export starter dummy variable and the dummy variables for $t = 4$ to $t = 6$ are very small and statistically not significantly different from zero.[10] These findings are consistent with the results from the descriptive statistics reported in Table 1.

Next, we apply an alternative approach to test for wage (and productivity) enhancing effects of starting to export. This is motivated by the problem that faster wage growth of plants which have just entered the export market (compared to plants that keep selling their products on the domestic market only) would not necessarily reflect a causal effect of exporting on wages. It could well be the case that better paying (and more productive) firms self-select into the export starting group, but would have experienced higher wage growth even without starting to export. However, we cannot observe the latter scenario (i.e. the wage developments of today's export starters if they had not started to export), which is the well-known problem of the missing counterfactual situation.[11]

This closely resembles a situation familiar from the evaluation of active labor market programs (or any other form of treatment of units): If participants, or treated units, are not selected randomly from a population but are selected or self-select according to certain criteria, the effect of a treatment cannot be evaluated by comparing the average performance of the treated and the non-treated. Since

[10]While the insignificance of the interaction terms could be due to the small number of export starters, the very small point estimates found here and in the following regressions should not be a consequence of small sample size.

[11]Although the regression results discussed above do not show a difference in wage growth between export starters and non-exporters, these estimates may be biased due to the self-selection of export starters.

each unit (plant or person) either did participate or not, we lack the required information about its performance in the counterfactual situation. A way out is to construct a control group in such a way that every treated unit is matched to an untreated unit that was as similar as possible (ideally, identical) at the time before the treatment. Differences between the two groups (the treated, and the matched non-treated) after the treatment can then be attributed to the treatment (for a comprehensive discussion, see Heckman, LaLonde and Smith 1999). The use of a matching approach to search for effects of starting to export on wages (and other dimensions of firm performance, including productivity) has been pioneered by Wagner (2002), and it has been used in a growing number of empirical studies (surveyed in Wagner, 2007) ever since.

In the present study, export starters in year $t = 4$ were matched with "statistical twins" from the large group of non-exporters, based on characteristics of the plants in $t = 1$ (three years before the starters begin to export). Matching was implemented by nearest neighbor propensity score matching.[12] The propensity score was estimated from a probit regression of a dummy variable indicating whether or not a plant is an export starter in year $t = 4$ on a set of variables (all measured at $t = 1$) that are considered as determinants of the probability to start to export, and are related to the average wage paid in the firm. Details are given in Table A1 in the Appendix. The balancing property (which requires an absence of statistically significant differences between the treatment group and the control group in the covariates after matching) is satisfied. The differences in the means of the variables used to compute the propensity score were never statistically significant between the starters and the matched non-exporters (see Table A2 in the Appendix). The common support condition (which requires that the propensity score of a treated observation is neither higher than the maximum nor lesser than the minimum propensity score

[12]Alternative matching procedures have also been carried out (using three and five nearest neighbors, kernel matching), but the (unreported) results were similar to those discussed in the next section.

of the controls) was imposed by dropping export starters whose propensity score is higher than the maximum or lower than the minimum propensity score of the non-exporters.

This matching approach leads to 59 (out of 70) export starters for which a non-exporting twin-plant could be found. These 59 pairs constitute our so-called matched sample made up of 118 plants. The plant-level regressions of average daily wages and of sales per employee discussed above were repeated for data from this matched sample; results are reported in columns 2 and 4 of Table 2. By construction (due to the successful matching), neither wages nor productivity differ significantly between export starters and non-exporting plants in $t = 1$, and the same holds for the other years before the export start in $t = 4$.

In the matched sample, the estimated regression coefficients of the interaction terms of the export starter dummy variable with the dummy variables for the years $t = 4, t = 5$, and $t = 6$ turn out to be statistically insignificant at any conventional level in both the wage and the productivity regression. Therefore, in line with the findings from the descriptive statistics reported in Table 1 and from the regressions using the full sample of plants reported in columns 1 and 3 of Table 2, we find no evidence for hypothesis *H*2 which argues that exporting increases productivity and thus wages due to learning-by-exporting.

### 3.3. *Individual-level wage regressions*

The plant-level estimations presented in Section 3.2 may suffer from aggregation bias since individual heterogeneity which influences wages cannot be controlled for. Therefore, we replicate the empirical investigation for wages using data at the individual level, controlling for both observed employer and employee characteristics.[13] Like in the plant-level analysis we consider two samples

[13]Due to the lack of information for productivity at the individual level, this replication is possible for the wage equations only.

of plants — the full sample of all plants, and the matched sample made up of export starters and matched non-exporters.

Results for the full sample of 3,587 plants and all 242,879 employees, meaning a total of 819,076 observations, are reported in column 1 of Table 3. The estimated coefficient of the export starter dummy variable is positive and highly statistically significant. It is also large from an economic point of view, pointing to an export starter wage differential of 6.9 percent in $t = 1$ (i.e. three years before the start) which does not significantly change in the following two years ($t = 2$ and $t = 3$). These results are strongly in favor of hypothesis *H*1 according to which higher wages in exporting firms are due to self-selection of better paying firms into export markets.[14]

In contrast, hypothesis *H2* (according to which wages and productivity increase after starting to export due to learning-by-exporting effects) is hardly supported by our data. In the full sample, only the interaction term for $t = 6$ is positive and (albeit weakly) significant, indicating that the wage change of export starters exceeds the wage change of non-exporters by 3 percent. However, turning to the results of the matched sample (column 3), we do not find any evidence in favor of a wage increase after starting to export, because all interaction terms are insignificant.

In order to see whether the covariation between wages and exports differs when conditioning on plant productivity, we have repeated the regressions for the full and the matched sample with the logarithm of sales per employee included as an additional regressor (see columns 2 and 4 of Table 3). While this robustness check does not change the results in the matched sample, in the full sample the magnitude and statistical significance of the export starter dummy is reduced. This is further evidence that the observed export wage premium (largely) reflects self-selection of more productive firms into export markets (as proposed by hypothesis *H1*).

[14]As before, the control variables all have the expected signs, and most of them are statistically significant.

Table 3. Individual level wage regressions (OLS); all employees; Germany (Dependent variable: logarithm of daily wage)

| Explanatory variables | Full sample | | Matched sample | |
|---|---|---|---|---|
| Export starter (dummy: 1 = yes) | 0.069<br>[2.37]** | 0.036<br>[1.54] | −0.028<br>[1.04] | −0.031<br>[1.29] |
| Dummy ($t = 2$) × export starter | −0.008<br>[0.88] | −0.006<br>[0.70] | −0.020<br>[1.50] | −0.025<br>[1.57] |
| Dummy ($t = 3$) × export starter | −0.016<br>[0.80] | 0.017<br>[0.77] | 0.001<br>[0.07] | −0.005<br>[0.31] |
| Dummy ($t = 4$) × export starter | −0.005<br>[0.32] | 0.020<br>[0.95] | −0.006<br>[0.31] | −0.018<br>[1.03] |
| Dummy ($t = 5$) × export starter | 0.014<br>[0.96] | 0.030<br>[1.25] | −0.018<br>[0.77] | −0.027<br>[1.22] |
| Dummy ($t = 6$) × export starter | 0.030<br>[1.88]* | 0.061<br>[2.53]** | 0.006<br>[0.24] | −0.006<br>[0.35] |
| Logarithm of sales per employee | | 0.095<br>[11.35]*** | | 0.073<br>[4.48]*** |
| Plant size dummies (number of employees; reference: 1–9) | | | | |
| 10–19 | 0.100<br>[4.52]*** | 0.091<br>[4.64]*** | 0.125<br>[1.98]** | 0.145<br>[2.56]** |
| 20–49 | 0.085<br>[4.92]*** | 0.081<br>[5.27]*** | 0.131<br>[2.03]** | 0.131<br>[2.33]** |
| 50–99 | 0.079<br>[4.04]*** | 0.076<br>[4.25]*** | 0.108<br>[1.60]* | 0.077<br>[1.32] |
| 100–199 | 0.086<br>[3.78]*** | 0.085<br>[4.15]*** | 0.121<br>[1.79]* | 0.111<br>[1.93]* |
| 200–499 | 0.112<br>[4.74]*** | 0.110<br>[5.24]*** | 0.176<br>[2.42]** | 0.152<br>[2.46]** |
| 500–999 | 0.105<br>[3.80]*** | 0.111<br>[4.55]*** | −0.001<br>[0.01] | −0.074<br>[0.95] |
| 1000 and more | 0.062<br>[0.82] | 0.077<br>[1.37] | | |
| Works council (dummy: 1 = yes) | 0.105<br>[7.37]*** | 0.076<br>[5.65]*** | 0.071<br>[1.78]* | 0.064<br>[2.14]** |
| Collective agreement (reference: no collective agreement) | | | | |
| at sectoral level (dummy: 1 = yes) | 0.019<br>[1.35] | 0.022<br>[1.78]* | 0.005<br>[0.23] | 0.015<br>[0.69] |

*(Continued)*

Table 3. (*Continued*)

| Explanatory variables | Full sample | | Matched sample | |
|---|---|---|---|---|
| at firm level | 0.003 | 0.006 | 0.001 | 0.003 |
| (dummy: 1 = yes) | [0.22] | [0.46] | [0.04] | [0.21] |
| Plant belongs to a larger | 0.072 | 0.043 | 0.096 | 0.072 |
| unit (dummy: 1 = yes) | [5.79]*** | [3.53]*** | [3.57]*** | [3.21]*** |
| New production technology | 0.037 | 0.020 | 0.028 | 0.016 |
| (dummy: 1 = yes) | [4.53]*** | [2.70]*** | [2.15]** | [1.34] |
| Eastern Germany | −0.283 | −0.277 | −0.363 | −0.385 |
| (dummy: 1 = yes) | [4.04]*** | [4.35]*** | [5.05]*** | [6.22]*** |
| Age of employee (in years) | 0.026 | 0.025 | 0.035 | 0.035 |
| | [29.28]*** | [29.19]*** | [11.43]*** | [11.73]*** |
| Age squared (divided by 100) | −0.029 | −0.027 | −0.037 | −0.037 |
| | [28.54]*** | [27.78]*** | [10.56]*** | [10.67]*** |
| Tenure of employee (in years) | 0.024 | 0.022 | 0.017 | 0.015 |
| | [13.46]*** | [15.60]*** | [5.52]*** | [5.34]*** |
| Tenure squared | −0.057 | −0.051 | −0.033 | −0.029 |
| (divided by 100) | [10.13]*** | [11.49]*** | [3.47]*** | [3.05]*** |
| Female (dummy: 1 = yes) | −0.156 | −0.150 | −0.155 | −0.146 |
| | [18.10]*** | [19.07]*** | [9.92]*** | [10.22]*** |
| Non-German | −0.074 | −0.073 | −0.111 | −0.111 |
| (dummy: 1 = yes) | [7.38]*** | [7.28]*** | [4.55]*** | [4.31]*** |
| Without apprenticeship or *Abitur* (ref. group) | | | | |
| Apprenticeship, no | 0.139 | 0.136 | 0.152 | 0.159 |
| *Abitur* (dummy: 1 = yes) | [13.60]*** | [14.26]*** | [5.87]*** | [6.32]*** |
| No Apprenticeship, with | 0.181 | 0.152 | 0.295 | 0.300 |
| *Abitur* (dummy: 1 = yes) | [7.85]*** | [6.49]*** | [6.29]*** | [6.69]*** |
| Apprenticeship and | 0.335 | 0.319 | 0.315 | 0.315 |
| *Abitur* (dummy: 1 = yes) | [26.10]*** | [25.53]*** | [7.71]*** | [7.60]*** |
| Technical college degree | 0.486 | 0.463 | 0.474 | 0.480 |
| (dummy: 1 = yes) | [32.35]*** | [35.11]*** | [16.13]*** | [16.74]*** |
| University degree | 0.568 | 0.534 | 0.491 | 0.494 |
| (dummy: 1 = yes) | [31.76]*** | [34.30]*** | [14.21]*** | [14.68]*** |
| Education unknown | 0.099 | 0.111 | 0.111 | 0.134 |
| (dummy: 1 = yes) | [3.35]*** | [4.16]*** | [2.53]** | [3.36]** |
| Master craftsman, foreman | 0.195 | 0.193 | 0.143 | 0.156 |
| (dummy: 1 = yes) | [26.25]*** | [26.37]*** | [7.77]*** | [9.09]*** |
| Constant | 3.165 | 2.122 | 3.519 | 2.726 |
| | [41.29]*** | [19.78]*** | [28.35]*** | [13.72]*** |

(*Continued*)

Table 3. (*Continued*)

| Explanatory variables | Full sample | | Matched sample | |
|---|---|---|---|---|
| Observations | 819,076 | 714,093 | 48,879 | 44,414 |
| Employees | 242,879 | 222,144 | 13,134 | 12,763 |
| Plants | 3,587 | 3,444 | 118 | 118 |
| $R^2$ | 0.580 | 0.607 | 0.601 | 0.620 |

*All employees* comprise *stayers* (workers which work for the respective plant in all six years of the data window) as well as employees which join/leave the plant during the observed six years. Regressions also include 37 sectoral dummies, 9 urbanization dummies, 15 regional dummies, 11 year dummies as well as 5 dummies for the respective periods $t$. $|t|$ -statistics in parentheses, based on robust standard errors adjusted for clustering at the plant-level. *Full sample* refers to all observations with no missing values in the covariates. *Matched sample* refers to observations of employees from plants which have been selected via nearest neighbor propensity score matching, where the propensity score has been obtained from a probit on export starting.

We also take into account that the selection effect only controls for time-invariant differences between export starters and non-exporters and their employees. Any changes in the workforce (due to hirings and separations) are by definition not absorbed by the selection effect. If quitters and joiners are non-random with respect to the introduction of the export activity, we may obtain a biased estimate of our hypothesis *H2*. We control for this by (additionally) looking only at wages of individuals who remain in the respective plant in all six years observed (*stayers*), the results of which are reported in Table 4.

The findings for stayers closely resemble those for all employees. We find an export starter wage premium of 5.9 percent (column 1). However, neither in the estimations based on all plants nor in the regressions including stayers in matched plants only the interaction terms of the export starter dummy and the dummy variables for the years $t = 4, t = 5$, and $t = 6$ are ever statistically significant. Higher wages in exporting plants thus do not seem to be induced by export activities.[15]

[15]In a further regression for *stayers*, we conditioned on covariates fixed at $t = 1$ because one could argue that some observables might themselves respond to the start of the export activity. However, the results of this estimation did not alter our conclusions.

Table 4. Individual level wage regressions (OLS); stayers only; Germany (Dependent variable: logarithm of daily wage)

| Explanatory variables | Full sample | | Matched sample | |
|---|---|---|---|---|
| Export starter | 0.059 | 0.031 | −0.028 | −0.036 |
| (dummy: 1 = yes) | [2.05]** | [1.26] | [1.03] | [1.41] |
| Dummy ($t = 2$) × | 0.001 | −0.011 | −0.006 | −0.011 |
| export starter | [0.20] | [0.97] | [0.67] | [0.96] |
| Dummy ($t = 3$) × | 0.003 | 0.026 | 0.006 | 0.010 |
| export starter | [0.32] | [1.26] | [0.47] | [0.77] |
| Dummy ($t = 4$) × | 0.006 | 0.024 | 0.004 | −0.002 |
| export starter | [0.58] | [1.28] | [0.31] | [0.14] |
| Dummy ($t = 5$) × | 0.012 | 0.019 | −0.007 | −0.010 |
| export starter | [1.09] | [0.86] | [0.41] | [0.56] |
| Dummy ($t = 6$) × | 0.017 | 0.040 | 0.001 | 0.012 |
| export starter | [1.39] | [1.56] | [0.07] | [0.66] |
| Logarithm of sales | | 0.084 | | 0.072 |
| per employee | | [10.02]*** | | [4.09]*** |
| Plant size dummies (number of employees; reference: 1–9) | | | | |
| 10–19 | 0.103 | 0.098 | 0.119 | 0.124 |
| | [7.76]*** | [7.69]*** | [1.60]* | [1.91]* |
| 20–49 | 0.137 | 0.134 | 0.171 | 0.159 |
| | [10.33]*** | [10.42]*** | [2.22]** | [2.31]** |
| 50–99 | 0.135 | 0.132 | 0.160 | 0.120 |
| | [8.84]*** | [8.92]*** | [2.02]** | [1.68]* |
| 100–199 | 0.163 | 0.153 | 0.177 | 0.152 |
| | [8.90]*** | [8.65]*** | [2.24]** | [2.14]** |
| 200–499 | 0.178 | 0.167 | 0.243 | 0.203 |
| | [9.29]*** | [9.12]*** | [2.91]*** | [2.75]*** |
| 500–999 | 0.180 | 0.173 | 0.139 | 0.152 |
| | [8.12]*** | [8.44]*** | [1.41] | [1.86]* |
| 1000 and more | 0.126 | 0.134 | | |
| | [1.87]* | [2.63]*** | | |
| Works council | 0.083 | 0.062 | 0.046 | 0.036 |
| (dummy: 1 = yes) | [6.06]*** | [7.76]*** | [1.14] | [1.09] |
| Collective agreement (reference: no collective agreement) | | | | |
| at sectoral level | 0.036 | 0.040 | −0.002 | 0.006 |
| (dummy: 1 = yes) | [2.54]** | [3.21]*** | [0.10] | [0.29] |

*(Continued)*

Table 4. (*Continued*)

| Explanatory variables | Full sample | | Matched sample | |
|---|---|---|---|---|
| at firm level | 0.028 | 0.019 | −0.011 | −0.007 |
| (dummy: 1 = yes) | [1.75]* | [1.21] | [0.63] | [0.42] |
| Plant belongs to a | 0.056 | 0.035 | 0.091 | 0.067 |
| larger unit (dummy: 1 = yes) | [4.04]*** | [2.60]*** | [3.50]*** | [2.91]*** |
| New production technology | 0.030 | 0.019 | 0.017 | 0.001 |
| (dummy: 1 = yes) | [4.39]*** | [2.99]*** | [1.37] | [0.12] |
| Eastern Germany | −0.198 | −0.215 | −0.259 | −0.405 |
| (dummy: 1 = yes) | [4.26]*** | [5.28]*** | [3.80]*** | [6.26]*** |
| Age of employee | 0.020 | 0.019 | 0.031 | 0.031 |
| (in years) | [16.02]*** | [16.10]*** | [8.70]*** | [8.85]*** |
| Age squared | −0.021 | −0.021 | −0.033 | −0.033 |
| (divided by 100) | [14.92]*** | [14.78]*** | [8.28]*** | [8.27]*** |
| Tenure of employee | 0.012 | 0.013 | 0.018 | 0.016 |
| (in years) | [6.10]*** | [6.36]*** | [5.27]*** | [4.75]*** |
| Tenure squared | −0.019 | −0.020 | −0.038 | −0.033 |
| (divided by 100) | [3.16]*** | [3.42]*** | [3.66]*** | [3.06]*** |
| Female | −0.149 | −0.143 | −0.129 | −0.129 |
| (dummy: 1 = yes) | [17.61]*** | [19.09]*** | [7.25]*** | [7.10]*** |
| Non-German | −0.069 | −0.070 | −0.097 | −0.090 |
| (dummy: 1 = yes) | [8.06]*** | [8.13]*** | [3.58]*** | [3.27]*** |
| Without apprenticeship or *Abitur* (ref. group) | | | | |
| Apprenticeship, no | 0.129 | 0.129 | 0.160 | 0.162 |
| *Abitur* (dummy: 1 = yes) | [12.58]*** | [12.10]*** | [6.74]*** | [7.30]*** |
| No Apprenticeship, with | 0.255 | 0.231 | 0.291 | 0.307 |
| *Abitur* (dummy: 1 = yes) | [10.37]*** | [9.01]*** | [4.00]*** | [4.29]*** |
| Apprenticeship and | 0.323 | 0.314 | 0.320 | 0.316 |
| *Abitur* (dummy: 1 = yes) | [21.80]*** | [20.53]*** | [7.24]*** | [7.19]*** |
| Technical college | 0.460 | 0.450 | 0.488 | 0.490 |
| degree (dummy: 1 = yes) | [28.60]*** | [28.67]*** | [16.60]*** | [17.88]*** |
| University degree | 0.516 | 0.497 | 0.483 | 0.479 |
| (dummy: 1 = yes) | [28.97]*** | [29.90]*** | [15.28]*** | [15.40]*** |
| Education unknown | 0.079 | 0.096 | 0.106 | 0.105 |
| (dummy: 1 = yes) | [4.03]*** | [5.27]*** | [2.09]** | [2.33]** |
| Master craftsman, | 0.182 | 0.180 | 0.139 | 0.151 |
| foreman (dummy: 1 = yes) | [21.92]*** | [21.63]*** | [7.27]*** | [8.53]*** |

(*Continued*)

Table 4. (*Continued*)

| Explanatory variables | Full sample | | Matched sample | |
|---|---|---|---|---|
| Constant | 3.218 | 2.261 | 3.585 | 2.835 |
| | [54.68]*** | [19.73]*** | [26.77]*** | [13.22]*** |
| Observations | 417,222 | 367,584 | 28,092 | 25,491 |
| Employees | 69,530 | 67,118 | 4,682 | 4,682 |
| Plants | 3,046 | 2,925 | 116 | 116 |
| $R^2$ | 0.568 | 0.588 | 0.622 | 0.630 |

*Stayers* are workers which work for the respective plant in all six years of the data window. Regressions also include 37 sectoral dummies, 9 urbanization dummies, 15 regional dummies, 11 year dummies as well as 5 dummies for the respective periods $t$. $|t|$-statistics in parentheses, based on robust standard errors adjusted for clustering at the plant-level. *Full sample* refers to all observations with no missing values in the covariates. *Matched sample* refers to observations of employees from plants which have been selected via nearest neighbor propensity score matching, where the propensity score has been obtained from a probit on export starting.

## 4. Conclusions

Using a rich set of German linked employer–employee panel data, we have demonstrated that the exporter wage premium does already exist in the years before plants start to export, and that it does not increase in the years after exporting started. According to our results, higher wages in exporting plants that are found after controlling for observed and unobserved employer and employee characteristics are due to self-selection of more productive, better paying plants into export markets. This empirical finding is in accordance with the recent theoretical literature on exporting by heterogeneous firms (pioneered by Melitz 2003) which postulates that only the more productive firms in an industry can bear the extra costs of entering foreign markets.

Our empirical results imply that the so-called exporter wage premium is labeled misleadingly since it may not be caused by export activities. At least in the case of Germany, one of the major exporting countries in the world, exporting does not seem to make firms more productive or lead to higher wages. One may, however, argue that it takes some time before the positive effects of exporting are fully realized, and that the period of two years after starting to export observed here is too short for investigating the presence or not of wage effects. Future research that can use data for a longer period will be able to provide empirical evidence on this. Furthermore, it would be interesting to see whether our finding can be replicated for other countries using linked employer–employee panel data. This sort of data provides information that should be tapped more intensively in order to gain additional insights in international firm activities.

## Acknowledgments

We thank two anonymous referees and the participants of the 2008 Annual Congress of the *Verein für Socialpolitik* in Graz for their helpful comments.

## References

Akerlof, G. A. and J. L. Yellen, (Eds.) (1986). Efficiency Wage Models of The Labor Market. Cambridge, England: Cambridge University Press.

Akerlof, G. A. and J. L. Yellen (1990). The Fair Wage — Effort Hypothesis and Unemployment. *Quarterly Journal of Economics* 105, 255–283.

Alcalá, F. and P. J. Hernández (2007). Firm Characteristics, Labor Sorting, and Wages. Universidad de Murcia, mimeo, January.

Alda, H., S. Bender and H. Gartner (2005). The Linked Employer-Employee Dataset Created From the IAB Establishment Panel and the Process-Produced Data of the IAB (LIAB). *Schmollers Jahrbuch/Journal of Applied Social Science Studies* 125, 327–336.

Amiti, M. and D. R. Davis (2008). Trade, Firms, and Wages: Theory and Evidence. National Bureau of Economic Research Working Paper No. 14106, June.

Baldwin, J. and W. Gu (2003). Export-Market Participation and Productivity Performance in Canadian Manufacturing. *Canadian Journal of Economics* 36, 634–657.

Bernard, A. B. and J. B. Jensen (1995). Exporters, Jobs, and Wages in U.S. Manufacturing: 1976–1987. *Brookings Papers on Economic Activity. Microeconomics* 67–119.

Bernard, A. B. and J. B. Jensen (1999). Exceptional Exporter Performance: Cause, Effect, or Both? *Journal of International Economics* 47, 1–25.

Bernard, A. B. and J. Wagner (1997). Exports and Success in German Manufacturing. *Weltwirtschaftliches Archiv/Review of World Economics* 133, 134–157.

Breau, S. and D. L. Rigby (2006). Is There Really an Export Wage Premium? A Case Study of Los Angeles Using Matched Employee-employer Data. Center for Economic Studies, Bureau of the Census, Washington, DC, Working Paper CES 06-06, February.

Crespi, G., C. Criscuolo and J. Haskel (2008). Productivity, Exporting, and the Learning-by-Exporting Hypothesis: Direct Evidence from UK Firms. *Canadian Journal of Economics* 41, 619–638.

Davis, D. R. and J. Harrigan (2007). Good Jobs, Bad Jobs, and Trade Liberalization. National Bureau of Economic Research Working Paper 13139, May.

Egger, H. and U. Kreikemeier (2008), Fairness, Trade, and Inequality. CESIFO Working Paper No. 2344, July.

Egger, H. and U. Kreikemeier (2009). Firm Heterogeneity and the Labour Market Effects of Trade Liberalization. *International Economic Review* 50(1), 187–216.

Fehr, E. and S. Gächter (2000). Fairness and Retaliation: The Economics of Reciprocity. *Journal of Economic Perspectives* 14, 159–181.

Fryges, H. and J. Wagner (2010). Exports and Profitability — First Evidence for German Manufacturing Firms. *The World Economy* 33(1), in press.

Greenaway, D. and D. Kneller (2007). Firm Heterogeneity, Exporting and Foreign Direct Investment: A Survey. *Economic Journal* 117, F134–F161.

Heckman, J. J., R. J. LaLonde and J. A. Smith (1999). The economics and econometrics of active labor market programs. In: Ashenfelter, O. C. and D. Card (Eds.), *Handbook of Labor Economics*, Vol. 3A, Amsterdam: North-Holland, 1865–2097.

Helpman, E., O. Itskhoki and S. Redding (2008). Inequality and Unemployment in a Global Economy. National Bureau of Economic Research Working Paper No. 14478, November.

International Study Group on Exports and Productivity (ISGEP), 2008. Understanding Cross-Country Differences in Exporter Premia: Comparable Evidence for 14 Countries. *Review of World Economics* 144(4), 596–635.

Melitz, M. J. (2003). The Impact of Trade on Intra-industry Reallocations and Aggregate Industry Productivity. *Econometrica* 71, 1695–1725.

Munch, J. R. and J. R. Skaksen (2008). Human Capital and Wages in Exporting Firms, *Journal of International Economics* 75, 363–372.

Schank, T. C. Schnabel and J. Wagner (2007). Do Exporters Really Pay Higher Wages? First Evidence From German Linked Employer-Employee Data. *Journal of International Economics* 72, 52–72.

Shapiro, C. and J. E. Stiglitz (1984). Equilibrium Unemployment as a Worker Discipline Device. *American Economic Review* 74, 433–444.

Wagner, J. (2002). The Causal Effect of Exports on Firm Size and Labor Productivity: First Evidence from a Matching Approach. *Economics Letters* 77, 287–292.

Wagner, J. (2007). Exports and Productivity: A Survey of the Evidence From Firm-Level Data. *The World Economy* 30, 60–82.

## Appendix

Table A1. Determinants of export starting, probit estimation; Germany (Dependent variable is a dummy for export starters: 1 = yes)

| Explanatory variables | Coefficient | Z-value |
|---|---|---|
| Logarithm of average wage | 1.090 | [2.88]*** |
| Logarithm of total sales per employee | 0.101 | [0.84] |
| Plant size dummies (number of employees; reference: 1–9) | | |
| 10–19 | 0.524 | [1.92]* |
| 20–49 | 0.794 | [2.95]*** |
| 50–99 | 1.112 | [3.54]*** |
| 100–199 | 1.619 | [4.94]*** |
| 200–499 | 1.127 | [2.94]*** |
| 500–999 | 1.291 | [2.48]*** |
| Works council (dummy: 1 = yes) | 0.244 | [1.16] |
| Collective agreement (reference: no collective agreement) | | |
| at sectoral level (dummy: 1 = yes) | −0.276 | [1.48] |
| at firm level (dummy: 1 = yes) | −0.005 | [0.02] |
| Plant belongs to a larger unit (dummy: 1 = yes) | −0.181 | [0.83] |
| New production technology (dummy: 1 = yes) | 0.230 | [1.31] |
| Eastern Germany (dummy: 1 = yes) | 0.532 | [2.33]** |
| Average age of employees (in years) | −0.210 | [1.41] |
| Average age squared (divided by 100) | 0.278 | [1.50] |
| Average tenure of employees | 0.031 | [0.45] |
| Average tenure squared (divided by 100) | −0.337 | [0.77] |
| Proportion within total workforce of plant: | | |
| Female workers | 0.500 | [1.36] |
| Workers with apprenticeship, no *Abitur* | −0.410 | [1.49] |
| Workers without apprenticeship, with *Abitur* | −0.801 | [0.25] |
| Workers with apprenticeship and *Abitur* | 0.600 | [0.72] |
| Workers with technical college degree | −0.406 | [0.41] |
| Workers with university degree | 0.508 | [0.78] |
| Master craftsman | −0.564 | [0.36] |
| Constant | −9.682 | [.] |
| Number of plants | 2,329 | |
| $X^2(52)$ | 177.10 | *** |
| Pseudo-$R^2$ | 0.310 | |

All covariates dated at $t = 1$. Regressions also include sectoral and year dummies. */**/*** denotes statistical significance at the 10 percent, 5 percent, 1 percent, level. Number of plants is lower than the respective figure reported in Tables 2 and 3, since the latter also comprise-plants which have missing values in the first year (and thus do not enter the probit regression), but with complete information in at least one of the other years.

Table A2. Mean values of variables for export starters and non-exporters

| Variable[b] | All plants | | | Matched plants | | |
|---|---|---|---|---|---|---|
| | Export starters ($N = 68$)[c] | Non-exporters ($N = 3,413$)[c] | *p*-value[a] | Export starters ($N = 59$) | Non-exporters ($N = 59$) | *p*-value[a] |
| Logarithm of average wage | 4.272 | 4.041 | 0.00 | 4.248 | 4.264 | 0.79 |
| Logarithm of total sales per employee | 12.243 | 11.818 | 0.00 | 12.251 | 12.467 | 0.21 |
| Establishment size (number of employees) | 105.60 | 60.03 | 0.00 | 106.70 | 92.42 | 0.57 |
| Works council (dummy: 1 = yes) | 0.471 | 0.214 | 0.00 | 0.441 | 0.458 | 0.86 |
| Collective agreement at the sectoral level (dummy: 1 = yes) | 0.500 | 0.491 | 0.89 | 0.475 | 0.407 | 0.46 |
| Collective agreement at the firm level (dummy: 1 = yes) | 0.103 | 0.098 | 0.90 | 0.119 | 0.169 | 0.44 |
| Plant belongs to a larger unit (dummy: 1 = yes) | 0.191 | 0.126 | 0.18 | 0.186 | 0.186 | 1.00 |
| New production technology (dummy: 1 = yes) | 0.809 | 0.704 | 0.04 | 0.797 | 0.831 | 0.64 |
| Eastern Germany (dummy: 1 = yes) | 0.485 | 0.485 | 1.00 | 0.508 | 0.475 | 0.72 |
| Average age of employees (in years) | 40.208 | 38.630 | 0.01 | 40.119 | 39.889 | 0.79 |
| Average Tenure of employees | 5.640 | 4.833 | 0.06 | 5.625 | 5.789 | 0.79 |
| Proportion within total workforce of plant: | | | | | | |
| Female workers | 0.251 | 0.381 | 0.00 | 0.262 | 0.252 | 0.82 |
| Workers with apprenticeship, no *Abitur* | 0.663 | 0.731 | 0.05 | 0.672 | 0.661 | 0.84 |
| Workers without apprenticeship, with *Abitur* | 0.006 | 0.004 | 0.42 | 0.004 | 0.004 | 0.83 |
| Workers with apprenticeship and *Abitur* | 0.034 | 0.024 | 0.26 | 0.036 | 0.034 | 0.84 |

(*Continued*)

Table A2. *(Continued)*

| | All plants | | | Matched plants | | |
|---|---|---|---|---|---|---|
| Variable[b] | Export starters ($N = 68$)[c] | Non-exporters ($N = 3,413$)[c] | $p$-value[a] | Export starters ($N = 59$) | Non-exporters ($N = 59$) | $p$-value[a] |
| Workers with technical college degree | 0.042 | 0.023 | 0.07 | 0.038 | 0.036 | 0.88 |
| Workers with university degree | 0.063 | 0.027 | 0.07 | 0.050 | 0.060 | 0.67 |
| Master craftsman | 0.025 | 0.023 | 0.66 | 0.027 | 0.034 | 0.58 |

[a]Two-sample $t$-test (with unequal variance) of the hypothesis that the difference in the mean is equal to zero.
[b]Information refers to the first year a plant is observed ($t = 1$), i.e. three years before the (potential) export start. Sample may be lower for some variables due to missing values.
[c]Numbers differ slightly from those reported in Table 1 (70 resp. 3,517) since the latter also includes plants which have missing values in covariates in $t = 1$.

# PART IV

# International Trade and Profits

Chapter 7

# Exports and Profitability — First Evidence for German Manufacturing Firms

Helmut Fryges and Joachim Wagner

## 1. Motivation

A huge and emerging literature on the microeconometrics of international trade demonstrates that exporting firms are more productive than otherwise identical firms that sell in the national market only (see Bernard *et al.* (2007) for the United States, Mayer and Ottaviano (2007) for European countries, Wagner (2007a) for a survey of studies from countries all over the world, and The International Study Group on Exports and Productivity (2008) for strictly comparable results from 14 countries). Exporting firms have to bear extra costs due to, among others, market research, adaptation of products to local regulations, or transport costs. These extra costs are one reason for a self-selection of the more productive firms in international markets. Furthermore, exporting firms tend to pay higher wages than non-exporting firms (see Schank, Schnabel and Wagner (2007) for a survey). Germany, one of the leading actors on the world market for goods, is a case in point: After controlling for observable and unobservable firm characteristics, productivity is significantly and substantially higher in exporting than in non-exporting firms (Wagner 2007b), and compared to identical non-exporting firms exporting firms pay significantly and substantially higher wages to workers with the same observable and unobservable characteristics (Schank, Schnabel and Wagner 2007).

A question that has (to the best of our knowledge) not been investigated in this literature is whether the productivity advantage of exporting firms does lead to a profitability advantage of exporters compared to otherwise identical non-exporters, even when exporters are facing extra costs and pay higher wages. Profitability is a performance dimension that is not investigated empirically in the literature dealing with the microeconometrics of international trade (see the recent survey papers by Bernard *et al.* (2007) and by Mayer and Ottaviano (2007)).[1]

The situation differs when the literature on international management is considered. Here, empirical investigations of the relationship between internationalization (measured by the percentage of exports in total sales, or by various other indicators including foreign assets to total assets, or the number of foreign subsidiaries) and firm performance (measured by various accounting indicators like return on assets, or return on equity) have a long tradition lasting at least 40 years. This literature has produced a great number of studies based on various methods. Glaum and Oesterle (2007, p. 308) recently argued that these empirical studies have come to heterogeneous and sometimes contradictory results. Similarly, Ruigrok, Amann and Wagner (2007, p. 350) state that the findings generated by this research stream have been inconclusive and contradictory. In a meta-analysis that covers 36 studies, Bausch and Krist (2007) find a positive and statistically significant overall relationship between internationalization and firm performance, although the effect size is small in magnitude. Furthermore, they find evidence that this relationship is highly context-dependent, and that R&D intensity, product diversification, country of origin, firm age, and firm size significantly affect performance gains attributable to internationalization (see Bausch and Krist (2007), p. 337).

[1]Note that the recent paper by Asiedu and Freeman (2007) has a different focus — it examines the within-region effect of globalization, i.e. the extent to which the level of globalization in the region in which a firm operates affects its performance.

Given that the samples used in these studies from the literature on international management tend to be small cross-section samples that do not allow to control for unobserved heterogeneity by including fixed firm effects, and that various measures of both internationalization and performance are used (see Bausch and Krist (2007), p. 332), we cannot find an answer to our question — whether the productivity advantage of exporting firms does lead to a profitability advantage of exporters compared to otherwise identical non-exporters even when exporters are facing extra costs and pay higher wages — from this literature. One might argue that theoretically (and logically) it is assumed that exporting is profitable in the long run, as firms would choose to forgo it otherwise. While this is true, we are interested in the size of the effect of exports and profits, and how it varies with the share of exports in total sales, and we look at short run effects.

This chapter contributes to the literature by using unique, recently released nationally representative high-quality longitudinal data for German enterprises to conduct the first comprehensive empirical study on the relationship between exports and profitability. We document a positive profitability differential of exporters compared to non-exporters that is statistically significant, though rather small, when observed firm characteristics and unobserved firm specific effects are controlled for. In contrast to nearly all empirical studies on the relationship between productivity and exports, we do not find any evidence for self-selection of more profitable firms into export markets. Due to the sampling frame of the data used, we cannot test the hypothesis that firms which start exporting perform better in the years after the start than their counterparts which do not start. Instead, we use a newly developed continuous treatment approach and show that exporting improves the profitability almost over the whole range of the export–sales ratio. This means that the usually observed higher productivity of exporters is not completely absorbed by the extra costs of exporting or by higher wages paid by internationally active firms. This evidence presented here for Germany, a leading actor in the world market for manufactured goods, is interesting on its own, and it can serve as a benchmark for future studies using comparable data from other countries.

The rest of the chapter is organized as follows: Section 2 introduces the newly available data set. Section 3 presents results from descriptive comparisons of exporting and non-exporting firms. Section 4 reports estimations of exporter profitability premia after controlling for observed and unobserved differences between exporters and non-exporters. Section 5 investigates the causal effect of exporting on profitability using the recently developed generalized propensity score (GPS) methodology.

## 2. Data

The data used in this study are merged from two surveys conducted by the German Statistical Offices. One source is a monthly report for establishments in manufacturing industries that covers all local production units that have at least 20 employees itself or that belong to an enterprise with a total of at least 20 employees. Information from the monthly surveys is either summed up for a year, or average values for a year are computed, and a panel data set is built from annual data. A detailed description of these data is given in Konold (2007). For this project, the information collected at the establishment level has been aggregated at the enterprise level to match the unit of observation from the second source of data used here, the cost structure survey for enterprises in the manufacturing sector. This survey is carried out annually as a representative random sample survey (stratified according to the number of employees and the industries) of around 18,000 enterprises. While all enterprises with 500 or more employees are included in each survey, a stratified random sample of smaller firms with 20–499 employees is drawn that remains in the survey sample for four years in succession and that is replaced by a new stratified random sample afterwards. Therefore, data from the cost structure survey can be used to build an unbalanced panel containing all enterprises with at least 500 employees (in a year) plus a sample of smaller firms with a rotating panel design. A detailed description of the cost structure survey can be found in Fritsch, Hennchen and Stephan (2004).

Data from the two sources are matched using the enterprise identifier available in both surveys. The resulting panel used in this study covers the years from 1999 to 2004.[2] These data are confidential but not exclusive. They can be used by researchers on a contractual basis via controlled remote data access inside the research data centres of the German Statistical Offices (see Zühlke *et al.* (2004) for details).[3]

## 3. Descriptive Analysis

As a first step in our empirical investigation, we compare the profitability of exporting and non-exporting firms. Information on exports is based on data taken from the monthly report for establishments in manufacturing industries, and an enterprise is considered to be an exporter in a year if at least one of its establishments (or, in case of single-establishment enterprises, the enterprise itself) reported a positive amount of sales to a customer in a foreign country or to a German export trading company. The share of exporters in all enterprises was about 70 percent in 1999 and about 75 percent in 2004. Figure 1 shows that in 1999 the distribution of the share of exports in total sales was highly skewed — most of the exporters sold a relatively small share of their total production abroad, and only some firms exported a very high share.[4]

Using information from the cost structure surveys, the rate of profit of a firm is computed as a rate of return, defined as gross firm surplus (computed as gross value added at factor costs minus gross wages and salaries minus costs for social insurance paid by

[2]The data are available for 1995–2004. Due to the introduction of a new industry classification, new samples were drawn after two years in 1997 and in 1999. This leads to a highly unbalanced panel when data for 1995–2004 are used (see Brandt, Dittrich and Konold (2008), p. 221), and these data are not useful for the empirical investigation performed here. Furthermore, information on employees in R&D is available from 1999 onwards only.

[3]To facilitate replication the Stata do-files used in the computations are available from the authors upon request.

[4]The figures look identical for all other years; graphs are available on request.

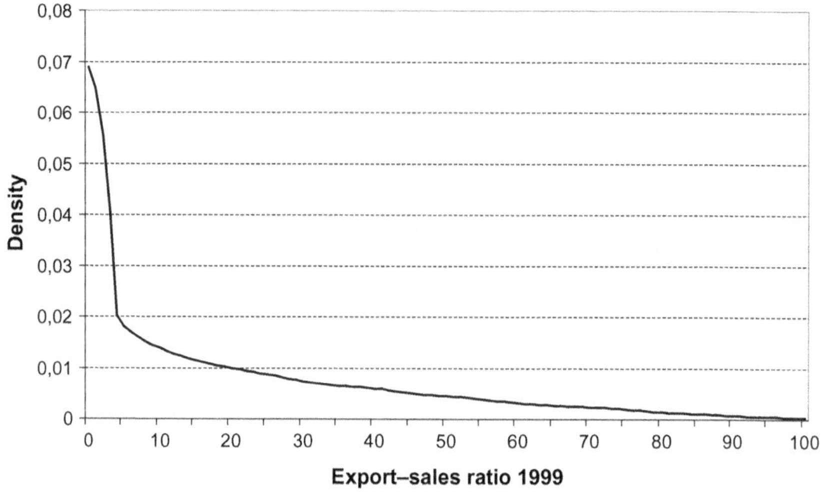


Fig. 1. Kernel density estimate of the share of exports in total sales, 1999

the firm) divided by total sales (net of VAT) minus net change of inventories.[5]

Our profit measure is a measure for the price–cost margin which, under competitive conditions, should on average equal the required rental on assets employed per money unit of sales (see Schmalensee (1989), p. 960f.). Differences in profitability between firms, therefore, can follow from productivity differences, but also from different mark-ups of prices over costs and from differences in the capital intensity. Given that our dataset does not have information on the capital stock employed by the firms in our econometric investigations we control for differences in the capital intensity by including a complete set of industry dummy variables at the most disaggregated (4-digit) level.

Table 1 reports the mean and selected percentiles of the distribution of the rate of profit for exporting and non-exporting enterprises for each year between 1999 and 2004. The mean and the median is

[5]Note that the dataset does not have any information on the capital stock, or the sum of assets or equity, of the firm, so that it is not possible to construct profit indicators based thereon like return on assets or return on equity.

Table 1. Rate of profit (percentage) in exporting and non-exporting enterprises (1999–2004)[1]

| Year | | Number of enterprises | Mean | Standard deviation | p1[2] | p25[2] | p50[2] | p75[2] | p99[2] |
|---|---|---|---|---|---|---|---|---|---|
| 1999 | Exporters | 11726 | 12.84 | 13.88 | −21.06 | 5.06 | 11.22 | 19.24 | 55.20 |
| | Non-Exporters | 5049 | 12.42 | 13.90 | −20.58 | 4.76 | 10.98 | 19.11 | 54.28 |
| 2000 | Exporters | 11744 | 12.90 | 13.64 | −17.89 | 5.04 | 11.03 | 19.15 | 54.80 |
| | Non-Exporters | 4890 | 11.76 | 13.60 | −20.05 | 4.22 | 10.17 | 18.04 | 53.07 |
| 2001 | Exporters | 11241 | 12.29 | 13.70 | −19.39 | 4.55 | 10.49 | 18.55 | 54.35 |
| | Non-Exporters | 4412 | 11.24 | 13.04 | −19.42 | 3.66 | 9.81 | 17.26 | 51.50 |
| 2002 | Exporters | 10885 | 11.84 | 13.52 | −20.09 | 4.05 | 10.07 | 17.95 | 53.25 |
| | Non-Exporters | 4098 | 10.56 | 12.94 | −21.48 | 3.17 | 8.97 | 17.01 | 49.94 |
| 2003 | Exporters | 11911 | 11.82 | 14.13 | −20.20 | 4.29 | 10.08 | 18.18 | 52.90 |
| | Non-Exporters | 4005 | 11.14 | 12.86 | −18.27 | 3.77 | 9.76 | 17.67 | 49.69 |
| 2004 | Exporters | 11776 | 12.37 | 14.03 | −20.50 | 4.76 | 10.64 | 18.51 | 52.59 |
| | Non-Exporters | 3954 | 11.53 | 12.60 | −18.84 | 4.13 | 9.97 | 17.67 | 49.69 |

[1] For definition of the rate of profit see text.
[2] p1, p25, p50, p75 and p99 are the first, $25^{th}$, $50^{th}$, $75^{th}$ and $99^{th}$ percentile of the distribution of the rate of profit.

higher for exporters compared to non-exporters in every year, and with the exception of the first percentile in three of the six years this holds for the other percentiles of the distribution of the rate of profit reported here, too.

According to the results from a *t*-test (that does not assume equal variances for both groups of enterprises) reported in Table 2, the difference in the mean value is highly statistically significant in five years. Note, however, that this difference in the rate of profit is rather small; it rarely exceeds 1 percentage point with a mean of the rate of profit for exporters around 12 percent.

If one looks at differences in the mean value for two groups only, one focuses on just one moment of the profitability distribution. A stricter test that considers all moments is a test for stochastic dominance of the profitability distribution for one group over the

Table 2. Tests for differences in the rate of profit between exporting and non-exporting enterprises (1999–2004)[1]

| Year | *t*-test for difference in the mean (*p*-value)[2] | Kolmogorov–Smirnov test (*p*-value)[3] | | |
|---|---|---|---|---|
| | | Difference: yes | Exporters > Non-Exporters | Non-Exporters > Exporters |
| 1999 | 0.075 | 0.044 | 0.023 | 0.997 |
| 2000 | 0.000 | 0.021 | 0.011 | 0.997 |
| 2001 | 0.000 | 0.016 | 0.009 | 0.911 |
| 2002 | 0.000 | 0.004 | 0.002 | 0.992 |
| 2003 | 0.005 | 0.015 | 0.008 | 0.961 |
| 2004 | 0.000 | 0.007 | 0.004 | 0.955 |

[1]For definition of the rate of profit see text.
[2]The *t*-test does not assume equal variances for both groups. A *p*-value of 0.05 (or smaller) indicates that the null hypothesis of equal mean values for exporters and non-exporters can be rejected at an error level of 5 percent (or less).
[3]The rate of profit is measured as the deviation from the mean value in the 4-digit industry; see text. A *p*-value of 0.05 (or smaller) indicates that the hypothesis mentioned in the header of the column cannot be rejected at an error level of 5 percent (or less), meaning that
— the distributions of the rate of profit differ between exporting and non-exporting enterprises.
— the distribution of the rate of profit for exporting enterprises first order stochastically dominates the distribution of the rate of profit for non-exporting enterprises.
— the distribution of the rate of profit for non-exporting enterprises first order stochastically dominates the distribution of the rate of profit for exporting enterprises.

profitability distribution for another group. More formally, let $F$ and $G$ denote the cumulative distribution functions of profitability for exporters and for non-exporters. Then first order stochastic dominance of $F$ relative to $G$ means that $F(z) - G(z)$ must be less or equal zero for all values of $z$, with strict inequality for some $z$. Whether this holds or not is tested non-parametrically by adopting the Kolmogorov–Smirnov test (see Conover (1999), p. 456ff.). Furthermore, exporters and non-exporters are not equally distributed over the industries, and the level of the rate of profit might vary across industries due to, for example, differences in the degree of competition or regulation. To control for the different industries, for the Kolmogorov–Smirnov test, the rate of profit of a firm is calculated as the deviation from the mean value in the 4-digit industry.

The Kolmogorov–Smirnov test is used here to test three hypotheses, i.e. that the distributions of the rate of profit are different for exporting and non-exporting enterprises, that the distribution of the rate of profit for exporting enterprises first order stochastically dominates the distribution of the rate of profit for non-exporting enterprises, and that distribution of the rate of profit for non-exporting firms first order stochastically dominates the distribution of the rate of profit for exporting firms. Results reported in Table 2 show that the first two hypotheses cannot be rejected at a 5 percent level, while the third hypothesis is clearly rejected.

A comparison of the rate of profit between exporting and non-exporting firms neglects that exporters distinguish from each other with respect to the share of total sales they generate abroad (the so-called export–sales ratio or export intensity). Fryges and Wagner (2008a) showed that the relationship between labor productivity growth and the export–sales ratio is nonlinear. Thus, it can be expected that similar to the relationship between the export–sales ratio and labor productivity growth, the firms' profitability also varies between firms with different export intensities. Table 3 displays the rate of profit for enterprises within different classes of the export–sales ratio. The descriptive results demonstrate that enterprises that exhibit a higher export–sales ratio tend to have

Table 3. Rate of profit (percentage) for firms in different classes of the export–sales ratio (1999 and 2004)[1]

| Year | | Number of enterprises | Mean | Standard deviation | p1[2] | p25[2] | p50[2] | p75[2] | p99[2] |
|---|---|---|---|---|---|---|---|---|---|
| 1999 | 0 percent | 5049 | 12.42 | 13.90 | −20.58 | 4.76 | 10.98 | 19.11 | 54.28 |
| | >0 percent and ≤5 percent | 2340 | 12.22 | 13.70 | −21.06 | 4.77 | 10.48 | 18.30 | 53.84 |
| | >5 percent and ≤10 percent | 1329 | 11.97 | 14.61 | −33.16 | 4.43 | 10.32 | 18.34 | 53.48 |
| | >10 percent and ≤20 percent | 2093 | 12.96 | 13.58 | −16.89 | 4.76 | 10.48 | 18.73 | 56.49 |
| | >20 percent and ≤50 percent | 3921 | 13.19 | 13.46 | −19.17 | 5.34 | 11.76 | 19.61 | 55.20 |
| | >50 percent | 2043 | 13.31 | 14.66 | −28.91 | 5.44 | 12.22 | 20.27 | 57.48 |
| 2004 | 0 percent | 3954 | 11.53 | 12.60 | −18.84 | 4.13 | 9.97 | 17.67 | 49.69 |
| | >0 percent and ≤5 percent | 1906 | 10.89 | 14.90 | −24.50 | 3.88 | 9.70 | 16.86 | 52.50 |
| | >5 percent and ≤10 percent | 1123 | 11.38 | 13.43 | −25.35 | 4.18 | 9.88 | 17.22 | 48.36 |
| | >10 percent and ≤20 percent | 1935 | 11.95 | 13.66 | −18.87 | 4.25 | 9.63 | 17.31 | 54.42 |
| | >20 percent and ≤50 percent | 4021 | 12.82 | 13.76 | −17.33 | 5.35 | 11.13 | 19.01 | 51.96 |
| | >50 percent | 2791 | 13.42 | 14.18 | −22.41 | 5.27 | 11.78 | 20.01 | 54.71 |

[1]For definition of the rate of profit see text. Results for 2000–2003 are available on request.
[2]p1, p25, p50, p75 and p99 are the first, $25^{th}$, $50^{th}$, $75^{th}$ and $99^{th}$ percentile of the distribution of the rate of profit.

higher levels of the rate of profit. However, for all years covered by our dataset the mean profitability of firms that export only a small share of their total sales (less than 5 percent) falls below that of non-exporting firms. For the two years 1999 and 2004, firms that export more than 5 percent and not more than 10 percent of their total sales also show a mean rate of profit smaller than the comparable rate of non-exporting firms. Enterprises with an export–sales ratio of more than 10 percent exhibit a rate of profit that, on average, exceeds the profitability of firms without any exports and that increases with the export intensity. Moreover, Table 3 shows that the standard deviation of the rate of profit also tends to increase with the export–sales ratio. In both 1999 and 2004, the 1$^{st}$ percentile of the rate of profit of those enterprises that sell more than half of their total sales abroad is smaller than the 1$^{st}$ percentile of non-exporters. This points out that intense export activities are not only associated with a higher mean rate of profit but also with a higher risk of losses.

The results from the descriptive comparison of exporters and non-exporters reported here indicate that exporting enterprises are more profitable than non-exporting enterprises not only on average, but over the whole distribution of the rate of profit. The statistically significant difference, however, is small from an economic point of view. Moreover, the rate of profit tends to increase with the firms' export–sales ratio. However, firms that export only a very small share of their total sales exhibit a rate of profit that falls below that of non-exporting firms.[6]

## 4. Exporter Profitability Premia

The next step in our empirical investigation consists of the estimation of the so-called exporter profitability premia that indicate the *ceteris paribus* difference in profitability between exporting and non-exporting enterprises, controlling for other characteristics of the enterprises. In analogy with the now standard approach in the

[6]The exclusion of the enterprises with the 1 percent lowest and highest values for the rate of profit leads to the same conclusions; the tables are available on request.

microeconometric literature on exports and productivity (see The International Study Group on Exports and Productivity (2008)), pooled data are used to regress the rate of profit on the export activity of the enterprise plus a set of control variables including firm size (measured as the number of employees and its squared value), share of employees in R&D, and a full set of interaction terms of the year of observation and the 4-digit industry the enterprise is active in.[7]

Export activity of an enterprise is measured in four different ways, i.e. by a dummy variable that takes on the value of one if an enterprise is an exporter (and zero otherwise), by the share of exports in total sales, by the share of exports in total sales and its squared value, and by the share of exports in total sales plus its squared and its cubic value. While the dummy variable for exporting firms tests for the presence or not of an exporter profitability premium *per se*, the estimated coefficient of the share of exports in total sales shows whether or not this premium increases with an increase in the relative importance of exports for an enterprise. The quadratic terms test for the presence or not of a so-called threshold of internationalization — whether the positive effects vanish and become even negative when the optimal share of exports in total sales is exceeded because increasing costs of exporting exceed the extra benefits. The cubic term tests for an s-shaped relationship between profitability and the share of exports in total sales that is suggested in recent studies from the international management literature.[8]

Results for empirical models using pooled data without fixed enterprise effects are reported in columns 1–4 of Table 4. According

[7]The set of control variables used is motivated by the evidence reported by Bausch and Krist (2007, p. 337) from their meta-analysis of results from the literature in international management. The authors find that the relationship between firm performance and internationalization is highly context-dependent, and that R&D intensity, product diversification, country of origin, firm age, and firm size significantly affect performance gains attributable to internationalization. While country of origin does not matter in our study using data for Germany only, information on firm age and product diversification in exporting is not available in the data at hand.

[8]See Contractor (2007) for a discussion of this s-shaped relationship in a longitudinal perspective that investigates the relationship between internationalization and performance when a firm increases its international activities over time.

Table 4. Exports and profits: Evidence from regression models (1999–2004) Endogenous variable: Rate of profit (percentage)

| | | Pooled data | | | | Fixed enterprise effects | | | |
|---|---|---|---|---|---|---|---|---|---|
| Exogenous variable | Model | 1 | 2 | 3 | 4 | 5 | 6 | 7 | 8 |
| Exporter | ß | 0.962 | | | | 0.298 | | | |
| (Dummy; 1 = yes) | p | 0.000 | | | | 0.210 | | | |
| Share of exports in total | ß | | 0.031 | 0.065 | 0.049 | | 0.030 | −0.005 | 0.048 |
| sales (percentage) | p | | 0.000 | 0.000 | 0.000 | | 0.000 | 0.728 | 0.072 |
| Share of exports in total | ß | | | −0.0005 | 0.0001 | | | 0.0005 | −0.001 |
| sales (squared) | p | | | 0.000 | 0.815 | | | 0.021 | 0.109 |
| Share of exports in total | ß | | | | 4.48e-6 | | | | 0.0001 |
| sales (cubic) | p | | | | 0.132 | | | | 0.037 |
| Number of employees | ß | 0.001 | 0.001 | 0.001 | 0.001 | −4.5e-5 | −0.0001 | −0.0001 | −0.0001 |
| | p | 0.000 | 0.000 | 0.000 | 0.000 | 0.833 | 0.644 | 0.733 | 0.706 |
| Number of employees | ß | −3.78e-9 | −3.41e-9 | −3.37e-9 | −3.36e-9 | −1.24e-9 | −1.50e-9 | −1.36e-9 | −1.14e-9 |
| (squared) | p | 0.000 | 0.000 | 0.000 | 0.000 | 0.295 | 0.205 | 0.249 | 0.232 |
| Share of employees | ß | −0.015 | −0.032 | −0.032 | −0.032 | −0.002 | −0.004 | −0.004 | −0.005 |
| in R&D | p | 0.298 | 0.027 | 0.026 | 0.027 | 0.935 | 0.856 | 0.827 | 0.825 |
| Constant | ß | 11.284 | 11.366 | 11.148 | 11.192 | −0.012 | −0.011 | −0.012 | −0.012 |
| | p | 0.000 | 0.000 | 0.000 | 0.000 | 0.611 | 0.615 | 0.614 | 0.614 |
| Interaction terms of year and 4-digit industry | | included | included | included | included | included | included | included | included |
| Number of observations | | 95644 | 95644 | 95644 | 95644 | 95644 | 95644 | 95644 | 95644 |
| $R^2$ | | 0.083 | 0.084 | 0.084 | 0.084 | 0.0002 | 0.002 | 0.001 | 0.001 |

to the results in column 1, exporting firms have a rate of profit that is 1 percentage point higher *ceteris paribus* than in non-exporting firms (a difference that matches the order of magnitude showing up in the descriptive analysis that does not control for firm size, R&D intensity, and industry and time effects reported in Table 1), and from column 3 we see that the pattern of the relationship between export intensity and profitability is inversely u-shaped with an estimated maximum at a level of exports to sales of 65 percent. According to column 4, there is no evidence for an s-shaped relationship.[9]

When unobserved firm heterogeneity[10] is controlled for by including fixed enterprise effects a different picture emerges. From column 5, we see that exporting *per se* is not accompanied by higher profits — the estimated coefficient of the exporter dummy variable is statistically insignificant at any conventional level. This, however, is simply due to the fact that the exporter status variable has very low within firm variance over time. Column 6 shows that there is a statistically significant relationship of exporting and profitability that increases with a rise in the share of exports in total sales. According to this result, an increase in the exports to sales ratio of 10 percentage points is accompanied by an increase in the profit rate by 0.3 percentage points. Therefore, a firm that exports 50 percent of its products has on average a rate of profit that is 1.5 percentage points higher than a firm from the same industry and size, and with the same share of employees in R&D, that does not export at all.[11]

---

[9]The conclusions are identical when the enterprises with the 1 percent lowest and highest value for the rate of profit were excluded from the calculations; tables are available on request.

[10]These characteristics may include such factors as the age of the firm, the geographical scope of exports, financial constraints, or the degree of risk aversion and international orientation of the managers.

[11]From the models with fixed enterprise effects we do not have any evidence that the relationship between the share of exports in total sales and profitability is nonlinear. While the estimated coefficient for the quadratic term in column 7 and for the cubic term in column 8 are both statistically different from zero at an error level of 5 percent (pointing to nonlinearity), this does not hold when the enterprises with the 1 percent lowest and highest values for the rate of profit were excluded from the calculations; detailed results are available on request.

The exporter premia detected by estimating regression models using pooled data for exporters and non-exporters cannot be interpreted as indicators for a positive causal effect of exporting on profitability. On the one hand, it might well be the case that there is self-selection of more productive and, net of any higher costs related to exporting, more profitable firms into exporting. On the other hand, exporting might increase profitability by learning from foreign customers and competitors, by realizing scale effect on markets larger than the national market, or by earning monopoly rents from firm specific advantages on more than one market. Obviously, for any given firm both directions of causality might be important.

Again following the now standard approach in the microeconometric literature on exports and productivity (see The International Study Group on Exports and Productivity (2008)), the next step in our empirical investigation, therefore, consists in testing whether we can document any self-selection of more profitable firms into exporting. To do so, we identify a group of firms that did not export over a time span of the three years $t-3$ to $t-1$. Some of these firms started to export in year $t$ (these are called export starters of cohort $t$), some did not (these are called non-starters of cohort $t$). We then compare the export starters and the non-starters of cohort $t$

— in the year $t$
— three years back in year $t-3$.

Given that our data set covers the year 1999–2004, we can investigate three cohorts for $t = 2002$, 2003, and 2004. Results are reported in Table 5. It turns out that export starters are not more profitable than non-starters in $t$, the year of start. For the cohort 2002, we even have (although somewhat week) evidence from both the $t$-test and the Kolmogorov–Smirnov test that the non-starters have a higher level of the rate of profit than the starters.

The *ex-ante* profitability premia in year $t-3$ is the estimated regression coefficient of a dummy variable (taking the value one for export starters in $t$, and zero for non-starters) from an OLS-regression of the rate of profit in $t-3$ on this dummy, controlling

Table 5. Rate of profit in export starters and non-starters in the start year and three years before start

| | Cohort of starters | 2002 | 2003 | 2004 |
|---|---|---|---|---|
| Number of enterprises | Starters | 159 | 307 | 138 |
| | Non-starters | 3497 | 3172 | 2854 |
| Rate of profit in start year (percentage): | Starters | 11.16 (0.92) | 12.61 (14.15) | 11.22 (11.29) |
| Mean (standard deviation) | Non-starters | 12.94 (0.22) | 12.23 (13.06) | 11.72 (12.89) |
| $t$-test for difference in the mean[1] | $p$-value | 0.062 | 0.650 | 0.618 |
| Kolmogorow–Smirnov test[2] | | | | |
| — Difference: yes | $p$-value | 0.077 | 0.422 | 0.383 |
| — Starters > Non-starters | $p$-value | 0.922 | 0.229 | 0.215 |
| — Non-starters > Starters | $p$-value | 0.046 | 0.744 | 0.276 |
| Profit premia of export | ß | −1.554 | 0.392 | 1.378 |
| starters (percentage points)[3] | $p$-value | 0.105 | 0.642 | 0.157 |

[1]The $t$-test does not assume equal variances for both groups. A $p$-value of 0.05 (or smaller) indicates that the null- hypothesis of equal mean values for export starters and non-starters in the start year can be rejected at an error level of 5 percent (or less).
[2]A $p$-value of 0.05 (or smaller) indicates that the hypothesis stated in the first column of the row cannot be rejected at an error level of 5 percent (or less), meaning that
— the distributions of the rate of profit differ between export starters and non-starters in the start year.
— the distribution of the rate of profit for export starters first order stochastically dominates the distribution of the rate of profit for non-starters in the start year.
— the distribution of the rate of profit for non-starters first order stochastically dominates the distribution of the rate of profit for export starters in the start year.
[3]The profit premia is the estimated regression coefficient of a dummy variable (taking the value 1 for export starters, and 0 for non-starters) from an OLS-regression of the rate of profit on this dummy, controlling for the number of employees and its squared value, the share of employees in R&D in all employees, and a complete set of 4-digit industry dummy variables, all measured three years before the export start.

for firm size (number of employees and number of employees squared), share of employees in R&D, and the 4-digit industry, all measured in year $t-3$.[12] This coefficient is never significantly different from zero. Therefore, we conclude that in contrast to nearly all empirical studies on the relationship between productivity and

[12]At first sight it might confuse that we regress the rate of profit in $t-3$ on a dummy variable measured later in year $t$. Note, however, that this regression is not meant to "explain" past profits by today's exports — it is just a way to test whether or not profits did differ between today's starters and today's non-exporters three years before the start.

exports, we have no evidence for self-selection of more profitable firms into exporting. However, as a caveat we add that the number of starters in the cohorts tends to be small, and that this may contribute to imprecise estimates of any profitability differences.

When the rate of profit between exporting and non-exporting firms does differ at a point in time — and this is the case according to both the descriptive evidence reported in Section 3 and the results of the econometric investigation presented in Table 4 — and when there is no evidence for self-selection of more profitable firms into export activities, this points to positive effects of exporting on the rate of profit. However, due to the sampling frame of the data used we cannot test the hypothesis that firms which start exporting perform better in the years after the start than their counterparts which do not start. As pointed out in Section 2, the cost structure survey that is the basis for the computation of the profit rate is a survey based on a stratified random sample with a rotating panel design, and all but the largest firms with 500 and more employees in the sample usually are replaced every four years. Therefore, it is not possible to follow the cohorts of starters from 2002 or 2003 over the next year(s).

## 5. Causal Effect of Exports on Profitability

In the last step of our analysis, we examine whether there is a causal effect of a firm's export activity on its rate of profit. As stated in the previous section, we cannot evaluate post-entry differences in profitability between export starters and non-starters due to the panel design of the German cost structure survey. Nonetheless, the question of whether exports improve profitability is crucial for our analysis. Since we demonstrated that there is no evidence for self-selection of more profitable firms into the export market, the absence of a causal effect of exports on profitability would suggest that a firm's international business activities and its rate of profit are unrelated. In this case, exporting may result in a higher labor productivity but this increase is then completely absorbed by higher wages and higher costs related to exporting.

The hypothesis of a positive causal effect of exporting on profitability is tested using a newly developed econometric technique, the GPS methodology recently developed by Imbens (2000) and Hirano and Imbens (2004). The GPS methodology was introduced to the literature examining the export-performance relationship by Fryges (2008) and applied by Fryges and Wagner (2008a) who estimated the relationship between exports and labor productivity growth using a sample of German manufacturing firms.

The GPS methodology has a number of advantages compared to other econometric techniques. Firstly, the GPS method allows for continuous treatment, i.e. different levels of the firms' export–sales ratio. In this way, we are able to determine the causal relationship between profitability and the export–sales ratio (the treatment) at each value of firms' export intensity in the interval from 0 to 1. Thus, the second important advantage of the GPS method is that it enables us to identify the entire function of the rate of profit over all possible values of the continuous treatment variable. This property of the GPS methodology might be important in our case. The OLS regression of the determinants of the rate of profit in Table 4 pointed out that there might be a nonlinear relationship between profitability and the share of exports in total sales — at least if we restrict ourselves on the estimations without unobserved heterogeneity. Fryges and Wagner (2008a) showed that the relationship between the export–sales ratio and labor productivity growth is nonlinear and that exporting causally affects labor productivity growth only within a sub-interval of the domain of the share of exports in total sales. The GPS methodology is flexible allowing to test how the causal impact of exporting on profits varies along the range of the export–sales ratio from 0 to 1.

Thirdly, the continuous treatment approach allows us to analyze the level of the export intensity at which profitability is maximized (or minimized) or whether the relationship between the export–sales ratio and the rate of profit exhibits turning points or discontinuities (*cf.* Flores 2004). A detailed description of the GPS methodology is presented in Appendix A.1.

Using the GPS methodology, we do not compare export starters vs. non-starters. Export starters that have entered the foreign market during the previous year generally show a very small export–sales ratio. Thus, restricting the analysis to export starters precludes a reliable estimation of the causal effect of medium-sized and large export–sales ratios on profitability. Our causal analysis in this section therefore includes export starters as well as firms that export for decades. We estimate the causal effect of the export–sales ratio measured in period $t$ on the rate of profit in $t + 1$.[13] In this way, the GPS method is an appropriate econometric technique that provides an analysis of the causal effect of exporting on profitability despite the fact that, due to data restrictions, we cannot follow cohorts of starters over the next years after foreign market entry.

Hirano and Imbens (2004) suggest a three-stage approach to implement the GPS method. In the first stage, the conditional distribution of the treatment variable given the covariates is estimated. In our case, the distribution of the treatment variable, i.e. the export–sales ratio, is highly skewed. In particular, it has many limit observations at the value zero, representing firms without any exports. The latter group of firms decided that their optimal volume of exports was 0. Following Wagner (2001, 2003), we apply the fractional logit model developed by Papke and Wooldridge (1996) to estimate the export intensity of the firms in our sample.[14] In the second stage of the GPS method the conditional expectation of outcome (rate of profit in our case) is modeled as a function of the treatment and the (estimated) GPS. In the last stage, we estimate

[13]In a previous version of this chapter, we estimated the contemporaneous effect of the export–sales ratio in $t$ on the rate of profit in $t$ (Fryges and Wagner (2008b)). The results are very similar to those discussed in this section. However, estimating the contemporaneous effect raises the problem that wages per employee that are included in the fractional logit estimation of the export–sales ratio (see below) are endogenous since wages are a component of our measure of profitability. This problem is solved when the lagged effect of the export–sales ratio on profitability is estimated.

[14]Hirano and Imbens (2004) use a normal distribution for (the logarithm of) the treatment variable of their model. However, they emphasize that more general models may be considered.

a dose-response function that depicts the conditional expectation of profitability given the continuous treatment (export–sales ratio) and the GPS, evaluated at any level of the continuous treatment variable in the interval from 0 to 1.

As stated above, we first estimate the conditional distribution of the export–sales ratio given the covariates, applying the fractional logit model. The exogenous covariates of the fractional logit model include firm size (measured as the log of number of employees and its squared value), the log of wages and salaries per employee, the share of employees in R&D, and the log of the firms' lagged labor productivity (measured as sales per employee in $t-1$). The average wage per employee is used to proxy differences in firms' human capital. A firm with a highly qualified human capital and with extensive R&D activities is likely to generate intangible assets (e.g. a technologically superior product) leading to a competitive advantage of the firm over its (international) rivals and enabling the firm to realize a high export intensity. The lagged labor productivity is included as a covariate in order to account for self-selection of more productive firms into the international market. While we did not find any evidence for a self-selection effect of more profitable firms (see Section 4), most studies in the literature confirm the self-selection hypothesis of firms with higher labor productivity (*cf.* Wagner (2007a) for a survey and The International Study Group on Exports and Productivity (2008) for an international comparison). Thus, firms with a higher labor productivity in $t-1$ are expected to generate a higher share of total sales abroad. The model was estimated with pooled data for 1999–2004, and the set of covariates finally contains a full set of interaction terms of the year of observation and the 4-digit industry the enterprise is active in.

The results of the fractional logit model are presented in Table 6.[15] Firm size has a significantly positive effect on the export–sales ratio. The significantly negative sign of the squared value of

[15]The sample we used to estimate the fractional logit model is restricted to those firms for which data on profitability in $t+1$ is available in the dataset. Due to the sampling frame of our dataset, this reduces significantly the number of observations compared to Table 4.

Table 6. Determinants of the export–sales ratio (endogenous variable) — results of the fractional logit model

| Exogenous variable | | Pooled data |
|---|---|---|
| Number of employees (log) | ß | 0.790 |
| | *p* | 0.000 |
| Number of employees (squared) (log) | ß | −0.049 |
| | *p* | 0.000 |
| Share of employees in R&D | ß | 2.231 |
| | *p* | 0.000 |
| Wage per employee (log) | ß | 0.611 |
| | *p* | 0.000 |
| Labor productivity (sales per employee) in $t-1$ (log) | ß | 0.302 |
| | *p* | 0.000 |
| Constant | ß | −13.351 |
| | *p* | 0.000 |
| Interaction terms of year and 4-digit industry | | included |
| Number of observations | | 60,957 |
| Log-likelihood | | −20,544.43 |
| $R^2$ | | 0.410 |

the number of employees, however, shows the familiar picture that the export–sales ratio tends to increase with firm size at a decreasing rate.[16] As hypothesized, firms with a higher average wage per employee and a higher share of employees in R&D realize a higher export intensity, reflecting the importance of a firm's intangible assets by which a firm is able to create a competitive advantage over its international rivals. The lagged labour productivity is also positively correlated with the share of exports in total sales: Firms that exhibited a higher labor productivity in the past are able to bear the additional costs of exporting and to extend their international business activities. It can also be argued that more productive firms have a competitive advantage when compared with their

[16]The negative sign of the squared value of the number of employees actually points out to an inversely u-shaped relationship between the export–sales ratio and the number of employees. However, the estimated maximum of this relationship lies at 3,177 employees. Since only few firms in Germany (less than 1 percent) have a number of employees that exceeds the estimated maximum, our results should better be interpreted to indicate that the export–sales ratio increases with firm size but with a decreasing rate.

(foreign) counterparts. Thus, more productive firms are more likely to generate a higher share of total sales abroad.

The fractional logit model is estimated in order to calculate the GPS. As Imbens (2000) shows, adjusting for the GPS removes all the bias associated with differences in covariates between treated (exporting) and non-treated (non-exporting) firms. This allows us to identify a possibly causal influence of the (lagged) export–sales ratio on profitability. This is done by calculating pairwise treatment effects: we compare the expected rate of profit at one deliberately chosen export–sales ratio with the estimated value of profitability at another deliberately chosen export intensity. If the difference in these two expected rates of profits is significantly positive (negative) a hypothetical switch between the two deliberately chosen export–sales ratios at which the rate of profit is measured increases (decreases) firms' profitability. Since the GPS methodology controls for differences in covariates, the increase (decrease) in the rate of profit can be interpreted as a causal effect of the varying export–sales ratio on profitability (see Appendix A.1 for more details). The dose-response function that represents the expected profitability conditional on the export–sales ratio and the GPS is depicted in Figure 2.

Overall, the estimated dose-response function shows an inversely u-shaped relationship between profitability in $t + 1$ and firms' export–sales ratio in $t$. The maximum value of the rate of profit is reached at an export–sales ratio of 49 percent, where the expected value of the rate of profit amounts to 13.5 percent. Establishments that do not export show an expected rate of profit of 11.1 percent. Calculating the pairwise treatment effect reveals that at an export–sales ratio of 49 percent profitability is significantly larger than at an export intensity of zero ($p$-value: 0.000). In other words, at an export–sales ratio of 49 percent a firm's export activities have a causal effect on the rate of profit. The difference in the expected rate of profit accounts for 2.4 percentage points.

In order to find out whether profitability is positively improved by a firm's export activities over the whole range of the export–sales

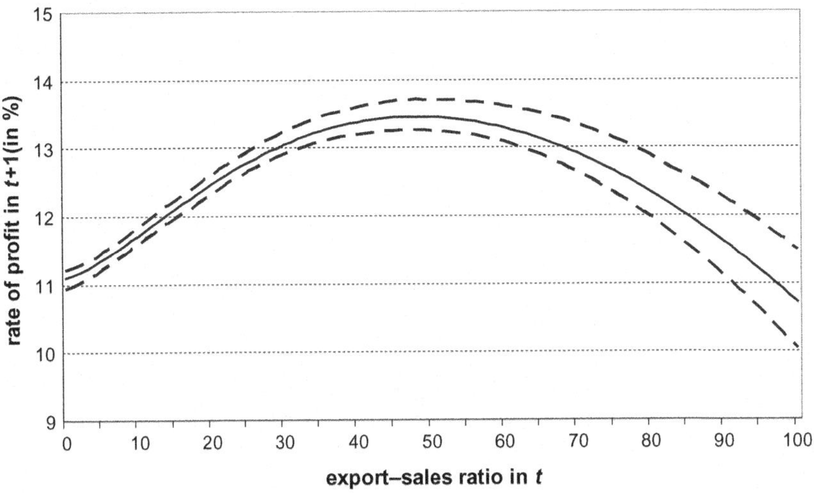


Fig. 2. Estimated dose-response function
**Solid lines:** estimated conditional expectation of firms' profits in $t+1$ given the export–sales ratio in $t$ and the estimated generalized propensity score (GPS).
**Dotted lines:** simulated 90 percent confidence interval, using the $5^{th}$ and $95^{th}$ percentiles of the bootstrap distribution (100 replications).

ratio or whether the effect is restricted to a sub-interval of the domain of the share of exports in total sales, we calculated pairwise treatment effects at each export intensity from 1 to 100 percent, always comparing the expected value of the rate of profit in the case of exporting with the respective value of non-exporting firms. According to conventional t-tests at the 5 percent level of significance, exporting increases profitability almost over the whole range of the export–sales ratio. Even firms that generate a very small share of their total sales in the international market do show a rate of profit that exceeds that of non-exporting firms. This result corresponds to that obtained by Fryges and Wagner (2008a) who demonstrate that exporting increases labor productivity growth even for firms with very small export–sales ratios. Thus, learning from foreign customers and competitors is relevant and the positive effect of learning-by-exporting is not completely absorbed, e.g. by higher wages or by the costs of entry into a foreign market, even if firms carry out only limited export activities.[17]

As already discussed above, the rate of profit is maximized at an export-sales ratio of 49 percent. Beyond this threshold of internationalization, firms exhibit a decrease in profitability compared to firms with lower export intensities. This decrease might be a result of additional costs of exporting, for instance, due to rising costs of coordination and control of a firm's export activities or higher transportation costs due to the increasing geographical distance of the foreign markets a firm has entered. Furthermore, according to results reported in Fryges and Wagner (2008a) the dose-response function for the impact of the export–sales ratio on productivity growth shows a very similar inversely u-shaped pattern, suggesting that productivity dynamics may play a part in the specific shape of the profit dose-response function. Note, however, that both dose-response functions cannot be compared straightforwardly because in Fryges and Wagner (2008a) we used establishment-level data from one German federal state (Lower Saxony) only while the data used in this study are enterprise-level data for Germany as a whole.

Nevertheless, the rate of profit for firms of which the export intensity exceeds the threshold of internationalization is still significantly higher than the profitability of non-exporting firms — provided that the firms realize an export–sales ratio of 89 percent or more. Firms that generate an export intensity of at least 89 percent do not benefit from a higher rate of profit if compared with non-exporting firms. Thus, there is a sub-interval of the domain of the export–sales ratio where exporting does not

[17]As discussed in Section 2, differences in the rate of profit might also be explained by varying mark-ups of prices over costs. Firms that possess a competitive advantage over their (international) rivals, due to, for instance, intense R&D activities or a highly qualified human capital, might be able to realize a higher mark-up. However, differences in profitability that result from intense R&D activities or a highly qualified human capital (and consequently from a higher mark-up) have been eliminated since we included these variables in the vector of covariates of the fractional logit model estimated in the first step of the GPS methodology. Thus, the different rates of profit depicted by the estimated dose-response function can primarily be interpreted as an effect of differences in labor productivity resulting from learning-by-exporting.

significantly improve profitability. However, there are only very few exporters in our sample (less than three percent) that realize an export intensity that lies in the range between 89 and 100 percent. Therefore, we can conclude that almost all exporters in the German manufacturing sector benefit from their international business activities in terms of an increased rate of profit.

The results we obtained in this section are very similar to those described in Section 4. At least, the estimation results without fixed enterprise effects as reported in columns 1–4 of Table 4 show an inversely u-shaped relationship between profitability and the export–sales ratio. Based on the results in Table 4, the estimated threshold value of internationalization amounts to 65 percent, whereas, according to the estimated dose-response function the rate of profit reaches its maximum at an export–sales ratio of 49 percent. According to the results in Section 4, the difference in profitability between exporting and non-exporting firms is rather small. The analysis based on the estimated dose-response function can confirm this result: the maximum difference in the rate of profit is 2.4 percentage points. The advantage of the continuous treatment approach applied in the section is that we can prove that differences in profitability are caused by differences in the share of exports in total sales. Furthermore, the dose-response function shows that firms with very high export intensities do not benefit from their export activities — at least not in terms of an increase in the rate of profit.

## 6. Conclusion

The relationship between productivity and a firm's export activities has been studied extensively in the literature on the microeconometrics of international trade. Stylized facts point out that exporting firms exhibit a higher productivity and higher wages. Econometric analyses proved that there is a self-selection of the more productive firms into the international market. A question that has not been investigated so far is whether the productivity advantage of exporting firms does lead to a profitability advantage of exporters compared to non-exporting firms even when exporters are facing extra costs and pay higher wages.

Looking at profitability instead of productivity is more appropriate from a theoretical point of view, too. Even if productivity and profitability are positively correlated (which tends to be the case) productivity is, as was recently pointed out by Foster, Haltiwanger and Syverson (2008, p. 395), only one of several possible idiosyncratic factors that determine profits. Success of firms in general, and especially survival, depends on profitability. Often profitability is viewed both in theoretical models of market selection and in empirical studies on firm entry and exit as a positive monotonic function of productivity, and selection on profits then is equivalent to selection on productivity. In empirical studies, the use of productivity instead of profitability is usually due to the fact that productivity is easily observed in the datasets at hand while profitability is not. Fortunately, our recently released dataset on German manufacturing firms is rich enough to allow to measure profitability.

Our findings illustrate that using profitability sheds new light on the relationship between exports and firm performance. We demonstrate that exporters show a positive profitability differential compared to non-exporters and that this differential is statistically significant, though rather small. However, in contrast to nearly all empirical studies on the relationship between productivity and exports, we find no evidence for self-selection of more profitable firms into export activities. Conversely, exporting has a positive causal effect on profitability almost over the whole domain of the export–sales ratio from 0 to 1. The only exceptions are firms that realize an export–sales ratio of 89 percent and more.

The maximization of the rate of profit is one of the main objectives of a firm. This chapter shows that exporting leads to a higher rate of profit. This means that the higher productivity usually observed in the group of exporting firms is not completely absorbed by higher wages and higher costs related to exporting. However, the positive effect of exporting on profitability varies along the range of the export–sales ratio. The effect reaches its maximum for firms that generate 49 percent of their total sales abroad and it is zero for firms with very high export intensities. As a rule, therefore, we conclude that exporting pays for German manufacturing firms. Open questions, however, are the role played by different destinations and by the characteristics of these export-markets, and the importance of the number and the quality of products exported for the relationship between exports and profitability. These questions that cannot be examined due to restrictions of the dataset we have at hand are subject of future research.

## Acknowledgment

All computations for this study were done inside the Research Data Centre of the Statistical Office of Berlin. A first version of this chapter was presented at the workshop of the International Study Group on Exports and Productivity at Nottingham University in February 2008. Furthermore, this chapter was presented at the Applied Micro Workshop at Pennsylvania State University in September 2008, while Helmut Fryges was visiting Penn State University during the fall semester 2008. Helpful suggestions by Mark Roberts, James Tybout and other participants of the Applied Micro Workshop are highly acknowledged. Comments from two anonymous referees helped us to improve the paper.

## References

Asiedu, E. and J. A. Freeman (2007). The Effect of Globalization on the Performance of Small- and Medium-Sized Enterprises in the United States: Dos Owners' Race/Ethnicity Matter? *American Economic Review Papers and Proceedings* 97(2), 368–372.

Bausch, A. and M. Krist (2007). The Effect of Context-Related Moderators on the Internationalization-Performance Relationship: Evidence from Meta-Analysis. *Management International Review* 47(3), 319–347.

Bernard, A. B., B. J. Jensen, S. J. Redding and P. K. Schott (2007). Firms in International Trade. *Journal of Economic Perspectives* 21(3), 105–130.

Brandt, M., S. Dittrich and M. Konold (2008). Wirtschaftsstatistische Längsschnitt daten für die Wissenschaft. *Wirtschaft und Statistik* 3/2008, 217–224.

Conover, W. J. (1999). *Practical Nonparametric Statistics* Third Edition. New York: Wiley.

Contractor, F. J. (2007). Is International Business Goof for Companies? The Evolutionary or Multi-Stage Theory of Internationalization vs. the Transaction Cost Perspective. *Management International Review* 47(3), 453–475.

Flores, C. A. (2004). Estimation of Dose-Response Functions and Optimal Doses with a Continuous Treatment. Job Market Paper, University of California, Berkeley.

Foster, L., J. Haltiwanger and C. Syverson (2008). Reallocation, Firm Turnover, and Efficiency: Selection on Productivity or Profitability? *American Economic Review* 98(1), 394–425.

Fritsch, M., B. Görzig, O. Hennchen and A. Stephan (2004). Cost Structure Surveys for Germany. *Schmollers Jahrbuch/Journal of Applied Social Science Studies* 124(4), 557–566.

Fryges, H. (2008). The Export-Growth Relationship: Estimating a Dose-Response Function. *Applied Economics Letters*, forthcoming.

Fryges, H. and J. Wagner (2008a). Exports and Productivity Growth — First Evidence from a Continuous Treatment Approach. *Review of World Economics/Weltwirtschaftliches Archiv* 144(4), 695–722.

Fryges, H. and J. Wagner (2008b). Exports and Profitability — First Evidence for German Manufacturing Firms. ZEW Discussion Paper 08-085, Mannheim.

Glaum, M. and M.-J. Oesterle (2007). 40 Years of Research on Internationalization and Firm Performance: More Questions than Answers? *Management International Review* 47(3), 307–317.

Hennart, J.-F. (2007). The Theoretical Rationale for a Multinationality–Performance Relationship. *Management International Review* 47(3), 423–452.

Hirano, K. and G. W. Imbens (2004). *The Propensity Score with Continuous Treatments.* In: Gelman, A. and X.-L. Meng (Eds.), Applied Bayesian Modeling and Causal Inference from Incomplete-Data Perspectives, Chichester: Wiley, pp. 73–84.

Imbens, G. W. (2000). The Role of the Propensity Score in Estimating Dose-Response Functions. *Biometrika* 87(3), 706–710.

Konold, M. (2007). New Possibilities for Economic Research through Integration of Establishment-level Panel Data of German Official Statistics. *Schmollers Jahrbuch/Journal of Applied Social Science Studies* 127(2), 321–334.

McCullagh, P. and J. A. Nelder (1989). *Generalized Linear Models*, Second edition. New York: Chapman and Hall.

Mayer, T. and G. I. P. Ottaviano (2007). *The Happy Few: The Internationalisation of European Firms. New Facts Based in Firm-Level Evidence.* Brussels: Bruegel.

Papke, L. E. and J. M. Wooldridge (1996). Econometric Methods for Fractional Response Variables with an Application to 401(K) Plan Participation Rates. *Journal of Applied Econometrics* 11(4), 619–632.

Rosenbaum, P. R. and D. B. Rubin (1983). The Central Role of the Propensity Score in Observational Studies for Causal Effects. *Biometrika* 70(1), 41–55.

Ruigrok, W., W. Amann and H. Wagner (2007). The Internationalization-Performance Relationship at Swiss Firms: A Test of the S-Shape and Extreme Degree of Internationalization. *Management International Review* 47(3), 349–368.
Schank, T., C. Schnabel and J. Wagner (2007). Do Exporters Really Pay Higher Wages? First Evidence from German Linked Employer–Employee Data. *Journal of International Economics* 72(1), 52–74.
Schmalensee, R. (1989). Inter-Industry Studies of Structure and Performance. In: Schmalensee, R. and R. D. Willig (Eds.), Handbook of Industrial Organization, Vol. II, Amsterdam: North-Holland, pp. 951–1009.
The International Study Group on Exports and Productivity (2008). Understanding Cross-Country Differences in Exporter Premia — Comparable Evidence for 14 Countries. *Review of World Economics/Weltwirtschaftliches Archiv* 144(4), 596–635.
Wagner, J. (2001). A Note on the Firm Size — Export Relationship. *Small Business Economics* 17(4), 229–237.
Wagner, J. (2003). Unobserved Firm Heterogeneity and the Size-Exports Nexus: Evidence from German Panel Data. *Review of World Economics* 139(1), 161–172.
Wagner, J. (2007a). Exports and Productivity: A Survey of the Evidence from Firm Level Data. *The World Economy* 30(1), 60–82.
Wagner, J. (2007b). Exports and Productivity in Germany. *Applied Economics Quarterly* 53(4), 353–373.
Zühlke, S., M. Zwick, S. Scharnhorst and T. Wende (2004). The research data centres of the Federal Statistical Office and the Statistical Offices of the *Länder*. *Schmollers Jahrbuch/Journal of Applied Social Science Studies* 124(4), 567–578.

## Appendix

### A.1. The GPS Method

This chapter applies the GPS method developed by Imbens (2000) and Hirano and Imbens (2004). The GPS method allows for continuous treatment, that is, in our case, different levels of firms' export–sales ratios. It is a generalization of the binary treatment propensity score methodology as derived by Rosenbaum and Rubin (1983).

The key assumption of the GPS method is a generalization of the strong unconfoundedness assumption made by Rosenbaum and Rubin (1983) for binary treatments (*cf.* Imbens (2000)). Let the treatment $D$ take on values in the interval $\mathrm{D} = [d_0, d_1]$. Assignment to treatment $D$ is *weakly unconfounded*, given a vector of pre-treatment variables $X$, if

$$Y(d) \perp D | X \quad \text{for all } d \in \mathrm{D}, \tag{1}$$

with $Y(d)$ as the outcome associated with treatment level $d$. It is important to note that this assumption does not require joint independence of all potential outcomes $\{Y(d)\}_{d \in \mathrm{D}}$. Instead, weak unconfoundedness only requires pairwise independence of the treatment with each of the potential outcomes. In other words, the random variable $D$ (the treatment) is assumed to be conditionally independent with the random variable $Y$ (the outcome), measured at an arbitrarily chosen treatment level $d$.

Let further $r(d, x)$ be the conditional density of the treatment given the covariates:

$$r(d, x) = f_{D|X}(d|x). \tag{2}$$

Then the GPS is defined as $R = r(D, X)$ (Hirano and Imbens (2004), p. 74). Assuming that assignment to treatment $D$ is weakly unconfounded given pre-treatment variables $X$, it can be proved that for every treatment level $d$

$$f_D(d|r(d, X), Y(d)) = f_D(d|r(d, X)), \tag{3}$$

i.e. assignment to treatment $D$ is unconfounded given the GPS (Hirano and Imbens (2004), p. 75). Equation (3) shows that the conditional density of the treatment level at $d$ is calculated using the GPS at the corresponding level of the treatment. Thus, the GPS methodology uses as many propensity scores as there are levels of the treatment.

In the case of binary treatment, Rosenbaum und Rubin (1983) demonstrate that conditioning on the one-dimensional propensity score (i.e. the conditional probability of receiving the treatment given pre-treatment variables) is sufficient to remove all the bias associated with differences in pre-treatment variables between treated and non-treated individuals or firms. With continuous treatment, Hirano and Imbens (2004) prove that adjusting for the GPS eliminates any biases associated with differences in the pre-treatment variables. Assuming that assignment to treatment $D$ is weakly unconfounded given pre-treatment variables $X$ und using the result from equation (3), it can be shown that

$$\eta(d,r) = E[Y(d)|r(d,X) = r] = E[Y|D = d, R = r] \quad \text{and} \tag{4}$$

$$\mu(d) = E[\eta(d, r(d,X))] = E[Y(d)]. \tag{5}$$

Thus, the bias-removing property is obtained in two steps. In the first step, the conditional expectation of the outcome $Y$ is estimated as a function of the treatment $D$ and the GPS $R$, $\eta(d,r) = E[Y|D = d, R = r]$. Hirano and Imbens (2004) stress, however, that the regression function $\eta(d,r)$ does not have a causal interpretation. In the second step, the conditional expectation $\eta(d,r)$ is averaged over the GPS evaluated at a particular level of the treatment, $\mu(d) = E[\eta(d, r(d,X))]$. This leads to an estimation of the dose-response function $\mu(d)$ at any level or dose of the continuous treatment variable.

Hirano and Imbens (2004) suggest a three-stage approach to implement the GPS method. In the first stage, the conditional distribution of the treatment variable given the covariates is estimated. In our case, the distribution of the treatment variable $D$, i.e. the firms' export–sales ratios, is highly skewed. In particular, it has many limit observations at the value zero, representing firms without any international sales. Following Wagner (2001, 2003), we apply the fractional logit model developed by Papke and Wooldridge (1996) to estimate the export intensity of the firms in our sample. Papke and Wooldridge assume that, for all observations $i$, the expected value of $D_i$ conditional on a vector of covariates $X_i$ is given by

$$E(D_i|X_i) = F(X_i\beta), \tag{6}$$

with $0 < F(X_i\beta) < 1$ for all $X_i\beta \in \mathrm{R}$, ensuring that the predicted values of $D_i$ lie in the interval (0, 1). Nevertheless, Equation (6) is defined even if $D_i$ takes the limit observations zero or one. The function $F(\cdot)$ is assumed to be the cumulative distribution function (cdf) of the logistic distribution:

$$F(X_i\beta) \equiv \Lambda(X_i\beta) \equiv \frac{\exp(X_i\beta)}{1+\exp(X_i\beta)}. \tag{7}$$

Papke and Wooldridge propose a quasi-maximum likelihood estimator (QMLE) of $\beta$. The estimation procedure maximizes the

Bernoulli log-likelihood function given by

$$l_i(\beta) \equiv D_i \cdot \log[\Lambda(X_i\beta)] + (1 - D_i) \cdot \log[1 - \Lambda(X_i\beta)], \quad (8)$$

using the generalized linear models (GLM) framework developed by McCullagh and Nelder (1989). The estimated GPS based on the Bernoulli log-likelihood function defined in Equation (8) is then given by

$$\hat{R}_i = [\Lambda(X_i\hat{\beta})]^{D_i} \cdot [1 - \Lambda(X_i\hat{\beta})]^{(1-D_i)}. \quad (9)$$

In the second stage of Hirano and Imbens' GPS methodology the conditional expectation of outcome $Y_i$ (the rate of profit in our case) is modelled as a function of the treatment $D_i$ and the (estimated) generalised propensity score $\hat{R}_i$. Following Hirano and Imbens, we use a quadratic approximation for the conditional expectation of $Y_i$:

$$E[Y_i|D_i, \hat{R}_i] = \alpha_0 + \alpha_1 \cdot D_i + \alpha_2 \cdot D_i^2 + \alpha_3 \cdot \hat{R}_i + \alpha_4 \cdot \hat{R}_i^2 + \alpha_5 \cdot D_i \cdot \hat{R}_i. \quad (10)$$

Equation (10) corresponds to Equation (4) and is estimated by OLS. As Hirano and Imbens point out, the estimated regression coefficients $\hat{\alpha}$ do not have any direct meaning and will therefore not be reported in Section 5 for reasons of space.

In the last stage of the GPS method, the average expected outcome at treatment level $d$ is estimated, using the regression coefficients $\hat{\alpha}$ from the second stage of the GPS method:

$$\widehat{E[Y(d)]} = \frac{1}{N}\sum_{i=1}^{N}(\hat{\alpha}_0 + \hat{\alpha}_1 \cdot d + \hat{\alpha}_2 \cdot d^2 + \hat{\alpha}_3 \cdot \hat{r}(d, X_i) + \hat{\alpha}_4 \cdot \hat{r}(d, X_i)^2 + \hat{\alpha}_5 \cdot d \cdot \hat{r}(d, X_i)), \quad (11)$$

with $N$ as the number of observations. Equation (11) corresponds to Equation (5). In order to obtain an estimate of the entire dose-response function, Equation (11) is calculated at each export intensity $d$ in the interval from 0 to 1. Hirano and Imbens (2004) state that asymptotic normality for the estimator in Equation (11) can be proved. However, following the same procedure as Hirano and Imbens, the confidence intervals of the dose-response functions in this paper are determined via bootstrapping.

Applying the GPS methodology, we do not calculate the effect of the treatment *per se* , that is, we do not compare the potential outcome for non-treated individuals or firms with that for all treated entities simply allowing for different levels or doses of the treatment variable. Instead, the dose-response function we estimate shows the average potential outcome at each dose of the treatment and how average responses vary along the interval $D = [d_0, d_1]$. From this curve we can calculate pairwise treatment effects of the form (*cf.* Flores 2004):

$$E(\Delta^{d'd''}) = E[Y(d') - Y(d'')] \quad \text{for } d', d'' \in D. \tag{12}$$

In other words, we estimate the average response of outcome at one particular treatment level and compare this outcome with the average outcome at any other, deliberately chosen treatment level. Since the GPS model controls for differences in pre-treatment variables, potential differences between the average outcomes at two deliberately chosen levels of treatment can be interpreted as a causal effect of varying doses of the continuous treatment variable.

## Chapter 8

# Exports and Profitability — First Evidence for German Business Services Enterprises

Alexander Vogel and Joachim Wagner

**Abstract**

We use the unique recently released German business services statistics panel to conduct the first comprehensive empirical study on the relationship between exports and profitability for the business services sector. We document a negative profitability differential of services exporters compared to non-exporters that is statistically significant, though rather small, when observed firm characteristics and unobserved firm specific effects are controlled for. We find that export-starters in services are less profitable than non-starters, even two years before they begin to export, pointing to self-selection of less profitable firms into export markets. We use a recently developed continuous treatment approach to investigate the causal impact of exports on profits. The estimated dose-response function shows an s-shaped relationship between profitability in 2005 and firms' export–sales ratio in 2004. Enterprises with a very small share of exports in total sales have a lower rate of profit than non-exporting firms. Then, with an increase in export intensity the rate of profit increases, too. However, even at the maximum the average profitability of the exporters is not, or only slightly, higher than the average rate of profit of the non-exporting firms. Given that Germany is one of the leading actors in the world market for services, the evidence provided here is interesting on its own. Furthermore, it can serve as a benchmark for future studies using comparable data for firms from services industries in other countries.

*Keywords*: Exports, profitability, business services enterprises, Germany

**JEL Classification:** F14, D21, L80

## 1. Motivation

For manufacturing firms, a huge and emerging literature on the microeconometrics of international trade provides evidence for a number of stylized facts: Exporting firms are more productive than otherwise identical firms that sell in the national market only.[1] Exporting firms have to bear extra costs due to, among others, market research in foreign countries, adaptation of products to local regulations, or transport costs. These extra costs are one reason for a self-selection of the more productive firms on international markets. Furthermore, exporting firms tend to pay higher wages than non-exporting firms.[2]

While this empirical evidence for manufacturing firms is widely known for some time now, comparable information for firms from services is scarce and of a more recent vintage. Vogel (2009a) finds that in Germany — that ranked as No. 3 on the world market for services exports in 2007 (Bundesministerium für Wirtschaft und Technologie 2009) — exporting firms from the business services sector have a significantly and substantially higher productivity than non-exporting firms, and pay significantly and substantially higher wages, after controlling for firm size and industry.

Does the productivity advantage found for exporting firms lead to a profitability advantage, or is it compensated by the extra costs facing exporters and by higher wages paid? Research in this topic has only recently started in a paper by Fryges and Wagner (2009).[3] For German manufacturing enterprises, they document

---

[1]See Bernard *et al.* (2007) for the U.S., Mayer and Ottaviano (2008) for European countries, Wagner (2007) for a survey of studies from countries all over the world, and The International Study Group on Exports and Productivity (2008) for strictly comparable results from 14 countries.

[2]See Schank, Schnabel and Wagner (2007) for a survey.

[3]Note that in the literature on international management the empirical investigation of the relationship between internationalization and firm performance has a long tradition. However, given that the samples used in these studies tend to be small cross-section samples that do not allow to control for unobserved heterogeneity by including fixed firm effects, and that various measures of both internationalization and performance are used (see Bausch and Krist (2007), p. 332), we cannot find an answer to our question — whether the productivity advantage of exporting services firms does lead to a profitability advantage of exporters

that the positive profitability differential of exporters compared to non-exporters is statistically significant, though rather small, when observed firm characteristics and unobserved firm specific effects are controlled for. In contrast to nearly all empirical studies on the relationship between productivity and exports, Fryges and Wagner do not find any evidence for self-selection of more profitable firms into export markets. However, they show that exporting improves the profitability almost over the whole range of the export–sales ratio. Only firms that generate 90 percent and more of their total sales abroad do not benefit from exporting in terms of an increased rate of profit. This means that the usually observed higher productivity of exporters is not completely absorbed by the extra costs of exporting or by higher wages paid by internationally active firms from manufacturing industries.

Comparable evidence for firms from services is lacking. This chapter contributes to the literature by using the unique recently released German business services statistics panel to conduct the first comprehensive empirical study on the relationship between exports and profitability for the business services sector. Unless otherwise stated, business services are defined in this chapter as NACE divisions 72 (computers and related activities, including, among others, hardware and software consultancy, data processing, software publishing and database activities), 73 (research and development), and 74 (other business activities, including, for example, business, management and tax consultancy, advertising, legal activities, market research, and architectural and engineering activities). Even though the business services sector covers a wide range of activities, business services are traded more than most other services,[4] and these activities have in common that they provide primarily intermediate inputs.

---

compared to otherwise identical non-exporters even when exporters are facing extra costs and pay higher wages — from this literature (see Fryges and Wagner (2009) for an overview).

[4]According to the German balance of payments, business services (defined as advertising, engineering, commercial and computer services) have by far the highest trade volume of any service other than travel and transport (*cf.* Deutsche Bundesbank (2009)). In addition, Jensen and Kletzer (2006) classified nearly all business services as tradable, based on the geographic concentration of service activities in the United States.

Our investigation considers export activities defined as the first, the second and the fourth mode of delivery mentioned in the General Agreement on Trade in Services (see WTO (1994), p. 285). Thus, our export measure covers cross-border delivery of services (using e.g. new forms of telecommunication and information technology), services that are used by foreign clients at the domestic location of the supplier, and services that are supplied by natural persons in the foreign country. Mode 3 (i.e. the provider produces the service in a foreign subsidiary after foreign direct investment) is not considered in our analysis.

To investigate the relationship between exports and profitability, we follow the now standard approach in the microeconometric literature on exports and productivity (see The International Study Group on Exports and Productivity (2008)). First, we document a negative profitability differential of services exporters compared to non-exporters that is statistically significant, though rather small, when observed firm characteristics and unobserved firm specific effects are controlled for. Based on these negative export profitability premia, we analyze in the second step a possible self-selection of less profitable firms into export markets and find that export-starters in services are less profitable than non-starters, even two years before they begin to export. Finally, we analyze the effect of exporting on profitability. Unfortunately, the data used in our empirical study cover the years 2003–2005 only. Therefore, we cannot test whether services firms that started to export performed better or worse in the years after the start than their otherwise identical counterparts that did not start to export. Instead, we use a recently developed continuous treatment approach (described in detail in Section 6) to investigate the causal impact of exports on profits. The estimated dose-response function for all business services sectors (NACE 72–74) shows an s-shaped relationship between profitability in 2005 and firms' export–sales ratio in 2004, and the same picture is found when looking at the more disaggregated two-digit NACE level separately. Enterprises with a very small share of exports in total sales have a lower rate of profit than non-exporting firms. Then, with an increase in export intensity the rate of profit increases, too. However, even at the maximum of the dose-response function the average profitability of the exporters is not or only slightly higher than the average rate of profit of the non-exporting firms. Beyond the maximum, firms exhibit a decrease in profitability compared to firms with lower export intensities. This decrease might be a result of additional costs of exporting, for instance, due to rising costs of coordination and control of a firm's export activities or higher travel or transportation costs due to the increasing geographical distance of the foreign markets a firm has entered.

These findings for German service sector exporters stand in stark contrast to the results from the investigation of exporters from German manufacturing industries reported by Fryges and Wagner (2009). Given that Germany is one of the leading actors in the world market for both goods and services, the evidence provided here is interesting on its own. Furthermore, it can serve as a benchmark for future studies using comparable data from other countries.

The rest of the chapter is organized as follows: Section 2 introduces our data base, the German statistics on business services. Section 3 presents results from descriptive comparisons of exporting and non-exporting business services firms. Section 4 reports estimations of exporter profitability premia after controlling for observed and unobserved differences between exporters and non-exporters. Section 5 documents whether differences between export starters and non-exporters exist even before the future exporters start to export and Section 6 investigates the causal effect of exporting on profitability using the recently developed generalized propensity score (GPS) methodology. Section 7 concludes.

## 2. Data

To investigate the relationship between export and profitability of German business services enterprises, we use the business services statistics (*Strukturerhebung im Dienstleistungsbereich*) established by the German Federal Statistical Office and the statistical offices of the Federal States (*Länder*). The statistics were first compiled for the year 2000 on the initiative of the European Union. The data covers the enterprises and professions (*Freie Berufe*) of the NACE divisions I (transport, storage and communication) and K (real estate, renting and business activities) with an annual turnover of 17,500€ or more. A stratified random sample is used to select the enterprises. The stratification is based on the federal states, 4-digit industries, and 12 size ranges (in terms of turnover or employees). For 2005, the following sample sizes are drawn from the three industries analyzed in this paper: 18.3 percent of all statistical units from the NACE division 72 (computer and related activities), 36.9 percent of all statistical units from the NACE division 73 (research and development) and 12.6 percent of all statistical units from the NACE division 74 (other business activities). Because the same enterprises that participated in 2003 also participated in 2004 and 2005, it is possible to merge the cross-sectional datasets to a panel dataset that covers the years 2003–2005.

The business services statistics include, among other data, information about the economic sector, the number of persons employed (not including temporary workers), total turnover, salaries and wages, and export — defined as turnover for business with companies located abroad, including exports to foreign affiliates. Unfortunately, information on the target countries of exports is not included in the statistics and we cannot distinguish between service and goods exports as well as the different types of services exported by the firm. Also, no information is obtained about other forms of companies' activities abroad, such as cooperation, direct investments, exports via commercial presence or imports. Furthermore, small enterprises with an annual turnover lower than 250,000 € are given a shorter questionnaire, so important information, such as information about export activities, is missing for these enterprises. As a result, only enterprises with an annual turnover over 250,000 € are considered for the analyses.

These data are confidential but not exclusive. They can be used by researchers on a contractual basis via controlled remote data access inside the research data centres of the German Statistical

Offices (see Zühlke *et al.* (2004) for details).[5] For more details about the dataset, see Vogel (2009b).

## 3. Descriptive Analysis

### 3.1. *Export participation of business services firms*

The enterprises' export activities are measured by the export intensity, defined as the percentage of exports in total turnover. Regarding all business services industries, the share of exporters in all enterprises was about 14 percent in 2003 and about 16 percent in 2005.[6] Table 1 shows that in both years the distribution of the export intensity was highly skewed — most of the exporters sold a relatively small share of their total production abroad, and only a few firms exported a very high share. Looking at the more disaggregated industry level, the highest export participation was in the research and development sector (about 36 percent in 2005), followed by computer and related activities (about 25 percent in 2005).[7]

### 3.2. *Profitability of exporting and non-exporting firms*

As a first step in our empirical investigation, we compare the profitability of exporting and non-exporting business services firms. The rate of profit of a firm is computed as a rate of return, defined as gross firm surplus (computed in line with the definition of the European Commission (1998) as gross value added at factor costs minus gross wages and salaries minus costs for social insurance

[5]To facilitate replication the Stata do-files used in the computations are available from the first author upon request.

[6]Note that only enterprises with a turnover greater than 250,000 € are considered. We do not have information about the export participation of small business services firms.

[7]To explain the high export participation in the research and development sector it has to be mentioned that privately organized entities, owned by German research institutions such as the Max Planck Society, the Fraunhofer Society, Helmholtz Association of National Research Centres, and public research institutions of the Federal and Länder governments are included. Usually, these institutions are intensively integrated in international networks (see Eickelpasch (2008)).

Table 1. Export activities of business services enterprises 2003 and 2005 — share of exporting enterprises in all enterprises (percentage)

| Year | Export intensity | All business services (NACE 72 to 74) | Computer and related activities (NACE 72) | Research and development (NACE 73) | Other business activities (NACE 74 without 74.1 and 74.2) | Business consultancy, market research, etc* (NACE 74.1) | Architectural and engineering activities (NACE 74.2) |
|---|---|---|---|---|---|---|---|
| | | Share of exporting enterprises on all enterprises in percentages | | | | | |
| 2003 | 0% | 86.29 | 75.39 | 65.90 | 87.79 | 86.96 | 90.99 |
| | > 0% and < 5% | 6.38 | 10.00 | 8.47 | 6.10 | 6.97 | 3.14 |
| | ≥ 5% and < 10% | 1.92 | 4.04 | 5.22 | 1.53 | 1.71 | 1.35 |
| | ≥ 10% and < 25% | 2.22 | 4.23 | 5.64 | 1.66 | 1.93 | 2.13 |
| | ≥ 25% and < 50% | 1.58 | 3.67 | 6.47 | 1.44 | 1.20 | 0.94 |
| | ≥ 50% and < 75% | 0.79 | 1.57 | 4.27 | 0.81 | 0.57 | 0.49 |
| | ≥ 75% | 0.82 | 1.10 | 4.02 | 0.67 | 0.67 | 0.95 |
| 2005 | 0% | 84.32 | 74.45 | 63.96 | 85.87 | 85.73 | 87.31 |
| | > 0% and < 5% | 7.05 | 9.52 | 9.00 | 7.15 | 7.12 | 4.80 |
| | ≥ 5% and < 10% | 2.06 | 3.95 | 5.53 | 1.57 | 1.71 | 2.02 |
| | ≥ 10% and < 25% | 2.66 | 5.47 | 7.03 | 2.31 | 2.10 | 2.14 |
| | ≥ 25% and < 50% | 1.80 | 2.94 | 6.35 | 1.47 | 1.56 | 1.72 |
| | ≥ 50% and < 75% | 0.97 | 1.76 | 3.78 | 0.81 | 0.86 | 0.70 |
| | ≥ 75% | 1.13 | 1.92 | 4.35 | 0.82 | 0.92 | 1.31 |

*Note*: (*) NACE code 74.1 includes legal, accounting, book-keeping and auditing activities; tax consultancy; market research and public opinion polling; and business and management consultancy.
Only enterprises of the NACE division 72 to 74 with a turnover greater than € 250,000 are considered. All values are weighted with cross-sectional weights. The 1st and 99th percentiles of the rate of profit distribution are excluded from all computations.

paid by the firm) divided by total sales (net of VAT) minus net change of inventories.[8]

$$\text{rate of profit} = \frac{\begin{array}{c}\text{gross value added} - \text{gross wages}\\ - \text{cos ts for social insurance}\end{array}}{\text{total sales} - \text{net change of inventories}}.$$

Our profit measure is a measure for the price–cost margin which, under competitive conditions, should on average equal the required rental on assets employed per money unit of sales (see Schmalensee 1989, p. 960f.). Differences in profitability between firms, therefore, can follow from productivity differences, but also from different mark-ups of prices over costs and from differences in the capital intensity. Given that our data set does not have information on the capital stock employed by the firms in our econometric investigations, we control for differences in the capital intensity by including a complete set of industry dummy variables at the most disaggregated (4-digit) level.[9]

Table 2 reports the mean and selected percentiles of the distribution of the rate of profit for all business services enterprises within different classes of the export intensity. In contrast to the evidence from the manufacturing sector (see Fryges and Wagner (2009)) the descriptive results show that non-exporting enterprises tend to have a higher rate of profit than exporters. This holds for the mean profitability and for almost all considered percentiles. The results indicate that the mean profitability (or the percentiles of the profitability distribution) of firms that export only a small share of their total sales (less than 10 percent) falls below that of non-exporting firms. The pattern over the higher export intensity classes, however, does not reveal any clear pattern.

[8]Note that the data set does not have any information on the capital stock, or the sum of assets or equity, of the firm, so that it is not possible to construct profit indicators based thereon like return on assets or return on equity.

[9]One important problem with the profitability measurement we use, arises due to the fact that two main components of profitability, profits and capital costs, need not to show a monotone relationship between each other. This may bias the results.

Table 2. Rate of profite (percentage) for enterprises in different classes of the export intensity (2003 and 2005) — All Business Services

| | | All business services (NACE division 72 to 74) | | | | | | | |
|---|---|---|---|---|---|---|---|---|---|
| | | | Rate of profit (in percent) | | | | | | |
| Year | Export intensity | Number of enterprises | Mean | Standard deviation | p1 | p25 | p50 | p75 | p99 |
| 2003 | 0% | 19,279 | 27.46 | 25.96 | −33.80 | 8.65 | 25.27 | 44.44 | 90.80 |
| | > 0% and < 5% | 1,759 | 25.13 | 23.72 | −25.79 | 7.51 | 21.60 | 42.62 | 84.63 |
| | ≥ 5% and < 10% | 521 | 23.90 | 27.00 | −42.28 | 4.79 | 20.49 | 42.27 | 81.29 |
| | ≥ 10% and < 25% | 669 | 19.25 | 25.48 | −40.99 | 4.12 | 16.09 | 34.24 | 91.21 |
| | ≥ 25% and < 50% | 423 | 23.50 | 27.72 | −40.43 | 4.88 | 19.14 | 41.94 | 91.17 |
| | ≥ 50% and < 75% | 205 | 18.63 | 28.99 | × | 4.14 | 18.53 | 36.66 | × |
| | ≥ 75% | 220 | 14.43 | 27.79 | × | 2.05 | 13.65 | 26.38 | × |
| 2005 | 0% | 20,416 | 25.16 | 26.67 | −41.06 | 5.62 | 22.28 | 42.81 | 90.40 |
| | > 0% and < 5% | 2,033 | 21.20 | 23.81 | −31.13 | 4.38 | 16.88 | 36.84 | 77.09 |
| | ≥ 5% and < 10% | 620 | 17.06 | 22.74 | −34.87 | 1.82 | 12.97 | 30.75 | 79.71 |
| | ≥ 10% and < 25% | 810 | 18.67 | 27.62 | −71.82 | 1.85 | 13.23 | 39.27 | 82.57 |
| | ≥ 25% and < 50% | 521 | 17.27 | 27.28 | −59.16 | 1.54 | 12.40 | 32.46 | 89.79 |
| | ≥ 50% and < 75% | 238 | 22.66 | 30.12 | × | 3.47 | 23.89 | 42.91 | × |
| | ≥ 75% | 296 | 19.99 | 30.23 | × | 2.58 | 14.75 | 40.16 | × |

*Note*: (x) Due to the small number of observations these values were not revealed for publication by the statistical office. Only enterprises of the NACE division 72 to 74 with a turnover greater than € 250,000 are considered. All values (except the number of enterprises) are weighted with cross-sectional weights. The 1$^{st}$ and 99$^{th}$ percentiles of the rate of profit distribution are excluded from all computations.

## 4. Exporter Profitability Premia

The next step in our empirical investigation consists of the estimation of the so-called exporter profitability premia that indicate the *ceteris paribus* difference in profitability between exporting and non-exporting enterprises, controlling for other characteristics of the enterprises. In analogy with the now standard approach in the microeconometric literature on exports and productivity (see The International Study Group on Exports and Productivity (2008)), pooled data are used to regress the rate of profit on the export activity of the enterprise plus a set of control variables including firm size (measured as the number of employees and its squared value), and a full set of interaction terms of the year of observation and the 4-digit industry the enterprise is active in.

Export activity of an enterprise is measured in four different ways, i.e. by a dummy variable that takes on the value of one if an enterprise is an exporter (and zero otherwise), by the share of exports in total sales, by the share of exports in total sales and its squared value, and by the share of exports in total sales plus its squared and its cubic value. While the dummy variable for exporting firms tests for the presence of an exporter profitability premium *per se*, the estimated coefficient of the share of exports in total sales shows whether this premium increases with an increase in the relative importance of exports for an enterprise. The quadratic terms test for the presence of a so-called threshold of internationalization — whether the positive effects vanish and become even negative when the optimal share of exports in total sales is exceeded, because increasing costs of exporting exceed the extra benefits. The cubic term tests for an s-shaped relationship between profitability and the share of exports in total sales that is suggested in recent studies from the international management literature.[10]

---

[10]See Contractor (2007) for a discussion of this s-shaped relationship in a longitudinal perspective that investigates the relationship between internationalization and performance when a firm increases its international activities over time.

For all business services (NACE divisions 72–74), the results based on empirical models using pooled data without fixed enterprise effects are reported as Models 1–4 in Table 3. According to the results in Model 1, exporting firms have a rate of profit that is nearly 4 percentage points lower *ceteris paribus* than in non-exporting firms (a difference that matches the order of magnitude showing up in the descriptive analysis that does not control for firm size, and industry and time effects, reported in Table 2), and from Model 3 we see that the pattern of the relationship between export intensity and profitability is u-shaped with an estimated minimum at a level of exports to sales of 56 percent. According to Model 4, there is evidence for an-shaped relationship, with an estimated inflection point at an export intensity level of 55 percent, a minimum at 32 percent, and a maximum at an export intensity of 78 percent. In both the quadratic and cubic function, there exists no export intensity level where exporters have a higher predicted rate of profit than the average *ceteris paribus* profitability level of non-exporters.

If unobserved firm heterogeneity[11] is controlled for by including fixed enterprise effects,[12] we still find a negative relationship between exporting and the rate of profit. From Models 5 and 6, we see that the estimated coefficients of the exporter dummy and the export intensity variable are negative and statistically significant at a usual level. Exporters have on average a rate of profit that is 0.7 percentage points lower ceteris paribus than in non-exporting enterprises, and an increase in the exports–sales ratio of 10 percentage points is accompanied by a decrease in the profit rate by 0.3 percentage points. However, from the models with fixed enterprise

[11] These characteristics may include such factors as the age of the firm, the geographical scope of exports, financial constraints, or the degree of risk aversion and international orientation of the managers.

[12] To control for unobserved heterogeneity we estimate a fixed-effects model using the Stata xtreg, fe command. This procedure is equivalent to a regression that includes an indicator variable for each firm, allowing for a different intercept term for each firm (see e.g. Nichols (2007) for an intuitive description).

Table 3. Exports and Profits: Evidence from Regression Models (2003–2005), All Business Services (NACE Divisions 72 to 74) Endogenous Variable: Rate of Profit (Percentage)

| | | Pooled Data | | | | Fixed enterprise effects | | | |
|---|---|---|---|---|---|---|---|---|---|
| Exogenous variable | Model | 1 | 2 | 3 | 4 | 5 | 6 | 7 | 8 |
| Exporter | ß | −3.82 | | | | −0.71 | | | |
| (Dummy; 1 = yes) | p-value | 0.000 | | | | 0.052 | | | |
| Export intensity | ß | | −0.0737 | −0.2259 | −0.4105 | | −0.0286 | −0.0599 | −0.0906 |
| (percentage) | p-value | | 0.000 | 0.000 | 0.000 | | 0.021 | 0.119 | 0.206 |
| Export intensity | ß | | | 0.002 | 0.00906 | | | 0.000385 | 0.00155 |
| (squared) | p-value | | | 0.000 | 0.000 | | | 0.381 | 0.526 |
| Export intensity | ß | | | | −0.000055 | | | | −0.000009 |
| (cubic) | p-value | | | | 0.000 | | | | 0.631 |
| Number of employees | ß | −0.00494 | −0.00525 | −0.00517 | −0.00513 | −0.00186 | −0.00188 | −0.00185 | −0.00185 |
| | p-value | 0.000 | 0.000 | 0.000 | 0.000 | 0.232 | 0.230 | 0.235 | 0.236 |
| Number of employees | ß | $2.28e-07$ | $2.39e-07$ | $2.36e-07$ | $2.35e-07$ | $4.49e-8$ | $4.51e-8$ | $4.46e-8$ | $4.45e-8$ |
| (squared) | p-value | 0.001 | 0.001 | 0.001 | 0.001 | 0.189 | 0.186 | 0.191 | 0.192 |
| Constant | ß | 20.99 | 20.57 | 20.71 | 20.77 | 17.27 | 17.28 | 17.31 | 17.31 |
| | p-value | 0.000 | 0.000 | 0.000 | 0.000 | 0.000 | 0.000 | 0.000 | 0.000 |
| Interaction terms of year and 4-digit industry | | included | Included | included | Included | included | included | included | Included |
| Number of observation | | 72,139 | 72,139 | 72,139 | 72,139 | 72,139 | 72,139 | 72,139 | 72,139 |
| $R^2$ | | 0.124 | 0.122 | 0.123 | 0.123 | 0.002 | 0.001 | 0.001 | 0.001 |

*Note*: Only enterprises of the NACE division 72 to 74 with a turnover greater than € 250,000 are considered. The p-values are based on cluster robust standard errors. The $1^{st}$ and $99^{th}$ percentiles of the rate of profit distribution are excluded from all computations.

effects we do not have any evidence that the relationship between the share of exports in total sales and profitability is nonlinear.[13]

When we look at the more disaggregated industry level, we find almost similar results in terms of signs and significance levels (see Table 4).[14] The highest difference concerning the rate of profit between exporting and non-exporting enterprises exists in the economic branch of architectural and engineering activities. Here, based on the pooled regression model exporters have a rate of profit that is 7 percentage points lower than the profitability level of non-exporters, and even in the model with fixed effects, exporters show an economically and a statistically significant lower profitability level of nearly 3 percentage points.

The negative exporter premia found in regression models using pooled data for exporters and non-exporters cannot be interpreted as indicators for a negative causal effect of exporting on profitability:

On the one hand, it might be the case that there is self-selection of less profitable firms into exporting, because exports are viewed as a chance to raise the rate of profit above the level that can be earned on the national market. Further, Vogel (2009a) shows for West German business services firms a self-selection into export markets of firms' that pay higher average wages, that reflects the importance of intangible assets by which it is possible to create a competitive advantage over national and international rivals. Particularly in the labor-intensive business services sector, firms need highly qualified human capital to generate competitive advantages in the form of customer specific superior products. However, it is more difficult to absorb the higher average wages that are related with the need for highly qualified human capital by means of the

[13]Note, however, that this regression is not meant to "explain" profits. The dataset is not rich enough for estimating a complete model of profitability. Our empirical model is just a way to test whether or not profits did differ between exporters and non-exporters, or by export intensity.

[14]Due to space restrictions, only the estimated coefficients of the exporter dummy are presented in Table 4.4. The more detailed tables that include also the estimated coefficients of the share of exports in total sales are available on request.

Table 4. Profit Premia of Exporters (2003–2005): Evidence from Regression Models by Service Industries

| | | All business services (NACE 72 to 74) | Computer and related activities (NACE 72) | Research and development (NACE 73) | Other business activities (NACE 74 without 74.1 and 74.2) | Business consultancy, market research, etc* (NACE 74.1) | Architectural and engineering activities (NACE 74.2) |
|---|---|---|---|---|---|---|---|
| | | Profit premia (percentage points) of exporters (2003–2005)** | | | | | |
| Profit Premia of exporters (pooled model 2003 to 2005) | ß | −3.82 | −3.23 | −2.94 | −2.72 | −3.35 | −7.32 |
| | p-value | 0.000 | 0.000 | 0.050 | 0.000 | 0.000 | 0.000 |
| Profit Premia of exporters (fixed effects model 2003 to 2005) | ß | −0.71 | −1.68 | −1.06 | −0.96 | 0.78 | −2.88 |
| | p-value | 0.052 | 0.034 | 0.646 | 0.142 | 0.195 | 0.024 |
| Number of observations | | 72,139 | 11,800 | 2,010 | 26,405 | 23,227 | 8,697 |

*Note*: (*) NACE code 74.1 includes legal, accounting, book-keeping and auditing activities; tax consultancy; market research and public opinion polling; and business and management consultancy.
(**) Only enterprises of the NACE division 72 to 74 with a turnover greater than € 250,000 are considered. The profit premia are estimated regression coefficients of a dummy variable (taking the value one for exporters, and zero for non-exporters) from an OLS-regression on the rate of profit on this dummy, controlling for the number of employees and its squared value, and a full set of interaction terms of year and 4-digit industry dummies. The p-values are based on cluster robust standard errors. The 1st and 99th percentiles of the rate of profit distribution are excluded from all computations.

firms' higher productivity. Thus, we would expect a self-selection of enterprises that pay higher wages, are more productive, but are less profitable.[15]

On the other hand, exporting might decrease profitability by higher additional costs related to export activities itself, or due to the fact that foreign services markets are more competitive. Compared to the manufacturing sector one would expect that cultural and language differences represent barriers and costs that are more critical in the business services sector since, because of the high level of interaction between user and provider, exporters of services must have good language skills, a high level of intercultural competence, and the ability to customize and adapt services to the specific market (*cf.* McLaughin and Fitzsimmons (1996), Winstead and Patterson (1998)). Regulatory barriers, like the need for locally recognized professional qualifications or other country-specific requirements, can also affect the fixed costs of entering an export market and the variable costs of servicing that market to a greater extent for service enterprises than for manufacturing enterprises (cf. Kox and Nordås (2007)).

Both directions of causality are possible. In the following, therefore, Section 5 investigates whether export starters are less profitable than non-exporters, even before they begin to export and Section 6 analyzes the causal effect of a firm's export activity on its rate of profit.

## 5. Pre-Entry Profitability Premia of Export Starters

Again following the now standard approach in the microeconometric literature on exports and productivity (see The International Study Group on Exports and Productivity (2008)), the next step in our empirical investigation consists of testing whether we can document that enterprises that begin to export are less profitable than non-exporters, even before they begin to export. To do so, we identify a group of firms that did not export over a time span of the

---

[15]Note that in this case one would expect a profitability level of export starters that is smaller than that of non-exporters, but not a negative rate of profit of export starters.

two years $t-2$ to $t-1$. Some of these firms started to export in year $t$ (these are called export starters of cohort $t$), some did not (these are called non-starters of cohort $t$). We then compare the export starters and the non-starters of cohort $t$

— in year $t$, and
— two years back in year $t-2$.

Given that our data cover the years 2003–2005, we can investigate the cohort for $t = 2005$ only. Results are reported in Table 5.

First, we compute the *ceteris paribus* percentage profitability difference between export starters and non-starters in 2005, the year of start. In line with the above presented pooled regression results, in all considered industries export starters are less profitable than non-starters in $t$. However, this negative profit premium for export starters is not statistically significant in NACE section 73 (research and development; where the number of observations is very small) and NACE section 74.1 (business consultancy, market research, etc.).

Second, the *ex-ante* profitability premia in the year 2003 ($t-2$) is the estimated regression coefficient of a dummy variable (taking the value one for export starters in 2005, and zero for non-starters) from an OLS-regression of the rate of profit in 2003 on this dummy, controlling for firm size (number of employees and number of employees squared), and the 4-digit industry, all measured in the year 2003.[16] This coefficient is negative for all considered industries and statistically significant (at least at the 5 percent level) for enterprises with architectural and engineering activities (NACE 74.2), and for other business activities (NACE 74 without 74.1 and 74.2). Therefore, we conclude that in contrast to nearly all empirical studies on the relationship between productivity and exports we have no evidence for self-selection of more profitable firms into exporting. In fact, we even have evidence that two years

[16] At first sight, it might confuse that we regress the rate of profit in $t-2$ on a dummy variable measured later in year $t$. Note, however, that this regression is not meant to "explain" past profits by today's exports — it is just a way to test whether or not profits did differ between today's starters and today's non-exporters two years before the start.

Table 5. Profit Premia of Firms that Start to Export in 2005: Evidence from Regression Models by Service Industries

| | | All business services (NACE 72 to 74) | Computer and related activities (NACE 72) | Research and development (NACE 73) | Other business activities (NACE 74 without 74.1 and 74.2) | Business consultancy, market research, etc* (NACE 74.1) | Architectural and engineering activities (NACE 74.2) |
|---|---|---|---|---|---|---|---|
| Profit premia (percentage points) of enterprises that start to export in 2005** | | | | | | | |
| Profit premia of export starters in the start year | ß | −2.18 | −3.64 | −1.77 | −3.73 | −2.12 | −8.71 |
| | p-value | 0.012 | 0.049 | 0.765 | 0.009 | 0.165 | 0.000 |
| Pre-entry profit premia of export starters two years before start | ß | −3.97 | −0.35 | −0.65 | −2.94 | −0.63 | −6.24 |
| | p-value | 0.000 | 0.846 | 0.874 | 0.050 | 0.681 | 0.016 |
| Number of observations | | 12,915 | 1,763 | 253 | 5,095 | 4,157 | 1,647 |

*Note*: (*) NACE code 74.1 includes legal, accounting, book-keeping and auditing activities; tax consultancy; market research and public opinion polling; and business and management consultancy.
(**) Only starters (enterprises with no export activities in 2003 and 2004, but export activities in 2005) and non-starters (enterprises that do not export between 2003 and 2005) of the NACE division 72 to 74 with a turnover greater than € 250,000 are considered. The profit premia are estimated regression coefficients of a dummy variable (taking the value one for export starters, and zero for non-starters) from an OLS-regression on the rate of profit on this dummy, controlling for the number of employees and its squared value, and a set of 4-digit industry dummies. The p-values are based on robust standard errors. The 1st and 99th percentiles of the rate of profit distribution are excluded from all computations.

before the export starters begin to export, the non-starters have a higher level of profit than the starters. Regarding the coefficient for all business services (NACE 72–74), the difference is not only statistically significant but also economically large. Thus, in 2003 ($t - 2$) the rate of profit of the non-starters is on average four percentage points higher than the profitability of the export starters.

The negative profitability premium of exporters that was found in both the descriptive analyses reported in Section 3.2 and as a result of the econometric investigation presented in Tables 3 and 4 could be caused also by negative effects of exports on the rate of profit (e.g. by higher additional costs or more competitive markets). However, due to the time frame of the data used we cannot test the hypothesis that firms which started to export performed worse in the years after the start compared to their counterparts that did not start. As pointed out in Section 2, the German business services statistics panel covers only the years 2003–2005. Therefore, it is not possible to follow the cohort of starters from 2005 over the next year(s).

## 6. Causal Effect of Exports on Profitability

In the last step of our analysis, we examine whether there is a causal effect of a firm's export activity on its rate of profit. As stated in the previous section, we cannot evaluate post-entry differences in profitability between export starters and non-starters due to the time frame of the German business services statistics. Nonetheless, the question of whether exports have a negative effect on profitability is crucial for our analysis.

The hypothesis of a negative causal effect of exporting on profitability is tested using the GPS methodology recently developed by Imbens (2000) and Hirano and Imbens (2004). The GPS methodology was introduced to the literature examining the export–performance relationship by Fryges (2008) and applied by Fryges and Wagner (2008, 2009) who estimated the relationship between exports and labour productivity growth, and the relationship between exports and profitability using a sample of German manufacturing firms.

The GPS methodology has a number of advantages compared to other econometric techniques. First, the GPS method allows for continuous treatment, i.e. different levels of the firms' export–sales ratio. In this way, we are able to determine the causal relationship between profitability and the export–sales ratio (the treatment) at each value of firms' export intensity in the interval from 0 to 1. Thus, the second important advantage of the GPS method is that it enables us to identify the entire function of the rate of profit over all possible values of the continuous treatment variable. This property of the GPS methodology might be important in our case. The OLS regression of the determinants of the rate of profit in Table 3 pointed out that there might be a nonlinear relationship between profitability and the share of exports in total sales — at least if we restrict ourselves on the estimations without unobserved heterogeneity. The GPS methodology allows to test how the causal impact of exporting on profits varies along the range of the export–sales ratio from 0 to 1.

Thirdly, the continuous treatment approach allows us to analyze the level of the export intensity at which profitability is maximized (or minimized) or whether the relationship between the export–sales ratio and the rate of profit exhibits turning points or discontinuities (cf. Flores (2004)). A detailed description of the GPS methodology is presented in Fryges and Wagner (2009, Appendix A.1).

Using the GPS methodology, we do not compare export starters versus non-starters. Export starters that have entered the foreign market during the previous year generally show a very small export–sales ratio. Thus, restricting the analysis to export starters precludes a reliable estimation of the causal effect of medium-sized and large export–sales ratios on profitability. Our causal analysis in this section therefore includes export starters as well as firms that export for decades. We estimate the causal effect of the export–sales ratio measured in period $t$ on the rate of profit in $t+1$.[17] In this

---

[17]We do not estimate the contemporaneous effect of the export–sales ratio in $t$ on the rate of profit in $t$, because this raises the problem that wages per employee that are included in the fractional logit estimation of the export–sales ratio (see below) are endogenous since wages

way, the GPS method is an appropriate econometric technique that provides an analysis of the causal effect of exporting on profitability despite the fact that, due to data restrictions, we cannot follow cohorts of starters over the next years after foreign market entry.

Hirano and Imbens (2004) suggest a three-stage approach to implement the GPS method. In the first stage, the conditional distribution of the treatment variable given the covariates is estimated. In our case, the distribution of the treatment variable, i.e. the export–sales ratio, is highly skewed. In particular, it has many limit observations at the value 0, representing firms without any exports. The latter group of firms decided that their optimal volume of exports was zero. Following Wagner (2001, 2003), we apply the fractional logit model developed by Papke and Wooldridge (1996) to estimate the export intensity of the firms in our sample.[18] In the second stage of the GPS method, the conditional expectation of outcome (rate of profit in our case) is modeled as a function of the treatment and the (estimated) GPS. In the last stage, we estimate a dose-response function that depicts the conditional expectation of profitability given the continuous treatment (export–sales ratio) and the GPS, evaluated at any level of the continuous treatment variable in the interval from 0 to 1.

As stated above, we first estimate the conditional distribution of the export–sales ratio given the covariates, applying the fractional logit model. The exogenous covariates of the fractional logit model include firm size (measured as the log of number of employees and its squared value), the log of wages and salaries per employee, the log of the firms' lagged labor productivity (measured as sales per employee in $t-1$), the share of part-time employees,[19] and

are a component of our measure of profitability. This problem is solved when the lagged effect of the export–sales ratio on profitability is estimated.

[18]Hirano and Imbens (2004) use a normal distribution for (the logarithm of) the treatment variable of their model. However, they emphasize that more general models may be considered.

[19]The information on the number of employees is not stated in full-time equivalent units. This difference has to be considered while interpreting the coefficients of the log of number of employees, the average wage, and the labor productivity variable, because the values of these variables are underestimated in the case of enterprises with a high share of part-time

the share of purchased goods and services for resale on total turnover.[20] The average wage per employee is used to proxy differences in firms' human capital, because of the high level of interaction between user and provider, particularly in the service sector, employees must have good language skills and a high level of intercultural competence to establish and maintain certain contacts with the foreign market (*cf.* McLaughlin and Fitzsimmons (1996), Winstead and Patterson (1998)). Further, a firm with a highly qualified human capital is likely to generate intangible assets (e.g. a technologically superior product or customer-specific superior products) leading to a competitive advantage of the firm over its (international) rivals and enabling the firm to realize a high export intensity. In order to control whether using the average wage per employee is misleading, we employ available information on the proportion of employees who work part time.

The lagged labour productivity is included as a covariate in order to account for self-selection of more productive firms into the international market. While we did not find any evidence for a self-selection effect of more profitable firms (see Section 5), most studies in the literature about the manufacturing sector confirm the self-selection hypothesis of firms with higher labor productivity (*cf.* Wagner (2007) for a survey) and also for the German business services sector evidence for self-selection of more productive firms is found (*cf.* Vogel (2009a)).[21] Thus, firms with a higher labor productivity in $t-1$ are expected to generate a higher share of total

employed persons. To minimize this problem, the share of part-time employed persons is included in the estimation as a control variable.

[20]The share of turnover represented by goods and services that were purchased explicitly for resale in the same condition as received is included in our model to control for a possible effect of products and services that are not produced by the company itself on the export and export intensity decision. Unfortunately, we cannot distinguish between purchased goods for resale and purchased services for resale. Thus, we cannot directly control for the effect that a high export intensity might reflect a high share of purchased goods for resale (that might be easier to export than services). However, we use this control variable at least as a proxy for this effect and expect therefore a positive coefficient.

[21]Concerning the turnover per employed person Vogel (2009a) finds for West German business services enterprises significant differences between enterprises beginning to export and those that are not. Further, also positive pre-entry premia in terms of value added per employed person are found in the dataset, but these premia were not statistically significant.

sales abroad. The model was estimated for the export intensity in $t = 2004$, and the set of covariates finally contains 4-digit industry and legal status dummies, and an Eastern Germany dummy.

The results of the fractional logit model are presented in Table 6.[22] Firm size has a positive effect on the export–sales ratio; in the sectors research and development, architectural and engineering activities, and other business activities this effect, however, is not statistically significant. The negative sign of the squared value of the number of employees is insignificant in all of the considered industries. As hypothesized, firms with a higher average wage per employee have a higher export intensity, reflecting the importance of a firm's intangible assets by which it is able to create a competitive advantage over its international rivals. Except for architectural and engineering activities, this effect is significant in all business services industries. The lagged labor productivity is also positively correlated with the share of exports in total sales: firms that exhibited a higher labor productivity in the past are able to bear the additional costs of exporting and to extend their international business activities. It can also be argued that more productive firms have a competitive advantage when compared with their (foreign) counterparts. Thus, more productive firms are more likely to generate a higher share of total sales abroad. However, in the industries in computer and related activities, and research and development the positive coefficients are not significant at any conventional level.

The fractional logit model is estimated in order to calculate the GPS. As Imbens (2000) shows, adjusting for the GPS removes all the bias associated with differences in covariates between treated (exporting) and non-treated (non-exporting) firms. Thus, in the second stage of Hirano and Imbens' GPS methodology, the conditional expectation of the rate of profit in 2005 (outcome) is modeled as a function of the export intensity in 2004 (treatment) and the

[22]The sample we used to estimate the fractional logit model is restricted to those firms for which data on profitability in 2005 $(t + 1)$ and data on labor productivity in 2003 $(t - 1)$ is available in the data set. Due to the sampling frame of our data set, this reduces significantly the number of observations compared to Table 4.

Table 6. Determinants of the Export-Sales Ratio 2004 (Endogenous Variable) — Results of Fractional Logit Models

| | | All business services (NACE 72 to 74) | Computer and related activities (NACE 72) | Research and development (NACE 73) | Other business activities (NACE 74 without 74.1 and 74.2) | Business consultancy, market research, etc* (NACE 74.1) | Architectural and engineering activities (NACE 74.2) |
|---|---|---|---|---|---|---|---|
| Number of employees (log) | ß | 0.2896 | 0.2970 | 0.2554 | 0.0601 | 0.5194 | 0.3255 |
| | p-value | 0.001 | 0.073 | 0.348 | 0.713 | 0.007 | 0.307 |
| Number of employees (squared) (log) | ß | −0.0135 | −0.0094 | −0.0170 | 0.0076 | −0.0412 | −0.0052 |
| | p-value | 0.222 | 0.651 | 0.625 | 0.689 | 0.107 | 0.887 |
| Wage per employee (log) | ß | 0.3453 | 0.3895 | 0.5972 | 0.3697 | 0.3453 | −0.0531 |
| | p-value | 0.000 | 0.035 | 0.015 | 0.002 | 0.005 | 0.861 |
| Part-time workers (in percent) | ß | 0.0006 | 0.0080 | 0.0009 | −0.0031 | 0.0039 | −0.0100 |
| | p-value | 0.728 | 0.065 | 0.875 | 0.315 | 0.224 | 0.114 |
| Labour productivity (value added per employee) in t-1 (log) | ß | 0.3244 | 0.1407 | 0.1322 | 0.2417 | 0.4386 | 0.5475 |
| | p-value | 0.000 | 0.178 | 0.472 | 0.000 | 0.000 | 0.000 |
| Purchased goods and services for resale (in percent of turnover) | ß | 0.0002 | −0.0083 | −0.0038 | −0.0014 | 0.0011 | 0.0099 |
| | p-value | 0.920 | 0.017 | 0.665 | 0.607 | 0.760 | 0.014 |

| | | | | | | | |
|---|---|---|---|---|---|---|---|
| Constant | ß | −10.8828 | −8.8485 | −11.5688 | −9.4074 | −14.0707 | −10.2949 |
| | p-value | 0.000 | 0.000 | 0.000 | 0.000 | 0.000 | 0.002 |
| Eastern-Germany, Legal status, and 4-digit industry dummies | | included | included | included | included | included | included |
| Number of observations | | 16,520 | 2,735 | 465 | 6,195 | 5,111 | 2,014 |

*Note*: (*) NACE code 74.1 includes legal, accounting, book-keeping and auditing activities; tax consultancy; market research and public opinion polling; and business and management consultancy.
Only enterprises of the NACE division 72 to 74 with a turnover greater than € 250,000 are considered. The p-values are based on robust standard errors. The 1st and 99th percentiles of the rate of profit distribution are excluded from all computations.

estimated GPS. To approximate the predictor for the conditional expectation of the outcome, we use a polynomial function with a cubic term of the treatment variable and a cubic term of the estimated GPS. In the last stage of the GPS method, the average expected outcome at each export intensity (treatment level) in the interval from 0 to 1 is estimated, using the regression coefficients from the second stage of the GPS method. Thus, we obtain an estimate of the entire dose-response function that shows the average potential outcome at each dose of the treatment and how average responses vary along the interval from 0 to 1. The confidence intervals of the dose-response functions in this chapter are determined via bootstrapping.[23]

The dose-response function that represents the expected profitability conditional on the export–sales ratio and the GPS is depicted in Figure 1.

Due to the fact that only a small number of firms in the data set have an export intensity that is greater than 50 percent (see Table 2), we restrict our interpretation on the export intensity interval from 0 to 50 percent. The estimated dose-response function for all business services sectors (NACE 72–74) shows an s-shaped relationship between profitability in 2005 and firms' export–sales ratio in 2004. The maximum value of the rate of profit is reached at an export–sales ratio of 44 percent, where the expected value of the rate of profit amounts to 18.5 percent. Enterprises that do not export show an expected rate of profit of 17.7 percent. The same picture arises when looking at the more disaggregated industry level: In enterprises with a very small share of exports in total sales the rate of profit falls below the profitability level of non-exporting firms. Then, with increasing export intensity the rate of profit increases, too. However, even at the maximum the average profitability of the exporters is at most slightly higher than the average rate of

[23]Computations were done using Stata 10 and the Stata package for the estimation of dose-response functions (see Bia and Mattei (2008)) that was adjusted by the authors concerning the use of the fractional logit model in the first step of the GPS method.

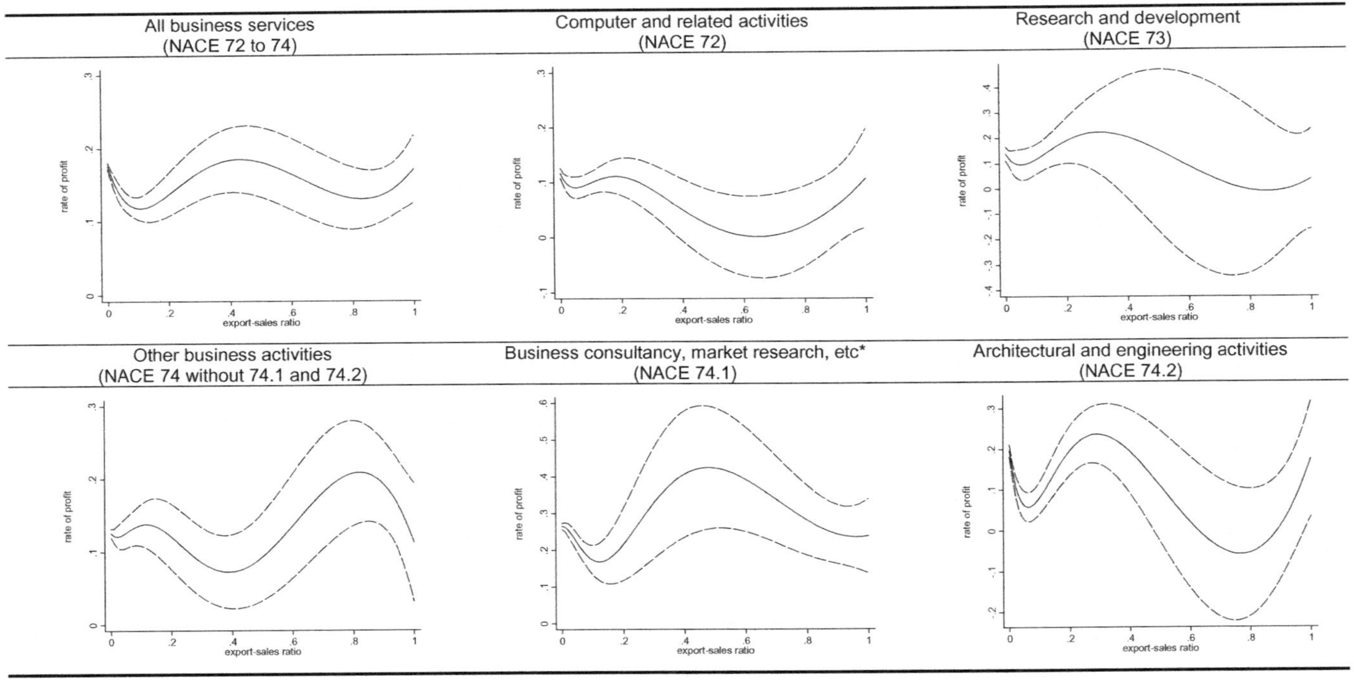


Fig. 1. Estimated Dose-Response Functions of the Treatment Export Intensity in 2004 on the Outcome Rate of Profit in 2005

*Note*: The solid lines indicate the estimated conditional expectation of enterprises' profits given the export intensity in t and the estimated generalised propensity score (GPS). The dotted lines indicate the simulated confidence bounds at 95% level (based on bootstrapping with 100 replications). Only enterprises of the NACE division 72 to 74 with a turnover greater than €250,000 are considered. The 1st and 99th percentiles of the rate of profit distribution are excluded from all computations. (*) NACE code 74.1 includes legal, accounting, book-keeping and auditing activities; tax consultancy; market research and public opinion polling; and business and management consultancy.

profit of the non-exporting firms.[24] Beyond the maximum, firms exhibit a decrease in profitability compared to firms with lower export intensities. This decrease might be a result of additional costs of exporting, for instance due to rising costs of coordination and control of a firm's export activities, or higher travel or transportation costs due to the increasing geographical distance of the foreign markets a firm has entered.

The results we obtained in this section are very similar to those described in Section 4. At least, the estimation results without fixed enterprise effects as reported in Models 1–4 of Table 3 show an s-shaped relationship between profitability and the export–sales ratio. Based on the estimated function for all business services industries on Model 4, the rate of profit reaches its maximum for an export–sales ratio of 78 percent, whereas, according to the estimated dose-response function the rate of profit reaches its maximum for an export intensity of 44 percent. According to the results of Section 4, even at the maximum, exporters have a lower predicted rate of profit than the average profitability level of non-exporters. By contrast, the analysis based on the estimated dose-response function shows a profitability level of exporters at the maximum that is slightly higher than the profitability level of non-exporters. However, due to the fact that this difference is smaller than 1 percentage point and that only a few firms in the business service sector have a export intensity that is higher than 40 percent, this difference is not economically relevant.

## 7. Conclusion

This chapter presents descriptive evidence and results from econometric investigations that suggest that — contrary to firms from manufacturing industries — German firms in business services

[24]Exceptions are the business consultancy, market research, sector etc. (NACE 74.1) and the research and development sector (NACE 73), where the profitability level of exporters at the maximum is 16 percentage points or 8 percentage points, respectively higher than the value of non-exporters. However, note that the bootstrapped confidence intervals are very large at the maximum of these two sectors.

industries do not benefit from exporting in terms of a higher rate of profit. Given that exporting firms are more productive than non-exporting firms in both manufacturing and services industries in Germany, the results suggest that in the services sector (but not in manufacturing) any cost advantage due to higher productivity might be "eaten up" by higher costs related to export activities, or by higher wages paid in exporting compared to non-exporting firms.

We document that the negative profitability differential of services exporters compared to non-exporters is very small when observed firm characteristics and unobserved firm specific effects are controlled for. Therefore, at least regarding profitability, exporting seems to be a business that is neither better nor worse than selling on the national market. This might seem to be a rather counterintuitive result at first sight, but in a more and more globalized world where firms compete in more and more markets, this is what one would expect, at least in open markets and in the long run. The estimated dose-response function shows an s-shaped relationship between profitability and firms' export–sales ratio. Enterprises with a very small share of exports in total sales have a lower rate of profit than non-exporting firms. Then, with an increase in export intensity the rate of profit increases, too. This might be interpreted as follows: If services firms that start to export do so by exporting a small share of their total sales only they will face a decline in their rate of profit due to extra costs caused by export activities. If the share of exports in total sales increases over time,[25] profits will rise up to the level earned on the national market — or the firms will leave the export market. Unfortunately, however, it is not possible to test whether this interpretation holds with the short panel of service firms available.

Given that Germany is one of the leading actors in the world market for both goods and services, the evidence provided here is interesting on its own. Furthermore, it can serve as a benchmark

[25] See Contractor (2007) for a discussion why firms increase its international activities over time.

for future studies using comparable data for firms from services industries in other countries.

## Acknowledgment

All computations were performed inside the Research Data Centre of the Statistical Office of Berlin/Brandenburg using Stata 10. To facilitate replication all do-files are available from the first author on request. Many thanks go to two anonymous referees and Alexander Eickelpasch for helpful comments as well as Ramona Voshage and Anja Malchin for running the dofiles in the Research Data Centre. Any remaining errors are our own.

## References

Bausch, A. and M. Krist (2007). The Effect of Context-Related Moderators on the Internationalization-Performance Relationship: Evidence from Meta-Analysis. *Management International Review* 47, 319–347.

Bernard, A. B., J. B. Jensen, Stephen J. Redding and Peter K. Schott (2007). Firms in International Trade. *Journal of Economic Perspectives* 21, 105–130.

Bia. M. and A. Mattei (2008). A Stata Package for the Estimation of the Dose-response Function through Adjustment for the Generalized Propensity Score. *The Stata Journal* 8, 354–373.

Bundesminsterium für Wirtschaft und Technologie (2009). Internationaler Dienstleistungshandel — Handelshemmnisse und Potenzial für Deutschland, Schlaglichter der Wirtschaftspolitik, Ausgabe 04-2009, 13–17.

Contractor, F. J. (2007). Is International Business Good for Companies? The Evolutionary or Multi-Stage Theory of Internationalization vs. the Transaction Cost Perspective. *Management International Review* 47, 453–475.

Deutsche Bundesbank (2009). Balance of Payments, www.bundesbank.de.

Eickelpasch, A. (2008). Export Orientation of Service Companies on the Increase. *DIW Weekly Report* 4, 28–35.

European Commission (1998). Commission Regulation (EC) No. 2700/98 Concerning the Definitions of Characteristics for Structural Business Statistics, Brussels. *Official Journal of the European Communities* L344, 49–80.

Flores, C. A. (2004). Estimation of Dose-Response Functions and Optimal Doses with a Continuous Treatment. Job Market Paper, University of California, Berkeley.

Fryges, H. (2008). The Export-Growth Relationship: Estimating a Dose-Response Function. *Applied Economics Letters*, forthcoming.

Fryges, H. and J. Wagner (2009). Exports and Profitability — First Evidence for German Manufacturing Firms. *The World Economy*, forthcoming.

Fryges, H. and J. Wagner (2008). Exports and Productivity Growth — First Evidence from a Continuous Treatment Approach. *Review of World Economics, Weltwirtschaftliches Archiv* 144, 695–722.

Hirano, K. and G. W. Imbens (2004). The Propensity Score with Continuous Treatments. In: Gelman. A. and X.-L. Meng (Eds.), *Applied Bayesian Modeling and Causal Inference from Incomplete-Data Perspectives*, Chichester: Wiley, pp. 73–84.

Imbens, G. W. (2000). The Role of the Propensity Score in Estimating Dose-Response Functions. *Biometrika* 87, 706–710.

Jensen, J. B. and L. G. Kletzer (2006). Tradable Services: Understanding the Scope and Impact of Services Offshoring. In: Brainard, L. and S. M. Collins (Eds.), *Offshoring White-Collar Work — Issues and Implications*, Brookings Trade Forum 2005, pp. 75–134.

Kox, H. and H. K. Nordås (2007). Services Trade and Domestic Regulations. OECD Trade Policy Working Paper, 49.

Mayer. T. and G. I. P. Ottaviano (2008). The Happy Few: The Internationalisation of European Firms. New Facts Based in Firm-level Evidence. *Intereconomics* 43, 135–148.

McLaughlin, C. P. and J. A. Fitzsimmons (1996). Strategies for Globalizing Service Operations. *International Journal of Service Industry Management* 7, 43–57.

Nichols, A. (2007). Causal inference with observational data. *The Stata Journal* 7, 507–541.

Papke, L. E. and J. M. Wooldridge (1996). Econometric Methods for Fractional Response Variables with an Application to 401(K) Plan Participation Rates. *Journal of Applied Econometrics* 11, 619–632.

Schank. T., C. Schnabel and J. Wagner (2007). Do Exporters Really Pay Higher Wages? First Evidence from German Linked Employer–Employee Data. *Journal of International Economics* 72, 52–74.

Schmalensee, R. (1989). Inter-Industry Studies of Structure and Performance. In: Schmalensee, R. and R. D. Willig (Eds.), *Handbook of Industrial Organization*, Vol. II, Amsterdam: North-Holland, pp. 951–1009.

The International Study Group on Exports and Productivity (2008). Understanding Cross-Country Differences in Exporter Premia — Comparable Evidence for 14 Countries. *Review of World Economics/Weltwirtschaftliches Archiv* 144, 596–635.

Vogel, A. (2009a). Exporter Performance in the German Business Services Sector. *The Service Industries Journal*, forthcoming.

Vogel, A. (2009b). The German Business Services Statistics Panel 2003–2007. *Schmollers Jahrbuch/Journal of Applied Social Science Studies* 129, 515–522.

Wagner, J. (2001). A Note on the Firm Size — Export Relationship. *Small Business Economics* 17, 229–237.

Wagner, J. (2003). Unobserved Firm Heterogeneity and the Size-Exports Nexus: Evidence from German Panel Data. *Review of World Economics* 139, 161–172.

Wagner, J. (2007). Exports and Productivity: A Survey of the Evidence from Firm Level Data. *The World Economy* 30, 60–82.
Winsted, K. F. and P. G. Patterson (1998). Internationalization of Services: The Service Exporting Decision. *Journal of Services Marketing* 12, 294–311.
WTO (1994). General Agreement on Trade in Services. In: *Agreement Establishing the World Trade Organization*, Annex 1B.
Zühlke, S., M. Zwick, S. Scharnhorst and T. Wende (2004). The Research Data Centres of the Federal Statistical Office and the Statistical Offices of the Länder. *Schmollers Jahrbuch/Journal of Applied Social Science Studies* 124, 567–578.

## Chapter 9

# Exports, Imports and Profitability: First Evidence for Manufacturing Enterprises

Joachim Wagner

**Abstract**

This paper documents for the first time the relationship between profitability and three types of international trade activities — exports, imports, and two-way trade. It uses unique new representative data for manufacturing enterprises from Germany, one of the leading actors in the world market for goods, that merge information from surveys performed by the Statistical Offices and administrative data collected by the Tax Authorities. Descriptive statistics and regression analysis (with and without controlling for unobserved firm heterogeneity and the role of outliers) point to the absence of any statistically significant and economically large effects of trade activities on profits. This demonstrates that any productivity advantages of trading firms are eaten up by extra costs related to selling and buying in foreign markets.

*Keywords*: Exports, imports, profitability

**JEL Classification:** F14

## 1. Motivation

A huge literature demonstrates that firms engaged in international trade as exporters or importers are more productive than otherwise identical firms that sell or buy in the national market only. For exporting firms, this stylized fact has been found in a large number of empirical studies based on the establishment or enterprise level data from countries all over the world that were published since the pioneering paper by Bernard and Jensen (1995).[1] While the positive correlation of engagement in exports and productivity is uncontroversial, the direction of causality is not. In a nutshell, the results from empirical investigations can be sketched as follows. Many studies report evidence in favor of the so-called self-selection hypothesis. Future export starters tend to be more productive than future non-exporters years before they enter the export market, and often have higher *ex-ante* growth rates of productivity. The good firms go abroad. Evidence regarding the so-called learning-by-exporting hypothesis is somewhat more mixed. Results for post-entry differences in performance between export starters and non-exporters point to faster productivity growth for the former group in some studies only. Exporting does not necessarily improve firms.

While the causes and consequences of export and its mutual relationships with productivity are prominent topics in the recent literature on internationally active firms, imports are seldom dealt with. With new datasets that include information on imports at the firm level becoming available for more and more countries, a new literature is emerging that has a focus on the links between productivity and imports. A number of recently published empirical studies (surveyed in Wagner (2011)) based on data from a wide range of countries document the shares of firms that are exporters, importers, and two-way traders (that both export and import), or that sell or buy on the national market only, and they look at differences between these four types of firms. Differences in productivity and their relationship with different degrees of involvement in international trade are at the centre of these studies. Details aside, the big picture that emerges from this literature can be sketched as follows. There is a positive link between importing and productivity at the firm level, documented by a significant productivity differential between firms that import and firms that do not trade internationally; the same holds for exporting. Two-way traders are more productive than firms that either only import,

[1]See Greenaway and Kneller (2007) and Wagner (2007, 2011) for surveys.

or only export, or do not trade at all. Often, two-way traders are the most productive group of firms, followed by importers and then exporters, while firms selling or buying in the national market come last. We have evidence for self-selection of more productive firms into exporting from most of the studies that look at this issue; the evidence on learning-by-importing, however, is still rare and inconclusive.

That said, from the microeconometric literature on trade and productivity, two conclusions emerge than can be regarded as uncontroversial:

— Exporters and importers are more productive than firms that do not trade internationally.
— Firms engaged in international trade have to bear extra costs. Exporting firms have to pay for, among others, market research in foreign countries, adaptation of products to local regulations there, or transport costs. Furthermore, exporting firms tend to pay higher wages than non-exporting firms (see Schank, Schnabel and Wagner (2007, 2010)). Importing is associated with fixed costs that are sunk costs, because the import agreement is preceded by a search process for potential foreign suppliers, inspection of goods, negotiation, contract formulation, etc. Furthermore, there are sunk costs of importing due to the learning and acquisition of customs procedures. These extra costs are the reason for self-selection of more productive firms in international markets — only firms with a productivity that is high enough can be profitable when extra costs have to be covered.

A question that has been investigated in the literature on the microeconometrics of international trade only recently is whether the productivity advantage of exporting and importing firms does lead to a profitability advantage of firms that engage in international trade compared to otherwise identical non-trading firms even when exporters and importers are facing extra costs. This apparent gap in the literature on the microeconometrics of international trade comes as a surprise because maximization of profits (and not of productivity) is usually considered as a central goal for firms. Furthermore, looking at profitability instead of productivity is more appropriate from a theoretical point of view, too. Even if productivity and profitability are positively correlated (which tends to be the case), productivity is, as was recently pointed out by Foster, Haltiwanger and Syverson (2008, p. 395), only one of several possible idiosyncratic factors that determines profits. Success of firms in general, and especially survival, depends on profitability. Often profitability is viewed both in theoretical models of market selection and in empirical studies on firm entry and exit as a positive monotonic function of productivity, and selection on profits then is equivalent to selection on productivity. In empirical studies, the use of productivity instead of profitability is usually due to the fact that productivity is easily observed in the data sets at hand, while profitability is not. Fortunately, there are data sets that are rich enough to allow to measure profitability. Table 1 summarizes the findings from recent studies on trade and profits.

The number of studies on trade and profits is still small and the number of countries covered (all of which are member states of the EU) is even smaller. Results differ widely across the studies — from positive to no to negative profitability differences between exporters and non-exporters; from evidence for self-selection of more or less profitable firms into exporting to no evidence for self-selection at all; from no positive effects of exports on profits to positive effects. Remarkably, none of the studies listed in Table 1 looks at imports and profitability.

This chapter contributes to the literature by documenting for the first time the relationship between profitability and three types of international trade activities — exports, imports and two-way trade — for manufacturing enterprises. It uses a unique new representative data set from Germany, one of the leading actors in the world market for goods. The data were constructed by merging information from surveys performed by the Statistical Offices and administrative data collected by the Tax Authorities. To anticipate the most important results, descriptive statistics and regression analysis (with and without controlling for unobserved

Table 1. Micro-econometric studies on international trade and profits

| Country Author(s) (year of publication) | Period covered | Topics investigated | Methods used | Important findings |
|---|---|---|---|---|
| France Temouri, Vogel and Wagner (2011) | 2003–2007 | Exports and profitability in business services enterprises | Descriptive analysis; regression analysis; propensity score matching | Services exporters are more profitable than non-exporters. No evidence for self-selection of more profitable firms into exporting. No evidence for positive effects of exports on profitability. |
| Germany Fryges and Wagner (2010) | 1999–2004 | Exports and profitability in manufacturing enterprises | Descriptive analysis; regression analysis; generalized propensity score methodology | Exporters are more profitable than non-exporters, but difference is small; rate of profit tends to increase with export–sales ratio. No evidence for self-selection of more profitable firms into exports. Positive causal effect of exporting on profitability almost over the whole domain of the export–sales ratio. |
| Germany Vogel and Wagner (2010b) | 2003–2005 | Exports and profitability in business services enterprises | Descriptive analysis; regression analysis; generalized propensity score methodology | Services exporters are less profitable compared to non-exporters, though difference is small. Evidence for self-selection of less profitable services firms into exports. No positive causal effect of exports on profits. |

(*Continued*)

Table 1. (*Continued*)

| Country Author(s) (year of publication) | Period covered | Topics investigated | Methods used | Important findings |
|---|---|---|---|---|
| Germany Temouri, Vogel and Wagner (2011) | 2003–2007 | Exports and profitability in business services enterprises | Descriptive analysis; regression analysis; propensity score matching | Services exporters less profitable than non-exporters. Self-selection of less profitable firms into exports. No evidence for positive effects of exporting on profits. |
| Italy Amendolagine, Capolupo and Petragallo (2008) | 1995–2003 | Exports and performance in manufacturing firms | Regression analysis; propensity score matching | Profitability difference between exporters and non-exporters not reported. No evidence for self-selection of more profitable firms into exporting. Evidence for positive effects of exports on profits. |
| Italy Grazzi (2009) | 1989–2004 | Trade and profitability | Descriptive analysis; non-parametric comparison of distributions; regression analysis | No evidence for profitability differential between exporters and non-exporters over all; positive relation for some sectors, negative for others. |
| Netherlands Kox and Rojas-Romagosa (2010) | 1997–2005 | Exports and performance of manufacturing and services firms | Descriptive analysis; OLS and probit regression | Profitability higher in exporting firms. Evidence for self-selection of more profitable firms into exporting. No positive effects of exporting on profitability. |
| United Kingdom Temouri, Vogel and Wagner (2011) | 2003–2007 | Exports and profitability in business services enterprises | Descriptive analysis; regression analysis; propensity score matching | Services exporters do not differ in profitability compared to non-exporters. No evidence for self-selection of more profitable firms into exports. No evidence for positive effects of exporting on profits. |

firm heterogeneity and the role of outliers) point to the absence of any statistically significant and economically large effects of trade activities on profits. This demonstrates that the productivity advantages of trading firms are eaten up by extra costs related to selling and buying on foreign markets.

The rest of the chapter is organized as follows. Section 2 describes the new data set. Section 3 presents descriptive results. Section 4 reports OLS estimates for trader productivity premia based on pooled data and models with and without fixed enterprise effects. Section 5 controls for outliers in robust estimations with and without fixed effects. Section 6 concludes.

## 2. Data

The scarcity of comprehensive microeconometric studies on the links between profitability and trade activities is due to the fact that information on profits, exports, and imports (plus other firm characteristics that are needed as control variables like firm size and industry) are only rarely found in a single data set. Germany is a case in point. While readily available enterprise level data allow empirical investigations of the relation between exports and profitability (see Fryges and Wagner (2010), Vogel and Wagner (2010b)) and of the links between exports, imports, and productivity (see Vogel and Wagner (2010a)), none of these data sets contains information on both types of trade (exports and imports) and on profitability.

For this study, a tailor-made enterprise level data set was built that uses information from surveys performed by the Statistical Offices and from data collected by the Tax Authorities. The first source of data is the monthly report for establishments in manufacturing industries described in Konold (2007). This survey covers all establishments from manufacturing industries that employ at least 20 persons in the local production unit or in the company that owns the unit. Participation of firms in the survey is mandated in official statistics law. This survey is the source for information on the location of the firm in West Germany or East Germany, the industry affiliation, the export activity, and the number of employees (used to measure firm size). In this data set, export refers to the amount of sales to a customer in a foreign country plus sales to a German export trading company; indirect exports (for example, tyres produced in a plant in Germany that are delivered to a German manufacturer of cars who exports some of his products) are not covered by this definition. For this project, the information collected at the establishment level has been aggregated at the enterprise level to match the unit of observation from the second and third source of data used here.

The second source of data is the cost structure survey for enterprises in the manufacturing sector. This survey is carried out annually as a representative random sample survey stratified according to the number of employees and the industries (see Fritsch *et al.* (2004)). The sample covered by the cost structure survey represents a large part of all enterprises with at least 20 employees from manufacturing industries. About 45 percent of the enterprises with 20–499 employees and all enterprises with 500 and more employees are included in the sample.[2] While firms with 500 and more employees are covered by the cost structure survey in each year, the sample of smaller firms is part of the survey for four years in a row only. This survey is the source for information on profitability.

The third source of data is the German Turnover Tax Statistics Panel (described in detail in Vogel *et al.* 2008). This data set is based on the yearly turnover tax; all enterprises with a turnover that exceeds a rather low threshold (17,500 € since 2003) are covered in the data. This data set is the source of information about import activities of firms. Note, however, that imports are not directly recorded therein completely. Imports from EU member states are reported under the item of 'intra-community acquisitions'. The amount of imports from states beyond the EU is not included in

[2]For details, see the quality report for the cost structure survey published by the Federal Statistical Office that is available on the web: http://www.destatis.de/jetspeed/portal/cms/Sites/destatis/Internet/DE/Content/Publikationen/Qualitaetsberichte/VerarbeitendesGewerbeIndustrie/Kostenstruktur,property=file.pdf.

the turnover tax statistics. In this case, an import turnover tax is charged by the customs authorities. Nonetheless, this import turnover tax is deductible as input tax and therefore reported in the dataset. With this information, a dummy variable which shows whether the enterprise imports from non-EU states or not can be generated (taking the value 1 if the import turnover tax is greater than 0, and 0 if no import turnover tax is deducted as input tax).

The data from the three sources were linked by using the enterprise register system (*Unternehmensregistersystem*) that includes, among others, information on the unique enterprise identifier used in surveys conducted by the Statistical Offices and the unique turnover tax identifier used by the Tax Authorities. Data from the turnover tax statistics that are used to identify enterprises with imports are available for the years 2001–2007 (as of June 2011). Data from the cost structure survey that are used to compute turnover profitability are available for one sample of enterprises from 1999 to 2002 and for a different sample for 2003–2006. Data based on the monthly report of manufacturing establishments that are used to identify enterprises with exports (and for information on firm size and industry affiliation) are available for 1995–2008 (as of June 2011). The sample of enterprises used in the empirical investigation performed here consists of all enterprises for which information from all three surveys for the years 2003–2006 could be linked via the enterprise register system. Enterprises that do not have complete information for each year were dropped from the computations.[3]

[3]The merging of the data sets was done inside the research data center of the Statistical Office in Berlin-Brandenburg by Julia Höninger. Firms with incomplete information for any variable in at least one year were dropped from all computations because there are, on the one hand, by construction no entries due to the fact that the firms taking part in the cost structure survey were sampled before the start of the survey in 2003. On the other hand, exits cannot be identified because firms with information in, say, 2003 but not in 2004 might have closed down — they might have, however, relocated out of manufacturing (or out of Germany) or they might have shrunk below the cut-off point relevant for the monthly report or the cost-structure survey. Looking at the data from an unbalanced panel, however, is an appropriate robustness check. All calculations were repeated with the unbalanced panel. The big picture remains the same — trade activities do not have a positive and statistically significant effect

## 3. Descriptive Results

Based on the combined data from the three sources described in Section 2, it is possible to distinguish between four types of enterprises, namely, enterprises without trade, enterprises that only export, enterprises that only import and enterprises that both export and import. Table 2 reports the shares of these four types of enterprises in the samples for each year between 2003 and 2006 for West Germany and East Germany.[4] In West Germany, more than three in four enterprises are two-way traders, while the share of firms not engaged in trade at all is small and declines from 8.6 percent in 2003 to 7.2 percent in 2006. The share of firms that only export is about 4 percent and the share of firms that only import is about 12 percent. In East Germany, the share of two-way traders is smaller than in West Germany (around 60 percent). The share of firms that only import is about twice as high in East Germany as in West Germany, while the share of firms that only export is about the same. Note that the share of firms without any trade is much larger in East compared to West Germany.

The high share of internationally active firms in both parts of Germany may come as a surprise. Note, however, that the average number of employees in a firm tends to increase from no traders to only exporters to only importers to two-way traders (which is, however, not the case in East Germany when non-trading firms are compared to firms that only export) and that by construction the largest firms are oversampled in the data set used here because the cost structure survey includes all enterprises with at least 500 employees but only a stratified random sample of smaller firms.[5]

---

on profitability. Detailed results are not reported in the paper to economize on space, but are available on request.

[4]The West German and the East German economies still differ largely even many years after the unification in 1990, and this is especially true for international trade (see Wagner (2008a) for an analysis). Therefore, all empirical investigations are carried out separately for both parts of Germany here.

[5]For a comprehensive documentation of participation in trade in manufacturing firms from West and East Germany between 2001 and 2006 by size class, see Vogel *et al.* (2009).

Table 2. Profitability and participation in international trade — descriptive evidence for German manufacturing enterprises.

| | | No trade | | Only exports | | Only imports | | Exports and imports | |
|---|---|---|---|---|---|---|---|---|---|
| **West Germany** | | | | | | | | | |
| 2003 | Number of firms (percentage share) | 548 | (8.6 percent) | 271 | (4.2 percent) | 728 | (11.4 percent) | 4,859 | (75.9 percent) |
| | Average number of employees | 70.9 | | 80.0 | | 152.6 | | 396.0 | |
| | Rate of profit (percentage): mean | 8.64 | | 8.78 | | 8.94 | | 7.74 | |
| | Rate of profit (percentage): median | 8.52 | | 8.44 | | 7.94 | | 7.35 | |
| | Rate of profit: standard deviation | 10.92 | | 10.00 | | 8.37 | | 9.03 | |
| 2004 | Number of firms (percentage share) | 522 | (8.1 percent) | 242 | (3.8 percent) | 740 | (11.6 percent) | 4,902 | (76.5 percent) |
| | Average number of employees | 68.1 | | 72.2 | | 139.1 | | 391.6 | |
| | Rate of profit (percentage): mean | 9.54 | | 9.21 | | 8.77 | | 8.35 | |
| | Rate of profit (percentage): median | 9.35 | | 9.15 | | 7.92 | | 7.73 | |
| | Rate of profit: standard deviation | 9.42 | | 10.60 | | 9.11 | | 8.93 | |
| 2005 | Number of firms (percentage share) | 491 | (7.7 percent) | 240 | (3.7 percent) | 756 | (11.8 percent) | 4,919 | (76.8 percent) |
| | Average number of employees | 60.8 | | 77.3 | | 143.0 | | 385.9 | |
| | Rate of profit (percentage): mean | 8.98 | | 9.02 | | 8.90 | | 8.14 | |
| | Rate of profit (percentage): median | 8.86 | | 8.45 | | 8.35 | | 7.60 | |
| | Rate of profit: standard deviation | 9.82 | | 10.10 | | 9.89 | | 9.21 | |
| 2006 | Number of firms (percentage share) | 466 | (7.2 percent) | 231 | (3.6 percent) | 744 | (11.6 percent) | 4,965 | (77.5 percent) |
| | Average number of employees | 63.8 | | 74.8 | | 136.6 | | 383.4 | |
| | Rate of profit (percentage): mean | 9.53 | | 10.04 | | 8.87 | | 8.73 | |
| | Rate of profit (percentage): median | 9.53 | | 9.77 | | 8.12 | | 8.20 | |
| | Rate of profit: standard deviation | 10.28 | | 10.42 | | 9.74 | | 8.73 | |

*(Continued)*

Table 2. (*Continued*)

| | | No trade | | Only exports | | Only imports | | Exports and imports | |
|---|---|---|---|---|---|---|---|---|---|
| **East Germany** | | | | | | | | | |
| 2003 | Number of firms (percentage share) | 155 | (13.3 percent) | 60 | (5.2 percent) | 264 | (22.7 percent) | 683 | (58.8 percent) |
| | Average number of employees | 65.0 | | 56.9 | | 125.2 | | 179.2 | |
| | Rate of profit (percentage): mean | 10.70 | | 8.05 | | 10.51 | | 9.04 | |
| | Rate of profit (percentage): median | 10.03 | | 8.88 | | 8.98 | | 8.78 | |
| | Rate of profit: standard deviation | 10.20 | | 9.37 | | 9.55 | | 12.03 | |
| 2004 | Number of firms (percentage share) | 142 | (12.2 percent) | 57 | (4.9 percent) | 272 | (23.4 percent) | 691 | (59.5 percent) |
| | Average number of employees | 59.2 | | 56.6 | | 126.1 | | 178.7 | |
| | Rate of profit (percentage): mean | 10.41 | | 9.73 | | 10.62 | | 8.78 | |
| | Rate of profit (percentage): median | 9.36 | | 9.53 | | 9.42 | | 8.80 | |
| | Rate of profit: standard deviation | 9.87 | | 13.66 | | 10.69 | | 11.83 | |
| 2005 | Number of firms (percentage share) | 149 | (12.8 percent) | 55 | (4.7 percent) | 250 | (21.5 percent) | 708 | (60.9 percent) |
| | Average number of employees | 59.9 | | 57.8 | | 125.7 | | 174.5 | |
| | Rate of profit (percentage): mean | 10.59 | | 8.86 | | 9.98 | | 9.21 | |
| | Rate of profit (percentage): median | 9.23 | | 9.32 | | 8.41 | | 8.93 | |
| | Rate of profit: standard deviation | 10.35 | | 12.39 | | 9.62 | | 10.57 | |
| 2006 | Number of firms (percentage share) | 147 | (12.7 percent) | 48 | (4.1 percent) | 246 | (22.7 percent) | 721 | (62.0 percent) |
| | Average number of employees | 61.2 | | 61.3 | | 115.6 | | 176.2 | |
| | Rate of profit (percentage): mean | 10.41 | | 10.23 | | 9.75 | | 9.51 | |
| | Rate of profit (percentage): median | 9.55 | | 7.24 | | 8.28 | | 9.06 | |
| | Rate of profit: standard deviation | 8.71 | | 8.90 | | 9.26 | | 9.29 | |

The rate of profit of a firm is computed as a rate of return, defined as gross firm surplus (computed in line with the definition of the European Commission (1998) as gross value added at factor costs minus gross wages and salaries minus costs for social insurance paid by the firm) divided by total sales (net of VAT) minus net change of inventories:[6]

$$\text{rate of profit} = \frac{\text{gross value added} - \text{gross wages} \\ - \text{costs for social insurance}}{\text{total sales} - \text{net change of inventories}}. \quad (1)$$

This profit measure is a measure for the price-cost margin which, under competitive conditions, should on average equal the required rental on assets employed per money unit of sales (see Schmalensee (1989, p. 960f.)). Differences in profitability between firms, therefore, can follow from productivity differences, but also from different mark-ups of prices over costs and from differences in the capital intensity.[7] That said, a first look at the mean and the median values of the rate of profit for the different categories of firms in West Germany does not reveal a pattern that is consistent over the years. If anything, two-way traders tend to have the smallest values for the rate of profit. For East Germany, the pattern is even less obvious.

Results for a *t*-test for statistical significance of the difference in means between pairs of groups of firms are reported in Table 3. At a usual error level of 5 percent, the null-hypothesis of no difference cannot be rejected in all years for any pair of firms in West or East Germany; *p*-values of 0.050 or smaller are only found for four out of 24 tests in West Germany and for two out of 24 tests in East Germany. This indicates that the average rate of profit tends to be rather similar between the four groups of firms with different forms of international activities.

[6]Note that the data set does not have any information on the capital stock, or the sum of assets or equity, of the firm, so that it is not possible to construct profit indicators based thereon like return on assets or return on equity.

[7]Given that the data set does not have information on the capital stock employed by the firms in the econometric investigations in the following sections, differences in the capital intensity are controlled for by including industry dummy variables or enterprise fixed effects.

Table 3. Profitability difference between German manufacturing enterprises with different forms of participation in international trade

| | | No trade vs. only exports | No trade vs. only imports | No trade vs. exports and imports | Only exports vs. only imports | Only exports vs. exports and imports | Only imports vs. exports and imports |
|---|---|---|---|---|---|---|---|
| **West Germany** | | | | | | | |
| 2003 | $t$-test ($p$-value)[1] | 0.852 | 0.598 | 0.064 | 0.823 | 0.095 | 0.000 |
| | $K$–$S$-test ($p$-values)[2] | 0.252 | 0.218 | 0.001 | 0.900 | 0.165 | 0.012 |
| | | 0.625 | 0.109 | 0.761 | 0.537 | 0.990 | 0.996 |
| | | 0.135 | 0.222 | 0.001 | 0.726 | 0.083 | 0.006 |
| 2004 | $t$-test ($p$-value)[1] | 0.679 | 0.150 | 0.006 | 0.567 | 0.220 | 0.245 |
| | $K$–$S$-test ($p$-values)[2] | 0.859 | 0.019 | 0.000 | 0.136 | 0.027 | 0.694 |
| | | 0.531 | 0.397 | 0.805 | 0.245 | 0.361 | 0.986 |
| | | 0.501 | 0.009 | 0.000 | 0.073 | 0.014 | 0.365 |
| 2005 | $t$-test ($p$-value)[1] | 0.951 | 0.890 | 0.072 | 0.864 | 0.186 | 0.049 |
| | $K$–$S$-test ($p$-values)[2] | 0.636 | 0.534 | 0.010 | 0.816 | 0.152 | 0.095 |
| | | 0.792 | 0.370 | 0.767 | 0.464 | 0.786 | 0.960 |
| | | 0.346 | 0.272 | 0.005 | 0.490 | 0.076 | 0.047 |
| 2006 | $t$-test ($p$-value)[1] | 0.540 | 0.271 | 0.056 | 0.132 | 0.038 | 0.452 |
| | $K$–$S$-test ($p$-values)[2] | 0.844 | 0.088 | 0.004 | 0.148 | 0.031 | 0.119 |
| | | 0.489 | 0.831 | 0.756 | 0.874 | 0.775 | 0.662 |
| | | 0.680 | 0.044 | 0.002 | 0.080 | 0.016 | 0.060 |

| | | | | | | | |
|---|---|---|---|---|---|---|---|
| **East Germany** | | | | | | | |
| 2003 | *t*-test (*p*-value)[1] | 0.073 | 0.849 | 0.079 | 0.071 | 0.446 | 0.050 |
| | *K–S*-test (*p*-values)[2] | 0.302 | 0.192 | 0.201 | 0.320 | 0.801 | 0.405 |
| | | 0.591 | 0.105 | 0.108 | 0.179 | 0.462 | 0.989 |
| | | 0.170 | 0.402 | 0.136 | 0.930 | 0.800 | 0.215 |
| 2004 | *t*-test (*p*-value)[1] | 0.735 | 0.839 | 0.086 | 0.645 | 0.612 | 0.020 |
| | *K–S*-test (*p*-values)[2] | 0.955 | 0.893 | 0.108 | 0.654 | 0.389 | 0.016 |
| | | 0.626 | 0.547 | 0.618 | 0.367 | 0.643 | 0.895 |
| | | 0.753 | 0.539 | 0.059 | 0.703 | 0.213 | 0.009 |
| 2005 | *t*-test (*p*-value)[1] | 0.359 | 0.562 | 0.142 | 0.531 | 0.840 | 0.289 |
| | *K–S*-test (*p*-values)[2] | 0.498 | 0.886 | 0.221 | 0.851 | 0.531 | 0.421 |
| | | 0.909 | 0.889 | 0.880 | 0.506 | 0.292 | 0.313 |
| | | 0.280 | 0.532 | 0.119 | 0.630 | 0.772 | 0.224 |
| 2006 | *t*-test (*p*-value)[1] | 0.903 | 0.475 | 0.261 | 0.733 | 0.592 | 0.733 |
| | *K–S*-test (*p*-values)[2] | 0.350 | 0.508 | 0.526 | 0.837 | 0.424 | 0.588 |
| | | 0.721 | 0.814 | 0.843 | 0.496 | 0.234 | 0.316 |
| | | 0.200 | 0.277 | 0.283 | 0.541 | 0.500 | 0.446 |

[1]The t-Test is a test for difference in mean values of profitability (no equal variances for both groups of firms is assumed); a *p*-value of 0.050 (or smaller) indicates that the null-hypothesis that the difference is zero can be rejected at an error level of 5 percent (or smaller).

[2]The K-S-Test is the Kolmogorov–Smirnov test for equality of distributions of profitability. The first *p*-value reported is for a test of the null-hypothesis that the two distributions are equal; a *p*-value of 0.050 (or smaller) indicates that the null-hypothesis that the two distributions are equal can be rejected at an error level of 5 percent (or smaller). The second and the third *p*-value are for tests of first-order stochastic dominance of one profitability distribution over the other. If the second *p*-value is (smaller than) 0.050 there is evidence (at an error level of 5 percent or less) for dominance of the profitability distribution of the second group of firms over the first, and vice versa in case of the third *p*-value.

A test for differences in the mean values, however, can only be a first step in a comparison of these groups of firms. As Moshe Buchinsky (1994, p. 453) put it: "'On the average' has never been a satisfactory statement with which to conclude a study on heterogeneous populations." An empirical study of heterogeneous firms should look at differences in the whole distribution of the variables under investigation between groups of firms, not only at differences at the mean. The hypothesis that the distribution of profits for one group of firms stochastically dominates the respective distribution of the comparison group can be tested by the Kolmogorov–Smirnov test. This non-parametric test for first order stochastic dominance of one distribution over another was introduced into the literature on the microeconometrics of international firm activities by Delgado, Farinas and Ruano (2002). Let $F$ and $G$ denote the cumulative distribution functions of a variable for two groups of firms, firms that do not trade and firms that only export. First order stochastic dominance of $F$ relative to $G$ is given if $F(z) - G(z)$ is less or equal zero for all $z$ with strict inequality for some $z$. Given two independent random samples of firms from each group, the hypothesis that $F$ is to the right of $G$ can be tested by the Kolmogorov–Smirnov test based on the empirical distribution functions for $F$ and $G$ in the samples (for details, see Conover (1999, p. 456ff.)).

The results for the Kolmogorov–Smirnov test are reported in Table 3. Using an error level of 5 percent, the test indicates that in East Germany the distributions of profit rates do not differ between the four types of firms with the exception of firms that only import compared to firms that export and import in one year, 2004 (where the results points to a difference in distributions that is in favor of the firms that only import). The big picture in West Germany is only slightly different. The Kolmogorov–Smirnov tests point to differences in the distributions of the profit rate at an error level of 5 percent or lower in 8 out of 24 cases. However, only when firms that do not trade at all are compared to two-way traders, results are the same for all four years and always in favor of the firms that do not trade at all. However, even if these differences are significant statistically they are rather small from an economic point of view (on average, the difference is less than 1 percentage point over the years).

The bottom line from the descriptive evidence presented in this section, then, is that the rate of profit does not vary systematically with the way a firm is engaged in international trade. This picture is very much different from the results reported by Vogel and Wagner (2010a) for a comparison of productivity (and not profitability) between groups of firms with different degrees of involvement in international trade. They find that compared to firms that do not trade at all two-way traders do have the highest productivity premium, followed by firms that only export, while firms that only import have the smallest premium. However, up to now only raw profitability differentials have been looked at without controlling for industry specific shocks or macroeconomic shocks that differ between years. Furthermore, neither effects due to differences in firm size nor other influences that might be important for profitability besides international trade have been controlled for. This is done in the econometric analyses in the next two sections.

## 4. Trader Profitability Premia

After a first look at descriptive statistics and tests for the statistical significance of differences in the rate of profit and its distribution between firms with different forms of engagement in international trade, the next step of the empirical investigation of the links between profitability and trade is the estimation of the so-called trader profitability premia. These premia are the difference in profitability between firms that do not trade and firms from each of the three types of traders (only exporters, only importers and two-way traders) after controlling for other firm characteristics and factors that might influence profitability. While the data at hand are not rich enough to estimate an empirical model for profitability, the approach used here follows the standard approach in the microeconometrics of international firm activities (described in detail in Wagner (2007)) and estimates the premia with a regression that controls for firm size (measured by the number of employees and

Table 4. Estimation results for trader profitability premia

| Variable | | West Germany | | East Germany | |
|---|---|---|---|---|---|
| | | Pooled OLS | Fixed effects | Pooled OLS | Fixed effects |
| Only exports (Dummy; 1 = yes) | ß | 0.300 | −1.166 | −1.736 | −0.807 |
| | *p* | 0.608 | 0.068 | 0.163 | 0.591 |
| Only imports (Dummy; 1 = yes) | ß | −0.167 | −0.064 | −0.057 | −0.788 |
| | *p* | 0.688 | 0.133 | 0.940 | 0.280 |
| Exports and imports (Dummy; 1 = yes) | ß | −0.700 | −0.962 | −1.471 | −0.302 |
| | *p* | 0.074 | 0.081 | 0.047 | 0.775 |
| Number of employees | ß | −0.00030 | −0.00048 | 0.0028 | 0.0042 |
| | *p* | 0.000 | 0.412 | 0.063 | 0.206 |
| Number of employees (squared) | ß | 2.11e-9 | 1.88e-9 | −4.10e-7 | −4.82e-7 |
| | *p* | 0.003 | 0.453 | 0.057 | 0.144 |
| Year dummy variables | | included | included | included | included |
| 2-digit industry dummies | | included | not included | included | not included |
| Number of observations | | 25,624 | 25,624 | 4,648 | 4,648 |

*Note*: Standard errors for the pooled model are estimated using the firm as a cluster; standard errors for the fixed effects model are robust against heteroskedasticity and within-panel serial correlation in the idiosyncratic error term.

its squared value to take care of a nonlinear relation) and industry affiliation (to control for industry specific shocks on the demand or supply side and to proxy differences in the unobserved capital intensity between industries). The empirical model is estimated using pooled data for the years 2003–2006, and year dummy variables are included to control for macroeconomic shocks and business cycle conditions.

In a first step, this model is estimated by OLS. Results are reported in columns one and three of Table 4 for West Germany and East Germany, respectively. For West Germany, the point estimates of the trader profitability premia are tiny (below 1 percentage point) and never statistically significant at a conventional error level of 5 percent. For East Germany, only the estimated premium for the two-way traders is statistically significantly different from zero at an error level of 5 percent. This premium is negative, pointing to a profitability disadvantage of two-way traders compared to firms that do not trade, and having a value of −1.5 percentage points it is relevant from an economic point of view.[8]

These results for the trader premia computed by OLS, however, are only conditional on observed firm characteristics included in the empirical model. They cannot deal with the role of unobserved (and sometimes unobservable) characteristics — like a unique product, or superior quality of the management of a firm — that might be correlated with the observed characteristics. Here, one might expect that selling and buying on international markets is related to the quality of the products of a firm, the international orientation of the management and other firm specific characteristics that are not included in the empirical model. If this is the case, the estimated values for the trader premia are biased. The workhorse in empirical studies faced with this problem is an empirical model that includes fixed effects to control for time invariant unobserved firm characteristics that might be correlated with the variables in that empirical model.

In a second step, therefore, the empirical model is estimated with fixed enterprise effects. Results are reported in columns two and four of Table 4. Compared to the results from the OLS estimates without fixed firm effects, the big picture is the same for West Germany. For East Germany, controlling for unobserved firm heterogeneity leads to an estimated two-way trader premium that is no longer statistically significantly different from zero (and a point estimate that is much smaller). The bottom line so far, then, is that results point to the absence of any statistically significant and economically large effects of trade activities on profits.

One crucial problem in any application of the fixed effects strategy is that in the estimation of the coefficients only the within variation of variables over time is used. Therefore, in the empirical model for the estimation of trader premia with fixed firm effects, the

[8]As a robustness check the same models were estimated with industry dummies at the 4 digit-level instead of the 2 digit-level. The conclusions remain unchanged; details are available from the author on request.

coefficients for the premia are only identified by information from firms that changed their trader status at least once between 2003 and 2006. In our sample, this is the case for 821 (or 12.8 percent of all firms) in West Germany and 275 (or 23.7 percent of all firms) in East Germany.[9] These status switchers that start or stop to export or import do differ from firms that continue (not) to export or import.[10] This means that in the empirical model with fixed firm effects, the trader premia are estimated using a sample of firms that is different from the population of firms (or a representative random sample of this population). Given that here the conclusions from the empirical model with and without firm fixed effects with regard to significance, sign and size of the trader premia do not differ much, however, this is not a cause for concern.

## 5. Robust Estimates of Trader Profitability Premia

If one investigates a sample of heterogeneous firms, it often happens that some variables for some firms are far away from the other observations in the sample. For example, in the sample of firms that is analyzed here the value of the rate of profit is −17.8 percent at the 1st percentile, 8.5 percent at the median, and 33.9 percent at the 99th percentile for the firms not trading internationally in West Germany in 2003. The corresponding values for the other groups of firms in the other years are similar. The smallest and largest values of the rate of profit are even further away from the values of the bulk of enterprises — due to confidentiality of the firm level data, however, these extreme values cannot be reported. These extreme values might be the result of reporting errors (and, therefore, wrong), or due to idiosyncratic events (think of the bankruptcy of a customers that causes a large loss in one year), or due to firm behavior that is vastly different from the

[9]In West Germany, 331 firms did not trade in all four years, 108 exported only, 494 imported only and 4,642 firms exported and imported in each year. The respective numbers of firms in East Germany are 91, 19, 160, and 617, respectively.

[10]See Wagner (2008b) for evidence on this for export starters and export stoppers in Germany.

behavior of the majority of firms in the sample. Observations of this kind are termed outliers. Whatever the reason may be, extreme values of profitability may have a large influence on the mean value of profitability computed for the different groups of firms in the sample, on the tails of the distribution of the rate of profit, and on the estimates of the trader premia. Conclusions with regard to the differences in profits between non-traders and the various groups of trading firms, therefore, might be influenced by a small number of firms with extremely high or low values of profits.

Researchers from the field of microeconomics of international firm activities usually are aware of all of this. Given that due to confidentiality of the firm level data single observations as a rule cannot be inspected closely enough to detect and correct reporting errors, or to understand the idiosyncratic events that lead to extreme values, a widely used procedure to keep these extreme observations from shaping the results is to drop the observations from the top and bottom 1 percent of the distribution of the variable under investigation. A case in point is the international comparison study on the exporter productivity premium by the International Study Group on Exports and Productivity (ISGEP) (2008, p. 610).

Dropping the firms from the top and the bottom 1 percent of the profitability distribution and comparing the results of empirical investigations with and without these firms with extremely high or extremely low values of profitability might be considered as a first and useful step to check the sensitivity of results. However, although this approach seems to be rather popular it is in some sense arbitrary. Why the top and bottom 1 percent? Why not choose a larger or smaller cut-off point? There are alternative approaches to deal with extreme observations (outliers) that are substantiated in statistics. Following Rousseeuw and Leroy (1987), we distinguish three types of outliers that influence the OLS estimator: vertical outliers, bad leverage points, and good leverage points. Verardi and Croux (2009, p. 440) illustrate this terminology in a simple linear regression framework (the generalization to higher dimensions is straightforward) as follows: "Vertical outliers are those observations that have outlying values for the corresponding error term (the $y$-dimension), but are not outlying in the space of explanatory variables (the $x$-dimension). Their presence affects the OLS estimation and, in particular, the estimated intercept. Good leverage points are observations that are outlying in the space of explanatory variables, but that are located close to the regression line. Their presence does not affect the OLS estimation, but it affects statistical inference because they do deflate the estimated standard errors. Finally, bad leverage points are observations that are both outlying in the space of explanatory variables and located far from the true regression line. Their presence significantly affects the OLS estimation of both the intercept and the slope."

Full robustness can be achieved by using the so-called MM-estimator that takes care of these three types of outliers and that can resist contamination of the data set of up to 50 percent of outliers (i.e. that has a breakdown point[11] of 50 percent compared to 0 percent for OLS). A discussion of the details of this estimator is beyond the scope of this chapter (see Verardi and Croux (2009) for this estimator and for Stata commands to compute it). Suffice it to say here that this estimator combines a breakdown point of 50 percent with a high efficiency (the degree of which can be chosen by the researcher). Explicit formulas for the estimator are not available; it is computed by numerical optimization.

Table 5 reports results for the trader premia computed using the MM-estimator (via `mmregress`) and pooled data without fixed firm effects in columns 1 and 3.[12] Results differ compared to the results reported in Table 4 for the same empirical model estimated by conventional OLS and disregarding the potential influence of outliers. For West Germany, the negative profitability premia of firms that only import and of two-way traders are now statistically significantly different from zero at an error level of much less than 5 percent (although still small and less than 1 percentage point).

[11]The breakdown point of an estimator is the highest fraction of outliers that an estimator can withstand, and it is a popular measure of robustness.

[12]Computations were done using the ado-files provided by Verardi and Croux (2009) with the efficiency parameter set at 0.7 as suggested there based on a simulation study; details are available on request.

Table 5. Robust estimation results for trader profitability premia

| Variable | | West Germany | | East Germany | |
|---|---|---|---|---|---|
| | | Pooled OLS | Fixed effects | Pooled OLS | Fixed effects |
| Only exports | ß | −0.338 | 0.298 | −0.989 | −0.072 |
| (Dummy; 1 = yes) | *p* | 0.384 | 0.288 | 0.182 | 0.890 |
| Only imports | ß | −0.650 | 0.072 | 0.020 | 0.201 |
| (Dummy; 1 = yes) | *p* | 0.022 | 0.699 | 0.970 | 0.560 |
| Exports and imports | ß | −0.977 | 0.083 | 0.015 | −0.533 |
| (Dummy; 1 = yes) | *p* | 0.000 | 0.736 | 0.976 | 0.224 |
| Number of employees | ß | −0.00062 | −0.00059 | −0.00071 | 0.0050 |
| | *p* | 0.000 | 0.096 | 0.229 | 0.008 |
| Number of employees | ß | 1.53e-08 | 2.38e-9 | 4.97e-8 | −5.16e-7 |
| (squared) | *p* | 0.000 | 0.151 | 0.562 | 0.031 |
| Year dummy variables | | included | included | included | included |
| 2-digit industry dummies | | included | not included | included | not included |
| Number of observations | | 25,624 | 22,056 | 4,648 | 3,969 |

*Note*: See text for the robust methods used to estimate the empirical models.

For East Germany, all the estimated premia are not statistically significant at any conventional level — the point estimate for the premium for two-way trades now is positive (although tiny). These results illustrate that outliers do have a large impact on the estimation results here.

The models in columns 1 and 3 of Table 5 do not control for unobserved heterogeneity by including firm fixed effects. A highly robust MM-estimator for panel data with fixed effects has been proposed recently by Bramati and Croux (2007). While a discussion of details of this estimator is beyond the scope of this chapter, the underlying idea is to center the series of observations for a firm in a similar way to what is generally done when applying the within transformation that is used to estimate a fixed effects model. The difference here is that the series are centered by removing the median instead of demeaning because the mean is largely distorted by outliers. Having centered the series, a robust estimator can be applied to deal with atypical individuals. The outcoming results will be comparable to those of a fixed effects estimator but will not be distorted by the presence of atypical individuals.

Verardi and Wagner (2011) apply this newly developed method to the estimation of exporter productivity premia for firms from manufacturing industries in West Germany. Using the xtregrob-command for Stata developed for this chapter,[13] the empirical models for the trader premia were estimated with firm fixed effects. Results are reported in columns 2 and 4 of Table 5. It turns out that in the data for West Germany, 3,568 observations (or 13.9 percent) were identified to be outliers; the respective number of outliers in the data for East Germany is 679 (or 14.6 percent). Dropping these outliers and estimating the empirical model with fixed effects using the reduced samples leads to estimated values for the trader premia that are never statistically significantly different from zero at any conventional error level in West or East Germany.

The bottom line, then, is the same as the one based on results that do not take the presence of outliers into account. The results point to the absence of any statistically significant and economically large effects of trade activities on profits.[14] This demonstrates that any productivity advantages of trading firms are eaten up by extra costs related to selling and buying in foreign markets.

## 6. Concluding Remarks

This chapter documents for the first time the relationship between profitability and three types of international trade activities — exports, imports, and two-way trade. Using unique new representative data for manufacturing enterprises from Germany, one of the leading actors in the world market for goods, the findings reported

[13]The Stata-code and a file describing the use of the command is now available from the web; see: repec.wirtschaft.uni-giessen.de/~repec/RePEc/jns/Datenarchiv/v231y2011i4/y231y2011i4p546_557/.

[14]Given this absence of any evidence for a positive profitability premium of trade activities, it makes no sense to investigate the direction of causality between trade and profitability (i.e. to test for self-selection of more profitable firms into trade and for positive effects of trade on profits). It should be noted that both tests are not possible with the data at hand anyway due to the very small number of trade starters in a year and the short time span of four years.

on the absence of any statistically significant and economically large effects of trade activities on profits hopefully add to the big picture on the relation between international firm activities and firm performance.

However, several caveats should be pointed out that might help to put the results reported here into perspective. First of all, the data used do not contain any information on the amount of imports from beyond the European Union. Therefore, the role of the difference in the exports to sales ratio and the imports to sales ratio between trading firms cannot be investigated; especially, it is not possible to investigate the causal effects of trading on profits with a dose-response approach (see Fryges and Wagner (2010)). Furthermore, there is no information on the type of goods imported. Imports of different kinds can be expected to be linked to profitability in different ways. While there might be no link between imports of raw materials that cannot be produced in Germany at all (like oil or iron ore) and profits, imports of intermediate products that are cheaper than similar goods produced in Germany or imports of capital goods that incorporate advanced technologies not available in machines produced in Germany might well have a positive effect on price and non-price competitiveness of firms and, therefore, on profits. Due to other limitations in the data, further open questions include the role played by different export destinations and by the characteristics of these export-markets, and the importance of the number and the quality of products exported, for the relationship between exports and profitability.

Given these (data driven) limitations of the study, the results cannot be considered as pointing to stylized facts — they should be taken as a first step and as stimulation for replication and extensions with (richer) data from other countries.

**Acknowledgment**

Comments by an anonymous referee that helped to improve an earlier version are gratefully acknowledged. All computations for this study were done inside the research data center of the Statistical

Office of Berlin-Brandenburg. Many thanks to Julia Höninger for her help with the data, for running my Stata do-files and for checking the output for violation of privacy. The firm level data used are confidential but not exclusive; see Zühlke *et al.* (2004) for a description of how to access the data. To facilitate replication the Stata do-files are available from the author on request.

## References

Amendolagine, Vito, Rosa Capolupo and Nadia Petragallo (2008). Export Status and Performance in a Panel of Italian Manufacturing Firms. Università degli Studi Bari Dipartomento di Scienze Economiche S.E.R.I.E.S Working Paper No. 27.

Bernard, Andrew B. and J. Bradford Jensen (1995). Exporters, Jobs, and Wages in U.S. Manufacturing: 1976–1987. *Brookings Papers on Economic Activity, Microeconomics* 1, 67–119.

Buchinsky, Moshe (1994). Changes in the U.S. Wage Structure 1963–1987: Application of Quantile Regression. *Econometrica* 62(2), 405–458.

Conover, W. J. (1999), *Practical Nonparametric Statistics*. Third edition. New York: John Wiley.

Delgado, Miguel A., Jose C. Farinas and Sonia Ruano (2002). Firm Productivity and Export Markets: A Non-parametric Approach. *Journal of International Economcis* 57(2), 397–422.

European Commission (1998). Commission Regulation (EC) No. 2700/98 Concerning the Definitions of Characteristics for Structural Business Statistics, Brussels. *Official Journal of the European Communities* L344, 49–80.

Foster, Lucia, John Haltiwanger and Chad Syverson (2008). Reallocation, Firm Turnover, and Efficiency: Selection on Productivity or Profitability? *American Economic Review* 98(1), 394–425.

Fritsch, Michael, Bernd Görzig, Ottmar Hennchen and Andreas Stephan (2004). Cost Structure Surveys for Germany. *Journal of Applied Social Science Studies* 124(4), 557–566.

Fryges, Helmut and Joachim Wagner (2010). Exports and Profitability: First Evidence for German Manufacturing firms. *The World Economy* 33(3), 399–423.

Grazzi, Marco (2009). Trade and Profitability: Is there an Export Premium? Evidence from Italian manufacturing firms. LEM Working Paper Series 2009/16, October.

Greenaway, David and Richard Kneller (2007). Firm Heterogeneity, Exporting and Foreign Direct Investment. *Economic Journal* 117, F134–F161.

International Study Group on Exports and Productivity (ISGEP) (2008). Understanding Cross-Country Differences in Exporter Premia: Comparable Evidence for 14 Countries. *Review of World Economics* 144(4), 596–635.

Konold, Michael (2007). New Possibilities for Economic Research through Integration of Establishment-level Panel Data of German Official Statistics. *Journal of Applied Social Science Studies* 127(2), 321–334.

Kox, Henk L. M. and Hugo Rojas-Romagosa (2010). Exports and Productivity Selection Effects for Dutch Firms. *De Economist* 158(3), 295–322.

Rousseeuw, Peter J. and Annick M. Leroy (1987). *Robust Regression and Outlier Detection*. New York: John Wiley and Sons.

Schank, Thorsten, Claus Schnabel and Joachim Wagner (2007). Do Exporters Really Pay Higher Wages? First Evidence from German Linked Employer–Employee Data. *Journal of International Economics* 72(1), 52–74.

Schank, Thorsten, Claus Schnabel and Joachim Wagner (2010). Higher Wages in Exporting Firms: Self-Selection, Export Effect, or Both? First Evidence from Linked Employer–Employee Data. *Review of World Economics* 146(2), 303–322.

Schmalensee, Richard (1989). Inter-Industry Studies of Structure and Performance. In: Schmalensee, R. and R. D. Willig, (Eds.), Handbook of Industrial Organization, Vol. II, Amsterdam: North-Holland, pp. 951–1009.

Temouri, Yama, Alexander Vogel and Joachim Wagner (2011). Self-selection into Export Markets by Business Services Firms — Evidence from France, Germany and the United Kingdom. Aston Business School and Leuphana University Lueneburg, Mimeo, March.

Verardi, Vincenzo and Christophe Croux (2009). Robust Regression in Stata. *The Stata Journal* 9(3), 439–453.

Verardi, Vincenzo and Joachim Wagner (2011). Robust Estimation of Linear Fixed Effects Panel Data Models with an Application to the Exporter Productivity Premium. *Jahrbücher für Nationalökonomie und Statistik* 231(4), 546–557.

Vogel, Alexander and Stefan Dittrich (2008). The German Turnover Tax Statistics Panel. *Journal of Applied Social Science Studies* 128(4), 661–670.

Vogel, Alexander and Joachim Wagner (2010a). Higher Productivity in Importing German Manufacturing Firms: Self-selection, Learning from Importing, or Both? *Review of World Economics* 145(4), 641–665.

Vogel, Alexander and Joachim Wagner (2010b). Exports and Profitability — First Evidence for German Business Services Enterprises. *Applied Economics Quarterly* 56(1), 7–30.

Vogel, Alexander, Joachim Wagner, Florian Burg and Stefan Dittrich (2008). Zur Dynamik der Export- und Importbeteiligung deutscher Industrieunternehmen. Empirische Befunde aus dem Umsatzsteuerpanel 2001 bis 2006. *Wirtschaft und Statistik* 11, 1109–1116.

Wagner, Joachim (2007). Exports and Productivity: A Survey of the Evidence from Firm-Level Data. *The World Economy* 30(1), 60–82.

Wagner, Joachim (2008a). A Note Why More West than East German Firms Export. *International Economics and Economic Policy* 5(4), 363–370.

Wagner, Joachim (2008b). Export Entry, Export Exit and Productivity in German Manufacturing Industries. *International Journal of the Economics of Business* 15(2), 169–180.

Wagner, Joachim (2011). International Trade and Firm Performance: A Survey of Empirical Studies Since 2006. University of Lueneburg Working Papers in Economics 210, August (forthcoming, *Review of World Economics*).

Zühlke, Sylvia, Markus Zwick, Sebastian Scharnhorst and Thomas Wende (2004). The Research Data Centres of the Federal Statistical Office and the Statistical Offices of the *Länder. Journal of Applied Social Science Studies* 124(4), 567–578.

# PART V

# International Trade and Firm Survival

Chapter 10

# Exports, Imports and Firm Survival: First Evidence for Manufacturing Enterprises in Germany

Joachim Wagner

**Abstract**

This paper investigates the links between firm survival and three types of international trade activities — exports, imports and two-way trade. It uses unique new representative data for manufacturing enterprises from Germany, one of the leading actors in the world market for goods. The chapter contributes to the literature by providing the first evidence on the role of imports and two-way trading for firm survival in a highly developed country. The results indicate a strong positive link between firm survival on the one hand and imports and two-way trading on the other hand, while exporting alone does not play a role for exiting the market or not.

*Keywords*: Exports, imports, firm survival

**JEL Classification:** F14

## 1. Motivation

Since the publication of the Brookings Paper by Bernard and Jensen (1995), a large and still growing empirical literature emerged that discusses the mutual links between international trade and firm performance.[1] The most prominent topic in this literature is the

[1]See Wagner (2012a) for a survey of recent empirical studies.

relationship between productivity and exports,[2] not least due to the central role played by productivity in the Melitz (2003) model of an exporting firm and the many variants of this model that are at the core of what is labelled the *new new international trade theory*. More recently, empirical investigations looked beyond exports and investigated the links between imports and productivity,[3] or the relationships between productivity and both exports and imports.[4] Stakeholders in firms, however, care for other dimensions of firm performance, too. Workers care for working conditions in general and especially for wages. Shareholders are interested in stock prices, dividends and profits. All of them care for the long-run development of the firm and for firm survival as the ultimate goal. The links between international trade and firm survival are the topics of this chapter.

Why should we expect that international trade activities and firm survival are linked, and in which direction should we expect these links to work? To start with, exporting can be considered as a form of risk diversification through spread of sales over different markets with different business cycle conditions or in a different phase of the product cycle (see Hirsch and Lev (1971)). Therefore, exports might provide a chance to substitute sales at home by sales abroad when a negative demand shock hits the home market and would force a firm to close down otherwise. Furthermore, Baldwin and Yan (2011, p. 135) argue that non-exporters are in general less efficient than exporters (younger, smaller and less productive) and that, as a result, one expects that non-exporters are more likely to fail than exporters.

As regards imports, imported intermediate inputs or capital goods might be cheaper and/or technically more advanced than inputs bought on the national market. Gibson and Graciano (2011) argue that the benefit of using imported inputs lies in a combination

---

[2]For surveys, see Greenaway and Kneller (2007) and Wagner (2007).

[3]Studies include Amiti and Konings (2007), Kasahara and Rodrigue (2007), Halpern Koren and Szeode (2009) and Vogel and Wagner (2010).

[4]Studies include Andersson, Lööf and Johansson (2008), Kasahara and Lapham (2008), Muûls and Pisu (2009), Altomonte and Békés (2009) and Castellani, Serti and Tomasi (2010).

of the relative price and the technology embodied in the inputs. Imports, therefore, lead to an increase in price competitiveness and non-price competitiveness of importers compared to firms that do not import. Furthermore, there is empirical evidence for a positive link of imports and productivity (discussed in Vogel and Wagner (2010)), documented by a significant productivity differential between firms that import and firms that do not trade internationally. Therefore, the probability to survive can be expected to be higher for importers than for non-importers, *ceteris paribus*.

Firms that both export and import can be expected to benefit from the positive effects of both forms of international trade on firm survival. Furthermore, two-way traders tend to be more productive than firms that either only import, or only export, or do not trade at all (see Vogel and Wagner (2010)). Therefore, we expect the probability of firm exit to be smaller for two-way traders than for firms that only export or only import.

A small number of recent empirical studies look at the role of international trade activities in shaping the chances for survival of firms; Wagner (2012a) summarizes this literature.[5] As a rule, the estimated chance of survival is higher for exporters, and this holds after controlling for firm characteristics that are positively associated with both exports and survival (like size, age and productivity). This might point to a direct positive effect of exporting on survival. To the best of my knowledge, López (2006), Gibson and Graciano (2011) and Namini, Facchini and López (2011) are the only empirical studies on imports and survival. All three studies use data for Chile. These studies find that importers are less likely to exit than non-importers. However, López (2006) reports that exporters are more likely to survive only if they import intermediate inputs. Exporting *per se*, therefore, does not seem to decrease the probability of plant failure. In the light of the empirical evidence for a positive link of imports and productivity, the positive link

[5]This literature looks at the survival of exporting and non-exporting firms on the home market; studies that investigate the determinants of surviving as an exporter on the export market include Ilmakunnas and Nurmi (2010) and Wagner (2008a, 2012b).

between imports and firm survival does not come as a surprise. The same holds for the positive link between two-way trading (i.e. importing and exporting) and survival. However, in light of the evidence for a positive link between exporting and survival found in the other studies surveyed in Wagner (2012a) (that do not deal with the role of imports), the finding that in Chile exporting *per se* does not seem to decrease the probability of plant failure is a puzzle.

This chapter contributes to the literature by providing the first evidence on the role of exports, imports and two-way trade for firm survival in a highly developed country, Germany, one of the leading actors in the world market for goods. It uses unique new representative data for manufacturing enterprises that merge information from surveys performed by the Statistical Offices and administrative data collected by the Tax Authorities. To anticipate the most important result, the analysis reveals a strong positive link between firm survival on the one hand and imports and two-way trading on the other hand, while exporting alone does not play a role for exiting the market or not.

The rest of the chapter is organized as follows. Section 2 describes the new data set. Section 3 presents descriptive results. Section 4 reports probit estimates for trader survival premia for four cohorts of exits of enterprises.[6] Section 5 concludes.

## 2. Data

This study uses a tailor-made enterprise-level data set that contains information from surveys performed by the Statistical Offices and from data collected by the Tax Authorities. The first source of data is the monthly report and the annual report for establishments in mining, quarrying, and manufacturing industries described in

[6]Given the data used in this study (described in Section 2) and the definition of exits and survivors (discussed in Section 3) applied here the time span of the study covers only four years (2001–2004). Therefore, it is not appropriate to apply methods from survival analysis (see Esteve-Pérez, Mánez-Castillejo and Sanchis-Llopis (2008) for a study of the role of exports in determining the survival of small firms using discrete time proportional hazard models that account for unobserved individual heterogeneity).

Konold (2007). These two surveys together cover all establishments from manufacturing industries that employ at least 20 persons in the local production unit or in the company that owns the unit as a whole. Participation of firms in the surveys is mandated in official statistics law. Participation in these surveys is used to identify surviving and exiting firms (discussed in detail in Section 3). These surveys are also the source for information on the location of the firm in West Germany or East Germany, the industry affiliation, information on whether a firm exports or not, labour productivity (measured as sales per employee) and the number of employees (used to measure firm size). Furthermore, given that the data start with the year 1995 these surveys are used to distinguish between old firms (that were already covered in 1995) and new firms (that entered the surveys in 1996 or later). Note that in this data set export refers to the amount of sales to a customer in a foreign country plus sales to a German export trading company; indirect exports (for example, tyres produced in a plant in Germany that are delivered to a German manufacturer of cars who exports some of his products) are not covered by this definition. For this project, the information collected at the establishment level has been aggregated at the enterprise level to match the unit of observation from the second and third source of data used here.

The second source of data is the German Turnover Tax Statistics Panel (described in detail in Vogel and Dittrich (2008)). This data set is based on the yearly turnover tax; all enterprises with a turnover that exceeds a rather low threshold (17,500 € since 2003) are covered in the data.[7] This data set is the source of information whether a firm imports or not. Note, however, that imports are not directly recorded therein completely. Imports from EU member states are reported under the item of 'intra-community acquisitions'. The amount of imports from states beyond the EU is not included in the turnover tax statistics. In this case, an import turnover tax is charged by the customs authorities. Nonetheless, this import turnover tax is deductible as an input tax and, therefore, reported in

[7]In 2001 this threshold was 16,617 € and in 2002 it was 16,620 €.

the dataset. From this information we know whether the enterprise imports from non-EU states or not.

The third source of data is the survey of products (*Produktionsstatistik*). This survey, the German version of what is elsewhere in Europe referred to as *PRODCOM*, is used to distinguish between firms that produce only one product (single-product firms) and firms that produce more than one product (multi-product firms).

The data from the three sources were linked by using the enterprise register system (*Unternehmensregistersystem*) that includes, among others, information on the unique enterprise identifier used in surveys conducted by the Statistical Offices and the unique turnover tax identifier used by the Tax Authorities. Data from the turnover tax statistics are available for the years 2001–2007. Data based on the monthly report of manufacturing establishments and on the survey of products are available for 1995–2008. The sample of enterprises used in the empirical investigation performed here consists of all enterprises for which information from all three sources for the years 2001–2007 could be linked via the enterprise register system.[8]

## 3. Descriptive Results

A firm is identified as an exit in year $t$ if it has reported to either the monthly report or the annual report for establishments in mining, quarrying and manufacturing industries in year $t$, but not in the three years after year $t$ — i.e. if it was active in a part of year $t$ but no longer than December 31 of year $t$. A surviving firm reported to the monthly report or the annual report in each year between $t$ and $t+3$. This means that a firm gets a 1 for the exit indicator in period $t$ if the firm is no longer present in the data in period $t+1, t+2$ and $t+3$, and firms that are still present in periods $t+1, t+2$ and $t+3$ get a 0. Therefore, a firm that exited soon after the end of year $t$ is not

[8]The merging of the data sets was done inside the research data center of the Statistical Office in Berlin-Brandenburg by Julia Höninger.

included in the comparison group of surviving firms — survivors stay in the market for (at least) the next three years.

It should be noted that the definition of firm exit used here is not without problems. First of all, if a firm relocates outside Germany or changes its activities from mining, quarrying and manufacturing to services or agriculture, it no longer reports to the monthly report or the annual report for establishments in mining, quarrying and manufacturing industries and, therefore, is considered as an exit. To the best of my knowledge and according to information from employees in official statistics that are in charge of preparing the data used here this is only rarely the case. Second, firms that shrink below the threshold of 20 employees in the local production unit or in the company that owns the unit are no longer obliged to report to the survey (but often do so at least for some years anyway). If they do not report three years in a row, they are considered as exits here but are in fact survivors. Note that neither a change of the legal form of the firm nor a change in the ownership (due to a merger or an acquisition) nor a relocation of the firm inside Germany leads to an erroneous classification of a firm as an exit, because the identification number of the firm used in official statistics will not change. Unfortunately, it is not possible to investigate further the data for firms identified as exits according to the definition used here due to the strict confidentiality of the firm-level data. A certain degree of fuzziness, therefore, remains, and this should be kept in mind when putting the results from the empirical investigation into perspective.

The numbers of exits from the cohorts of the years 2001–2004 and the percent share of exits in all firms (exits plus survivors) in these years are reported in Table 1 for West Germany and Table 2 for and East Germany.[9] This share of exits is declining from 8.94 percent in 2001 to 6.33 percent in 2004 in West Germany. In East Germany the

[9]The West German and the East German economies still differ largely even many years after the unification in 1990, and this is especially true for international trade (see Wagner (2008b) for an analysis). Therefore, all empirical investigations are carried out separately for both parts of Germany here.

Table 1. Exit cohorts 2001–2004: Descriptive statistics for West Germany

| Cohort | 2001 | 2002 | 2003 | 2004 |
|---|---|---|---|---|
| Number of exits | 2,626 | 2,441 | 2,178 | 1,827 |
| Share of exits (percent) | | | | |
| — in all firms | 8.94 | 8.09 | 7.40 | 6.33 |
| — in firms that do not trade | 17.62 | 13.39 | 12.90 | 10.86 |
| — in firms that only export | 10.90 | 10.26 | 9.63 | 8.92 |
| — in firms that only import | 4.55 | 5.96 | 6.75 | 4.50 |
| — in firms that export and import | 2.94 | 3.70 | 2.80 | 2.51 |
| — in firms with less than 50 employees | 12.77 | 12.04 | 11.46 | 9.29 |
| — in firms with 50–249 employees | 5.52 | 4.44 | 3.54 | 3.68 |
| — in firms with 250–499 employees | 5.95 | 4.85 | 4.05 | 4.38 |
| — in firms with 500 and more employees | 5.10 | 3.97 | 4.15 | 2.76 |
| — in firms that started before 1996 | 6.97 | 6.56 | 5.97 | 5.18 |
| — in firms that started in 1996 or later | 14.01 | 11.11 | 9.97 | 8.18 |
| — in firms with only one product | 8.75 | 9.73 | 8.32 | 6.91 |
| — in firms with two or more products | 9.06 | 7.04 | 6.80 | 5.94 |
| — in firms from the lower third of the distribution of labor productivity | 15.89 | 13.57 | 12.42 | 10.58 |
| — in firms from the middle third of the distribution of labor productivity | 5.39 | 5.31 | 4.89 | 3.96 |
| — in firms from the upper third of the distribution of labor productivity | 5.67 | 5.52 | 5.06 | 4.54 |

*Note*: For a definition of exits and survivors see text.

exits rates were higher than in West Germany in each year and there was no decline in exits over time.

Based on the combined data from the three sources described in Section 2, it is possible to distinguish between four types of enterprises, namely enterprises without trade, enterprises that only export, enterprises that only import and enterprises that both export and import. Shares of firms from these groups are reported in Table 3. Participation in international trade is lower among East German than among West German firms. In West Germany, firms that both export and import are the largest group of firms in all four years, followed by firms that only export, firms that do not trade at all and firms that only import. In East Germany, firms that do not

Table 2. Exit cohorts 2001–2004: Descriptive statistics for East Germany

| Cohort | 2001 | 2002 | 2003 | 2004 |
|---|---|---|---|---|
| Number of exits | 561 | 682 | 605 | 568 |
| Share of exits (percent) | | | | |
| — in all firms | 9.80 | 11.19 | 9.88 | 9.41 |
| — in firms that do not trade | 16.47 | 17.16 | 16.06 | 16.00 |
| — in firms that only export | 10.32 | 15.23 | 12.47 | 11.25 |
| — in firms that only import | 3.96 | 5.14 | 4.88 | 5.08 |
| — in firms that export and import | 2.96 | 2.96 | 3.23 | 3.19 |
| — in firms with less than 50 employees | 13.35 | 15.13 | 13.64 | 13.26 |
| — in firms with 50–249 employees | 5.64 | 6.36 | 5.39 | 5.27 |
| — in firms with 250–499 employees | 6.19 | 7.49 | 6.28 | 3.17 |
| — in firms with 500 and more employees | 2.91 | 7.63 | 4.88 | 1.60 |
| — in firms that started before 1996 | 8.25 | 9.10 | 8.23 | 6.59 |
| — in firms that started in 1996 or later | 11.42 | 13.00 | 11.11 | 11.29 |
| — in firms with only one product | 9.67 | 12.39 | 10.73 | 10.45 |
| — in firms with two or more products | 10.85 | 10.39 | 9.28 | 8.64 |
| — in firms from the lower third of the distribution of labor productivity | 17.12 | 19.17 | 17.78 | 16.62 |
| — in firms from the middle third of the distribution of labor productivity | 7.10 | 7.28 | 6.51 | 6.02 |
| — in firms from the upper third of the distribution of labor productivity | 5.47 | 7.38 | 5.63 | 5.85 |

*Note*: For a definition of exits and survivors see text.

trade form the largest group, followed by two-way traders, firms that only export and firms that only import.

In both parts of Germany, two-way traders had the smallest share of exits of all four groups of firms, followed by firms that only imported and firms that only exported, while the share of exits was highest among non-trading firms. Descriptive statistics point to a lower risk of exit among firms that are active on international markets.

Participation in international trade is related to firm characteristics that are linked to firm exit and survival, and that should be controlled for when investigating the links between trade activities and survival. While this issue is tackled in the following section of the chapter, the rest of this section will give some information on

Table 3. Shares of firms from various groups in all firms (percent)

| | 2001 | | 2002 | | 2003 | | 2004 | |
|---|---|---|---|---|---|---|---|---|
| Part of German | West | East | West | East | West | East | West | East |
| Firms that do not trade | 25.25 | 39.16 | 24.79 | 38.26 | 23.16 | 34.56 | 22.34 | 33.02 |
| Firms that only export | 26.79 | 18.96 | 26.93 | 20.04 | 27.68 | 21.07 | 27.56 | 20.75 |
| Firms that only import | 9.80 | 15.88 | 9.80 | 15.64 | 9.47 | 16.06 | 9.63 | 16.63 |
| Firms that export and import | 38.16 | 26.00 | 38.48 | 26.06 | 39.69 | 28.31 | 40.47 | 29.60 |
| Firms with less than 50 employees | 47.05 | 54.32 | 48.03 | 54.36 | 47.94 | 54.10 | 47.25 | 53.73 |
| Firms with 50–249 employees | 41.22 | 40.26 | 40.61 | 39.98 | 40.61 | 40.25 | 41.44 | 40.54 |
| Firms with 250–499 employees | 6.58 | 3.67 | 6.42 | 3.73 | 6.45 | 3.64 | 6.41 | 3.66 |
| Firms with 500 and more employees | 5.14 | 1.75 | 4.93 | 1.94 | 5.00 | 2.01 | 4.90 | 2.07 |
| Firms that started before 1996 | 71.99 | 51.04 | 66.34 | 46.33 | 64.18 | 42.85 | 61.56 | 39.98 |
| Firms that started in 1996 or later | 27.91 | 48.96 | 33.66 | 53.67 | 35.82 | 57.15 | 38.44 | 60.02 |
| Firms with only one product | 39.24 | 40.64 | 39.14 | 40.00 | 39.55 | 41.40 | 40.11 | 42.48 |
| Firms with two or more products | 60.76 | 59.36 | 60.86 | 60.00 | 60.45 | 58.60 | 59.88 | 57.52 |

the share of exits in firms by size class, firm age, number of products and productivity.[10]

*Firm size*: Audretsch (1995, p. 149) mentions as a stylized fact from many empirical studies on exits that the likelihood of firm exit apparently declines with firm size (usually measured by the number of employees in a firm). This is theoretically linked to the hypothesis of "liability of smallness" from organizational ecology. A small size can be interpreted as a proxy variable for a number of unobserved firm characteristics, including disadvantages of scale,

[10]Unfortunately, other firm characteristics that might be important for both firm survival and international trade like innovation activities (see Esteve-Pérez, Mánez-Castillip and Sanchis-Llopis (2008)) and financial variables (see Görg and Spaliara (2009)) cannot be included here due to lack of information in the data.

higher restrictions on the capital market leading to a higher risk of insolvency and illiquidity, disadvantages of small firms in the competition for highly qualified employees and lower talent of management (Strotmann 2007).

Results reported in Tables 1 and 2 show a pattern of the rate of exit across firm size classes (measured by the number of employees) that is broadly in line with this hypothesis. The share of firms from the four size classes in West Germany and East Germany in each cohort is reported in Table 3. Note that large firms are much more often found in West Germany than in East Germany.

*Firm age*: Audretsch (1995, p. 149) mentions as another stylized fact from many empirical studies on exits that the likelihood of firm exit apparently declines with firm age, too. This positive link between firm age and probability of survival is labelled "liability of newness" and it is related to the fact that older firms are "better" because they spent a longer time in the market during which they learned how to solve the range of problems facing them in day-to-day business.

Tables 1 and 2 indicate that, in line with this hypothesis, the rate of exit is smaller in older firms (founded before 1996) than in younger firms that started in 1996 or later. Not surprisingly, the share of old firms is much larger in West Germany than in East Germany; see Table 3.

*Product diversification*: On a theoretical level, the existence of multi-product enterprises has been explained by pointing to the reduction of risk and uncertainty that can be reached by diversification across product markets (Jovanovic and Gilbert, 1993, p. 199f.; Lipczynski and Wilson, 2001, p. 324f.). Demand shocks or new competitors may have a negative impact on sales and profits in a product market in an unpredictable manner. A single-product firm, therefore, is highly vulnerable to adverse shocks that hit their market. A multi-product firm can substantially reduce this vulnerability, at least if the risks on the various product markets are randomly distributed or negatively correlated. Consequently, we would expect that, other things equal, higher levels of product diversification are positively related to a higher probability of survival. To the best of my knowledge, however, this hypothesis has not been tested empirically for Germany before.[11]

As is shown in Tables 1 and 2, the rate of exits is higher among single-product firms than among firms that produce two or more products in three out of four cohorts in both parts of Germany. This descriptive evidence is broadly in line with the theory sketched above.

*Productivity:* In theoretical models for the dynamics of industries with heterogeneous firms, including Jovanovic (1982), Hopenhayn (1992), and Ericson and Pakes (1995), productivity differentials play a central role for entry, growth, and exit of firms. In equilibrium growing and shrinking, exiting and entering firms that have different productivities are found in an industry. These models lead to hypotheses that can be tested empirically. Hopenhayn (1992) considers a long-run equilibrium in an industry with many price-taking firms producing a homogeneous good. Output is a function of inputs and a random variable that models a firm-specific productivity shock. These shocks are independent between firms, and are the reason for the heterogeneity of firms. There are sunk costs to be paid at entry, and entrants do not know their specific shock in advance. Incumbents can choose between exiting or staying in the market. When firms realized their productivity shock they decide about the profit maximizing volume of production. The model assumes that a higher shock in $t + 1$ has a higher probability the higher the shock is in $t$. In equilibrium, firms will exit if for given

[11] Using data from the United States Bernard and Jensen (2007) report that the probability of failure is lower for multi-product plants than for single-product plants after controlling for other plant characteristics including size, age and exporter status. Braakmann and Wagner (2011a) use German firm-level longitudinal data to investigate the relationship between product diversification and the stability of sales and employment. They find that contrary to portfolio theoretic considerations more diversified firms exhibit a higher variability of sales and employment. However, the effects are negligibly small from an economic point of view. Furthermore, Braakmann and Wagner (2011b) find that an increase in the degree of product diversification has a negative impact on profitability when observed and unobserved firm characteristics are controlled for. This helps to understand the fact that about 40 percent of all firms are single-product firms according to a detailed classification of products (see Table 3 for the cohorts of firms investigated here), and that multi-product enterprises with a large number of goods are a rare species.

prices of output and inputs the productivity shock is smaller than a critical value, and production is no longer profitable.

Farinas and Ruano (2005, p. 507f.) argue that this model leads to the following testable hypothesis: Firms that exit in year $t$ were in $t-1$ less productive than firms that continue to produce in $t$. They test this hypothesis using panel data for Spanish firms. The hypothesis is supported by the data. Wagner (2009) replicates the study by Farinas and Ruano with panel data for West and East German firms from manufacturing industries. For the cohorts of exit from 1997 to 2002 the results are in line with the results for Spain.

As is shown in Tables 1 and 2, the rate of exit is much higher among firms from the lower third of the productivity distribution than among the more productive firms. Table 3 shows that the average productivity is lower among exits than among surviving firms. While this is in line with the theory sketched above, it should be noted that exits can be found among the most productive firms, too.

Furthermore, it should be pointed out that productivity is related to the trader status of a firm. Vogel and Wagner (2010) use data for manufacturing enterprises from West and East Germany and look at productivity differentials between groups of firms. Two-way traders do have the highest productivity, followed by firms that only import and firms that only export, while firms that do not trade internationally have the smallest productivity. These productivity differentials are observed even after controlling for unobservable firm heterogeneity in a fixed-effects model; in this case, however, the productivity premium over firms that do not trade is higher for exporters than for importers.

## 4. Trader Survival Premia: Results from Probit Estimates

The second step in the empirical investigation of the links between firm survival and participation in international trade consists in the estimation of trader survival premia. These premia are defined as the difference of the probability to exit between firms that did not

Table 4. Probit estimates of determinants of firm exits: West Germany

| | | 2001 | | 2002 | |
|---|---|---|---|---|---|
| Exit cohort | | Model 1 | Model 2 | Model 1 | Model 2 |
| Firms that only export | ß | −0.023** | −0.00066 | −0.026*** | −0.006** |
| | *p* | (0.026) | (0.937) | (0.000) | (0.022) |
| Firms that only import | ß | −0.064*** | −0.056*** | −0.049*** | −0.041*** |
| | *p* | (0.000) | (0.000) | (0.000) | (0.000) |
| Firms that export and import | ß | −0.103*** | −0.078*** | −0.091*** | −0.066*** |
| | p | (0.000) | (0.000) | (0.000) | (0.000) |
| Firms with 50 to 249 employees | ß | | −0.039*** | | −0.051*** |
| | *p* | | (0.000) | | (0.000) |
| Firms with 250 to 499 employees | ß | | −0.023** | | −0.034** |
| | *p* | | (0.042) | | (0.000) |
| Firms with 500 and more employees | ß | | −0.027*** | | −0.040*** |
| | *p* | | (0.000) | | (0.000) |
| Firms that started before 1996 | ß | | −0.033*** | | −0.025** |
| | *p* | | (0.000) | | (0.000) |
| Firms with two or more products | ß | | −0.006 | | −0.013*** |
| | *p* | | (0.177) | | (0.000) |
| Labor productivity (sales per employee; 1000 €) | ß | | −0.00014*** | | −0.00008 |
| | *p* | | (0.000) | | (0.045)** |
| Number of firms | | 29,355 | 29,355 | 30,127 | 30,127 |
| Firms that only export | ß | −0.024*** | −0.004 | −0.015*** | −0.002 |
| | *p* | (0.000) | (0.296) | (0.010) | (0.751) |
| Firms that only import | ß | −0.038*** | −0.029** | −0.038*** | −0.033*** |
| | *p* | (0.000) | (0.000) | (0.000) | (0.000) |
| Firms that export and import | ß | −0.093*** | −0.067*** | −0.077*** | −0.060*** |
| | *p* | (0.000) | (0.000) | (0.000) | (0.000) |
| Firms with 50–249 employees | ß | | −0.053*** | | −0.038*** |
| | *p* | | (0.000) | | (0.000) |
| Firms with 250–499 employees | ß | | −0.034*** | | −0.025*** |
| | *p* | | (0.000) | | (0.000) |
| Firms with 500 and more employees | ß | | −0.033*** | | −0.037*** |
| | *p* | | (0.000) | | (0.000) |
| Firms that started before 1996 | ß | | −0.019*** | | −0.013*** |
| | *p* | | (0.000) | | (0.000) |

(*Continued*)

Table 4. (*Continued*)

| | | 2003 | | 2004 | |
|---|---|---|---|---|---|
| Exit cohort | | Model 1 | Model 2 | Model 1 | Model 2 |
| Firms with two or | ß | | −0.005 | | −0.002 |
| more products | *p* | | (0.156) | | (0.565) |
| Labor productivity | ß | | −0.0006** | | $-2.37e-6$ |
| (sales per | *p* | | (0.047) | | (0.799) |
| employee; 1000 €) | | | | | |
| Number of firms | | 29,392 | 29,392 | 28,820 | 28,820 |

*Note*: The entries in the table are the marginal effects (ß) und the *p*-values (*p*). The reference categories for the dummy variables are: firms that do not trade; firms with less than 50 employees; firms that started in 1996 or later; firms with only one product. All models include a constant plus a full set of 2-digit-level industry dummy variables. Standard errors are adjusted for clusters at 2-digit-level industries. *, ** and *** indicate statistical significance at 10, 5 and 1 percent level, respectively.

trade at all and firms from one of the three groups of traders (firms that only export, firms that only import and two-way traders). To document these premia two empirical models were estimated by Probit for firms from each cohort of exits and from the respective control group of surviving firms. Model 1 includes a dummy variable taking the value 1 for exits and the value 0 for survivors as the endogenous variable; three dummy variables for firms that only export, firms that only import and two-way traders plus a full set of 2-digit-level industry dummy variables and a constant are included as exogenous variables. Model 2 augments Model 1 by including a set of other variables that are expected to be related to firm exit and survival, i.e. dummy variables for three firm size classes (using firms from the smallest size class as the reference category), for old firms and for multi-product firms plus labor productivity (measured as sales per employee).[12]

[12]Note that these empirical models are not to be considered as models that explain the exit decision of the firms. The data at hand are not rich enough for that kind of empirical investigation. The empirical models are only used to indicate the *ceteris paribus* difference in the exit probability of firms with different forms of international trade activities, following

Table 5. Probit estimates of determinants of firm exits: East Germany

| | | 2001 | | 2002 | |
|---|---|---|---|---|---|
| Exit cohort | | Model 1 | Model 2 | Model 1 | Model 2 |
| Firms that only export | ß | −0.036*** | −0.018 | −0.012 | 0.004 |
| | *p* | (0.002) | (0.146) | (0.243) | (0.676) |
| Firms that only import | ß | −0.079*** | −0.071*** | −0.084*** | −0.078*** |
| | *p* | (0.000) | (0.000) | (0.000) | (0.000) |
| Firms that export and import | ß | −0.099*** | −0.083*** | −0.117*** | −0.104*** |
| | *p* | (0.000) | (0.000) | (0.000) | (0.000) |
| Firms with 50–249 employees | ß | | −0.044*** | | −0.062*** |
| | *p* | | (0.000) | | (0.000) |
| Firms with 250–499 employees | ß | | −0.025 | | −0.040*** |
| | *p* | | (0.221) | | (0.005) |
| Firms with 500 and more employees | ß | | −0.045** | | −0.039 |
| | *p* | | (0.014) | | (0.110) |
| Firms that started before 1996 | ß | | −0.003 | | −0.015* |
| | *p* | | (0.722) | | (0.076) |
| Firms with two or more products | ß | | 0.005 | | −0.005 |
| | *p* | | (0.312) | | (0.425) |
| Labor productivity (sales per employee; 1000 €) | ß | | −0.00022** | | 0.00001*** |
| | p | | (0.024) | | (0.002) |
| Number of firms | | 5,712 | 5,712 | 6,082 | 6,082 |
| Firms that only export | ß | −0.026*** | −0.003 | −0.033*** | −0.009 |
| | *p* | (0.000) | (0.721) | (0.000) | (0.175) |
| Firms that only import | ß | −0.076*** | −0.065*** | −0.073*** | −0.060*** |
| | *p* | (0.000) | (0.000) | (0.000) | (0.000) |
| Firms that export and import | ß | −0.106*** | −0.084*** | −0.105*** | −0.078*** |
| | *p* | (0.000) | (0.000) | (0.000) | (0.000) |
| Firms with 50–249 employees | ß | | −0.053*** | | −0.044*** |
| | *p* | | (0.000) | | (0.000) |
| Firms with 250–499 employees | ß | | −0.024 | | −0.040*** |
| | *p* | | (0.183) | | (0.006) |
| Firms with 500 and more employees | ß | | −0.034 | | −0.056*** |
| | *p* | | (0.170) | | (0.007) |

*(Continued)*

a standard approach used in empirical studies from the microeconometrics of international firm activities (see Wagner (2007)).

Table 5. (*Continued*)

| Exit cohort | | 2003 Model 1 | 2003 Model 2 | 2004 Model 1 | 2004 Model 2 |
|---|---|---|---|---|---|
| Firms that started before 1996 | ß | | −0.005 | | −0.021*** |
| | *p* | | (0.403) | | (0.000) |
| Firms with two or more products | ß | | −0.003 | | −0.013** |
| | *p* | | (0.714) | | (0.025) |
| Labor productivity (sales per employee; 1000 €) | ß | | −0.00024*** | | −0.00025*** |
| | *p* | | (0.000) | | (0.001) |
| Number of firms | | 6,109 | 6,109 | 6,023 | 6,023 |

*Note*: The entries in the table are the marginal effects (ß) und the *p*-values (*p*). The reference categories for the dummy variables are: firms that do not trade; firms with less than 50 employees; firms that started in 1996 or later; firms with only one product. All models include a constant plus a full set of 2-digit-level industry dummy variables. Standard errors are adjusted for clusters at 2-digit-level industries. *, ** and *** indicate statistical significance at 10, 5 and 1 percent level, respectively.

Results are reported in Table 4 for West Germany and in Table 5 for East Germany.[13] The estimated coefficients from a Probit model cannot easily be used for statements about the size of the *ceteris paribus* effect of a change of the value of an exogenous variable (e.g. being a two-way trader or not) on the value of the endogenous variable (the probability of exit), because the size of this effect depends on both the value of the exogenous variable under consideration and on the values of all other variables in the model (see Long and Freese (2001), p. 87ff.). To put it differently, the estimated size of the change in the probability of exit due to a change in the value of one exogenous variable depends on where we start. In the tables, therefore, the estimated marginal effects are reported. For a continuous variable, the marginal effect is the estimated change in the probability of exit due to a one unit change in the value of that variable when the values of all variables in the model are at

[13]Descriptive statistics for variables included in the empirical models are reported in the Table A.1.

the mean of the sample used for the estimation of the model. For a dummy variable, the marginal effect is the change in the probability of exit when this dummy variable takes on the value 1 instead of the value 0 (and when the values of all other exogenous variables in the model are fixed at the sample mean).

From the results of the Probit estimates, we have strong evidence for a negative link between the probability of exit and both importing and two-way trading in all four cohorts in West Germany and in East Germany. Both in Model 1 (without control variables) and Model 2 (with control variables), the estimated regression coefficients for the dummy variables indicating that a firm is an "only importer" or a "two-way trader" have a negative sign, they are highly statistically significant, and the estimated marginal effects point to a reduction of the risk of exit that is large. For example, according to results from Model 2 for the cohort 2001 in West Germany importing only reduces the risk of exit by 5.6 percentage points and two-way trading reduces it by 7.8 percentage points. Risk reduction is always larger for two-way traders than for firms that only import according to the point estimates of the marginal effects; however, this difference is statistically significantly different from zero at an error level of 5 percent or smaller for the cohorts 2002–2004 in West Germany only (see Table 6).

Table 6. Test for significant differences between coefficients from probit estimates for different types of internationally active firms

| Exit cohort | | 2001 | 2002 | 2003 | 2004 |
|---|---|---|---|---|---|
| Firms that only export vs. | West Germany | 0.000 | 0.000 | 0.000 | 0.000 |
| Firms that only import | East Germany | 0.000 | 0.000 | 0.000 | 0.000 |
| Firms that only export vs. | West Germany | 0.000 | 0.000 | 0.000 | 0.000 |
| Firms that export and import | East Germany | 0.000 | 0.000 | 0.000 | 0.000 |
| Firms that only import vs. | West Germany | 0.677 | 0.000 | 0.000 | 0.001 |
| Firms that export and import | East Germany | 0.696 | 0.062 | 0.132 | 0.397 |

*Note*: The entries in the table are the prob-values from a test of $H_0$: the difference between the estimated probit regression coefficients for the two types of internationally active firms is zero against $H_1$: the difference between the estimated probit regression coefficients for the two types of internationally active firms is different from zero. For the empirical models see the respective Model 2 in Tables 4 and 5.

Contrary to the findings for two-way trading and importing, exporting *per se* is not negatively related to the probability of exit. The estimated probit regression coefficient for the dummy variable indicating that a firm is an "only exporter" is statistically significantly different from zero when controlling for the role of firm size, firm age, number of products and productivity in Model 2 only for the cohort 2002 in West Germany — and here the marginal effect is tiny pointing to a reduction of the risk of exit by 0.6 percentage points.

By and large, the results for the control variables reported for Model 2 tend to be in line with the descriptive statistics reported above and with the expectations based on theoretical reasoning.[14]

## 5. Discussion

This chapter provides the first evidence on the role of exports, imports and two-way trade for firm survival in a highly developed country. Results from the microeconometric analysis point to a strong positive link between firm survival on the one hand and imports and two-way trading on the other hand, while exporting alone does not play a role for exiting the market or not.

The finding of this chapter that imports are more important in affecting firm survival than exports is not surprising given the recent evidence on the importance of imports for firm performance.[15] At first sight, however, the result that in Germany exports *per se* are not positively related to firm survival seem to contradict both theoretical reasoning and the findings from other empirical studies. As stated in Section 1, exporting can be considered as a form of risk diversification through spread of sales over different markets with different business cycle conditions or in a different phase of the product cycle. Therefore, exports might provide a

[14]As a robustness check computations were performed using rare events logit (see King and Zeng (2001a), (2001b)), too. All results are remarkably similar; to economize on space, the tables are available on request.

[15]See Castellani, Serti and Tomasi (2010), Goldberg *et al.* (2010a, 2010b), Bas and Strauss-Kahn (2010), Damijan, Konings and Polanec (2011) and Vogel and Wagner (2010).

chance to substitute sales at home by sales abroad when a negative demand shock hits the home market and would force a firm to close down otherwise. Furthermore, non-exporters are in general less efficient than exporters (younger, smaller and less productive) and, as a result, one expects that non-exporters are more likely to fail than exporters. In line with this reasoning, empirical studies (summarized in Wagner (2012a)) as a rule find that the estimated chance of survival is higher for exporters, and this holds after controlling for firm characteristics that are positively associated with both exports and survival (like size, age, productivity).

However, as regards the findings from other empirical studies remember that (with the exception of the studies using data from Chile) imports are ignored therein. This means that two-way traders and firms that only export are classified in one group called exporters. For this group of firms, the link between survival and trade is positive for Germany, too. Probit estimates for empirical models that only include a dummy variable indicating whether a firm is an exporter or not and that do not control for import activity show a statistically highly significant negative coefficient of the exporter dummy variable (in models with and without control variables for firm size, firm age, number of products and productivity) for all four cohorts of exits in West and East Germany.[16] However, looking at both exports and imports separately does reveal more insights into the link between foreign trade and firm survival, and is, therefore, important for understanding the role of international trade activities in shaping the chances to survive in the market or not.[17]

[16]Details are not reported here to economize on space but are available from the author on request.

[17]It should be noted that the missing positive link between exports without imports and firm survival is not due to the fact that firms exporting are marginal exporters only that exporting only a small share of their production. In West Germany, in 2001, the share of exports in total sales was 25.1 percent on average for the firms that were exporters only, compared to 27.8 percent for firms that were exporters and importers. Differences in the share of exports in total sales between these two groups of firms were of the same order of magnitude in the other years and in East Germany. Details are available on request.

Given that Germany is one of the big players on the world market for goods and that international linkages of German manufacturing enterprises are extremely important for the short and for the longer run development of the economy, the empirical evidence presented in this chapter is interesting on its own. It would be even more interesting to see whether the pattern revealed for West Germany and East Germany is the same in other highly developed economies, and if not, why there is a difference. A replication and extension[18] of this study with data for other countries, therefore, is suggested as a step on the thorny road from estimation results in one study to the finding of stylized facts. These stylized facts then could be used both to guide economic policy makers in an evidence-based way and to motivate the building of theoretical models that are based on "realistic" assumptions.[19]

## Acknowledgments

I thank the German Research Foundation for financial support under project WA 610/5-1 "Firm exit" (*Betriebsschließungen*). Earlier versions were presented at the ISGEP 2011 Workshop, at the German Bundesbank and in the research seminar of the Institute of Economics at Leuphana University Lüneburg. Comments from participants at these presentations, from Claus Schnabel and Daniel Fackler and from two referees are gratefully acknowledged. Special thanks go to Julia Höninger and Florian Köhler for pointing out problems related to the identification of firm exits with the turnover tax statistics data; their comments lead to a complete revision of an earlier version that circulates as a working paper, see Wagner (2011b). The usual disclaimer applies. All computations for this

[18]One way to extend this study is to consider the role of the share of exports in total sales and the ratio of imports to total sales for firm survival; unfortunately, this information is not available for Germany (see Section 2). Another line of extension should consider the differences between firms that exported and/or imported for several years and firms that just started to trade or just stopped to trade (see Görg and Spaliara (2009)); unfortunately, the period covered by the data for Germany is not long enough for this exercise (again, see Section 2).

[19]See Wagner (2011a) for a discussion of these issues.

study were done inside the research data center of the Statistical Office of Berlin-Brandenburg. The firm level data used are confidential but not exclusive; see Zühlke *et al.* (2004) for a description of how to access the data. To facilitate replication the Stata do-files are available from the author on request.

## References

Amiti, Mary, and Jozef Konings (2007). Trade Liberalization, Intermediate Inputs and Productivity: Evidence from Indonesia. *American Economic Review* 97(5), 1611–1638.

Andersson, Martin, Hans Lööf and Sara Johansson (2008). Productivity and International Trade: Firm-Level Evidence from A Small Open Economy. *Review of World Economics/Weltwirtschaftliches Arciv* 144(4), 774–801.

Altomonte, Carlo and Gábor Békés (2009). Trade Complexity and Productivity. Discussion Paper MT-DP 2009/14, Institute of Economics, Hungarian Academy of Sciences.

Audretsch, David B. (1995). *Innovation and Industry Evolution*. Cambridge, MA: Cambridge University Press.

Baldwin, John and Beiling Yan (2011). The Death of Canadian Manufacturing Plants: Heterogeneous Responses to Changes in Tariffs and Real Exchange Rates. *Review of World Economics/Weltwirtschaftliches Archiv* 147(1), 131–167.

Bas, Maria and Vanessa Strauss-Kahn (2010). Does Importing More Inputs Raise Exports? Firm-level Evidence from France. MPRA Paper 27315. Munich Personal RePEc Archive University Library of Munich.

Bernard, Andrew B. and J. Bradford Jensen (1995). Exporters, Jobs, and Wages in U.S. Manufacturing: 1976–1987. *Brookings Papers on Economic Activity, Microeconomics* 1, 67–119.

Bernard, Andrew B. and J. Bradford Jensen (2007). Firm Structure, Multinationals, and Manufacturing Plant Deaths. *Review of Economics and Statistics* 89(2), 193–204.

Braakmann, Nils and Joachim Wagner (2011a). Product Diversification and Stability of Employment and Sales: First Evidence from German Manufacturing Firms. *Applied Economics* 43(27), 3977–3985.

Braakmann, Nils and Joachim Wagner (2011b). Product Diversification and Profitability in German Manufacturing Firms. *Jahrbücher für Nationalökonomie und Statistik* 231(3), 326–335.

Castellani, Davide, Francesco Serti and Chiara Tomasi (2010). Firms in International Trade: Importers' and Exporters' Heterogeneity in Italian Manufacturing Industry. *The World Economy* 33(3), 424–457.

Damijan, Joze P., Jozef Konings and Saso Polanec (2011). Import Churning and Export Performance of Multi-product Firms. LICOS Discussion Papers 277/2011, Centre for Institutions and Economic Performance, K. U. Leuven.

Ericson, Richard and Ariel Pakes (1995). Markov-Perfect Industry Dynamics: A Framework for Empirical Work. *Review of Economic Studies* 62, 53–82.

Esteve-Pérez, Silviano, Juan A. Mánez-Castillejo and Juan A. Sanchis-Llopis (2008). Does a "Survival-by-Exporting" Effect for SMEs Exist? *Empirica* 35(1), 81–104.

Farinas, Jose C. and Sonia Ruano (2005). Firm Productivity, Heterogeneity, Sunk Costs and Market Selection. *International Journal of Industrial Organization* 23, 505–534.

Gibson, Mark J. and Tim A. Graciano (2011). Costs of Starting to Trade and Costs of Continuing to Trade. Washington State University, mimeo, January.

Görg, Holger and Marina-Eliza Spaliara (2009). Financial Health, Exports, and Firm Survival: A Comparison of British and French Firms. Kiel working paper 1568, Kiel Institute for the World Economy Kiel.

Goldberg, Pinelopi K., Amit Khandelwal, Nina Pavcnik and Petia Topolova (2010a). Imported Intermediate Inputs and Domestic Product Growth: Evidence from India. *Quarterly Journal of Economics* 125(4), 1727–1767.

Goldberg, Pinelopi K., Amit Khandelwal, Nina Pavcnik and Petia Topolova (2010b). Multi-product Firms and Product Turnover in the Developing World: Evidence from India. *Review of Economics and Statistics* 92(4), 1042–1049.

Greenaway, David and Richard Kneller (2007). Firm Heterogeneity, Exporting and Foreign Direct Investment. *Economic Journal* 117, F134–F161.

Halpern, Laszlo, Miklos Koren and Adam Szeidl (2009). Imported Inputs and Productivity. CeFiG Working Papers 8, Center for Firms in the Global Economy Budapest.

Hirsch, Seev and Baruch Lev (1971). Sales Stabilization through Export Diversification. *Review of Economics and Statistics* 53(2), 270–277.

Hopenhayn, Hugo (1992). Entry, Exit, and Firm Dynamics in Long Run Equilibrium. *Econometrica* 60(5), 1127–1150.

Ilmakunnas, Pekka and Satu Nurmi (2010). Dynamics of Export Market Entry and Exit. *Scandinavian Journal of Economics* 112(1), 101–126.

Jovanovic, Boyan (1982). Selection and the Evolution of Industry. *Econometrica* 50, 649–670.

Jovanovic, Boyan and Richard J. Gilbert (1993), The Diversification of Production. *Brookings Papers on Economic Activity, Microeconomics* (1), 197–247.

Kasahara, Hiroyuki, and Beverly Lapham (2008). Productivity and the Decision to Import and Export: Theory and Evidence. CESIfo Working Papers 2240, Ifo Institute for Economic Research, Munich.

Kasahara, Hiroyuki and Joel Rodrigue (2007). Does the Use of Imported Intermediates Increase Productivity? Plant-level Evidence. *Journal of Development Economics* 87(1), 106–118.

King, Gary and Langche Zeng (2001a). Logistic Regression in Rare Events Data. *Political Analysis* 9(2), 137–163.

King, Gary and Langche Zeng (2001b). Explaining Rare Events in International Relations. *International Organization* 55(3), 693–715.

Konold, Michael (2007). New Possibilities for Economic Research through Integration of Establishment-level Panel Data of German Official Statistics. *Journal of Applied Social Science Studies* 127(2), 321–334.

Lipczynski, John and John Wilson (2001). *Industrial Organisation. An Analysis of Competitive Markets*. Harlow, England: Prentice Hall.

Long, J. Scott and Jeremy Freese (2001). *Regression Models for Categorical Dependent Variables using Stata*. College Station, TX: Stata Press.

López Ricardo A. (2006). Imports of Intermediate Inputs and Plant Survival. *Economics Letters* 92(1), 58–62.

Melitz, Mark J. (2003). The Impact of Trade on Intra-Industry Reallocations and Aggregate Industry Productivity. *Econometrica* 71(6), 1695–1725.

Muûls, Mirabelle, and Mauro Pisu (2009). Imports and Exports at the Level of the Firm: Evidence from Belgium. *The World Economy* 32(5), 692–734.

Namini, Julian Emami, Giovanni Facchini and Ricardo López (2011). Export Growth and Factor Market Competition: Theory and Evidence. CEPR Discussion Paper 8256, Centre for Economic Policy Research, London.

Strotmann, Harald (2007). Entrepreneurial Survival. *Small Business Economics* 28(1), 87–104.

Vogel, Alexander and Stefan Dittrich (2008). The German Turnover Tax Statistics Panel. *Journal of Applied Social Science Studies* 128(4), 661–670.

Vogel, Alexander and Joachim Wagner (2010). Higher Productivity in Importing German Manufacturing Firms: Self-Selection, Learning from Importing, or Both? *Review of World Economics/Weltwirtschaftliches Archiv* 145(4), 641–665.

Wagner, Joachim (2007). Exports and Productivity: A Survey of the Evidence from Firm-Level Data. *The World Economy* 30(1), 60–82.

Wagner, Joachim (2008a). Export Entry, Export Exit and Productivity in German Manufacturing Industries. *International Journal of the Economics of Business* 15(2), 169–180.

Wagner, Joachim (2008b). A Note on Why More West than East German Firms Export. *International Economics and Economic Policy* 5(4), 363–370.

Wagner, Joachim (2009). Entry, Exit and Productivity: Empirical Results for German Manufacturing Industries. *German Economic Review* 11(1), 78–85.

Wagner, Joachim (2011a). From Estimation Results to Stylized Facts: Twelve Recommendations for Empirical Research in International Activities of Heterogeneous Firms. *De Economist* 159(4), 389–412.

Wagner, Joachim (2011b). Exports, Imports and Firm Survival: First Evidence for Manufacturing Enterprises in Germany. IZA Discussion Paper 5924, Institute for the Study of Labor Bonn.

Wagner, Joachim (2012a). International Trade and Firm Performance: A Survey of Empirical Studies Since 2006. *Review of World Economics/Weltwirtschaftliches Archiv* 148(2), 235–267.

Wagner, Joachim (2012b). The Post-Entry Performance of Cohorts of Export Starters in German Manufacturing Industries. *International Journal of the Economics of Business* 19(2), 169–193.

Zühlke, Sylvia, Markus Zwick, Sebastian Scharnhorst and Thomas Wende (2004). The Research Data Centres of the Federal Statististical Office and the Statistical Offices of the Länder. *Schmollers Jahrbuch/Journal of Applied Social Science Studies* 124(4), 567–578.

# Appendix 1

Descriptive statistics for variables included in the empirical models

| | | 2001 | | 2002 | | 2003 | | 2004 | |
|---|---|---|---|---|---|---|---|---|---|
| West Germany | | Exits | Survivors | Exits | Survivors | Exits | Survivors | Exit | Survivors |
| Dummy Variables: | | | | | | | | | |
| Firms that only export | mean | 0.327 | 0.262 | 0.342 | 0.263 | 0.360 | 0.270 | 0.388 | 0.268 |
| Firms that only import | mean | 0.050 | 0.103 | 0.072 | 0.100 | 0.086 | 0.095 | 0.068 | 0.098 |
| Firms that export and import | mean | 0.126 | 0.407 | 0.176 | 0.403 | 0.150 | 0.417 | 0.160 | 0.421 |
| Firms with 50–249 employees | mean | 0.255 | 0.428 | 0.223 | 0.422 | 0.194 | 0.423 | 0.241 | 0.426 |
| Firms with 250–499 employees | mean | 0.044 | 0.068 | 0.039 | 0.067 | 0.035 | 0.067 | 0.044 | 0.065 |
| Firms with 500 and more employees | mean | 0.029 | 0.054 | 0.024 | 0.052 | 0.028 | 0.052 | 0.021 | 0.051 |
| Firms that started before 1996 | mean | 0.562 | 0.736 | 0.538 | 0.674 | 0.517 | 0.652 | 0.504 | 0.623 |
| Firms with two or more products | mean | 0.616 | 0.607 | 0.529 | 0.616 | 0.556 | 0.608 | 0.562 | 0.601 |
| Labor productivity | mean | 103.96 | 143.63 | 111.35 | 141.90 | 113.02 | 145.44 | 136.08 | 153.30 |
| (sales per employee; 1000 €) | std. dev. | 137.48 | 174.99 | 147.96 | 168.76 | 160.37 | 185.00 | 454.14 | 212.13 |

(Continued)

*(Continued)*

| | | 2001 | | 2002 | | 2003 | | 2004 | |
|---|---|---|---|---|---|---|---|---|---|
| East Germany | | Exits | Survivors | Exits | Survivors | Exits | Survivors | Exit | Survivors |
| Dummy variables: | | | | | | | | | |
| Firms that only export | mean | 0.200 | 0.188 | 0.273 | 0.191 | 0.266 | 0.205 | 0.248 | 0.203 |
| Firms that only import | mean | 0.064 | 0.169 | 0.072 | 0.167 | 0.079 | 0.170 | 0.090 | 0.174 |
| Firms that export and import | mean | 0.078 | 0.280 | 0.069 | 0.285 | 0.093 | 0.304 | 0.100 | 0.316 |
| Firms with 50–249 employees | mean | 0.232 | 0.421 | 0.227 | 0.422 | 0.220 | 0.423 | 0.227 | 0.424 |
| Firms with 250–499 employees | mean | 0.023 | 0.038 | 0.025 | 0.039 | 0.023 | 0.038 | 0.012 | 0.039 |
| Firms with 500 and more employees | mean | 0.005 | 0.019 | 0.013 | 0.020 | 0.010 | 0.021 | 0.004 | 0.022 |
| Firms that started before 1996 | mean | 0.430 | 0.519 | 0.377 | 0.474 | 0.357 | 0.436 | 0.280 | 0.412 |
| Firms with two or more products | mean | 0.599 | 0.593 | 0.557 | 0.605 | 0.550 | 0.590 | 0.528 | 0.580 |
| Labor productivity | mean | 77.84 | 118.33 | 179.04 | 122.19 | 80.10 | 128.26 | 83.84 | 134.03 |
| (sales per employee; 1000 €) | std. dev. | 108.52 | 168.02 | 1613.1 | 182.91 | 91.11 | 187.54 | 89.64 | 184.63 |

*Note*: For a definition of exits and survivors see text. All variables with the exception of labour productivity are dummy variables coded as 1 if the firm belongs to the category and 0 else; the means reported in the table, therefore, indicate the percentage share of firms from a category in all exits and all survivors, respectively, in the year.

## Chapter 11

# Risk or Resilience? The Role of Trade Integration and Foreign Ownership for the Survival of German Enterprises during the Crisis 2008–2010

Joachim Wagner and John P. Weche Gelübcke

**Abstract**

This is the first study of the link between internationalization and firm survival during the 2008–2009 crisis in Germany, a country which was hit relatively lightly compared to other countries. Moreover, it is the first study which looks at the role of importing, exporting and FDI simultaneously in the context of a global economic recession. We use a tailor-made representative data set that covers all enterprises from the manufacturing sector with at least 20 employees. Our most striking result is to demonstrate the disadvantage of exporting for the chances of survival of a firm during the crisis in Western Germany. Importing instead reveals a positive correlation with survival and firms that both export and import do not show a different exit risk relative to non-traders. A plausible explanation is that in a global recession, deteriorating markets abroad cause demand losses for exporters and improved conditions on factor markets which result in an advantage for firms sourcing from factor markets abroad. Two-way traders do not show a link with exit risk, supporting the idea that they were able to outweigh their losses from exporting with their gains from importing, in what could be called an export–import hedge. Furthermore, we cannot support the hypothesis that foreign multinationals are more volatile during times of economic crisis.

*Keywords*: Exports, imports, foreign ownership, firm survival, economic crisis, Germany

**JEL Classification:** F23, L60

## 1. Introduction

Germany is one of the economies most integrated into the international division of labor. Only a few years ago, Germany was considered the world's leading export nation in terms of the total value of its exported goods. In 2012, Germany was the third largest exporter, and, at the same time, the third largest importer, demonstrating a considerable level of trade integration (World Trade Organization 2013, Appendix Table 1.2). From the dimension of foreign direct investment (FDI), only United States, Hong Kong, the UK, and France had a larger inward FDI stock than Germany and direct investments of German multinationals abroad made Germany rank fourth in terms of outward FDI stocks in 2010 (UNCTAD 2011, Annex Table I.2).

Although trade integration generally enables welfare-increasing efficiency gains and the exploitation or generation of firms' competitive advantages, the recent global economic crisis, which started in 2008–2009, shed light also on the negative aspects of economic internationalization. For example, Kleinert, Martin and Toubal (2012) investigate the transmission of economic shocks within multinational firms' affiliate networks and Wagner (2013a) finds that idiosyncratic shocks to only a few internationalized large firms characterized the export collapse in German manufacturing. The recent economic crisis is an appropriate event for evaluating the general hypothesis of whether or not negative idiosyncratic shocks, such as a shrinking world demand or decreasing availability of investment funds, affect internationalized firms to a greater extent than nationally oriented competitors. In other words, whether internationalization increases an individual firm's vulnerability in times of economic deterioration.

The link between firm performance and international activities has been the subject of a huge strand of the empirical literature since the seminal work by Bernard and Jensen (1995).[1] Apart from other dimensions of firm performance, such as productivity and

[1]See Wagner (2012) for a survey of recent studies.

profitability, survival chances are a key aspect of firm performance which is of high importance to all stakeholders. Developments in trade theory have given an additional incentive to study firm survival in the context of international trade, since the so-called *new new trade theory* predicts a considerable impact of trade on industry structure, meaning in particular that less productive firms leave the market (see Melitz (2003) and Helpman (2013)). Previous work on internationalization and firm closure can be separated into that referring to trade activities, including exporting and importing, and that referring to FDI and foreign ownership.[2]

To start with the trade criterion, why should exporting activities be linked to firm survival? Exporting can be considered a form of risk diversification through the spread of sales over different markets with different business cycle conditions or being in different phases of the product cycle (see Hirsch and Lev (1971)). Therefore, exports might provide a chance to substitute sales abroad for sales at home when a negative demand shock to the home market would have otherwise forced a firm to close down. Furthermore, Baldwin and Yan (2011) argue that non-exporters are in general less efficient than exporters (younger, smaller and less productive) and that, as a result, one expects that non-exporters are more likely to fail than exporters.

Regarding imports, imported intermediate inputs or capital goods might be cheaper and/or technically more advanced than inputs bought on the national market. Gibson and Graciano (2011) argue that the benefit of using imported inputs lies in a combination of the relative price and the technology embodied in the inputs. Imports, therefore, lead to an increase in price competitiveness and non-price competitiveness of importers compared to firms that do not import. Furthermore, there is empirical evidence of a positive link between imports and productivity (discussed in Vogel and Wagner (2010)), documented by a significant productivity differential between firms that import and firms that do not

[2]For a more detailed survey of these two parts of the literature, see Wagner (2011, 2013b) and Wagner and Weche Gelübcke (2012). The following summary is based on these publications.

trade internationally. Therefore, the probability of surviving can be expected to be higher for importers than for non-importers, *ceteris paribus*.

Firms that both export and import can be expected to benefit from the positive effects of both forms of international trade on firm survival. Furthermore, two-way traders tend to be more productive than firms that either only import, or only export, or do not trade at all (see Vogel and Wagner 2010). Therefore, we expect the probability of firm exit to be smaller for two-way traders than for firms that only export or only import.

Surveying the empirical literature on the link between the international trade activities of a firm and its survival chances, Wagner (2011 and 2013b) concludes that the survival chances of exporters are generally higher even after controlling for individual firm characteristics, such as size, age and productivity. His results for Germany show that importers and two-way traders have lower probabilities of closure, but that exporting does not seem to lower the exit risk.

Regarding foreign ownership ties, Baldwin and Yan (2011) argue that from a theoretical point of view the relation between foreign ownership and firm exit is not clear. On the one hand, foreign-owned firms may have access to superior technologies belonging to their foreign owners that might increase their efficiency and lower the risk of exit. The greater propensity to invest in R&D found in foreign-owned firms in Germany might lead to more innovation, improved competitiveness in Germany and in foreign markets, and might therefore increase the chances of survival. On the other hand, Baldwin and Yan (2011) point out that foreign-owned firms are less rooted in the host country economy and that they can shift their activities to another country when the local economy deteriorates. This should increase the probability of shutdown compared to nationally-owned firms.

Empirical studies reveal that the evidence is ambiguous and highly country dependent: Foreign-owned firms turn out to be more likely to exit in some countries and less likely in other countries. The only studies for Germany, by Andrews *et al.* (2012)

and by Wagner and Weche Gelübcke (2012), conclude that there is a higher exit risk for foreign firms than for domestically-owned firms when only dependent subsidiaries are considered, but that foreign-owned firms do not differ when also domestically-owned independent firms and group heads are part of the control group.

Firm-level studies on the link between firms' international status and their exit risk in the context of an economic crisis are rare. Narjoko and Hill (2007) investigate firm survival during the 1997–1998 Indonesian crisis and find export orientation and foreign ownership to be highly significant determinants of both survival and recovery. Although a local crisis is never without an impact on other countries in an integrated economic world and the distinction between a *local* and a *global* economic crisis cannot be straightforward, it is a major feature of the recent economic crisis 2008–2009 that it can be characterized as a global phenomenon rather than a local one.[3] This has a significant impact on theoretical considerations regarding the link between international exposure and performance. For example, in a local crisis framework, exporting would be clearly seen as risk diversifying and, therefore, as a measure for overcoming economic slow-downs. In contrast, if a crisis ramifies mainly abroad, export orientation would be regarded as much more risky than a focus on domestic sales. The underlying problem is twofold: (i) firms are usually not able to perfectly substitute sales abroad with sales at home and (ii) firms are normally not able to shrink rapidly in reaction of a deteriorating demand as they may expand in prospering times. Therefore, a shift to the home market cannot be regarded as a perfect alternative for most exporting firms, although it may serve as an easing factor. Alfaro and Chen (2012) find multinational subsidiaries worldwide to have been more resilient during the 2008–2009 global crisis. The key determinants turn out to be a vertical production link with the parent company

[3]When we talk about the impact of the recent economic crisis in the context at hand, we refer mainly to the aspect of a shrinking demand for manufactured products. It is known that such a demand shock happened in many of the German export markets and that the general demand in Germany was relatively stable, for example, due to stable employment levels.

and being more closely linked in financial terms. Godart, Görg and Hanley (2012) focus on Ireland and conclude that foreign firms were not more likely to exit than domestically-owned firms during the crisis. Amendola *et al.* (2012) bring together the aspects of trade relatedness, foreign ownership and outward FDI as determinants for firm survival over the crisis with Italian data. Their findings point to more volatile multinational subsidiaries and more resilient Italian exporters. It is self evident that there are other factors shaping the survival chances in times of economic downturn. An important feature of economic distress is an increase in interest rates and a potential "credit crunch". Consequently, Abildgren, Vølund Buchholst and Staghøj (2013) stress the importance of bank links in shaping survival chances. They use data on Danish non-financial firms and find a higher default probability of firms with links to "weak" banks during the crisis, but they do not focus on the role of internationalization.[4]

The contribution of our paper is to provide the first empirical study of the link between internationalization and firm survival during the 2008–2009 crisis in Germany. Hence, it is the first study for a country which was hit relatively lightly compared to other countries, and whose domestic demand experienced a relatively lesser decline. Furthermore, it is the first analysis adding the role of input sourcing and importing activities to FDI and export status. We use a tailor-made representative dataset that merges information from surveys performed by the German statistical offices, from administrative data collected by the Tax Authorities, and from a commercial data provider. The data covers all enterprises from the manufacturing sector with at least 20 employees. We have been able to study the link between international integration and firm exits during non-crisis years previously with the same data (Wagner 2013b; Wagner and Weche Gelübcke 2012) and are therefore able to compare the results from the crisis period with those from a

[4]Naidoo (2010) also looks at firms' behavior during the recent crisis and specifically at the role played by marketing. His analysis of Chinese export oriented SMEs reveals a positive correlation between marketing innovations and the perceived likelihood of survival.

non-crisis period. Our previous studies focus on different aspects of international integration (Wagner (2013b) on trade integration; Wagner and Weche Gelübcke (2012) on foreign ownership) which are combined in the study at hand. Both studies were performed when data on the crisis period had not been available.

To anticipate the most important results, exporting appears to negatively affect survival chances in western Germany during the crisis. Importing instead reveals a positive correlation with survival and firms that both export and import do not show a different exit risk relative to non-traders. A plausible explanation is that in a global recession, deteriorating markets abroad cause demand losses for exporters and improved conditions in factor markets, something which results in an advantage for firms sourcing abroad. Furthermore, foreign subsidiaries do not show any different exit probabilities than German firms, therefore not supporting the hypothesis of more volatile multinationals. In Eastern Germany, all our indicators for different aspects of internationalization remain statistically insignificant.

The rest of the paper is organized as follows. Section 2 describes the dataset and the definitions of the variables. Section 3 presents the descriptive results. Section 4 gives the probit estimates of survival premia dependent on several aspects of internationalization and other firm-level characteristics. Section 5 concludes.

## 2. Data and Variables

This study uses a tailor-made enterprise level dataset that contains information from surveys performed by the German statistical offices, from data collected by the Tax Authorities, and from a commercial data provider.

The first source of data is the monthly and annual reports for establishments in mining, quarrying and manufacturing industries described in Konold (2007). These surveys cover all establishments from the mining, quarrying and manufacturing industries that employ at least 20 people in the local production unit or in the company that owns the unit as a whole. The participation of firms in the survey is mandated by law. Participation in this survey is used to identify surviving and exiting firms (discussed in more detail below). This survey is also the source for information on the location of the firm in Western Germany or Eastern Germany, industry affiliation, whether a firm exports or not, labor productivity (measured as sales per employee), and the number of employees (used to measure firm size). Furthermore, given that the data start with the year 1995, this survey is used to distinguish between old firms (that were already covered by the survey in 1995) and new firms (that entered the survey in 1996 or later). Note that in this dataset, export refers to the amount of sales to a customer in a foreign country plus sales to a German export trading company; indirect exports (for example, tires produced in a plant in Germany that are delivered to a German manufacturer of cars who exports some of its products) are not covered by this definition. For this project, the information collected at the establishment level has been aggregated at the enterprise level to match the unit of observation from the other sources of data used here.

The second source of data is the German Turnover Tax Statistics Panel (described in detail in Vogel and Dittrich (2008)). This data set is based on the yearly turnover tax: All enterprises with a turnover that exceeds a rather low threshold (17,500 EUR since 2003) are covered. This data set informs us whether a firm imports or not. Note, however, that imports are not directly recorded therein completely. Imports from EU member countries are reported under the item of "intra-Community acquisitions". The amount of imports from countries outside the EU is not included in the turnover tax statistics. In this case, an import turnover tax is charged by the customs authorities. Nonetheless, this import turnover tax is deductible as an input tax, and is therefore reported in the data set. From this information, we know whether the enterprise imports from non-EU countries or not.

The third source of data is the survey of products (*Produktionsstatistik*). This survey is used to distinguish between firms that produce only one product and multi-product firms.

Information on the foreign ownership status of a firm is based on data from the commercial database MARKUS, a joint product of the commercial data providers Bureau van Dijk and Creditreform. This database reports whether an enterprise is an affiliate, group head or independent entity, and whether the group head of an affiliate is located abroad. Starting with the reporting year 2007, this information was linked to the German enterprise register system (*Unternehmensregistersystem*) by the German Federal Statistical Office (see Weche Gelübcke (2011) for details). A firm is regarded as foreign owned if it is an affiliate with a group head located in a foreign country and if more than 50 percent of the voting rights of the owners or more than 50 percent of the shares are controlled (directly or indirectly) by a firm or a person/institution located outside Germany.

The data from these sources were linked by using the enterprise register system that includes, among other things, information about the unique enterprise identifier used in the surveys conducted by the statistical offices and the unique turnover tax identifier used by the Tax Authorities. Our data covers the years from 2007 to 2010. The global financial crisis started in 2007 and unfolded its impact on the real economy in the last quarter of 2008. Since we are interested in the economic crisis that followed the financial crisis (although these two aspects are of course not easy to separate) we try to start our analysis immediately before the crisis unfolded its real economic impact. Since we use yearly data, to start our analysis in 2007 seems too far from the major breakout at the end of 2008 and 2008 may already be affected by the economic crisis. We decided to start the analysis in 2008 as we assume firm exits to appear with a certain lag after the economic impact and we therefore call 2008 the pre-crisis period.

A firm is identified as an exit if it has reported to either the monthly report or the annual report for establishments in mining, quarrying and manufacturing industries in 2008 but not in the recovery year 2010. Consequently, we assume the identified firms to have exited the market at some point in 2009 or 2010.

It should be noted that the definition of *firm exit* used here is not without problems. First of all, if a firm relocates outside Germany or changes its activities from mining, quarrying, or manufacturing to services or agriculture, it no longer reports to the monthly report or the annual report for establishments in mining, quarrying, and manufacturing industries and, therefore, is considered as an exit. To the best of our knowledge and according to information from the employees in the official statistical office who are in charge of preparing the data used here, this is only rarely the case.

Second, the industry classification of the monthly reports and the Turnover Tax Statistics was subject to changes in the year 2009. This means that some identified exits may not be real exits but rather firms which became classified as being outside the scope of the surveys used here in 2009. Therefore we had to exclude the whole of those industries which experienced such re-classifications, namely the publishing sector and the recycling sector.[5]

Third, firms that shrink below the threshold of 20 employees in the local production unit or in the company that owns the unit are no longer obliged to report to the survey (but often do so at least for some years anyway), and if they did not report in 2009 or 2010 they are considered as exits here but are in fact survivors. To reduce the uncertainty in the classification of a firm as an exit related to the threshold of 20 employees, we excluded all firms below a threshold of 30 employees in 2008.[6] Note that neither a change in the legal form of the firm nor a change in the ownership (due to a merger or an acquisition) nor a relocation of the firm inside Germany leads to an erroneous classification of a firm as an exit, because the identification number of the firm used in official statistics will not change. Unfortunately, it is not possible to investigate further the data for firms identified as exits according to the definition used here due to the strict confidentiality of the firm level data. A certain

---

[5]Within the publishing sector, there were 2,371 observations dropped from the sample, including 33 exits. In the recycling sector, there were 191 observations and no exits. For the descriptive statistics of the final sample, see Section 3.

[6]All estimates are also reported without this additional threshold in the Appendix 1.

degree of fuzziness, therefore, remains, and this should be kept in mind when putting the results from the empirical investigation into perspective.

## 3. Descriptive Results

The final sample contains information about 36,183 enterprises, of which 288 left the market in the years 2009 or 2010. The overall exit rate in our sample is hence below 1 percent. This seems very low compared to other results for the pre-crisis period from the same data base by Wagner and Weche Gelübcke (2012), who report an exit rate of 2.77 percent for the 2007 exit cohort. This huge difference is mainly due to the exclusion of firms with less than 30 employees and points to higher exit rates among small firms, which is in line with theoretical considerations that assume a "liability of smallness" due to, for instance, disadvantages of scale, more restrictive access to capital markets and a lower level of management skills (Audretsch 1995: 149; Strotmann 2007). Even after excluding firms with below 30 employees from our sample, still 76 percent of exiting firms had between 30 and 50 employees (see Table 1).

Surprisingly, the descriptive statistics in Table 1 also reveal that only 25 percent of exits were firms without any trade activities and 67 percent of exiting firms reported either solely export activities or export and import activities in 2008. Only 8 percent of exits happened within the group of only importing firms. This somehow contradicts the general expectation of only domestically oriented firms' being more likely to exit than internationally oriented firms due to risk diversification and generally higher productivity levels. In this respect, the picture appears to be different from the pre-crisis evidence, which shows an exit rate among non-trading firms that is almost twice the exit rate among firms that are involved in exporting activities (Wagner and Weche Gelübcke 2012). However, if we consider the risk diversification reasoning in the light of a global crisis it may not be too surprising to see exporting firms more vulnerable.

Table 1. Descriptive statistics for 2008

| | Survivors | | Exits | |
|---|---|---|---|---|
| | Number of firms | Share (in percent) | Number of firms | Share (in percent) |
| All firms | 35,895 | 99.20 | 288 | 0.80 |
| **Number of employees** | | | | |
| <50 | 16,101 | 44.86 | 218 | 75.69 |
| 50–249 | 15,893 | 44.28 | 62 | 21.53 |
| 250< | 3,901 | 10.87 | 8 | 2.78 |
| **International trade** | | | | |
| No trade | 7,365 | 20.52 | 70 | 24.31 |
| Exports only | 10,235 | 28.51 | 97 | 33.68 |
| Imports only | 3,557 | 9.91 | 24 | 8.33 |
| Exports and imports | 14,738 | 41.06 | 97 | 33.68 |
| **Ownership** | | | | |
| Foreign owned | 3,437 | 9.58 | 20 | 6.94 |
| Domestic independent | 16,837 | 46.91 | 163 | 56.60 |
| Domestic dependent | 14,160 | 39.45 | 101 | 35.07 |
| Domestic group head | 1,461 | 4.07 | 4 | 1.39 |
| **Firm age** | | | | |
| Founded before 1996 | 17,594 | 49.02 | 122 | 42.36 |
| Founded after 1996 | 18,301 | 50.98 | 166 | 57.64 |
| **Labor productivity** | | | | |
| Bottom 1/3 | 11,855 | 33.03 | 137 | 47.57 |
| Middle 1/3 | 11,960 | 33.32 | 80 | 27.78 |
| Top 1/3 | 12,080 | 33.65 | 71 | 24.65 |
| **Number of products** | | | | |
| One | 13,859 | 38.61 | 138 | 47.92 |
| Two and more | 22,036 | 61.39 | 150 | 52.08 |
| **Region** | | | | |
| Western | 29,360 | 81.79 | 242 | 84.03 |
| Eastern | 6,535 | 18.21 | 46 | 15.97 |

The figures of exits by ownership categories in Table 1 do not surprise. The major share of exiting firms (57 percent) was labeled *independent entity* and was therefore not part of any domestic or foreign enterprise group. Only 7 percent of exits were foreign subsidiaries, supporting the assumption that affiliates of multinationals have higher survival chances due to a network effect and access to internal resources.

Furthermore, younger and less productive firms show higher exit rates, in line with the assumption of a "liability of newness" due to a lack of experience in the particular market (Audretsch 1995: 149) and the predictions by theoretical models of industrial dynamics, such as Jovanovic (1982), for the role of firms' productivity levels for entry, exit and growth. The number of products seem to have little influence on the exit rate as both categories — one-product firms and two or more product firms — show similar exit rates. Multi-product firms are generally regarded as the more resilient firms because they are diversified across product markets and thus are able to reduce their sales default risk (e.g. Jovanovic and Gilbert (1993) and Lipczynski and Wilson (2001): 324f).

Totally, 84 percent of exiting firms were located in Western Germany, which reflects almost exactly the share of observations in the total sample located in Western Germany, which is 82 percent.

## 4. Results from Probit Estimates

To go beyond the descriptive evidence about the role of internationalization in the survival chances of firms during times of crisis, we estimate the probability of firm exits in a nonlinear binomial probit model.[7] We estimate the conditional probability of firm $i$ leaving the market, $EXIT$, during the period $t+1$ (2009–2010), conditioned on a set of firm-level characteristics $X$ in the pre-crisis period $t$ (2008). The model can be written as follows, with $\Phi$ as the standard normal distribution:

$$Pr(EXIT_{it+1} = 1) = \Phi(x\beta) = \Phi(\alpha + \delta X'_{it} + \epsilon_{it}).$$

In a first version of the model above, we include only indicator variables for the different aspects of internationalization as firm-level characteristics (Model 1). In particular, we include three indicator

[7]Unfortunately, we do not have information on the exact age of an individual firm in the data. Therefore, we cannot work with hazard rates or survival analysis in general.

variables: The first takes the value '1' if a firm only exports, the second, if it only imports, the third if it both exports and imports (two-way traders), and the fourth indicates whether a firm is under foreign control. A next version of the model adds other covariates motivated in the previous section (Model 2). We include two dummies for size: One for medium-sized firms (50–249 employees), and one for large firms (more than 250 employees), a dummy variable indicating whether or not a firm was established before 1996, and another, indicating whether or not a firm is a multi-product seller. Moreover, we add labor productivity (measured in 1,000 EUR). All these covariates are likely to be correlated with a firm's probability of survival. A third version of our model includes additional indicators that consider whether a firm is an independent entity or if a firm is a group head, controlling other subsidiaries located in Germany or abroad (Model 3). The reference group here is thus the group of firms which are controlled by a German group head, in other words, the group of domestic dependent firms. All versions include industry dummies at the 2-digit level to control for general differences between sectors and are estimated separately for western and eastern Germany to account for regional differences.[8]

Table 2 reports the average marginal effects (AMEs) of our probit estimates for Western and Eastern Germany separately. Instead of calculating a marginal effect only at one specific value of a variable or at a hypothetical sample mean, AMEs consider marginal effects along the entire distribution of a variable. If we only control for general differences across industries in Model 1, only being an importer and being a two-way trader lowers the exit risk of firms in Western Germany during the crisis years. Being an importer (a two-way trader) in the pre-crisis period lowers the risk of exit in the following period by 0.6 (0.2) percentage points relative to firms without trade activities and *ceteris paribus*. Although the absolute values of the marginal effects for both variables seem to be fairly

[8]Even more than 20 years after German reunification in 1990, the eastern and western regions of Germany still differ markedly in economic terms. This has recently been confirmed by a 2011 report on Eastern Germany's economic situation and perspectives, carried out by leading German research institutes (IWH 2011).

Table 2. Probit estimates of firm exits in 2009 and 2010

| | Western Germany | | | | Eastern Germany | | | |
|---|---|---|---|---|---|---|---|---|
| | (1) | (2) | (3) | (4) | (1) | (2) | (3) | (4) |
| Only exporters | 0.002 | 0.004** | 0.004** | 0.002 | −0.001 | −0.0004 | −0.0004 | −0.0001 |
| | (1.00) | (2.25) | (2.20) | (0.78) | (0.27) | (0.12) | (0.12) | (0.04) |
| Only importers | −0.006** | −0.005** | −0.005* | −0.005 | 0.0002 | 0.001 | 0.001 | −0.0001 |
| | (2.26) | (1.98) | (1.95) | (1.14) | (0.05) | (0.11) | (0.16) | (0.04) |
| Two-way traders | −0.002* | 0.001 | 0.001 | −0.001 | −0.003 | −0.002 | −0.002 | 0.003 |
| | (1.89) | (0.49) | (0.52) | (0.31) | (0.74) | (0.47) | (0.42) | (0.58) |
| Foreign owned | −0.002 | 0.001 | 0.001 | 0.001 | −0.007 | −0.007 | −0.005 | −0.003 |
| | (1.11) | (0.61) | (0.51) | (0.46) | (1.11) | (1.03) | (0.80) | (0.65) |
| Independent | — | — | −0.0001 | −0.0002 | — | — | 0.003 | 0.002 |
| | | | (0.08) | (0.14) | | | (0.95) | (0.81) |
| Domestic group head | — | — | −0.002 | −0.002 | — | — | omitted | omitted |
| | | | (0.73) | (0.75) | | | | |
| 50–249 employees | — | −0.007*** | −0.007*** | −0.007*** | — | −0.008*** | −0.008*** | −0.005*** |
| | | (4.84) | (4.84) | (4.79) | | (3.06) | (2.88) | (3.61) |
| 250< employees | — | −0.012*** | −0.012*** | −0.012*** | — | −0.003 | −0.002 | −0.001 |
| | | (2.98) | (2.87) | (2.87) | | (0.52) | (0.37) | (0.19) |
| Established before 1996 | — | −0.001 | −0.001 | −0.001 | — | 0.001 | 0.002 | 0.001 |
| | | (1.55) | (1.52) | (1.48) | | (0.36) | (0.44) | (0.36) |
| Multi-product firms | — | −0.002** | −0.002** | −0.002** | — | −0.004* | −0.004 | −0.002** |
| | | (2.01) | (2.01) | (2.01) | | (1.68) | (1.62) | (1.97) |
| Labor productivity | — | $-8.72e-06$* | $-8.58e-06$* | −0.00002 | — | −9.78e-07 | −2.57e-07 | v5.42e-07 |
| | | (1.78) | (1.83) | (0.99) | | (0.34) | (0.10) | (0.63) |

*(Continued)*

Table 2. Probit estimates of firm exits in 2009 and 2010

| | Western Germany | | | | Eastern Germany | | | |
|---|---|---|---|---|---|---|---|---|
| | (1) | (2) | (3) | (4) | (1) | (2) | (3) | (4) |
| Only export * productivity | — | — | — | 0.00002 | — | — | — | $-1.07e-06$ |
| | — | — | — | (0.70) | — | — | — | (0.24) |
| Only import * productivity | — | — | — | $9.12e-06$ | — | — | — | $4.02e-06^{*}$ |
| | — | — | — | (0.24) | — | — | — | (1.80) |
| Two-way trader * productivity | — | — | — | 0.00002 | — | — | — | −0.00003 |
| | — | — | — | (0.63) | — | — | — | (1.08) |
| 2-digit industry dummies | yes | yes | yes | yes | yes | yes | yes | yes |
| Number of firms | 23,603 | 23,603 | 23,603 | 23,603 | 3,918 | 3,918 | 3,810 | 3,810 |

*Notes*: Reported are estimated AME with |z-values| in parentheses; Statistical significance at the 10 percent (*), 5 percent (**) and 1 percent (***) level; Standard errors are adjusted for 2-digit industry clusters.

small, their significance should not be neglected. All marginal effects here have to be interpreted in relation to the overall exit rate in Western Germany which is 0.8 percent (it is also 0.8 percent in the overall sample and 0.7 percent in the Eastern German sample). Considering the overall exit rate of the sample, 0.6 (0.2) percentage point change of the exit probability seems large. Engaging only in exports and being part of a foreign multinational network does not seem to have a statistically significant link with the exit probability during a global crisis. Pre-crisis results instead show exporting to be negatively correlated with exit risk (Wagner and Weche Gelübcke 2012). When adding additional covariates in Model 2, the estimates for the Western German sample give all control variables the expected negative sign and are statistically significant at common levels, except firm age, which is statistically insignificant. The control for these additional factors brings about a change in the significance of our trade variables and, other factors being held constant, exporting without importing is positively correlated with exit risk, which means that exporting firms are 0.4 percentage points more likely to exit if they do not import, than are non-trading firms. This result is surprising and supports the hypothesis that the diversification mechanism of exporting does not work during times of a global recession. Importing instead is correlated with a firm's default risk in the other direction. A possible explanation for this finding is that exporters rely on product prices on markets abroad and suffer from a decreasing demand and declining prices in export markets. Unfortunately, we do not have information about the specific destination markets of firms' exports and therefore cannot test the hypothesis that it is in fact those exits driving the results that have exported to deteriorating markets. This could be convincing, because, for example, some German exports go to China (almost 5 percent in 2009 and almost 6 percent in 2010, Destatis (2011): 473) which did not suffer a demand shock during the crisis and if it was German firms exporting to China that represent the exits in our sample, the hypothesis outlined above does not hold. On the other hand, firms obtaining their inputs from factor markets abroad benefit from exactly the same mechanism of decreasing demand and prices in the country providing these input factors. Therefore, it seems plausible that, in a global recession, German firms experienced losses through exporting and gains from importing. Two-way traders are not significantly correlated with exit risk anymore in our Model 2 estimates. This supports the explanation given above because firms which are engaged in both exporting and importing were probably able to outweigh their losses from exporting with their gains from importing.

As we have seen in Model 1 estimates, without controlling for other factors, *only exporting* does not show any statistically significant link with exit risk. Although we include other covariates than productivity in Model 3, it is likely that productivity plays a crucial role as a determinant for firm exits in combination with international trade as standard models of heterogeneous firms in international trade suggest (Melitz 2003). To consider this aspect, we estimate a fourth model with interaction terms of productivity and all trade indicators. The results in Table 2 demonstrate that productivity indeed plays a crucial role — in the sense that exits happen more often among low productive firms (*cf*. Table 1) — since the trade indicator coefficients all turn statistically insignificant.[9] This does not mean that the significant role of *only exporters* in Model 3 estimates is due to an omitted variable bias. Rather it shows that, according to standard theory, the low productive firms are less likely to compensate losses from sales penalties abroad.

Model 3 estimates for Western Germany do not change the picture regarding our trade indicators and it turns out that being part of an enterprise group, either domestic or foreign, does not matter for survival during the crisis in Germany, since not only does

[9]Considering interaction effects in nonlinear models is not without problems in terms of both magnitude (including the direction) and statistical significance (see Ai and Norton (2003)). To account for this we used the Stata *inteff* command suggested by Norton *et al*. (2004) and computed the corrected marginal effects and standard errors for Tables 2 and 3 but the result of insignificant interaction terms does not change (and even the importer productivity interaction for the Eastern German sample loses its statistical significance).

the foreign ownership dummy remain insignificant, but so do the dummies for being an independent entity or a group head.

The results for Eastern Germany in Table 2 reveal different results: they do not point to any significant influence of trade and ownership on survival chances.

## 5. Robustness

Beside the AMEs, there are other possible ways of calculating marginal effects, and this methodological change might change the results. To take into account this possibility, we additionally present marginal effects at the sample mean (MEM) in Table 3. The marginal effects in Table 3 differ only very slightly from those in Table 2, thereby supporting the robustness of our results. In general, we prefer the AMEs because they consider effects along the entire distribution and not only one hypothetical case as do the marginal effects at the sample mean. For a more detailed discussion of marginal effects, see Williams (2010) and Cameron and Trivedi (2010: 343ff).

Another issue is whether or not the exclusion of all firms with less than 30 employees from our analysis changes our results. To test this, we repeated the estimations with the sample including those small firms below the threshold of 30 employees in Table A.1. It turns out that exporting activities still exhibit a positive and statistically significant sign, supporting the validity of our finding regarding export activities. However, the coefficient of being an importer is no longer statistically significant, although its sign remains negative.

The descriptive statistics in Table 1 show that more than 99 percent of firms in our sample are survivors and that the distribution of our dichotomous dependent variable is therefore skewed with disproportionately many zeros. This asymmetric distribution is not considered in the symmetric probit model. Consequently, we estimate a binary response complementary log–log model that assumes a response curve which approaches one more sharply than zero and is commonly used in this context (Cameron and Trivedi

Table 3. Marginal effects at the sample mean for probit estimates

| | Western Germany | | | | Eastern Germany | | | |
|---|---|---|---|---|---|---|---|---|
| | (1) | (2) | (3) | (4) | (1) | (2) | (3) | (4) |
| Only exporters | 0.001 | 0.003** | 0.003** | 0.002 | −0.001 | −0.0003 | −0.0003 | −0.0001 |
| | (1.01) | (2.32) | (2.25) | (0.78) | (0.27) | (0.12) | (0.12) | (0.04) |
| Only importers | −0.006** | −0.004** | −0.004** | −0.004 | 0.0002 | 0.0004 | 0.001 | −0.0002 |
| | (2.39) | (2.03) | (2.00) | (1.16) | (0.05) | (0.11) | (0.16) | (0.04) |
| Two-way traders | −0.002* | 0.001 | 0.001 | −0.001 | −0.003 | −0.002 | −0.001 | 0.005 |
| | (1.92) | (0.49) | (0.52) | (0.31) | (0.75) | (0.47) | (0.41) | (0.52) |
| Foreign owned | −0.002 | 0.001 | 0.001 | 0.001 | −0.006 | −0.005 | −0.004 | −0.004 |
| | (1.14) | (0.62) | (0.51) | (0.46) | (1.15) | (1.06) | (0.82) | (0.64) |
| Independent | — | — | −0.0001 | −0.0001 | — | — | 0.002 | 0.003 |
| | | | (0.08) | (0.14) | | | (0.96) | (0.95) |
| Domestic group head | — | — | −0.002 | −0.002 | — | — | omitted | omitted |
| | | | (0.72) | (0.74) | | | | |
| 50–249 employees | — | −0.005*** | −0.005*** | −0.005*** | — | −0.006*** | −0.006*** | −0.008*** |
| | | (5.95) | (6.03) | (5.83) | | (4.00) | (3.59) | (2.90) |
| 250< employees | — | −0.009*** | −0.009*** | −0.009*** | — | −0.002 | −0.001 | −0.001 |
| | | (3.51) | (3.34) | (3.32) | | (0.51) | (0.36) | 0.20 |
| Established before 1996 | — | −0.001 | −0.001 | −0.001 | — | 0.001 | 0.001 | 0.001 |
| | | (1.50) | (1.47) | (1.45) | | (0.37) | (0.45) | 0.36 |
| Multi-product firms | — | −0.002* | −0.002* | −0.002** | — | −0.003* | −0.003 | −0.004 |
| | | (1.95) | (1.96) | (1.98) | | (1.76) | (1.64) | (1.60) |

*(Continued)*

Table 3. *(Continued)*

| | Western Germany | | | | Eastern Germany | | | |
|---|---|---|---|---|---|---|---|---|
| | (1) | (2) | (3) | (4) | (1) | (2) | (3) | (4) |
| Labor productivity | — | −6.67e-06* | −6.54e-06* | −0.00002 | — | −7.41e-07 | −1.92e-07 | 8.41e-07 |
| | | (1.85) | (1.89) | (1.00) | | (0.34) | (0.10) | (0.65) |
| Only export * productivity | — | — | — | 0.00001 | — | — | — | $-1.66e-06$ |
| | — | — | — | (0.71) | — | — | — | (0.24) |
| Only import * productivity | — | — | — | $6.90e-06$ | — | — | — | $6.25e-06^{***}$ |
| | — | — | — | (0.24) | — | — | — | (2.54) |
| Two-way trader * productivity | — | — | — | 0.00001 | — | — | — | −0.0001 |
| | — | — | — | (0.63) | — | — | — | (0.87) |
| 2-digit industry dummies | yes | yes | yes | yes | yes | yes | yes | yes |
| Number of firms | 23,603 | 23,603 | 23,603 | 23,603 | 3,918 | 3,918 | 3,810 | 3,810 |

*Notes*: Reported are estimated marginal effects at the sample mean (MEM) with $|z\text{-values}|$ in parentheses; Statistical significance at the 10 percent (*), 5 percent (**) and 1 percent (***) level; Standard errors are adjusted for 2-digit industry clusters.

2010: 460).[10] The results of complementary log–log model estimates do not change the results from our probit estimates as the positive coefficient for only exporters for the Western German sample remains statistically significant as well as the negative coefficient for only importers. Both coefficients are statistically insignificant in the Eastern German sample and if we consider interaction terms between productivity and trade indicators (Model 4).

## 6. Concluding Remarks

We provide the first study on the internationalization–firm-survival link during the 2008–2009 crisis in Germany, a country which was hit relatively lightly compared to other countries. Moreover, it is the first study which, in the context of a global economic recession, looks simultaneously at the roles of importing, exporting, and FDI. We use a tailor-made representative data set that merges information from surveys performed by the German statistical offices, from administrative data collected by the Tax Authorities, and from a commercial data provider. The data covers all enterprises from the manufacturing sector with at least 20 employees.

Our most striking result is to demonstrate a disadvantage of exporting for the survival chances of a firm during a global economic recession. Importing instead reveals a positive correlation with survival, but firms that both export and import do not show a different exit risk relative to non-traders. A plausible explanation is that in a global recession, deteriorating markets abroad cause demand losses for exporters (either in terms of price or magnitude) and improved conditions in factor markets, something which results in an advantage for firms sourcing from factor markets abroad. In other words, German firms experienced losses through exporting and gains from importing. Two-way trading is not significantly correlated with exit risk. This supports the explanation

[10]As mentioned earlier, we are not able to apply survival analysis and therefore the model here is not to confuse with a complementary log–log specification of the hazard rate in survival models (see Jenkins (2005)).

given above, because firms which are engaged in both exporting and importing were probably able to outweigh their losses from exporting with their gains from importing, something which could be called an "export–import hedge." However, these findings apply only to Western Germany, as all our indicator variables for the several aspects of internationalization remain insignificant in the Eastern German sample.

Furthermore, foreign subsidiaries do not show any different exit probabilities than German firms. Therefore, we cannot support the hypothesis that foreign firms and/or foreign multinationals are more volatile during times of economic crisis.

A limitation of our study is that the identification of exits remains somewhat fuzzy and that we have to believe the data processing staff that the applied identification is an appropriate mean to reduce this fuzziness to a minimum. As a more general limitation of our study it is important to keep in mind that, although we look at a time period of three years, we cannot fully exploit the panel character of our data and our study therefore suffers from all the usual shortcomings of cross-sectional data. In particular these are, for example, the existence of unobserved time-invariant heterogeneity and a potential reverse causality. Nevertheless, we can conclude that internationalization as such is not correlated with a firm's resilience or exit risk during the 2008–2009 economic crisis in Germany. It was rather the specific mode of trade integration that mattered for the survival of firms. There is a wealth of other key variables whose response to the crisis should also be accounted for when judging the crisis resilience of firms from a broader perspective. Such variables are for example, employment levels, profitability and the number of products, but since the focus of this study is on firm exits, the exploitation of those is left for future research.

## References

Abildgren, Kim, Birgitte Vølund Buchholst and Jonas Staghøj (2013). Bank-firm Relationships and the Survival of Non-financial Firms During the Financial

Crisis 2008–2009. European Central Bank Working Paper Series, 1516, February.

Ai, Chunrong and Edward C. Norton (2003). Interaction Terms in Logit and Probit Models. *Economics Letters* 80, 123–129.

Alfaro, Laura and Maggie Chen (2012). Surviving the Global Financial Crisis: Foreign Ownership and Establishment Performance. *American Economic Journal: Economic Policy* 4(3), 30–55.

Amendola, Adalgiso, Anna Maria Ferragina, Rosanna Pittiglio and Filippo Reganati (2012): Are Exporters and Multinational Firms More Resilient Over A Crisis? First Evidence for Manufacturing Enterprises in Italy. *Economics Bulletin* 32(3), 1914–1926.

Andrews, Martyn, Lutz Bellmann, Thorsten Schank and Richard Upward (2012). Foreign-owned Plants and Job Security. *Review of World Economics* 148(1), 89–117.

Audretsch, David B. (1995). *Innovation and Industry Evolution*. Cambridge, MA and London, England: Cambridge University Press.

Baldwin, John and Beiling Yan (2011). The Death of Canadian Manufacturing Plants: Heterogeneous Responses to Changes in Tariffs and Real Exchange Rates. *Review of World Economics* 147(1), 131–167.

Bandick, Roger (2010). Multinationals and Plant Survival. *Review of World Economics* 146(4), 609–634.

Bernard, Andrew B. and J. Bradford Jensen (1995). Exporters, Jobs, and Wages in U.S. Manufacturing: 1976–1987. *Brookings Papers on Economic Activity, Microeconomics* 1, 67–119.

Cameron, Adrian C. and Pravin K. Trivedi (2010). *Microeconometrics using Stata*. revised edition, Stata Press.

[Destatis] Statistisches Bundesamt (2011). Statistisches Jahrbuch 2011, Wiesbaden.

Gibson, Marc J. and Tim A. Graciano (2011). *Costs of Starting to Trade and Costs of Continuing to Trade*. mimeo: Washington State University.

Godart, Olivier, Holger Görg and Aoife Hanley (2012). Surviving the Crisis: Foreign Mutinationals Versus Domestic Firms in Ireland. *The World Economy* 35(10), 1305–1321.

Helpman, Elhanan (2013). Foreign Trade and Investment: Firm-Level Perspectives. Economica Coase Lecture Working Paper, April.

Hirsch, Seev and Baruch Lev (1971). Sales Stabilization through Export Diversification. *Review of Economics and Statistics* 53(2), 270–277.

IWH, DIW, ifo Dresden, IAB, HOF, and RWI (2011): Wirtschaftlicher Stand und Perspektiven für Ostdeutschland. Studie im Auftrag des Bundesministeriums des Innern. Halle (Saale).

Jenkins, Stephen P. (2005). *Survival Analysis*. Mimeo: University of Essex. Available at https://www.iser.essex.ac.uk/files/teaching/stephenj/ec968/pdfs/ec968lnotesv6.pdf.

Jovanovic, Boyan (1982). Selection and the Evolution of Industry, *Econometrica* 50, 649–670.

Jovanovic, Boyan and Richard J. Gilbert (1993). The Diversification of Production, *Brookings Papers on Economic Activity, Microeconomics* 1993(1), 197–247.

Kleinert, Jörn, Julien Martin and Farid Toubal (2012). The Few leading the Many: Foreign Affiliates and Business Cycle Comovement, Federal Reserve Bank of Dallas. Globalization and Monetary Policy Institute Working Paper No. 116, May.

Konold, Markus (2007). New Possibilities for Economic Research through Integration of Establishment-level Panel Data of German Official Statistics. *Schmollers Jahrbuch/Journal of Applied Social Science Studies* 127(2), 321–334.

Lipczynski, John and John Wilson (2001). *Industrial Organisation. An Analysis of Competitive Markets*, Harlow, England etc.: Prentice Hall.

Melitz Marc (2003): The Impact of Trade on Intra-industry Reallocations and Aggregate Industry Productivity. *Econometrica* 71(6), 1695–1725.

Nahm, Matthias (2011). Inward-FATS Auslandskontrollierte Unternehmen in Deutschland 2008, *Wirtschaft und Statistik*, September 2011, 899–906.

Naidoo, Vikash (2010). Firm Survival through a Crisis: The Influence of Market Orientation, Marketing Innovation and Business Strategy, *Industrial Marketing Management* 39(8), 1311–1320.

Narjoko, Dionisius and Hal Hill (2007). Winners and Losers during a Deep Economic Crisis: Firm-level Evidence from Indonesian Manufacturing, *Asian Economic Journal* 21(4), 343–368.

Norton, Edward C., Hua Wang, and Chunrong Ai (2004). Computing Interaction Effects and Standard Errors in Logit and Probit Models, *The Stata Journal* 4(2), 154–167.

Strotmann, Harald (2007). Entrepreneurial Survival, *Small Business Economics* 28(1), 87–104.

UNCTAD (2011), United Nations Conference on Trade and Development World Investment Report 2011, Geneva: UNCTAD.

Vogel, Alexander, Joachim Wagner (2010). Higher Productivity in Importing German Manufacturing Firms: Self-selection, Learning from importing, or Both? *Review of World Economics* 145(4), 641–665.

Vogel, Alexander, Stefan Dittrich (2008). The German Turnover Tax Statistics Panel. *Schmollers Jahrbuch/Journal of Applied Social Science Studies* 128(4), 661–670.

Wagner, Joachim (2013a). The Microstructure of the Great Export Collapse in German Manufacturing Industries, 2008/2009. *Economics — The Open Access, Open Assessment E-Journal* 7(5).

Wagner, Joachim (2013b). Exports, Imports and Firm Survival: First Evidence for Manufacturing Enterprises in Germany. *Review of World Economics* 149(1), 113–130.

Wagner, Joachim (2012). International Trade and Firm Performance: A Survey of Empirical Studies since 2006. *Review of World Economics* 148(2), 235–267.

Wagner, Joachim (2011). Exports, Imports and Firm Survival: First Evidence for Manufacturing Enterprises in Germany, University of Lüneburg Working Paper Series in Economics No. 211, August.

Wagner, Joachim and John P. Weche Gelübcke (2012). Foreign Ownership and Firm Survival: First Evidence for Enterprises in Germany. *International Economics* 132(4), 117–139.

Weche Gelübcke, John P. (2013). The Performance of Foreign Affiliates in German Manufacturing: Evidence from a new Database. *Review of World Economics* 149(1), 151–182.

Weche Gelübcke, John P. (2011). Ownership Patterns and Enterprise Groups in German Structural Business Statistics, *Schmollers Jahrbuch/Journal of Applied Social Science Studies* 131(4), 635–647.

Williams, Richard (2010). Using the Margins Command to Estimate and Interpret Adjusted Predictions and Marginal Effects, *The Stata Journal* 12(2), 308–331.

World Trade Organization (2013). World Investment Report 2013, Geneva: World Trade Organization.

# Appendix 1

Table A.1. Probit estimates of firm exits without size threshold

| | Western Germany | | | | Eastern Germany | | | |
|---|---|---|---|---|---|---|---|---|
| | (1) | (2) | (3) | (4) | (1) | (2) | (3) | (4) |
| Only exporters | −0.0001 | 0.003* | 0.003* | 0.002 | −0.004 | −0.002 | −0.002 | −0.003 |
| | (0.05) | (1.80) | (1.76) | (0.97) | (1.23) | (0.74) | (0.73) | (0.66) |
| Only importers | −0.004** | −0.003 | −0.003 | −0.005*** | 2.35e-06 | 0.001 | 0.001 | 0.001 |
| | (2.15) | (1.45) | (1.42) | (3.06) | (0.00) | (0.33) | (0.40) | (0.24) |
| Two-way traders | −0.004*** | 0.0001 | 0.0002 | 0.0003 | −0.003 | −0.001 | −0.001 | 0.010 |
| | (2.95) | (0.10) | (0.14) | (0.16) | (0.75) | (0.18) | (0.13) | (1.12) |
| Foreign owned | −0.002 | 0.002 | 0.002 | 0.002 | −0.006 | −0.005 | −0.004 | −0.003 |
| | (1.62) | (0.91) | (0.76) | (0.88) | (1.06) | (0.75) | (0.56) | (0.41) |
| Independent | — | — | −0.0001 | −0.0002 | — | — | 0.003 | 0.004 |
| | | | (0.04) | (0.13) | | | (1.01) | (1.08) |
| Domestic group head | — | — | −0.003 | −0.003 | — | — | omitted | omitted |
| | | | (1.01) | (0.91) | | | | |
| 50–249 employees | — | −0.01*** | −0.01*** | −0.011*** | — | −0.01*** | −0.011*** | −0.009*** |
| | | (6.72) | (6.96) | (6.97) | | (2.89) | (2.70) | (2.67) |
| 250< employees | — | −0.017*** | −0.02*** | −0.016*** | — | −0.003 | −0.003 | −0.001 |
| | | (3.65) | (3.51) | (3.45) | | (0.53) | (0.39) | (0.15) |
| Established before 1996 | — | −0.001 | −0.001 | −0.001 | — | 0.001 | 0.002 | 0.001 |
| | | (1.57) | (1.49) | (1.50) | | (0.45) | (0.54) | (0.42) |
| Multi-product firms | — | −0.002* | −0.002* | −0.002* | — | −0.011*** | −0.005*** | −0.005*** |
| | | (1.73) | (1.73) | (1.71) | | (2.85) | (2.86) | (2.76) |

(*Continued*)

Table A.1. (*Continued*)

| | Western Germany | | | | Eastern Germany | | | |
|---|---|---|---|---|---|---|---|---|
| | (1) | (2) | (3) | (4) | (1) | (2) | (3) | (4) |
| Labor productivity | — | −7.08e-06 | −6.96e-06 | −0.00002** | — | −8.16e-06 | −6.49e-06 | −8.66e-07 |
| | | (1.35) | (1.40) | (2.17) | | (0.92) | (0.74) | 0.21 |
| Only export * productivity | — | — | — | 0.00001 | — | — | — | −1.06e-06 |
| | — | — | — | (1.05) | — | — | — | (0.11) |
| Only import * productivity | — | — | — | 0.00002** | — | — | — | 3.67e-06 |
| | — | — | — | (2.28) | — | — | — | (0.61) |
| Two-way trader * productivity | — | — | — | 3.82e-06 | — | — | — | −0.0001 |
| | — | — | — | (0.35) | — | — | — | (1.30) |
| 2-digit industry dummies | yes | yes | yes | yes | yes | yes | yes | yes |
| Number of firms | 29,367 | 29,367 | 29,367 | 29,367 | 5,415 | 5,415 | 5,269 | 5,269 |

*Notes*: Reported are estimated AME with |*z*-values| in parentheses; Statistical significance at the 10 percent (*), 5 percent (**) and 1 percent (***) level; Standard errors are adjusted for 2-digit industry clusters.

Table A.2. Complementary log–log model estimates

| | Western Germany | | Eastern Germany | |
|---|---|---|---|---|
| | (3) | (4) | (3) | (4) |
| Only exporters | 0.611** | 0.211 | 0.024 | 0.044 |
| | (2.09) | (0.44) | (0.05) | (0.09) |
| Only importers | −0.743* | −0.941 | 0.117 | 0.030 |
| | (1.78) | (1.19) | (0.17) | (0.04) |
| Two-way traders | 0.108 | −0.219 | −0.186 | 0.901 |
| | (0.51) | (0.51) | (0.29) | (0.62) |
| Foreign owned | 0.192 | 0.176 | −0.857 | −0.659 |
| | (0.65) | (0.58) | (0.74) | (0.56) |
| Independent | −0.037 | −0.052 | 0.450 | 0.430 |
| | (0.22) | (0.29) | (0.85) | (0.76) |
| Domestic group head | −0.389 | −0.385 | omitted | omitted |
| | (0.77) | (0.75) | | |
| 50–249 employees | −1.053*** | −1.055*** | −1.132*** | −1.106*** |
| | (4.76) | (4.75) | (2.71) | (2.73) |
| 250< employees | −1.923** | −1.938*** | −0.184 | −0.042 |
| | (2.58) | (2.59) | (0.22) | (0.05) |
| Established before 1996 | −0.142 | −0.132 | 0.266 | 0.212 |
| | (1.18) | (1.13) | (0.52) | (0.43) |
| Multi-product firms | −0.357** | −0.358** | −0.531 | −0.527 |
| | (2.06) | (2.06) | (1.56) | (1.58) |
| Labor productivity | −0.001* | −0.005 | −0.00004 | 0.0001 |
| | (1.68) | (1.13) | (0.09) | (0.81) |
| Only export * productivity | — | 0.004 | — | −0.0002 |
| | | (0.89) | | (0.20) |
| Only import * productivity | — | 0.003 | — | 0.001** |
| | | (0.40) | | (2.34) |
| Two-way trader * productivity | — | 0.004 | — | −0.009 |
| | | (0.82) | | (0.84) |
| 2-digit industry dummies | yes | yes | yes | yes |
| Number of firms | 23,603 | 23,603 | 3,810 | 3,810 |

*Notes*: Reported are estimated coefficients with |*z*-values| in parentheses; Statistical significance at the 10 percent (*), 5 percent (**) and 1 percent (***) level; Standard errors are adjusted for 2-digit industry clusters; Sample is restricted to enterprises with more than 30 employees.

PART VI

# Credit Constraints and International Trade

## Chapter 12

# Credit Constraints and Exports: A Survey of Empirical Studies Using Firm Level Data

Joachim Wagner

**Abstract**

Business managers are well aware of the fact that credit constraints can hamper or even prevent exporting. Economists only recently started to incorporate these arguments in theoretical models of heterogeneous firms and to test the implications of these models econometrically with firm-level data. Starting with the pioneering study by Greenaway, Guariglia and Kneller (*Journal of International Economics*, 2007), a growing number of empirical papers looked at the links between financial constraints and export activities using data at the level of the firm. This chapter presents a tabular survey of 32 empirical studies that cover 14 different countries plus five multi-country studies. The big picture can be summarized as follows: Financial constraints are important for the export decisions of firms — exporting firms are less financially constrained than non-exporting firms. Studies that look at the direction of this link usually report that less constrained firms self-select into exporting, but that exporting does not improve financial health of firms. The chapter argues that the results at hand should not be considered as stylized facts that can guide policy makers in an evidence-based way and suggests a strategy to further improve our knowledge in this area.

*Keywords*: Credit constraints, exports, empirical studies, literature survey

**JEL Classification:** F14

## 1. Motivation

Business managers are well aware of the fact that credit constraints can hamper or even prevent exporting. The reason is that exporting involves extra costs to enter foreign markets (e.g. for the acquisition of information about a target market, for the adaption of products to foreign legal rules or local tastes, for instruction manuals in a foreign language and for setting up a distribution network) that often have to be paid up front and that to a large extent are sunk costs. Firms need sufficient liquidity to pay for these costs, and constraints in the credit market may be binding. Furthermore, it tends to take considerably more time to complete an export order and to collect payment after shipping compared to a domestic order, and this increases exporters' working capital requirement. The higher risk of export activities (including exchange rate fluctuations and the risk that contracts cannot be as easily enforced in a foreign country) adds to these liquidity requirements. Therefore, whether a firm is financially constrained or not can be considered as one of the characteristics of a firm that are relevant for the decision to export.

While this is common knowledge for practitioners, economists only recently started to incorporate these arguments in theoretical models of heterogeneous firms and to test the implications of these models econometrically with firm-level data. Chaney (2013), Muuls (2008) and Manova (2013) introduce credit constraints into the seminal model of heterogeneous firms and trade by Melitz (2003) to discuss the role of these frictions for the export decision.[1] In the Chaney (2013) model, firms must pay extra costs in order to access foreign markets, and if they face liquidity constraints to finance these costs, only those firms that have sufficient liquidity are able to export. The Muuls (2008) model has the same implication — firms are more likely to be exporters if they are less credit-constrained. In the Manova (2013) model, firms that are more affected by credit

[1] A detailed discussion of the theoretical models is far beyond the scope of this empirical chapter; for a synopsis, see Egger and Kesina (2013) and Minetti and Zhu (2011).

constraints participate less likely in export markets, and if they do, they export less.

The basic idea that financial constraints matter for the export decision of a firm and the implications of the recent formal theoretical models are taken to firm-level data in a number of microeconometric studies for developed and developing countries. This chapter surveys these studies and puts the results into perspective.

It should be noted that there are a few papers dealing with topics of credit constraints and international firm activities besides exports. This literature includes papers that discuss the relationship between imports and credit constraints (Bas and Berthou 2011; Muuls 2012) and the impact of financial constraints on the decision to engage in foreign direct investment and on foreign affiliate sales (Buch *et al.* 2009). Given the focus of this survey on credit constraints and exports, this related literature will not be discussed here.[2]

## 2. A Survey of Empirical Studies on Financial Constraints and Exports at the Firm Level

Starting with the pioneering study by Greenaway, Guariglia and Kneller (2007), a growing number of empirical papers looked at the links between financial constraints and export activities using data at the level of the firm. Table 1 is a tabular survey of 32 empirical studies that cover 14 different countries plus five multi-country studies.[3] As of today, we have evidence for countries that differ widely in the level of economic development. While the studies use different measures of financial constraints and apply different econometric methods to investigate the links between these constraints and export activities, the big picture[4] can be summarized as

[2]For an up-to-date discussion of findings on the role of financial constraints for various other dimensions of firm behavior and firm dynamics, see Bottazzi, Secci and Tamagni (2014).

[3]The tabular survey does not include studies with aggregate data. Furthermore, studies that use firm-level data to investigate related but different topics are excluded. For a short discussion of this literature, see the working paper version of this paper (Wagner 2013).

[4]There are a few notable exceptions, see Stiebale (2011) for France, Arndt, Buch and Mattes (2012) for Germany, Lancheros and Demirel (2012) for India and Akarim (2013) for Turkey;

Table 1. Empirical studies on exports and financial constraints with firm-level data

| Country Authors (year) | Data | Measures of financial constraints | Methods | Important findings |
|---|---|---|---|---|
| **High Income Economies** | | | | |
| **Belgium** | | | | |
| Muuls (2008) | Trade and balance sheet data for manufacturing firms 1999–2005 | Yearly measure of credit-worthiness of firms from a credit insurer (Coface International) | Descriptive statistics; linear probability model with/without fixed firm effects, fixed-effects OLS | Firms more likely to be exporters if they have higher productivity levels and lower credit constraints. Credit constraints important for extensive but not for intensive margin of trade in terms of destinations. |
| Muuls (2012) | Manufacturing firms, 1999–2007 | Credit score measure (as in Muuls 2008) | Descriptive statistics; linear probability model with/without fixed firm effects, fixed-effects OLS | Firms with lower credit constraints more likely to exports and import, to export and import more, and more products to and from more countries. |

| | | | | |
|---|---|---|---|---|
| **Czech Republik** | | | | |
| Manole and Spatareanu (2010) | Sample of 365 manufacturing firms, 1994–2003 | Cash flow, liquidity ratio, leverage ratio | Fixed-effects OLS, system GMM IV | Exporters less financially constrained; less constrained firms self-select into exporting, but exporting does not alleviate firms' financial constraints. |
| **France** | | | | |
| Bellone *et al.* (2010) | Balance sheet data and DIANE database for manufacturing Firms, 1993–2005 | Liquidity ratio, leverage ratio, index based on seven variables (size, profitability, liquidity, cash flow generating ability, solvency, trade credit over total assets, repaying ability) | OLS, random effects probit, dynamic GMM, discrete time duration model, Heckman two-step model | Export starters have a significant *ex-ante* financial advantage compared to non-exporters. No significant improvement in financial health of firms that started to export. |
| Askenazy, *et al.* (2011) | Customs data; profit and loss data; balance sheet data. Firms from manufacturing, 1995–2007 | Liquidity ratio; inverse trade credit ratio; equity to asset ratio; dummy indicating whether firm has defaulted to its trade creditors | Negative binomial models | Credit constraints have negative influence on number of newly served destinations. Higher probability of export exit associated with credit constraints. |

(*Continued*)

Table 1. (*Continued*)

| Country Authors (year) | Data | Measures of financial constraints | Methods | Important findings |
|---|---|---|---|---|
| Stiebale (2011) | Sample of firms from manufacturing from AMADEUS, 1998–2005 | Liquidity ratio, long term debt/total assets, short term debt/current assets, cash flow/capital, earnings before interest and tax payments/interest payment | Dynamic probit, GMM, dynamic random effects Tobit | No evidence that financial constraints matter for export decision. |
| Bellone, Bernini and Guillou (2013) | Customs and balance sheet data, 1997–2007 | Firms' leverage (total debt over total assets), covarage ratio (pre-tax profits over interest rates payments), Musso and Schiavo score | Pooled OLS and FE (IV) | Financially healthier exporters sell expensive varieties on foreign markets. |
| **Germany** | | | | |
| Buch *et al.* (2010) | Enterprise level data from Dafne and MiDi, 2002–2006 | Cash flow, debt ratio | Probit, OLS (no fixed effects models) | Positive impact of cash flow on probability to export and export volume; debt ratio insignificant. |
| Arndt, Buch and Mattes (2012) | Establishment level data; cross-section for 2004–2005 | Self-reported financial constraints (from interview) | Two-step Heckman selection model | Self-reported financial constraints have no impact on firms' internationalization decisions. |

| | | | | |
|---|---|---|---|---|
| Wagner (2014) | Enterprise level data, 2007–2009 | Credit-rating score by leading credit rating agency | Probit and fractional logit models | Positive but weak link between between credit-rating score and exports. Weak evidence that credit-constrained firms are less likely to start to export. No evidence of difference in scores between firms that stopped to export and continuous exporters. |
| **Italy** | | | | |
| Forlani (2010) | Small and medium enterprises, 1998–2000, 2001–2003 (two cross sections) | Firms clustered into different groups according to their relative level of leverage | Probit, OLS | Probability of export start affected by cash stock for constrained firms. Exporters that increase number of destinations show higher liquidity. No evidence that export start improves firm's financial health. |
| Minetti and Zhu (2011) | Sample of 4,680 manufacturing firms, 2001 | Binary indicator based on answer to survey question about denied credits | Descriptive statistics, probit, bivariate probit, IV probit, OLS, 2SLS | Probability of exporting and foreign sales lower for credit rationed firms. |
| Secchi, Tamagni and Tomasi (2011) | Customs information on exports plus register data for manufacturing firms, 2000–2003 | Official credit rating issued by an independent institution (used after transformation into a dummy variable for constrained/unconstrained firms) | Descriptive statistics; 2-stage Heckman-type procedure for panel data models | Limited access to external capital narrows scale of foreign sales, exporters' product scope and number of trade partners. |

(*Continued*)

Table 1. (*Continued*)

| Country Authors (year) | Data | Measures of financial constraints | Methods | Important findings |
|---|---|---|---|---|
| Caggese and Cunat (2013) | Sample of small and medium manufacturing firms, 1995–2003 | Binary indicator based on answers to survey questions about credits; various instruments measuring regional financial development and based on relationship lending literature | IV regressions | Constrained firms less likely to export when financing constraints are instrumented. Financial constraints do not affect percentage of sales exported. Financing constraints affect negatively number of export destination regions. |
| Ciani and Bartoli (2013) | 7,436 small and medium sized firms, 2002–2010 | Binary indicator based on answer to survey questions about denied credits; credit rating score | Probit, OLS, ordered probit, IV | Credit constrained firms are less likely to increase output quality for export market. Credit constraints important for extensive and intensive margins. |
| Tamagni (2013) | Population of limited firms in manufacturing, 2000–2003 | Credit rating score, perceived as an official rating | Heckman type 2-stage approach for panel data with selection | Limited access to external capital narrows scale of foreign sales, exporters' product scope and number of trade partners. |
| **Portugal** | | | | |
| Silva (2011) | Panel of manufacturing firms, 1996–2003 | Approximation of credit constraints by financial score built on eight variables based on balance sheet information | Propensity score matching with difference in differences | New exporters show significant improvements in their financial situation. |

| | | | | |
|---|---|---|---|---|
| **Sweden** | | | | |
| Halldin (2012) | Panel of manufacturing Firms, 1997–2006 | Degree of collateralizable assets | Probit (pooled cross-section, random effects panel probit) | Tangible assets are an important determinant of export entry. |
| **UK** | | | | |
| Greenaway, Guariglia and Kneller (2007) | Panel of 9,292 manufacturing firms, 1993–2003 | Liquidity ratio (current assets less current liabilities over total assets); leverage ratio (ratio of short-term debt to current assets); Quiscore (likelihood of company failure over next 12 months; not used in econometric estimates) | Descriptive statistics; pooled probit, random-effects probit, fixed-effects, GMM, dynamic random effects probit, dynamic GMM | Positive link between firms' financial health and export status. No evidence that firms enjoying good *ex-ante* financial health are more likely to start exporting. Participation in exporting improves firms' *ex-post* financial health. |
| Görg and Spaliara (2013) | Manufacturing firms, FAMA date base, 2000–2009 | Liquidity (current assets less current liabilities over total assets); leverage (short-term debt to assets ratio) | Complementary log–log model | Deterioration in the financial position of firms increased the hazard of export exit. |

(*Continued*)

Table 1. (*Continued*)

| Country Authors (year) | Data | Measures of financial constraints | Methods | Important findings |
|---|---|---|---|---|
| **Upper Middle Income Economies** | | | | |
| **Argentina** | | | | |
| Espanol (2007) | Data for sample of manufacturing firms, 1992, 1996, 1998, 2001 | Dummy indicating whether firm was inhibited to innovate because of financial restrictions (1998–2001); proportion of innovation financed by banking system (1992–1996) | Probit | Access to financial markets and not facing financial restrictions to innovate have positive impact on export decision. |
| Castagnino, D'Amato and Sangiácomo (2012) | 38,207 firms, 2001–2006 | Firms debt with domestic banks and with foreign creditors (assume firms without access to bank financing are rationed) | Descriptive statistics, probit | Having more access to bank credit facilitates firms' entry into export markets. Access to foreign financing seems to matter for success in foreign markets. |
| **China** | | | | |
| Du and Girma (2007) | Data for domestic private firms from manufacturing, 1999–2002 | Bank loans normalized by total assets | IV-Tobit | Access to bank loans is associated with greater export market orientation. |

| | | | | |
|---|---|---|---|---|
| Li and Yu (2009) | Firm-level data from manufacturing, 2000–2007 | Firm's interest expenditures used as proxy for firm's capacity to borrow | OLS, fixed-effects, Poisson pseudo-ML fixed-effects, IV fixed-effects | Firms with fewer credit constraints export more. |
| Manova, Wei and Zhang (2011) | Customs data for all internationally active firms, 2005 | Financial vulnerability measured at sector level (average over the 1980–1999 period for median U.S. firm in each sector) | Firm fixed-effects for firms active in more than one sector | Limited credit availability hinders firms' trade flows (export sales, export product scope, number of export destinations). |
| Egger and Kesina (2013) | Census data for firms, 2001–2005 (average values over years used) | Long-run dept-to-capital ratio, financial-costs-to-liquid-funds ratio, liquid-asset-to-capital ratio, ratio of surplus of profits over long run debts to total assets | Logit, fractional logit | Credit constrained firms are less likely to export and have lower shares of exports in total sales. |
| **Thailand** | | | | |
| Cole, Elliott and Virakul (2010) | Manufacturing firms, 2001–2004 | Liquidity ratio, leverage ratio | Pooled probit | Financial health has a significant influence on a firm's export decision. |
| **Turkey** | | | | |
| Akarim (2013) | Firms traded at ISE stock exchange, 2000–2011 | Financial variables (total short term debt over total debts or total assets; leverage ratio, etc.) | Panel logit model | No significant relationship between liquidity and leverage ratios and the export probability of firms. |

(*Continued*)

Table 1. (*Continued*)

| Country Authors (year) | Data | Measures of financial constraints | Methods | Important findings |
|---|---|---|---|---|
| **Lower Middle Income Economies** | | | | |
| **Egypt** | | | | |
| Kiendrebeogo and Minea (2012) | Unbalanced panel of 2,387 manufacturing firms from World Bank's Enterprise Surveys database, 2003–2008 | Self-assessment indicators of financial constraints; composite indicator of financial health, based on ratio of net income to total assets and share of new investment financed by equity; credit related variables in a robustness check | Pobit (pooled, random effects, dynamic random effects) for export participation; OLS fixed effects, Amemiya-MaCurdy, system GMM for export/sales ratio; Gamma RE and Normal RE for hazard rate of export start | Financial constraints reduce export participation, and have a negative impact on export intensity and the hazard rate of entry into exporting. |
| **India** | | | | |
| Ito and Terada-Hagiwara (2011) | Sample of 6,000 manufacturing firms, 1996–2008 | Cash flow/total assets, debt-to-asset ratio, ratio of retained profits to total assets | Random effects probit, OLS | Firms with higher amount of net cash flow and smaller debt-to-asset ratios are more likely to become exporters. |
| Nagaraj (2011) | Balance sheet and financial statement data, manufacturing firms, 1989–2008 | Liquidity = (current assets − current liabilities)/total assets; Leverage = Short term debt/current assets | Probit, IV-GMM, system GMM | New exporters have better financial health than non-exporters; financial health cause, not effect of exports. Share of exports in total sales not dependent on financial health. |

| | | | | |
|---|---|---|---|---|
| Lancheros and Demirel (2012) | Indian service firms, 1999–2007 | Stock of long-term debt over total assets; flow of short-term borrowing over total assets | IV Probit and Tobit; system GMM | No evidence that access to any particular source of finance influences the decision to export or the amount exported. |
| **Multi-Country Studies** | | | | |
| 9 developing and emerging countries Berman and Héricourt (2010) | World Bank Enterprise Survey Data, some 5,000 firms, between 1998 and 2004 | Ratio of total debt over total assets; ratio of cash flow over total assets | Probit, OLS, 2SLS (Note: No investigation for single countries) | Access to finance important for export t entry, but not for continuation decision or for size of exports. Productivity only important for export start if firm has sufficient access to external finance. |
| 28 East European and Central Asian countries Wang (2010) | World Bank Enterprise Survey Data, 3,392 firms, between 2002 and 2009 | Financially constrained firms applied for loans but got rejected, or did not apply for loans because of too high costs | Descriptive statistics, pooled Probit, random effects probit, fixed effects LPM, RE LPM, Heckman Selection model (Note: No investigation for single countries) | Probability of exporting higher among firms with no financial constraints; unconstrained firms tend to export more. |

(*Continued*)

Table 1. (*Continued*)

| Country Authors (year) | Data | Measures of financial constraints | Methods | Important findings |
|---|---|---|---|---|
| 18 developing countries Fauceglia (2011) | World Bank Enterprise Survey Data, 9,072 firms between 2002 and 2005 | Liquidity ratio (current over total assets) | Probit, OLS, 2SLS, Heckman selection model (Note: No investigation for single countries) | Positive effect of firms' liquidity on export propensity larger for firms in financially less developed countries. Credit constraints do not constitute determinants for export revenues for existing exporters. |
| 27 transition economies (East Europe and Central Asia) Bernini (2012) | BEEPS data (waves II, III, IV), 25,086 firms (6,890 interviewed in more than one year) | Self-reported degree of financial constraints — size of obstacle in access to finance | Ordered probit, OLS, FE (Note: No investigation for single countries) | Findings suggest that export activities improve *ex-post* firms' access to credit by signaling their resilience to domestic and foreign competition. |
| 6 Latin American Countries Hasan (2013) | World Bank Enterprise Survey data, 1,501 firms, 2006 and 2008 | Answer to survey question about availability of outside commercial bank or financial institution | Probit, OLS, IV (Note: No investigation for line of credit from private single countries) | Credit availability significant for the decision to export, but not significant in determining the volume of exports. |

*Note*: The classification of economies by income follows The World Bank's World Development Report 2014; see p. 295 there. In the groups the studies are listed in alphabetical order of the countries covered and in chronological order of the publication year in a country. Studies that cover more than one country are listed at the end of the table

follows: Financial constraints are important for the export decisions of firms — exporting firms are less financially constrained than non-exporting firms. Studies that look at the direction of this link usually[5] report that less constrained firms self-select into exporting, but that exporting does not improve financial health of firms.

## 3. What have We Learned and Where Do We Go from Here?

A bird's eye view on the literature on credit constraints and exports that emerged since the pioneering study by Greenaway, Guariglia and Kneller (2007) suggests that financial constraints are important for the export decisions of firms — exporting firms are less financially constrained than non-exporting firms — and that less constrained firms self-select into exporting, but that exporting does not improve financial health of firms. Can these findings be considered as a basis to discuss the need for policy measures that aim to improve access to credits for firms that intend to start or to expand export activities at the extensive or intensive margins? From my reading of the literature, the answer should be "no". To guide policy makers in an evidence-based way, stylized facts are needed that are valid over time and space (or at least for a selected country). Empirical evidence from the studies surveyed in this chapter does not pass this test for four reasons:

— First, given that financial constraints are not directly observable for an applied econometrician who works with data for a sample of firms, empirical research has to rely on indirect measures. From Table 1, it is obvious that the way credit constraints are measured does differ widely across the studies listed. Therefore, results from these studies are not comparable. Furthermore, there is evidence that not all measures for

note that other studies using data for France, Germany and India report results that are in line with the big picture of a negative link between credit constraints and export activities.

[5] An exception is the study by Greenaway, Guariglia and Kneller (2007) for the UK that reports an opposite result.

financial constraints used can be considered as valid measures. Farre-Mensa and Ljungqvist (2013) recently evaluated how well five popular measures from the finance literature (that are based on balance-sheet data and that have been used in some of the studies listed in Table 1, too) identify firms that are financially constraint. They report that none of these five measures identifies firms that behave as if they were constrained.

An alternative way to measure credit constraints that has been used in studies for Belgium (Muuls 2008; 2012), Germany (Wagner 2014) and Italy (Secchi, Tamagni and Tomasi 2011; Tamagni 2013) is the use of a credit rating score supplied by a credit rating agency. Compared to other widely used measures that are based on balance sheets information or subjective assessments collected in surveys, this score mirrors the credit market experts' view on the creditworthiness of a firm, and it is heavily relied upon by banks and firms in their day-to-day decisions. Usually a score is based on a number of firm characteristics, including liquidity, turnover, capital structure, information on payment behavior, legal form, industry, firm age, productivity and firm size. Muuls (2008) argues that although the score is clearly endogenous to the firm's performance and characteristics, it is not directly affected by its exporting behavior, given that exports are not used in constructing the index. Important advantages are that the score is determined independently by a private firm, is firm-specific, varies over time on an annual basis and allows for a measure of the degree of credit constraints, rather than classifying firms as constrained or not. Given that evidence on the link between exports and credit constraints that is based on credit scores is hitherto limited to three (highly developed) countries empirical results at hand should not be considered as stylized facts.

— Second, results are not comparable across studies due to differences in the empirical models used. Any comparison that goes beyond a qualitative comparison of results for different countries or time periods and that looks at the size of the effects can only be based on results from identically specified empirical models that use the same type of data.

— Third, results are limited due to the availability of sound measures of credit constraints for smaller firms (that form the bulk of firms that do not yet export and that might be hit hardest by credit constraints).

— Fourth, the number of export status switchers in the samples used often tends to be small and the time span the data are available for usually is not long enough to investigate the direction of causality between exporting and credit constraints in a convincing way or to apply panel econometric methods to control for unobserved time-invariant firm characteristics.

Therefore, the results at hand should not be considered as stylized facts that can guide policy makers in an evidence-based way. One way to proceed[6] would be to analyze in one study different datasets from different periods of time and/or different countries, and to perform what is called a *within-study replication* (Hamermesh 2007, p. 730). This approach of within-study replication is especially attractive. If work is done by a single researcher (or a single research team), the chances that all the details of the empirical study are identical (or at least very similar) across the data sets tend to be quite high. In most cases, however, firm-level data are strictly confidential, and as a rule these data can only be used on computers located inside the statistical agencies that are in charge of collecting the data. The data cannot cross borders, and often they cannot be accessed by citizens of a foreign country (who are not liable to jurisdiction in case of violation of privacy in the country where the data are located). Within-study replication using firm-level data from various countries, therefore, usually cannot be performed by one author (or a team of authors) from one country.

A way out is to form a team of researchers who are located in different countries, each of whom does have access to firm level data from her or his country, to agree on a unified empirical

[6] For a comprehensive discussion of this topic, see Wagner (2011).

approach, and to perform a within-study replication where strictly comparable results for each country are produced by the author(s) from that country.[7] Based on the discussion of the literature covered in this survey, I argue that this empirical approach should adopt a credit rating score as the most appropriate measure of financial constraints of firms; that information on this score should be collected for a large sample of smaller firms, too, because many of these smaller firms do not yet export and might be hit hardest by credit constraints; and that data should be collected for time span that is long enough to investigate the direction of causality between financial constraints and export activities in a convincing way and to control for unobserved firm heterogeneity.

## Acknowledgment

I thank two anonymous referees for helpful comments on an earlier version. The usual disclaimer applies.

## References

Akarim, Y. D. (2013). The Impact of Financial Factors on Export Decisions: The Evidence from Turkey. *Economic Modelling* 35, 305–308.

Arndt, C., C. M. Buch and A. Mattes (2012). Disentangling Barriers to Internationalization. *Canadian Journal of Economics* 45, 41–63.

Askenazy, P., A. Caldera, G. Gaulier and D. Irac (2011). Financial Constraints and Foreign Market Entries or Exits: Firm-Level Evidence from France. *Banque de France Document de Travail* No. 328, April.

Bas, M. and A. Berthou (2011). The Decision to Import Capital Goods in India: Firms' Financial Factors Matter. CEPII Working Paper No. 2011-06, March.

Bellone, F., M. Bernini and S. Guillou (2013). Financial Constraints and Export Quality: Evidence from France. Mimeo.

[7]Some years ago, teams of researchers from some 15 countries joined to form the *International Study Group on Exports and Productivity* and to apply the approach of within-study replication using confidential firm level longitudinal data from various countries. The study looks at cross-country differences in exporter productivity premia estimated by using comparable data and a unified empirical approach (ISGEP 2008). This approach might act as a template for future research in the links between financial constraints and exports that might help to generate the stylized facts needed to inform both scientific research and policy makers in an evidence-based way.

Bellone, F., P. Musso, L. Nesta and S. Schiavo (2010). Financial Constraints and Firm Export Behaviour. *The World Economy* 30, 347–373.

Berman, N. and J. Héricourt (2010). Financial Factors and the Margins of Trade: Evidence from Cross-Country Firm-Level Data. *Journal of Development Economics* 93, 206–217.

Bernini, M. (2012). Competitive Pressure, Export Status and Financial Constraints in Transition Economies. University of Trento, mimeo.

Bottazzi, G., A. Secci and F. Tamagni (2014). Financial Constraints and Firm Dynamics. *Small Business Economics* 42, 99–116.

Buch, C. M., I. Kesternich, A. Lipponer and M. Schnitzer (2009). Financial Constraints and the Margins of FDI. University of Munich Department of Economics Discussion Paper No. 2009-17, August.

Buch, C. M., I. Kesternich, A. Lipponer and M. Schnitzer (2010). Exports versus FDI revisited: Does finance matter? Deutsche Bundesbank Discussio Paper Series 1: Economic Studies, No. 03/2010.

Caggese, A. and V. Cunat (2013). Financing Constraints, Firm Dynamics, Export Decisions, and Aggregate Productivity. *Review of Economic Dynamics* 16, 177–193.

Castagnino, T., L. D'Amato and M. Sangiácomo (2012). How do Firms in Argentina get Financing to Export? *Banco Central de la República Afgentina, Investigaciones Económicas*, Working Paper 2012|58, November.

Chaney, T. (2013). Liquidity Constrained Exporters. National Bureau of Economic Research NBER Working Paper 19170, June.

Ciani, A. and F. Bartoli (2013). Export Quality Upgrading and Credit Constraints. Mimeo, August.

Cole, M. A., R. J. R. Elliott and S. Virakul (2010). Exporting and Financial Health: A Developing Country Perspective. Department of Economics, University of Birmingham, mimeo.

Du, J. and S. Girma (2007). Finance and Firm Export in China. *Kyklos* 60, 37–54.

Egger, P. and M. Kesina (2013). Financial Constraints and Exports: Evidence from Chinese Firms. *CESifo Economic Studies* 59, 676–706.

Espanol, P. (2007). Exports, Sunk Costs and Financial Restrictions in Argentina during the 1990s. Paris School of Economics Working Paper No. 2007-01, January.

Farre-Mensa, J. and A. Ljungqvist (2013). Do Measures of Financial Constraints Measure Financial Constraints? National Bureau of Economic Research NBER Working Paper 19551, October.

Fauceglia, D. (2011). Credit Constraints, Firm Exports and Financial Development: Evidence from Developing Countries. University of St. Gallen, mimeo, August.

Forlani, E. (2010). Liquidity Constraints and Firm's Export Activity. *Université Catholique des Louvain* — CORE, mimeo, April.

Görg, H. and M.-E. Spaliara (2013). Export Market Exit, Financial Pressure and the Crisis. Kiel Institute for the World Economy, Kiel Working Papers No. 1859, August.

Greenaway, D., A. Guariglia and R. Kneller (2007). Financial Factors and Exporting Decisions. *Journal of International Economics* 73, 377–395.

Halldin, T. (2012). External Finance, Collateralizable Assets and Export Market Entry. The Royal Institute of Technology Centre of Excellence for Science and Innovation Studies — CESIS Electronic Working Paper Series No. 268, March.

Hamermesh, D. S. (2007). Viewpoint: Replication in Economics. *Canadian Journal of Economics* 40, 715–733.

Hasan, S. M. (2013). Credit Constraints, Technology Choice and Exports — A Firm Level Study for Latin American Countries. Mimeo.

International Study Group on Exports and Productivity (ISGEP) (2008). Understanding Cross-Country Differences in Exporter Premia: Comparable Evidence for 14 Countries. *Review of World Economics* 144, 596–635.

Ito, H. and A.Terada-Hagiwara (2011). An Analysis of the Effects of Financial Market Imperfections on Indian Firm's Exporting Behavior. Department of Economics, Portland State University, mimeo, May.

Kiendrebeogo, Y. and A. Minea (2012). Financial Factors and Manufacturing Exports: Theory and Firm-level Evidence from Egypt. CERDI, *Etudes et Documents*, E2012.21

Lancheros, S. and P. Demirel (2012). Does Finance Play a Role in Exporting for Service Firms? Evidence from India. *The World Economy* 35, 44–60.

Li, Z. and M. Yu (2009). Export; Productivity, and Credit Constraints: A Fim-Level Empirical Investigation of China. Hitotsubashi University Research Unit for Statistical and Empirical Analysis in Social Schiences (Hi-Stat) Discussion Paper Series 098, December.

Manole, V. and M. Spatareanu (2010). Exporting, Capital Investment and Financial Constraints. *Review of World Economics* 146, 23–37.

Manova, K. (2013). Credit Constraints, Heterogeneous Firms, and International Trade. *The Review of Economic Studies* 80, 711–744.

Manova, K., S.-J. Wei and Z. Zhang (2011). Firm Exports and Multinational Activity under Credit Constraints. National Bureau of Economic Research NBER Working Paper Series 16905, March.

Melitz, M. J. (2003). The Impact of Trade on Intra-Industry Reallocations and Aggregate Industry Productivity. *Econometrica* 71, 1695–1725.

Minetti, R. and S. Chun Zhu (2011). Credit Constraints and Firm Exports: Microeconomic Evidence from Italy. *Journal of International Economics* 83, 109–125.

Muuls, M. (2008). Exporters and Credit Constraints. A Firm-Level Approach. National Bank of Belgium Working Paper Research No. 139, September.

Muuls, M. (2012). Expoerters, Importers and Credit Constraints. Centre for Economic Performance CEP Discussion Paper No. 1169, October.

Nagaraj, P. (2011). Financial Constraints and Export Participation. Graduate Center, City University of New York, mimeo.

Secchi, A., F. Tamagni and C. Tomasi (2011). Export Activities under Financial Constraints: Margins, Quantities and Prices. Laboratory of Economics and Management Sant'Anna School of Advanced Studies LEM Working Paper Series 2011/24, December.

Silva, A. (2011). Financial Constraints and Exports: Evidence from Portuguese Manufacturing Firms. *International Journal of Economic Sciences and Applied Research* 4, 7–19.

Stiebale, J. (2011). Do Financial Constraints Matter for Foreign Market Entry? A Firm-level Examination. *The World Economy* 34, 123–153.

Tamagni, F. (2013). Exporting Under Financial Constraints: Margins, Switching Dynamics and Prices. *Scuola Superiore Sant'Anna* LEM, mimeo, February.

Wagner, J. (2011). From Estimation Results to Stylized Facts. Twelve Recommendations for Empirical Research in International Activities of Heterogeneous Firms. *De Economist* 159, 389–412.

Wagner, J. (2013). Credit Constraints and Exports: A Survey of Empirical Studies using Firm-Level Data. University of Lüneburg Working Paper Series in Economics No. 288, December.

Wagner, J. (2014). Credit Constraints and Exports: Evidence for German Manufacturing Enterprises. *Applied Economics* 46, 294–302.

Wang, X. (2010). Financial Constraints and Exports. Department of Economics, University of Wisconsin, mimeo, October.

## Chapter 13

# Credit Constraints and Margins of Import: First Evidence for German Manufacturing Enterprises

Joachim Wagner

**Abstract**

This study uses tailor-made enterprise-level data for 2008–2010 from various sources for firms from manufacturing industries to test for the link between credit constraints, measured by a credit rating score provided by a leading credit rating agency, and imports in Germany for the first time. We find empirical evidence that a better credit rating score is positively related to extensive margins of import — firms with a better score have a higher probability to import, they import more goods and they source from more countries of origin. The intensive margin of imports — the share of imports in total sales — is found not to be related to credit constraints.

*Keywords*: Credit constraints; imports; Germany

**JEL Classification:** F14

## 1. Introduction

Access to sufficient credit at reasonable costs can play a decisive role for firms that decide to participate in international trade or not. Export and import activities both involve extra costs related to the entry into a foreign market. These costs often have to be paid in advance, and firms have to have sufficient liquidity to do so. Credit market constraints may be binding in a situation like this. Furthermore, international trade activities are often more risky than doing business with firms inside the own country due to, e.g. exchange rate fluctuations or less easily enforceable contracts, and this leads to further liquidity requirements. Therefore, financial constraints can be considered as relevant for export or import decisions.

While practitioners of international business are well aware of this, economists only recently started to investigate the links between credit constraints and international trade. The focus of this literature is on exports. Chaney (2013), Muuls (2008) and Manova (2013) introduce credit constraints into the seminal model of heterogeneous firms and trade by Melitz (2003) to discuss the role of these frictions for the export decision.[1] In these models, firms that are financially constrained are less likely to export. Starting with the pioneering study by Greenaway, Guariglia and Kneller (2007), this hypothesis has been tested in a number of studies that use firm-level data from a broad range of countries. Wagner (2013a) surveys 32 empirical studies that cover 14 different countries plus five multi-country studies. The central findings in this literature can be summarized as follows: Exporting firms are less financially constrained than non-exporting firms. Studies that look at the direction of this link usually report that less constrained firms self-select into exporting, but that exporting does not improve financial health.

Both the theoretical models and the microeconometric studies that investigate the links between financial constraints and international trade focus nearly exclusively on exports. However, the arguments for a role of financial constraints in the decision to engage in international trade discussed above do hold for imports, too. Import activities involve extra costs related to the entry into foreign markets that often have to be paid in advance, and firms have to have (access to) sufficient liquidity to cover these costs. Moreover, imports may have to be paid in advance of delivery, and usually there is a time span between the payment for imported

[1] A detailed discussion of the theoretical models is far beyond the scope of this empirical paper; for a synopsis, see Egger and Kesina (2013) and Minetti and Zhu (2011).

inputs and revenues generated from selling the goods produced with these inputs. Firms need either financial means generated inside the firm itself or bank credits to finance these imports. Therefore, a better credit rating score of the type used here (described in detail in Section 2) can be expected to be positively related to import activities for three reasons: First, by construction, liquidity of the firm is used to compute the value of the credit rating score. Second, the score mirrors the credit market experts' view of the creditworthiness of the firm. Therefore, the score value plays a role in the decision over a credit application, and it influences the rate of interest a firm has to pay. Third, the score value can be used by potential trading partners in foreign countries to decide whether and to which conditions they would be willing to do business with a firm.

To the best of my knowledge, only two papers consider the role of financial constraints for the import decision of a firm. Muuls (2012) uses data for Belgian manufacturing firms from 1999 to 2007 to analyze the links between credit constraints and trade. Note that she looks at exports and imports, while this chapter concentrates on imports (for evidence on exports and credit constraints in Germany, see Wagner (2014)). Credit constraints are measured by credit scores from an independent credit insurance company, and this measure is rather similar to the one used in this chapter (that is discussed in detail in Section 2). The most important findings from Muuls (2012) can be summarized as follows: Firms with lower credit constraints have a higher probability to export or to import. Furthermore, firms with a better credit rating export and import more. Results differ for the extensive margins of exports and imports. While credit constraints are positively associated with the total number of export destinations, this is not true in the case of products. Conversely, the number of countries of origin is not correlated with credit constraints whilst the number of imported products is.

Bas and Berthou (2012) use data for Indian firms from 1997 to 2006 to investigate the link between financial constraints and imports of capital goods. They develop a simple model of foreign technology adoption that shows that credit constraints do hinder firms from importing capital goods if financial markets are not perfect. They find that firms with a lower leverage and higher liquidity are more likely to import capital goods.

The small number of empirical studies on the links between imports and financial constraints may come as a surprise. One reason for this might be that data for imports at the firm level are not widely available. Fortunately, this is no longer the case for Germany. Using newly available and tailor-made data for 2008–2010 that are merged from various sources, this chapter contributes to the small empirical literature on the links between financial constraints and imports by providing first evidence for enterprises from manufacturing industries in Germany, one of the leading importers of goods worldwide.[2]

To anticipate the most important results, we find that less credit constrained firms with a better credit rating score have a higher probability to import, and that they import more goods and from more countries of origin, while the share of imports in total sales is not related to credit constraints.

## 2. Data and Measurement Issues

This chapter uses a unique newly constructed data set that merges high-quality data at the enterprise level from various sources for the period 2008–2010. Data are based on information on imports collected for the statistics on foreign trade and on data from surveys performed by the German Statistical Offices. These data are merged with a score that measures the creditworthiness of the firm and that is supplied by the leading German credit-rating agency, *Creditreform*. The data used are described in detail in this section.

*Imports*: Data on imports are based on customs' records about goods imported from countries outside the European Union (EU) and on information delivered by firms about imports from EU

[2]According to the World Trade Organization's World Trade Report 2012 Germany holds Rank 3 among the importers with a share of 6.8 percent in world merchandise imports; see World Trade Organization (2012), p. 30.

member countries (that exceed a reporting threshold of 400.000 €). These transaction-level data were aggregated at the level of the importing enterprise by the German Statistical Office for the first time for the reporting year 2009. These data are available for the reporting year 2010, too. The data include information at the firm level about the value of all imports, the number of different goods imported (measured at the 8-digit level of classification) and the number of countries of origin. These firm-level data are the basis for the aggregate figures of goods imported reported by the Statistical Office.[3]

*Credit rating score*: The extent of financial constraints faced by a firm is measured by various variables in the literature (see Musso and Schiavo (2008) for a discussion and Wagner (2013a) for a survey of the literature that looks at financial constraints and exports). There is evidence that not all measures for financial constraints used can be considered as valid measures. Farre-Mensa and Ljungqvist (2013) recently evaluated how well five popular measures from the finance literature that are based on balance-sheet data identify firms that are financially constraint. They report that none of these five measures identifies firms that behave as if they were constrained. An alternative way to measure credit constraints that has been used in studies for Belgium (Muuls 2008, 2012), Germany (Wagner 2014) and Italy (Secchi, Tamagni and Tomasi 2011; Tamagni 2013) is the use of a credit rating score supplied by a credit rating agency. Compared to other widely used measures that are based on balance sheets information or subjective assessments collected in surveys, this score mirrors the credit market experts' view on the creditworthiness of a firm, and it is heavily relied upon by banks and firms in their day-to-day decisions. Usually, a score is based

[3]For information on the share of countries of origin and the type of products imported, in total imports see Statistisches Bundesamt (2012), p. 411ff. Note that in 2010, 68 percent of imports originated in Europe (56 percent in the EU), 9 percent in America and 20.5 percent in Asia. The 10 most important countries of origin were China, The Netherlands, France, United States, Italy, United Kingdom, Austria, Belgium, Switzerland and Russia. As regards types of imported goods, the shares in 2010 were 31 percent for intermediate goods, 29.5 percent for capital goods, 15.7 percent for consumer non-durables, 11.5 percent for energy, and 3.7 percent for consumer durables.

on a number of firm characteristics, including liquidity, turnover, capital structure, information on payment behavior, legal form, industry, firm age, productivity and firm size. Although the score is clearly endogenous to the firm's performance and characteristics, it is not directly affected by its importing behavior, given that imports are not used in constructing the index. Important advantages are that the score is determined independently by a private firm, is firm-specific, varies over time on an annual basis and allows for a measure of the degree of credit constraints rather than classifying firms as constrained or not (see Muuls (2008, 2012)).

In this study, we use the credit rating score supplied by *Creditreform*, the leading credit rating agency in Germany. The score is based on 15 firm characteristics, including liquidity, turnover, capital structure, information on payment behavior, legal form, industry, firm age, productivity and firm size (for details, see Rossen (2012)). The score takes values from 100 to 600, where *Creditreform* suggests that 100 to 149 should be considered as excellent, 150–199 as very good, 200–249 as good, 250–299 as medium, 300–349 as weak, 350–419 as high risk of failure, and firms with a score of 420 or more are classified as firms that should not be considered as partners in trade and credit relations.

Data on the credit rating score of manufacturing enterprises were supplied by *Creditreform*. For several firms the information is updated during a year. The information supplied always refers to the last update during the reporting year. These data from *Creditreform* are used for the first time in this chapter to investigate the link between credit constraints and imports.

In the econometric investigation on the relation between imports and the credit rating score, information on a number of firm characteristics that are known to be related to import activities is included as control variables.[4] Information on these control variables is based on the report for establishments in manufacturing industries, a survey conducted regularly by the German statistical offices. This

[4]Given that these variables are used as control variables only they are not discussed in detail here.

survey covers all establishments from manufacturing industries that employ at least 20 persons in the local production unit or in the company that owns the unit. Participation of firms in the survey is mandated in official statistics law. For this study, the information collected at the establishment level has been aggregated at the enterprise level (see Malchin and Voshage (2009) for details). The following control variables are included:

*Firm size*: The positive relationship between imports and firm size qualifies as a stylized fact (for evidence from German manufacturing firms see Vogel and Wagner (2010)). Firm size is measured here by the number of employees. To take care of a nonlinear relationship the number of employees is included in squares, too.

*Productivity*: The positive relationship between imports and productivity is another stylized fact that has been documented in a number of recent empirical studies surveyed in Wagner (2012a). Germany is a case in point. Importing firms are more productive than comparable non-importing firms (see Vogel and Wagner (2010)), and both the number of products imported and the number of countries imported from are positively linked to productivity (Wagner 2012b). Productivity is measured here as labor productivity and defined as total turnover per employee. Information on the capital stock of the firms is not available in the data, so more elaborate measures of total factor productivity cannot be used in this study.

*Human capital intensity*: The quality of the workforce of a firm is positively related to the quality and innovativeness of the products produced. Firms that produce high-quality innovative products can be expected to source more often and to a larger extent for high-quality materials and capital goods on foreign markets, too. Therefore, human capital intensity and import activities are positively related. Human capital intensity is measured here by the average wage per employee. Information on the qualification of the employees is not available in the data, but Wagner (2012c) demonstrates that the average wage is indeed a good proxy variable for the qualification of the workforce in German manufacturing firms.

*Industry*: Dummy variables for 2-digit-industries are included in the empirical models to control for industry specific effects like competitive pressure, policy measures, demand shocks, etc.

The data from the three sources were merged inside the research data center of the statistical office. For West Germany,[5] we have information on import activities in 2009 and on the credit rating score (plus information on the control variables) in 2008 for 5,748 firms, 3,462 (or 60.22 percent) of which are importers; the respective numbers for 2010/2009 are 5,893 firms and 3,589 (or 60.9 percent) importers. Descriptive statistics for the two samples are reported in the Table A.1. It is known that larger firms have a much higher chance to be rated by the credit rating agency. Given that firm size and import activity are highly positively related, the high share of importers in the samples comes as no surprise. To take care of this oversampling of larger firms, the number of employees is included as a control variable in the empirical models.

## 3. Credit Rating Score and Margins of Import: Econometric Investigation

The considerations about the link between the credit rating score — a higher value of which by construction indicates a lower degree of creditworthiness and a higher degree of credit constraints — and import activities of a firms lead to six empirically testable hypotheses:

**H1**: *Firms with a higher credit rating score are less likely to import.*
**H2**: *Firms with a higher credit rating score will import less.*
**H3**: *Firms with a higher credit rating score will import a smaller number of goods.*

[5]There are still large differences between enterprises from manufacturing industries in West Germany and in former communist East Germany even some 20 years after the unification back in 1990, and this holds especially for international trade (see Wagner (2008)). Both parts of Germany have to be investigated separately. Given the small number of firms from East Germany in the sample we focus on West German firms in this study only.

**H4**: *Firms with a higher credit rating score will import from a smaller number of countries.*
**H5**: *Firms with a higher credit rating score are less likely to start to import.*
**H6**: *Firms with a higher credit rating score are more likely to stop to import.*

These six hypotheses will be tested empirically in turn in this section. Here, the credit rating score is treated as a continuous variable that may take values between 100 and 600. As a robustness check, the hypotheses will be tested again in Section 4 by applying the classification of the score value into seven credit rating classes (following the classification suggested by the credit rating agency *Creditreform*) from "excellent" to "not to be considered as partner in trade".

As a first step in the empirical investigation of H1 — that states that firms with a higher credit rating score are less likely to import — the credit rating scores of importers and non-importers are compared. Table 1 reports mean values and percentiles of the scores for both groups of firms for the two years under investigation. The average score is smaller for importers than for non-importers in both years — importers are judged to be better (because a smaller value of the score indicates a better performance). The difference in means is statistically highly different from zero according to a *t*-test. This result is in line with H1. The difference between the two groups, however, is only 5 score points and this is small from an economic point of view given the average level of about 200 points for both groups.

The percentiles of the score distributions for the groups indicate that firms are highly heterogeneous within the groups. Results that point to score differences at the (unconditional) mean might not tell the whole story. As Moshe Buchinsky (1994, p. 453) put it: "'On the average' has never been a satisfactory statement with which to conclude a study of heterogeneous populations." An empirical study of heterogeneous firms should look at differences in the whole distribution of the variable under investigation between

Table 1. Credit rating score for importers and non-importers

| | No. of firms | Mean | sd | p1 | p10 | p50 | p90 | p99 |
|---|---|---|---|---|---|---|---|---|
| Importer in 2009; credit rating score at end of 2008 | 3,483 | 194.53 | 38.56 | 108 | 147 | 196 | 246 | 293 |
| Non-importer in 2009; credit rating score at end of 2008 | 2,311 | 199.87 | 38.86 | 116 | 154 | 200 | 249 | 299 |
| $H_0$: Mean (Importer) = Mean (Non-importer); prob-value of $t$-test | 0.000 | | | | | | | |
| Kolmogorov–Smirnov tests for differences in distribution; prob-value | | | | | | | | |
| $H_0$: Distributions do not differ for importers and non-importers | 0.000 | | | | | | | |
| $H_0$: Non-importers have larger credit rating scores | 0.996 | | | | | | | |
| $H_0$: Importers have larger credit rating scores | 0.000 | | | | | | | |
| Importer in 2010; credit rating score at end of 2009 | 3,605 | 200.40 | 41.26 | 113 | 153 | 200 | 252 | 304 |
| Non-importer in 2010; credit rating score at end of 2009 | 2,316 | 205.61 | 41.31 | 120 | 159 | 203 | 257 | 309 |
| $H_0$: Mean (Importer) = Mean (Non-importer); prob-value of $t$-test | 0.000 | | | | | | | |
| Kolmogorov–Smirnov tests for differences in distribution; prob-value | | | | | | | | |
| $H_0$: Distributions do not differ for importers and non-importers | 0.000 | | | | | | | |
| $H_0$: Non-importers have larger credit rating scores | 0.999 | | | | | | | |
| $H_0$: Importers have larger credit rating scores | 0.000 | | | | | | | |

*Note*: p1, p10, etc. is the 1$^{st}$, 10$^{th}$ etc. percentile of the distribution of the credit rating score. The $t$-test is a two-sample test with unequal variances.

groups of firms, not only at differences at the mean. The empirical strategy used here, therefore, applies a non-parametric test for first order stochastic dominance of one distribution over another that was introduced into the empirical literature on international trade activities of firms by Delgado, Farinas and Rvano (2002). Let $F$ and $G$ denote the cumulative distribution functions of credit rating scores for two groups of firms (say, firms that import and firms that do not import). Fist order stochastic dominance of $F$ relative to $G$ is given if $F(z) - G(z)$ is less or equal zero for all $z$ with strict inequality for some $z$. Given two independent random samples of firms from each group, the hypothesis that $F$ is to the right of $G$ can be tested by the Kolmogorov–Smirnov test based on the empirical distribution functions for $F$ and $G$ in the samples. Note that this tests not only for differences in the mean credit rating score of both groups but for differences in all moments of the distribution. Results for the Kolmogorov–Smirnov test reported in Table 1 clearly indicate that the distributions of the credit rating scores do indeed differ between importers and non-importers and that importers have smaller (i.e. better) score values not only at the mean but over the whole score distribution. Again, the result is in favor of H1.

Results reported in Table 1 are for unconditional comparisons of mean values and distributions of the credit rating scores of importing and non-importing firms. In a second step H1 is tested controlling for other firm characteristics that are linked to imports. To do so an empirical model is estimated with a dummy variable that takes the value 1 if a firm is an importer in year $t$ (and 0 otherwise) as the dependent variable and the credit rating score at the end of year $t - 1$ plus control variables — the number of employees as a measure of firm size (also included in squares), labor productivity, the average wage per employee to proxy human capital intensity and a set of two-digit industry dummy variables — that are all measured in year $t - 1$ as independent variables. Results are reported in Table 2 in column 1 for a probit model. In both years the probability of being an importer is higher *ceteris paribus* for firms with a smaller (i.e. better) credit rating score. This is again in line with H1.

Table 2. Credit rating score and imports: Regression results

| Dependent variable method | | Importer-Dummy (1 = yes) probit | Share of imports in total sales Fractional Logit Model |
|---|---|---|---|
| 2009 | | | |
| Credit rating score | ß | −0.0008 | 0.00008 |
| 2008 | *p* | 0.000 | 0.909 |
| Labor productivity | ß | 3.89*e* − 9 | 2.37*e* − 8 |
| 2008 | *p* | 0.488 | 0.305 |
| Number of employees | ß | −7.90*e* − 6 | 0.000059 |
| 2008 | *p* | 0.332 | 0.001 |
| Number of employees | ß | 1.76*e* − 10 | −4.36*e* − 10 |
| (squared) 2008 | *p* | 0.160 | 0.012 |
| Wage per employee | ß | −3.14*e* − 7 | 3.52*e* − 6 |
| 2008 | *p* | 0.625 | 0.102 |
| Number of firms | | 5,748 | 5,748 |
| 2010 | | | |
| Credit rating score | ß | −0.0007 | −0.0004 |
| 2009 | *p* | 0.000 | 0.497 |
| Labor productivity | ß | −2.34*e* − 8 | −1.27*e* − 8 |
| 2009 | *p* | 0.124 | 0.807 |
| Number of employees | ß | −0.00001 | 0.00004 |
| 2009 | *p* | 0.220 | 0.017 |
| Number of employees | ß | 2.29*e* − 10 | −3.07*e* − 10 |
| (squared) 2009 | *p* | 0.138 | 0.047 |
| Wage per employee | ß | −1.81*e* − 6 | 4.15*e* − 6 |
| 2009 | *p* | 0.012 | 0.135 |
| Number of firms | | 5,891 | 5,893 |

*Note*: The empirical models include 2-digit industry dummy variables and a constant. ß is the estimated regression coefficient, *p* is the prob-value; for the Probit model marginal effects are reported.

The estimated marginal effects, however, are tiny. A decrease of the credit rating score by 40 points (which is equal to about one standard deviation) increases the probability of being an importer by about 0.03 percentage points. Even a change by 100 score points changes the estimated probability by less than 0.1 percentage points. From an economic point of view, therefore, the statistically highly significant coefficient of the credit score variable is next to zero.

We next turn to a test of H2 that states that firms with a higher credit rating score will import less, i.e. they will have a lower import to sales ratio. To test H2 an empirical model is estimated with the share of imports in total sales in year $t$ as the dependent variable and the credit rating score at the end of year $t-1$ plus control variables — the number of employees as a measure of firm size (also included in squares), labor productivity, the average wage per employee to proxy human capital intensity and a set of two-digit industry dummy variables — that are all measured in year $t-1$ as independent variables. The dependent variable, the share of imports in total sales, is a percentage variable that is limited between 0 and 100 percent, and that has a lot of observations at the lower bound because some 40 percent of all firms in the samples used here do not import at all. Papke and Wooldridge (1996) showed that for a fractional response variable of this type, and using cross-section data, a fractional logit estimator is appropriate.[6]

The results from fractional logit regressions are reported in column 2 of Table 2. The estimated coefficient for the credit rating score is statistically insignificant at any conventional level, and the point estimates have different signs in both years. Therefore, results are not in line with H2.

In the next step, we turn to the hypotheses H3 and H4 that are related to the extensive margins of imports with regard to the number of goods imported and the number of countries imported from. H3 states that firms with a higher credit rating score will import a smaller number of goods. To test this hypothesis, an empirical model is estimated by OLS that has the number of different goods imported by a firm as the dependent variable and the credit rating score value plus the set of control variables used in the empirical models to test H1 and H2 as independent variables. Results are reported in column 1 of Table 3. The

[6]Wagner (2001) introduced this estimation strategy into the literature on the determinants of trade activities of firms, and discusses the flaws related to alternative approaches like Tobit or two-step estimators. For a comprehensive recent discussion of estimation strategies for fractional response variables with a non-ignorable probability mass at zero see Ramalho, Ramalho and Murteira (2010).

Table 3. Credit rating score and extensive margins of imports: Regression results

| Dependent variable Method | | Number of goods imported OLS | Number of countries imported from OLS |
|---|---|---|---|
| 2009 | | | |
| Mean/p1/p99 | | 51/1/345 | 16/1/55 |
| Credit rating score | ß | −0.130 | −0.034 |
| 2008 | $p$ | 0.000 | 0.000 |
| Labor productivity | ß | −2.50$e$ − 6 | −2.65$e$ − 7 |
| 2008 | $p$ | 0.432 | 0.711 |
| Number of employees | ß | 0.049 | 0.004 |
| 2008 | $p$ | 0.000 | 0.000 |
| Number of employees | ß | −3.17$e$ − 7 | −3.02$e$ − 8 |
| (squared) 2008 | $p$ | 0.000 | 0.000 |
| Wage per employee | ß | 0.0006 | 0.0001 |
| 2008 | $p$ | 0.022 | 0.019 |
| Number of firms | | 3,462 | 3,462 |
| 2010 | | | |
| Mean/p1/p99 | | 55/1/357 | 16/1/51 |
| Credit rating score | ß | −0.061 | −0.021 |
| 2009 | $p$ | 0.032 | 0.000 |
| Labor productivity | ß | −9.85$e$ − 6 | −1.82$e$ − 6 |
| 2009 | $p$ | 0.002 | 0.008 |
| Number of employees | ß | 0.051 | 0.0044 |
| 2009 | $p$ | 0.000 | 0.000 |
| Number of employees | ß | −3.42$e$ − 7 | −3.15$e$ − 8 |
| (squared) 2009 | $p$ | 0.000 | 0.000 |
| Wage per employee | ß | 0.001 | 0.0002 |
| 2009 | $p$ | 0.000 | 0.000 |
| Number of firms | | 3,589 | 3,589 |

*Note*: The empirical models include 2-digit industry dummy variables and a constant. ß is the estimated regression coefficient, $p$ is the prob-value. Mean, p1 and p99 is the average number of goods (countries) and the first and the 99$^{th}$ percentile of the distribution of the number of goods (countries).

estimated regression coefficients have the expected sings, and they are statistically different from zero at an error level of 3.2 percent or better. In both years the estimated effect of the credit rating score is large. A change in the score value by 40 points (that corresponds to one standard deviation, see Table 1) is related to an estimated change of the number of goods imported by 5 in 2009 and 2.5 in 2010. Firms on average import about 50 different goods, so the estimated effect can be considered to be relevant from an economic point of view, too. Results, therefore, are in line with H3.

H4 states that firms with a higher credit rating score will import from a smaller number of countries. To test this hypothesis an empirical model is estimated by OLS that has the number of different countries of origin as the dependent variable and the credit rating score value plus the same set of control variables used in the empirical models to test H3 as independent variables. Results are reported in column 2 of Table 3. The estimated regression coefficients have the expected sings, and they are statistically highly significant. In both years the estimated effect of the credit rating score is large. A change in the score value by 40 points is related to an estimated change of the number of countries imported from by 1.4 in 2009 and 0.84 in 2010. Firms on average import from 16 countries, so the estimated effect can be considered to be relevant from an economic point of view, too. These results are in line with H4.

In the final step, we turn to the hypotheses H5 and H6 that consider the decision of a firm to start or to stop importing. Import starters are defined as firms that did not report any imports in 2009 but did report imports in 2010. Import stoppers are firms that did report imports in 2009 but did not report imports in 2010. This definition of starters and stoppers is a bit fuzzy due to the reporting threshold that applies in the collection of the data for the statistics of foreign trade. The group of import starters includes firms which imported in 2009 from countries inside the EU only but which had not to report because the amount of imports was below the reporting threshold of 400.000 €. A similar point applies to firms classified as import stoppers that continued to import from EU member countries only in 2010, but which had not to report any longer because the sum of imports was below the threshold value.

That said, it should be noted that the number of both import starters and import stoppers is tiny in the sample used here. From the 2,310 firms that did not import in 2009 only 118 (or 5.1 percent) started to import in 2010, and from the 3,611 firms that did import in 2009 only 124 (or 3.4 percent) stopped to import in 2010. These small numbers of starters and stoppers are a consequence of the fact that large firms are oversampled in the samples used here because larger firms have a much higher chance to be rated by the credit rating agency.

H5 states that firms with a higher credit rating score are less likely to start to import. Results reported in the upper panel of Table 4 are not in line with this hypothesis. Contrary to H5, the average value of the credit rating score of import starters is higher than the score on non-starters. This difference in means, however, is not statistically significantly different from zero at any conventional error level according to a *t*-test, and the Kolmogorov–Smirnov test does not reject the hypothesis of no difference in the credit score distribution for both groups of firms.

Results from a probit model with a dummy variable for import starters as the dependent variable and the credit rating score plus the set of control variables used before as independent variables that are reported in column 1 of Table 5 lead to an identical conclusion. Contrary to H5 there is no evidence that firms with a higher credit rating score are less likely to start to import.

H6 states that firms with a higher credit rating score are more likely to stop to import. Results reported in the lower panel of Table 4 are in line with this hypothesis. The average value of the credit rating score of import stoppers is higher than the score on non-stoppers. This difference in means is statistically highly significant according to a *t*-test, and the Kolmogorov–Smirnov test does indicate that the distribution of credit rating scores for export-stoppers stochastically dominates the distribution for firms that continue to import. Results from a probit model with a dummy variable for import stoppers as the dependent variable and the credit rating score plus the set of control variables used before as independent variables that are reported in column 2 of Table 5 lead to an identical conclusion. In line with H6 there is evidence that firms with a higher credit rating score are more likely to stop to

Table 4. Credit rating score for import starters, non-importers, import stoppers and importers

| | No. of firms | Mean | sd | p1 | p10 | p50 | p90 | p99 |
|---|---|---|---|---|---|---|---|---|
| Import starters in 2010; credit rating score at end of 2009 | 118 | 212.42 | 51.07 | ### | 169 | 206 | 263 | ### |
| Non-importers in 2009 and 2010; credit rating score at end of 2009 | 2,192 | 205.19 | 40.72 | 120 | 159 | 203 | 255 | 304 |
| $H_0$: Mean (Import starters) = Mean (Non-importers); prob-value of *t*-test | 0.113 | | | | | | | |
| Kolmogorov–Smirnov tests for differences in distribution; prob-value | | | | | | | | |
| $H_0$: Distributions do not differ for import starters and non-importers | 0.283 | | | | | | | |
| $H_0$: Non-importers have larger credit rating scores | 0.163 | | | | | | | |
| $H_0$: Import starters have larger credit rating scores | 0.570 | | | | | | | |
| Import stoppers in 2010; credit rating score at end of 2009 | 124 | 212.92 | 50.32 | ### | 161 | 205 | 283 | ### |
| Importers in 2009 and 2010; credit rating score at end of 2009 | 3,487 | 200.00 | 40.84 | 113 | 153 | 200 | 252 | ### |
| $H_0$: Mean (Import stoppers) = Mean (Importers); prob-value of *t*-test | 0.006 | | | | | | | |
| Kolmogorov–Smirnov tests for differences in distribution; prob-value | | | | | | | | |
| $H_0$: Distributions do not differ for import stoppers and Importers | 0.060 | | | | | | | |
| $H_0$: Import stoppers have larger credit rating scores | 0.038 | | | | | | | |
| $H_0$: Importer have larger credit rating scores | 0.990 | | | | | | | |

*Note*: p1, p10, etc. is the first, tenth, etc. percentile of the distribution of the credit rating score. The t-test is a two-sample test with unequal variances. ### indicates a confidential value (due to small number of cases).

Table 5. Credit rating score, import start and import stop: Regression results

| Dependent variable method | | Import starter (Dummy, 1 = yes) probit | Import stopper (Dummy, 1 = yes) probit |
|---|---|---|---|
| Credit rating score | ß | 0.00013 | 0.00020 |
| 2009 | *p* | 0.195 | 0.001 |
| Labor productivity | ß | −3.18*e* − 9 | −4.49*e* − 9 |
| 2009 | *p* | 0.839 | 0.601 |
| Number of employees | ß | −0.0000328 | −8.05*e* − 7 |
| 2009 | *p* | 0.051 | 0.928 |
| Number of employees | ß | 6.61*e* − 10 | −5.13*e* − 10 |
| (squared) 2009 | *p* | 0.061 | 0.667 |
| Wage per employee | ß | −1.14*e* − 6 | 2.39*e* − 7 |
| 2009 | *p* | 0.016 | 0.438 |
| Number of firms | | 2,201 | 3,494 |

*Note*: The empirical models include 2-digit industry dummy variables and a constant. ß is the estimated marginal effect, *p* is the prob-value.

import. The estimated marginal effect indicates, however, that the statically significant coefficient is rather small from an economic point of view. An increase in the credit rating score by 40 points increases the probability to stop to export by 0.13 percentage point which points to a weak relationship between the credit rating score and the decision to stop to import.

However, it should be pointed out that due to the small number of import status switchers in the sample over a short period of two years, the results reported for links between credit rating scores and starting or stopping to import should not be considered as reliable.

The bottom line, then, is that we find empirical evidence that a better credit rating score is positively related to extensive margins of import. On the one hand, firms with a better score have a higher probability to import. While statistically highly significant, this link is, however, is not relevant from an economic point of view according to the size of the estimated marginal effects of a change in the credit rating score on the probability to export. On the other hand, firms with a better credit rating score import more goods and they source from more countries of origin. This link is not only statistically highly significant — according to the estimated marginal effects it is relevant from an economic point of view, too. Firms that import many goods and from many countries have to cover extra costs related to import activities many times, and financial constraints are more important for such firms than for firms that are marginal importers only according to the number of goods imported and the number of countries imported from.

Contrary to these findings, the intensive margin of imports — the share of imports in total sales — is found not to be related to credit constraints. In light of the results found for the link between the credit rating score and both the number of goods imported and the number of countries imported from, this might be due to the fact that a given total value of imports of a firm can be the results of a wide range of import transaction that cover a small or a large number of different goods imported from a small or a large number of countries.

## 4. Robustness Checks

### 4.1. *Credit rating scores classes*

In this section, the six hypotheses on the links between the credit rating score of a firm and its import activities that were tested in Section 3 are tested again in a robustness check that uses the classification of the score value into seven credit rating classes suggested by the credit rating agency *Creditreform*, instead of treating the score as a continuous variable. The score takes values from 100 to 600, and *Creditreform* suggests that 100–149 should be considered as excellent, 150–199 as very good, 200–249 as good, 250–299 as medium, 300–349 as weak, 350–419 as high risk of failure, and firms with a score of 420 or more are classified as firms that should not be considered as partners in trade and credit relations.

Table 6 documents the distribution of the various types of firms considered in this study (importer, non-importer, import starter, non-starter, import stopper, non-stopper) over the seven credit rating score classes. About 80 percent of all firms from each of these types are in class 2 (very good) or class 3 (good), and most

Table 6. Distribution of types of firms over credit rating score classes

| Credit rating score class | Credit rating score | Importer 2009 | Non-importer 2009 | Importer 2010 | Non-importer 2010 | Importer starter 2010 | Non-starter 2010 | Import stopper 2010 | Non-stopper 2010 |
|---|---|---|---|---|---|---|---|---|---|
| | Share of firms from credit rating score class in year $t-1$ in group of firms (percentage) | | | | | | | | |
| 1 Excellent | 100–149 | 10.74 | 8.52 | 8.54 | 7.56 | ### | 7.57 | 7.26 | 8.80 |
| 2 Very good | 150–199 | 44.44 | 40.72 | 40.86 | 36.14 | 40.37 | 36.18 | 35.48 | 40.81 |
| 3 Good | 200–249 | 36.55 | 40.80 | 39.36 | 43.09 | 42.37 | 43.34 | 38.71 | 39.26 |
| 4 Medium | 250–299 | 7.67 | 8.96 | 10.10 | 11.49 | 11.86 | 11.36 | 13.71 | 10.04 |
| 5 Weak | 300–349 | 0.49 | 0.78 | 0.78 | 1.34 | ### | 1.28 | 2.42 | 0.75 |
| 6 High risk of failure | 350–419 | ### | ### | ### | ### | ### | ### | 2.42 | 0.23 |
| 7 Not to be considered as partner in trade | 420–600 | ### | ### | ### | ### | ### | ### | 0.00 | 0.11 |
| Total number of firms | | 3,483 | 2,311 | 3,605 | 2,316 | 118 | 2,192 | 124 | 3,487 |

*Note*: ### indicates a confidential value (less than three firms) or a value that has to be treated as confidential to prohibit the calculation of a confidential value. For a definition of import starter, non-starter, import stopper and non-stopper see text.

of the remaining firms are classified as medium (class 4) or, to a somewhat lesser extent, excellent. Firms in the three lowest credit rating score classes are rare — in some cases there are less than three firms of a type in a class so that the exact number of observations is confidential.

The empirical models used to test the hypotheses H3–H6 are identical to the models used in Section 3 with one exception. The credit rating score is no longer included as one continuous variable. Instead, the empirical models have six dummy variables for the credit rating score classes 2–7, using the left-out highest score class 1 (excellent) as the reference category.

For H1 and H2 the same big picture emerges that is reported in Table 2 in Section 3 based on the continuous score variable. From column 1 we see that firms from a better score class have a higher probability to import. The negative relationship between a worse score class and the probability to import is statistically significant for firms in the $3^{rd}$, $4^{th}$ and $5^{th}$ class (compared to the reference category of firms that are rated as excellent).[7] The marginal effects, however, are again rather low. The estimated probability that a firm from the score class "medium" is an importer is only 0.9 (0.7) percentage points smaller than the probability for a firm from the score class "excellent" in 2009 (2010). Results reported in column 2 indicate that, in line with results stated in Table 2, the credit rating score class is not related to the amount of imports.

For H3 and H4, too, results based on credit rating score classes are similar to results based on the continuously measured score. In line with results reported in Table 3, results in Table 8 show that both the number of goods imported and the number of countries imported from is higher among firms from a better credit rating score class.[8]

[7]Results for the score classes 6 and 7 should not be interpreted because they are based on one or two observations only. This caveat applies to estimation results reported in Table 8, too.

[8]H5 and H6 were tested using the credit rating score classes, too. However, due to problems with the sample used, the results are not reliable and are not reported here. Details are available from the author on request.

Table 7. Credit rating score class and imports: Regression results

| Dependent variable method | | Importer-Dummy (1 = yes) probit | | Share of imports in total sales Fractional Logit Model | |
|---|---|---|---|---|---|
| Year | | 2009 | 2010 | 2009 | 2010 |
| Credit rating score class | | | | | |
| Very good | ß | −0.036 | −0.005 | 0.006 | 0.017 |
| | *p* | 0.128 | 0.854 | 0.941 | 0.840 |
| Good | ß | −0.079 | −0.054 | −0.068 | 0.018 |
| | *p* | 0.001 | 0.031 | 0.421 | 0.834 |
| Medium | ß | −0.090 | −0.069 | 0.153 | 0.042 |
| | *p* | 0.004 | 0.024 | 0.208 | 0.703 |
| Weak | ß | −0.168 | −0.159 | −0.176 | −0.557 |
| | *p* | 0.050 | 0.022 | 0.633 | 0.048 |
| High risk | ß | −0.135 | −0.109 | 0.184 | −0.315 |
| of failure | *p* | 0.518 | 0.410 | 0.691 | 0.424 |
| Not to be considered | ß | −0.340 | 0.069 | −4.328 | 0.368 |
| as partner In trade | *p* | 0.220 | 0.705 | 0.000 | 0.336 |
| Labor productivity | ß | 4.13*e* − 9 | −2.24*e* − 8 | 2.44*e* − 8 | −1.08*e* − 8 |
| | *p* | 0.466 | 0.133 | 0.297 | 0.836 |
| Number of employees | ß | −8.15*e* − 6 | −0.00001 | 0.00006 | 0.00004 |
| | *p* | 0.318 | 0.227 | 0.001 | 0.013 |
| Number of employees | ß | 1.79*e* − 10 | 2.28*e* − 10 | −4.24*e* − 10 | −3.23*e* − 10 |
| (squared) | *p* | 0.155 | 0.138 | 0.013 | 0.040 |
| Wage per employee | ß | −3.12*e* − 7 | −1.79*e* − 6 | 3.50*e* − 6 | 4.17*e* − 6 |
| | *p* | 0.625 | 0.013 | 0.106 | 0.134 |
| Number of firms | | 5,748 | 5,891 | 5,748 | 5,893 |

*Note*: All independent variables are lagged values for year $t-1$. The empirical models include 2-digit industry dummy variables and a constant. ß is the estimated regression coefficient, *p* is the prob-value; for the Probit model marginal effects are reported. The reference category for the credit rating class is "excellent"; for a definition of the classes see text and Table 6.

## 4.2. *Negative binomial regressions*

In a further robustness check, the empirical models for the number of goods imported and the number of countries imported from were estimated using a negative binomial regression model that explicitly takes care of the fact that both variables are count

Table 8. Credit rating score class and extensive margins of imports: Regression results

| Dependent variable method | | Number of goods imported OLS | | Number of countries imported from OLS | |
|---|---|---|---|---|---|
| Year | | 2009 | 2010 | 2009 | 2010 |
| Mean/p1/p99 | | 51/1/345 | 55/1/357 | 16/1/55 | 16/1/51 |
| Credit rating score class | | | | | |
| Very good | ß | −7.286 | −7.917 | −1.656 | −1.873 |
| | *p* | 0.080 | 0.075 | 0.006 | 0.005 |
| Good | ß | −13.116 | −10.445 | −3.532 | −3.268 |
| | *p* | 0.002 | 0.018 | 0.000 | 0.000 |
| Medium | ß | −10.835 | −9.212 | −3.552 | −2.798 |
| | *p* | 0.049 | 0.082 | 0.000 | 0.000 |
| Weak | ß | −20.424 | −10.073 | −4.971 | −4.613 |
| | *p* | 0.016 | 0.275 | 0.004 | 0.003 |
| High risk | ß | −84.170 | −28.111 | −5.496 | −4.937 |
| of failure | *p* | 0.354 | 0.462 | 0.699 | 0.337 |
| Not to be considered | ß | ### | 32.618 | ### | 4.969 |
| as partner In trade | p | ### | 0.056 | ### | 0.135 |
| Labor productivity | ß | −2.26*e* − 6 | −9.55*e* − 6 | −2.26*e* − 7 | −1.73*e* − 6 |
| | *p* | 0.480 | 0.003 | 0.753 | 0.011 |
| Number of employees | ß | 0.049 | 0.051 | 0.004 | 0.004 |
| | *p* | 0.000 | 0.000 | 0.000 | 0.000 |
| Number of employees | ß | −3.19*e* − 7 | −3.42*e* − 7 | −2.99*e* − 8 | −3.12*e* − 8 |
| (squared) | *p* | 0.000 | 0.000 | 0.000 | 0.000 |
| Wage per employee | ß | 0.0006 | 0.001 | 0.0001 | 0.0002 |
| | *p* | 0.027 | 0.000 | 0.023 | 0.000 |
| Numnber of firms | | 3,462 | 3,589 | 3,462 | 3,589 |

*Note*: All independent variables are lagged values for year $t - 1$.The empirical models include 2-digit industry dummy variables and a constant. ß is the estimated regression coefficient, $p$ is the prob-value. The reference category for the credit rating class is "excellent"; for a definition of the classes see text and Table 6. Mean, p1 and p99 is the average number of goods (countries) and the first and the 99$^{th}$ percentile of the distribution of the number of goods (countries). ### indicates a confidential value (that is based on one or two observations only).

variables with positive integer values only. Results are reported in Tables 9 and 10. The big picture that results from this robustness check is identical to the results from the OLS regressions documented in Tables 3 and 8.

Table 9. Credit rating score and extensive margins of imports: Results for negative binomial regression models

| Dependent variable method | | Number of goods imported negative binomial regression | Number of countries imported from negative binomial regression |
|---|---|---|---|
| 2009 | | | |
| Mean/p1/p99 | | 51/1/345 | 16/1/55 |
| Credit rating score | ß | −0.002 | −0.0019 |
| 2008 | *p* | 0.000 | 0.000 |
| Labor productivity | ß | −1.28*e* − 7 | −3.54*e* − 8 |
| 2008 | *p* | 0.021 | 0.338 |
| Number of employees | ß | 0.00063 | 0.0003 |
| 2008 | *p* | 0.000 | 0.000 |
| Number of employees | ß | −4.62*e* − 9 | −2.15*e* − 9 |
| (squared) 2008 | *p* | 0.000 | 0.000 |
| Wage per employee | ß | 0.000018 | 0.000011 |
| 2008 | *p* | 0.000 | 0.000 |
| Number of firms | | 3,462 | 3,462 |
| 2010 | | | |
| Mean/p1/p99 | | 55/1/357 | 16/1/51 |
| Credit rating score | ß | −0.0009 | −0.0011 |
| 2009 | *p* | 0.017 | 0.000 |
| Labor productivity | ß | −2.16*e* − 7 | −1.03*e* − 7 |
| 2009 | *p* | 0.001 | 0.022 |
| Number of employees | ß | 0.0007 | 0.0003 |
| 2009 | *p* | 0.000 | 0.000 |
| Number of employees | ß | −5.08*e* − 9 | −2.26*e* − 9 |
| (squared) 2009 | *p* | 0.000 | 0.000 |
| Wage per employee | ß | 0.0002 | 0.00001 |
| 2009 | *p* | 0.000 | 0.000 |
| Number of firms | | 3,589 | 3,589 |

*Note*: The empirical models include 2-digit industry dummy variables and a constant. ß is the estimated regression coefficient, *p* is the prob-value. Mean, p1 and p99 is the average number of goods (countries) and the first and the 99$^{th}$ percentile of the distribution of the number of goods (countries).

## 4.3. *Augmented empirical models*

As another robustness check (and following the suggestions of a referee), the empirical models were augmented by the following control variables: a dummy variable indicating whether the firm is

Table 10. Credit rating score class and extensive margins of imports: Results for negative binomial regression models

| Dependent variable method | | Number of goods imported negative binomial regression | | Number of countries imported from negative binomial regression | |
|---|---|---|---|---|---|
| Year | | 2009 | 2010 | 2009 | 2010 |
| Mean/p1/p99 | | 51/1/345 | 55/1/357 | 16/1/55 | 16/1/51 |
| Credit rating score class | | | | | |
| Very good | ß | −0.140 | −0.133 | −0.076 | −0.080 |
| | *p* | 0.011 | 0.018 | 0.015 | 0.015 |
| Good | ß | −0.266 | −0.190 | −0.193 | −0.166 |
| | *p* | 0.000 | 0.001 | 0.000 | 0.000 |
| Medium | ß | −0.216 | −0.213 | −0.192 | −0.158 |
| | *p* | 0.010 | 0.002 | 0.000 | 0.000 |
| Weak | ß | −0.293 | −0.206 | −0.260 | −0.293 |
| | *p* | 0.213 | 0.403 | 0.058 | 0.009 |
| High risk | ß | 0.073 | −0.075 | 0.129 | −0.181 |
| of failure | *p* | 0.901 | 0.834 | 0.814 | 0.560 |
| Not to be considered | ß | ### | 0.611 | ### | 0.310 |
| as partner In trade | *p* | ### | 0.005 | ### | 0.041 |
| Labor productivity | ß | $-1.28e-7$ | $-2.12e-7$ | $-3.32e-8$ | $-9.95e-8$ |
| | *p* | 0.020 | 0.001 | 0.357 | 0.026 |
| Number of employees | ß | 0.00063 | 0.00066 | 0.0003 | 0.0003 |
| | *p* | 0.000 | 0.000 | 0.000 | 0.000 |
| Number of employees | ß | $-4.59e-9$ | $-5.04e-9$ | $-2.14e-9$ | $-2.24e-9$ |
| (squared) | *p* | 0.000 | 0.000 | 0.000 | 0.000 |
| Wage per employee | ß | 0.000018 | 0.000018 | 0.00001 | 0.00014 |
| | *p* | 0.000 | 0.000 | 0.000 | 0.000 |
| Number of firms | | 3,462 | 3,589 | 3,462 | 3,589 |

*Note*: All independent variables are lagged values for year $t-1$. The empirical models include 2-digit industry dummy variables and a constant. ß is the estimated regression coefficient, $p$ is the prob-value. The reference category for the credit rating class is "excellent"; for a definition of the classes see text and Table 6. Mean, p1 and p99 is the average number of goods (countries) and the first and the 99$^{th}$ percentile of the distribution of the number of goods (countries). ### indicates a confidential value (that is based on one or two observations only).

an exporter or not — alternatively, the share of exports in total sales of a firm was used to control for exports; three dummy variables that indicate whether the firm is a foreign-owned firm (that belongs to at least 50 percent to a firm that is located in a foreign country), whether the firm is controlled by a German firm (i.e. whether it belongs to a group headed by a German firm), and whether the firm is a German firm that is head of a group and that controls other German firms, using independent German firms as the reference group; and a set of dummy variables that indicate the German federal state the firm is located in.

The big picture that emerges from the results for these augmented models is the same as the one reported for the more parsimonious specifications. For example, for 2009 in the augmented model the estimated marginal effect for the credit rating score on the probability that the firm is an importer is −0.0005 (with a $p$-value of 0.000) instead of −0.0008 (as reported in Table 2). For the number of goods imported, the estimated regression coefficient of the credit rating score is −0.162 instead of −0.130 (as reported in Table 3), and for the number of countries imported from, the coefficient is −0.037 instead of −0.034 (with identical $p$-values).

## 5. Conclusions

This study uses tailor-made enterprise-level data for 2008–2010 from various sources for firms from manufacturing industries to test for the link between credit constraints, measured by a credit rating score provided by a leading credit rating agency, and imports in Germany for the first time. We find empirical evidence that a better credit rating score is positively related to extensive margins of import — firms with a better score have a higher probability to import, they import more goods and they source from more countries of origin. The intensive margin of imports — the share of imports in total sales — is found not to be related to credit constraints.

To put these results into perspective, two characteristics of the enterprise-level data used in this study should be pointed out. First, the way credit constraints are measured can be considered as convincing. While the credit rating score used is clearly endogenous to the firm's performance and characteristic, it is not directly affected by its importing behavior, given that imports, are not used in constructing the index. Important advantages are that the score is determined independently by a private firm and is not based on subjective assessments, it is firm-specific, varies over time on an annual basis and allows for a measure of the degree of credit constraints rather than classifying firms as constrained or not. Second, while the measure for credit constraints is very suitable for the study of the links between credit constraints and imports, the sample used is less so. As said in Section 2 smaller firms are underrepresented because the credit rating score is not available for these firms. Connected to this shortcoming is the small number of import starters and import stoppers. Smaller firms do more often switch in and out of importing. For these firms credit constraints might be more important, than for larger firms who often generate enough liquidity to cover the extra costs of importing.

Furthermore, the empirical investigation is limited to the analysis of data from two cross-section samples only. This limitation is due to the fact that as of today the transactions-level data aggregated to the firm level are available for the reporting years 2009 and 2010 only. On the one hand, this limitation hinders the use of panel data and panel econometric models than could be used to control for unobserved time invariant firm characteristics that might be correlated with the credit rating score and, therefore, might lead to biased estimates of the coefficients of the score variables. On the other hand, it should be kept in mind that the two years investigated here are special periods with regard to imports. After the severe collapse of international trade during the Great Recession in 2009 global trade flows rebounded strongly in 2010. The value of total German imports declined by 17.5 percent in 2009 compared to 2008, and this was followed by an increase in imports by 19.9 percent in 2010 (see Wagner (2013b) for details). The links between import activities and credit rating scores might look quite different in periods that are characterized by much less turbulence on the international goods markets.

The results of this first empirical study on the links between credit rating scores and import activities of firms in Germany, one of the most important actors in the world market for goods, are interesting in itself and as a contribution to the small literature on credit constraints and imports. However, given the shortcomings mentioned, the results presented here should not be used as a basis to discuss the need for any policy measures to improve the access to credits for firms that intend to start or expand import activities.

## Acknowledgments

I thank two anonymous referees for helpful comments on an earlier version. All computations were performed inside the research data center of the Statistical Office of Berlin-Brandenburg. I thank Rafael Beier, Florian Köhler and Julia Höninger for preparing the project-specific data set that merges data from the statistics of foreign trade, from surveys performed by official statistics and data from a private credit rating agency. The enterprise-level data from official statistics are confidential but not exclusive; see www.forschungsdatenzentrum.de for information on how to access the data. The data from the credit rating agency are proprietary; details are available from the author on request. To facilitate replications the Stata do-files used to compute the results reported in this chapter are available on request.

## References

Bas, Maria and Antoine Berthou (2012). The Decision to Import Capital Goods in India: Firms' Financial Factors Matter. *The World Bank Economic Review* 26(3), 486–513.

Buchinsky, Moshe (1994). Changes in the U.S. Wage Structure 1963–1987: Application of Quantile Regression. *Econometrica* 62(2), 405–458.

Chaney, Thomas (2013). Liquidity Constrained Exporters. National Bureau of Economic Research NBER Working Paper 19170, June.

Delgado, Miguel A., Jose C. Farinas and Sonia. Ruano (2002). Firm Productivity and Export Markets: A Non-parametric Approach. *Journal on International Economics* 57(2), 397–422.

Egger, Peter and Michaela Kesina (2013). Financial Constraints and Exports: Evidence from Chinese Firms. *CESifo Economic Studies* 59(4), 676–706.

Farre-Mensa, Joan and Alexander Ljungqvist (2013). Do Measures of Financial Constraints Measure Financial Constraints? National Bureau of Economic Research NBER Working Paper 19551, October.

Greenaway, David, Alessandra Guariglia and Richard Kneller (2007). Financial Factors and Exporting Decisions. *Journal of International Economics* 73(2), 377–395.

Malchin, Anja and Ramona Voshage (2009). Official Firm Data for Germany. *Schmollers Jahrbuch/Journal of Applied Social Science Studies* 129(3), 501–513.

Manova, Kalina (2013). Credit Constraints, Heterogeneous Firms, and International Trade. *Review of Economic Studies* 80(4), 711–744.

Melitz, Mark J. (2003). The Impact of Trade on Intra-Industry Reallocations and Aggregate Industry Productivity. *Econometrica* 71(6), 1695–1725.

Minetti, Raoul and Susan Chun Zhu (2011). Credit Constraints and Firm Exports: Microeconomic Evidence from Italy. *Journal of International Economics* 83(1), 109–125.

Musso, Patrick and Stefano Schiavo (2008). The Impact of Financial Constraints on Firm Survival and Growth. *Journal of Evolutionary Economics* 18(2), 135–149.

Muuls, Mirabelle (2008). Exporters and Credit Constraints. A Firm-Level Approach. National Bank of Belgium Working Paper Research No. 139, September.

Muuls, Mirabelle (2012). Exporters, Importers and Credit Constraints. CEP Discussion Paper No. 1169, October.

Papke, Leslie E. and Jeffrey M. Wooldridge (1996). Econometric Methods for Fractional Response Variables with an Application to 401(k) Plan Participation Rates. *Journal of Applied Econometrics* 11(6), 619–632.

Ramalho, Esmeralda A., Joaquim J. S. Ramalho and José M. R. Murteira (2010). Alternative Estimating and Testing Empirical Strategies for Fractional Regression Models. *Journal of Economic Surveys* 25(1), 19–68.

Rossen, Jörg (2012). Verfeinerte Bonitätsbewertung für das Kreditrisikomanagement. *KSI – Krisen-, Sanierungs- und Insolvenzberatung* 1/2012, 22–26.

Secchi, Angelo, Federico Tamagni and Chiara Tomasi (2011). Export Activities Under Financial Constraints: Margins, Quantities and Prices. Laboratory of Economics and Management Sant'Anna School of Advanced Studies LEM Working Paper Series 2011/24, December.

Statistisches Bundesamt (2012). Statistisches Jahrbuch Deutschland. Wiesbaden: Statistisches Bundesamt.

Tamagni, Federicio (2013). Exporting Under Financial Constraints: Margins, Switching Dynamics and Prices. Scuola Superiore Sant'Anna LEM, mimeo, February.

Vogel, Alexander and Joachim Wagner (2010). Higher Productivity in Importing German Manufacturing Firms: Self-Selection, Learning from Importing, or Both? *Review of World Economics* 145(4), 641–665.

Wagner, Joachim (2001). A Note on the Firm Size — Export Relationship. *Small Business Economics* 17(4), 229–237.

Wagner, Joachim (2008). Why More West than East German Firms Export. *International Economics and Economic Policy* 5(4), 363–370.

Wagner, Joachim (2012a). International Trade and Firm Performance: A Survey of Empirical Studies Since 2006. *Review of World Economics* 148(2), 235–267.

Wagner, Joachim (2012b). Productivity and the Extensive Margins of Trade in German Manufacturing Firms: Evidence from a Non-Parametric Test. *Economics Bulletin* 32(4), 3061–3070.
Wagner, Joachim (2012c). Average Wage, Qualification of the Workforce and Export Performance in German Enterprises: Evidence From *KombiFiD* Data. *Journal of Labour Market Research* 45(2), 161–170.
Wagner, Joachim (2013a). Credit Constraints and Exports: A Survey of Empirical Studies Using Firm Level Data. University of Lüneburg Working Paper Series in Economics No. 288, December.
Wagner, Joachim (2013b). Extensive Margins of Imports in the Great Import Recovery in Germany, 2009/2010. *Economics Bulletin* 33(4), 2732–2743.
Wagner, Joachim (2014). Credit Constraints and Exports: Evidence for German Manufacturing Enterprises. *Applied Economics* 46(3), 294–302.
World Trade Organization (2012). *World Trade Report 2012*. Geneva: WTO Publications.

## Table A.1

Table 11. Descriptive statistics

| Variable | Mean | sd | p1 | p50 | p99 |
|---|---|---|---|---|---|
| [2008/2009; Number of firms: 5,748] | | | | | |
| Importer (Dummy, 1 = yes) 2009 | 0.6022 | 0.4895 | 0 | 1 | 1 |
| Imports/total sales 2009 | 0.0930 | 0.1581 | 0 | 0.0229 | 0.8310 |
| Credit rating score 2008 | 196.52 | 38.62 | 112 | 197 | 296 |
| Labor productivity (sales/employee; Euro) 2008 | 321,537 | 1,362,519 | 55,956 | 217,749 | 1,467,826 |
| Number of employees 2008 | 465.71 | 2, 544.71 | 27 | 210.33 | 3,576.08 |
| Human capital intensity (wage/employee; Euro) 2008 | 39,507 | 11,395 | 16,875 | 38,856 | 67,005 |
| [2009/2010; Number of firms: 5,893] | | | | | |
| Importer (Dummy, 1 = yes) 2010 | 0.6092 | 0.4880 | 0 | 1 | 1 |
| Imports/total sales 2010 | 0.1027 | 0.1680 | 0 | 0.0262 | 0.8666 |
| Credit rating score 2009 | 202.38 | 41.39 | 116 | 201 | 309 |
| Labor productivity (sales/employee; Euro) 2009 | 275,118 | 1,038,344 | 46,112 | 187,747 | 1,356,743 |
| Number of employees 2009 | 453.70 | 470.81 | 26 | 204.08 | 3,704.50 |
| Human capital intensity (wage/employee; Euro) 2009 | 38,324 | 10,210 | 16,841 | 37,469 | 67,237 |

PART VII

# Extensive Margins of Exports and Imports

Chapter 14

# Trading Many Goods with Many Countries: Exporters and Importers from German Manufacturing Industries

Joachim Wagner

## 1. New Data on Exports and Imports of German Manufacturing Firms

Germany is one of the leading actors in the international markets for goods. According to the *World Trade Report 2011* published by the World Trade Organization, it was number three (after China and the United States) in the ranking of countries by the value of both exports and imports in merchandise trade in 2010 (see Word Trade Organization (2011), Appendix Table 3). International trade is of high relevance for the German economy as a whole, for its regions, industries and firms. Reliable information on international trade activities, therefore, is important for empirical analyses in many areas of economics including business cycles, structural change and economic growth.

Data on total exports and imports, and on exports and imports by goods traded and countries trades with, are published on a regular basis by the German Statistical Office. While these published aggregate data from official statistics are important for a bird's-eye view of international activities, disaggregated data for the actors on international markets — the firms trading goods with partners in foreign countries — are needed for any in-depth analyses of the causes and consequences of exports and imports.

Empirical studies for Germany that use comprehensive firm-level data from the surveys of the statistical offices hitherto focus on exports from manufacturing firms; only most recently imports have been investigated, too.[1] The firm-level data used in these empirical investigations identify firms that export or import, but they do not cover any information about the goods traded and the countries of destination or origin of the goods. In other words, we know from these data *who* trades *how much*, but not *what* and *with whom*.

Information on the goods traded internationally and on the countries with which these goods are traded[2] is available from the statistic on foreign trade (*Außenhandelsstatistik*). This statistic is based on two sources. One source is the reports by German firms on transactions with firms from countries that are members of the European Union (EU); these reports are used to compile the so-called *Intrahandelsstatistik* on intra-EU trade. The other source is transaction-level data collected by the customs on trade with countries outside the EU (the so-called *Extrahandelsstatistik*).[3] Data in the statistic of foreign trade are transaction-level data, i.e. they relate to one transaction of a German firm with a firm located outside Germany at a time. Published data from this statistic report exports or imports aggregated at the level of goods traded and by country of destination or origin.

For the reporting year 2009, these transaction-level data have been aggregated at the level of the exporting or importing firm for the first time. For each exporting or importing firm that reported either to the statistic on intra-EU trade, or to the statistic on trade with countries outside the EU, we know from these data, among others, the number of goods exported and imported and the

[1]For surveys of this literature, see Wagner (2011, 2012).

[2]Note that in Germany information on international trade in services is compiled by the German Central Bank (*Deutsche Bundesbank*) to build the balance of services trade (*Dienstleistungsbilanz*).

[3]Note that firms with a value of exports to and imports from EU-countries that does not exceed 400,000 € in 2009 do not have to report to the statistic on intra-EU trade. For trade with firms from non-member countries all transactions that exceed 1,000 € are registered. For details see Statistisches Bundesamt, Qualitätsbericht Außenhandel, January 2011.

number of countries exported to and imported from.[4] Furthermore, the values of these transactions are known.

Using the firms' registration number for turnover tax statistics, these data were matched with the enterprise register system (*Unternehmensregister-System*). For enterprises from manufacturing industries this matching made it possible to add information (that is taken from a regular survey of manufacturing firms) on industry affiliation, total turnover and the number of employees.[5] The new data on export and import activities of firms from German manufacturing industries are used in this chapter to uncover new facts and to test theoretical hypotheses of the relationship between a core dimension of firm performance, namely productivity, and the number of goods traded and countries traded with.

## 2. Five Facts for Exporters and Importers from German Manufacturing Industries

Based on the newly available data for 2009 that is built from transaction-level information five empirical facts are uncovered.

*Fact 1: Many firms export and import simultaneously.*

Results reported in Table 1 show that many manufacturing enterprises in West Germany and in East Germany[6] are simultaneously active on the international market as exporters and importers. This holds for four in five firms in West Germany and for three

[4]Note that information for firms with a value of exports to and imports from EU-countries that does not exceed 400,000 € in 2009 is not covered in the data (see Footnote 2). Small exporters and importers that trade with EU-countries only are therefore under represented in the sample. Presumably, many of these are firms that trade only one good (or a very small number of goods) with one country (or a very small number of countries).

[5]Preparation of the data set was done inside the research data center of the German Federal Statistical Office by Christopher Gürke.

[6]The economy differs between West Germany and the former communist East Germany even some 20 years after unification in 1990, and this holds especially for exports (see Wagner (2008a) for a detailed analysis). Therefore, all computations were performed for West Germany and East Germany separately.

Table 1. Exporter and importer in German manufacturing industries, 2009

| | West Germany | | East Germany | |
|---|---|---|---|---|
| Type of enterprise | Number | Share (percent) | Number | Share (percent) |
| Exporter or importer | 12,919 | 100.00 | 2,261 | 100.00 |
| Exporter | 11,949 | 92.49 | 1,958 | 86.60 |
| Importer | 11,370 | 88.01 | 1,945 | 86.02 |
| Exporter only | 1,549 | 11.99 | 316 | 13.98 |
| Importer only | 970 | 7.51 | 303 | 13.40 |
| Exporter and importer | 10,400 | 80.50 | 1,642 | 72.62 |

*Source*: Research Data Center of the German Statistical Office, Foreign Trade Statistics 2009, own calculations.

in four firms in East Germany. Firm characteristics that distinguish exporters from non-exporters, therefore, often distinguish importers from non-importers, too, and vice versa.

*Fact 2: While many firms trade only a small number of different goods, many firms trade a large number of different goods.*

It can be seen from Table 2 that many firms concentrate their export or import activities on a small number of goods.[7] p1, p10, etc. are the percentiles from the distribution of the number of goods traded and the number of countries traded with. The median firm (that is in p50) exports 7 goods in West Germany and 5 goods in East Germany, while it imports 13 goods in West Germany and 10 goods in East Germany. However, there are many firms in both parts of Germany that trade a large number of different goods, too. In West Germany, some 1,200 firms that are in the highest percentile (and that cover 1 percent of the 11,929 exporting firms) export more than 300 goods or import more than 200 goods. In East Germany, some 200 firms export or import more than 130 goods. Note that both the number of exported goods and the number of imported goods is on average considerably larger in West Germany than in East Germany.

[7] A good is an 8-digit number from the official nomenclature for the statistics of foreign trade.

Table 2. Exporter and importer in german manufacturing industries by number of goods and number of countries, 2009

| | | Number of firms | Mean | *p*1 | *p*10 | *p*25 | *p*50 | *p*75 | *p*90 | *p*99 |
|---|---|---|---|---|---|---|---|---|---|---|
| **West Germany** | | | | | | | | | | |
| Number of goods | Exporter | 11,929 | 27.8 | 1 | 1 | 3 | 7 | 23 | 68 | 306 |
| | Importer | 11,363 | 29.3 | 1 | 2 | 5 | 13 | 32 | 67 | 237 |
| Number of countries | Exporter | 11,788 | 20.7 | 1 | 2 | 6 | 16 | 29 | 46 | 89 |
| | Importer | 11,135 | 10.18 | 1 | 1 | 3 | 7 | 14 | 22 | 46 |
| **East Germany** | | | | | | | | | | |
| Number of goods | Exporter | 1,953 | 12.31 | 1 | 1 | 2 | 5 | 11 | 28 | 136 |
| | Importer | 1,942 | 19.8 | 1 | 1 | 3 | 10 | 23 | 46 | 148 |
| Number of countries | Exporter | 1,921 | 13.7 | 1 | 1 | 3 | 9 | 19 | 33 | 67 |
| | Importer | 1,890 | 7.95 | 1 | 1 | 3 | 6 | 11 | 17 | 33 |

*Source*: Research Data Center of the German Statistical Office, Foreign Trade Statistics 2009, own calculations.

*Fact 3: While many firms trade only with firms from a small number of countries, many firms trade with firms from a large number of countries.*

Like in the case of the number of products traded many firms concentrate their export or import activities on firms from a small number of countries. Table 2 shows that the median firm (that is in p50) exports to 16 countries in West Germany and to 9 countries in East Germany, while it imports from 7 countries in West Germany and from 6 countries in East Germany. However, there are many firms in both parts of Germany that trade with firms from a large number of different countries, too. Note that the number of countries exported to is considerably larger in West Germany than in East Germany on average, while the number of countries imported from is of a similar order of magnitude.[8]

[8]The number of exporters and importers reported in Table 2 differs from the figures reported in Table 1 and between the figures reported for "number of goods" and "number of countries" because trade with certain goods and trade with certain countries are kept secret by request of the trading firms. The value of these confidential transactions is, however,

*Fact 4: Exports and imports are highly concentrated.*

While there are thousands of exporting and importing manufacturing firms in Germany, a small share of these firms are responsible for the lion's share of international trade. More than half of total exports and imports in West Germany and East Germany stem from the largest 50 trading firms (see upper panel of Table 3). This high degree of concentration of international trade is found for other countries, too (see World Trade Organization (2008), p. 54); Bernard *et al.* (2011, p. 10) call it one of the striking feature of international trade data.

*Fact 5: Exports and imports are dominated by firms that trade many goods with many countries.*

While thousands of firms trade only a small number of goods with firms from a small number of countries, firms that trade many goods with many countries are responsible for the lion's share of both exports and imports. Table 3 shows that the largest traders trade on average a very large number of goods with firms from a very large number of countries. Furthermore, Table 3 reports (in the lower panel) that enterprises that trade 10 or more goods with 10 or more countries have a share of higher that 90 percent in total exports and imports in West Germany while their share in all trading enterprises is less than 40 percent. The figures for East Germany are somewhat smaller but still large.

Fact 5 can help to understand Fact 4. Bernard *et al.* (2011, p. 10) argue that "(o)ne reason why international trade is so concentrated is that larger exporters not only export more of a given product to a given destination than smaller exporters, but also export more products to more destinations." According to the findings reported here, the same holds for imports.

---

included in the sum of all exports and imports, and it is known that the firm exported and imported (but not what and/or with whom). Therefore, for a small number of traders with a known number of goods traded the number of countries traded with is not known, and vice versa.

Table 3. Concentration in exports and imports by German manufacturing enterprises, 2009

| Type of enterprise | Share of largest 3 traders in total trade (in percent) | 10 | 50 | 100 |
|---|---|---|---|---|
| **West Germany** | | | | |
| Exporter | 24.7 | 44.1 | 57.5 | 63.3 |
| Average number of goods | 1447.7 | 1225.0 | 542.24 | 406.5 |
| Average number of countries | 158.0 | 133.0 | 101.8 | 87.4 |
| Importer | 23.5 | 42.1 | 59.9 | 66.6 |
| Average number of goods | 1096.3 | 1076.5 | 473.6 | 339.6 |
| Average number of countries | 95.0 | 85.1 | 54.7 | 47.0 |
| **East Germany** | | | | |
| Exporter | 17.1 | 31.3 | 54.0 | 64.5 |
| Average number of goods | 60.7 | 86.2 | 57.3 | 44.6 |
| Average number of countries | 52.7 | 55.7 | 38.7 | 33.5 |
| Importer | 26.4 | 42.0 | 64.2 | 74.1 |
| Average number of goods | 284.3 | 220.9 | 111.3 | 83.8 |
| Average number of countries | 36.7 | 33.2 | 23.2 | 20.5 |

| | Enterprises that trade 10 or more goods with 10 or more countries: Number of enterprises | Share in total trade (in percent) | Share in all enterprises (in percent) |
|---|---|---|---|
| **West Germany** | | | |
| Exporter | 4,678 | 91.1 | 39.1 |
| Importer | 4,331 | 93.1 | 38.1 |
| **East Germany** | | | |
| Exporter | 439 | 67.8 | 22.4 |
| Importer | 565 | 85.1 | 29.0 |

*Source*: Research Data Center of the German Statistical Office, Foreign Trade Statistics 2009, own calculations.

## 3. Productivity Premia for Multi-product and Multi-country Traders

### 3.1. *Four hypotheses on productivity and firms' international trade activities by number of products and number of countries*

What makes the difference between a firm that sales many products and that trades with many countries on the one hand, and a firm that trades only some products and that trades only with some countries on the other hand? Economic theory, and results from econometric studies that use micro-level data to investigate the international trade decisions of firms empirically, point to an important role of productivity.

Productivity — the efficiency with which firms turn inputs (labor, physical capital, energy, materials, managerial know-how) into outputs (goods, services) — is important for the competitiveness of firms, regions and countries on local, national and international markets. Productivity is an important driver of growth and welfare. Therefore, the study of productivity has been a core topic in economics for a long time. Empirical studies that use firm-level micro-data to investigate the determinants and consequences of productivity differentials between firms, however, are of a more recent vintage. A case in point is the literature dealing with the links between productivity and international firm activities. This literature started with a Brookings paper by Bernard and Jensen (1995) that documents a positive exporter productivity premium in US manufacturing industries — exporters are more productive that non-exporting firms of the same size from the same narrowly defined industry. This paper started a literature. Afterwards economists all over the world used firm-level micro data to investigate productivity differences between exporting and non-exporting firms and the direction of causality between export activity and firm-level productivity (see Wagner (2007) for a survey). This literature on the *Micro-econometrics of International Trade* inspired theorists to develop what is now labeled the *New New Trade Theory* where heterogeneous firms that differ in productivity are at the heart of the theoretical models (see the canonical model by Melitz (2003) and the recent survey by Redding (2011)).

There are two alternatives but not mutually exclusive hypotheses why exporters can be expected to be more productive than non-exporting firms (see Bernard and Jensen (1999) and Bernard and Wagner (1997)). The first hypothesis points to self-selection of the more productive firms into export markets. The reason for this is that there exist additional costs of selling goods in foreign countries. The range of extra costs include transportation costs, distribution or marketing costs, personnel with skill to manage foreign networks, or production costs in modifying current domestic products for foreign consumption. These costs provide an entry barrier that less successful firms cannot overcome. Furthermore, the behavior of firms might be forward-looking in the sense that the desire to export tomorrow leads a firm to improve performance today to be competitive on the foreign market, too. Cross-section differences between exporters and non-exporters, therefore, may in part be explained by *ex-ante* differences between firms: The more productive firms become exporters. The second hypothesis points to the role of learning-by-exporting. Knowledge flows from international buyers and competitors help to improve the post-entry performance of export starters. Furthermore, firms participating in international markets are exposed to more intense competition and must improve faster than firms who sell their products domestically only. Exporting makes firms more productive.

Wagner (2007) gives a synopsis of findings from 54 empirical studies published between 1995 and 2006 that use firm-level data from 34 countries and that investigate the relationship of exports and productivity. Among the countries covered are highly industrialized countries, countries from Latin America and Asian countries, transition economies and least developed countries. Given this wide range of countries the big picture is amazingly clear-cut: With only a few exceptions exporters are found to have higher productivity, and often higher productivity growth, and this tends to hold after controlling for observed plant characteristics (like industry and size), too. Exporters are better.

The findings for pre-entry differences often present evidence in favor of the self-selection hypothesis: Future export starters tend to be more productive than future non-exporters years before they enter the export market, and often have higher *ex-ante* growth rates of productivity. The good firms go abroad. Evidence regarding the learning-by-exporting hypothesis is somewhat more mixed: Results for post-entry differences in performance between export starters and non-exporters point to faster productivity growth for the former group in some studies only. Exporting does not necessarily improve firms.

According to findings from this literature on exports and productivity, an important reason for the positive productivity differential between exporters and non-exporters is self-selection of more productive plants on export markets. Furthermore, there is evidence for a market driven selection process in which exporters that have low productivity fail as a successful exporter, while only those that are more productive continue to export (Wagner 2008b). The reason for this is that there exist additional costs of selling goods in foreign countries. To repeat, the range of extra costs include transportation costs, distribution or marketing costs, personnel with skill to manage foreign networks, or production costs in modifying current domestic products for foreign consumption. This implies that firms that export to a larger number of foreign markets have to be more productive than firms that serve a smaller number of foreign markets only, because at least some of the extra costs mentioned recur for each market (e.g. preparing a user's manual in another language, or checking the relevant national laws). Lawless (2009) presents a simple theoretical model that builds on the seminal contributions by Melitz (2003) and Chaney (2008) and that has this testable prediction. Furthermore, it seems plausible to assume that the larger the number of markets the higher will be (at least, on average) the distance related costs of exporting an exporter has to bear and that market entry costs differ across markets. This leads to a first hypothesis to be tested with the newly available data for international trade activities of German manufacturing firms[9]:

*H1: The number of export markets served by a firm increases with firm productivity.*

While the causes and consequences of export and its mutual relationships with productivity are prominent topics in the recent literature on internationally active firms, imports are seldom dealt with. As Bernard *et al.* (2007, p. 123) recently put it, "(t)he empirical literature on firms in international trade has been concerned almost exclusively with exporting, largely due to limitations in datasets.... As a result, the new theories of heterogeneous firms and trade were developed to explain facts about firm export behavior and yield few predictions (if any) for firm import behavior."

In the literature, arguments for both a positive impact of productivity on importing (which is in accordance with self-selection of more productive firms into import markets) and for a positive impact of importing on productivity ('learning-by-importing') are discussed. To start with the arguments in favor of self-selection of more productive firms into importing it is pointed out that the use of foreign intermediates increases a firm's productivity but, due to fixed costs of importing, only inherently highly productive firms import intermediates. Importing is associated with fixed costs that are sunk costs, because the import agreement is preceded by a search process for potential foreign suppliers, inspection of goods, negotiation, contract formulation, learning about legal rules and regulations for doing business in a foreign country, etc. Furthermore, there are sunk costs of importing due to the learning and acquisition of customs procedures (see Kasahara and Lapham (2008), Andersson, Lööf and Johansson (2008), Castellani, Serti and Tomasi (2010)).

As regards learning-by-importing, it is stated that there are strong arguments in favor of a causal effect of imports on productivity, because by importing a firm can exploit global specialization

[9]For a survey of empirical evidence for other countries (including Belgium, Ireland, Italy, Japan, Slovenia, Spain and Sweden) that is in line with this hypothesis see Wagner (2012).

and use inputs from the forefront of knowledge and technology. Proponents of this view point to the literature on international technology diffusion that advances imports as an important vehicle for knowledge and technology transfer. Furthermore, importing intermediate products allows a firm to focus resources and to specialize on activities where it has particular strengths. Importers may improve productivity by using higher quality foreign inputs or by extracting technology embodied in imported intermediates and capital goods. Furthermore a variety effect is mentioned (in which the broader range of available intermediates contributes to production efficiency) and a quality effect caused by imported intermediates that might be of better quality than local ones.

From a theoretical point of view, therefore, the direction of causality between productivity and importing can run from one of the two sides or from both sides simultaneously. With new datasets that include information on imports at the firm level becoming available for more and more countries, a new literature is emerging that has a focus on the links between productivity and imports. Details aside, the big picture that emerges from this literature can be sketched as follows (see Wagner (2012) for a survey): There is a positive link between importing and productivity at the firm level, documented by a significant productivity differential between firms that import and firms that do not trade internationally. We have evidence for self-selection of more productive firms into importing from most of the studies that look at this issue; the evidence on learning-by-importing, however, is still rare and inconclusive.

If, as is argued above, importing is associated with fixed costs that are sunk costs, because the import agreement is preceded by a search process for potential foreign suppliers, learning about legal rules and regulations for doing business in a foreign country, and acquisition of customs procedures, among others, these sunk costs emerge for each country a firm imports from. This implies that firms that import from a larger number of foreign markets have to be more productive than firms that import from a smaller number of foreign markets only. This leads to a second hypothesis to be tested with the newly available data for international trade activities of German manufacturing firms:

*H2: The number of countries a firm imports from increases with firm productivity.*

Recently, a new literature started that looks at an alternative measure of the extensive margin of trade besides the number of destination countries for exports or countries of origin for imports, namely the number of products exported and imported, and its relationship to firm performance. Muuls and Pisu (2009) find for Belgium that productivity is also increasing as the number of products exported or imported rises. Similarly, Silva, Afonso and Africano (2010) show that Portuguese firms that export or import a larger number of products are more productive. These relationships are interpreted to be suggestive that fixed costs of trade are incurred for each new product a firm starts to trade internationally.[10] This leads to a third and a fourth hypothesis to be tested with the newly available data for international trade activities of German manufacturing firms:

*H3: The number of goods a firm exports increases with firm productivity.*

*H4: The number of goods a firm imports increases with firm productivity.*

### 3.2. *Empirical estimates for productivity premia for multi-product and multi-country traders from German manufacturing industries*

The four hypotheses outlined above refer to the empirical relationship of firm productivity on the one hand, and the number of countries traded with and the number of goods traded on the other hand. While information on the number of goods imported and exported, and on the number of countries exported to and imported from, is available from the statistics of foreign trade, information on firm productivity is not. As stated in Section 1, using

[10]Note that the direction of causality between the number of traded products and productivity is not investigated in these studies.

the firms' registration number for turnover tax statistics the data from the statistics of foreign trade were matched with the enterprise register system (*Unternehmensregister-System*). For enterprises from manufacturing industries this matching makes it possible to add information (that is taken from a regular survey of manufacturing firms) on total turnover and on the number of employees. Based thereon the amount of average sales per employee is computed, and this is the measure of labor productivity used in the empirical investigation of the four hypotheses.

Productivity is measured as labor productivity because information on the capital stock of a firm is not available, so more elaborate measures of total factor productivity cannot be used in this study. However, Bartelsman and Doms (2000, p. 575) point to the fact that heterogeneity in labor productivity has been found to be accompanied by similar heterogeneity in total factor productivity in the reviewed research where both concepts are measured. In a recent comprehensive survey, Syverson (2011) argues that high-productivity producers will tend to look efficient regardless of the specific way that their productivity is measured. Furthermore, Foster, Haltiwanger and Syverson (2008) show that productivity measures that use sales (i.e. quantities multiplied by prices) and measures that use quantities only are highly positively correlated. In my view, these three arguments justify the use of labor productivity as a suitable measure for productivity at the firm level.

As a first step in the empirical investigation of the four hypotheses derived above, we look at the average labor productivity in firms by number of goods traded and number of countries traded with. To do so, firms are grouped into four categories according to the number of goods and number of countries: Firms that trade only one good or with one country only, firms that trade "a few" goods or with "a few" countries (where " a few" is defined as two to five), firms that trade "several" goods or with "several" countries (where "several" is defined as six to nine), and firms that trade "many" goods or with "many" countries (where "many" are defined as 10 or more). Results reported in Table 4 are in line with the four hypotheses. Firm productivity increases over the number

Table 4. Productivity by number of traded goods and number of countries traded with, German manufacturing enterprises, 2009

| | West Germany | | East Germany | |
|---|---|---|---|---|
| | Share in all firms (percent) | Productivity (Average sales per employee (€)) | Share in all firms (percent) | Productivity (Average sales per employee (€)) |
| Number of goods exported | | | | |
| 1 | 14.02 | 149,347 | 19.35 | 136,000 |
| 2–5 | 28.51 | 167,023 | 36.10 | 171,004 |
| 6–9 | 13.31 | 179,204 | 15.11 | 194,541 |
| 10 or more | 44.16 | 210,322 | 29.44 | 206,072 |
| Number of goods imported | | | | |
| 1 | 7.84 | 138,317 | 12.46 | 144,611 |
| 2–5 | 20.12 | 167,658 | 21.72 | 155,106 |
| 6–9 | 13.34 | 172,608 | 14.94 | 178,493 |
| 10 or more | 58.70 | 213,809 | 50.88 | 217,166 |
| Number of countries exported to | | | | |
| 1 | 8.11 | 148,854 | 12.70 | 123,671 |
| 2–5 | 15.36 | 169,513 | 24.78 | 176,231 |
| 6–9 | 11.21 | 183,835 | 13.38 | 181,316 |
| 10 or more | 65.32 | 194,608 | 49.14 | 195,151 |
| Number of countries imported from | | | | |
| 1 | 10.85 | 131,406 | 14.97 | 114,476 |
| 2–5 | 28.19 | 168,805 | 30.11 | 167,748 |
| 6–9 | 20.49 | 196,491 | 23.39 | 194,009 |
| 10 or more | 40.47 | 229,236 | 31.53 | 245,731 |

*Source*: Research Data Center of the German Statistical Office, Foreign Trade Statistics 2009, own calculations.

of goods exported and imported, and over the number of countries exported to and imported from, in West Germany and in East Germany. Productivity differences are large from an economic point of view if the "marginal" traders with only one traded good and one country of destination or origin are compared to firms from the other groups, especially with "power traders" that trade 10 or more goods and with 10 or more countries.

Following the now standard approach to investigate the links between productivity and international trade activities (outlined in Wagner (2007)) the next step of the empirical analysis consists in the estimation of the so-called productivity premia of firms with different numbers of goods traded and different numbers of countries traded with. These productivity premia are computed from the estimated coefficients of dummy variables for firms with 2–5, 6–9 and 10 or more goods traded (or countries traded with) from an OLS regression of the log of labor productivity on these dummy variables (taking firms that trade only one good or with one country only as the reference group) plus the number of employees (also included in squares) and a full set of 2-digit industry dummy variables and a constant. This regression model is not meant to be an empirical model to explain labor productivity at the firm level[11]; the data set used here is not suited at all for such an exercise. The regression model is just a vehicle to test for, and estimate the size of, productivity premia of multi-product and multi-country traders from German manufacturing industries over firms that trade only one good or with one country only while controlling for other firm characteristics that are available in the data, namely firm size and industry affiliation. The premia are reported as percentages, computed from the estimated regression coefficients ß as (exp(ß) − 1)*100.

Results for estimated productivity premia for manufacturing enterprises from West Germany and East Germany by number of traded goods and number of countries traded with are reported in Table 5. All premia are positive, statistically significant at an error level of 5 percent or (usually much) better, large from an economic point of view, and increasing over the number of goods traded and the number of countries traded with. These results are fully in line with the four hypotheses.

In a robustness check, all regressions were estimated using the fully robust MM-estimator (see Verardi and Croux (2009) for details) to take care of the possible role of extreme observations, or

[11]Note that productivity differences at the firm level are notoriously difficult to explain empirically. "At the micro level, productivity remains very much a measure of our ignorance." (Bartelsman and Doms (2000), p. 586)

Table 5. Productivity premia by number of traded goods and number of countries traded with, German manufacturing enterprises, 2009*

| | West Germany | | East Germany | |
|---|---|---|---|---|
| | Productivity premium (in percent) | Significance ($p$-value) | Productivity premium (in percent) | Significance ($p$-value) |
| Number of goods exported | | | | |
| 2–5 | 11.63 | 0.000 | 13.88 | 0.001 |
| 6–9 | 19.72 | 0.000 | 22.14 | 0.000 |
| 10 or more | 39.10 | 0.000 | 34.99 | 0.000 |
| Number of goods imported | | | | |
| 2–5 | 12.75 | 0.000 | 10.52 | 0.052 |
| 6–9 | 25.86 | 0.000 | 22.14 | 0.001 |
| 10 or more | 49.18 | 0.000 | 43.33 | 0.000 |
| Number of countries exported to | | | | |
| 2–5 | 13.88 | 0.000 | 19.72 | 0.000 |
| 6–9 | 25.86 | 0.000 | 25.86 | 0.000 |
| 10 or more | 46.23 | 0.000 | 43.33 | 0.000 |
| Number of countries imported from | | | | |
| 2–5 | 20.92 | 0.000 | 24.61 | 0.000 |
| 6–9 | 43.33 | 0.000 | 43.33 | 0.000 |
| 10 or more | 68.20 | 0.000 | 71.60 | 0.000 |

*Source*: Research Data Center of the German Statistical Office, Foreign Trade Statistics 2009, own calculations.

*See text for details on the enterprises covered. The reported productivity premia are based on the estimated coefficients of dummy variables for firms with 2–5, 6–9 and 10 or more goods traded (or countries traded with) from an OLS regression of the log of labor productivity on these dummy variables (taking firms that trade only one good or with one country as the reference group), plus the number of employees (also included in squares) and a full set of 2-digit industry dummy variables and a constant. The premia are computed from the estimated coefficients ß as (exp(ß) — 1)*100. The $p$-values are based on heteroscedasticity-robust standard error estimates.

outliers. Results are rather similar and lead to identical conclusions (see Table A.1).[12]

[12]In a further robustness check the empirical models were estimated with the number of products (or the number of countries) plus the squared values of these variables instead of the

## 4. Conclusions

This chapter uses newly available data on the number of goods exported and imported, and on the number of countries traded with, by enterprises from manufacturing industries in Germany. It documents that foreign trade is dominated by firms that trade multiple goods with multiple countries, and that a small number of very large multiple-goods multiple-country exporters and importers play a decisive role in shaping exports and imports of one of the most important actors in the world market for goods. Firms that trade many goods or that trade with many countries are much more productive than firms of the same size from the same industry that trade some goods or trade with some countries only.

An open question is the direction of causality between firm productivity and the number of goods traded or the number of countries traded with. Is the productivity premium of multiple-goods multiple-countries traders due to self-selection of more productive firms in more international markets (due to fixed costs that recur for every new good traded and for every new country traded with and that can only be covered profitably by more productive firms) or due to higher learning-by-trading effects when more goods are traded in more markets? We know from the literature on trade and firm performance how to tackle these issues empirically when it comes to investigate the productivity premium of exporters or importers over firms that do not trade internationally (see the

dummy variables for firms with 2–5, 6–9 and 10 or more goods traded (or countries traded with). In the OLS regressions the estimated coefficient of the squared term is statistically different from zero at an error level of 5 percent in one of eight cases only. The coefficients of the number of goods and the number of countries are all positive, but not statically significant at a usual error level for the number of goods imported. Fully robust MM-regressions lead to no significant coefficients for the squared term and to positive and significant estimated premia for the number of goods and countries in all regressions with data from West German firms, while a significant increase in productivity in East Germany is only found for the number of countries imported from. Tables with the results are available on request. The more flexible specification using dummy variables is able to capture the highly nonlinear relationship between productivity and the number of goods traded/number of countries traded with much better than the second-order polynomial specification that imposes a restriction on the functional form of this relation.

surveys by Wagner (2007, 2012)). Application of these empirical approaches, however, needs data for (at least) four years. Therefore, due to the lack of these data for Germany this question has to remain open for several years.

## Summary

In Germany, for the reporting year 2009, transaction-level data on exports and imports of goods have been aggregated at the level of the exporting or importing firm for the first time. In these data the number of goods exported and imported and the number of countries exported to and imported from is reported, together with the values of these cross-border transactions. This chapter uses these newly available data for firms from manufacturing industries to uncover new facts and to test theoretical hypotheses of the relationship between a core dimension of firm performance, namely productivity, and the number of goods traded and countries traded with.

## Acknowledgment

All computations were done at the Research Data Centre of the German Statistical Office. I thank Christopher Gürke for preparing the data, running my Stata do-files and checking the results for any violation of privacy. The enterprise level data used are confidential but not exclusive; see http://www. forschungsdatenzen trum.de/nutzungsbedingungen.asp for any details regarding the access to the data.

## References

Andersson, M., H. Lööf and S. Johansson (2008). Productivity and International Trade: Firm Level Evidence from a Small Open Economy. *Review of World Economics/Weltwirtschaftliches Archiv* 144, S. 774–S. 801.

Bartelsman, E. J. and M. Doms (2000). Understanding Productivity: Lessons from Longitudinal Micro Data. *Journal of Economic Literature* 38, S. 569–S. 594.

Bernard, A. B. and J. B. Jensen (1995), Exporters, Jobs, and Wages in U.S. Manufacturing: 1976–1987. Brookings Papers on Economic Activity, *Microeconomics* 1, S. 67–S. 119.

Bernard, A. B. and J. B. Jensen (1999). Exceptional Exporter Performance: Cause, Effect, or Both? *Journal of International Economics* 47, S. 1–S. 25.

Bernard, A. B., J. B. Jensen, S. J. Redding and P. K. Schott (2007). Firms in International Trade. *Journal of Economic Perspectives* 21, S. 105–S. 130.

Bernard, A. B., J. B. Jensen, S. J. Redding and P. K. Schott (2011). The Empirics of Firm Heterogeneity and International Trade. National Bureau of Economic Research NBER Working Paper 17627, November.

Bernard, A. B. and J. Wagner (1997). Exports and Success in German Manufacturing. *Review of World Economics/Weltwirtschaftliches Archiv* 133, S. 134–S. 157.

Castellani, D., F. Serti and C. Tomasi (2010). Firms in International Trade: Importers' and Exporters' Heterogeneity in the Italian Manufacturing Industry. *The World Economy* 33, S. 424–S. 457.

Chaney, T. (2008). Distorted Gravity: The Intensive and Extensive Margins of International Trade. *American Economic Review* 98, S. 1707–S. 1721.

Foster, L., J. Haltiwanger and C. Syverson (2008). Reallocation, Firm Turnover, and Efficiency: Selection on Productivity or Profitability? *American Economic Review* 98, S. 394–S. 425.

Kasahara, H. and B. Lapham (2008). Productivity and the Decision to Import and Export: Theory and Evidence. CESifo Working Papers 2240, Ifo Institute for Economic Research, Munich.

Lawless, M. (2009). Firm Export Dynamics and the Geography of Trade. *Journal of International Economics* 77, S. 245–S. 254.

Melitz, M. J. (2003). The Impact of Trade on Intra-Industry Reallocations and Aggregate Industry Productivity. *Econometrica* 71, S. 1695–S. 1725.

Muuls, M. and M. Pisu (2009), Imports and Exports at the Level of the Firm: Evidence from Belgium. *The World Economy* 32, S. 692–S. 734.

Redding, S. J. (2011). Theories of Heterogeneous Firms and Trade. *Annual Review of Economics* 3, S. 77–S. 105.

Silva, A., O. Afonso and A. P. Africano (2010). Economic Performance and International Trade Engagement: The Case of Portuguese Manufacturing Firms. FEP Working Paper 369, Universidade de Porto, Faculdade de Economia do Porto.

Syverson, C. (2011). What Determines Productivity? *Journal of Economic Literature* 49, S. 326–S. 365.

Verardi, V. and C. Croux (2009). Robust Regression in Stata. *The Stata Journal* 9, S. 439–S. 453.

Wagner, J. (2007). Exports and Productivity: A Survey of the Evidence from Firm-Level Data. *The World Economy* 30, S. 60–S. 82.

Wagner, J. (2008a). A Note Why More West than East German Firms Export. *International Economics and Economic Policy* 5, S. 363–S. 370.

Wagner, J. (2008b). Export Entry, Export Exit and Productivity in German Manufacturing Industries. *International Journal of the Economics of Business* 15, S. 169–S. 180.

Wagner, J. (2011). Exports and Firm Characteristics in Germany: A Survey of Empirical Studies (1991 to 2011). *Applied Economics Quarterly* (in press).

Wagner, J. (2012). International Trade and Firm Performance: A Survey of Empirical Studies Since 2006. *Review of World Economics/Weltwirtschaftliches Archiv*, 148, S. 235–S. 267.

World Trade Organization (2008). World Trade Report 2008. Trade in a Globalizing World. Geneva: WTO Publications.

World Trade Organization (2011). World Trade Report 2011. The WTO and Preferential Trade Agreements: From Co-existence to Coherence. Geneva: WTO Publications.

## Appendix

Table A.1. Productivity premia by number of traded goods and number of countries traded with, German manufacturing enterprises, 2009*

| | West Germany | | East Germany | |
|---|---|---|---|---|
| | Productivity premium (in percent) | Significance (*p*-value) | Productivity premium (in percent) | Significance (*p*-value) |
| **Number of goods exported** | | | | |
| 2–5 | 8.33 | 0.000 | 10.52 | 0.017 |
| 6–9 | 18.53 | 0.000 | 19.72 | 0.001 |
| 10 or more | 36.34 | 0.000 | 33.64 | 0.000 |
| **Number of goods imported** | | | | |
| 2–5 | 12.75 | 0.000 | 13.88 | 0.009 |
| 6–9 | 27.12 | 0.000 | 24.61 | 0.000 |
| 10 or more | 50.68 | 0.000 | 50.68 | 0.000 |
| **Number of countries exported to** | | | | |
| 2–5 | 11.63 | 0.000 | 10.52 | 0.049 |
| 6–9 | 24.61 | 0.000 | 19.72 | 0.001 |
| 10 or more | 43.33 | 0.000 | 40.49 | 0.000 |
| **Number of countries imported from** | | | | |
| 2–5 | 19.72 | 0.000 | 23.37 | 0.000 |
| 6–9 | 41.91 | 0.000 | 46.23 | 0.000 |
| 10 or more | 69.89 | 0.000 | 68.20 | 0.000 |

*Source*: Research Data Center of the German Statistical Office, Foreign Trade Statistics 2009, own calculations.

*See text for details on the enterprises covered. The reported productivity premia are based on the estimated coefficients of dummy variables for firms with 2–5, 6–9 and 10 or more goods traded (or countries traded with) from an MM-regression of the log of labor productivity on these dummy variables (taking firms that trade only one good or with one country as the reference group), plus the number of employees (also included in squares) and a full set of 2-digit industry dummy variables and a constant. The premia are computed from the estimated coefficients ß as (exp(ß) — 1)*100.

PART VIII

# Methods of Empirical Analysis of Heterogeneous Exporters and Importers

Chapter 15

# From Estimation Results to Stylized Facts: Twelve Recommendations for Empirical Research in International Activities of Heterogeneous Firms

Joachim Wagner

**Abstract**

Heterogeneous firms are at the heart of both the *New New International Trade Theory* and the *Micro-econometrics of International Firm Activities.* One important aim of microeconometric studies is to uncover stylized facts that hold over space and time, and that can both inspire theoretical models that are based on "realistic" assumptions, and inform policy debates in an evidence-based way. Which results from the thousands of empirical estimates reported in the literature on the microeconometrics of international firm activities do we consider as convincing? Based on my own experience from the last 20 years, I use the opportunity of this chapter to make 12 recommendations that, hopefully, will help to find the right way on the thorny road from estimation results to stylized facts. I will deal with the following topics: comparisons of means vs. comparisons of distributions; extremely different firms, or outliers; unobserved heterogeneity; simultaneous occurrence of differences across quantiles, outliers, and unobserved heterogeneity; heterogeneous effects of international firm activities on firm performance; replication; within-study replication by international research teams; meta-analysis; and talking to practitioners.

*Keywords*: International firm activities, heterogeneous firms, stylized facts, robust statistics, replication, meta analysis

**JEL Classification:** F14, C21, C23

## 1. Motivation

Some 15 years ago, economists working on empirical investigations of international trade issues started to recognize that trade is performed by firms, and that these internationally active firms differ from firms that are not engaged in international markets. Furthermore, they realized that firms are heterogeneous, and that the representative firm is a myth.[1] During the following years, a comprehensive literature emerged that formed the field of *Microeconometrics of International Firm Activities*. Economists all over the world used large comprehensive sets of firm-level data collected by the statistical agencies to investigate the differences between firms with different forms of international activities, and the causes and consequences of these international activities.[2]

These empirical studies inspired a number of theoretical papers that model the behavior of heterogeneous firms in open economies.[3] This literature emerged to what is now labeled the *New New International Trade Theory*. Some of these theoretical papers developed testable hypotheses that led to microeconometric studies with results that bounced back to theory. The mushrooming growth of this literature indicates that this is a fertile ground for both theoretical and empirical analyses.

One important aim of empirical studies in this field of economics (and in other fields as well) is to uncover stylized facts that hold over space and time, and that can both inspire theoretical models that are based on "realistic" assumptions, and inform policy debates in an evidence-based way. Which results from the thousands of empirical estimates reported in the literature on the

---

[1]Pioneering papers in this field include Bernard and Jensen (1995) and Wagner (1995). Note that this has been recognized by business economists active in empirical research in the field of international management for a long time; see the papers collected in the five volume set edited by McNaughton and Bell (2009) where the first paper included dates from 1978.

[2]For partial surveys of this empirical literature, see Greenaway and Kneller (2007), López (2005), and Wagner (2007).

[3]The canonical paper in this literature is Melitz (2003) who explicitly motivates his theoretical model by referring to findings in the microeconometric literature; see Helpman (2006) for a survey.

microeconometrics of international firm activities do we consider as convincing? Based on my own experience from the last 20 years, I use the opportunity of this lecture to make 12 recommendations that, hopefully, will help to find the right way on the thorny road from estimation results to stylized facts. I will deal with the following topics: comparisons of means vs. comparisons of distributions (Section 2); extremely different firms, or outliers (Section 3); unobserved heterogeneity (Section 4); simultaneous occurrence of differences across quantiles, outliers and unobserved heterogeneity (Section 5); and heterogeneous effects of international firm activities on firm performance (Section 6). The final section deals with a number of topics that are relevant for empirical work with microdata in general, namely replication, meta-analysis and talking to practitioners.

## 2. Comparison of Means vs. Comparison of Distributions

Heterogeneous firms are at the heart of both the *New New International Trade Theory* and the *Micro-econometrics of International Firm Activities*. The implications of firm heterogeneity for empirical analyses, however, are not always fully taken into account. One important aspect here is the frequent use of (unconditional or conditional) means for different groups of firms — say, exporters and firms selling on the national market only — as a basis for comparisons. A case in point is the well-known fact that in almost all countries and periods examined, exporters are significantly more productive than non-exporters on average (see Wagner (2007)). This fact is usually documented by comparing the mean of productivity for the two groups of firms, using either a statistical test for the significance of differences in (unconditional) means of exporting and non-exporting firms, or by performing a test for the statistical significance of the estimated regression coefficient of a dummy variable indicating the exporter status of a firm in an empirical model that controls for industry affiliation and firm size (i.e. the difference in the conditional mean).

As a first step this is fine, But one should not stop here. As Buchinsky (1994: 453) put it: "'On the average' has never been a satisfactory statement with which to conclude a study on heterogeneous populations." An empirical study of heterogeneous firms should look at differences in the whole distribution of the variable under investigation between groups of firms, not only at differences at the mean.

To illustrate this point, I will look at productivity differences between exporters and firms selling in the national market only. The data used were collected from personal interviews with firm owners or top managers. The population covered encompasses all manufacturing establishments with at least five employees in the German state of Lower Saxony. From this population, a random sample (stratified by industry and size classes) was interviewed. Detailed information on the data set and how it can be accessed by researchers is given in Gerlach, Hübler and Meyer (2003). The survey has information on whether or not a plant was an exporter in 1995. One great advantage of this survey for the exercise performed here is that, in using these data I am allowed to do things that are impossible for me to do using the confidential firm-level data from official statistics that are usually used for empirical investigations on international activities of German firms. For instance, I can report results for minimum and maximum values of variables that are by definition values for single firms and, therefore, cannot be revealed when using the data from official statistics.

Table 1 reports figures for labor productivity (defined as sales per employee)[4] for exporters and non-exporters.[5] As expected, exporters are on average more productive than non-exporters. This difference in the unconditional mean is statistically highly significant (with a *p*-value of 0.007), and it is large from an economic point of view (66,178 DEM, or 30.22 percent, in favor of the exporters). However, the mean value of a variable might be

[4]Note that the figures are in Deutschmark (DEM) because they refer to 1995; it might help to get an impression about what is behind these figures if a rule of thumb is applied, and all values in Deutschmark are divided by 2 to get the approximate amount in Euro.

[5]All computations were performed using Stata 11.0; see StataCorp (2009).

Table 1. Productivity differences between exporters and non-exporters — full sample

| | Exporters | Non-Exporters |
|---|---|---|
| Number of firms (share in all firms) | 377 (61 percent) | 241 (39 percent) |
| Labor productivity (Sales in Deutschmark per employee) | | |
| Mean | 285,163 | 218,985 |
| (Standard Deviation) | (327,911) | (272,110) |
| Test for difference in means ($p$-value) | 0.007 | |
| Percentiles | | |
| 1 percent | 60,000 | 50,000 |
| 5 percent | 100,000 | 74,783 |
| 10 percent | 120,000 | 85,714 |
| 25 percent | 154,429 | 120,000 |
| 50 percent | 216,216 | 164,286 |
| 75 percent | 307,692 | 234,286 |
| 90 percent | 500,000 | 366,667 |
| 95 percent | 666,667 | 462,500 |
| 99 percent | 1,166,667 | 928,000 |
| Smallest values | 31,250 | 33,333 |
| | 53,763 | 35,294 |
| | 58,333 | 50,000 |
| | 60,000 | 50,000 |
| Largest values | 1,166,667 | 750,000 |
| | 1,634,021 | 928,000 |
| | 2,542,373 | 1,037,500 |
| | 5,000,000 | 3,837,209 |
| Skewness | 9.224 | 10.116 |
| Kurtosis | 121.311 | 131.568 |

Kolmogorov–Smirnov test for equality of distribution functions

| | $p$-value |
|---|---|
| $H_0$: Equality of distributions | 0.000 |
| $H_0$: Productivity of non-exporters is larger | 0.000 |
| $H_0$: Productivity of exporters is larger | 0.998 |

heavily influenced by a small number of extremely large or small observations, especially if the number of firms is fairly small like in the exercise performed here.

A look at selected percentiles of the productivity distribution for exporters and for non-exporters reported in Table 1 reveals that both exporters and non-exporters are highly heterogeneous with regard to their productivity. The largest value is 160 (115) times the smallest value for exporters (non-exporters). Exporters do have a higher productivity than non-exporters at each percentile, and not only at the mean. The hypothesis that the productivity distribution of exporters stochastically dominates the productivity distribution of non-exporters can be tested by the Kolmogorov–Smirnov test (see Delgado, Farinas and Ruano (2002). Results reported in the lower panel of Table 1 show that according to this test the two productivity distributions do differ, and that the null hypothesis that productivity is higher among exporters cannot be rejected at any conventional error level, while the null hypothesis that the productivity is higher among non-exporters has to be rejected at any error level. These results based on a comparison of distributions are more convincing when firms are heterogeneous. My first recommendation, therefore, is:

> *R1: In a comparison of groups of heterogeneous firms do not only test for differences in mean values — look at differences at percentiles of the distributions, and test for differences between distributions, too.*

Empirical studies on international firm activities usually go beyond a comparison of (unconditional) mean values for groups of firms and look at differences between firms controlling for firm characteristics by using regression analysis, i.e. they look at differences in the conditional mean value. Taking the example of productivity differences between exporting and non-exporting firms, researchers often are interested in the *ceteris paribus* difference in productivity between exporters and non-exporters that are of the same size and from the same industry. This exporter productivity premium is estimated by a regression of the (log of) labor productivity on a dummy variable that takes on the value of 1, if a firm is an exporter plus a set of control variables.[6] Results reported in the upper left corner of Table 2 show that the estimated exporter premium, conditional on firm size and industry affiliation, is 33.79 percent in our example (and larger than the unconditional premium that is 30.22 percent according to the figures reported in Table 1).

If we acknowledge that firms are heterogeneous, we have reasons to suspect that the conditional difference in labor productivity between exporting and non-exporting firms does not need to be the same for all firms. For example, it might be the case that the productivity difference between exporters and non-exporters of the same size and from the same industry is higher for firms at the lower end of the productivity distribution. If we are interested in the size of the exporter premium, and if we regress the log of labor productivity on an exporter dummy variable and a set of control variables using ordinary least squares (OLS), there is no room for firm heterogeneity of this kind. OLS assumes that the conditional distribution of productivity, given the set of firm characteristics included in the regression, is homogeneous. This implies that no matter what point on the conditional distribution is analyzed, the estimates of the relationship between productivity (the dependent variable) and the firm characteristics (the independent variables) are the same.

If one wants to test the empirical validity of the assumption made by OLS, and if one is interested in the evaluation of the size of the exporter premium at different points of the conditional productivity distribution, one has to apply a different estimation technique that is tailor-made for this — quantile regression (see Koenker and Hallock (2001)). The estimated regression coefficients can be interpreted as the partial derivative of the conditional

[6]See e.g. International Study Group on Exports and Productivity (ISGEP) (2008) for comparable results for 14 countries and Kox and Rojas-Romagosa (2010) for first results for Dutch firms. Note that this regression equation is not meant to be an empirical model to explain labor productivity at the firm level; the data set at hand here is not rich enough for such an exercise. It is just a vehicle to test for, and estimate the size of, the exporter premium controlling for other firm characteristics. Furthermore, note that productivity differences at the firm level are notoriously difficult to explain empirically. "At the micro level, productivity remains very much a measure of our ignorance." (Bartelsman and Doms 2000, p. 586).

Table 2. Exporter productivity premium (percent) — full sample

| | | OLS-estimates | Quantile regression estimates | | | | |
|---|---|---|---|---|---|---|---|
| | | | 0.10 | 0.25 | 0.50 | 0.75 | 0.90 |
| Exporter premium (percent) | | 33.79 | 24.52 | 24.37 | 20.06 | 31.54 | 28.45 |
| | *p* | 0.000 | 0.008 | 0.001 | 0.008 | 0.000 | 0.000 |

*Note*: The exporter productivity premium is calculated from the estimated regression coefficients of the exporter dummy variable ß as 100*($e^{ß}$ — 1). The *p*-values for quantile regression estimates are based on standard errors bootstrapped with 500 replications. All regressions include the number of employees (also in squares) and 17 two-digit industry dummy variables.

Tests for coefficient equality between pairwise quantiles and across all quantiles

| | | | | | | | |
|---|---|---|---|---|---|---|---|
| A: Pairwise | | | | | | | |
| | *p*-value | | *p*-value | | *p*-value | | *p*-value |
| 0.10 vs. 0.25 | 0.987 | 0.25 vs. 0.50 | 0.580 | 0.50 vs. 0.75 | 0.220 | 0.75 vs. 0.90 | 0.777 |
| 0.10 vs. 0.50 | 0.699 | 0.25 vs. 0.75 | 0.512 | 0.50 vs. 0.90 | 0.460 | | |
| 0.10 vs. 0.75 | 0.597 | 0.25 vs. 0.90 | 0.746 | | | | |
| 0.10 vs. 0.90 | 0.787 | | | | | | |
| B: Joint test for all quantiles | | *p*-value = 0.810 | | | | | |

*Note*: The null hypothesis is that the coefficients are equal between pairwise quantiles (Panel A) and across all quantiles (Panel B). Test statistics are based on the variance–covariance matrix of the coefficients of the system of quantile regressions used to compute the estimates for the exporter productivity premia reported in the upper panel of this table. *p*-values for the *f*-values are reported.

quantile of the dependent variable (here: labor productivity) with respect to a particular regressor (e.g. being an exporter or not). For each quantile it can be shown whether the effect of a particular independent variable is positive or negative, and how large this effect is compared to other quantiles. This provides information about the heterogeneity of plant behavior.

Estimation results for the exporter productivity premium from quantile regressions are reported in the upper panel of Table 2. The estimated exporter premium is statistically different from zero, positive, and large from an economic point of view for all quantiles. The premium varies across the different quantiles, and there seems to be a u-shaped pattern showing a higher premium at both ends of the conditional productivity distribution than at the median. According to the results of tests for coefficient equality between pairwise quantiles and across all quantiles reported in the lower panel of Table 2, however, these differences between the estimated exporter premia are never statistically different from zero.

The bottom line, then, is that the relationship between exporting and labor productivity is the same at each point of the conditional productivity distribution.[7] These results that are based on a comparison across different quantiles of the conditional distribution are more convincing than OLS results when firms are heterogeneous. My second recommendation, therefore, is:

> *R2: In a comparison of groups of heterogeneous firms do not only test for differences in conditional mean values estimated by OLS (or any other econometric method that focuses on the conditional mean of a dependent variable) — look at differences at quantiles of the conditional distribution using quantile regression, and test for differences between quantiles, too.*

[7]Bellone, Guillou and Nesta (2010) report a similar finding for a sample of firms from France, while Yasar, Nelson and Rejesus (2006) find for Turkish firm-level data that the exporter productivity premium increases as one moves from the lower tail to the upper tail of the distribution.

## 3. Extremely Different Firms (Outliers)

If one investigates a sample of heterogeneous firms it often happens that some variables for some firms are far away from the other observations in the sample. For example, in the sample of exporting and non-exporting firms that is analyzed here, according to Table 1 there are a few firms with labor productivity values that are extremely low or extremely high compared to the mean values. These extreme values might be the result of reporting errors (and, therefore, wrong), or due to idiosyncratic events (like in the case of a shipyard that produces a ship over a long time and that reports the sales in the year when the ship is completed and delivered), or due to firm behavior that is vastly different from the behavior of the majority of firms in the sample. Observations of this kind are termed outliers. Whatever the reason may be, extreme values of labor productivity may have a large influence on the mean value of labor productivity computed for the exporters and non-exporters in the sample, on the tails of the distribution of labor productivity, and on the estimates of the exporter premium. Conclusions with regard to the productivity differences between exporters and non-exporters, therefore, might be influenced by a small number of firms with extremely high or low values of productivity, and the same is true for any other empirical investigation using data for a sample of heterogeneous firms.

Researchers from the field of microeconomics of international firm activities usually are aware of all of this. Given that due to confidentiality of the firm-level data single observations as a rule cannot be inspected closely enough to detect and correct reporting errors, or to understand the idiosyncratic events that lead to extreme values, a widely used procedure to keep these extreme observations from shaping the results is to drop the observations from the top and bottom 1 percent of the distribution of the variable under investigation. A case in point is the international comparison study on the exporter productivity premium by the International Study Group on Exports and Productivity (ISGEP 2008, p. 610).

To illustrate the effects of trimming the sample this way all computations for Tables 1 and 2 were repeated for a sample without the observations from the top and bottom 1 percent of the productivity distribution. Results are reported in Tables 3 and 4.

Table 3 reveals that the share of exporters and non-exporters is the same in both samples. Mean values of labor productivity are lower for both groups of firms, and the same holds for the standard deviations. A *t*-test for differences in productivity means again rejects the null-hypothesis of no difference. The difference in the unconditional mean of productivity is large from an economic point of view (55,016 DEM, or 26.62 percent, in favor of the exporters), but is considerably smaller than for the whole sample (66,178 DEM, or 30.22 percent). This illustrates that the mean value of a variable might be heavily influenced by a small number of extremely large or small observations.

Exporters do have a higher productivity than non-exporters at each percentile, and not only at the mean, after trimming the sample, too. Furthermore, results of the Kolmogorov–Smirnov test are again in line with the hypothesis that the productivity distribution of exporters stochastically dominates the productivity distribution of non-exporters.

The exporter productivity premium that is estimated by an OLS regression of the (log of) labor productivity on a dummy variable that takes on the value of 1 if a firm is an exporter, plus a set of control variables is reported in the upper left corner of Table 4 for the trimmed sample. The estimated premium, conditional on firm size and industry affiliation, is 28.51 percent — considerably lower than the 33.79 percent premium estimated using the full sample.

Estimation results for the exporter productivity premium from quantile regressions are reported in the upper panel of Table 4. Results are in line with results reported for the complete sample. The bottom line, then, is that the big picture of the relationship between exporting and labor productivity that is sketched using the complete sample and the trimmed sample without the top and bottom 1 percent observations from the distribution of labor productivity is the same in our example. The unconditional and the

Table 3. Productivity differences between exporters and non-exporters — sample without top and bottom one percent of productivity distribution

| | Exporters | Non-Exporters |
|---|---|---|
| Number of firms (share in all firms) | 371 (61 percent) | 236 (39 percent) |
| Labor productivity (Sales in Deutschmark per employee) | | |
| Mean | 261,667 | 206,651 |
| (Standard Deviation) | (165,912) | (138,654) |
| Test for difference in means ($p$-value) | 0.000 | |
| Percentiles | | |
| 1 percent | 67,283 | 62,500 |
| 5 percent | 100,000 | 75,000 |
| 10 percent | 120,000 | 93,333 |
| 25 percent | 154,429 | 125,540 |
| 50 percent | 215,517 | 165,686 |
| 75 percent | 307,190 | 235,000 |
| 90 percent | 461,794 | 366,667 |
| 95 percent | 608,273 | 462,500 |
| 99 percent | 878,378 | 750,000 |
| Smallest values | 58,333 | 53,846 |
| | 60,000 | 38,824 |
| | 66,667 | 62,500 |
| | 67,283 | 64,000 |
| Largest values | 878,378 | 723,077 |
| | 909,091 | 750,000 |
| | 1,066,667 | 928,000 |
| | 1,066,667 | 1,037,500 |
| Skewness | 2.033 | 2.616 |
| Kurtosis | 7.928 | 12.544 |

Kolmogorov–Smirnov test for equality of distribution functions

| | $p$-value |
|---|---|
| $H_0$: Equality of distributions | 0.000 |
| $H_0$: Productivity of non-exporters is larger | 0.000 |
| $H_0$: Productivity of exporters is larger | 0.997 |

Table 4. Exporter productivity premium (percent) — Sample without top and bottom one percent of productivity distribution

| | | OLS-estimates | Quantile regression estimates 0.10 | 0.25 | 0.50 | 0.75 | 0.90 |
|---|---|---|---|---|---|---|---|
| Exporter premium (percent) | | 28.51 | 22.29 | 18.95 | 19.17 | 29.35 | 28.74 |
| | $p$ | 0.000 | 0.003 | 0.005 | 0.004 | 0.001 | 0.003 |

*Note*: The exporter productivity premium is calculated from the estimated regression coefficients of the exporter dummy variable ß as $100^*(e^{ß} - 1)$. The $p$-values for quantile regression estimates are based on standard errors bootstrapped with 500 replications. All regressions include the number of employees (also in squares) and 17 two-digit industry dummy variables.

Tests for coefficient equality between pairwise quantiles and across all quantiles

A: Pairwise

| | $p$-value | | $p$-value | | $p$-value | | $p$-value |
|---|---|---|---|---|---|---|---|
| 0.10 vs. 0.25 | 0.672 | 0.25 vs. 0.50 | 0.976 | 0.50 vs. 0.75 | 0.200 | 0.75 vs. 0.90 | 0.952 |
| 0.10 vs. 0.50 | 0.739 | 0.25 vs. 0.75 | 0.297 | 0.50 vs. 0.90 | 0.390 | | |
| 0.10 vs. 0.75 | 0.532 | 0.25 vs. 0.90 | 0.432 | | | | |
| 0.10 vs. 0.90 | 0.620 | | | | | | |

B: Joint test for all quantiles $p$-value = 0.771

*Note*: The null hypothesis is that the coefficients are equal between pairwise quantiles (Panel A) and across all quantiles (Panel B). Test statistics are based on the variance–covariance matrix of the coefficients of the system of quantile regressions used to compute the estimates for the exporter productivity premia reported in the upper panel of this table. $p$-values for the $f$-values are reported.

conditional exporter premium, however, is smaller for the firms in the trimmed sample.

Dropping the firms from the top and the bottom 1 percent of the productivity distribution and comparing the results of empirical investigations with and without these firms with extremely high or extremely low values of labor productivity might be considered as a first and useful step to check the sensitivity of results. However, although this approach seems to be rather popular it is in some sense arbitrary. Why the top and bottom 1 percent? Why not choose a larger or smaller cut-off point? There are alternative approaches to deal with extreme observations (outliers) that are substantiated in statistics, and we will turn to these methods now.

One approach that is advocated in the literature has already been applied in our exercise. Quantile regression is often used to deal with outliers. Quantile regression at the median is identical to least absolute deviation (LAD) regression that minimizes the sum of the absolute values of the residuals rather than the sum of their squares (as in OLS). This estimator is also known as the $L_1$, or median regression, estimator. Results reported in Tables 2 and 4 demonstrate that this estimator is indeed robust with respect to the inclusion of observations with extreme values of labor productivity — the estimated exporter premium at the median of the conditional labor productivity distribution is 20.06 percent for the full sample and 19.17 percent for the sample without the observations from the top and the bottom 1 percent of the productivity distribution.

LAD regression, however, is not a panacea against outliers. To see why, following Rousseeuw and Leroy (1987) we distinguish three types of outliers that influence the OLS estimator: vertical outliers, bad leverage points, and good leverage points. Verardi and Croux (2009, p. 440) illustrate this terminology in a simple linear regression framework (the generalization to higher dimensions is straightforward) as follows: "Vertical outliers are those observations that have outlying values for the corresponding error term (the $y$-dimension) but are not outlying in the space of explanatory variables (the $x$-dimension). Their presence affects the

OLS estimation and, in particular, the estimated intercept. Good leverage points are observations that are outlying in the space of explanatory variables but that are located close to the regression line. Their presence does not affect the OLS estimation, but it affects statistical inference because they do deflate the estimated standard errors. Finally, bad leverage points are observations that are both outlying in the space of explanatory variables and located far from the true regression line. Their presence significantly affects the OLS estimation of both the intercept and the slope."

Using this terminology, one can state that the median regression estimator protects against vertical outliers but not against bad leverage points (Verardi and Croux 2009, p. 441; Koenker 2005, p. 268). Another quite popular robust estimator is the M-estimator proposed by Huber (1964) that generalizes median regression to a wider class of estimators.[8] However, as pointed out by Verardi and Croux (2009, p. 442), this estimator can only identify isolated outliers and is inappropriate when clusters of outliers exist where one outlier can mask the presence of another, and the initial values for the algorithm is not robust to bad leverage points.

Full robustness can be achieved by using the so-called MM-estimator that can resist contamination of the data set of up to 50 percent of outliers (i.e. that has a breakdown point[9] of 50 percent compared to 0 percent for OLS). A discussion of the details of this estimator is beyond the scope of this chapter (see Verardi and Croux (2009)).

Table 5 reports results for the exporter premium computed for the sample of 618 firms described above using OLS and LAD regression (already reported in Table 2) plus results estimated using the Huber M-estimator and the MM-estimator.[10] Furthermore, given that the MM-estimator (like LAD and the Huber M-estimator) uses

[8]This estimator is implemented in Stata via the command rreg.

[9]The breakdown point of an estimator is the highest fraction of outliers that an estimator can withstand, and it is a popular measure of robustness.

[10]Computations were done using the ado-files provided by Verardi and Croux (2009) with the efficiency parameter set at 0.7 as suggested there based on a simulation study; details are available on request.

Table 5. A comparison of OLs and robust estimates of the exporter productivity premium

| | OLS-estimate | Median regression estimate | Huber M-estimate | MM-estimate | OLS-estimate without outliers |
|---|---|---|---|---|---|
| Exporter premium (percent) | 33.79 | 20.06 | 25.85 | 15.53 | 19.52 |
| $p$ | 0.000 | 0.008 | 0.000 | 0.008 | 0.000 |

*Note*: The exporter productivity premium is calculated from the estimated regression coefficient of the exporter dummy variable ß as 100*(e$^{ß}$ − 1). Median regression is the quantile regression for the 0.50 quantile; the $p$-value is based on standard errors bootstrapped with 500 replications. The Huber M-estimate uses the rreg-command implemented in Stata. The MM-estimate uses mmregress (Verardi and Croux 2009) with the efficiency set at 0.7. The OLS-estimate without outliers uses the sample without the 53 outliers (31 vertical outliers that are not outlying in the space of explanatory variables and 22 bad leverage points) identified by the MM-estimator. All regressions include the number of employees (also in squares) and 17 two-digit industry dummy variables.

all 618 observations but a weighting scheme, results for an OLS estimation for a sample without the outliers detected by the MM-estimator are reported in the last column, too.[11]

The estimated labor productivity premium is statistically highly significant and large from an economic point of view for all estimators applied. The estimated size, however, differs considerably. The estimated premium from the fully robust MM-estimator is considerably lower than the values from both OLS and LAD applied to the full or the trimmed sample (see Table 4). In my view it is important to document the extent to which estimation results are influenced by extreme observations. Given that the presence of outliers can be expected to be the rule in data sets for heterogeneous firms my third recommendation is:

> *R3: Carefully check how your results are influenced by firms that are very much different from the mass of firms in your sample. Report results based on OLS and on the MM-estimator.*

[11]Note that it is not possible to state the efficiency of the estimator when these outliers are dropped; results are reported to document the effect on the point estimate only.

## 4. Unobserved Heterogeneity

The last two sections dealt with the consequences of observed firm heterogeneity for microeconometric studies of international firm activities. Firm heterogeneity, however, might be caused by factors that are either not observed by the researcher and that, therefore, are not included in the empirical model, or that are unobservable to a researcher. A case in point with regard to the exporter productivity premium is management quality (see Syverson (2010, p. 14) and the recent study by Bloom and Van Reenen (2010)).

In the data sets used to empirically investigate international firm activities variables that measure management quality are missing. This would not pose a big problem if management quality would be uncorrelated with the other variables included in the empirical model (e.g. the exporter status) — of course it would not be possible to investigate the role of management quality for productivity differences between firms empirically, but the estimated coefficient for the exporter dummy variable would be an unbiased estimate of the exporter productivity premium (given all other assumptions for the applicability of OLS are fulfilled). However, one would not expect that management quality is uncorrelated with either the exporter status or other variables like firm size. Not controlling for management quality then leads to biased estimates for the exporter premium.

A standard solution for this problem that is widely used in the literature on the microeconometrics of international firm activities is the estimation of fixed effects models for panel data. Using pooled cross-section time-series data for firms and including fixed firm effects in the empirical model allows to control for time invariant unobserved firm heterogeneity, and to estimate the coefficients for the time variant variables that are included in the models without any bias caused by the non-inclusion of the unobserved variables that are correlated with these included variables. A case in point is the paper by ISGEP (2008), where in Table 4 exporter productivity premia are reported based on empirical models with and without fixed effects. If fixed firm effects are added to control for time invariant unobserved heterogeneity the point estimates of the exporter productivity premia are much smaller compared to the results based on pooled data only.

Thus, unobserved firm heterogeneity does matter. However, before dropping the estimates based on pooled data without fixed effects one should remember that by construction the estimated coefficients of the exporter status variable from the empirical models with fixed firm effects are identified by observations only that change their exporter status (at least once) during the period under investigation. This exporter status of a firm tends to be highly persistent over adjacent years. Table 6 illustrates this with evidence from German manufacturing enterprises over the two-year periods from (1995/1996) to (2005/2006). On average, some 93 percent of all enterprises that did not export in a year did not export in the following year, and the share of firms that exported in year $t + 1$ among the exporting enterprises in year $t$ is even higher.

Furthermore, we know that firms that enter or exit the export market are different from firms that persistently stay in or out of it. Using a panel of German manufacturing establishments Wagner (2008) finds that firms that stop exporting in year $t$ were in $t - 1$ less productive than firms that continue to export in $t$, and that firms that start to export in year $t$ are less productive than firms that export both in year $t - 1$ and in year $t$. This means that the coefficient of the exporter status variable that gives us the estimate for the exporter productivity premium is in a sense estimated for quite different samples when models with and without firm fixed effects are used. Therefore, both estimates with and without fixed effects should be reported, and they should be amended by a table that documents the share of different patterns of export participation in the whole sample over time.

A similar argument holds when the share of exports in total sales instead of the exporter status is included in an empirical model to estimate the productivity premium of higher export intensity. A case in point is again the paper by ISGEP (2008), where in Table 5 such exporter productivity premia are reported based on empirical models with and without fixed effects. If fixed firm effects are added

Table 6. Firm transitions in the German export market, 1995–2006

| | 20–49 workers | | | | 50–249 workers | | | | 250–499 workers | | | | +499 workers | | | |
|---|---|---|---|---|---|---|---|---|---|---|---|---|---|---|---|---|
| Year $t$ status | No exports | | Exports | | No exports | | Exports | | No exports | | Exports | | No exports | | Exports | |
| Year $t+1$ Status | No Exports | Exports | No Exports | Exports | No Exports | Exports | No Exports | Exports | No Exports | Exports | No Exports | Exports | No Exports | Exports | No Exports | Exports |
| Average 1995–2006 | 0.9346 | 0.0654 | 0.0448 | 0.9552 | 0.9267 | 0.0733 | 0.0234 | 0.9766 | 0.9280 | 0.0720 | 0.0119 | 0.9881 | 0.9321 | 0.0679 | 0.0110 | 0.9890 |

*Note*: The value of each figure is the proportion of firms in each year $t$ statuses (exports–no exports) that chooses each of the two possible statuses in year $t+1$.

to control for time invariant unobserved heterogeneity the point estimates of the exporter productivity premia are much smaller compared to the results based on pooled data only.

Again, unobserved firm heterogeneity does matter. However, before dropping the estimates based on pooled data without fixed effects one should keep in mind that by construction, the estimated coefficients of the export share variable in the model with fixed firm effects uses only the information on the change of the share of exports in total sales within the firms over the time span included in the panel. While we have good reasons to suspect that this share tends to vary over time, it is an open question how large this variation over time within firms is compared to the variation of the share of exports between firms. Information on the relative importance of the within variation and the between variation is helpful to put the estimates with and without fixed firm effects into perspective, because in the fixed-effects model the coefficient of a regressor with little within variation will be imprecisely estimated (and will be not identified if there is no within variation at all). A table reporting overall, between, and within variance for any variable used in the empirical model should be included and discussed (see Cameron and Trivedi (2009, p. 239) for an example).

It seems appropriate to mention a dilemma here that is well known to applied researchers. Usually, the within variation that is needed to identify the coefficient of a regressor tends to increase with the length of the panel used in the estimation. A long panel covering many years, therefore, might be considered to be a better basis for empirical investigations than a short panel for only some years. However, the fixed effects that control for unobserved firm heterogeneity are by assumption time invariant, and this assumption seems more appropriate in shorter than in longer panels. A case in point is the quality of the management of a firm mentioned at the beginning of this section to motivate the application of fixed effects regression methods when investigating heterogeneous firms econometrically. The assumption that management quality does not vary over time seems more convincing in the short run than in the long run (if only because bad management quality can be expected to lead to either market exit or to a new and better (or at least, different) group of in the longer run). The empirical researcher, therefore, is facing a trade-off — usually, the longer the panel, the larger is the within variation in the regressors, but the less appropriate is the assumption of time invariant unobserved heterogeneity. The only solution for this dilemma seems to be an exogenous event that leads to large enough variation in the observed regressors in a short time span.

This leads to my fourth recommendation:

*R4: If panel data are used, report results for pooled data with and without fixed effects, and document time patterns for discrete variables plus the within and between variation of continuous variables.*

## 5. Differences Across Quantiles, Outliers, and Unobserved Heterogeneity: Three Challenges at a Time

As a next step, we will discuss the different aspects of working with data for heterogeneous firms that have been discussed separately in Sections 2–4 simultaneously. Is it possible to tackle all three problems — different effects at different (conditional) quantiles of the distribution of a variable under consideration, outliers, and unobserved heterogeneity — simultaneously? Is there such a thing as a highly robust quantile regression estimator for fixed effects models? To the best of my knowledge, the answer as of today is "unfortunately, no" — but there is progress to report.

As regards outliers and unobserved heterogeneity, Verardi and Croux (2009, p. 452) point out that "(i)n particular, development of robust procedures for panel-data and time-series models would be of major interest for applied economic research." A highly robust MM-estimator for panel data with fixed effects has been proposed recently by Bramati and Croux (2007). While a discussion of details of this estimator is beyond the scope of this chapter the underlying idea is to center the series of observations for a firm in a similar way to what is generally done when applying the within transformation that is used to estimate a fixed-effects model.

The difference here is that the series are centered by removing the median instead of demeaning because the mean is largely distorted by outliers. Having centered the series, a robust estimator can be applied to deal with atypical individuals. The outcoming results will be comparable to those of a fixed effects estimator but will not be distorted by the presence of atypical individuals.

Verardi and Wagner (2010) apply this newly developed method to the estimation of exporter productivity premia for firms from manufacturing industries in West Germany and compare the results to those from using the standard fixed effects estimator. The empirical study uses pooled data for the years 1995–2006. The dependent variable is the log of labor productivity (defined as sales per employee; in Euro). Two empirical models are estimated that differ in the way exports are measured — either as a dummy variable that takes the value of one if an enterprise is an exporter in a year (Model 1), or as the share of exports in total sales in a year and its squared valued (Model 2). Both empirical models include the number of employees and its squared value plus year dummy variables and a constant.

For both models 3.07 percent of the enterprises are identified to be outliers (1,060 in case of Model 1 and 1,052 in Model 2), and this holds for 12.42 percent (or 37,666) observations in the case of Model 1 and for 12.36 percent (or 37,497) observations in the case of Model 2. Dropping these outliers leads to a drastic change in the estimation results for the exporter productivity premium and to a dramatic change in the conclusions drawn: While the estimated exporter premium is statistically highly significant and large from an economic point of view, taking on a value of 13.43 percent, this estimate (while still statistically highly significant) drops to 0.997 percent when the same model is estimated using the robust fixed-effects method. According to the results from the robust fixed-effects regression there is no such thing as a large exporter productivity premium! Comparing the results for Model 2, the conclusions drawn do differ between the standard and the robust fixed-effects regression, too: While productivity is rising at a decreasing rate with an increase in the share of exports according to the results from the standard fixed-effects estimation there is no such pattern revealed from the robust fixed-effects regression, and the increase of productivity with an increase in the share of exports in total sales is much less pronounced. This demonstrates that outliers can drive results from an empirical study with heterogeneous firms.

As regards quantile regression (that takes care of differences at the different quantiles of the conditional distribution, and that is robust to outliers in the dependent variable) recently Powell (2009) developed a method for unconditional quantile regression for panel data with exogenous or endogenous regressors.[12] Powell and Wagner (2011) apply this approach to estimate the exporter productivity premium at quantiles of the productivity distribution for manufacturing enterprises in Germany. They find that the exporter productivity premium is positive, statistically significant, larger at the bottom end, and of a relevant order of magnitude over the whole productivity distribution when unobserved firm characteristics are controlled for in a fixed-effects quantile regression. These are important new insights that lead to my fifth recommendation:

*R5: If panel data are used, report results for pooled data with fixed effects using the standard fixed-effects estimator plus both the quantile regression fixed-effects estimators and the highly robust fixed-effects estimator.*

## 6. Heterogeneous Effects of International Firm Activities on Firm Performance

When firms are heterogeneous we have reasons to suspect that any effect of international firm activities on firm performance — like the effect of exporting on productivity growth or profitability — will vary across the firms under consideration. This is illustrated by results I found in a survey of exporting firms from the region I live in (see Wagner (2009)): For example, strong positive effects of

[12] A discussion of the details of this estimator is far beyond the scope of this chapter; see Powell (2009) for details.

exports on profits are reported by half of the firms only, while more than one-third argued that there is a small positive effect only, and 13 percent reported no positive effect at all. Similar results are found for other dimensions of firm performance. While the probability to find a strong positive effect increases with an increasing share of exports in total sales, other firm characteristics (including size, years of export experience, and research and development activities) are not related to positive export effects.[13]

In the literature on the causal effects of international firm activities on firm performance this heterogeneity of effects is often ignored. The standard approach — that has been pioneered by Wagner (2002) and Girma, Greenaway and Kneller (2003) and that has been applied in a large number of studies ever since — uses propensity score matching to uncover what is known as the *average treatment effect on the treated* (ATT). In a nutshell[14] this ATT is the average difference in a performance dimension (say, productivity growth) that can be observed between firms that started to engage in an activity (say, exporting) and firms that did not, while the firms from the two groups of starters and non-starters are made of matched pairs, or statistical twins, that were identical (or at least as similar as possible) in all characteristics that are relevant for the probability to start exporting and for the outcome variable in the year before some of the firms started to export.

This standard approach looks at the average treatment effect on the treated. To repeat an argument put forward in Section 2 above, as a first step this is fine, but one should not stop here. To quote Buchinsky (1994: 453) again: "'On the average' has never been a satisfactory statement with which to conclude a study on heterogeneous populations." An empirical study of heterogeneous firms should also consider the variation in the effect of exporting (or any other form of international firm activity) over the treated firms.

---

[13] Kneller and Pisu (2010) report results from a survey of UK firms on the returns to exporting and report differences between firms regarding these effects, too.

[14] A discussion of the details of the method used to estimate the ATT is beyond the scope of this paper; see Wagner (2002) and the literature cited therein.

One approach that makes a step in this direction, and that has been applied to the analysis of causal effects of international firm activities on firm performance, is not to consider the effects of a discrete treatment (like exporting or not) but of a continuous treatment (like exporting a different share of the total product of a firm). In this approach not an average treatment effect on the treated is estimated but a dose-response function is computed that shows the effect of a specific dose of a treatment (a given share of exports in total sales) on an indicator of firm performance (like productivity growth or profitability). Pioneering studies using this continuous treatment approach in the field of microeconometrics of international firm activities are Fryges (2009), Fryges and Wagner (2008, 2010), and Vogel and Wagner (2010).[15] This approach turns out to be a powerful tool to uncover heterogeneous effects of international firm activities on firm performance. For example, Fryges and Wagner (2008) find that exporting improves labor productivity growth only within a sub-interval of the range of firms's export–sales ratios.

These considerations lead to my sixth recommendation:

> *R6: A study of the causal effects of international firm activities on firm performance should not only look at the average effect — it should consider the variation of this effect over the range of the extent of this activity.*

## 7. The Role of Replication, Meta-analysis and Talking to Practitioners in Empirical Work with Micro-data

In the final section of this chapter a number of topics that are relevant for empirical work with micro-data in general are dealt with, starting with a discussion of the role of replication. Everybody who ever produced estimation results is aware of the fact that only a tiny fraction of these results is documented in tables of working

[15] A discussion of the details of the method used to estimate a dose-response function is beyond the scope of this chapter; see Fryges and Wagner (2008) and the literature cited therein.

papers, and often an even smaller fraction is published in the final version of a paper. The published results are not a random sample of all the variants that came out of the printer, they are a highly selected sample made of those results we as researchers consider to be the most suitable — be it because they are the ones that are most in line with our priors, or the most statistically significant, or whatever. Given that we all are aware of this publication bias, we usually tend to be reluctant to trust published results (at least, those from others).

If a paper carefully performed an empirical investigation, taking all the recommendations given above into account, does it show more than that the results reported are possible results? Can the results be taken as a reliable guide for evidence-based policy recommendations? In most of the times (if not at any time) in my opinion the answer should be "no". Besides the publication bias mentioned above, errors can occur at every stage of an empirical investigation (not to mention that it is easy to fake numbers reported in tables), and the data used can be non-representative in many ways (that are often not obvious for the researcher and even less for the reader), taken from a specific part of the population of all firms at a specific point in time sampled in a specific way. Therefore, my seventh recommendation is:

*R7: Never consider results based on one sample of firms from one country and from one period of time as a stylized fact.*

Replication can be most helpful on the long way from isolated estimation results to stylized facts. In this context, replication can take on two different forms. The first one is related to the reproducibility of a set of published results, and it is termed *pure replication* by Hamermesh (2007, p. 716). To qualify as a scientific contribution a published result must be reproducible. As Vinod and McCullough (2003, p. 888) put it, "(r)eplication is the cornerstone of science. Research that cannot be replicated is not science, and cannot be trusted either as part of the profession's accumulated body of knowledge or as a basis for policy."

Results that can be trusted must be reproducible by the original investigator (and by any other person with the technical skills needed) even after a considerable amount of time. This might seem to be self-evident, but many of us know that it is not (see Hamermesh (2007) for examples). Moreover, more and more journals demand that the material used to produce results in a published paper is submitted to a data archive, and this should make replication of results an easy task.

However, as Frey, Eichenberger and Frey (2009, p. 154) argue "(in) economics, to replicate the work published by others, and to reveal mistakes, usually is not a promising strategy, because the scholars exposed are likely to be among the referees". But this depends on the editors, and the mere possibility that it is easy to replicate published results, and to demonstrate the degree of fragility of it, should work as an incentive to publish only robust and reliable results. Making all details of the computations done for an empirical study easily available to other researchers, therefore, is highly recommended:

> *R8: Always make the program files and the data used in an empirical study available for replication and extensions. If the data are confidential, give detailed information how they can be accessed by other researchers.*

The second type of replication besides *pure replication* is named *scientific replication* by Hamermesh (2007, p. 727); this approach means "re-examining an idea in some published research by studying it using a different data set chosen from a different population from that used in the original paper". Results generated from data for one economy in one period cannot generally be expected to hold for another economy or the same economy in another period due to differences in institutions or its changes over time, or to time and region specific shocks. "If our theories are intended to be general, to describe the behavior of consumers, firms, or markets independent of the social or broader economic context, they should be tested using data from more than just one economy" (Hamermesh 2007, p. 728). To put it differently, and again quoting Hamermesh (2000, p. 376), "the credibility of a new finding that is based on carefully analyzing two data sets is far more than twice that of a result based only on one."

The literature on the microeconometrics of international firm activities is a case in point. Much of it started with the Brookings paper by Bernard and Jensen (1995) that used data from the U.S., and the empirical approach introduced in this paper (and in later papers by the authors) has been applied by others using similar data from many other countries ever since (see the survey by Wagner (2007)). These replication studies that often gave rather similar results over space and time all contributed to the big picture we now have on the causes and consequences of international activities of heterogeneous firms. Scientific replication studies of this type provide valuable steps on the way from estimation results to stylized facts.

A problem with this type of replication studies, however, is that the incentives for performing them are often quite low. As Hamermesh (2000, p. 376) puts it, "(t)here is little or no reward to replication", not least because "(n)o editor of a major journal is likely to publish replications of previous original pieces" (Hamermesh 2007, p. 731). But my experience shows that more and more referees and editors of good field journals and general journals are willing to recognize the value added provided by papers that report evidence on the validity or not of an empirical result reported in other studies. This leads to my recommendation number nine:

*R9: Recognize the important role of scientific replication studies that re-examine ideas from published research using different data sets from different countries and periods — and do this as an author, as a referee, and as an editor.*

One way scientific replication is performed by a number of authors in different studies investigating the same topic. Another way to perform it is that one author in one study analyzes different data sets from different periods of time and/or different countries, and it is named *within-study replication* in this case (Hamermesh 2007, p. 730). This approach of within-study replication is especially attractive. First of all, it provides evidence on the empirical validity of a finding beyond a specific point in time and space from the outset of the publication of the original study, and not after an often large time span due to lags in recognition, preparation and publication related to replication studies. Second, if work is done by a single researcher (or a single research team) the chances that all the details of the empirical study are identical (or at least very similar) across the data sets tends to be quite high.

In most cases, however, firm-level data are strictly confidential, and as a rule these data can only be used on computers located inside the statistical agencies that are in charge of collecting the data. The data cannot cross borders (not even in a united Europe where borders are hard to recognize when you cross them by car or train), and often they cannot be accessed by citizens of a foreign country (who are not liable to jurisdiction in case of violation of privacy in the country where the data are located). Within-study replication using firm-level data from various countries, therefore, usually cannot be performed by one author (or a team of authors) from one country.

A way out is to form a team of researchers who are located in different countries, each of whom does have access to firm-level data from her or his country, to agree on a unified empirical approach, and to perform a within-study replication where strictly comparable results for each country are produced by the author(s) from that country. The pioneering study of this type of within-study replication by an international research team in the field of microeconometrics of international firm activities is Bernard, Jensen and Wagner (1997). This study reports directly comparable results on the differences between exporters and non-exporters for the United States and Germany. Recently, teams of researchers active in this field from some 15 countries joined to form the *International Study Group on Exports and Productivity* and to apply the approach of within-study replication using confidential firm-level longitudinal data from various countries. The study looks at cross-country differences in exporter productivity premia estimated by using comparable data and a unified empirical approach (ISGEP 2008).

In my view results from this type of replication studies demonstrate that it surely pays to coordinate the approach used in empirical research *ex-ante* among the researchers involved. Therefore, my recommendation number 10 is:

> *R10: If within-study replication is not possible for you due to limitations of access to firm-level data from several countries join with teams from various countries to perform ex-ante coordinated studies using a unified approach.*

The next topic to be discussed is the use of meta-analysis as a tool to uncover stylized facts. Ideas from an emerging literature often tend to be analyzed empirically in a large number of scientific replication studies over the years after the original study has been published. A case in point from the microeconometrics of international firm activities is the literature on the relationship between exports and productivity that grew out of the original paper by Bernard and Jensen (1995). One way to tease out general facts about this and any other topic (assuming such facts exist) is to collect all the results and prepare a survey article (see Hamermesh 2007, p. 731). I did this for the literature on exports and productivity that was published until the end of 2006 and summarized the core results in a table (see Wagner 2007). A bird's-eye view on this collection of results revealed both striking similarities and differences.

If a comprehensive survey of empirical studies on a topic reveals that the effect under investigation tends to be rather similar across space and time, this might be viewed as evidence for the existence of a stylized fact that can be used to guide both economic theory and economic policy. If results differ considerably among the various studies using data from different periods and countries, the next task on the agenda is to find out why they differ.

Obvious suspects that can cause differences in results between empirical studies include, among others, different sampling frames (Are establishments or enterprises used as the unit of analysis? Is the lower bound of the number of employees in a unit identical across the samples?), different definitions of variables (Is productivity measured as sales per employee, value added per employee, or one of several estimates for total factor productivity?), and different specification of the empirical model (Is firm size controlled for by including the squared value of employees? Is unobserved heterogeneity controlled for in a fixed-effects model?). The within-study approach to replication recommended in the section above takes care of these causes for cross-study differences in results.

If results differ across space and time when a unified approach in the form of a within-study replication has been conducted in a promising way to investigate these differences is to perform a meta-analysis. This approach regresses the variable under consideration — say, the exporter premium found for a country *j* — on characteristics of that country *j* that are considered as possible determinants of the premium (e.g. the average tariff rate, or distance to trading partners). A pioneering application of this approach in the literature on the microeconometrics of international firm activities can be found in ISGEP (2008).[16] This study demonstrates that a meta-analysis can be a powerful tool to summarize what we can learn from all the replication studies, and that it can help to uncover the stylized facts that are needed to inform both theoretical modeling and policy debates.

This leads to my recommendation number 11:

> *R11: Use a meta-analysis to understand why empirical results differ across space and time, and to uncover stylized facts that can help to inform theoretical modeling and policy debates.*

While all my recommendations given so far deal with aspects of how to take care of heterogeneity in the analysis of large sets of firm

[16]Meta-analyses from this literature that are not based on estimation results from a within-study replication include Görg and Strobl (2001), Martins and Yang (2008) and Tingvall and Ljungwall (2010). Florax, de Groot and de Mooij (2002) review the method of meta-analysis and illustrate its potential use in applied economic policy analysis. Recent examples from different fields of economics include Abreu, de Groot and Florax (2005), de Dominicis, Florax and de Groot (2008) and Koetse, de Groot and Florax (2009).

data, I would like to add one final recommendation that aims at a different point:

> *R12: From time-to-time leave your office and your computer, and go out to talk to decision makers that care about international firm activities in their day-to-day work.*

Freeman (1989, p. xi) pointed out that "(g)etting the opinions of the subjects of our research is also the only advantage we have over physicists. Quarks and gluons do not talk about what they do or why ...". While many economist doubt that we can learn much from field work of this type, others state that "learning by asking those who are doing" (Blinder 1990) can be important. Akerlof (2007, p. 28) argued in his Nobel-lecture: "In contrast to reliance on statistical testing, disciplines other than economics typically put much greater weight on a naturalistic approach. This approach involves detailed case studies. Such observation of the small often has been the key to understanding of the large."

The combination of qualitative case studies and quantitative analysis that amalgamates microeconometric investigations of firm-level data with discussions with actors inside the firms has recently been labeled *pin factory* or *insider econometrics* (see Freeman and Shaw (2009), p. 3) — where the term pin factory refers to Adam Smith's famous example of the division of labor, and insider econometrics refers to the use of information that is only available to persons with detailed knowledge of the firm. The list of insider econometric studies is long and growing (see Ichniowski and Shaw (2009)). From my own experience I can tell that it is true that you can learn a lot from talking to people who are active in international business. Theorists might get ideas for topics to model and for assumptions to make, and applied econometricians should not forget to check their findings outside academia.

In his Nobel-lecture Heckman (2001, p. 674 and p. 732) pointed out that "(t)he most important discovery [from microeconometric investigations, *J.W.*] was the evidence on the pervasiveness of heterogeneity and diversity in economic life. ... The evidence from microeconomic data has already had a substantial effect on the development of macroeconomic theory, which is slowly abandoning the representative agent paradigm." International economics is a case in point. Over the past decade the *New New International Trade Theory* and the *Micro-econometrics of International Firm Activities* considerably changed the way economists think about firms that are active on international markets. In this chapter I offer recommendations that, hopefully, will contribute to a more complete recognition of firm heterogeneity in the empirical part of this venture.

## Acknowledgment

Many thanks to Vincenzo Verardi for his cooperation on the application of the robust estimator for fixed-effects models, to David Powell for his cooperation on the application of the quantile regression estimatior for fixed-effects models, and to Nils Braakmann and Christian Pfeifer for helpful remarks on an earlier draft. Earlier versions were presented as an invited lecture at the DIME–ISGEP International Workshop on Firm Selection and Country Competitiveness in Nice-Cote-d'Azur in March 2010, as a keynote paper at the Sixth Danish International Economics Workshop, Aarhus, June 3–4, 2010, and as a keynote lecture at the international conference "Productivity and Internationalisation — A Micro-data approach", The Hague, September 1–3, 2010. I thank participants and two referees for helpful comments. All remaining errors are mine.

## References

Abreu, Maria, Henri L. F. de Groot and Raymond J. G. M. Florax (2005). A Meta-analysis of ß-convergence: The Legendary 2%. *Journal of Economic Surveys* 19(3), 389–420.

Akerlof, George A. (2007). The Missing Motivation in Macroeconomics. *American Economic Review* 97(1), 5–36.

Bartelsman, Eric J. and Mark Doms (2000). Understanding Productivity: Lessons from Longitudinal Micro Data. *Journal of Economic Literature* XXXVIII(3): 569–594.

Bellone, Flora, Sarah Guillou and Linel Nesta (2010). To What Extent Innovation Accounts for Firm Export Premia? University of Nice — Sophia Antipolis, mimeo, February.

Bernard, Andrew B. and J. Bradford Jensen (1995). Exporters, Jobs, and Wages in U.S. Manufacturing: 1976–1987. Brookings Papers on Economic Activity, *Microeconomics* 1, 67–119.

Bernard, Andrew B., J. Bradford Jensen and Joachim Wagner (1997). The good go abroad: Evidence from longitudinal micro data on German and U.S. exporers. In: Laaksonen, S. (Ed.), *The Evolution of Firms and Industries*. Helsinki: Statistics Finland, p. 489–500.

Blinder, Alan S. (1990). Learning By Asking Those Who Are Doing. *Eastern Economic Journal* XVI(4), 297–306.

Bloom, Nicholas and John Van Reenen (2010). Why Do Management Practices Differ across Firms and Countries? *Journal of Economic Perspectives* 24(1), 203–224.

Bramati, Caterina Maria and Christophe Croux (2007). Robust Estimators for the Fixed Effects Panel Data Model. *Econometrics Journal* 10(3), 521–540.

Buchinsky, Moshe (1994). Changes in the U.S. Wage Structure 1963–1987: Application of Quantile Regression. *Econometrica* 62(2), 405–458.

de Dominicis, Laura, Raymond J. G. M. Florax and Henri L. F. de Groot (2008). A Meta-Analysis on the Relationship between Income Inequality and Economic Growth. *Scottish Journal of Political Economy* 55(5), 654–682.

Delgado, Miguel A., Jose C. Farinas and Sonia Ruano (2002). Firm Productivity and Export Markets: A Non-parametric Approach. *Journal on International Economics* 57(2), 397–422.

Florax, Raymond J. G. M., Henri L. F. de Groot and Ruud A. de Mooij (2002). Meta-analysis. Tinbergen Institute Discussion Paper TI 2002-041/3.

Freeman, Richard B. (1989). *Labour Markets in Action*. New York: Harvester Wheatsheaf.

Freeman, Richard B. and Kathryn L. Shaw (2009). Introduction. In: Freeman, R. B. and Kathryn L. Shaw (Eds.), *International Differences in the Business Practices and Productivity of Firms*. Chicago and London: University of Chicago Press.

Frey, Bruno S., Reiner Eichenberger and René L. Frey (2009). Editorial Ruminations: Publishing Kyklos. *Kyklos* 62(2), 151–160.

Fryges, Helmut (2009). The Export-Growth Relationship: Estimating a Dose-Response Function. *Applied Economics Letters* 16, 1855–1859.

Fryges, Helmut and Joachim Wagner (2008). Exports and Productivity Growth: First Evidence from a Continous Treatment Approach. *Review of World Economics* 144(4), 695–722.

Fryges, Helmut and Joachim Wagner (2010). Exports and Profitability — First Evidence for German Manufacturing Firms. *The World Economy* 33(3), 399–423.

Gerlach, Knut, Olaf Hübler and Wolfgang Meyer (2003). The Hannover Firm Panel (HFP). *Schmollers Jahrbuch/Journal of Applied Social Science Studies* 123(3), 463–470.

Girma, Sourafel, David Greenaway and Richard Kneller (2003). Export Market Exit and Performance Dynamics: A Causality Analysis of Matched Firms. *Economics Letters* 83(3), 317–324.

Görg, Holger and Eric Strobl (2001). Multinational Companies and Productivity Spillovers: A Meta-Analysis. *Economic Journal* 111, F723–F739.

Greenaway, David and Richard Kneller (2007). Firm Heterogeneity, Exporting and Foreign Direct Investment. *Economic Journal* 117, F134–F161.

Hamermesh, Daniel S. (2000). The Craft of Labormetrics. *Industrial and Labor Relations Review* 53(3), 363–380.

Hamermesh, Daniel S. (2007), Viewpoint: Replication in Economics. *Canadian Journal of Economics* 40(3), 715–733.

Heckman, James. J. (2001). Micro Data, Heterogeneity, and the Evaluation of Public Policy: Nobel Lecture. *Journal of Political Economy* 109(4), 673–748.

Helpman, Elhanan (2006). Trade, FDI, and the Organization of Firms. *Journal of Economic Literature* XLIV, 589–630.

Huber, Peter J. (1964). Robust Estimation of a Location Parameter. *Annals of Mathematical Statistics* 35(1), 73–101.

Ichniowski, Casey and Kathryn L. Shaw (2009). Insider Econometrics: Empirical Studies of How Management Matters. National Bureau of Economic Research NBER Working Paper 15618, December.

International Study Group on Exports and Productivity (ISGEP) (2008). Understanding Cross-Country Differences in Exporter Premia: Comparable Evidence for 14 Countries. *Review of World Economics* 144(4), 596–635.

Kneller, Richard and Mauro Pisu (2010). The Returns to Exporting: Evidence from UK Firms. *Canadian Journal of Economics* 43(2), 494–519.

Koenker, Roger and Kevin F. Hallock (2001). Quantile Regression. *Journal of Economic Perspectives* 15, 143–156.

Koetse, Mark J., Henri L. F. de Groot and Raymond J. G. M. Florax (2009). A Meta-Analysis of the Investment-Uncertainty Relationship. *Southern Economic Journal* 76(1), 283–306.

Kox, Henk L. M. and Hugo Rojas-Romagosa (2010). Exports and Productivity Selection Effects for Dutch Firms. *De Economist* 158(3), 295–322.

López, Ricardo A. (2005). Trade and Growth: Reconciling the Macroeconomic and Microeconomic Evidence. *Journal of Economic Surveys* 19(4), 623–648.

Martins, Pedro S. and Yong Yang (2008). The Impact of Exporting on Firm Productivity: A Meta-Analysis of the Learning-by-Exporting Hypothesis. *Review of World Economics* 145(3), 431–445.

McNaughton, Rod B. and Jim Bell (Eds.) (2009). *Entrepreneurship and Globalization*, Vols. 1–5, Los Angeles: Sage.

Melitz, Mark J. (2003). The Impact of Trade on Intra-Industry Reallocations and Aggregate Industry Productivity. *Econometrica* 71(6), 1695–1725.

Powell, David (2009). Unconditional Quantile Regression for Panel Data with Exogenous or Endogenous Regressors. RAND Working Paper WR-710, October.

Powell, David and Joachim Wagner (2011). Low Productive Exporters and High Productive Non-exporters. The Exporter Productivity Premium along the Productivity Distribution in German Manufacturing Enterprises. Mimeo, February.

Rousseeuw, Peter J. and Annick M. Leroy (1987). *Robust Regression and Outlier Detection*. New York: John Wiley and Sons.

StataCorp (2009). *Stata. Release 11. Statistical Software*. College Station, TX: StataCorp.

Syverson, Chad (2010). What Determines Productivity? National Bureau of Economic Research NBER Working Paper 15712, January.

Tingvall, Patrik Gustavsson and Christer Ljungwall (2010). Is China different? A Meta-Analysis of Export-led Growth. Stockholm School of Economics, CERC Working Paper 15, April.

Verardi, Vincenzo and Christophe Croux (2009). Robust Regression in Stata. *The Stata Journal* 9(3), 439–453.

Verardi, Vincenzo and Joachim Wagner (2010). Robust Estimation of Linear Fixed Effects Panel Data Models with an Application to the Exporter Productivity Premium. University of Lueneburg Working Paper Series in Economics No. 168, April.

Vinod, Hrishikesh D. and Bruce D. McCullough (2003). Verifying the Solution from a Nonlinear Solver: A Case Study. *American Economic Review* 93(3), 873–892.

Vogel, Alexander and Joachim Wagner (2010). Exports and Profitability — First Evidence for German Business Services Enterprises. *Applied Economics Quarterly* 56(1), 7–30.

Wagner, Joachim (1995). Exports, Firm Size, and Firm Dynamics. *Small Business Economics* 7(1), 29–39.

Wagner, Joachim (2002). The Causal Effects of Exports on Firm Size and Labor Productivity: First Evidence from a Matching Approach. *Economics Letters* 77(2), 287–292.

Wagner, Joachim (2007). Exports and Productivity: A Survey of the Evidence from Firm-Level Data. *The World Economy* 30(1), 60–82.

Wagner, Joachim (2008). Export Entry, Export Exit and Productivity in German Manufacturing Industries. *International Journal of the Economics of Business* 15(2), 169–180.

Wagner, Joachim (2009). Exporte und Firmenerfolg: Welche Firmen profitieren wie vom internationalen Handel? *AStA — Wirtschafts- und Sozialstatistisches Archiv* 3(2), 109–122.

Yasar, Mahmut, Carl H. Nelson and Roderick Rejesus (2006). Productivity and Exporting Status of Manufacturing Firms: Evidence from Quantile Regressions. *Review of World Economics* 142(4), 675–694.

Lightning Source UK Ltd.
Milton Keynes UK
UKOW04n1151280616

277237UK00001B/6/P

9 789813 109681